Too Cheap to Meter

SUNY Series in Radical Social
and Political Theory

Roger S. Gottlieb, Editor

Too Cheap to Meter

An Economic and Philosophical Analysis
of the Nuclear Dream

Steven Mark Cohn

State University of New York Press

Published by
State University of New York Press, Albany

For information, address State University of New York
Press, State University Plaza, Albany, N.Y., 12246

Production by Diane Ganeles
Marketing by Dana Yanulavich

Library of Congress Cataloging-in-Publication Data

Cohn, Steve.
    Too cheap to meter : an economic and philosophical analysis of the
nuclear dream / Steven Mark Cohn.
        p.   cm. — (SUNY series in radical social and political
theory)
    Includes bibliographical references and index.
    ISBN 0-7914-3389-7 (hc : alk. paper). — ISBN 0-7914-3390-0 (pb :
alk. paper)
    1. Nuclear industry.   2. Nuclear energy—Social aspects.
I. Title. II. Series.
HD9698.A2C57   1997
333.792′4—DC20   96-41499
                                                      CIP

10 9 8 7 6 5 4 3 2 1

For Betty and Morris George Cohn,
One Last Time.

Contents

Part III: The Competitive Context

Part IV: Conclusion

List of Tables and Figures

TABLES

FIGURES

Acknowledgments

It is a real pleasure to thank the many people who have helped me in my studies of nuclear power. Some of them differ with my assessment of the technology but were generous in helping me explore it. Any errors in the text are of course my responsibility.

From my years at the University of Massachusetts and Denver University, I thank Harry Bloch, Sam Bowles, Joe Bowring, Gerry DuGuay, Nancy Folbre, Peter Hayes, Ed King, and Lyuba Zarsky for their aid early in the project. From Oak Ridge National Laboratory, I thank Robin Cantor, David Feldman, the late Martin Katzman, and Anthony Turhollow. From the Department of Nuclear Engineering at MIT, I thank Eric Eiverson, Michael Golay, Richard Lester, Marvin Miller, Eugene Skolnikoff, Xing Yan, and most especially, Larry Lidsky.

Many thoughtful people in the anti-nuclear movement have aided my research. I especially thank Charles Komanoff, Bob Pollard, and staff members of the Nuclear Information Resource Service and Critical Mass.

Others to whom thanks is owed include Melissa Ames, David Amor, Peter Bailley, Bruce Biewald, Jeff Clark, Angela Fillenwarth, Jim Manwell, Maliha Safri, Sam Smucker, and Rich Stout. David Lewis and Blair Sandler provided insightful editing. The index was prepared by Carol Inskip, and the cover was designed by David Lewis. A special thanks to Nancy Eberhardt, Larry Cohn, and the late Betty Cohn for help of all kinds.

I'd also like to acknowledge research support from Knox College's faculty research and Lilly Grant funds; the DOE's Oak Ridge Science Semester summer research funds, the University of Chicago's "Occasional Fellowship" program, and a special thanks to the Department of Nuclear Engineering at MIT for inviting an avowed skeptic about nuclear power to take a sabbatical as a Visiting Research Associate.

Thanks also to the librarians at numerous libraries, especially Knox College. This list is necessarily incomplete, as one incurs intellectual debts to informal conversations and other kinds of assistance during a long project that elude formal lists. But a thanks just the same to these anonymous helpers.

Acknowledgment and gratitude are also extended to the following publishers for permission to quote from their works:

Richard Tybout, "The Economics of Nuclear Power"; *American Economic Review* 47, 2; pp. 359–360.

From NUCLEAR, INC. by Mark Hertsgaard. Copyright © 1983 by Mark Hertsgaard. Reprinted by permission of Pantheon Books, a division of Random House, Inc.

The excerpt from "Nuclear Safety (IV): Barriers to Communication" by Robert Gillette is reprinted with permission from *Science*, September 22, 1972, pp. 1081–1082. The two excerpts from "Nuclear Safety (I): The Roots of Dissent" by Robert Gillette are reprinted with permission from *Science*, September 1, 1972, page 771 and page 773, respectively. Copyright 1972 American Association for the Advancement of Science.

Excerpts from *Nucleus*, 16:1, Spring 1994 article titled "The Fight for Nuclear Power Safety," page 2. Permission granted by the Union of Concerned Scientists.

Excerpts from *Scientific and Managerial Manpower in Nuclear Industry* by James W. Kuhn. Copyright © 1966 by Columbia University Press. Reprinted with permission of the publisher.

Excerpt reprinted from "Nuclear Safety Regulation: Lessons from U.S. Experience" by Victor Gilinsky published in *Energy Policy* (20) 8. Copyright 1992, pages 706 and 707, with kind permission from Elsevier Science Ltd., The Boulevard, Langford Lane, Kidlington OX5 1GB, UK.

Portions of material reprinted with permission from *Power Engineering*, Vol. 91, No. 7, July 1987, page 4.

Portions of "Pioneer in Radiation Sees Risk Even in Small Doses" by Matthew L. Wald, December 8, 1996, page A-1. Copyright © 1996 by The New York Times Co. Reprinted by permission.

Figure 13.1 reprinted with permission from "Least-Cost Climatic Stabilization" by Amory B. Lovins and L. Hunter Lovins, July 31, 1991.

Figure 13.2 taken from Nordhaus' article "To Slow or Not to Slow" from the *Economic Journal* 101 (1991), page 929. Copyright: Royal Economic Society. Reprinted with permission from Blackwell Publishers.

Figure 13.3 reprinted with permission from *Policy Implications of Greenhouse Warming*. Copyright © 1991 by the National Academy of Sciences. Courtesy of the National Academy Press, Washington, D.C.

Excerpts taken from "Energy Strategy: The Road Not Taken?" by Amory B. Lovins. Reprinted by permission of *Foreign Affairs*, March/April 1996. Copyright © 1996 by the Council on Foreign Relations, Inc.

Quote from the article "Containment of a Reactor Meltdown" by Jan Beyea and Frank von Hippel, Vol. 38, No. 7. August/September 1982, reprinted by permission of *The Bulletin of the Atomic Scientists*, copyright 1992 by the Educational Foundation for Nuclear Science, 6042 South Kimbark Avenue, Chicago, Illinois 60637, USA. A one-year subscription is $36.00.

Excerpts from "G.E.'s Costly Ventures Into the Future" by Allan T. Demaree, *Fortune*, October 1970 reprinted with permission from the publisher.

Excerpts from "Wind Energy Comes of Age in California" by Paul Gipe, July 1989. Reprinted by permission.

Excerpts from "What the Fight is All About" by Michael McCally, September 1990, reprinted by permission of *The Bulletin of Atomic Scientists*, copyright © 1990 by the Educational Foundation for Nuclear Science, 6042 South Kimbark Avenue, Chicago, Illinois 60637, USA. A one-year subscription is $36.00.

Abbreviations

ABWR	advanced boiling water reactor
ACRS	Advisory Committee on Reactor Safeguards
AEC	Atomic Energy Commission
A-E-C (firm)	architect-engineering-construction (firm)
AFBC	atmospheric fluidized bed combustion
AIF	Atomic Industrial Forum
AP-600 (reactor)	advanced passive 600 (reactor)
Bkwh	billion kilowatt hours
BM	biomass
BTU	British thermal unit
BWR	boiling water reactor
C	Celsius (or carbon)
CC	combined cycle
CFCs	chlorofluorocarbons
C/kwh	Carbon per kilowatt hour
c/kwh	cents per kilowatt hour
DoD	Department of Defense
DOE	Department of Energy
DSM	demand side management
$/tC	dollars per ton carbon
ECCS	emergency core cooling system
EIS	environmental impact statement
ERDA	Energy Research and Development Administration
FBC	fluidized bed combustion
FCR	fixed charge rate
FGD	flue gas desulfurization
FOI	freedom of information
GDP	gross domestic product
GHG	greenhouse gas
GT	gas turbine
GTCC	gas turbine combined cycle

GW	gigawatt
GWe	gigawatt electric
HDR	hot dry rock
HLW	high level nuclear waste
HLWD	high level nuclear waste disposal
HTGR	high temperature gas reactor
IGCC	integrated gasification combined cycle
IOU	investor owned utility
IPP	independent power producer
JCAE	Joint Committee on Atomic Energy
/KW	per kilowatt
/kwh	per kilowatt hour
LC	learning curve
LLW	low level nuclear waste
LLWD	low level nuclear waste disposal
LMFBR	liquid metal fast breeder reactor
LMR	liquid metal reactor
LNG	liquefied natural gas
LWR	light water reactor
MHTGR	modular high temperature gas reactor
MIT	Massachusetts Institute of Technology
M/kwh	mills per kilowatt hour
MMBTU	millions of BTUs
mr	millirem
MRS	monitored retrievable storage
MT/yr.	metric ton per year
MW	megawatt
NEPA	National Environmental Policy Act
NOx	nitrogen oxides
NPC	nuclear planning context
NRC	Nuclear Regulatory Commission
NSF	National Science Foundation
NSSS	nuclear steam supply system
O&M	operation and maintenance
OT	Official Technology
OTA	Office of Technology Assessment
PC	planning context
PFBC	pressurized fluidized bed combustion
PIUS (reactor)	Process Inherent Ultimately Safe (reactor)
PMC	professional managerial class
Pu	plutonium
PURPA	Public Utilities Regulatory Policies Act

PV	photovoltaic (or pressure vessel)
PWR	pressurized water reactor
Quad	quadrillion BTUs
R&D	research and development
rem	rad equivalent man
RET	renewable energy technology
SBWR	simplified boiling water reactor
SERI	Solar Energy Research Institute
SIPI	Scientists Institute for Public Information
SO2	sulfur dioxide
ST	solar thermal
TA	technological aesthetics
tC/yr.	ton Carbon per year
TG (or T-G)	turbine generator
TMI	Three Mile Island
TVA	Tennessee Valley Authority
TWH	terawatt hours
UCS	Union of Concerned Scientists
VOC	volatile organic compound

Chapter 1

Introduction

A Personal Journey

When I first became interested in nuclear power in the mid-1970s, its fortunes were much brighter than they are today. Defenders of nuclear energy pointed to the market's apparent endorsement of the technology (over 200 plants ordered by 1974) as *prima facie* evidence of its economic viability and technological superiority. I was more skeptical about the desirability of nuclear power, and after participating in the protests against the Seabrook nuclear plant, was led to ponder how market organized technical change might promote "inappropriate" technologies. This question evolved into an economics Ph.D. dissertation on the political-economic history of nuclear power (1986), a year's research at Oak Ridge National Laboratory (1988–1989), a sabbatical year as a Visiting Research Associate in the Department of Nuclear Engineering at MIT (1992–1993) and, finally, this book.

Reinforcing my original skepticism about nuclear power was a general distrust of technological determinism. I was skeptical of theories of innovation that analogized technological evolution to the inevitable sequence of mathematical theorems so inexorably derived in high school geometry classes. I was also skeptical of Panglossian economic theories that tended to reduce market-governed technical choices to the optimal expression of technical rationality. My instinct was to look for how social contexts influenced technical decisions about nuclear power. My goal was to develop analytical techniques to illuminate these influences. The task proved a complex and engaging project. I hope that readers can share the fascination I've felt in unpacking the diverse ways that ideology, institutional structures, distributions of power, and other products of social contexts have influenced market responses to nuclear power.

The assertion that social contexts *infuse* what appear to be "technically driven" decisions does not deny that "nature" and engineering constraints play key roles in shaping technological evolution, nor does it imply that market-organized technical change is generally a bad idea. The claim does,

1

however, assert that market-structured technical change is laden with social *as well* as technical inputs, and it questions simple policy recommendations that counsel "leaving innovation to the the market." As will be demonstrated in the text, the issue is not *whether* socio-political-ideological phenomena influence technological evolution, but *how* and to what degree. When these forces are understood, the "leave it to the market" mantra of the Reagan and Bush administrations that promised "pure technological change" appears as naive as King Canute's legendary order to the tides to cease their advance.

How To Read This Book

This book is intended for two major audiences: those interested in the history and future of nuclear power, and those interested in social theory. I hope to convince members of the first group that attention to methodological and philosophical issues in social theory has very practical implications for understanding nuclear power history and forecasting its future. I wish to convince the second group that the nuclear power experience provides an excellent context for exploring important methodological and conceptual debates in social theory.

It is my hope that the book weaves together its concrete and theoretical foci in a way that maintains the interests of its two audiences. There will be sections, however, that go into more detail than some readers of each audience might find necessary for their purposes. I have tried to identify such passages with a brief note and to avoid including in them material necessary for understanding later sections.

In order to further guide readers to those notes most likely to be of interest to them, I have used a footnoting system designed to signal whether the note is a simple source citation, a more detailed elaboration of a concrete nuclear power issue, or a further exploration of a social science issue. Notes in square brackets (e.g., [1]) are reference citations. Notes in angled brackets (e.g., <1>) elaborate concrete issues related to nuclear power, while notes in squiggly brackets (e.g., {1}) pertain to social theory issues.

Nuclear Power Issues

For those readers primarily interested in the technical aspects of the nuclear power debate, the book offers a detailed analysis of the history and future of nuclear power. Part I of the text analyzes the reasons for the rapid expansion of nuclear power during 1954–1974 (chapters 2–5) and its subsequent collapse from 1974–1995 (chapter 6). Part II (chapters 7–10) explores the key issues within the nuclear sector that will shape its future. The chapters focus on expected future nuclear power costs, likely government R&D, subsidy, and regulatory policy, and the debate between proponents of evolutionary light water and passively safe reactor designs over which is the most promising route to a second nuclear era.

Part III (chapters 11–13) analyzes the factors outside the nuclear sector that will most influence nuclear power's future. The chapters focus on the level of future energy demand, the expected economics of non-nuclear energy options, and the implications of greenhouse hazards. Part IV (chapter 14) summarizes the book's findings.

Nuclear Power and Social Theory

The book's theoretical framework emphasizes two aspects of technological evolution to highlight the way social contexts have influenced nuclear power's history and future. The first is the potential for path dependency in technological competition, and the second is the paradigmatic nature of technology assessment.

Path Dependency

The potential for positive feedback in technological development implies that the outcome of technological competition can be determined by early path choices. Technologies gaining a head start in economic development may be able to transform initial advantages into permanent market dominance if they are able to capture path dependent cost reductions, such as:

- standardization and mass production economies

- learning curve cost reductions

- reduced risk premiums in capital markets

- the fruits of system-wide efficiencies (such as payoffs from investments in complementary technologies)

- the benefits of bureaucratic momentum

- the benefits of institutional accommodation to the social needs of the technology

While a few authors have insightfully explored some of these phenomena (see, for example, Bupp and Derian 1981, Morone and Woodhouse 1989, and Cowan 1990), analysis has most frequently concentrated on the first two factors rather than the full socio-technical process. There has also been a tendency to neglect the implications of path dependency for the behavior of corporate, political, and other participants in technical change. Such oversights have deflected attention from some important implications of path dependency, such as the links between path dependency and the polarization of energy sector debates.

The "Planning Context" - "Official Technology" framework developed in chapter 2 is specifically designed to grapple with path dependency and the impact of social contexts on technological development. The analysis demonstrates how ideological beliefs, institutional biases, etc. can significantly shape technical evolution if linked to positive feedback. The findings parallel some of the conclusions of contemporary "chaos theory" concerning the sensitivity of system outcomes to small changes in initial conditions.

The Planning Context-Official Technology framework introduced in chapter 2 develops three related concepts for analyzing technological evolution: (1) a "Planning Context" (PC); (2) "Technological Aesthetics" (TA); and (3) an "Official Technology" (OT). A *Planning Context* is a decision making environment defined in four dimensions: by the identities and political-economic objectives of its participants, by the context's ideological milieu, by the context's institutional structures, and by the nature of existing technical information. A planning context functions like a scientific paradigm, in that it defines the conceptual framework that informs decision making. The PC concept goes beyond categories of discourse, however, to include the material circumstances shaping and shaped by the discourse.

The second concept, *Technological Aesthetics*, refers to engineering intuitions and other subjective judgments about technological trajectories that are generally untestable but still play important roles in technology assessment. These judgments often represent collective traditions (such as those of professional societies, protest movements, or corporate subcultures) rather than random individual beliefs and thus are intertwined with larger institutional and ideological histories.

The third related concept of an *Official Technology* refers to a technology that enjoys strong state support, the sponsorship of a significant representative of private capital, the promoted aura of "the coming technology," and the capture of path dependent advantages. The book's analysis of nuclear power history demonstrates that the decision to choose one particular technology over another can be underdetermined by technical variables, due to the early presence of incomplete information and path dependent effects. Thus in the early stages of decision making, different technologies may be able to win enduring market dominance if they are able to capture OT status. By emphasizing the influence of non-technically determined planning context phenomena, such as technological aesthetics, on which of several competing technologies captures OT benefits, the analysis highlights how social contexts can influence market-organized technical evolution.

The PC-OT framework also illuminates the character of technological competition. The framework's image of technological change challenges conventional economic theory's "passive" image of the firm as a "technology-taker." The PC-OT approach replaces older images of companies methodically trying to *discover* a priori technically determined development paths, with a new image of companies racing to *create* or *capture* path dependent OT status for technologies in which they possess a competitive advantage. The victor's prize is a stream of surplus profits (quasi rents) on technologically-specific capital (such as staff technical expertise, long lived plant and equipment, marketing networks, mineral rights, etc.).

Put more generally, "PC-OT analysis" seeks to uncover the socio-political variables influencing technical change by tying official technologies to particular planning contexts and their sponsoring dynamics. The book's analysis of this process follows a three step strategy:

Step one identifies the four dimensions of the planning context that produces a technical change by specifying the context's political-economic participants, its ideological milieu, its institutional structure, and its available technical information.

Step two analyzes how advocates of different development paths attempt to achieve critical mass or OT status for their favored option and how various ideological and institutional factors influence the success of their efforts.

Step three calculates the impact of promotional support on the micro-economic competitiveness of the victorious "Official Technology."

Chapters 2–5 of this book use the PC-OT framework's three step logic to unravel the origins of nuclear expansion 1950–1974. Chapter 6 explores the sociological origins of the shifting character of the nuclear planning context after the mid-sixties and ties these changes to nuclear power's eventual loss of OT status and economic competitiveness. Later chapters employ many of the same concepts to explore the potential impact of social contexts and path dependent phenomena on future energy sector developments.

Sociology of Knowledge Concerns

The book's second focus vis-à-vis social theory involves the implications of sociology of knowledge concerns for technology assessment. The analysis shows why attention to epistemological issues is critical for an understanding of nuclear power debates. Using Thomas Kuhn's concept of paradigmatic discourse, the book explores:

(1) why nuclear power cost forecasting and hazard assessment debates persist and are unlikely to be resolved in the foreseeable future by appeal to empirical data or available theory;

(2) why nuclear power costs and safety hazards have been traditionally underestimated;

(3) the parallels between nuclear power and alternative energy technology assessment; and

(4) the "technological aesthetics" that differentiate nuclear optimists from nuclear pessimists.

Put in terms more familiar to economists, the analysis explores the implications of bounded rationality and unfalsifiable assumptions for technology assessment. The book also raises some broader epistemological issues not usually addressed by economists or engineers.

By noting the inevitable tendency for constrained realms of discourse to organize technology assessment, and further by linking these constraints to the impact of social contexts, the analysis adds another dimension to the avenues by which social contexts infuse technical decisions.

Because Kuhn's theory of scientific knowledge plays such a large role in my analysis of nuclear power, it may be helpful to review the major aspects of his work that are relevant to technology assessment.[1] Kuhn asserts that scientific inquiry is always conducted within a paradigm or conceptual framework. Paradigms are said to influence the data attended to, the abstractions used to organize data, the character of research agendas, the responses to anomalous findings, and the boundaries of legitimate questions. He writes:

"What a man sees depends both upon what he looks at and also upon what his previous visual-conceptual experience has taught him to see. In the absence of such training there can only be, in William James's phrase, 'a bloomin' buzzin' confusion'" (p. 113).

". . . one of the things a scientific community acquires with a paradigm is a criterion for choosing problems that, while the paradigm is taken for granted, can be assumed to have solutions. To a great extent these are the only problems that the community will admit as scientific or encourage its members to undertake. Other problems, including many that had previously been standard, are rejected as metaphysical, as the concern of another discipline, or sometimes as just too problematic to be worth the time. A paradigm can, for that matter, even insulate the community from those socially important problems that are not reducible to the puzzle form, because they cannot be stated in terms of the conceptual and instrumental tools the paradigm supplies" (p. 37).

I shall return many times in the course of this book to the issue of how such paradigms have influenced the development of nuclear power. The discussion will link the character of particular planning contexts to the construction of specific paradigms for assessing nuclear power, and tie the reasoning style of particular paradigms to specific conclusions about nuclear energy, be it judgments about nuclear hazards, nuclear cost forecasting, or analyses of nuclear power's competition.

Kuhn argues that paradigms define themselves by establishing templates for generating analogies. One learns a paradigm by studying these templates which embody the paradigm's solutions to classical problems. The paradigm advances by extending these solutions (or shared exemplars) to new problems.

Key to Kuhn's epistemology is his claim that paradigms operate at the level of perception as well as interpretation. Like a pair of spectacles (and/or a specialized language), a paradigm conditions the way practitioners *see* (and/or conceptualize) the world. All observations and deductions conditioned within the paradigm are therefore theory laden.

Debate about Kuhn's claims has often centered on his discussion of the way paradigm changes or scientific revolutions occur. He argues that the timing and direction of these gestalt shifts is underdetermined by available data. He does not claim that paradigm choices are irrational, or undisciplined by judgments about a theory's relative simplicity, consistency, scope, etc. He does claim that after ensuring logical consistency, and competitive, rather than absolute consistency with available data, (as all theories will contain puzzling inconsistencies or anomalies), judgments can differ about the relative promise of competing gestalts. He writes,

"Observation and experience can and must drastically restrict the range of admissible scientific belief, else there would be no science.

But they cannot alone determine a particular body of such belief. An apparently arbitrary element, compounded of personal and historical accident, is always a formative ingredient of the beliefs espoused by a given scientific community at a given time" (p. 4).

It is such open-endedness and ambiguity that Kuhn's positivist critics have found the most troubling. In a famous postscript to *The Structure of Scientific Revolutions*, Kuhn adds,

"Debates over theory-choice cannot be cast in a form that fully resembles logical or mathematical proof. . . . Nothing about that relatively familiar thesis implies either that there are no good reasons for being persuaded or . . . that the reasons for choice are different from those usually listed by philosophers of science: accuracy, simplicity, fruitfulness, and the like. What it should suggest, however, is that such reasons . . . [can] be differently applied. . . . There is no neutral algorithm for theory-choice, no systematic decision procedure which, properly applied, must lead each individual in the group to the same decision" (pp. 199–200).

I will return to these observations in later chapters, when analyzing the open-ended nature of energy sector debates between "soft" and "hard" path energy advocates and when discussing intra-nuclear sector debates between proponents of "evolutionary light water reactors" and those who favor "passive safety reactor" designs.

The ambiguity involved in technology assessment and cost forecasting for new energy technologies is analogous to the uncertainties Kuhn found to accompany judgments about the relative fertility of alternative research paradigms. While assessments are not made arbitrarily, the evaluation of a theory in terms of its scope, consistency, simplicity, or fecundity, necessarily involves a weighting and aggregation that defies a priori, deterministic rules. "What is simple?" and "What is fertile?" in scientific paradigms, and "What is promising?" in technological paradigms, are more ambiguous questions than "What is the freezing point of water?" Such judgments necessarily involve "technological aesthetics."

By "technological aesthetics" I mean judgments about aspects of a technology where measurement is qualitative rather than quantitative and subject to "tastes." Relatedly, Kuhn writes, ". . . there is also another sort of consideration that can lead scientists to reject an old paradigm in favor of a new. These are arguments, rarely made entirely explicit, that appeal to the individual's sense of the appropriate or the aesthetic—the new theory is said to be 'neater,' 'more suitable,' or 'simpler,' than the old" (Kuhn 1970, 155).

With respect to nuclear power this can be analogized to judgments about what is an "appropriate technology". Nuclear enthusiasts perceive the technology as the obvious next step in an energy heritage that has already progressed through wood, coal, and oil/natural gas. Indeed, from this perspective, nuclear power's energy intensity (BTU per pound of fuel) and fuel abundance (assuming reprocessing and breeder designs) make it one of the few appropriate technologies for continuing industrial civilization. Cost containing technical fixes are assumed to be available for all conceivable engineering problems. Critics, on the other hand, attack nuclear power as an "inappropriate technology" analogizing its use to "cutting butter with a chain saw." They expect the economic implications of increased efforts to minimize reactor accident probabilities and other hazards, such as nuclear weapons proliferation, to overwhelm any cost saving innovations. Neither side sees very much appealing or attractive in the metaphors and images constructed by the other.

We shall see similar instances of conflicting technological aesthetics in the discussion of different assessments of energy sector alternatives to nuclear power, found in chapter 12.

Extending Kuhn's observations concerning scientific revolutions, Clark (1987) suggests that technological paradigms very rarely collapse solely from internal contradiction. Instead, paradigm shifts require both internal anomalies and external alternatives. The recent attention to reactor designs without the thermal instability of light water reactors (and the accompanying hazard complications), may provide such an alternative inside the nuclear community. Significant leaders of nuclear opinion (Alvin Weinberg formerly at Oak Ridge National Laboratory and Lawrence Lidsky at MIT, for example) are currently taking a more critical view of the future of light water reactors than was prevalent before the expansion of alternative nuclear development paths.

Overview of the Book and Chapter Summaries

As the book is lengthy, it seems appropriate to provide a preview of upcoming chapters. These summaries offer a roadmap for situating individual chapters within the book's overall logic. Part I (chapters 2–6) analyzes the history of nuclear power 1950–present. Chapter 2 outlines the four dimensions of the planning context overseeing nuclear power decision making from 1950–1970 and details the promotional mechanisms used by nuclear power's private sector sponsors to seek OT status for the technology. The chapter analyzes the historical conjuncture created by the period's ideological milieu, institutional structure, corporate growth strategies, national political dynamics, and available technical information. While many parts of the story have been told elsewhere, the analysis adds several new threads (such as greater elaboration of the early support of nuclear initiatives by segments of the utility industry than has been commonly noted) and weaves the history together in novel ways, designed to highlight the impact of path dependency, constrained realms of discourse, and social contexts on nuclear development. The implications of this history are used later in the text to recommend policy responses to current nuclear power choices.

Chapter 3 analyzes the mechanisms used by nuclear power's public sector sponsors to promote OT status for the technology. Particular attention is paid to the factors facilitating massive R&D spending for nuclear power 1954–1974. The analysis uses the PC-OT framework to develop a Kuhnian model of private sector energy research that divides R&D activities into periods of "normal" and "revolutionary" research. The analysis demonstrates how social contexts can condition the timing and direction of "revolutionary" departures. The second part of chapter 3 explores the long list of subsidies, cost deferments, and risk shifting measures given the nuclear industry by its state sponsors.

Chapter 4 uses insights from the sociology of knowledge to analyze the impact of the nuclear planning context on nuclear power hazard assessment and cost forecasting. In a detailed study of the extraordinary history of nuclear cost underestimation and briefer analyses of routine radiation release, thermal pollution, and reactor accident hazard assessment, this section explores how contextual factors imposed an optimistic bias on technical realms of discourse. The analysis demonstrates how the nuclear planning context conditioned the data available, the methodologies used to analyze the data, and the research attention given to anomalous information in the nuclear cost forecasting and hazard assessment fields. Much like direct subsidies, the results were extremely helpful to nuclear power in its competition with alternative energy options. The discussion also briefly illustrates how the gradual restructuring of the nuclear planning context from the mid-sixties forward (vis-à-vis participants, institutions, etc.) altered the technical frames of reference organizing nuclear power information.

Chapter 5 assesses the overall impact of nuclear promotionalism on nuclear power's market position from 1954 to 1974. The chapter analyzes the impact on nuclear power costs of direct nuclear power assistance (such as R&D spending), in-kind aid (such as accident liability protections), and the technology's induced capture of OT status and accompanying path dependent economies (such as the capture of mass production economies). The analysis also highlights the qualitative impact of the OT process as a whole, noting how OT dynamics created the great bandwagon market of 1966–1967, triggered massive oil company investment in the nuclear fuel industry in the late-sixties, stunted European efforts to develop alternative nuclear technologies to U.S. light water reactor designs, and retarded coal based economic options in the U.S.

The chapter concludes by discussing the ability of the PC-OT framework to reinforce and operationalize Amory Lovins' dichotomy between hard and soft energy paths. Using the PC-OT framework, Lovins' mutual exclusivity assertion can be disaggregated into discrete testable claims, a task he never fully addresses. Lovins' "technical incompatibilities" are analogized to the economic level of the PC-OT framework and represent the extent to which phenomena like economies of scale, learning curve efficiencies, system-wide positive externalities, and interdependent risk premiums characterize the energy sector. Lovins' "social incompatibilities" are analogized to the PC-OT framework's attention to the social construction of constraining realms of discourse and planning context logics.

Chapter 6 uses the PC-OT framework to explain the collapse of the nuclear power industry from 1975 to 1995. The beginning of chapter 6 parallels chapter 2's analysis of the nuclear planning context from 1954–1974. The discussion specifies the changing character of the *participants* in nuclear planning, the *ideological beliefs* facilitating collective action, the *institutional structures* organizing nuclear decision making, and the *technical conditions* surrounding nuclear choices. The chapter stresses how the interactive logic of the above changes reconstituted the basis for nuclear planning in a manner equal to a paradigm shift. The chapter thus offers a "structuralist epistemology" that locates the origins of shifting judgments about nuclear hazards, costs, and competition in social structural changes.

Part II of the book shifts the focus into the present. Chapters 7–9 explore the issues within the nuclear sector that will shape nuclear power's future. Chapter 7 explains why there are large disagreements between nuclear industry and nuclear critics' cost projections for new nuclear plants. The chapter returns to the sociology of knowledge issues discussed in chapter 4's analysis of the history of nuclear cost forecasting. It demonstrates that the nuclear industry's current optimism rests on the same methodological assumptions that produced past forecasting errors.

Chapter 8 explores the cloudy future of nuclear energy R&D and the prospects for continued public subsidy of the technology. The chapter demonstrates that without OT status nuclear power's large scale and hazardous nature (requiring both expensive demonstration projects and careful regulatory review before deploying innovations) leave it disadvantaged in R&D competition with small scale technologies that have shorter turnaround times for technical experiments.

The analysis highlights the paradigmatic character of R&D assessment and demonstrates how technological aesthetics can influence judgments about potential R&D payoffs. The chapter contrasts the technological aesthetics governing current energy planning, which favor technologies offering planning flexibility, marginal rather than radical change, and environmental protection, with the OT period's technological aesthetics, which favored technologies with long run growth potentials, centralized administrative formats, and novel scientific bases.

Chapter 9 discusses the likely direction of future NRC regulatory policy and the implications of changing electric utility regulations for the future of nuclear power. Extending the Kuhnian approach to technology assessment highlighted earlier, the chapter's detailed analysis of current radiation hazard and reactor safety debates presents these controversies as paradigm debates over modes of safety analysis. While acknowledging that the data is inconclusive about the seriousness of nuclear hazards, the chapter supports safety skepticism and foresees little public support for relaxation of current safety regulations.

The discussion of utility sector issues foresees little chance of a return to the OT period's regulatory regime which appeared to promise automatic recovery of utility investments in new generating plants. The analysis projects an increasing role for independent power producers (IPPs) in the electricity generating market and expects regulatory changes, such as Integrated Resource Planning (which requires increased utility attention to energy demand management and alternative energy options) to make future utility nuclear plant purchases more difficult.

Chapter 10 explores the intra-nuclear industry debate between advocates of evolutionary light water and passively safe reactor designs over the most attractive technological development path for the nuclear industry. The chapter outlines the strengths and weaknesses of each approach with respect to reactor safety, plant economics, and miscellaneous factors (such as proliferation resistance) and demonstrates the paradigmatic character of judgments about the designs' relative merits. The chapter concludes that only passively safe reactors have a chance of recapturing public confidence in nuclear power, a prerequisite for any second nuclear era.

Part III of the book analyzes issues external to the nuclear sector that will influence nuclear energy's future. Chapter 11 addresses energy demand issues, especially the competition faced by nuclear power from increased energy efficiency investments. The chapter briefly reviews the history of energy demand forecasting and reemploys insights from the sociology of knowledge to understand past and current energy demand forecasting debates.

Chapter 12 analyzes the economics of fossil fuel and renewable energy alternatives to nuclear power. Cheap natural gas and coal-fired electricity (~4.5–6 c/kwh) are expected until at least 2010, with large reductions in renewable energy costs anticipated by 2030. The economics of wind and biomass renewable energy sources seem especially promising and even now appear to underprice nuclear power at favorable sites. As a result nuclear energy is found to have to achieve costs of less than 6 c/kwh (versus my expectation of costs of 7.5–8.5 c/kwh) to regain market attention. The chapter highlights the impact of technological aesthetics on assessments of non-nuclear energy alternatives and the importance of path dependent cost reductions to many of the technologies' economic prospects.

Chapter 13 focuses on the problem of global warming as the future of nuclear power has been increasingly linked to possible "greenhouse" constraints on fossil fuel use. The chapter reviews the science of the greenhouse effect, current cost estimates of the damages potentially caused by climate change, and the projected costs of different abatement responses, including increased reliance on nuclear power. The analysis finds that large uncertainties surround estimates in all of these fields. The final part of the chapter adds political consideration to the mix, and speculates on likely policy responses to greenhouse concerns and their implications for future nuclear power development.

Chapter 14 summarizes the book's findings and discusses the implications of the book's PC-OT organized history of nuclear power for debates in economic and social theory.

Part I

History

Chapter 2

The Nuclear Planning Context (NPC)

Introduction

This chapter develops step one of the Planning Context-Official Technology (PC-OT) framework's three-step process for analyzing the history of nuclear power. It specifies the planning context that promoted nuclear power's early expansion, identifying its major participants and their strategic objectives, the status of relevant technical information, and the ideological and institutional variables that conditioned how participants pursued their objectives. The analysis illuminates how sociopolitical phenomena (what we have been calling social rather than technical variables) infused what are often taken to be technically determined behavior, such as engineering expectations and market outcomes. The chapter also begins Step two of the PC-OT framework's three-step analysis, looking at how nuclear power's private sponsors promoted nuclear expansion.

NPC: Ideological Dimension[1]

During the 1950s and 1960s, popular culture nurtured a political-economic consensus in favor of nuclear power development. The most important ideological phenomena facilitating nuclear expansion were: (1) cold war beliefs; (2) a widespread public trust in business and government leaders; (3) tendencies for consumerist (as opposed to ecologist) responses to technological opportunity; and (4) a popular faith in "science," blending into a technological hubris among engineering and corporate professionals that minimized potential nuclear hazards.

Cold war dynamics promoted nuclear power as a national security measure and vehicle for competition with the Soviets. The McCarthyite climate of the fifties also discouraged research into nuclear power hazards. Concern over the radiation dangers of atomic testing, for example, was often attacked

17

as subversive (Wasserman 1982, 303; Metzger 1972, 125). The cold war also contributed to the general weakness of left leaning social critics during this period, tending to discourage independent review of corporate planning and to reduce public concern about the concentrated character of nuclear markets.

Government and corporate promoters of nuclear power were able to tap the public's buoyant faith in business and political leaders through the mid-sixties. In 1964, for example, only 22% of those surveyed agreed with the statement, "You cannot trust government to do right most of the time." In 1980, 70% agreed with such a statement. Similar patterns were recorded in public perceptions of business trustworthiness (Morone and Woodhouse 1989, 89) and confidence in spokespersons for scientific institutions (Mazur 1981, 48, Balogh 1991, 17).[2] The period of enhanced business credibility was especially helpful in transforming corporate marketing claims about nuclear economics into the conventional wisdom.

Faith in the ability of science and technology to unambiguously and quickly solve social and economic problems during the 1950s and 1960s is nicely reflected in the founding document of Students for a Democratic Society (SDS) in 1962. The statement contrasts sharply with student activists' subsequent hostility towards nuclear power. The 1962 Port Huron Statement declared,

> Our monster cities, based historically on the need for mass labor, might now be humanized, broken into smaller communities, powered by nuclear energy, arranged according to community decisions. . . . a desire for human fraternity may now result in blueprints of civic paradise (Miller 1987, 364–5).

A similar utopian strain animated many nuclear scientists who perceived nuclear energy as a Faustian bargain for global affluence. Describing images that animated AEC Director Glen Seaborg and Oak Ridge Lab Director Alvin Weinberg, Spencer Weart writes,

> Ungainly cities, those 'great clots of humanity' would wither away leaving only centers for thought and art, while industry would be handled by reactor complexes buried safe and invisible beneath meadows. Oak Ridge leader Alvin Weinberg proudly explained that this was precisely the dream of a world set free that he had learned from H.G. Wells (Weart 1988, 302–304).[3]

A 1967 Westinghouse pamphlet on nuclear power similarly declared, (it) will give us all the power we need and more. That's what it's all about. Power seemingly without end. Power to do everything man is destined to do. We have found what might be called *perpetual youth* (Hilgartner et al. 1982, 190).

Alongside broad cultural beliefs, the technological aesthetics governing engineering and corporate planning helped to generate positive assessments of nuclear power. The two most important technological intuitions involved a tendency to underestimate the novelty of and safety challenge posed by nuclear technology [4] and a tendency to overestimate the payoffs to megawatt scaling (i.e., large plant size).

Closely related to the first belief was a willingness to select reactor development strategies based on non-safety criteria (such as fuel conservation or nearness to prototype construction) under the assumption that adequate reactor safety, waste disposal, or proliferation safeguards could be ensured later in the design process; a willingness to "learn on the job" (to begin actual plant construction with very incomplete designs); and a willingness to rely on complicated engineered safety features (such as system redundancy or the emergency core cooling system) rather than passive or inherent safety features (such as remote siting, low power densities, and natural cooling) to avoid serious accidents. The end product of these beliefs was the Rube Goldberg safety system that burdens existing plants.

Reactor designers' preference for large nuclear plants grew out of fossil fuel experience. The relatively unreflective pursuit of MW scaling economies has led to many regrettable investment and safety risks. The tendency to transfer practices automatically from fossil fuel plants to nuclear plants has encouraged other oversights, such as insufficient attention to the implications of nuclear plant construction materials for nuclear plant decommissioning costs.

Weinberg (1990) has also suggested that engineers' fascination with the glamour of high tech systems and a distrust of technologies involving changes in social institutions and cultural habits (e.g., energy conservation initiatives) spurred high tech supply side planning initiatives (p. 27). Hirsh finds that even in the relatively conservative utility industry, for example, "(b)ig, 'neat' and exciting technologies often caught their (utility engineers) imaginations, distracting them from purely economic considerations" (Hirsh 1989, 71). Nuclear projects thus came to be perceived as vehicles for capturing professional prestige among the utilities' management staff.

On a more immediate level, utility planners also worried about technological exhaustion for fossil fired generating technologies. They feared that materials limitations were precluding further increases in steam temperature and pressure, which traditionally had been a main avenue for increasing energy conversion efficiencies and lowering generating costs. The industry was thus encouraged to take a close look at nuclear experimentation.

Interestingly, there were some significant cultural beliefs and technological aesthetics infusing popular and engineering imaginations that posed potential obstacles to rapid nuclear development. Alongside popular fascination with the atom, for example, was: (1) a deep-seated cultural dread of radiation hazards, linked by Spencer Weart to ancient images of transmutation and more modern images of mad scientists and mushroom clouds; (2) Americans' historical distrust of experts and ambivalence towards technologies denaturing the environment; and (3) populist and federalist traditions favoring decentralized political institutions. Among utility engineers there had been a tendency to avoid radical innovative leaps in favor of evolutionary change, a design-by-experience as opposed to a design-by-extrapolation approach (Hirsh 1989, 63).

These countercurrents were submerged as nuclear promoters assembled a critical mass of social support for nuclear technology and subsequently constructed assessment centers in industry, the National Laboratories, and nuclear engineering departments that were dominated by technological aesthetics congenial with nuclear power expansion. Chapter 4 explores how nuclear cost forecasting and hazard assessment were influenced by the supportive intellectual environment these institutions created.

Cultural ambivalence towards nuclear energy quietly persisted, however, emerging publicly in the late 1960s and early 1970s when a different social context permitted different bundles of cultural beliefs to reach critical mass and capture social influence. We will return to the politicization of nuclear ambivalence in chapter 6's discussion of the anti-nuclear movement.

Conclusion

The cultural context of the 1950s and 1960s facilitated the creation of a highly centralized, promotionally-oriented government structure for managing nuclear policies. It also helped generate widespread optimism about the ease of containing nuclear hazards and the expected costs of nuclear power that was resistant to empirical challenge. These conditions insulated government nuclear support from political challenge and created a context conducive to long term private investment.

The dichotomous history of public responses to nuclear power (its early embrace and subsequent rejection) also demonstrates that there can be conflicting ideological traditions in a society that can serve as bases for collective action. Conjunctural factors, such as political alliances, historical accidents, and institutional design can sometimes be decisive in determining which combination of available cultural beliefs serves as the basis for political-economic decisions.

NPC: Institutional Dimensions

The most important institutional arrangements facilitating the expansion of nuclear power involved the centralized and insulated character of early government nuclear policy making. A similar phenomenon has characterized other nations' nuclear programs and often reflects the technology's military lineage and tradition of secrecy. Centralization avoided the policy delays common in more open environments and the possibility of pluralist dilution of pro-nuclear programs. In the U.S., the centralization was embodied in three measures: the preemption of state and local regulatory authority by federal regulations (established by the 1946 and 1954 Atomic Energy Acts and reaffirmed in the Northern States decision in 1971); the concentration of congressional authority in the Joint Committee on Atomic Energy (JCAE); and concentration of executive authority in the Atomic Energy Commission (AEC). The Joint Committee was virtually the only congressional committee with legislative jurisdiction empowered to hold substantive hearings on nuclear-related subjects. This monopoly was used to discourage the technology's critics from testifying at legislative hearings and mobilizing the investigatory powers of congress for critical review. The JCAE also acted as its own conference committee making it procedurally difficult to amend its legislative recommendations (Bupp and Derian 1981, 189).

The AEC exercised similarly centralized control over the executive dimensions of public policy. Of particular importance was nuclear power's early insulation from regulation by less sympathetic government agencies like the Public Health Service or Department of Labor. The AEC used its control over research funds, classification authority, and joint monopoly with the JCAE on official credibility, to manage the nuclear information environment in a promotional manner.

Judicial review was the one avenue for formal political activity not controlled by nuclear advocates. Early opposition to the technology often entered the planning context through this gap. The invulnerability of the French and Soviet programs to similar legal challenge contributed significantly to their lengthier expansion.

Other regulatory and institutional habits that facilitated nuclear expansion included: (1) the character of utility regulation, which created an apparently self-financing, expansionary industry, with powerful ties to financial capital; (2) the inbred character of nuclear sector training, which created a pool of commonly socialized professionals and subsequently linked university research agendas to prevailing industry technical choices[5]; and (3) the character of client relationships among the utilities, heavy electrical equipment suppliers, and utility industry consulting firms, which tended to vest planning power in the equipment suppliers.

NPC: Available Technical Information

It is difficult to portray the large nuclear power investments of the 1950s and 1960s as responses to planners' concern about available energy supply. Popular expectations anticipated minimal environmental and scarcity constraints on fossil fuel consumption and funded very little R&D in non-nuclear, non-fossil fuel energy development during most of this period.[6]

The respected 1958 National Planning Association study, *Nuclear Energy and the U.S. Fuel Economy 1955–1980*, for example, was relatively sanguine about the adequacy of conventional energy supplies (Teitelbaum 1958, 31, 84–5). As early as 1955 the Association's nuclear project reported,

"Middle East oil reserves are so huge and production costs so low that substantial increases in output . . . can be accomplished without substantial increases in cost. . . . Moreover, the availability of petroleum products from oil shale at prices not substantially higher than from crude is expected to deter the rise of oil prices in the U.S. for some time" (Joint Committee on Atomic Energy 1956b, 50). The report added, "Coal reserves in the U.S. are ample for centuries" (p. 54).[7]

In a private presidential briefing in 1959, the AEC indicated, "For our own economy, with but few exceptions, we do not need atomic energy power in the foreseeable future" (Balogh 1991, 178). In 1962, the widely-cited AEC study *Civilian Nuclear Power—A Report to the President* foresaw falling coal fired generating costs for the next forty years (JCAE 1968, 188, 220, 227). The Cambel study of U.S. energy R&D in 1964 concluded, "The findings of this staff study indicate no grounds for serious concern that the Nation is using up its stocks of fossil fuels too rapidly; rather there is the suspicion that we are using them up too slowly" (Cambel 1964, 54). Representatives of the conventional fuel industries and utilities testified annually during the 1950s that no pressing need existed for alternative energy development (Mullenbach 1963, 79).

While the 1952 President's Commission on Materials Policy (the Paley Commission) and the AEC's Putnam report in 1953 made economic cases for rapid nuclear development, the former placed an equal emphasis, and the latter a strong emphasis, on the simultaneous need for solar R&D. These recommendations were entirely ignored. Solar research received less than 1% of the nuclear budget during the next twenty years (Holloman and Grenon 1975, 83). Most of this sum was related to NASA's space projects. Alternative fossil fuel resources, such as innovative coal based technologies and shale oil, were also neglected (Mullenbach 1963, 90–91, 94–95, 320).

The major demand side rationale for large nuclear power R&D involved the explosive long term implications of unchecked exponential growth in energy demand. The enormous energy consumption levels suggested by the Putnam report in 1953 and the AEC Report to the President in 1962, both relied on demand forecasts relatively unchecked by feedback from energy price increases on energy efficiency.[8] It is highly unlikely that decision makers would have relied on such speculative long term projections without other underlying motives for supporting nuclear power development. The tenuousness of the demand side arguments for large nuclear investment, suggest that they were secondary rationales used to reinforce decisions made for other reasons. The private sector's failure to fund non-petroleum, non-nuclear energy development, reinforces the impression that the purely economic case for aggressive energy R&D was uncompelling.[9]

If not spurred by fears of energy scarcity, could nuclear energy investments (1955–1970) have been spurred by expectations of very low nuclear power generating costs? Yes and no. While there was certainly enough technical information about nuclear energy available to justify a modest and even an active nuclear power R&D program, there was very little basis for massive commercialization investments. One of the continuing ironies of nuclear power development has been that scientific, economic, and public interest in the technology have focused on long term rationales (such as energy scarcity and greenhouse hazard insurance) while public policy and corporate market strategies have focused on short term outcomes. The dichotomy is at the root of many of the technology's problems, such as the commercialization of premature designs with unconvincing safety features and uncertain economics.

As detailed in chapter 4, massive uncertainties have always accompanied nuclear cost forecasting. Through the late 1960s, there were no operating experience data from which to derive cost estimates for commercial-sized nuclear plants. Popular projections were based on optimistic scaling and learning curve assumptions. These predictions gave only cursory attention to the economic implications of containing nuclear externalities, such as accident hazards and thermal pollution. Waste disposal and decommissioning uncertainties were totally ignored in economic forecasts. The degree of indeterminacy introduced by these and other unknowns is evidenced by the more than 500% real cost increase in expected nuclear construction costs from 1963 to 1983, and the downgrading by 25% of expected plant capacity rates.[10]

The bottom line is that there was no compelling economic case for large public or private investments in commercial nuclear power plants in the 1950s and 1960s. The available technical information justified an active R&D program and perhaps some speculative risk taking by nuclear power entrepreneurs. Classic expected value calculations, however, need to be supplemented by some other motives or model of market behavior to explain the level of observed public and private nuclear power spending.

NPC Participants: The State

Government support was central to nuclear power's capture of Official Technology status. Government aid reflected cold war priorities and deference to the growth strategies of a number of large energy firms, rather than cost benefit calculations of the economic payoffs to nuclear energy R&D.

The early character of American nuclear policy was dominated by military concerns, focusing first on the development of atomic and hydrogen bombs, second on the production of significant amounts of weapons grade material, and finally on the development of reactors for naval and aircraft propulsion. During the mid-fifties the civilian side of U.S. nuclear technology grew as a by-product of military research. Civilian projects benefited directly from military experience and indirectly from the political support they received in anticipation of the military spinoffs that a healthy civilian nuclear sector might produce. The National Security Council, for example, proclaimed in 1953 that the early development of civilian nuclear power was a prerequisite for the national security goal of maintaining American dominance in the atomic field (Allen 1977, 30; Balogh 1991, 102).[11] The martial stamp is also borne by the French, British, and Russian atomic energy programs and helps explain the popularity of early nuclear power development efforts in the absence of a compelling economic logic.

Alongside promoting civilian nuclear power for its direct military spinoffs, the government sought to enhance U.S. international prestige and to extend U.S. dominance of nuclear weaponry by promoting and funding the Atoms for Peace program. The program promised easy access to American technology and U.S. stockpiles of enriched uranium in exchange for foreign

rians have emphasized the political influence of atomic scientists. This interpretation often seems to ascribe too much political clout to scientists and too much independence to government bureaucracies. When bureaucratic or scientific interests collided with cold war or corporate priorities, the latter generally triumphed. The prestigious scientist-laden General Advisory Committee, for example, lost much of its influence and was removed from the area of general policy making when it opposed the rapid development of the hydrogen bomb (Orlans 1967, 184–187). The AEC's first chairman, David Lilienthal, and its General Manager were similarly forced from office by a series of McCarthy-like hearings held by Senator Hickenlooper. Lilienthal has noted that the skepticism of some members of the General Advisory Committee concerning the feasibility of civilian nuclear power was ignored, while voices urging full-scale development were publicized (Lilienthal 1963, 98). A selective attention to scientific opinion also prevailed in the radiation and accident hazard areas. (See chapter 4.)

While the cold war consensus promoted nuclear expansion, even it was constrained by corporate priorities. Chief among these was the concern that nuclear power not become a Trojan horse for government ownership of key industries.[18] The tilt of state policy toward nuclear development thus reflected complex planning context interactions, rather than the unilateral fancy of nuclear scientists, the turf decisions of interested bureaucracies, or the simple assertion of military priorities.

NPC Participants: The Reactor Vendors[19]*

One of the legacies of the military atom was the creation of a group of powerful nuclear contractors with an interest in promoting a civilian version of the technology. The two most important firms were Westinghouse and General Electric. Despite enormous technical and economic uncertainties and the expectation of continued stiff competition from coal-fired electricity, the vendors had, by the late 1960s, committed well over a billion dollars to nuclear power development and assumed market risks rivaled only by commercial jet aircraft manufacturers and the U.S. computer industry (Little 1968, 24). The claim is not that the firms' nuclear commitments were demonstrably unsound, but that they were highly speculative. They were undertaken prior to the accumulation of definitive knowledge of nuclear's com-

---

*All costs in this section and throughout the remainder of the chapter are expressed in historical dollars unless otherwise specified.

mercial potential. The companies' goal was to transform their self-interested development choice into a self-fulfilling economy-wide prophecy.

Direct corporate involvement with nuclear energy began during World War II. While initial government nuclear contracts did not involve significant profits, they offered firms an information and expertise monopoly that created possibilities for massive commercial returns in the future. AEC contracting policies concentrated nuclear projects among very few firms. Besides managing the AEC's nine weapons material production reactors at Hanford, G. E. personnel staffed the AEC's $100 million Knolls research and development laboratory in Schenectady (Mullenbach 1963, 116). Westinghouse administered the AEC's $50 million Bettis lab in Pittsburgh and the naval reactor testing facility in Idaho. Both companies benefited greatly from their prime contracting for the nuclear navy. Westinghouse in particular gained enormous experience and commercial credibility from its successful design of the reactors for the majority of the navy's submarines (Little 1968, 140). Using its aircraft carrier reactor design, the company served as AEC contractor for the nation's first commercial power reactor at Shippingport, Pennsylvania in 1954. The company also received over 60% of the subsidized megawattage of the AEC's Power Reactor Demonstration Program (1956–1965) (Little 1968, 316). Though the AEC was quite aware of the oligopoly implications of its contracting policies, it resisted pressures for change in order to speed nuclear development.[20]

The nature of technical change in the nuclear sector raised the possibility that Westinghouse and G. E. could transform their initial headstart into permanent technological leadership. Because of the rapidly evolving character of the sector, contractor experience was built upon staff experience and general expertise rather than upon licenses or circumventable patents. The character of continuous innovation suggested a cumulative learning curve, like that in the turbine generator (T-G) industry. Westinghouse and G. E. could thus hope to maintain their nuclear leadership through the same high R&D/sales strategy they had employed in the T-G industry (Sultan 1974, 226–233).

Besides giving the companies a large headstart in technical matters, the firms' military contracts established valuable bureaucratic linkages and goodwill with the AEC. As the industry grew, AEC and contractor bureaucracies evolved collectively.[21] Over time a partnership emerged, illustrated by the "administrative contract" which committed the commission and contractor to a common project without specifying precise responsibilities. The relationship strengthened the firms' credibility with the utilities as reactor suppliers and long term maintenance resources (Little 1968, 22). It also insured that the companies' viewpoints would gain commission attention.

The duo's historical client relationships with the utilities also lent credibility to the firms' optimistic cost predictions and allowed them to mobilize traditional utility partners in the innovation process (Little 1968, 83, 361). In return for expected future discounts, for example, select utilities often served the equipment vendors as vehicles for de facto demonstration projects (Sultan 1974, 288–289). U.S. firms also enjoyed the advantage of traditional client relations with foreign utilities located in countries within the postwar U.S. sphere of influence, such as the Philippines, Japan, and Taiwan.

G. E. and Westinghouse were also well situated to capture popularly expected nuclear scale and vertical integration economies due to their: (1) access to strong internal and external financing; (2) organizational experience in coordinating large projects; (3) linked domination of the turbine-generator market; and (4) strong existing research laboratories.

The payoffs to Westinghouse and G. E.'s advantages in nuclear markets if nuclear power captured OT status were potentially enormous. In 1971, for example, the AEC estimated that total domestic expenditures for atomic power plants would top 100 billion dollars by 1985 and approximate 11 billion dollars annually thereafter (Dawson 1976, 141). Based on mid-seventies plant component and market share statistics, about 15% of these revenues would have been expected to accrue to the two firms. The former president of Westinghouse's Power Division gave an even more optimistic assessment of his company's potential nuclear revenues in 1973, stating, "Between now and the year 2000, the potential return to Westinghouse, just assuming it maintains its present share [38%] of the reactor market, could be $300 billion" (*Business Week* 2/24/73, 68). To put these numbers in perspective, G. E.'s total sales in 1968 were $7.7 billion, Westinghouse's sales were $2.9 billion.

From the dawn of the nuclear age, the two firms recognized their self-interest in nuclear expansion. The first director of Westinghouse's atomic division, for example, indicates, "Our perception of nuclear energy's commercial potential certainly accounted for a large part of our interest in the Navy work" (Hertsgaard 1983, 21). Other interviews with Westinghouse officials reveal that nuclear programs quickly assumed the highest priority in company planning (James Kuhn 1966, 93; Hewlett and Duncan 1974, 93, 97–98) and may have led the firm to sacrifice market share in the key turbine and aircraft industries (James Kuhn 1966).

G. E.'s interest in civilian nuclear power also animated its naval work (Hewlett and Duncan 1974, 35, 82). In the early sixties the firm established a Growth Council to construct a long term investment strategy. G. E. executives indicated in a *Fortune* interview that the company was searching for markets with anti-trust acceptable growth potential (i.e., markets with massive capital requirements and technologically determined economies of scale or other natural barriers to entry) (*Fortune* 10/70, 93). Nuclear power seemed an ideal solution as it also offered a chance to capitalize on G. E.'s AEC contract experience.

Based on similar reasoning, G. E. had constructed a $20 million reactor research complex in Pleasanton, California, in the late fifties (Nehrt 1966, 259). It also contracted (at an expected loss of $15–$20 million, all mid-fifties $) to build the Dresden I reactor for a consortium of utilities headed by Commonwealth Edison (*Fortune* 10/70, 91). The company's demand that the utilities decline government subsidy assistance freed G. E. from the extra limitations on patentable innovation and proprietary information that government participation entailed. The company built the Humboldt Bay plant in the early sixties under similar patent terms. It agreed to share its research results with the AEC in return for government funding at the Big Rock plant in Michigan, only after considerable Commission pressure (Nehrt 1966, 259–260). The cost of such information disclosure has proved minor. The relevant technical expertise and marketing advantages gained from the projects appear to have been institutionally embodied. As Nehrt's study of reactor development 1954–1962 concludes, the evidence is "that it is not patent rights nor the published technical data which are important. Rather it is the technological know-how, built up within the company carrying out the research and development for the USAEC, which is of value . . ." (Nehrt 1966, 330, see also Orlans 1967, 48).

Despite G. E.'s sense of technical success, the company received only three domestic orders from 1955 to 1962 and feared a massive devaluation of its expertise or "organizational capital." As the G. E. vice president in charge of the Growth Council, John McKitterick, recalls,

> "We had a problem like a lump of butter sitting in the sun. . . . If we couldn't get orders out of the utility industry, with every tick of the clock it became progressively more likely that some competing technology would be developed that would supersede the economic viability of our own. Our people understood this was a game of massive stakes, and that if we didn't force the utility industry to put those stations on line, we'd end up with nothing" (*Fortune* 10/70, 93).

In effect, G. E. perceived the development process in OT terms, and as a result, (to be followed quickly by Westinghouse) offered the "turnkey" contract, which offered the utilities fully constructed power plants at a fixed price. Both G. E. and Westinghouse perceived the contracts as loss leader extensions of their R&D programs. Though complete data has never been released, most conventional estimates suggest losses in the 800 million dollar to billion dollar range, with per unit subsidies of about 50% on the thirteen plants.[22] General Atomics appears to have lost a similar amount on its nuclear programs, with at least half of this sum tied to the Fort Saint Vrain turnkey plant.[23] The 1968 A. D. Little study also estimates that through the mid-sixties about half of the non-turnkey reactor sales were sold at bargain prices (Little 1968, 23). The vendors also extended various performance warranties, including the absorption of the cost of regulatory escalation in the licensing process (Little 1968, 153; Pringle and Spigelman 1981, 269). Similarly bold guarantees were extended foreign purchasers (Nehrt 1966, 276). European LWR vendors appear to have adopted similar pricing (Bupp and Derian 1981, 87). Framatome, for example, funded four loss leader plants in 1970 and 1971 (Pringle and Spigelman 1981, 354).

Westinghouse's marketing strategy also guaranteed twenty-seven utilities an eighty million pound supply of uranium at an average price of $9.50/lb. (*Nuclear Industry* 7/77; Duffy and Adams 1978, 29). Partly due to the uranium producers cartel, the market price had risen to more than $40/lb. by the end of 1977. As a result, Westinghouse was forced to renege on its multi-billion dollar contracts. The company has since been engaged in a series of lawsuits totaling $2.5 billion. Though more cautious than Westinghouse, G. E. reportedly lost $500 million through similar guarantees (Duffy and Adams 1978, 34).

Though the turnkey losses were apparently larger than expected, the promotional strategy proved successful. The subsidized plants literally transformed the industry from an idea into a concrete reality. They laid the psychological groundwork for what Philip Sporn has called the "great bandwagon market" of 1966–1967. During this period the utilities contracted for fifty-eight plants, increasing ordered nuclear capacity from 2,000 megawatts (MW) to 45,000 MW (AEC 1971a). In the words of G. E. Vice President Bertram Wolfe, "The turnkeys made the light water reactor a viable product. . . . They got enough volume in the business that we could build an engineering staff, standardize our product, and put up facilities to mass-produce things so that the cost went down. That way we got over this tailor-made, one-of-a-kind, high-cost plant" (Hertsgaard 1983, 43).

As intended, the subsidies also drove out most of the competition.[24] In 1954 there had been some twenty firms seeking a foothold in the reactor field. This number had fallen to ten by 1959, and only four or five remained shortly after the turnkey plants (Allen and Melnik 1970, 392).

Besides investing in reactor capital equipment and loss-leader marketing strategies, the companies actively pursued vertical integration opportunities. By the mid- to late-seventies, G. E. was: the seventh largest holder of domestic uranium reserves; the fourth largest uranium miller; one of five fuel fabricators; one of four reactor vendors; one of two nuclear turbine-generator vendors; one of three fuel reprocessing firms; a partner with Exxon in a major fuel enrichment R&D project; and a major nuclear weapons contractor.

By the late seventies Westinghouse was similarly diversified. While less active than G. E. in the mining and milling end of the fuel cycle, the company was more active in the engineering and enrichment areas. It also subcontracted fewer aspects of its nuclear steam supply system (Hayes and Zarsky 7/84, 21).

The breeder reactor offered the greatest growth potential for both companies. Its internally-generated fuel source and massive capital costs ensured an Exxon-like role for its contractors if adopted as part of an all-electric economy. From very early in nuclear development, visions of a breeder-fired energy sector animated the AEC's promotional strategy and the duopoly's long run plans. G. E., for example, fell behind Westinghouse in the light water reactor market because it initially sought to jump directly to breeder designs. In 1968, Westinghouse indicated breeder development was its number one R&D project (*New York Times* 4/4/68, 76).

Complementing their market activities, G. E. and Westinghouse promoted nuclear expansion by influencing the informational, ideological, and political environments surrounding energy planning. The firms' technical expertise and the AEC's decision not to create an independent research capacity in many areas left the vendors with significant functional authority in regulatory matters.[25] Despite egregious exceptions, the firms probably acted in good faith in the vast majority of technical matters. The problems created by their technical optimism reflect the dangers posed by insulated research environments rather than purposeful deceit. The firms' successful promotion of excessively optimistic cost projections is less innocent. (See chapter 4.) The companies have also intervened in the electoral process, contributing $215,000, for example, to help defeat the California and Maine anti-nuclear referendums (*Business Week* 6/7/76; *Groundswell* 9/80) and financed pro-nuclear public relations campaigns. Westinghouse, for example, has cultivated campus audiences.[26]

Rivalry Dynamics

Much like inter-technology competition for OT status, intra-nuclear industry competition for market share spurred nuclear investment. The electrical equipment manufacturers' experience in the turbine-generator market, where production costs were a declining function of market share, spurred aggressive sales campaigns and design choices geared towards winning immediate rather than long term results.[27] As early as 1948, the director of the AEC's Argonne National Laboratory complained that G. E.-Westinghouse competition was forcing hasty reactor choices (Hertsgaard 1983, 23). Describing the late 1950s, Commonwealth Edison Chairman Thomas Ayers, indicates, "Everybody was in there cutting each other's throats. . . . The people in the business were anxious to be up front in this new technology, so they were willing to offer plants or equipment at more favorable prices than otherwise. . . . In the big capital goods businesses, the thing you don't want to be is left behind" (Hertsgaard 1983, 34).[28] Rivalry dynamics within the nuclear steam supply system also spilled over into linked markets. Two firms, Babcock and Wilcox, and Combustion Engineering, for example, were pressured to enter the reactor market by the threat of Westinghouse and General Electric's cannibalization of the linked thermal equipment market. Due to vertical integration economies, the newcomers were forced to enter other areas of the nuclear field as well. In assessing market entry, the firms appear to have faced asymmetric risks. Participation in an unsuccessful nuclear industry threatened a large but one time loss. Failure to enter a viable nuclear industry threatened permanent market exclusion.

Describing what appears to be Babcock and Wilcox's decision-making, a company official stated,

> "Our concern was purely defensive. We had built equipment for energy transfer [for over sixty years], and we felt compelled to keep up to date with nuclear energy if we were to survive in our chosen field. . . . What alarmed us, however, was the decision by these two companies [Westinghouse and General Electric] to build their own components. We realized that they were organizing their facilities to include our part and share of the business. We decided immediately that we would have to jump all the way in and do it quickly if we were not to lose out" (James Kuhn 1966, 160,189).

Combustion Engineering Vice President William Connolly's explanation for his company's nuclear investment, reveals similar deference to gathering OT dynamics. Connolly indicates,

> "We went in at a time when the projections were that half of the additional installed capacity for the rest of the century would be nuclear. . . . That meant that the market for our most fundamental product, namely steam supply systems, would be literally cut in half if we stayed in only coal. So in order to protect our birthright as a company, we had to go in" (Hertsgaard 1983, 46).

The oil companies' nuclear fuel cycle investments in the late sixties and early seventies, which raised the likelihood of industry-wide surplus capacity, partially reflect a similar logic. Once established, the reactor market generated an internal momentum. Westinghouse's increasing consolidation of market leadership in the early 1960s led to G. E.'s 1963 turnkey offer. Westinghouse responded with similar terms. The scaling battles of the mid-sixties reflected similar dynamics. Because significant efficiencies were believed to accompany larger megawatt plants, the vendors rushed to offer the utilities larger and larger capacity designs in order to capture reactor orders and learning curve advantages. From most accounts, the technological leaps required were beyond the prudent management of the competing vendors.[29] The result was the employment of relatively expensive development and construction techniques and the toleration of potential safety hazards (Hertsgaard 1983, Bodde 1975).

In a late-seventies interview, for example, Babcock and Wilcox official James Deddens admitted that companies would sometimes "go out on a technical limb" to win orders. "When you get into that kind of competitive situation . . . (Deddens indicated) you may sell something that hasn't been tested as thoroughly as it would be today" (Hertsgaard 1983, 64). More than ten years earlier, James Kuhn's discussants from what appears to be Babcock and Wilcox similarly acknowledged ". . . (the company) went out and got orders and then we tried to get the people to do the work . . . We didn't really know what was involved in our research and development program" (Kuhn 1966, 164–166). The scaling race was finally stopped by AEC intervention, in the form of a licensing ceiling of 1300 MW (Hertsgaard 1983 64).[30]

The A. D. Little study of 1968 found the same dynamics spilling over into research and development and investment in a new generation of reactors. The study reported, ". . . the five current thermal reactor manufacturers are all participating in breeder reactor design and development. At least part of the reason for this is that in order to be considered progressive suppliers by current utility customers, it is almost essential that these manufacturers also participate in the development of expected future generation reactor types. The same is true for participants in a number of other segments of the industry . . ." (p. 401).

Considering the implications of competition in the heavy electrical equipment industry more generally, Sultan writes,

> "Many economists worry about the 'quiet life' and technological sluggishness which they suspect to be a pervasive tendency in oligopolistic market structures. In recent years the problem seems more often to have been the reverse: oligopolies in high-technology settings have been too willing to escalate the technological competition, and to promise products and technologies that do not yet exist

and which will be rushed to the customer in untested form . . ." (Sultan 1974, 224).

Summary

Nuclear power's market characteristics, its technically determined oligopolistic market structure, open-ended growth potential, and opportunities for cooperative development through existing arrangements between public and private bureaucracies, attracted strong support from General Electric and Westinghouse. The companies sought to transform their competitive advantages in the nuclear field into extraordinary profits (realized quasi-rents). In particular they sought to capitalize on their relative monopoly on military reactor design experience; marketing advantages due to existing client relationships with the utilities and federal energy bureaucracy; and greater access to nuclear scale, vertical integration, and learning curve efficiencies. Even though both companies already possessed strong market positions in fossil fuel fired generation, the potential prize in nuclear markets was much greater. As G. E.'s 1972 annual report noted,

> "Our potential revenue base in a nuclear plant, for example, is some six times that of a fossil fuel plant because we can supply the reactor, the fuel, and fuel re-loads, as well as turbine-generators and their auxiliary equipment" (Nader and Abbotts 1979, 265).

G. E. and Westinghouse's behavior demonstrates how modern corporate planning encourages technical innovation in areas already organized by large corporations or amenable to such management. The large firm's access to retained earnings, external financing, and the public bureaucracies organizing state planning, facilitates oligopolistic-oriented technical change. Alongside nuclear power, for example, G. E.'s Growth Council committed the company to computer and jet aircraft production. Both of these choices reflected the same quest for capital intensive oligopolistic market investments.

NPC Participants: The Utilities

The utilities' nuclear purchases reflected aspects of advocacy-promotional planning by a group of fifteen or so activist pro-nuclear utilities,[31] a deference to the OT momentum generated by the reactor vendors and AEC-

JCAE by many passive utilities, and the growth oriented institutional and ideological context organizing utility decisions. The analysis contradicts the popularly-held belief that the utilities were dragged kicking and screaming into nuclear commitments by the federal government and reactor vendors.

The utility industry has been commonly portrayed as a technologically lazy one, composed of passive firms allocating only .025% sales to R&D, as opposed to a national average of 2% and a 4%–10% range in the most innovative sectors. This picture is misleading. While the utilities did not directly fund significant research, they encouraged the equipment manufacturers to pursue a high R&D/sales development strategy.[32] Many of the largest companies actively participated in the innovation process by self-consciously funding de facto demonstration plants.

From 1954–1963 the utilities participated in fourteen reactor projects at a total cost of more than $750 million (mixed historical $). About $300 million of this sum can be considered R&D spending (Cohn 1986, 129–132). The outlay is about twice that spent on R&D by the coal sector over the same years (Cohn 1986, 131–2). From 1965–1974 the utilities ordered a startling 223 nuclear plants (DOE 0438(91), 105–110), funding one of the most rapid growth curves for a new energy source in the history of the energy sector. The utilities' adoption of nuclear power appears modest only in comparison with the breakneck pace recommended by the AEC, JCAE, and nuclear industry.

The utilities' nuclear policies illustrate anew how corporate cultures and growth strategies, regulatory regimes, and technological aesthetics can influence the direction of technical change. The U.S. utility industry (1950–1974) involved a complex blend of public utility commission regulations, market competition within those regulations, management traditions, habits of client relationships with equipment suppliers and consultants, and informal linkages to regional planning initiatives involving state and local governments, local energy consuming industries, local nuclear power related industries, and the banks who finance much of the utilities' long term debt. The utilities' support for nuclear expansion reflected pro-nuclear inputs from all of these phenomena.

Nuclear Power and Utility Growth Strategies

Nuclear power's central power station format, growth potential, and capital intensity encouraged a number of large utilities to promote nuclear expansion as a vehicle for their own expansion. Towards the end of the 1960s, concern over potential environmental constraints on coal usage and fears of diminishing returns to fossil fuel R&D also spurred some utility interest in nuclear technologies.[33]

Since the early twentieth century the corporate culture of the utility industry has celebrated increased electricity provision as a social good and sales growth as a business strategy. Abetted by technological change and scale economies that created falling long run marginal costs, utility executives actively promoted increased electricity demand. The latter permitted new plant construction (and new equipment sales and R&D financing for the electric equipment manufacturers) which further lowered electricity costs, spurring additional demand and a new cycle. Richard Hirsh (1989) writes,

> ". . . utility engineers clung to the popular views associated with the liberating power of electricity . . . . [G]rowth constituted an essential element of the grow-and-build strategy. Individually and collectively (through the National Electric Light Association—an industry trade organization), utilities pursued the goal of growth by engaging in a series of publicity and propaganda activities throughout the years . . ." (33).

> "The biggest concerted promotional push began in 1956 with the 'Live Better Electrically' campaign. Conceived of by the General Electric Company . . ." (51).

> "Utility journals exhorted, 'Sell or Die!' and 'Sell—and Sell—and Sell'. . . . Meanwhile in a famous 'Inventing Our Future' speech in 1964, Sporn noted that 'the most important elements that determine our loads are not those that happen, but those that we project—that we invent—in the broad sense of the term 'invention.' You have a control over such loads: you invent them, and then you can make plans for the best manner of meeting them'" (53).

Coupled with an engineering ideology that celebrated technical progress and a tendency for managerial salaries and prestige to be correlated with firm size, the industry's history created a powerful momentum for growth-oriented decision-making.[34] The widespread expectation of enormous electricity markets if generating costs could be kept from rising steeply and the utilities' apparently guaranteed ability to recover outlays for de facto demonstration plants, made "risk-taking" in pursuit of new generating technology an attractive option. More than any other foreseeable technology, nuclear power seemed to promise the possibility of an all-electric economy, replete with electric heating, electric cars, and nuclear desalinization.

Several formal and informal aspects of electric utility regulation similarly encouraged nuclear initiatives. The technology's capital intensity recommended nuclear power to utility planners because ratebase regulation allowed only flow through recovery for operating expenses (basically labor and fuel) and cost-plus for capital outlays. As long as the allowed rate of return was higher than financing charges, firms had an incentive to invest in capital intensive generating choices.[35]

Public Utility Commissions' rate adjustment policies may have also encouraged nuclear orders by encouraging risk taking in capital contracting (Burness et al. 5/80). The investor owned utilities (IOUs) could expect quick recovery for cost overruns, and belated, if any, regulatory recapture of cost underruns. The decline in regulatory tolerance of overruns since 1974 has sharply discouraged nuclear orders.

Rivalry Dynamics

The character of competition in the utility sector also spurred nuclear initiatives. Although electric generation and distribution was a regulated market with fixed service areas, utilities competed to attract new industry to their geographic region, and to capture an institutional slot in an increasingly concentrated industry. As in the electric equipment field, rivalry dynamics created an asymmetric perception of the risks associated with laggard or excessive nuclear investment. Fear of potentially enduring disadvantage within an economical nuclear technology dominated fear of short term losses from potentially inefficient nuclear plants. This dynamic operated most intensely amidst the rivalry between publicly-owned and investor-owned utilities, high and low fossil fuel cost regions, and large and small utilities.

The large IOUs were attracted to the technology by anticipated scale economies. Industry and government cost projections have generally predicted reductions of 20% or more for doublings in nuclear plant size.[36] The inability to take advantage of such scaling economies foreshadowed increased absorption of small publicly-owned municipal utilities by systems able to finance and integrate into their grid large megawatt projects. Commenting on the implications of nuclear power for the structure of the utility industry in 1969, the chairman of Commonwealth Edison (the nation's most nuclear-oriented utility) declared,

> ". . . big plants, big transmission lines and big distribution systems are more economical. . . . Nuclear tends to accelerate this trend toward bigness. . . . The continued existence of small operators and small plants may not be threatened but the economic gap between these and large generating complexes certainly will grow. . . ." (J. Harris Ward, "Nuclear Energy and the Electric Power Industry,"

Proceedings of the 1967 Conference, Atomic Industrial Forum, 297–298).

The most ambitious utilities may have perceived nuclear power as a medium for absorbing fairly large competitors and emerging as a "mega-utility."[37] Over the last 50 years the private production and distribution of electricity has followed the classic pattern (with interruptions) of centralization of most of American industry. In 1927 there were 2135 separate IOUs, in 1945 about 1000, and in 1970 about 300 (Senate Judiciary Committee 1970, 410). In the late 1960s, the president of the largest utility holding company predicted that there would be only 12–15 mega-utilities within 50 years (*Fortune* 11/69). Many recent institutional reforms proposed for the nuclear sector have called for similar concentration, as is the case with nuclear power generation in England, France, and Japan.

Learning curve competition among large utilities (who act as their own power plant construction engineers) may have similarly encouraged early nuclear orders, just as efforts to "get in on the ground floor" spurred some political entities (like New York State) to encourage their utilities to invest in nuclear plants. High cost fossil fuel regions, such as New England and New York, also promoted nuclear development as a means for reducing their energy cost disadvantage.

The most important rivalry, however, was between public and private power. The IOUs had historical reasons to be wary of the growth of a public sector nuclear electricity industry. Public power had grown from 5% of all electricity generated in the U.S. in 1933 to nearly 25% in 1960. Its advance had been spearheaded by the the the TVA, which the AEC's first chairman, David Lilienthal, had directed. The military aspects of nuclear power had produced a legacy of information classification and government ownership along the nuclear fuel cycle that threatened to extend to electricity production.

Although the AEC was ideologically committed to transferring nuclear technology to the private sector, the commission's top priority was rapid nuclear development. The AEC and the nuclear industry were thus quick to use fears of nuclear TVAs to promote private investment. AEC Chairman Lewis Strauss warned in 1957

". . . if industry does not submit acceptable proposals for reactor plants of the types considered ready for full-scale demonstration and construction, the commission will request funds to initiate such projects under complete federal financing" (JCAE 1957, 16; see also JCAE 1956c, 36–39; and AIF, *Forum Memo* 1/57, 3).[38]

In response to these pressures the IOUs lobbied Congress against public nuclear power. The utilities also increased their own nuclear spending (Mullenbach 1963, 139,104). As early as 1955 the *Wall Street Journal* reported

> "The United States with abundant cheap coal and oil, really has no urgent need for atomic power. Officials of the companies which make reactors say frankly most of their utility company customers have no early expectation of cutting costs by building atom plants; their primary motive is to stake this out as an area of private rather than public power" (*Wall Street Journal* 8/22/55, 1).[39]

Interestingly, similar private/public sector competition also seems to have spurred private nuclear initiatives in Japan and Germany (Pringle and Spigelman 1981, 323–324, 541).

Besides reflecting their own growth strategies, the utilities' nuclear initiatives often reflected the planning visions of local business interests and their public sector sponsors. The first commercial nuclear power project was initiated in 1954 by agreement between the AEC and Duquesne Light to build the government-owned Shippingport reactor, using Westinghouse's naval reactor design.[40] Duquesne's nuclear initiative represented a planning thrust by Pittsburgh's concentrated energy interests (Westinghouse, the city's energy-intensive metallurgical industry, and local banks) to facilitate the development of a new Westinghouse-dominated energy technology. The regulated cash flow of Pittsburgh's local utility was used as the financial instrument for the development project (Sneddon, "Nuclear Web" series, *Beaver County Times* 12/23–31/74). Duquesne has traditionally had a close relationship with Westinghouse, purchasing all seven of its turbine generators from the company during 1948–1962, and additional reactors in 1967 and 1971.

A Brief History of Utility Nuclear Investments

The history of utility nuclear spending during 1955–1969 reveals its costliness and strategic motives. Utility initiatives can be divided into four clusters: (1) the first IOU financed and owned projects (1955–1963); (2) the three rounds of the AEC's Power Reactor Demonstration Program (1955–1963); (3) the turnkey years (12/63–1966); and (4) the bandwagon market (1966–1969).[41]

IOU Owned Plants 1955–1963

From 1955 to 1959 the utilities funded four private sector reactors. The plants were not expected to produce least cost power.[42] Explaining the motives behind the investments, economist Richard Tybout wrote in 1957,

". . . Why might so much nuclear capacity be installed when it will result in costs above those of alternative conventional facilities? . . . the incentive [is] to gain know-how. . . . There is evidence that just such an approach is being taken by designers of nuclear reactors and equipment, but this does not take care of our present problem, for the contract prices entered into by supply firms were used as a starting point for the 1960 nuclear cost figures. . . . To explain the installation of high-cost nuclear capacity, we must turn to the electric power industry itself. . . . [T]he operation of a full-scale electric power station at a cost above that of alternative methods in order to advance technology is something of an extension of the research concept . . ." (Tybout 1957, 359–360).

The fifth and only other nuclear plant to be completely financed by the utilities before the turnkey orders was Niagara Mohawk's Nine Mile Point project, purchased in 1963. It was generally expected to have higher generating costs than available fossil fuel alternatives (Cohn 1986, 200) and was undertaken as a technology-promoting investment. Like its predecessors, the company soon announced an ambitious follow-up nuclear expansion plan.[43] Like Duquesne's Westinghouse reactor purchases, Niagara's Nine Mile Point order of a G. E. reactor can be linked to the vendor's operation of major turbine-generator and nuclear facilities in the utility's service area.[44]

Nine Mile Point also reflected the nuclear promotionalism and corporate planning vision of New York's Governor Nelson Rockefeller, whose family had very early ties to the nuclear industry.[45] As governor, Rockefeller attempted to make New York State a center for nuclear technology, partially in an effort to overcome the state's disadvantaged position within a fossil fueled economy,[46] and partially because the technology's limitless energy potential, capital intensiveness, large scaling economies, and advanced scientific base fit well with his financier-industrialist vision of progress.

Seconding Rockefeller's nuclear strategy was NY Power Authority Chairman Robert Moses, who asserted in 1961,

"Modern steam plants in the Ohio Valley, in western Pennsylvania and in the Southeast can produce power for about 4 or 5 mills. . . .

To produce power from the newest coal plants in the New York City area costs about 8 mills. . . . [W]ith power produced from coal, gas or oil New York can not hope to overcome this disadvantage. . . . But eventually power from nuclear fuels should be cheaper than coal. When atomic research has progressed to that point New York will again be able to compete with other areas in power costs."[47]

Building on G. E.'s existing New York activities, Rockefeller sought to win a synergistic economic advantage by promoting linked nuclear initiatives.[48] Included was support for power generation, fuel processing, materials transport, and desalinization projects. Efforts to coordinate nuclear promotion with the state's private sector were facilitated by the creation of a General Advisory Committee (chaired by G. E. Vice President Francis McCune) in the late fifties, and the IOU's joint formation of Empire State Atomic Development Associates (ESADA) in 1960. Like the New England Yankee Atomic and Connecticut Yankee projects (briefly discussed below), ESADA's activities represented a collective IOU response to regional fuel cost disadvantage and the threat of publicly owned nuclear power plants.[49]

State planning was aggressive. In 1959 the Office of Atomic Development sought to gain greater regulatory control over local atomic energy activities in order to facilitate private investment (JCAE 1960a, 359). In the same year, a nuclear research center was established at the University of Buffalo and a study undertaken to identify nuclear development projects worthy of state support (JCAE 1960a, 364). In 1960 plans were announced to promote the local siting of a nuclear fuel reprocessing plant, a high level waste disposal facility, a materials testing reactor, and a nuclear port facility. A program was also initiated to promote greater use of industrial isotopes (JCAE 1960a, 359–360). By the late-sixties, the state had given its nuclear development authorities license to float tax exempt bonds to subsidize private nuclear R&D, land use powers to facilitate nuclear siting, funds to develop nuclear desalinization (AEC 1968a, 11–12; AIF, *Nuclear Industry* 12/64, 43), and monies to subsidize the construction of a private fuel reprocessing facility.[50] Also proposed by Governor Rockefeller were subsidies for a fast breeder reactor project, a plutonium fuel fabrication facility, and permanent financing assistance for nuclear plant equipment.

Utility PRDP Projects 1955–1963

Like Rockefeller's NY initiatives and the utilities' spending for the first IOU owned and financed plants (1955–1963), the utilities' contributions to the government subsidized Power Reactor Demonstration Program (PRDP) (1955–1963) reflected a technology-forcing investment strategy. Several large IOUs and a group of multi-sized New England utilities participated in the PRDP plants.[51]

The Yankee Atomic PRDP project represented a collective R&D response by a group of New England utilities to the region's fossil fuel cost disadvantage.[52] As the consortium's president, William Webster, told the JCAE in 1955,

> "New England has no natural deposits of coal or oil, and must import its requirements of these fuels, resulting in relatively higher fuel costs in its conventional thermal plants. For that reason *we feel a particular urgency to assist in the necessary next step toward the development of economically competitive atomic power* (emphasis added). . . . New England is also rich in the engineering skill and the technical industrial know-how necessary for the successful development of such a pioneer plant, and we are confident that we will have full and able support for our venture in this respect. In addition, we believe that the early installation of an atomic power plant will have an important stimulating effect in the New England industries most closely connected with the broader development of peacetime uses of atomic energy" (JCAE 1955, 594).

Detroit Edison's Fermi breeder project best illustrates the expansive nuclear vision behind many of the utilities' PRDP initiatives. The Fermi plant was the most technically ambitious PRDP proposal. The plant cost its private sector sponsors $110 million and eventually suffered a partial meltdown. The breeder design was simultaneously the most difficult engineering challenge and the most promising long run growth technology available to the utility industry. Even the normally optimistic AEC staff believed the project to be technically premature (Allen 1977, 51). The driving force behind the project was Walker Cisler, Detroit Edison's president and an ideological champion of private enterprise. In his battle to win support for the plant, and forestall government owned nuclear power plants, he warned that rejection meant, "We are headed down the socialist road" (Fuller 1975, 51).

The Turnkey Years (1963–1966) and Bandwagon Aftermath (1963–1969)

The turnkey period opened in December 1963 with G. E. slashing prices and guaranteeing capital costs for its Oyster Creek plant of $132/KW. Similar terms were maintained by G. E. and Westinghouse through 1966, and twelve turnkey (fixed price) contracts were signed. Another sixteen plants were purchased during the 1964–1966 period under non-turnkey, basically cost-plus, terms (AEC 1974a). As noted earlier, the turnkey discounts were crucial in persuading the utility industry of the validity of the promotional claims made for nuclear power by its vendor-government sponsors. Still, more than two-thirds of the twenty-eight turnkey plants sold were bought by utilities who had already participated in a private or PRDP nuclear project, suggesting that utility receptivity augmented the impact of the turnkey terms.

Throughout the 1954–1969 period a core group of approximately fifteen utilities played an "active-firm" role in winning Official Technology status for nuclear power. By purchasing de facto demonstration plants, and often publicly championing the competitiveness of the technology, the firms helped stimulate intra-industry rivalry dynamics and the capture of scale economies and learning curve cost reductions. Along with the AEC/JCAE and vendors, they fused their growth strategies into a critical mass development path.

The neglect and at times hostility of many large utilities towards energy options without economies of scale or those that would permit increased competition from non-central power station sources also reveals the impact of institutional self-interest on technical evolution.[53] Early nuclear pioneers, such as Consolidated Edison, PG&E, and Consumers Power, for example, exhibited disinterest and/or opposition to several alternative energy options. The IOUs similarly opposed conservation-oriented policies such as peak load pricing prior to the credit crunch of the mid-seventies (Gandara 1977, 81). Many accounts indicate that the utilities aggressively retarded cogeneration technologies, paying cogenerators less than competitive market values for grid feed-ins, charging them prejudiciously high back-up rates, and placing procedural obstacles in the way of grid hook-ups.[54] The research agenda of the utilities' collectively financed research institute, the Electric Power Research Institute (EPRI), during the OT years also reflected the industry's pursuit of centralized generating technologies. In 1980, for example, the Institute allocated funds in a 70:1 ratio for nuclear and solar projects, with most of its solar spending earmarked for centralized solar technologies (*Power Line* 10/81).

As chapter 12 demonstrates, a wide variety of previously ignored technologies, such as wind and biomass energy systems, now appear competitive with nuclear power. The economics of energy conservation seem even more favorable. The fact that these options only received utility attention after anti-nuclear protests and IOU financing difficulties sidetracked the nuclear option suggests the socially-determined character of technological realms of discourse.

OT Momentum: 1954–@1969

Externally generated OT momentum complemented the pro-nuclear utilities' internal motivations for nuclear investments. The AEC, JCAE, and reactor vendors' promotional campaigns helped induce a bandwagon psychology among passive firms.[55] The more than 3:1 ratio of average plant size ordered to the largest plant in operation through 1967, and more than 25:1 ratio of ordered nuclear capacity to operating nuclear capacity in 1969 (AEC 1974c), reveal the minimal data about actual (rather than predicted) nuclear plant costs available to utility decision makers prior to their nuclear commitments. The utilities' nuclear risk taking is especially surprising in the light of the industry's previous commitment to incremental, rather than large design and scaling changes.

Non-turnkey plants ultimately cost about 175% of predicted costs (in constant $). All plants, including turnkeys, were vulnerable to poor capacity performance and through 1990 the most common sized plants (800+ MW) performed at only 3/4 their expected capacity rate. Many of these units have also had to be expensively retrofitted to meet upgraded safety requirements and unexpected technical problems.[56] The utilities also faced uncertain fuel, maintenance, waste disposal, and reactor decommissioning costs.

While there was also a degree of uncertainty associated with fossil fuel generating costs, it was much smaller than that associated with nuclear power, due to the relative maturity of the two technologies and the known character of coal deposits. The asserted cost advantage of nuclear projects often rested on a claimed edge of only .5M/kwh (Perry 1977, 37; Zimmerman 1987, 90) or a differential of 5%–15%. The utilities' decision to contract for $13 billion (mixed historical $)[57] of nuclear capacity during 1963–1969 is thus puzzling without appeal to the logic of OT dynamics and related impact of bandwagon psychology.

Three factors left the utilities especially vulnerable to bandwagon pressures: 1) the biased character of the institutional environment dominating nuclear information production and circulation; 2) the perceived self-fulfilling prophecy character of nuclear cost optimism; and 3) the cyclical character of heavy electrical equipment purchasing. Most of these factors reflected the decision making context created by nuclear's sponsors, rather than the vagaries of imperfect information or random error. They were endogenous to the OT process.

The information on nuclear economics available to the utilities during the bandwagon years was dominated by vendor-AEC/JCAE promotional campaigns. Even nuclear skeptics like Sporn and the National Coal Association acknowledged as late as the mid-sixties that their cost projections relied primarily on vendor supplied material (JCAE 1968, 93; *Electrical World* 8/31/64). Vendor marketing activities, such as the loss-leader turnkeys, were partly responsible for mistaken cost expectations. More influential, however, was the impact of vendor-AEC dominance of nuclear power research. The pair's activities were directed towards finding technical solutions to known engineering problems, and not towards uncovering potential nuclear hazards. This focus was reflected in the kinds of data collected, the methodologies used to organize information, and the attention given to anomalous findings. The resulting research minimized the economic implications of the technology's negative externalities, and thus generated misleadingly optimistic cost projections (see chapter 4).

Many observers have also suggested that the electric utilities image as a staid, backwater industry made it difficult to recruit talented young engineers and MBAs after World War II (Hirsh 1989, 111–121). Numerous industry studies, salary surveys, and academic rankings in the fifties and sixties suggest that the best electrical engineering students were drawn to the aerospace and electronics industries, leaving the utilities ill prepared to challenge the optimism of the AEC and reactor vendors (ibid.).[58] The utilities' tendency to mistakenly assume only modest differences between fossil fuel and nuclear engineering requirements exacerbated the firms' manpower shortcomings.

The spread of nuclear optimism from the vendors and AEC to the utilities is a fascinating example of ideological diffusion. The optimism often came "embodied" in personnel previously employed (and socialized) by the vendors (James Kuhn 1966, 142) and/or AEC.[59] It was mediated through trade journals inundated with nuclear industry-AEC promotional literature. Utility staff members often participated in formal and informal AEC training programs and many received early hands-on experience within industry-wide demonstration projects like Fermi (James Kuhn 1966, 145). These individuals reproduced the promotional outlook of their training within their home firm, serving as instructors for new generations of nuclear personnel (James Kuhn 1966, 147). The utilities self-consciously pursued a very passive attitude towards the training process, choosing to prepare the minimal number of staff in the least expensive fashion. James Kuhn of Columbia's Graduate School of Business writes,

> "Before actual construction of a nuclear plant begins, none of the companies ever had more than a small handful of men, sometimes no more than one and usually no more than four, who had any exposure to, or experience with, nuclear technology. So small a number of 'experts' was sufficient in the eyes of the managers. To train or prepare any more employees in nuclear technology before a

company made a commitment to build a nuclear plant was both unnecessary and unwise. . . .

Even during the training period employees did not usually devote full time to courses or to on-the-job instruction. They usually worked at their jobs part time, except when away from the company at a national laboratory or reactor test station. One company, for example, required their engineers to work every other day alternating regular assignments with classroom studies. For less highly skilled personnel, studies might amount to no more than one class day a week or every two weeks. The instructors were usually the engineers who had trained at ORSORT, or at NRTS Idaho, or with the manufacturer" (146–147).[60]

By seeking merely to internalize the AEC-vendor message the utility industry minimized its capacity for independent judgment.[61] This trend may have been exacerbated by the IOU's pursuit of a de-skilling and routinization of the engineering and operating task. As James Kuhn writes, (approvingly)

"The companies are proceeding as Charles F. MacGowan of the Boilermakers Union predicted almost a decade ago: [app. 1954] 'American industry has many times developed its genius for breaking down complex operations such as operation of these plants. The highly trained technicians and engineers currently operating these experimental models will give way, I think, to especially trained skilled and semiskilled workers. They will not obviate the necessity for training those people, but it will greatly reduce the amount of training now required.' Where one would have found a nuclear power plant operated by graduate, highly trained engineers in its first months, within a few years one finds that the employees are mostly experienced, able men with no more than a high-school degree. The complex job of control has been broken down into routines that can be mastered by men without a highly technical educational background even if they do not fully understand the theoretical details of the process" (148).

Retrospectively, Kuhn, MacGowan, and the utilities' celebration of the industry's "lean manpower" policies seems ironic, as recent analyses have partially blamed inadequate training for nuclear plants' poor capacity rates.[62] GPU's manpower policies were held partially responsible for the seriousness of the Three Mile Island accident. Review of utility trade journals during 1954–1969 indicates that the industry had little appreciation of the magnitude of the engineering and quality control problems associated with the technology. Paralleling the vendors' experience in the rivalry induced scaling race, the IOU's financial investments outpaced their technical competence.

Self-Fulfilling Prophecy Dynamics

The credibility of vendor-AEC cost claims was reinforced by the utilities' acceptance of the logic of self-fulfilling prophecies. The clear commitment of the vendors and AEC/JCAE to develop the technology appeared to promise future economic viability independent of current technical assessment, through the capture of learning curve cost reductions, scale economies, and state regulatory and subsidy favors. It was assumed, for example, that future public and private R&D commitments would solve the waste disposal and decommissioning problems without significant financial hardship to the utilities. Early discouraging experience with nuclear construction costs and capacity performance was similarly neutralized by the vendors' appeal to future learning curve cost reductions (Bupp and Derian 1981, 46–47).

The self-fulfilling prophecy dynamic imbued nuclear power with the image of "the coming technology." Former AEC consultant John Hogerton writes,

"... (the dynamic) placed the burden of proof not on the new technology, where one would normally have expected it to be put, but on the old one [coal]. And even if a utility president took his staff's nuclear cost estimates with a grain of salt, he could still justify going ahead with a nuclear project on the grounds that it would give his organization essential training and experience in what seemed destined to be the coming technology" (Hogerton 1968, 29).[63]

The nuclear industry was quite aware of the importance of capturing OT momentum. Just prior to the bandwagon sales, for example, the Atomic Industrial Forum's membership journal highlighted the "psychological importance" of two 1965 reactor sales, noting, "there is presumably a point where the utilities' faith in the future of nuclear power becomes firm confidence in its present" (AIF, *Nuclear Industry* 9/65, 4). The inverse of this dynamic, the self-fulfilling pessimism inflicted on the economics of non-nuclear energy, was noted by Sporn in 1967. He argued that deference to expected nuclear cost declines discouraged investment in coal and rail sector improvements, and led directly to increased fossil fuel generating costs.[64] In 1963 the National Coal Association similarly asserted, "The coal industry's ability to finance new mines or mining equipment is adversely affected by unfounded claims for nuclear power and the financing of new conventional utility plants is also affected by the mistaken notion that nuclear power may obsolete them in a short time" (*Nucleonics* 5/63). Recall that a similar deference crippled the European nuclear industry's ability to compete with U.S. light water designs.

The utilities' interest in nuclear power as an avenue to long run industry expansion also seems to have dimmed the firms' criticism of government and reactor vendor forecasting excesses. Considated Edison President Louis Roddis, for example, indicated in 1974 that the utilities "did not want to criticize the nuclear industry because they were depending on it heavily as a future power source" (*New York Times* 2/3/74).

Summary: The Utility Industry and OT Dynamics

The PC-OT framework highlights the importance of five factors in explaining the utility industry's nuclear initiatives during 1954–1974: (1) the technology's congeniality with key IOU growth strategies and the expansionist corporate culture of the utility industry; (2) the nature of intra-industry rivalries (especially that between public and private power); (3) the utilities' vulnerability to vendor and AEC/JCAE promotional activity; (4) the self-fulfilling prophecy character of successful infrastructural innovation; and (5) the character of utility regulation, especially its tendency to reduce the perceived risks of technical innovation.

The history of utility nuclear initiatives illustrates how a regulated industry can transform its revenue flow into a financing mechanism for congenial technological change. While the outcome was unsatisfactory with respect to nuclear power, the institutional and ideological nexus had previously overseen more than half a century of impressive technological change. The main problem was that nuclear power "was different" from past fossil fuel technologies and the utilities were ill equipped to recognize that difference; to provide a check on the excessive optimism emanating from the reactor vendors and AEC/JCAE, or to "learn" from each other's experience.

NPC Participants: The Architect-Engineering-Construction Firms

Like the pro-nuclear utilities, several large architect-engineering-construction (A-E-C) firms were attracted to nuclear power by their comparative advantage in nuclear markets and pushed towards it by the promotional activities of the AEC, JCAE, and reactor vendors. Their behavior and role in nuclear development fits neatly into the PC-OT framework.

In 1968, A-E-C activities accounted for about 10% of nuclear plant costs. By the mid-eighties, rising safety system outlays had helped increase A-E-C shares to about 30% plant costs. The A-E-Cs generally act as the utility's agent and are employed under cost-plus rather than fixed price contracts. This convention insulates the firms from many of the economic risks associated with technical uncertainties.

Many characteristics of the A-E-C market predisposed it to domination by a few firms.[65] While many of those companies well-situated to capture market shares also enjoyed strong positions in fossil fuel power plant construction, nuclear power had extra appeal due to its larger growth potential, greater capital intensity, and higher barriers to entry. Thus, like the active IOUs and electric equipment manufacturers, the leading A-E-C firms had a self-interest in nuclear expansion. Bechtel was the largest of these firms and the subsequent discussion focuses on its behavior. The company has captured about 30% of all U.S. nuclear plant engineering-construction contracts. In the early 1970s, this market share was expected to generate annual revenues of half a billion dollars (1971$) by 1985 (AEC 1971a, 85).

As with G. E., Westinghouse, and the pro-nuclear utilities, the claim is not that Bechtel knowingly sought to impose an inefficient technology on the American economy. The argument is that it chose to use its political-economic resources to promote nuclear power to economic efficiency; i.e., to capture OT status for the technology. It also sought to ensure itself a dominant position within the technology.

Bechtel's Promotional Role

The company's promotional activities have included subsidizing utility nuclear R&D projects, assuming demonstration plant risks through turnkey contracting, proffering pro-nuclear advice to its utility and government clients, and engaging in pro-nuclear political initiatives. The company has also sought to hire key government sector nuclear personnel and to orient government policy to its advantage. As the 1968 Arthur D. Little study reported,

"Bechtel's interest in the nuclear field dates back to 1949. It grew out of a determination after World War II of Bechtel's management to gain a stronger participation in the utility business. Electric power was viewed as a growth industry . . ." (Little 1968, 291; see also McCartney 1988, 102).

By the mid-fifties Bechtel was devoting 10% of its pre-tax profits to nuclear development and training (McCartney 1988, 107). The company actively sought participation in early AEC research projects and assumed fixed price contracting risks and economic losses in several early private sector nuclear projects.[66] It has also participated in bold initiatives along the nuclear fuel cycle.[67] As Bechtel executive David Nerell indicated in 1984, "Building demonstration plants is a good way to get a jump on technologies that have big futures" (*Wall Street Journal* 10/16/84).

Bechtel has been equally active in the nuclear export area, serving as A-E-C for seventeen overseas reactors (Hertsgaard 1983, 122). It has also had exploratory discussions with U.S. and foreign officials about the construction of enrichment or reprocessing facilities in Japan and Brazil (Hertsgaard 1983, 81, 233).

Besides aggressively assisting nuclear development through R&D contributions and turnkey contracting, Bechtel has also promoted the technology through political initiatives. For example, it contributed $180,000 to help defeat the 1976 California anti-nuclear referendum (*Business Week* 6/7/76), lobbied heavily for utility rate hikes to fund California's nuclear projects (McCartney 1988, 215), and was a key founder of the very active pro-nuclear Committee on Energy Awareness (Hertsgaard 1983, 187, 201). Its major political influence, however, has probably been exercised more covertly through direct contacts with high ranking government officials. Bechtel executives are legendary for their revolving door employment at the highest levels of government.[68]

Bechtel staffers also influenced government policy in numerous technical/regulatory areas through the functional authority created by the firm's research capabilities and practical nuclear experience. Bechtel executive W. Kenneth Davis, for example, served as chairman of the Atomic Industrial Forum's 1961 Committee on Reactor Safeguards. He was probably involved in the Forum's successful recommendation to the AEC that the pessimistic results of the mid-sixties Brookhaven accident probabilities study be withheld from the public. Davis also chaired an important panel on energy supply and delivery for the National Academy of Sciences' influential study *Energy in Transition 1985–2010*. Bechtel staffers similarly performed some of the safety analyses underlying the widely cited 1975 Rasmussen Safety Study and participated in an internal review of the preliminary draft of the report (Nader and Abbotts 1979, 372). The promotional biases introduced through these activities were more subtle than those associated with the company's marketing efforts or high level policy lobbying. They reflect the technological aesthetics of mega-builders, self-selected into an activist construction firm.[69] Chapter 4 explores how these aesthetics influenced approaches to nuclear cost forecasting and hazard assessment.

Bechtel and the other A-E-Cs similarly influenced U.S. nuclear development in their role as utility advisors. As noted above, the scale economies involved with technology assessment encouraged the utilities to rely heavily on outside consultants for technical advice in making capital equipment purchases (Sultan 1974, 20; Kuhn 1966, 123; Little 1968, 361, 378). While it is difficult to acquire information about the content of utility A-E-C relations, the available evidence suggests the A-E-Cs did little to mute the promotional optimism emanating from the AEC/JCAE, reactor vendors, and pro-nuclear utilities. Published plant cost predictions by Bechtel assisted utilities, for example, have been, like all utility projections, notoriously overoptimistic. On the international front, Bupp and Derian have noted the promotional impact of Bechtel et al.'s excessively optimistic presentation to the 1971 Geneva Conference on The Peaceful Uses of Atomic Energy. They write,

". . . the remaining two co-authors were executives of Bechtel. . . . As a promotional document, the report was not especially objectionable, although it was no more informative than an advertisement in a trade journal. But it was objectionable to place such a report, which obscured the truth rather than illuminated it, in officially sanctioned and authoritatively sponsored technical literature. It was with self-serving documents like this one that the American nuclear industry created a persuasive illusion."

"The advertisements were undeniably effective. Manufacturers in the fragmented European nuclear industry began intense competition to become licensees of the American companies" (Bupp and Derian 1981, 83).

The Impact of OT Momentum on Bechtel

While Bechtel clearly had a promotional interest in nuclear expansion, it would be an oversimplification to interpret its optimistic cost predictions (especially those forwarded to its own clients) as self-serving propaganda. The basis for Bechtel's participation in the nuclear bandwagon is much more subtle and involves self-deception as well as self-interest. The errors are more errors of omission than commission and reflect the firm's participation in a socially created realm of discourse, which was bounded by a collective failure to investigate the economic implications of the technology's negative externalities and an engineering hubris that minimized the potential problems posed by the technology's extreme novelty. The combination resulted in flawed cost predicting models, which mistakenly assumed static regulatory standards and routine learning curve cost reductions. In 1960, for example, Bechtel confidently asserted "complete, accurate and reliable" cost projections for commercial-sized versions of reactor designs for which even modest-sized demonstration plants had yet to be built (JCAE 1960b, 611).

While Bechtel's willingness to participate in this discourse was influenced by its self-interest in nuclear expansion and insulation from the risks of overoptimism due to its cost-plus contracts, the existence of a pro-nuclear bounded rationality was the product of larger bandwagon-OT dynamics. Like the utilities' management, Bechtel planners were influenced by the promotional activities of the vendors, AEC and JCAE, and the fail-safe logic of self-fulfilling prophecy dynamics. They implicitly assumed that the political consensus behind the technology ensured the availability of economically acceptable engineering solutions to all potential technical problems.

Bechtel's behavior may have also been conditioned by pressures emanating from the vendors, AEC, JCAE, and large IOUs not to disrupt the technology's growth path. Recall, for example, former Consolidated Edison and AIF President Louis Roddis's assertion that the IOUs' interest in nuclear expansion had muted their own criticism of the vendors' excessive cost optimism. Jessup and Lamont staffers claim that the utilities' hostile reaction to their company's prescient 1976 study "Problems of Nuclear Power: Possible Implications for Investors" hurt the firm financially. In a phone conversation with congressional staffers, a company spokesman asserted that publication of the report had resulted in a partial blacklisting of the firm from utility underwriting. Company Vice President Schroeder Boulton added, ". . . we could be excluded from other offerings if we testified publicly".[70] Hertsgaard's interviews with industry officials suggest a similar picture. He notes,

"Many nuclear executives point out that even if they wanted to leave the business, they could not without severely damaging their corporate reputations and customer relationships. . . . The vendors are also keenly aware that many of the larger electric utilities want nuclear power to be at least an option later in the 1980s. . . . Under the circumstances, to abandon nuclear could cost a reactor manufacturer millions of dollars in non-nuclear sales. As one Babcock and Wilcox executive explained, 'We can't cut our own throats by leaving nuclear. We depend on the utility business'" (Hertsgaard 1983, 117).

In February 1984 the Congressional Office of Technology Assessment confirmed that some utilities were channeling their non-nuclear purchases to companies that continued to offer nuclear services (Office of Technology Assessment 1984, 183). The bitter anger directed at the Arthur D. Little

Company during the AIF's 1968 annual meeting (in response to the firm's carefully qualified public suggestion that the utilities may not have bargained as aggressively as possible with reactor vendors), reinforces this impression (Little 1968, 27–28; AIF, *Nuclear Industry* 11–12/68, 3,18–19).

Conclusion

Bechtel's role in creating the nuclear bandwagon was the result of a complex interaction between the company and the aforementioned participants in the nuclear planning context. A conjuncture of self-interest, rivalry dynamics, inter-industry deferences, and political pressures created a collective misperception of uncertainty. Bechtel helped both produce and consume its illusions. To Bechtel, with the freedom of action of a large privately held company,[71] and a corporate culture committed to "building things," nuclear power loomed like the pyramids, a prized agenda for a master builder. The planning context of the 1950s enabled men like Steve Bechtel, Ralph Cordiner of G. E., and Harris Ward of Commonwealth Edison to translate corporate agendas into social policy with entrepreneurial handshakes.

Describing Bechtel's participation in the NPC of the 1950s, Laton McCartney indicates that plans for one of the country's first commercial nuclear power plants (the Dresden 1 plant) were forged at a weekend retreat of the Business Council in the Blue Ridge Mountains in October 1953. McCartney writes,

> "During a break in the Homestead weekend, Steve (Bechtel) drew Cordiner aside and told him that his company had decided to earmark 10 percent of its pretax earnings for nuclear development and training. Cordiner was impressed; he had no idea Bechtel was so committed to nuclear power. Bechtel was in the nuclear game to stay, Steve added, going on to describe the work it had done already in developing EBR-a [an experimental reactor]. . . . Why not, he proposed, get beyond all the testing and endless discussion over which type of reactor was best for generating commercial power, and simply built (sic) a nuclear plant—not just another prototype, but an actual, full-scale, money-making plant that ran on atomic energy. Cordiner's eyes lit up. The proposal was bold, but Bechtel was talking sense.

> "By the end of the weekend, Bechtel and Cordiner had concluded a handshake agreement to go to the National Power Group

and ask which of its members was ready to stop talking and start building. When Commonwealth Edison of Chicago volunteered to build a plant at Dresden, Illinois, not far from its corporate headquarters, General Electric and Bechtel were in business" (McCartney 1988, 107–8).

The opening up of social planning to new participants, such as environmentalists and local citizens, in the aftermath of the social movements of the 1960s, would eventually challenge such planning initiatives.

NPC Participants: The Nuclear Fuel Vendors*

The firms of the nuclear fuel industry complete the list of participants in the nuclear planning context. Through 1965, the industry was a product of AEC promotionalism. The bandwagon market for nuclear plants (1966–1969) subsequently stimulated large investments in nuclear fuel supply by several important oil and chemical industry firms who were well positioned to benefit from nuclear expansion. By the mid-1970s, these firms and the major reactor vendors dominated nuclear fuel markets.

Through August 1964, private ownership of nuclear fuel was prohibited. The industry was a heavily subsidized stepchild of the AEC, created to serve the military program. It consisted of two sets of firms: uranium exploration-mining and milling companies, and AEC fuel processing contractors. In order to ensure an adequate supply of materials for the commission's weapons reactors and the nuclear navy, the AEC guaranteed a relatively high floor for uranium prices for five to ten year periods. It also extended numerous mining subsidies, including bounties for new discoveries, funds for mining and milling R&D, and monies for road construction to remote mining sites (Dawson 1976, 161). The industry drew participation mainly from mining companies and a few oil and chemical firms. As military needs were met, prior investments created pressures for expanded civilian nuclear development (Mullenbach 1963, 121–122).

In the fuel processing area, the AEC concentrated contracts among a few companies, many of whom subsequently sought to create commercial variants of their military expertise. The late 1960s were a turning point in fuel cycle developments. The bandwagon reactor sales (1966–1969) and fuel

---

*The nuclear fuel cycle begins with uranium exploration, mining and milling; proceeds through conversion, enrichment and fuel fabrication; and terminates with reprocessing and waste disposal. All but the last of these steps will be discussed below.

markets' expected scale and vertical integration economies triggered large rivalry-induced fuel cycle investments and the aggressive entry of the oil companies. This in turn encouraged further utility nuclear orders. After the Gina and Millstone plant sales in 1965, the Atomic Industrial Forum's membership journal reported:

> ". . . some feel that these two contracts confirm that nuclear power has entered a new phase. They point out, for example, that the volume of work to be done . . . assures that production of components and fuel and the supply of services will be expanded, and the basis for commercial operations strengthened, not only by the reactor manufacturers but in other important sectors of the industry, including fuel preparation, chemical reprocessing, pressure vessel manufacturing and uranium production. The result must be improvements in quality and economics that will increase the attractiveness of nuclear power" (*Nuclear Industry* 9/65, 4).

More formally expressed, the AIF anticipated nuclear power's capture of system-wide efficiencies, as reciprocal positive externalities accumulated from capital outlays in different aspects of the nuclear industry. The oil firms' investments thus offer another example of the self-fulfilling prophecy dynamics associated with nuclear power's emerging OT status. The opposite phenomenon, a self-fulfilling pessimism, was simultaneously weakening the coal sector, as complementary investments were retarded in rail and other interfacing technologies.

As predicted, the AEC reported growing oil industry interest in nuclear fuel activities in 1966.[72] The rivalry dynamics in the fuel reprocessing market nicely illustrate the expansionary pressures created by OT momentum. Recall that construction of the first commercial reprocessing facility was begun by NFS in 1963. The project was part of Governor Rockefeller's efforts to transform New York State into a nuclear center. It also enjoyed assistance from the AEC, including a five-year guarantee of government spent fuel and regulatory approval of the PUREX process (despite the process' liquid residual which posed problems for nuclear waste disposal).[73]

Pursuing vertical integration economies, G. E. received a construction permit for the second reprocessing project in 1967. As the Little study of 1968 noted, G. E.'s ability to offer utilities a complete reactor-fuel fabrication-reprocessing service gave the company a competitive edge in linked markets (187, 234–236). In pursuit of large scale economies, Allied announced plans in 1968 for a reprocessing facility five times the ton/day size of both G. E. and NFS's plants.[74] Subsequent competition for market share and scale efficiencies created pressures for excess capacity (Little 1968, 235, 245). More or less concurrent with Allied's 5 ton/day announcement, ARCO and National Lead indicated their interest in building similar sized facilities (Little 1968, 217; AIF, *Nuclear Industry* 10/68; AEC 1967b, 137). A year later Getty announced its intention to triple NFS's reprocessing capabilities (AIF, *Nuclear Industry* 6/69), and Exxon began a major reprocessing R&D program (Senate Judiciary Committee 1977, 170). G. E. also appears to have increased the size of its facility (Campbell 1988, 114). Completion of all these plants (independent of Exxon's program) would have produced a reprocessing supply of at least 19 tons/day by 1973, a capacity three times the available market (AIF, *Nuclear Industry* 5/68, 19, 41; AEC 1968b, 174–175). Even after National Lead and ARCO's withdrawal, surplus capacity persisted as a result of NFS, G. E., and Allied's construction programs (AIF, *Nuclear Industry* 5/68). The companies' willingness to spend $150 million (late-sixties mixed historical $) in the face of five to ten years of load short losses testifies to the power of scale competition. Even more impressive, however, is the firms' willingness to make such investments in the face of large technical and regulatory uncertainties.[75] All three plants eventually proved technical failures and are currently inoperative. Their aborted history presents another occasion where rivalry induced investments in nuclear power outpaced firms' technical competence.

The ability of nuclear power's sponsors to promote the technology to OT status was facilitated by nuclear's congeniality with the long run interests of major oil companies who had significant influence over energy policy during this period. While it might have been expected that the oil industry would mirror the coal industry's opposition to nuclear development, the different end uses served by the two fossil fuels left nuclear power a much more serious competitor for the coal industry's utility market than the oil industry's liquid fuel market. Once it was clear that nuclear could not provide a near term competitive energy source for air propulsion and auto electrification, the technology ceased to be a major threat to the petroleum industry (Mullenbach 1963, 334–336).[76]

The oil companies' massive capital base, extensive mineral rights holdings, large geological libraries, chemical processing expertise, and working relationships with existing public energy bureaucracies, left them in a strong position in uranium markets. As William Slick, senior Exxon Vice President indicated in 1977,

". . . exploration for, and mining and milling of uranium was a logical extension of Exxon's historical activities . . . diversification into the nuclear fuel cycle offers business opportunities that match Exxon's capabilities" (Senate Judiciary Committee 1977).

The Little study reached similar conclusions (Little 1968, 79). By the 1970s U.S. uranium markets were dominated by petroleum companies. The American Petroleum Institute estimated in 1977 that 72% of all known uranium reserves available at less than $20/lb were controlled by oil companies (Senate Committee on Energy and Natural Resources 1977, 323). Fifty-two percent of U.S. mining and milling capacity was similarly owned in 1978 (Chapman 1983, 214). Oil firms have also sought to capitalize on various competitive advantages they possess in fuel processing markets. As Exxon Vice President William Slick noted in 1977,

> ". . . activities in the nuclear fuel cycle are technologically intensive and capital intensive, with long lead times between investments and return of investment—a capital management environment similar to oil production and refining" (Senate Judiciary Committee 1977, 166).

Such activities also offer opportunities for vertical integration and close coordination with federal officials for which the oil companies are especially well suited.[77]

By the mid-seventies, the nuclear fuel industry was dominated by six oil firms (Kerr-McGee, Exxon, Gulf, Getty, ARCO, and Continental), three chemical firms (Union Carbide, Allied Chemical, and Goodyear), and four vertically integrated reactor vendors (Westinghouse, G. E., Combustion Engineering, and Babcock and Wilcox). These firms, along with Bechtel and the pro-nuclear utilities, comprised the core of the nuclear industry. Amidst the massive uncertainties surrounding energy sector investment, each firm's nuclear commitments were taken by other firms as rationales for further nuclear investment. By the late-sixties and early-seventies the technology's sponsors had established a seemingly self-perpetuating momentum.

OT Dynamics, Nuclear Power and Technical Change

This chapter analyzed the four dimensions of the nuclear planning context from 1950–1970. The NPC's key ideological variables were cold war sentiments, a popular faith in government and business leaders, a prioritizing of corporate-led economic growth, and a technological aesthetic that minimized nuclear hazard concerns and maximized the value of large, high-tech, limitless energy supply systems. The NPC's key institutional designs involved the centralized and insular structure of government nuclear regulation, the apparently self-financing mechanisms of the utility sector, and the oligopoly character of key nuclear power industries.

The NPC's major participants were the AEC and JCAE, four reactor vendors, fifteen or so pro-nuclear utilities, and a few large engineering-construction firms.[78] Pursuing various political objectives, long run growth strategies, and the logic of rivalry dynamics, these agents, both consciously and unconsciously, carved out a critical mass development path for the technology. The bandwagon markets of the late-sixties and early-seventies, and the oil companies' concurrent nuclear investments, testify to their success.

The implication of nuclear history is that the market's organization of technical change reflects social as well as technical variables. The market is not merely a medium of aggregation which translates engineering parameters into economic outcomes in the process of finding technically efficient solutions to engineering problems. Instead, it is an arena for integrating strategic behavior, ideological and institutional variables, and technical parameters. Activist firms create as much as discover development paths. The social variables defining planning contexts complement (and to some extent dominate) technical parameters as the determinants of the pattern of infrastructural technical change.

The nuclear planning context during the OT years was particularly well-defined and limited in participation.[79] The closed loop of the AEC, JCAE, and nuclear industry nicely illustrates Galbraith's notion of bureaucratic symbiosis as de facto economic planning. The only source of sustained criticism of nuclear promotion before 1970 was the coal sector, and its competitive small firm character and limited political clout during this period minimized its impact. Organized labor sporadically raised health and safety concerns and objections to nuclear industry concentration ratios, but never developed an independent perspective on nuclear power from that cultivated by the industry and AEC (AIF, *Forum Memo* 11/59, 37; *Nucleonics* 4/63, 20; Dawson 1976, 153; Mullenbach 1963, 25). Some voluntary organizations did arise around nuclear issues, but their efforts were generally limited to weapons-related concerns.

Besides delineating the dimensions of the NPC (1950–1970), chapter 2 explored the ways in which nuclear power's private sponsors sought to promote nuclear expansion. Chapters 3–5 will explore the promotional activities of nuclear power's government sponsors and the overall impact of public and private assistance to nuclear power on the technology's development.

The PC-OT framework is designed to highlight the impact of social contexts on technological change. It emphasizes the "historicity" of "technical" judgments by highlighting: (1) the impact of prior social contexts on the information available to decision makers, (2) the impact of historically created "Technological Aesthetics" on technology assessment, and (3) the impact of distributions of power and institutional formats on who influences technical choices and which technology captures scaling advantages.

By exploring the implications of path dependency, the framework illustrates how social contexts can shape technological opportunity. While market outcomes may appear inevitable after a technology cashes in its path dependent advantages, it is a retrospective inevitability. *Technically deterministic histories of technical change may, therefore, impose the future on the past and in so doing hide the imposition of the past on the future.* By highlighting the infusion of social contexts into what appear to be technically deterministic decisions, the OT framework invites inquiry into how social systems evolve and produce particular contexts for technical change.

Chapter 3

Government Regulation of Nuclear Power

This chapter focuses on the subsidy, R&D, and regulatory assistance given nuclear power by its public sector sponsors in an effort to win OT status for the technology. It also explores how the larger social context of the Nuclear Planning Context influenced public policy and economic decisions in these areas.

R&D Directions

One of the major ways that social contexts shape the direction of innovation is by influencing government research funding. Though precise figures for corporate R&D spending are proprietary information and unavailable, federal monies appear to have funded about 30%–40% of national energy R&D expenditures during the years of nuclear power expansion (1955–1975).[1] As table 3.1 indicates, military and space priorities have dominated government R&D programs for forty years. The energy sector's nuclear tilt can be partly seen as a by-product of this influence. Economist Nathan Rosenberg has linked the general direction of post-World War II technical advance to the shape of military research. He writes,

> ". . . the size and the direction of research efforts are increasingly the product of allocative decisions made within the public sphere . . . Much of the technological change in the past quarter century has been the result of intensive public efforts undertaken in the pursuit of goals formulated in relation to the needs of national security—jet propulsion, numerical control, computer technology, and electronics more generally, and atomic energy . . ." (Rosenberg 1972, 183).

From 1951–1974 the federal government spent more than $23 billion (1990$) on research related to light water reactors (Komanoff and Roelofs

Table 3.1
Distribution of Federal and Non-Federal R&D Spending
(1953, 1960–1978) Percentages

Year	Federal Total	Federal Defense related	Federal Space related	Federal Civilian related	Non-Federal
1953	54	48	1	5	46
1960	65	52	3	9	35
1961	65	50	6	9	35
1962	64	48	7	9	36
1963	66	41	14	11	34
1964	66	37	19	9	34
1965	65	33	21	11	35
1966	64	33	19	12	36
1967	62	35	14	13	38
1968	61	35	13	13	39
1969	58	34	11	13	42
1970	57	33	10	14	43
1971	56	32	9	15	44
1972	55	32	8	15	45
1973	53	31	7	15	47
1974	51	28	7	16	49
1975	51	27	7	17	49
1976	51	26	8	17	49
1977	50	25	7	18	50
1978	50	24	7	19	50

Source: National Science Foundation: *National Patterns of Science and Technology Resources 1981.*

1992, 44).[2] This total is about eight times the level of government spending for oil related R&D, fifteen times that expended for coal research, and fifty to one-hundred times the allocation for solar energy (see table 3.2). While nuclear power's share of government energy R&D has declined significantly since this period, the technology has still enjoyed the lion's share of research support.

The architectonic impact of federal R&D spending was multiplied by the traditional division of labor in public and private research financing. Across the economy, federal dollars have generally dominated basic research, accounting for 70% of total outlays 1960–1980 (NSF 1981, 26). In contrast, private spending has been directed towards funding marginal innovations within existing technologies. Case studies and qualitative reviews indicate that a similar pattern prevailed in the energy sector during the OT period (Cambel 1964; Herman 1977, 2; *New York Times* 7/4/76).[3]

Table 3.2
Federal Energy R&D Spending 1951–1974
(Millions of Historical Dollars)[1]

Year	Nuclear Power Reactors[2] converter	breeder	Coal[3]	Oil & Gas[4]	Solar[5]	Geo-thermal[6]	Conservation[7]
1951	26						
1952	34						
1953	55						
1954	61		11				
1955	67	4	"				
1956	113	6	"				
1957	213	7	"	11			
1958	276	6	"	12			
1959	306	9	"	27			
1960	361	0	"	20			
1961	408	0	"	19			
1962	357	0	"	20			
1963	358	0	11	21			
1964	331	0		72			
1965	334	0		69			
1966	287	42	16	47			
1967	283	55	19	46			
1968	315	81	21	71			
1969	260	98	34	47	50–100		minimal
1970	228	104	46	22	thru	7 thru	thru
1971	250	106	63	17	1971	1971	1971
1972	282	139		(less than 1 million/yr. for			
1973	332	161		renewables in early seventies}[8]			
1974	494	216	all fossil	79[9]	20[9]	0[9]	2[9]

Notes

1. It is not possible to draw upon sources utilizing common accounting procedures for all of the energy options during the 1951–1971 period. The statistics are thus not entirely comparable. Gaps in the table represent years not included in the sources cited.

2. Nuclear expenditures broken into conventional fission and breeder reactor categories. Totals exclude outlays for fusion research (Komanoff and Roelofs 1992, table 12, 43).

3. Coal outlays 1954–1963 based on Cambel 1964, 30–31; 1966–1972 outlays drawn from Senate Interior and Insular Affairs Committee 1974, 315–316 (assuming all Bureau of Mines expenditures for health and safety and all EPA outlays for controlling stack pollution were coal related).

4. Oil and gas outlays 1957–1969 drawn from National Science Foundation *Research and Development in Industry 1969*, 34, 96; 1970–1971 entries drawn from National Science Foundation *National Patterns of Science and Technology Resources 1981*, 44.

5. Holloman and Grenon (1975), 83.

6. Holloman and Grenon (1975), 79.

7. 1973 is the first year for which specific data for conservation expenditures seem to be available. Prior outlays were most likely minimal.

8. CRS 1991, 5.

9. CRS 1991, Energy R&D spending table.

Military funding for basic research related to nuclear reactors generated significant civilian spin-offs and broad interest in nuclear technologies. The opposite situation prevailed in many non-nuclear fields during 1950–1970 (Cambel 1964, xix; Perry 1973). A key 1964 R&D study noted the sensitivity of campus as well as corporate R&D activities to the direction of federal funds and the level of ideological support for different technologies, concluding,

> "In the universities, too, the glamour of certain disciplines and the relative ease of funding tend to accentuate space—and defense-oriented energy R&D. Although colleges and technological institutes are engaged in some education and research for civilian energy, the efforts are widely dispersed and diffused, and few, if any, of the academic groups concerned are of an intellectually critical size" (Cambel 1964, xix).

Ten years later another government report found little change in university research environments (Perry 1973, 55–56, 125, 134).

Nuclear power also enjoyed the lion's share of government funds and military spin-offs for applied research. The naval program was especially important, generating a reservoir of practical knowledge and pool of skilled manpower.[4] Federal support for large scale nuclear demonstration projects provided the last link in the nuclear R&D chain. Since many competing energy options involve costly prototypes, the skewing of federal demonstration funds towards nuclear projects (such as the Shippingport and Power Reactor Demonstration Program plants), gave the technology a significant edge.[5] The current lack of similar federal support for advanced reactors helps explain the inability of the industry to translate some innovative ideas into concrete projects.

Besides directly funding research, state policy created numerous incentives for private nuclear R&D, most often by minimizing associated risks. De facto efforts to involve private firms in the development process began with the concentrated contracting procedures of the AEC, which created a self-interest on the part of select corporations in nuclear power's technical success. Formal programs began with the Industrial Participation Studies in 1951 and the subsidies of the Power Reactor Demonstration Program in 1955.[6] All nuclear initiatives benefited from the limited liability provisions of the Price-Anderson Act, and the AEC's de facto commitment to dissolve potential nuclear bottlenecks. The latter served as an implicit form of technical insurance, guaranteeing that research gaps in the rest of the nuclear industry would not compromise the economic value of power plant investments. The DOE's draft nuclear power subsidy study rated this insurance more economically stimulating than direct funding, noting,

"The clear government commitment to the nuclear option has created a general reduction in uncertainty. The industry has been assured that the government will supply acceptable solutions to serious outstanding problems. The result has been a decrease in the rate of return required by nuclear investors, and a substantial amount of investment" (Bowring 1980, 30).

The government's naval demand and subsidy support for nuclear exports also offered "demand-pull" incentives for nuclear R&D.

Corporate and university/non-profit R&D programs comprise the private sector share of U.S. R&D planning. Corporate efforts are by far the most important.[7] University/non-profit projects are only significant in the basic research area,[8] and as already noted are more sensitive to corporate and federal policy than it might first appear. Conventional estimates of industry funding levels are contained in table 3.3.

Table 3.3
Estimated Energy R&D Outlays 1963 & 1964[1] (in millions 1979$)

Industry	1963 Govt.	1963 Industry	1974 Govt.	1974 Industry
Coal	25	25	151	14
Oil and Gas	91	766	13	994
Nuclear (fission)	479	205	667	*[2]
Nuclear (fusion)	59	7	126	*[2]
Electricity	2	356	11	426
Solar	7	2	17	*[2]
Magnetohydrodynamics	21	4	7	*[3]
Fuel Cells	18	21	*[3]	*[2]
Thermionics	15	5	*[3]	*[3]
Thermoelectricity	25	7	*[3]	*[3]
Pollution Control Technology	no 1963 listings		65	*[4]
Miscellaneous	no 1963 listings		14	*[3]
Totals	742	1398	1071	1434

1. Table based on tables 6.1 and 6.2 of the "Perry Report" (*Energy Research and Development - Problems and Prospects*, Senate Committee on Interior and Insular Affairs, 1973, 39–40). 1963 nuclear totals are lower than in table 3.1 due to less exhaustive accounting.
2. Included under electricity
3. Negligible
4. Included under oil and gas, and electricity.

While the figures for private spending reflect sources of funds rather than area of expenditure, they appear to be representative of research directions as well. The major exception involves the use of oil/gas industry funds for non-oil/gas energy related research, such as petrochemical R&D. The major weakness of the numbers is their failure to include multi-billion dollar nuclear outlays for development and demonstration projects, such as the reactor vendors' turnkey plants, or the utilities' early nuclear orders.

When amended to include such nuclear spending, the data indicate that the U.S. (1955–1975) had two privately funded energy R&D programs, an oil/gas tack led by the major oil companies and a nuclear program directed by the electric equipment manufacturers and utilities. While the IOUs' lack of regulatory support for earmarked R&D activities led to minimal (less than .5% sales) formal research outlays, their apparently guaranteed rate base recovery of capital expenditures facilitated de facto demonstration plant purchases.

Besides financing R&D activities, energy sector corporations influenced energy planning through their inputs to government decisions. Most visible was the direct clout of corporate lobbyists in electoral or legislative processes. The firms were also able to influence realms of practical and political discourse, and by extension, scientific agendas, through their regular professional interactions with key government agencies. This influence is nicely illustrated by a Harvard Business School study of the U.S. response to the energy crisis of the 1970s.

> "When the (energy) crisis broke in 1973, the country turned to the experts, the people who had spent their working lives trying to increase energy supplies through oil, gas, coal, and nuclear. Not surprisingly, these people forcefully advocated a rapid further build-up of conventional sources, and their voices were powerful. After all, they belonged to organizations set up to accomplish such tasks . . . Even if economic self-interest had not been involved, points of view, convictions, and experience acquired over many decades of working to provide more energy would naturally have caused these people to emphasize energy production rather than conservation . . . . Thus the energy suppliers pretty much shaped the terms of the debate, and established what was important and what was not" (Stobaugh and Yergin 1979, 140).

Much of the senior staff of the public sector's energy bureaucracies had also come from private sector energy firms.[9] Similar dynamics reinforced the "hands on influence" of corporate voices in other nations' R&D policy making.[10]

Technological Aesthetics and R&D Regimes

The pro-nuclear outlook of the AEC, JCAE, and nuclear industry eventually produced a mutually reinforcing complex of engineering hardware, planning institutions, and technological subcultures that facilitated continuing nuclear power R&D. Through self-selection, stylized experience, and socialization by corporate and/or technological subcultures, participants in an industry often share a common technological aesthetic. This was exaggerated in the nuclear field by the development of the technology within an insular and promotional environment. The nuclear industry's accretion of economic consultants, professional associations, trade journals, lobbyists, etc., immersed industry participants in a flow of self-promoting information. Nuclear power professionals often moved back and forth between the public and private sectors creating a seamless web of pro-nuclear opinion.

The technological realm of discourse accompanying nuclear power reproduced both technical information and a pro-nuclear power technological aesthetic. Recall from chapter 2, for example, that the utilities' purchase and staffing of nuclear reactors brought with it nuclear planning visions as well as nuclear plants. The elevation of nuclear practitioners to positions of influence in utility management and U.S. energy planning (as the AEC evolved into the Energy Research and Development Administration and the Department of Energy), tended to reinforce technological aesthetics favorable to nuclear research across the energy sector.

The planning vision promoting nuclear R&D involved overlapping expectations about future energy demand, the viability of alternative energy options, the nature of nuclear power hazards, and the behavior of nuclear power costs. Chapters 4, 11, and 12 develop a "sociology of knowledge"— explanation for the origins of pro-nuclear conclusions in these areas that highlight the linkages between socially nurtured technological aesthetics and technology assessment. The discussion below illustrates the kind of connections explored in these chapters and their implications for R&D decision making.

The starting point for aggressive nuclear R&D funding was the assumption of enormous growth in future energy demand. Relying less on formal analysis than recent market experience and intuition, nuclear enthusiasts expected electricity use to double every ten to fifteen years for the foreseeable future. There was a tendency to assume relatively fixed energy/GNP and electricity/GNP ratios and a reluctance to use social policy to dissolve institutional bottlenecks in the way of increased energy efficiency. Abundant energy was seen as a prerequisite for permanent economic growth and nuclear power as a prerequisite for abundant energy.

Nuclear planners were generally skeptical about the long run potential of non-nuclear energy technologies.[11] Fossil fueled systems were discounted heavily because of exhaustibility. Many renewable energy technologies (RETs) were dismissed because of their low-tech modesty and early stage of development.[12] Other RETs were rejected because of their low power densities (and accompanying large material and land needs), their decentralized formats (which was assumed to create management problems), and their inability to provide *limitless* energy.

The NPC's R&D assessments reflected a technological aesthetic that favored large, centralized, and apparently limitless energy sources. The judgments were tied to particular institutions and historical experience, and were infused with "technological tastes" as well as technical rationality. They were the product of a particular planning context and open to revision when that context changed. The flip side of the NPC's pessimism about non-nuclear energy options was a high-tech optimism about the ease of containing nuclear hazards and minimizing nuclear costs. Chapters 4 and 9 analyze the technical aesthetics behind this optimism.

The most interesting aspect of the tilt towards renewable technologies in the Carter administration in the late 1970s and the Clinton administration in the 1990s is the accompanying shift in technical opinion. The point is not that scientists and research engineers contrive results to suit political audiences, but that socio-political environments affect the problems scientists choose to work on and the methodologies employed to address them. Institutions that develop within one planning context, such as the AEC, may internalize its ideological vision and become independent perpetuators of that vision. It may take new institutions to reorient technological directions. The creation of these institutions is often the product of political change. One of the great successes of the alternative energy movement has been its ability to supplement older energy planning institutions with new ones, such as the Solar Energy Research Institute (now called the National Renewable Energy Laboratory), the Council on Environmental Quality, the Union of Concerned Scientists, the Rocky Mountain Institute, and so on.

An OT-Kuhnian Model of Energy Sector R&D Paradigms

Mixing Kuhnian categories from the history of science and economic models of rivalry dynamics, it is possible to complement our discussion of the technological aesthetics underlying nuclear power R&D with an OT model of corporate R&D behavior. The model divides R&D activities into years of "normal" research (paralleling Kuhn's notion of normal science) and "revolutionary" research (paralleling Kuhn's notion of scientific revolutions).[13] During normal periods, there is a strong tendency for corporate spending to be geared towards marginal innovation within existing technical contexts. Political-economic-scientific conjunctures can occur, however, which raise the possibility of "infrastructural paradigm shifts". During these periods incentives exist for corporate R&D risk taking and promotional planning.

Using the distinction between normal and revolutionary R&D periods, it is possible to divide U.S. energy R&D from 1950–1995 into five categories. Category 1 research refers to the bulk of R&D spending for traditional (mainly fossil fuel) energy sources. This research was geared primarily towards producing minor innovations directly related to the funder's existing market activities. It was dominated by oil/gas spending. Category 2 refers to the electric equipment manufacturers' and growth oriented utilities' promotional R&D support for nuclear power. It was a more speculative venture, geared towards winning OT status for a new technology. Category 3 research refers to "reactive" nuclear R&D, and represents a new round of "normal" research after nuclear power captured OT status. It includes R&D performed by the more passive utilities, oil companies, and firms threatened by the nuclear cannibalization of their industries. Category 4 refers to the R&D initiatives that followed the disestablishment of nuclear power as an OT by the mid-seventies. It represents a second round of revolutionary R&D activity. Its participants failed to win OT status for breeder reactors, synfuels or renewable energy paths, though all were seriously promoted by different advocates. Category 5 refers to the incrementalism of the 1980s and 1990s and represents another round of "normal R&D" focused on marginal changes within existing energy systems. The discussion below explores these categories in more detail.

Category 1: A McGraw-Hill study found that the bulk of corporate R&D projects were expected to payoff within five years (Mansfield 1968). They were perforce directed towards producing minor technical change, often for the purpose of product differentiation. This practice seems repeated in the energy sector (Cambel 1964, 34; Perry 1973, 20; *New York Times* 7/4/76; Freeman 1974, 11). Mansfield's case studies from the oil and coal industries, for example, found that funded projects generally had an expected payoff period of less than five years and a probability of success of about 75% (Mansfield 1975, 318).

Category 1 R&D imparts an inertia to technological evolution. It currently funds fossil fuel technologies and electricity oriented energy sources. Like the Highway Trust Fund (financed from a tax on gasoline), it tends to perpetuate existing infrastructural relationships and the influence of corporate planners on research directions.

The utility industry fought very hard in the early 1970s to maintain that influence. It responded to proposed legislation calling for a tax on electricity to finance a Federal Power Research and Development Board with the establishment of a utility funded and controlled research organization, the Electric Power Research Institute (EPRI). EPRI's initial policies reflected the industry's traditional growth oriented and increasingly pro-nuclear perspective (Hirsh 1989, 133–137).

Several public financing mechanisms, akin to the Highway Trust fund, strengthen existing energy technologies in comparison with unestablished ones. For example, the Gas Research Institute's (~$200 million/yr.) R&D program is funded by public levies on interstate gas transport (DOE 12/92, 52). A 1 M/kwh tax finances nuclear industry waste disposal R&D. Utility ratepayers also finance the NRC's ~$100 million/year nuclear safety R&D program. The energy conservation or wind power industries lack similar R&D funding mechanisms.

Category 2: Complementing the tendency for marginalist R&D behavior, the PC-OT framework implies the potential for speculative R&D activities, such as the reactor vendors' large in-house nuclear power research outlays and early loss leader plants, the utilities' nuclear power demonstration plant purchases, and Bechtel's nuclear power activities. The character of promotional R&D activities suggests that technical change will be biased towards technologies offering key corporations (or government bureaucracies) special profit opportunities (or political payoffs). *Fortune*'s account of G. E.'s decision to concentrate company investments in nuclear power, jet engines and computers, illustrates this bias. Category 2 research is facilitated by ideological and political contexts that permit active government support of chosen technologies.

Category 3: As nuclear power emerged as an Official Technology it stimulated bandwagon R&D support. Recall for example, the effect of the technology's "coming technology"—image on utility nuclear investments. The oil companies' late-1960s nuclear expenditures contain aspects of both category 2 and 3 behavior. Rivalry dynamics amongst the reactor vendors pressured firms to match the R&D of the most aggressive company. The entrance of the large fossil fuel furnace and boiler firms into the reactor market was similarly a defensive reaction.

Category 4: After the disestablishment of nuclear power as an Official Technology in the mid-seventies, the U.S. witnessed the beginning of a second round of revolutionary R&D. Although it initially appeared that synfuels or solar energy/energy efficiency might emerge with OT status, the country entered an ambiguous period within which no technology enjoyed the political support necessary for bold initiatives. Without the aid of OT status, support for breeder technologies declined drastically.

Category 5: Category 5 R&D represents a return to a regime of "normal" R&D. With the election of Ronald Reagan, government R&D funding for renewable energy and conservation was slashed. The latter fell 90% and the former 50% (FY 1981–FY 1990) (CRS 1/22/91). While the Reagan administration supported nuclear power ideologically, the strength of the anti-nuclear power lobby and the administration's market oriented economic policies precluded the kind of R&D and subsidy aid necessary to re-establish nuclear power as an Official Technology. The Senate killed the Clinch River Breeder in 1983. In the 1990s, cheap fossil fuels discouraged risk taking in energy R&D.

The Troubled Marriage of Short Term Commercialization Pressures and Long Term Breeder Reactor Development Strategies

Many of nuclear power's current difficulties have been exacerbated by R&D strategies that sacrificed long term design objectives to short term political and commercial pressures. Inter-technology competition for OT status, intra-nuclear sector competition for market share, and geopolitical pressures all combined to impose immature nuclear plant designs on the electricity sector. Chapter 2 has already discussed the premature adoption of the light water reactor as the work horse for the U.S. nuclear sector. Adding to the LWR's problems was the AEC's decision in the mid-sixties to shift the bulk of its R&D activities to the breeder reactor in preparation for a limitless nuclear sector.

Even while acknowledging the need for additional LWR research (especially with respect to reactor safety and the back end of the nuclear fuel cycle), the AEC deferred work in these areas in order to finance breeder reactor development. Breeder proponents continued to urge fast tracking even as the uranium scarcity argument for fuel breeding evaporated and proliferation concerns increased about breeder designs. The private contractors for the liquid metal fast breeder reactor (LMFBR), for example, resisted efforts to carefully test the reactor's components. Interviews with industry executives circa 1977 found that:

> "Westinghouse thinks that the ERDA program contains one unnecessary element. ERDA plans to build a testing complex for large LMFBR components, in order to bridge the gap from small to large plants. Westinghouse feels that the undertaking will take too much money. ERDA admits that the building and operation of that facility is now the main obstacle to more rapid commercialization of the technology. Malcolm Dyos (Westinghouse Manager of Commercial Plant Design) notes that Westinghouse has never tested entire large

systems of interacting components for nuclear reactors before installing them in plants. It does not believe such testing necessary. Instead, the company has carried out intensive tests on parts or scale models of the larger components. Dyos claims that, in general, past experience with breeder and non-breeder reactors, together with a considerable amount of design work, will be sufficient for scaling up LMFBR technology" (Herman 1977, 629).

In light of the massive problems encountered during the LWR scale-up, this confidence is disturbing. Equally wrong-headed, but typical of the period, was the company's economic forecast,

". . . Dyos thinks that the future of the LMFBR as the mainstay of U.S. power generation is assured. 'No one's going to kill the LMFBR. You have no choice. The LMFBR is the only new form of bulk electric power generation that will be in operation for the next several decades'" (Ibid., 630).

One of the great tragedies and scandals of nuclear power development has been commercialization of the technology at a time when the strength of its competition constantly pressured for economizing on safety expenditures and design completeness. Marginally competitive nuclear power is not an appropriate technology for achieving fuel diversity. As Weinberg has eloquently argued, reactors need to be designed such that routine and irregular operation do not create *incentives* for staff neglect of safety procedures. The Chernobyl accident provides a good example of what happens when important safety procedures seem to conflict with staff convenience. The same care needs to be taken with respect to the financial incentives for reactor owners. While there will always be economic pressures for cost reduction, these pressures need to be moderated and kept from forcing choices between corporate survival and public safety.

Conclusion

The massive tilt of U.S. energy R&D policy towards nuclear power in 1950–1974 midwifed a nuclear industry and stunted most non-nuclear energy R&D alternatives. It has taken two decades to reverse this direction. The premature commercialization of an incomplete technology created constant pressures for safety compromises and public subsidy.

Nuclear Power Subsidies & Cost Deferments*

Complementing nuclear power's dominance of federal R&D spending 1955–1975 were numerous other government subsidies. The aid was part of the AEC's "infant industry" development strategy under which it sought to reduce or defer nuclear power costs in order to buy time for the industry to capture path dependent cost advantages. Several nuclear fuel subsidies, for example, were legally contingent on the AEC finding the nuclear industry in a pre-commercial phase. The AEC continued to characterize nuclear plant investments as "without practical value" as late as 1970 in order to maintain this assistance and protect the nuclear industry from anti-trust review.

While it is difficult to estimate a precise dollar value for many subsidies, their combined impact reduced *expected* nuclear power generating costs by at least 50% during the OT years. The aid can be divided into operating and development assistance.[14] Operating subsidies reduced nuclear costs by more than 1.5 c/kwh through 1974. Development subsidies lowered costs by another third of a cent/kwh through 1974.[15] Annual totals for both types of subsidies appear in tables 3.4 and 3.5. The subsidies are striking for their large number, diverse forms, and economic significance. The aid can be further divided into direct expenditure subsidies, implicit subsidies (such as tax breaks and risk reducing measures), and cost deferring measures.

(The next three pages discuss mechanisms of nuclear subsidy. Readers uninterested in such details may wish to skip "Cost Deferments.")

Direct Expenditure Subsidies

The major direct expenditure subsidies were R&D outlays, uranium supply and enrichment subsidies, and regulatory subsidies. Annual nuclear power R&D funding levels are reproduced in table 3.4. Amortizing the expenditures yields a per kilowatt hour subsidy rate of about 2.5 M/kwh.[16]

Uranium subsidies were initiated to serve the military program. After the late-fifties, assistance was motivated by the civilian program. Prior to 1964, when all uranium sales had to be made to the AEC, the commission subsidized its mining and milling suppliers, undercharged its utility uranium customers, and over compensated reactor operators for plutonium (Pu) buybacks.[17] The plutonium program illustrates the general character of nuclear subsidies. Through 1963 the AEC subsidized nuclear fuel costs through

---

*All $ 1992$ unless otherwise noted.

Table 3.4
Development Subsidies (millions of 1992$)

Year	Basic[1] R&D	Related[2] Military R&D	Related[3] Miscellan. R&D	Uranium[4] Supply Assist.	Regulatory[5] Services R&D	Export[6] Assist.	Miscellan.[7] Assist.	Grand Totals
1950	19	30						49
1951	28	94						122
1952	33	130						163
1953	52	202						254
1954	96	183						279
1955	133	163						296
1956	239	250						489
1957	427	466	104					997
1958	660	479	104					1243
1959	797	437	104			58		1445
1960	1082	353	104		9		185	1733
1961	1247	364	104		11		185	1911
1962	1177	207	104	4	11	9	185	1697
1963	1134	233	104	22	13		185	1691
1964	1258		104	41	57	4	185	1649
1965	1217		167	56	65	13	185	1703
1966	960		167	67	72	102	185	1553
1967	897		268	78	89		185	1517
1968	938		268	85	100	63	185	1639

Year							
1969	720		268	93	102	20	185	1388
1970	588		268	96	109	87	185	1334
1971	614		268	96	109	54	185	1326
1972	683		268	96	146	464	185	1842
1973	759		268	96	196	427	185	1931
1974	997		268	104	216	161	185	1931
Sum	16,757	3,591	3,310	934	1,305	1,511	2,775	30,183
1975	167		268	17	2	215	185	854
1976	433		268	37	94		185	1017
1977	444		268	76	35	68	185	1076
1978	374		268	111	26	63	185	1027
1979	340		268	133	131	511	185	1568
Sum	18,515	3,591	4,650	1,308	1,593	2,368	3,700	35,725

1. Basic R&D expenditures are defined as federal R&D expenditures for non-breeder civilian reactor development (DOE 2/81, 19).

2. Military R&D expenditures related to civilian power development, as reported in the DOE study cited above.

3. R&D expenditures in nuclear biology and medicine, education and training, physical research, and program management, as calculated in Battelle Memorial Institute 1978, 117–124. Table entries based on levelized distribution, assuming one-third Battelle listed outlays expended 1957–1966 and two-third's 1967–1976. Statistics for 1977–1979 deduced from aggregate statistics found in the Battelle and DOE studies.

4. Uranium assistance outlays based on 1962–1974 carrying costs of DOE surplus uranium purchases (per Bowring 1980, 49, assuming 3% real carrying charges). 1975–1979 outlays represent National Uranium Resource Evaluation expenses (Bowring 1980, 49).

5. Regulatory costs 1960–1974 drawn from Battelle Memorial Institute 1978, 145; 1975–1979 costs drawn from DOE 2/81, 19. The development subsidy portion of regulatory expenditures was calculated by subtracting "operating subsidies" from total NRC expenditures, with the latter assumed to be 1 M/kwh times the year's kwh totals.

6. Export assistance totals refer to de facto subsidies contained in Export-Import Bank loans, per Nawab (1980), Appendix A.

7. Miscellaneous expenditure levels based on rationale developed in the text.

military purchase of the plutonium embedded in used reactor fuel. From 1964–1970 the AEC guaranteed Pu prices at levels that assumed widespread deployment of breeder reactors. This guarantee turned a nasty waste product into a valuable utility asset by shifting the uncertainties of the future demand for plutonium to public shoulders.[18] The AEC's "stretchout" uranium purchase program during 1962–1970 similarly reduced risk levels in the uranium industry.[19]

It is difficult to translate federal uranium activities into a per kilowatt hour subsidy. The programs' chief impact was to allay fears of supply bottlenecks. The effect of early guaranteed prices for reactor by-products of plutonium and irradiated uranium was also greater on expected than actual plant generating costs.

All enrichment facilities in the U.S. have been government owned. This has been due to the linkage between uranium enrichment and nuclear weapons material production, but probably would have occurred without proliferation concerns due to the large scale and expensiveness of gaseous diffusion enrichment plants and the reluctance of the private sector to invest in a technology without an assured market. Government enrichment subsidies have taken the form of below market pricing for enrichment services, de facto guarantees of enrichment supply (with the attendant risks of building facilities ahead of the market) and public liabilities for the cost uncertainties accompanying enrichment facilities' decommissioning. Through the OT period, pricing subsidies averaged about 2 M/kwh.[20] This figure excludes the cost of de facto enrichment supply guarantees, which prompted the DOE to invest $3.4 billion (historical $) in a new enrichment facility at Portsmouth Ohio that was later abandoned. It also excludes open ended costs for the decommissioning of existing enrichment facilities, which could exceed the utilities' $2.25 billion liabilities (see chapter 8) by billions of dollars.

Because of the special health hazards and national security issues associated with atomic energy, the development of nuclear power has involved significant federal regulatory expenditures. Subsidies tallied more than $9 billion through 1990.[21] Through 1974 operating subsidies averaged about 2 M/kwh, alongside development subsidies of about $1.25 billion.[22] The NRC began collecting more of its costs from industry clients in the mideighties. Since late-1990 the commission has been legally required to recover all of its regulatory costs from licensees.

Nuclear power's OT status also won the technology a myriad of special subsidies. In the 1960s, for example, the country's only nuclear merchant ship, the Savannah, received $3.5+ million per year in operating subsidies from the National Maritime Administration.[23] U.S. government support for international nuclear activity (excluding EximBank funds) totaled more than $400 million through 1977.[24] Other aid was funded on a local level, such as New York States' nuclear subsidies.[25]

Implicit Subsidies

The effect of nuclear power's OT status is seen in many aspects of the technology's tax treatment. In the late 1950s, the Office of Defense Mobilization authorized accelerated amortization certificates for utility nuclear projects. In the 1960s, New York State established a special authority to finance the purchase of nuclear fuel cores with tax exempt bonds for subsequent IOU leasing. The Treasury-IRS's initial approval of the procedure reflected the belief that Congress wished to encourage utility expansion.[26]

It is very difficult to quantify the per kwh impact of tax policy on nuclear costs. This is partly due to ambiguities about what constitutes a tax subsidy.[27] For the OT years it is estimated that nuclear generation enjoyed about a 1 M/kwh tax advantage over coal-fired generating alternatives.[28] This margin increased substantially from 1974 to 1984. The most important tax subsidies were the tax incentives given utilities for investment in all kinds of new generating plants. During the last thirty years the utilities have enjoyed accelerated depreciation schedules, shortened booklives, investment tax credits, and tax exempt pollution control bonds. These aids reduced nuclear plant capital costs by more than $26 billion (1990$) from 1950 through 1990.[29]

Many of the most important government nuclear subsidies involved risk reduction. This distorted the market's assessment of nuclear power. The AEC implicitly promised to resolve any unanticipated technical problems in the nuclear industry with R&D funds and to provide an assured nuclear fuel supply. The Commission also insulated the industry from uncertain nuclear accident liabilities, uncertain waste disposal and facility decommissioning costs, and foreign credit risks.

The most important risk shifting measure was the 1957 Price-Anderson Act, which discounted the technology's most serious weakness, potential accident hazards. If the economic implications of reactor accident risks had been acknowledged, nuclear technology might have evolved in the direction of the passively safe reactors discussed in chapter 10. The Price-Anderson Act established a $560 million (nominal $) ceiling on liability for nuclear accidents. During the 1950s, industry spokesmen and independent analysts agreed that private sector nuclear development would have likely stalled without liability protection.[30]

It is difficult to quantify the market value of the liability limit. A 1992 DOE study appears to endorse the 1990 findings of Dubin and Rothwell that projected a current subsidy rate of ~$28 million per plant per year (or ~5 M/kwh) and a $77 million subsidy per plant per year (or ~14 M/kwh) prior to the increase in industry accident liability to $7 billion in 1988.[31]

The Export-Import Bank (Exim) aided nuclear power by subsidizing loans and loan guarantees for U.S. nuclear exports. The market value of the aid was estimated to be $164 million (historical $) in 1975, roughly 25% of the Bank's aid to all U.S. exports that year.[32] Through 1975 about two-thirds of U.S. nuclear exports had received Eximbank aid.[33] The General Accounting Office indicated in 1973 that, " 'None of the nuclear power plants sold abroad since 1967 would have been ordered without Exim loans' "[34] By 1979 cumulative nuclear loans and financial guarantees totaled ~$6 billion and exceeded Bank support for any other product category.[35] Similar subsidies are enjoyed by other nations' nuclear industries.

Cost Deferments

AEC cost estimates served as the basis for nuclear waste disposal charges during the OT years. Projections were extremely low, tallying less than .2 M/kwh as late as 1973.[36] Recent DOE analyses assume a 1 M/kwh charge (matching the utilities' current payments into the DOE's waste disposal trust fund). The history of cost underestimation in the waste disposal area and repeated recommendations by the General Accounting Office that the fee be raised, suggest that it will not cover final waste disposal expenses (see chapter 7).<37> This analysis assumes a likely waste disposal cost of ~3 M/kwh, implying that future electricity consumers or the federal government will pick up a ~ 2 M/kwh tab for earlier nuclear power consumers.

Similar neglect and cost underestimation characterized nuclear facility decommissioning cost projections and derived consumer charges during the OT years. When nuclear plant decommissioning costs were included in ratepayer fees, they were trivial, akin to the DOE's mid-seventies' estimate of about .1 M/kwh.[38] Prior to the 1980s, most utilities appear not to have established sinking funds to finance future decommissioning obligations.[39] Current nuclear industry cost studies project decommissioning costs of .1–2 M/kwh. This analysis assumes final decommissioning costs of ~ 3 M/kwh (see chapter 7), implying a cost deferment of about 3 M/kwh. This figure probably under-represents the full impact of neglected decommissioning costs, as it includes only neglected power plant decommissioning costs.

Cost Deferment and Subsidy Totals

Nuclear power's annual operating and development aids are listed in tables 3.4 and 3.5. The assistance reduced nuclear generating costs by 2 c/kwh to 2.5 c/kwh during the OT period and exceeds the average projected

Table 3.5[1]

Operating Subsidies (92$)

Enrichment Services	~2 M/kwh ⎱ total ~3.5 M/kwh
Regulatory Services	~2 M/kwh ⎰
Price-Anderson Act	7–14 M/kwh
Backend Cost Deferment	~5 M/kwh
Tax Assistance[2]	~1 M/kwh
Totals	16.5–24 M/kwh

1. Rationale for subsidy rates explained in text.
2. Entry refers to nuclear/coal tax differential through 1974. Actual nuclear tax subsidies are larger.

generating costs for plants ordered during the OT years by 10%-33%. (See table 4.4) These figures probably underestimate the magnitude of subsidy assistance due to the difficulty of quantifying the market value of risk reductions. The subsidies' downpayment implications (e.g., the promise of additional research and guarantee of fuel supply continuity) are also incompletely captured. In an attempt to include a partial measure of the continuing commitment implied by nuclear power's OT status, OT period development expenditures include outlays through 1979. Subsequent spending, such as the multi-billion dollar outlays for the canceled Portsmouth enrichment facility or later DOE R&D funds, are not included in the subsidy totals.

The calculations distribute the subsidies over the period's projected nuclear kwh totals, rather than subsequent performance and current projections. Calculations based on actual experience would increase the subsidy rate by about .5 M/kwh, as the size of the nuclear sector is smaller than anticipated.

Without the subsidies almost all utility nuclear/coal comparisons would have tilted significantly in favor of coal. Recall, for example, that many of the rationales for ordering nuclear plants in the 1960s rested on alleged cost advantages of less than 3 M/kwh.[40] As a result, the nuclear industry fought hard to achieve minor cost reductions, seeking, for example, to site plants close to populated areas, in order to avoid modestly higher electricity transmission costs. In 1964, the AEC opposed legislation that would have reduced nuclear subsidies by .2–.4 M/kwh (1964$) (1–2 M/kwh 92 $), claiming the change would adversely effect the advanced reactor program.[41]

The sensitivity of development subsidy rates to the time horizon used to amortize the outlays reinforces the key role government research subsidies are likely to play in technical development. Because private firms are likely to employ relatively short planning horizons requiring quick R&D paybacks, it will be difficult for nongovernmentally favored technologies to compete with publicly financed options, even if the former are more cost effective in an engineering sense.[42] By analogy it will be difficult for technologies favored by small firms to compete with development paths favored by larger firms with lower credit costs and longer planning horizons.

Disestablishment and Eroding Subsidy Differentials

Like R&D support, many nuclear subsidies declined after the technology lost OT status. Perhaps most important was the defeat of new subsidy proposals designed to deter nuclear plant cancellations. President Ford was forced to veto one version of the Price-Anderson Act's extension in the mid-seventies due to a provision permitting immediate reconsideration. By 1988 Price-Anderson subsidies had fallen by more than 50% due to increased private insurance requirements. Enrichment subsidies were reduced during the Carter administration and NRC regulatory subsidies ended during the Bush administration. Congressional opposition increased to ExIm Bank's nuclear subsidies and forced withdrawal of bank support for a South Korean nuclear project in 1976.[43] Utility tax breaks for new generating plants were also reduced.

Most crucially, during a period of extreme utility financing difficulties, a series of new nuclear credit subsidy proposals were defeated. The most dramatic setback was congressional rejection of the proposed Energy Independence Authority (EIA). The EIA would have provided up to $100 billion for financing capital intensive energy projects. Testifying before the Senate Banking, Housing, and Urban Affairs Committee in April 1976, Vice President Rockefeller called for continued OT support for nuclear projects through the EIA, arguing:

> "In the case of energy we have the raw materials to achieve self-sufficiency. However, the normal functioning of our economy will not, because of the uncertainty of the risks involved, produce the capital investment required to fully develop these resources within a reasonable period of time. Private capital sources are—for good reason—reluctant to make capital available for domestic energy production projects because of the uncertainty of government regulation, cost and prices . . . Many projects, such as floating nuclear power plants, railroad reconstruction, or large pipelines, are of such size and scope that financing from the private sector alone may not be adequate. Because the electrical utilities have not been able to raise the financing necessary to construct them, ninety-two nuclear power plants have been canceled or postponed. . . ."[44]

Also rejected were: utility efforts to create a utility reconstruction finance corporation and other credit mechanisms, such as regional energy corporations and government guarantees of utility debt; Westinghouse's attempts to promote government purchase of 4–8 floating nuclear power plants for leasing to private utilities;[45] and Los Alamos director Agnew's suggestion that nuclear units be built for defense installations.[46] Similar efforts to utilize public credit mechanisms for nuclear construction were defeated on the state level. In New Hampshire, for example, the Clamshell Alliance successfully blocked efforts by the local utility company to establish a state energy corporation for purchase and subsequent leasing of part of the Seabrook plant.[47] In New York, environmental groups forced the state's Atomic and Space Development Authority to include research on non-nuclear energy sources.[48] Also defeated were several reprocessing plant bailout schemes, continued funding for the Clinch River Breeder reactor, and the Ford administration's proposal for government subsidy of private enrichment projects.

Pro-Nuclear Regulatory Incentives

Pro-nuclear regulatory incentives complete the R&D-subsidy-regulatory triad used by nuclear power's public sector sponsors to pursue OT status for the technology. The major regulatory aids during the OT years were pro-nuclear utility pricing and accounting procedures, sympathetic anti-trust review, infant industry regulation of nuclear power's negative externalities, and the general exercise of public authority to promote nuclear expansion.

Nuclear plant orders were encouraged by rate base formulas that favored capital intensive generating choices and regulatory precedents creating expectations of full recovery of unexpected cost overruns and undercapacity performances.[49] Accounting conventions were often adopted to facilitate utility expansion.[50] In contrast, utility regulations discouraged cogeneration, conservation, and solar energy options through the use of declining block rate structures and a failure to credit independent sources of electricity with a fair value for their grid feed-in.[51]

Both the AEC and Justice Department actively facilitated industry concentration in the nuclear sector, encouraging capital commitments by dominant firms. The AEC's focused contracting policies for R&D and facility administration created a strong "insider" advantage. The commission's characterization of all plants through 1970 as research reactors without "practical value," (and thus insulated from anti-trust review), similarly facilitated the dominance of nuclear generation by large IOUs. Indeed, the possibility that nuclear scale economies might subdue the small municipal utility helped mobilize IOU support for the technology in the sixties. In contrast, industrial cogeneration technologies were inhibited by antitrust policy, especially in the paper industry.[52]

The most important area of nuclear regulation was the treatment of the technology's negative externalities. The latter include routine radiation releases from reactor operation, extraordinary radiation releases from reactor accidents, thermal pollution, radwaste pollution, increased ease of nuclear weapons proliferation, and possible infringement on civil liberties.

Through the OT years, the AEC-JCAE adopted an infant industry regulatory strategy towards nuclear hazards with a heavy reliance on industry "self-regulation". Government policy reflected an underlying technological aesthetic that *posited* the existence of engineering solutions to all known *and unknown* nuclear safety problems. The strategy assumed that the technology's capture of OT status would guarantee resolution of all safety uncertainties by assuring open ended public R&D funding for hazard research and institutional accomodation to hazard containment needs. As RAND Corporation analyst Elizabeth Rolph wrote, "(the AEC's policy was to) . . . adopt the most conservative requirements *consistent with the commercial viability of the nuclear power reactor* (emphasis in original). The staff had no intention of seriously constraining its commercial use".[53]

The AEC and JCAE's infant industry strategy was reinforced by the period's fondness for the idea of industry self-regulation, the symbiotic relationship between the AEC and nuclear industry, and the latter's political clout. The vendors and utilities lobbied constantly for societal tolerance of large safety uncertainties.[54] As nine year NRC Commissioner Victor Gilinsky has observed,

> "We're still digging our way out of the problems created in the sixties. The original idea—and it was a flawed idea—was that we could operate on the basis of self-regulation. A system was set up that was not adequate to the task . . . There was a fairly deliberate policy of keeping the regulatory body weak . . ."[55]

While the level of government and industry safety consciousness was high compared to non-nuclear industries, it underestimated the distinctiveness of nuclear technology. The very thoughtfulness of the industry's hazard assessment program by conventional standards seemed to preclude openness to more radical assessments of safety research needs and equipment requirements. The reorientation of the NPC in the 1970s eventually challenged the regulatory strategy of the OT years and seriously increased hazard containment expenses (see chapter 4).

The varied form of regulatory assistance enjoyed by nuclear power illustrates the diffuse impact of state nuclear promotionalism. It also highlights the "signaling" function of public policy, which by suggesting a consensus development choice encourages private investment. Illustrative of these regulatory aids was the exercise of public property rights in nuclear's favor. The federal government owned approximately 90% of the western lands where uranium was initially sought, and prospectors were given favorable access to these sites.[56] The utilities were similarly assisted in power plant site selection.[57]

The AEC's fuel cycle regulations were designed to shift the risks of fluctuating nuclear fuel demand from the utilities to the AEC.[58] Federal regulations also protected the uranium and fuel reprocessing industries from foreign competition by embargoing private uranium importation through 1974[59] and forbidding reprocessing contracts with foreign firms. Domestic reprocessing firms were also offered guaranteed government markets and an end to the utilities' access to government facilities if private charges were reasonable.[60] Other AEC-JCAE policies before and during the OT years sought to minimize intervenor influence in legislative and licensing procedures, state and local government influence in nuclear affairs, the access of the media to nuclear information, and the financial robustness required for utility nuclear undertakings.

Regulatory Implications of Disestablishment

The anti-nuclear movement stimulated a general contraction in regulatory support. Analogous to the defeat of the Energy Independence Authority and other credit subsidies noted above, was the defeat of various proposals designed to facilitate ratepayer financing of incomplete nuclear construction.[61] The absence of full "Construction Work in Progress" (CWIP) funding was the direct result of anti-nuclear movement pressures and rate-payer backlash against the earlier rate increases caused by rising fossil-fuel prices.[62] The protest movement also undermined nuclear power's "performance insurance", as utility commissions began to disallow full recovery of nuclear cost overruns or project cancellations.[63] This change significantly increased the utilities' perception of the risks associated with the uncertainties of nuclear economics.

From the mid-seventies onward state and local governments also used their environmental protection, land use, and utility regulatory authorities to deter nuclear expansion.[64] At least ten states limited new nuclear construction until waste disposal and other problems were resolved,[65] and nearly one hundred localities banned or limited nuclear materials transport.[66] Numerous states limited ratepayer supported pro-nuclear advertising.[67] Post Three Mile Island regulation witnessed local veto of utility nuclear projects through non-cooperation in emergency planning.

Exacerbating nuclear's regulatory woes during this period was a simultaneous increase in regulatory support for non-nuclear energy options. The Public Utilities Regulatory Policies Act of 1978, for example, facilitated: increased payment to cogenerators, rate reform in the direction of marginal cost pricing (and thus the elimination of anti-solar and anti-conservation declining block rates),<68> and the funding of intervenor groups in utility proceedings. Additional legislation has required the utilities to provide conservation information to their customers.

Chapter 4

The Creation of Promotional Realms of Discourse: A Sociology of Nuclear Knowledge

Introduction

The degree to which technical information about nuclear power has reflected planning context orientations is striking and highlights the need for sociology of knowledge studies of technology assessment in order to understand the direction of technical change. This chapter focuses on how scholarly and popular realms of discourse about radiation hazards, serious reactor accident probabilities, nuclear plant thermal pollution burdens, and nuclear cost forecasts were influenced by the pro-nuclear cast of the NPC from ~1950–~1970. Similar analyses could have been performed for other nuclear power issues, such as nuclear weapons proliferation risks or waste disposal burdens.

Purposefully employing a common framework, the chapter explores how the NPC's technological aesthetics and AEC's infant industry attitude towards nuclear power regulation influenced:

1) the data base available for hazard assessment and cost forecasting;

2) the methodologies used to conceptualize hazard dangers and cost determination;

3) the level of scientific attention given anomalous or otherwise troubling findings; and

4) the regulatory and market reaction to existing and new information.

Subsequent discussion ties the gradual penetration of the nuclear planning context by environmentalists and other nuclear skeptics to a gradual recasting of the data, methodologies, and feedback loops governing nuclear hazard assessment and nuclear cost forecasting. The chapter provides a crucial link between the history of nuclear power and current debates about its future. Without an appreciation of the systematic tendency for excess optimism within the nuclear sector and the institutional habits that reproduce this bias, it is difficult to accurately assess current industry projections.

The chapter includes detailed endnotes on the specific ways that planning context biases influenced nuclear hazard assessment and cost forecasting in order to ground the chapter's more general claims about technology assessment. Readers uninterested in such details may skip these references without losing the thread of the general argument.

Radiation Hazard Assessment

Radiation Hazards: Data Base Constraints 1950–1970

Because the activities of the AEC were initially directed towards expanded weapons production and bomb testing, and then towards the rapid commercialization of nuclear power, the commission placed a relatively low priority on hazard data collection prior to and during the OT years. It ignored a National Academy of Sciences recommendation that a national record of radiation exposure histories be established.[1] Relatively little data was collected on the health history of nuclear industry workers[2] or populations exposed to high levels of fallout.[3] Minimal monitoring oversaw industry release levels.[4] The epidemiological data that was collected was marred by inconsistent and incomplete radiation measurement, a lack of timely attention to subsequent health problems, and insufficient recording of relevant complementary data (such as the population's smoking habits).[5]

As a result, a wide range of hazard claims were consistent with available epidemiological data through the OT years. This ambiguity permitted promotional optimism to dominate official hazard assessments. Through 1990, the accumulation of new information has tended to increase hazard estimates. The National Academy of Sciences' fifth report on the *Biological Effects of Ionizing Radiation* (BEIR V, 1990), for example, increased risk factors by three times over BEIR III (1980) *(New England Journal of Medicine, 2/14/91, 499)*.

Methodological Constraints 1950–1970

Centralized AEC-DOE control of radiation hazard data and research funding encouraged a methodological inbreeding that underestimated the scope of nuclear hazards. Illustrative of this tendency was: the early neglect of food chain avenues of radiation exposure,[6] the adoption of the now discredited threshold hypothesis,[7] the use of misestimated ratios of low to high level radiation for Hiroshima epidemiological studies,[8] an inattention to the fuel cycle's release of certain radioactive isotopes,[9] and the constraining of environmental burden estimates into arbitrarily narrow time periods compared with the lifespan of nuclear waste materials.[10]

AEC-DOE radiation hazard studies have also been criticized for underestimating: the "survivor bias" in Japanese bomb casualty studies,[11] the "healthy worker" bias in U.S. nuclear industry studies,[12] and the need to investigate mutagenic and non-cancerous radiation hazards.[13]

While some studies claiming to demonstrate radiation hazards have also suffered from methodological flaws[14] and extreme statements have been made by some nuclear power opponents, the nuclear industry's tendency to dismiss radiation critics as uninformed is unwarranted. Researchers such as Karl Morgan, John Gofman, and Alice Stewart have first class scientific and professional credentials. The debate over radiation hazards is not a debate between reason and fear as has often been the rhetorical device used by the industry to explain to itself and the public why controversy continues. It is a debate over how to interpret and respond to ambiguous findings.

The AEC-DOE's policy of denying independent researchers access to government data on radiation exposure and health histories in the nuclear weapons complex has been especially conducive to insular discourse. The most famous instance of this exclusion was the department's fourteen year refusal to allow Doctors Mancuso, Kneale, and Stewart access to follow up data on workers at the Hanford weapons plant after their initial findings suggested higher hazard levels than anticipated (*New York Times* 12/8/92). In defending its data monopoly, the DOE argued that release of the information " 'could lead to spurious and/or conflicting results that would confuse the public and generate irrational criticism that could further undermine public confidence in DOE' " (Geiger et al. 1992, 57).

While such heavy-handed efforts at "guided research" are the most obvious example of the impact of planning context variables on hazard assessment, the subtler socialization of a generation of health physicists and industry radiation professionals is probably more important. Describing the sociological context that has dominated radiation research, a 1979 article in *Science*, the journal of the American Association for the Advancement of Science, noted, "The radiation research community has lived almost entirely off the energy and defense establishments. The situation is conducive to a monolithic approach to research. . . . It also means that for anyone seeking objective scientific advice it is practically impossible to find someone knowledgeable who was not trained with AEC money" (Holden 1979, 156).[15]

Inattention to Anomalous information 1950–1970

Despite limited data and methodological constraints, findings at odds with the prevailing optimism concerning nuclear radiation hazards emerged during the fifties and early sixties. Both the AEC and industry, however, were able to minimize the social meaning of this material by not publicizing anomalous findings nor funding follow-up studies. A popular image of radiation concern as unpatriotic[16] and the difficulty of establishing cause and effect relationships in epidemiological studies allowed this policy to dominate information contexts.[17] The AEC also appears to have reinforced its position by engaging in professional reprisals against its scientific critics.[18]

Because there is natural variability in cancer rates, measurement error in worker radiation exposure and health history data, a long latency period between radiation exposure and malignancy, and a relatively small number of nuclear industry workers with limited radiation exposure levels, it is extremely difficult to derive definitive radiation hazard estimates from existing empirical data. Recent disagreements between DOE statisticians and DOE critics, for example, over projected radiation induced cancer fatalities at the Hanford weapons plant differ by only 150–200 deaths out of a sample of 35,000 (*New York Times* 12/8/92, 1).[19]

Throughout the 1950–1970 period (and in fact to this day), the AEC and nuclear industry have found available information consistent with the hypothesis that radiation hazards were relatively well understood and posed very little risk for the routine operation of nuclear facilities. Given the AEC and industry's additional assumption of very low reactor accident probabilities, a relatively low priority was placed on clarifying radiation effects. The burden of proof was placed on proving hazards rather than proving safety. If a study found an increase in some form of cancer in an exposed population, there was a tendency to ignore the results unless they could not have been due to random fluctuations in cancer rates.[20] Even when such clusters were found, there was a tendency to highlight alternative explanations for their appearance rather than potential "tip of the iceberg" implications. The commission's civilian power policies thus resembled its attitude towards the military atom and atomic bomb testing.

An alternative approach would have been to treat elevated cancer rates in small samples as suspicious warnings calling for increased research. Recent findings of excess cancers at Oak Ridge, after earlier studies relying on shorter follow-up periods painted a more reassuring picture, highlight the risks of premature epidemiological conclusions when dealing with hazards with long latency periods (Wing et al. 1991).

To date, the AEC's optimism prior to and during the OT period seems excessive by at least an order of magnitude. While this error is not large enough to make acknowledged radiation releases from *routine* nuclear plant operations a serious occupational or public health problem, it is large enough to alter the implications of large scale reactor accidents. Even with respect to routine nuclear sector activities (including uranium mining and waste disposal), there is enough uncertainty to warrant expanded epidemiological study of radiation effects (see chapter 9). From both a public health and public relations perspective, the AEC and DOE's greatest error may have been the tolerance of excessive uncertainty.

Lenient Regulatory Requirements

The realm of discourse created by the OT period's data and methodological constraints allowed the AEC and nuclear industry's infant industry perspective to dominate regulatory design. Radiation release standards were set with deference to the needs of the weapons testing program and light water reactor technology.[21] In many cases problems were solved by recourse to self-regulation. Radon levels in uranium mines during the 1950s were left unrestrained and commonly reached rates one hundred times current standards. Power plant emission limits during the 1960s were twenty times higher than in the 1980s.[22] Minimal regulations were imposed on the disposal of uranium mill tailings. Little attention was given to high level waste disposal questions. In defense of the AEC, it should be noted that given the Commission's optimistic technical assumptions, the AEC's regulatory decisions were sometimes conservative.[23]

Political Refocus: Shifting Regulatory Environments

After the mid- to late-1960s, the penetration of the nuclear planning context by nuclear critics reconstituted the data base available, methodologies employed, and attention given to anomalous findings in the radiation hazard area. The economic result was increased radiation containment expenditures. Although the radiation debate was conducted on a technical plain, it was conditioned by broader socio-political contexts. Its roots stretch back to the atomic testing debates in the 1950s. Key to hazard rethinking in both cases was the interaction between the technical critics of the AEC and a popular political movement.[24]

During the mid-sixties, critics gained a public platform for hazard discussion in sixteen radiation related plant licensing challenges (Rolph 1979,

113). Political pressures eventually forced the AEC to collect health data on soldiers exposed to fallout during the nuclear tests,[25] and civilians working in nuclear shipyards. The *Washington Post* used the Freedom of Information Act to release leukemia-fallout correlation data. The Kennedy Health Subcommittee fallout hearings revealed a pattern of information suppression. Public pressures similarly forced the AEC to investigate Ernest Sternglass' radiation hazard claims and to accept new findings by the commission's staff increasing radiation hazard estimates. Other nuclear critics forced rejection of the threshold hypothesis and the use of longer time periods in calculating radiation hazard burdens.

The controversies fueled efforts to transcend the JCAE-AEC's dominance of the federal government's nuclear regulatory and research apparatus. In 1967 the Department of Labor promulgated the first federal regulations limiting radon concentrations in U.S. uranium mines. In the early seventies the National Environmental Policy Act shifted some of the AEC's radiation related informational and regulatory functions to the Environmental Protection Agency (DOE 5/80, 104). In 1990, under the threat of a Freedom of Information lawsuit and pending congressional legislation to transfer radiation hazard research from DOE oversight to the Department of Health and Human Services, the DOE agreed to allow some independent researchers access to the department's epidemiological data on radiation exposure among weapons complex workers (Geiger et al. 1992, 22). Two years later the *New York Times* reported,

"The first independent study of the health records of 35,000 workers at a Government bomb plant in Washington State presents a new, more sinister picture of the risks of small doses of radiation.

This finding, by a pioneer in radiation epidemiology, Dr. Alice Stewart, follows her 14-year struggle to regain access to the health data. For decades, the Federal Government had limited access to scientists of its choosing. . . .

Dr. Stewart's study . . . concludes that 200 of the workers have lost or will lose years of their lives because of radiation-induced cancer. This contradicts earlier Government-sponsored studies that found no additional cancer deaths" (*New York Times* 12/8/92, 1).[26]

Dr. Rosalie Bertell found a similar tendency for independent epidemiological studies to find higher hazard levels than official nuclear power related agencies in Western Europe and Japan in the 1960s and 1970s (Bertell 1985, 7). Sadly, the International Atomic Energy Agency has also acted as a promotional arm of the nuclear industry, rather than an independent forum for technology assessment.

Economic Implications

The impact of escalating radiation concern on the cost of nuclear power is difficult to quantify. In addition to increasing outlays for radiation containment equipment, the concern stimulated efforts to strengthen siting distance criteria, quality control standards, and accident prevention efforts (Rolph 1979, 61,116,124). Among the first economic consequences of the radiation controversy were the radiation reduction agreements negotiated between intervenors in nuclear plant licensing hearings and the utilities in the late sixties and early seventies. Under the agreements the intervenors withdrew their licensing objections in return for a utility's upgrading of plant radiation release safeguards.[27] By 1970, political pressures forced the AEC to strengthen its radiation release guidelines (Rolph 1979, 113). The same year the National Environmental Policy Act transferred some radiation regulatory authority from the AEC to the EPA. By 1977, the EPA, following AEC precedents, had reduced permissible exposure levels at plant boundaries by twentyfold (Nader and Abbotts 1979, 75–6; Komanoff 1981, 113). The reduction required numerous plant design changes, including: the upgrading of waste holding tanks, air filtration systems, waste monitoring capabilities, waste protection during accident conditions, and occupational exposure protection.[28]

Table 4.1 records the declining level of recommended radiation expo-

Table 4.1
Changing Radiation Standards

Occupational Exposure	General Public Exposure
1934 30 rem/yr	
1949 15 rem/yr	
1957 5 rem/yr	1956 .50 rem/yr
1960 5 rem/yr	1960 .17 rem/yr
1977 5 rem/yr	
1987 5 rem/yr	1987 .10 rem/yr
1990 2 rem/yr*	

*recommended. (Recommendations from the International Commission on Radiological Protection (ICRP) have traditionally served as the basis of U.S. radiation exposure standards.) Current U.S. exposure limits remain at 5 rem/yr despite 1990 ICRP recommendations for a reduction to 2 rem/yr *Nucleonics Week* 4/8/93, 2.
From: Michael McCally, "What the Fight is All About," *Bulletin of the Atomic Scientists*, September 1990, 14.

sure in the U.S. The movement towards increasingly stringent regulations is even greater than suggested by the figures, as in many cases industry practices are regulated by even tighter "ALARA" (As Low As Reasonably Achievable) standards rather than permissible levels (Kocher 1991).[29] It should be noted that some of the decline has been due to the development of less expensive radiation reduction techniques as well as increased radiation hazard concerns. Chapter 9 reviews current debates about radiation hazard assessment and regulatory policy. The controversies are surprisingly similar to past debates.

Nuclear Plant Accident Hazards

As in the radiation hazard field, the AEC and nuclear industry believed reactor safety challenges were well understood and accident risks extremely small. The same pattern of constrained discourse that organized radiation hazard assessment organized accident probability analysis prior to and during much of the OT period.

Data Base Constraints (1950–1970)

Because of the AEC's confidence in existing reactor safety and belief that it could rapidly resolve any outstanding safety uncertainties, accident research held a relatively low priority in the AEC's development program (1950–1970). Safety studies received only modest funding[30] and were frequently delayed to speed other projects, such as breeder reactor development or quality assurance demonstration. To further economize, the AEC left much safety research and data collection to the nuclear industry, despite the firms' demonstrated reluctance to share information with the commission that would lead to new safety requirements (Campbell 1988, 58–59).[31]

Data collection was also limited by the location of safety R&D in the promotionally oriented Division of Reactor Development and Technology (RDT). In 1969 the commission's technical experts, the Advisory Committee on Reactor Safeguards (ACRS), expressed alarm over the lack of studies investigating potential core melting, fuel failure, and seismic stress problems (Rolph 1979, 94). Only limited attention was given to reactor operating experience as a source of safety information (Ford 1982, 200; Pollard 1979, 1–2).[32] By 1971, Robert Gillette reported,

". . . Scientists and engineers in the safety program have come to believe . . . that the AEC, in its eagerness to develop a thriving nuclear industry—and to get on with building the breeder reactors it has dreamed about for 20 years—has deliberately bypassed tough safety questions . . ." (Gillette 9/1/72, 771).[33]

The nuclear industry displayed even less interest than the AEC in uncovering safety hazards. During the JCAE's 1967 regulatory hearings, industry spokesmen strongly opposed funding for heuristic safety research, favoring instead studies designed to redress known hazards.[34] The minutes of a February 1968 ACRS meeting report, "The representatives of the reactor designers . . . expressed their opinions that their designs are adequately safe without further major R&D . . ." (Okrent 1981, 310, see also 194).[35]

Among the potential safety problems ignored were current concerns regarding the adequacy of meltdown containment systems[36], seismic stress[37] and fire hazard[38] response systems, and quality control.[39] Problems such as fuel densification, safety system crippling plant blackouts, endemic tube denting, steam corrosion cracking, and pressure vessel embrittlement were encountered during commercial operation rather than design research.[40]

Increased information has typically led to increased regulatory stringency and higher safety expenditures. For example, plants are now equipped with back-up fossil fuel generating capacity to guard against plant blackouts. The reliability of the backup system, however, eventually became a serious safety issue[41], illustrating a more general problem associated with nuclear safety: the potential for exponential difficulties to accompany linear increases in hazard information. A similar scenario accompanied efforts to reduce earthquake hazards, where the addition of "$150 million worth of snubbers, pipe supports, and engineering" (has generated new concerns, as the) "snubbers are unreliable and subject to frequent failure. . . . The resulting pipe work is now very rigid, and access to equipment for inspection or repair is less convenient" (Weinberg et al. 1985, 6). The economic result has been a negative learning curve for nuclear construction costs.[42]

Methodological Constraints (1950–1970)

As in early radiation research, methodological inbreeding generated a narrow consensus regarding accident probabilities. Five conceptual biases, all related to the adoption of a restricted definition of credible accident scenarios, lay behind the AEC-nuclear industry's initial optimism about accident probabilities.

1) The exclusion from hazard calculations of the impact of unanticipated events inside the reactor.

2) The characterization of various theoretically possible events as practically impossible, such as pressure vessel rupture or multiple failure initiated accidents.[43]

3) A minimization of the dangers of external disruptions such as tornadoes, earthquakes, and sabotage.

4) A minimization of the dangers of human error.[44]

5) The assumed bounding of accident scenarios by backstop defenses, such as the pressure vessel and ECCS.

In effect, the commission and industry began by excluding multiple-failure initiated and unexpected events from credible consideration; then positing a pervasive redundancy, the possibility of serious accidents was eliminated tautologically. New accident paths might be discovered, but their practical hazard implications were minimal.[45]

Misplaced optimism also characterized the commission's confidence in the ability of computer modeling to replace experimental data. As a result the AEC and industry failed to conduct adequate emergency core cooling system (ECCS) tests. Subsequent experience has found errors in the ECCS computer modeling codes as well as those used for seismic stress analysis.[46] Two senior AEC safety officials have characterized the commission's reliance on the codes as "a triumph of faith over reason" (Gillette 5/5/72, 498). They attribute this behavior to the pressures of "group think" and bureaucratic momentum.[47] Government safety experts have also tended to treat safety problems as solved when conceptual solutions have been theorized, rather than developed or deployed (Adato et al. 1987, 17).

Inattention to Anomalous Information (1950–1970)

As in the radiation hazard area, both the AEC and the nuclear industry were able to influence the policy implications of technical information by:

1) discouraging interest in findings that conflicted with policy optimism,

2) minimizing the opportunities for networking amongst nuclear skeptics, and

3) limiting public awareness of the safety concerns amongst the commission and industry's technical staffs.

One of the earliest examples of selective publication of information is the AEC's suppression of the the Advisory Committee on Reactor Safeguards' report on the FERMI breeder reactor in 1956. After political pressures forced the report's release, the AEC acknowledged there were unresolved safety issues associated with the FERMI project. The commission justified continuing reactor construction with an especially explicit statement of the technological optimisim underlying the entire nuclear enterprise. The commission indicated that it assumed,

> " '. . . that the gaps in knowledge which are discovered in the course of design can be corrected by design changes, and that those gaps in knowledge which are encountered only when the reactor is put into operation have negligible probability of making the reactor unsafe with containment' " (Hilgartner et al. 1982,112).

In the late fifties the U.S. decided against releasing information about the Russian nuclear accident in the Urals (Hilgartner et al. 1982, 112–117). In November 1974 the *New York Times* reported:

> ". . . memos and letters written by AEC and industry officials since '64, show (that the) AEC has repeatedly sought to suppress studies by its own scientists that found nuclear reactors are more dangerous than officially acknowledged or that raised questions about reactor safety devices" (New York Times Index 11/10/74).

Former AEC Commissioner Victor Gilinsky adds,

> "One result of the regulators' professional identification with the owners and operators of the plants in the battles over nuclear energy was a tendency to try to control information to disadvantage the anti-nuclear side" (Gilinsky 1992, 707).

The most publicized example of non-attention was the suppression of a major study of accident probabilities (the WASH-740-update) after the report calculated relatively high hazard estimates.[48] Critics charge that the

follow-up study, WASH 1400, was carefully designed to avoid similar difficulties. Quality control and quality assurance issues, for example, were excluded from analysis.[49]

The Advisory Committee on Reactor Safeguards (ACRS) served as the
chief technical check on AEC-nuclear industry safety decisions. The commission was able to mute ACRS safety initiatives, however, through its ability to appoint committee members[50] and to threaten disbandment.[51] The
social dynamics within the ACRS also tended to dilute critics' concerns
(Okrent 1981, 10). It appears that safety skeptics acquiesced to lax licensing
decisions in exchange for personal credibility in a long run battle for a grad-
ualist set of safety upgrades. In numerous cases, for example, the committee
agreed to refrain from public criticism of the AEC, in exchange for commission promises of new research or future regulatory upgrades.[52]

The information history of the emergency core cooling system (ECCS)
controversy mirrors, in microcosm, the information history of nuclear power.
Endnote 53 explores this history in detail.[53]

Political Refocus: Expanding Accident Hazard Data Bases

During the 1970s, environmentalist pressures forced the AEC to increase accident hazard R&D and to establish a Division of Reactor Safety
Research free from administrative control by the promotionally oriented Division of Reactor Development and Technology.[54] In 1973 the commission
reduced industry's participation in AEC safety research in order to reduce
the appearance of conflicts of interest (Campbell 1988, 70). In 1974 Congress replaced the AEC with the Energy Research and Development Administration and the NRC in an attempt to insulate regulatory and safety review
from promotional activities. Congress required the commission to investigate
new safety systems in 1977 (Okrent 1981, 314). Reactions to TMI overrode
long-standing industry opposition to research on how to minimize the impact
of core meltdowns (Okrent 1981, 314). The result of expanded inquiry has
usually been regulatory escalation.

Reorienting Methodological Assumptions

The coalescence of a critical mass of technically trained skeptics played
a central role in generating new methodological perspectives. Illustrative is
the impact of the Union of Concerned Scientists' activities on the ECCS

debate. Other UCS research led to the upgrading of reactor fire and earthquake hazard response systems, the adoption of improved equipment qualification levels, and the NRC's partial withdrawal of support for the Rasmussen safety study.[55] The Scientists Institute for Public Information (SIPI) played much the same role in the breeder reactor debate (Del Sesto 1979, 166–169).

Local anti-nuclear intervenors repeatedly demonstrated the NRC and utilities' neglect of site-specific geological conditions[56] and eventually forced a general review of earthquake standards. Other local efforts increased the AEC's attention to on-site quality control problems and reactor building support settling (Komanoff 1981, 60). The threat of intervenor cross-examination and design review pressured both the industry and AEC to upgrade their overall safety analysis (Rolph 1979, 124; see also DOE 5/80, 131). The intervenors also strengthened the ACRS' internal bargaining position with the AEC bureaucracy. The threat of public disclosure of ACRS safety concerns was more compelling when intervenor groups were likely to introduce such information into local licensing hearings and the national nuclear debate.[57]

Revising the Social Meaning of Technical Information

The anti-nuclear movement has also been able to gain public exposure for previously neglected research that raised questions about the adequacy of nuclear accident safeguards. Among the documents introduced into the public domain by Freedom of Information suits or pressures are: The WASH 740 Update, the AEC's "Task Force Report Study of the Reactor Licensing Process,"[58] the Nugget File,[59] the Reactor Safety Study Correspondence,[60] CIA information about the Russian nuclear accident in the Urals (Hilgartner et al. 1982, 113), NRC data on equipment qualification deficiencies[61] and a number of reports raising questions about reactor pipe integrity and plant sabotage hazards.[62] Additional information gained public review through the discovery powers granted nuclear critics in various hearings and other "open-government" legislation.[63]

One of the most important impacts of the protest movement was the creation of a social context more conducive to public dissent within the industry than the OT period's "team-player" environment. Whistle blowing by AEC officials, nuclear industry engineers, and on-site construction personnel has been a key source of regulatory escalation.[64]

Economic Impact

The integrated character of plant design makes it difficult to isolate the financial impact of particular regulatory upgrades.[65] The escalation is reflected, however, in the increased materials requirements for plant construction. Average cable, concrete, and piping requirements, for example, increased by 150% during 1971–1985. Craft labor requirements rose from 3.5 hrs/KW capacity in 1967 to 21.6 hrs/KW for 1982–1985 plants. Non-manual field and engineering services leaped from 1.3 hrs/KW to 9.2/hrs/KW (OTA 1984, 60–61). Escalating quality control requirements have been particularly costly, more than doubling, for example, the real 1975 cost of reactor steel supports without changing their physical dimensions.

Thermal Pollution Hazards

The OT Period

The history of waste heat regulation follows the same pattern of official neglect (1950–1970) and later concern that characterized the treatment of radiation and accident dangers. As in other hazard areas, only a limited data base was available in 1970 for estimating the thermal pollution burden to specific bodies of water.[66] Reactor designers initially paid little attention to thermal pollution problems (Nelkin 1971, 118). The AEC aggressively refused to consider the hazard in licensing review, resisted the JCAE's attempts to endow it with regulatory authority, and opposed efforts to apply thermal pollution standards to nuclear power plants (which produce about 40%–50% more heat per kwh than fossil fuel plants) without similar application to fossil fuel units (Walker 1989, 978–79). While the AEC did fund some thermal pollution research, its hostility towards thermal pollution concerns, encouraged hazard neglect. For example, after Cornell University personnel helped stimulate pressures for higher waste heat containment standards for the proposed Bell nuclear plant, former AEC Commissioner Frank Costagliola attacked "small academic groups who . . . degrade the competency of the AEC in the eyes of the public," and warned, "It is my opinion that the access our colleges and universities have to federal funds for the conduct of research is a privilege and not a right" (Nelkin 1971, 111).

Political Refocus

Initial skirmishes involved legal challenges during licensing proceedings. Little concern was evident before 1966, but from 1966–1971 fourteen plants were challenged on thermal pollution grounds (Rolph 1979, 105). The AEC parried such attacks by claiming it lacked jurisdiction to impose thermal constraints. As in the radiation release area, the intervenors' first victories involved agreements with individual utilities to increase expenditures to reduce thermal pollution in exchange for an end to intervenor protests.[67]

Widely publicized hearings before Senator Muskie's subcommittee on air and water pollution in 1968, an article in *Sports Illustrated* in 1969, and the Muskie Bill increasing nuclear power's thermal accountability facilitated thermal pollution protests (Walker 1989, 982–987). The balance of power between the utilities and intervenors swung significantly in the direction of the environmentalists with the Calvert Cliffs court decision in 1971 applying the National Environmental Policy Act (NEPA) to nuclear power plants. The court castigated the AEC for behavior that "makes a mockery of the act" (Lewis 1972, 282). Regulatory policy has increasingly required the use of cooling towers.

Cost estimates for cooling towers have varied. Walker (1989) cites costs of ~$9–$22 million (1979$) for a 1000 MW plant (p. 974). Cooling towers also slightly reduce net plant output.

Summary: Planning Contexts and Nuclear Hazard Assessment

Although precise figures are unobtainable, it is possible to estimate the cost of escalating health and environmental regulations. Deflating for general construction cost increases, nuclear construction costs grew from approximately $700/KW for non-turnkey plants coming on line before 1971 to $3,750–$4000/KW for plants entering service after 1982 (Komanoff 1981, 20; 1984, Table 1; Komanoff and Roelofs 12/92, 17, 74–75). About $600/KW of this increase represents the impact of higher market interest rates. Analyses completed in the mid-eighties suggested that regulatory streamlining, more efficient construction scheduling, standardization, and learning improvements could reduce future construction costs by $925/KW (OTA 1984, 67). The net result implies a $1525–$1775/KW safety and environmental upgrade. Early insulation from these charges, equal to

~3 c/kwh, can be considered another dimension of nuclear power's OT status. The tally would be even larger if the impact of OT informational-regulatory environments on capacity rates, fuel cycle costs, and O&M costs were included.

Nuclear power's regulatory treatment reflected the interactive logic of the period's nuclear planning context. As Table 4.2 indicates, this logic transcends conventional models of lobbying pressure and reflects the social creation of a realm of discourse. Planning context variables severely influenced the available data and methodologies used to assess hazards, the attention given to anomalous findings, and the regulatory reaction to technical information. The pattern of discourse addressing radiation hazards, accident probabilities, and thermal pollution during the OT period was repeated in other hazard areas, such as nuclear waste disposal and nuclear weapons proliferation.

Nuclear supporters have rejected claims of self-serving inattention to nuclear hazards. They point to the industry's self-interest in the safe operation of nuclear plants, as well as the moral character of AEC regulators. The PC-OT framework demonstrates that both factors are consistent with lax hazard regulations, if the latter is linked to constrained realms of technical discourse and a long run confidence in the ability of OT status to ensure successful resolution of hazard uncertainties.

The strength of the PC-OT planning context model is its ability to integrate a wide range of phenomena into a common framework of explanation. We have thus far looked at how the NPC infused R&D and hazard assessment paradigms. The next section develops a similar sociology of cost forecasting knowledge. The ability to link together changing realms of technical discourse in fields as diverse as emergency core cooling, food chain radiation hazards, thermal pollution, electricity demand forecasting (chapter 11), and biomass energy costs (chapter 12), illustrates the robustness of the PC-OT model.

The pattern of insular discourse surrounding nuclear power in the U.S. during the OT period was reproduced globally, often through spinoffs of the U.S. nuclear industry, such as Euratom and the International Atomic Energy Association. The continued dominance of many third world nuclear programs by true believers infused with the ideology of the OT period is especially worrisome in the light of Chernobyl. The risk of insular discourse in emerging technologies, such as biotechnology, is also suggested by the history of nuclear hazard assessment.

Table 4.2
Hazard Assessment Paradigms

OT Years (circa 1950–1970)	Protest Years (~1970–present)
Nuclear Power Radiation Hazards	

DATA

Lack of occupational exposure registry	Protest-controversy induced establishment of rad. exposure registry
Lack of rigorous study of nuclear industry cancer rates	Muckraking journalist spurred govt. study of cancer rates at Portsmouth naval yard
Lack of fallout and military exercise exposure data	Protest induced study of GI bomb test observers' cancer rates
Lack of vigorous monitoring of nuclear plant radiation	Citizen monitoring of nuclear plant radiation releases

METHODOLOGY

General lack of attention to cancer-nuclear power links	Protest induced increase in research on cancer linkages
Assumption of "threshold hypothesis"	Protest stimuli for exploration & adoption of cumulative linear hypothesis
Neglect of food chain avenue of human radiation exposure & some kinds of radioactive emissions	Inclusion of food chain exposure
Use of 1–30–100 yr. ceiling for calculating rad hazard burdens	Modest extension of hazard burden period towards actual decay period
Use of original Hiroshima Bomb Assessment data	Use of revised Hiroshima data, implying greater rad hazards
Incomplete attention to genetic damage hazards	Increased attention to genetic hazards

SOCIAL MEANING

Suppression of early fallout hazard concerns	Protest induced Senate hearings on early treatment of fallout info.
Suppression of early study linking higher leukemia rates to bomb tests	Protest induced attention to cancer rates among GIs exposed to bomb tests
Neglect of Utah sheep deaths and relative indifference to info. on uranium tailings hazards	Freedom of Information release of Radiation hazard related data

Nuclear Plant Accident and Thermal Pollution Hazards	

DATA

Limited accident hazard R&D	Protest induced expansion of accident hazard R&D
Limited collection of accident related empirical data	Congressionally mandated study of reactor operating experience
Prohibition of communication between regulatory and hazard research staffs	Protest stimulated establishment of administratively independent reactor safety division, with research capabilities
Limited attention to local seismic conditions	Local intervenor motivated study of site specific seismic issues
Limited data and planning attention to thermal pollution	Court required attention to thermal pollution and all environmental impacts

Table 4.2 (*Continued*)

OT Years (circa 1950–1970)	Protest Years (~1970–present)

| Nuclear Plant Accident and Thermal Pollution Hazards | |
OT Years	Protest Years

METHODOLOGY

Assumption of single failure initiated accident paths	Use of multiple failure accident paths
Reactor safety study (RSS) exclusion of unanticipated accident paths from hazard probabilities	UCS et al. stimulated, congressionally mandated review and partial rejection of RSS fault tree methodology
Minimization of externally initiated events for reactor safety	Intervenor stimulated increases in: attention to earthquakes, tornadoes, sabotage and other external hazards
Use of flawed computer codes to predict seismic stress	UCS-protest movement induced review of seismic stress formulas
Minimal attention to quality control problems	Protest induced attention to quality control issues
Use of backstop assumption to minimize implications of system failures	Protest induced recalculation of adequacy of ECCS and pressure vessel

SOCIAL MEANING

Public relations campaigns to trivialize accident dangers Suppression of: WASH-740 update on potential accident hazards, ACRS safety concerns, and CIA data about Soviet nuclear accidents	Fish bowl treatment of nuclear plant performance, congressionally ordered publication of abnormal occurrences and unresolved safety issues, increased whistle blowing; opening-up of ACRS proceedings; F.O.I. access to safety data. Controversy induced upgrading of ECCS, quality control, and other accident safeguards; reductions in thermal pollution

Nuclear Power Cost Forecasting*

The magnitude of nuclear cost forecasting errors during the OT period was extraordinary. Nuclear plants persistently cost about twice the inflation adjusted price predicted when they were purchased. The last forty-three plants coming on line in the U.S. (1983–present) cost more than $3.75 billion per 1000 MW, or more than six times the constant dollar sum projected in the mid-sixties, and generate electricity at ~10 c/kwh or more than five

---

*NB: All cost references in this section have been translated into 1992 $ using the GDP deflator, as reported in *The Economic Report of the President 1994*, 272–273.

times the average rate predicted from 1963–1972 (see tables 4.3 and 4.4). Costs were underestimated and performance over promised in almost all categories, from plant construction costs to plant decommissioning costs, from construction duration to plant capacity performance. The pattern of error is directly traceable to the logic of OT competition and the character of the Nuclear Planning Context.

The vendors and AEC were spurred to promote misleadingly optimistic cost expectations by inter-technology competition for OT status and/or intra-nuclear industry competition for market share. Even if partially contradicted by subsequent experience, misleadingly optimistic cost expectations could impart critical mass advantages to the nuclear sector and proselytizing firms. The utilities and their contractors (especially the architect-engineering-construction firms) were discouraged from critical cost review by their: expected cost-plus insulation from cost overrun penalties, self-interest in successful nuclear development, traditional reliance on the vendors' technical judgment, and deference to the self-fulfilling prophecy aspect of OT dynamics.[68] Eventually, a modified "emperor has no clothes" syndrome emerged, as many nuclear firms sought to protect prior nuclear investments by encouraging overall nuclear expansion.

Several ideological and institutional characteristics of the 1950–1965 period increased the industry's potential for self-deception by insulating the sector's cost forecasts from critical review.[69] Among these were: the classified or proprietary nature of early nuclear information, the dominance of "hands-on" experience by nuclear promoters, the relative absence of public

Table 4.3
Nuclear Power Predicted and Actual Costs (Constant 1992$)

Year of Prediction	1963–1968[1]	1969–1972[2]	1973–1974[3]	Actual Costs 1983–Present[4]
Capital Costs per Kilowatt	$537	$685	$1258	$3,750+
Total Generating Costs	17M/kwh	20M/kwh	39M/kwh	100–105M/kwh

1. 1963–1968 cost estimates: Burn 1967, 38; Perry 1977, 30, 35; *Fortune* 9/66; *Electrical World* 5/2/66; *New York Times* 4/10/66; Montgomery and Quirk 1978, 24; AEC 1968a; Little 1968.
2. 1969–1972 cost estimates: Montgomery and Quirk 1978, 24; AEC: 1970a, 1972b; House Committee on Interior and Insular Affairs 7/12/79, 226.
3. 1973–1974 cost estimates: AEC: 1973, 1974c; Montgomery and Quirk 1978, 24.
4. Actual Costs refer to projected costs for reactors entering service in the mid-eighties, see table 4.4.

Too Cheap to Meter

Table 4.4
Nuclear Plant Generating Costs: Prediction and Performance
('92 Mills/kwh, assuming constant real interest rates)

	Expected Costs[1] 1963–1972	Actual Costs Plants coming online 1983-Present
Overall generating costs M/kwh	18–18.5	~100
Capital Costs M/kwh	9.1	64
$/KW	648	~3,750[2]
capacity rates	75%	65%[3]
plant construction duration (years)	4.5	10–12 +[4]
fixed charge interest rate differential	0	.5(5)
Fuel Costs M/kwh (w/o waste disposal)	6.3	6.5[6]
Operation & Maintenance M/kwh (Including post operation capital additions)	2.5	20–22[7]
waste disposal M/kwh	.09	3.0[8]
Decommissioning Costs M/kwh	.09	3.0[8]
Miscellaneous	0	2[9]

1. Nuclear cost prediction entries are based on an averaging of actual cost forecasts. See table 4.3 for the sources used to calculate average capital cost and total cost predictions. For capacity rate forecasts see: AEC, 1960, 134; AEC 1968a, Montgomery and Quirk 1978, 52; *New York Times* 11/9/72, 73 and 3/9/75, 4; and the *Wall Street Journal* 5/3/73, 2. For plant construction duration predictions, see: AEC 1960, AEC 1968a, AEC 1970a, and AEC 1974b. For fuel cost predictions see Cohn 1986, 375–379. For O&M cost expectations, see: Ford Foundation 1977, 126; AEC 1974c, 20; House Government Operations Committee, 1977, 391; AEC 1971a, 91. For waste disposal and decommissioning cost forecasts, see: Dawson 1976, 145; Ford Foundation 1977, 122 and Ford Foundation 1979, 419; House Government Operations Committee, 1977, 329, 335, 391, 427; and Cohn 1986, 379–386.
2. Actual capital costs for plants coming on line 1983–1993 were closer to $3,900/kW (Komanoff and Roelofs 12/92, 9, 75), plus Comanche Peak 2. Since some of the latter plants' long construction periods were especially unusual, I've adjusted the total downwards.
3. Through 1990, U.S. commercial sized nuclear plants averaged 59% capacity rates (Komanoff and Roelofs 12/92, 18). Recent years have been much better. Given the probability of aging related declines in capacity rates in the future, lifetime rates of 65% for plants coming on line 1983–present seems generous.
4. Construction time for the seventeen plants entering service 1980–1984 averaged 10.1 years; durations increased to 12.2 years for the thirty plants entering service 1985–1989 (National Research Council 1992, 33). Plants coming on line in the 1990s probably averaged even longer construction durations.
5. The fixed charge rate (FCR) differential increases the average FCR used in the cost predicting cost calculations from .0923 to .0973, reflecting the market's imposition of a risk premium on nuclear credit offerings. The .0923 rate is based on the utilities' average real cost of capital 1955–1977 and Komanoff's algorithm for estimating FCRs from market interest rates (Komanoff 1981, 272). The 9.73% rate is lower than the utilities' actual capital costs after 1977 or the FCR used by the CEA in 1992 (10.3%) for nuclear cost forecasting. I've kept the rate low in order to avoid confusing macroeconomic cost forecasting errors (low interest rates) with nuclear sector forecasting errors.

interest group attention to utility issues, the "organization-man" outlook of nuclear sector personnel, the public's awed fascination with the atom, and the cold war.

Early nuclear power cost studies established a pattern that persisted until the late-seventies. Technical reports underestimated future engineering problems, and available warnings about cost trends were ignored. Social contexts infused the inevitable ambiguity of technology assessment with buoyant optimism. Economic analyses were almost always performed by self-interested advocates of nuclear expansion and frequently served more as marketing documents than forecasting models.

The overly optimistic and quickly pulled together Thomas report of 1946 served as a basis for a number of early economic studies and significantly influenced early business opinion.[70] The more cautious perspective of the General Advisory Committee (the AEC's chief technical resource) received less popular attention.[71] President Eisenhower's geopolitically motivated Atoms for Peace speech to the UN in 1953, and the U.S. presentations at the Geneva Conference on Atomic Energy in 1955 provided a second round of misleading nuclear optimism. In September of 1954, AEC Chairman Lewis Strauss urged science journalists to promote nuclear expansion, suggesting the possibility of "electricity too cheap to meter" (Ford 1982, 50). In the mid-fifties, forecasters predicted 1980 generating costs in the range of 1.85 to 3 c/kwh. The projections boldly assumed scale and learning cost reductions of 50% from the already optimistic predictions for plants then under construction.

In the early 1960s, industry's promotional forecasts spurred a third round of short run cost optimism. In mid-1961, G. E. and PG&E, a leading California utility, predicted costs of 2.8 c/kwh for their newly announced Bodega Bay plant.<72> In 1962, the AEC released *Civilian Nuclear Power—*

Table 4.4 footnotes continued

6. Nuclear fuel costs (excluding waste disposal) in the 1980s averaged ~7.5 M/kwh (1990$) (Komanoff and Roelofs 12/92, 21). They have recently been falling due largely to lower uranium and enrichment costs and improved plant performance. Fuel costs have been the major bright spot in nuclear economics and cost forecasting.

7. Komanoff and Roelofs report average O&M costs in the 1980s of 1.48 c/kwh (1990$) and capital additions of .89 c/kwh (1990$) (Komanoff and Roelofs 12/92, 19–20). The DOE calculated average O&M costs of ~$86/kW (1982$) or ~2.2 c/kwh (1992$) for 1985–1989, assuming 65% capacity rates (DOE/EIA 0547 5/91, 4).

8. See chapter 7 for the reasoning behind projected waste disposal and decommissioning costs.

9. Miscellaneous costs refer to indirect nuclear costs, such as higher transmission costs (due to siting penalties), reduced planning flexibility (due to long construction periods and large capacity increments), and increased spinning reserve requirements (due to relatively low capacity rates and large unit size).

A Report to the President. The widely cited study highlighted the convergence of manufacturers' cost estimates around 2.6 c/kwh (AEC 1962, 33–35).

The first turnkey contract was signed in December 1962 and appeared to confirm the AEC's optimism. Generating costs were projected to be about 1.67 c/kwh. Capital costs were *guaranteed* at $555/KW and projected to be less than $463/KW. From late 1962 to mid-1966 thirteen turnkey plants were sold, at a vendor subsidy of ~50%.[73] The loss leader strategy was very effective in promoting nuclear cost optimism and helped trigger the bandwagon market for non-turnkey plants in the mid- to late-sixties.

In 1968 the first of a new series of AEC costs studies (AEC 1968a) lent added credibility to the turnkey estimates. The study projected capital costs of $496/KW and overall generating costs of 1.57 c/kwh for plants under construction.[74] While acknowledging the possibility of regulatory escalation, the report was hopeful that learning and scale economies and duplicate plant sitings could contain costs.[75] The AEC's *Nuclear Industry* serial of 1969 continued this optimism.[76] By the 1970s, market experience with the first generation of full-sized reactors began to contradict early cost estimates. Non-turnkey plants gradually revealed a pattern of severe cost overruns. Plants beginning construction in 1966–1967 cost $900/KW versus predictions of $431/KW, while those begun during 1968–1969 cost $1535/KW versus predictions of $522/KW (DOE 1986, xvi). Despite these overruns, the AEC and nuclear industry's assurances that cost increases were over helped win new reactor orders.[77]

A Sociology of Knowledge Analysis of Cost Forecasting Errors

As in the hazard assessment area, the NPC influenced the data sought and available for economic analysis, the methodologies used to analyze this data, and the attention given to anomalous and inconvenient findings.

Data Constraints

The most important data constraints involved the paucity of empirical information about construction costs for large sized reactors, plant operating data, and waste disposal and decommissioning costs. The industry and its government sponsors convinced the public and capital markets to make massive investments in nuclear facilities on the basis of engineering projections rather than empirical experience from commercial sized plants.

Since earlier sections of this chapter discussed the information environments organizing nuclear radiation, accident, and thermal pollution hazard assessment, note 78 explains the informational environments surrounding waste disposal and decommissioning cost forecasting to further illustrate the kinds of data constraints clouding nuclear cost forecasting.[78]

Methodological Constraints

The key methodological assumptions bending cost forecasts towards excess optimism were:

(1) an underestimation of the novelty of nuclear technology, especially its distinctiveness from coal-powered plants

(2) the assumption of stable regulatory requirements

(3) the assumption of excessive learning curves

(4) the assumption of excessive standardization economies

(5) the assumption of excessive scaling economies from increases in nuclear plant size

(6) the neglect of several indirect costs of nuclear investment

and after the loss of OT status;

(7) the assumption of zero risk premiums in capital markets

(8) the assumption of continued subsidy and regulatory support at OT levels

The nuclear industry's underestimation of the novelty of nuclear technology encouraged premature increases in plant size and numerous design oversights, including: neglect of material embrittlement problems involving neutron bombardment, insufficient attention to cooling water chemistry and potential corrosion problems, a lack of appreciation of maintenance complexities and quality control problems, and a trivialization of waste disposal and decommissioning tasks. Forecasters' assumption of regulatory stability allowed industry planners to rely almost exclusively on engineering estimates of the cost of equipment able to meet *existing regulatory standards* in cost forecasting models. Despite continual regulatory escalation, contingency margins were kept relatively low.

The assumption of excessive cost reductions from routine learning, industry standardization, and increased plant size emphasizes the degree to which nuclear cost forecasting models and development strategies were based on the realization of *path dependent* cost reductions. Learning curve theory typically projects 10%–20% cost declines per doubling of cumulative output.[79] Similar assumptions in nuclear cost forecasting models predicted 50% reductions in nuclear costs from the mid-sixties to the turn of the century.[80] Many of these savings were not captured, as the expected size of the nuclear sector in the year 2000 fell from the ~1000 plants predicted by the AEC in the early-seventies to ~100 plants today. Increasing concern about the risks of serious nuclear accidents also caused the AEC and NRC to retard the pace of innovation in the nuclear sector by requiring extensive safety review before the deployment of new equipment and materials.[81]

Standardization became an explicit goal of the industry in the late-sixties and of the AEC in the early-seventies. In predicting large economies of scale attendant to standardization, the industry mistakenly assumed that an immature and rapidly changing technology was ready for standardization. Escalating AEC regulatory requirements, the surfacing of unexpected problems during plant operation, constant increases in new plant size, and corporate marketing strategies geared towards demonstrating technological leadership, inevitably frustrated standardization projects. Anti-trust constraints also inhibited plant designers from referencing particular companies' equipment.[82]

The assumption that nuclear costs would fall sharply as plant size increased was closely linked to the industry's mistaken tendency to generalize from fossil fuel experience. Industry cost models assumed scaling ratios that implied 13%–35% declines from a doubling in reactor size. Most planners anticipated about three doublings between the early-sixties and the year 2000, implying scaling cost reductions of 40%–60%. The scaling forecast was buttressed by engineering projections of the construction costs for different sized plants and the geometric logic of electricity economics (which projected costs as a function of area and performance as a function of volume).

In 1968 the AEC projected 3,000 MW plants to cost as much as 20% less than 1,000 MW units (AEC 1968a, ch. 3, 18). In August of 1968 James Lane of Oak Ridge National Laboratory foresaw plants of 2,000 MW on line by 1980 and 5,000 MW on line by 2000. In 1970, the Federal Power Commission predicted nuclear plants of 5,000 MW by 1980 and 10,000 MW by 1990 (Wilbanks 1984, 13).

While data limitations muddy the waters, most regression studies of actual nuclear capital cost behavior, have found only modest scaling savings (Phung 1987, ix). There appear to be five main reasons for the shortfall:

(1) the scaling process proved more difficult than expected

(2) the AEC regulatory staff capped plant size at 1,300 MW and linked the level of required safety features to potential accident burdens and thus MW size[83]

(3) larger plant size shifted an increasing fraction of plant construction activities from factory to on-site fabrication, lowering labor productivity and quality control

(4) increased megawattage lengthened construction time, with associated costs, such as financing costs, overwhelming direct construction cost savings[84]

(5) increased megawattage lowered capacity performance, thereby increasing capital costs per kilowatt hour.

To some degree, the MW scaling errors reflect the period's technological aesthetics, which tended to assume "bigger is better". It now appears that for large on-site fabrication projects, there may be a point at which management diseconomies of scale overwhelm materials economies of scale.

Among the indirect costs of nuclear investment ignored by the period's economic models were nuclear plants' curtailment of utility planning flexibility (due to their longer lead time), requirement of greater spinning reserves (due to their larger plant size and lower capacity performance), greater siting costs, and vulnerability to generic shutdown due to some unexpected technical problem in the sector as a whole.

Quantitatively, three factors contributed most to cost forecasting errors, the underestimation of nuclear hazard containment costs, a lack of attention to the novelty of nuclear activities, and excessive expectations of path dependent cost reductions. Over half of all cost overruns involved underestimation of hazard containment expenditures.

Inattention to Anomalous or Inconvenient Information

As already noted the AEC and industry forecasters tended to ignore the implications of early cost overrun experience and poor plant performance. Failed predictions were explained away with reference to "shakedown" problems, temporary bottlenecks, and special phenomena unlikely to reoccur. Industry forecasters were especially late in attending to the large economic implications of poor plant capacity performance and runaway O&M costs.

The ability of forecasters to maintain their long run expectations in spite of contradictory feedback is well illustrated by the testimony of a leading utility industry forecaster, Lewis Perl, in a 1985 Arkansas Public Utility Commission hearing:[85]

> Q: In what year did you first testify on this issue of trends in nuclear operating costs?
>
> A: . . . I think probably 1978 was the first time.
>
> Q: In which year did you first predict that cost escalation would end?
>
> A: In every year I predicted that it was ending. I have a remarkably consistent track record in that regard.
>
> Q: Good or bad?
>
> A: Well, I don't think it was bad. I think I was using perfectly good methodologies and coming to conclusions that after the fact turned out to be wrong, but I think that my conclusions during this period, at each point in time—I say this with neither pride or non-pride—was that the regulatory changes that had occurred in the past had driven up costs a lot, that it didn't seem to me like that the same changes were going to occur in the future and that the situation was stabilizing.
>
> I think there were always lots of facts out there to suggest that stability was there, and then additional events would occur to disabuse us of that conclusion.

Political Refocus

The growth of the anti-nuclear movement stimulated alternative approaches to nuclear cost forecasting.[86] Academe and state government also provided organizational contexts for rethinking nuclear economics.[87] As then Harvard Business School Professor Irvin Bupp noted in 1981,

> "One might have expected documentation of these cost increases to come from . . . the electric utilities that purchase and operate nuclear power plants. The utilities have the cost data and anecdotal experience necessary for such analysis, and presumably they would be ardently interested in learning industry cost trends. But, reluctant to buck what my colleague, Jean Claude Derian, and I have called

the 'extravagance of prophesy' that has long prevailed among nuclear power supporters, and wary about offering ammunition to its
critics, the nuclear industry has produced remarkably little analysis
of its economic misfortunes. Nor have the industry's official government and academic sponsors produced any objective analysis of
nuclear costs. That task has had to be assumed by outsiders" (Komanoff 1981, i).

Besides producing independent analysis, the anti-nuclear movement established its own network of dissemination. The movement's journals, newsletters, clipping services, reading lists, etc., were especially effective in reproducing at the local level the economic analyses developed by the groups'
professional and volunteer staffs. Local activists and national environmental
law firms injected the information into licensing, rate determination, and
legislative hearings. Demonstrations and teach-ins also publicized skeptic
findings. Eventually anti-nuclear groups gained credibility with the media as
information sources about future nuclear costs. Charles Komanoff, initially
with the Council on Economic Priorities, was especially successful in challenging the industry's nuclear plant construction cost models.[88] David
Comey of Business and Professional People for the Public Interest, played a
key role in turning popular attention to the economic implications of nuclear
power's high outage rates (i.e., low capacity rates). Other anti-nuclear researchers successfully challenged many utilities' electricity demand forecasts
during hearings on the need for new generating capacity (see chapters 6 and
11). Table 4.5 sums up the paradigm shift that anti-nuclear criticism helped
impose on nuclear cost forecasting. The import of increasing attention to
"outsider" economic analyses was slower nuclear expansion.[89]

Implications of Nuclear Power Cost Forecasting Experience

The history of nuclear power cost forecasting suggests several conclusions about the nature of technology assessment and the likely character of
future nuclear cost debates. Because nuclear cost prediction requires judgments about the technology's evolutionary potential (its capacity for spawn-
ing scale economies, mechanized operations, materials improvements, routinized learning, etc., and its economic vulnerability to unexpected technical
problems), cost debates are unlikely to be quickly resolved by appeal to past
cost experience. There exist no simple algorithms for translating empirical
data about a youthful technology into developmental forecasts and mature

Table 4.5
A Sociology of Nuclear Cost Information

	OT Years	*Protest Years*
DATA	Lack of significant empirical data re: plant construction costs and plant performance	Accumulation of cost overruns & poor performance data
	Absence of true turnkey costs	
	Inattention to backend costs (waste disposal and decommissioning)	Protest movement induced attention to backend issues
METHODOLOGY		
	Underestimation of novelty of nuclear technology, absence of nuclear risk premium	Popular and credit market risk aversion towards nuclear projects
	Static engineering-based cost models	Dynamic forecasting with regulatory escalation
	Excessive learning curve expectations	Negative learning coefficients, due to anticipation of unexpected problems during plant operation
	Excessive standardization expectations	Increasing skepticism about standardization economies
	Excessive megawatt scaling expectations	Absence of scaling economies
	Neglect backend costs	Inclusion backend costs
	Assumption of breeder-reprocessing backstop credits for plutonium	Treatment of Pu as burdensome waste product
	Expectation of continued OT regulatory & subsidy support	Pessimism about public support for nuclear power
SOCIAL MEANING		
	Popular acceptance of nuclear industry-AEC promotional cost estimates	Anti-nuclear pressure for attention to empirical cost experience
	Closure of JCAE-AEC forums to pessimistic economic testimony	Increased media & congressional attention to nuclear cost skeptics
	Expected utility insulation from cost-overrun, poor performance penalties	Increasing regulatory punishment for poor nuclear performance

industry cost profiles. It is difficult to conceive of empirical experience that would have falsified the path dependent view of nuclear optimists or allayed the concerns of cost pessimists. Both optimist and pessimist perspectives behaved like competing explanatory paradigms for interpreting and predicting nuclear cost behavior.

The history of nuclear cost forecasting supports many aspects of trajectory models of technical change. These models emphasize the evolutionary logic of technological systems. This discussion has emphasized the analogous logic of cost forecasting, noting how expectations of future developments can dominate empirical data in forecasting conclusions. Projected nuclear development paths have defined both practical avenues to cost reduction and *modes of cost analysis*. Like a powerful heuristic the posited path attuned forecasters to particular kinds of questions and information, and discouraged attention to others. Nuclear industry cost studies, for example, have often devoted more attention to minor aspects of fuel cost forecasting than to plant capacity performance, although the latter has had a much greater effect on generating costs. This focus reflects the history of nuclear planning (which initially assumed uranium scarcity) rather than the evolving character of forecasting needs.

Nuclear cost forecasting experience supports Norman Clark's claim that technological practice tends to produce communities of users socialized by habit and network into a shared outlook (Clark 1987). James Kuhn's observations about the common background and outlook of utility industry personnel discussed in chapter 2 nicely illustrate Clark's view. While Kuhn celebrated the practicality of nuclear industry officials (in contrast with the speculative curiosity of academics), his account also depicted individuals who were unlikely to challenge the conventional wisdom. Describing the vendors' staffs, he wrote,

".. . they were company men, trained to respect costs and schedules. Research was subordinated to practical engineering and the short-run view of the project superseded any long-run development perspectives . . . . [the men] were used to business discipline and willing to submit to it. Those who did not measure up moved to other positions in the company or to other organizations" (89).

Of the utilities he wrote,

".. . [Management] wanted men who intimately knew company standards and procedures . . . . They were old enough to be familiar with the utility business and to accept its values and outlook . . . . In every company the engineers chosen for training were looked upon as the most likely candidates for future managerial positions" (p. 149).

Summarizing his observations, Kuhn highlighted the importance of frames of references in technology assessment,

"The policy followed in making the initial selection of personnel to work in a technological area can be critical. The men called upon as advisors or used as managers and employees can determine the pace and direction of an organization's attack upon, and use of, a technology, fixing the perspective in which it is seen. . . . A developing technology appears to be in part an artifact of the men used by a company to work in it, not simply an objective body of knowledge. . . . Business managers and government officials might wisely recognize that in employing men, they obtain expertness and skill which are, however, accompanied by values and outlook not readily visible. . . ." (p. 98).

Unbeknownst to Kuhn, the nuclear industry's absorption of the promotional attitudes of the AEC and reactor vendors was to plague its economic analyses for the next two decades.

Contemporary theorists of bureaucratic behavior argue Kuhn's claim of paradigm laden expertise more generally. Leon Lindberg describes the paradoxical ability of highly trained personnel to maintain policy positions in conflict with existing data. Quoting the work of cybernetic theorist John Steinbrunner on the legacy of highly structured professional training, he writes,

"'With his beliefs established in a long-range framework and well anchored, his inference management mechanisms are able to handle the pressure of inconsistency in any short-term situation. Inferences of transformation and impossibility, the selective use of information, and other inconsistency management mechanisms are brought to bear for this purpose. Since the theoretical thought process is strongly deductive, and thus relatively less dependent upon incoming information in order to *establish* (in original) coherent beliefs, incoming information can be molded and even ignored or denied . . .'" (Lindberg 1977, 343).

There is frequently an accompanying tendency to dismiss "outsiders" as uninformed, as has been common in the nuclear industry. While one can sympathize with nuclear practitioners' belief that cost critics are unaware of an impressive list of accumulating engineering avenues to cost reduction, the optimists have similarly neglected areas of potential cost escalation. The consensus inside a paradigm can be misleading if it projects correlated confirmation as independent confirmation. Phung's finding that almost all studies of the impact of plant size on plant costs cited ORNL papers as a basic data source is archetypical in this regard (Phung 1987, 14). The pessimist literature tends to be similarly self-referenced.

The history of cost prediction at Oak Ridge National Laboratory provides a particularly interesting example of paradigmatic insularity. The forecasting was done by engineering economists, immersed in the lab's technical optimism about engineering hardware, rather than by social science trained economists. The engineers' professional milieu seems to have facilitated underestimation of the quality control and human factors-problems associated with nuclear power, the potential implications of regulatory escalation, and the dangers of insular discourse. Partially in response to these and similar oversights (e.g., an underestimation of the price elasticity of electricity demand), the lab began a social science program in the seventies, staffed heavily with academically trained economists. While the lab's cost forecasting model retained its engineering economics staff and optimistic format, other work by social science economists has been less confident of nuclear competitiveness.

Extending Thomas Kuhn's observations concerning scientific revolutions, Clark also suggests that technological paradigms very rarely collapse solely from internal contradiction. Paradigm shifts require both internal anomalies and external alternatives. The recent attention to reactor designs without the thermal instability of light water reactors (and the accompanying hazard complications), may provide such an alternative inside the nuclear community (see chapter 10).

As noted previously, the inherent uncertainty surrounding long run cost predictions and the potential for insular discourse, has interesting implications for the behavior of firms. Companies with competitive advantage in particular technologies have an incentive to promote misleadingly optimistic cost expectations about these technologies. To the extent that cost reductions are path dependent, these expectations can generate self-fulfilling prophecies. The payoff is high returns on the firm's technology specific capital. The ability of economic agents to influence the economic meaning of technological possibility erodes some of the "epistemological objectivity" Clark imputes to market functioning (Clark 1987, 90). Nuclear power experience is more supportive of Dosi's claim that

> "(g)iven the intrinsic uncertainty associated with their outcomes . . .
> it is hardly possible to compare and rank [technological alternatives] . . . *ex ante*. . . . the economic interests of the organizations involved in R&D in these new technological areas, (2) their technological history, the field of their expertise, etc.; (3) institutional variables . . . . All these factors are likely to operate as focusing forces upon defined directions of technological development. . . .

Proceeding in our parallel with epistemology, this resembles a world a la Feyerabend with different competing technological paradigms . . ." (Dosi 1982, 155).

Conclusion

The history of nuclear power hazard assessment and cost forecasting demonstrates that technology assessment can be dominated by paradigmatic realms of discourse that are resistant to critical review if protected from "outsiders." The lesson for policy makers and public participants in current nuclear power debates is that consumers of technical information need to be sensitive to sociology of knowledge concerns and evaluate technical claims in the light of institutional biases, both conscious and unconscious.

Chapter 5

Nuclear Power's OT Differential*

Previous chapters have analyzed how the nuclear planning context of the OT period promoted nuclear expansion by tilting R&D efforts, public subsidy, and regulatory incentives towards nuclear technologies, and promoting misleadingly optimistic expectations about the seriousness of nuclear hazards and the level of future generating costs. This chapter examines the benefits nuclear power gained from the capture of OT status and the related enjoyment of path dependent cost reductions, such as increased economies of scale, learning curve efficiencies, systemwide efficiencies, privileged access to capital markets, and bureaucratic momentum. The final sections examine the combined advantages nuclear power gained from promotional assistance and OT capture.

Scale and Learning Curve Efficiencies[1]

Learning curve cost reductions can be analogized to the capture of scale economies *over time*, while savings from mass production can be thought of as scale economies *at a point in time*. Both phenomena tie cost declines to sector growth. From the earliest days of the nuclear industry, the pursuit of scale and learning curve cost reductions has been a cornerstone of nuclear development strategy.[2] Although many expected learning cost reductions were never realized, several studies have found evidence of modest learning curve effects with respect to plant construction durations, direct construction costs, and capacity rates.[3] Actual learning curve payoffs have probably been greater than recognized, as reductions in the cost of handling old tasks have been masked by concurrent increases in expenditures to address new problems. There also appears to have been some standardization and capture of economies of scale within parts of the nuclear steam supply system and nuclear fuel cycle,[4] though again less than expected.

---

*All dollars are 1992$ unless otherwise specified.

Megawatt Scaling Effects

Nuclear promoters anticipated cost reductions through the construction of larger sized plants. As noted in chapter 4, this hope was unfulfilled.

The Capture of Systemwide Efficiencies

Nuclear promoters also anticipated several systemwide economies from sector expansion. Among these were: (1) multiple plant siting economies; (2) scaling economies captured at the industry rather than firm level; and (3) the benefits of investments in complementary technologies based on expectations of nuclear expansion. In 1968 the AEC foresaw capital cost declines of 9% from dual plant sitings (AEC 1968a, 2–3). In 1974 the commission increased expected savings to 10–15% (AEC 1974b, 74). Actual savings appear even greater. Komanoff found a surprising 28% cost reduction for plants expected to be completed in the mid-1980s (Komanoff 1984a, 11). The even larger savings alleged possible from nuclear complexes, replete with fuel reprocessing capabilities, have not been captured.

Nuclear power's enjoyment of OT status also generated some economies of scale in manpower training and increased private investment in complementary technologies, such as robotics[5] and long distance electricity transmission. Anticipation of nuclear expansion might have also encouraged increased research on electricity end-uses, such as electric cars.

Another aspect of systemwide efficiencies are joint product efficiencies. These cost reductions involve the shifting of some nuclear power costs to non-nuclear energy consumers. As noted earlier, nuclear power costs were initially lowered by the sale of plutonium waste products to the government as weapons material. Fuel cycle costs were also reduced by the scale economies in uranium enrichment made possible by the military program. More ambitious plans, like efforts to use waste heat from nuclear reactors for desalinization projects, have not been successful. While the integrated reactor vendors have captured some extra economic efficiency by entering both nuclear steam supply and nuclear fuel markets, efforts to capture broader economies of scope by developing new applications for nuclear expertise (such as the use of nuclear explosives for harbor engineering and fossil fuel recovery), have also failed.[6]

Scaling and Systemwide Efficiencies Summarized

The work of Oak Ridge researcher James Lane reflected the most expansive implications of OT status anticipated in the late-1960s. Assuming R&D improvements, learning curve efficiencies, mass production economies, megawatt scaling, increased industry competition, and breakthroughs in electricity transmission technology, Lane projected nuclear generating costs as low as 5.5 M/kwh for a 5,000 MW plant in the year 2000.[7] While nuclear economics have not evolved as optimistically as Lane surmised, I estimate that OT induced nuclear expansion induced at least 10%–20+% cost savings from learning curve and output scaling effects and 5%–10+% cost reductions from the capture of systemwide efficiencies.

Social Accommodation to Institutional Needs

Partly as a result of economies of scale with respect to the transaction costs of political action, the larger an industry is (all other things equal), the easier it is to arrange societal accommodation to its institutional requirements. Nuclear power's OT status and OT induced expansion facilitated several social adjustments to the technology's needs, such as renewal of the Price Anderson Act's limited liability provisions and efforts to circumvent state and local regulatory oversight of nuclear issues. The sacrifice of civil liberties to the needs of public safety in dealing with nuclear matters has similarly seemed a potential social cost of a large nuclear sector.[8]

Privileged Access to Capital Markets

Nuclear power's promotional assistance and capture of OT status also gave the technology privileged access to capital markets.[9] As Merrill Lynch Vice President Leonard Hyman has observed, ". . . the investor bestowed blanket confidence on the technology and the technicians behind it" (Hyman and Kelley 12/3/81). In addition to the Price Anderson Act, numerous government guarantees reduced nuclear investment risks. De facto government policy promised smooth fuel supply, trouble-shooting R&D, and congenial regulation. Promotional informational environments dulled investor skepticism.

It is difficult to estimate the additional cost of credit that nuclear projects would have incurred without OT status. Estimates range from minimal effects to interest rate premiums of more than 2%.[10] Table 5.1 illustrates the impact of various interest rate penalties on the costs of plants coming online after 1982.[11]

Table 5.1
The Impact of Increased Risk Premiums on Nuclear Costs[1]

| | Additional Interest Charge | | | | | |
	1%	2%	3%	4%	5%	6%
Fixed Charge Increment[2]	1.3%	2.7%	4.1%	5.6%	7.2%	8.8%
IDC Multiplier Increment[3]	4.5%	9.0%	14%	19%	24%	30%
Capital Cost M/kwh Increment[4]	11.1	24.1	38.9	54.6	72.2	91.6

1. Calculations assume average direct construction capital costs for mid-1980's plants of $3034/ KW (Komanoff 1984a).
2. See Komanoff 1981, 272 for formula used to calculate fixed charge rates (FCRs). Calculations assume a 2.8% base interest rate plus assigned interest rate penalty. Base case FCR = 9.23%.
3. See Komanoff 1981, 244 for the formula used to calculate the IDC multiplier. Calculations assume 94-month construction period. Base case (2.8% interest rate) IDC multiplier equals 11.6%.
4. Per kwh calculations assume 60% capacity rates.

Enjoyment of Bureaucratic Momentum

In 1968 former AEC consultant John Hogerton observed that utility markets had vested the benefit of the doubt in nuclear as opposed to coal technologies (Hogerton 1968, 29). Contemporary theorists of bureaucratic behavior argue that such planning assumptions are difficult to dislodge. Lindberg (1977) emphasizes this endurance in explaining the persistence of supply-side responses to the energy crisis in almost all advanced countries. Morone and Woodhouse (1989) tie the triumph of the LWR over more innovative reactor designs to a similar intellectual inertia (126–128). The concept of bureaucratic momentum is also implicit in the work of Bupp and Nader.

Calculating a Combined OT Differential

It is possible to estimate the sensitivity of nuclear economics to promotional activities by combining the market advantages gained by nuclear power from promotional assistance and OT capture. The dozens of calculations underlying the analysis are necessarily rough and categories may overlap on occasion, but taken together their implications are robust. One might raise or lower the estimated market value of several specific subsidies, learning curve benefits, institutional aids, etc., without changing the order of magnitude of OT impacts.

Nuclear plants ordered in 1963–1974 received an average OT benefit of at least 10 c/kwh. The plants enjoyed an average subsidy rate of 2.0–2.5 c/kwh.[12] Infant industry hazard regulation reduced the construction costs of plants on-line by 1972 by ~3 c/kwh[13] and other costs by more than 1 c/kwh.[14] The promotion of misleading cost optimism improved nuclear energy's competitive appearance by ~2.5 c/kwh (independent of the forecasting errors associated with the erosion of friendly regulation).[15] The capture of scaling and systemwide efficiencies, aided by OT status, reduced nuclear costs by an additional $15+\%-30+\%$, or approximately 1.5–3.0 c/kwh. Failure to capture as large as expected scaling efficiencies explains part of the reason for the 4 c/kwh forecasting errors cited above.

Summing all development aid for nuclear power (see table 5.2) yields a net benefit of 10–12 c/kwh. This total excludes the benefits of many aids which are especially difficult to quantify, such as privileged access to capital markets, social accommodation to the institutional needs of the technology, and the benefits of non-hazard related regulatory incentives.

Despite the conservative estimating procedures, the aid totals six times the expected cost of nuclear generation during the bandwagon market of the sixties. The benefits are more than twenty-five times the ~2.5 M/kwh expected nuclear cost advantage over coal generation, which publicly justified many nuclear orders (Perry 1977, 37; Zimmerman 1982, 308). As important

Table 5.2
Nuclear Power's OT Differential 1963–1974

Aid Categories	Economic Impact
Subsidy Assistance	2–2.5 c/kwh
Regulatory Protection	4 c/kwh
Forecasting Errors	2.5 c/kwh
Learning Curve & Scaling Benefits	1.5–3 c//kwh
Totals	10–12 c/kwh

as the aids' arithmetic sum was their dynamic and synergistic effects. Nuclear subsidies, for example, stimulated private capital commitments, which in turn made possible scale economies, and a cash flow basis for continued R&D. Regulatory incentives encouraged private capital commitments and the establishment of bureaucratic momentum, which facilitated the capture of systemwide efficiencies and social accommodation to the institutional needs of the technology.

A key aspect of the OT process is the risk reduction that accompanies OT status. This effect transcends marginal notions of differential credit costs, as it tends to define the entire context within which capital commitments are made. The process is pervasive and potentially self-perpetuating. On a technical level, OT status reduces engineering uncertainty by increasing R&D spending. On a socio-political level, OT dynamics reduce uncertainty by cementing political support amongst dependent corporate, labor, and consumer constituencies. In addition to reducing its own costs, nuclear's capture of OT status discouraged the development of competing options by denying them access to similar scale-induced efficiencies (see chapter 12).

The Macro/Micro Logic of Systemwide Planning Contexts

The best metaphor for depicting the impact of OT status on technical choice decisions is the planning context image of macro determined micro efficiencies. Amory Lovins has articulated this idea in terms of "hard and soft energy paths". He writes,

> "These two directions of development are mutually exclusive: the pattern of commitments of resources and time required for the hard energy path and the pervasive infrastructure that it accretes gradually make the soft path less and less attainable. That is, our two sets of choices compete not only in what they accomplish, but also in what they allow us to contemplate later. They are logistically competitive, institutionally incompatible, and culturally antithetical" (Lovins 1977, 49).

Without employing the formal language of political or economic theory, Lovins has focused on the natural monopoly characteristics of energy choices highlighted by the PC-OT framework. In addition he has emphasized the dynamic aspect of social life highlighted by Marxist and other holist social theories, wherein social contexts determine the shape of apparently naturally or technically determined constraints.

Employment of the PC-OT framework allows a disaggregation of Lovins' mutual exclusivity assertion into its constitutive parts, a task Lovins never systematically addresses. While his work is replete with individual examples of system incompatibilities and assertions of their general character, no formal model or accounting is presented to support this claim. The categories of the OT differential tallied in this chapter can be used to fill this gap.

Lovins divides the basis for mutual exclusivity between energy options into technical and social elements. The former can be compared with the economic level of PC-OT theory and represents the extent to which preemptive economies of scale, learning curve efficiencies, systemwide positive externalities, and interdependent risk premiums characterize the energy sector.

Describing the latter, the social basis for exclusivity, Lovins writes,

". . . (the two paths) are culturally incompatible. Each entails an evolution of perceptions that makes the other kind of world harder to imagine . . . . (They) are *institutionally* antagonistic. Each entails organizations and policy actions that inhibit the other . . . . (For example) the rigidity of some of our institutions, notably the utility sector, is a result of past commitments to a nascent hard path and is manifestly inhibiting proper consideration and implementation of a soft path . . ." (Nash 1979, 339–340).

In PC-OT terms the above incompatibilities refer to realms of discourse and planning context logics. Implicitly, Lovins asserts the mutually determining character of political, economic, and ideological phenomena. Though underdeveloped in his work, the ideas contain the seeds of a structuralist view of social life. Behind competing energy paths are competing planning contexts; and behind them are alternative sets of structurally given interests and outlooks.

In both Lovins' work and the PC-OT framework, the planning context metaphor highlights the role of social contexts in shaping technological change. The categories of OT dynamics facilitates quantification of path dependent theories of technical change.

Chapter 6

The Disestablishment of Nuclear Power as an Official Technology

Introduction

In 1967 the AEC foresaw one thousand nuclear plants on line in the U.S. by the year 2000. From 1967–1974 the utilities ordered one hundred and ninty-six new nuclear plants, appearing to confirm this projection.[1] Thereafter the market collapsed. All forty-one reactors ordered after 1973 were subsequently canceled. In fact more than two-thirds of all nuclear plants ordered after January 1970 were subsequently canceled.[2] This chapter analyzes the reasons for this dramatic reversal, applying the logic of the PC-OT framework.

The chapter develops a sociological study of the shifting character of the nuclear planning context and an epistemological study of the origins of shifting ideas about nuclear power. The analysis asserts a "structuralist epistemology," treating the data and conceptual frameworks used for energy planning as the products of social contexts. Three main points are argued: (1) that the social structure of American capitalism created the basis for a successful political challenge to the closed planning context that promoted nuclear expansion; (2) that the reorganization of the nuclear planning context (NPC) created an economic phenomenon analogous to a minor "scientific revolution," which restructured the entire framework for investor and popular thinking about energy planning; (3) and that this rethinking dissolved nuclear power's OT status and thereby eroded its economic competitiveness.

The Sociological Origins of the Anti-Nuclear Challenge

A number of general characteristics of American capitalism created the conditions for the development of the anti-nuclear movement, chief among these were:

1) The potential for independent political initiatives (outside the channels of corporate planning) by members of the professional-managerial class (PMC).

2) The relative openness of the U.S. political system to citizen initiatives.

3) The growth of the environmental movement.

4) The decline in influence of corporate-military planners and the increased credibility of "left" social critics in the wake of the Vietnam War and Watergate.

5) The popularity of free market ideology which can limit certain direct forms of government intervention in the economy (such as public ownership of productive industries).

Several additional factors more specific to the energy and nuclear industries facilitated efforts to restructure the NPC:

1) The evolution of significant opposition to nuclear power among PMC members within the environmental and consumer movements, and the vulnerability of the nuclear industry to such opposition,

2) The destabilization of the energy sector by the OPEC embargo and inflation-caused financing difficulties of the utilities in the 1970s (which retarded consolidation of nuclear power's OT status),

3) The submerged presence in popular culture of a demonic image for nuclear energy,

4) The resurfacing of potential problems in continued nuclear development (such as nuclear weapons proliferation and "unfair" foreign competition) for the technology's corporate and cold warrior promoters, and

5) the easier availability of alternatives to nuclear energy in the U.S. than in some other nations.

One of the implications of the history of nuclear power is that the direction of technical change and market evolution can be influenced by corporate development strategies and mass movements. The success of corporate initiatives within modern capitalism, such as those that established nuclear power as an official technology, are more common. Deflection of corporate planning requires the existence of alternative social networks to the common channels offered for collective action by the linkages between corporate and federal bureaucracies. The creation of such networks and alternative planning contexts is an enormous task. The actualization of the potential for nuclear protest depended on the interactive logic of a complex historical conjuncture. Like recessive genes, many of the causal factors that led to nuclear power's loss of OT status required joint presences to assert themselves. The theory of causality suggested by PC-OT explanations of market outcomes includes both deterministic and contingent elements. The PC-OT framework implies that social structures, like that of American capitalism, create the preconditions and probabilities of occurrence for a limited number of potential development paths. Which path is taken is somewhat contingent, dependent on external shocks, human agency, and historical accident, as well as underlying probabilities. Thus, while economic outcomes reflect the logic of social structures, situations can arise where slight differences in initial conditions can lead to large differences in economic outcomes, as they can permit the construction of alternative planning contexts and critical mass development paths. While all major capitalist countries experimented aggressively with nuclear power, different conjunctures in different countries led to different outcomes.

Critical Masses

Because there are economies of scale involved in information production and dissemination, as well as in political organizing, one can analogize the take off of a political movement to the assembling of a critical mass of social energy. Once gathered together a critical mass can: (1) facilitate information sharing and synergistic interactions; (2) socially reinforce whistle blowing and other protest behavior within hostile environments (as the growing anti-nuclear movement did for protesting officials within the nuclear industry and NRC), and most importantly; (3) transform otherwise fruitless gestures into acts of social consequence. As Mazur writes:

"The evolution of a protest into a mass movement is critical for public participation. . . . Most of us would have no effect working alone. . . . The options usually available to someone who wants to express his concerns are limited: either waste one's efforts on solitary protests with little chance of success, or join a currently-running protest movement and pool resources with other sympathetic souls" (Mazur 1981, 96).

The achievement of a critical mass of social energy is greatly facilitated by the presence of supportive ideological currents, that is, congenial value laden approaches to public policy questions.[3] Ideological perspectives provide predispositions to attend to different information and can either reinforce or undermine the momentum of corporate planning. Not surprisingly, the pro and anti-nuclear power movements have been animated by different ideological beliefs.

The pro-nuclear position has been imbued with a faith in science's ability to resolve all outstanding problems associated with nuclear power, a pessimism about the ability of non-nuclear technologies to fuel economic growth, cold war beliefs, a high level of trust in government and business leaders, an elevation of consumerist over ecologist values, and the rhetoric, if not the reality, of laisse-faire economic policies. The anti-nuclear movement has been supported by the left's anti-corporate and anti-centralization ideology,[4] a growing concern (especially amongst the PMC) for what Fred Hirsch calls the "social limits to growth,"[5] and a selective rather than a priori faith in the appropriateness of advanced technologies.[6] The combination tends to produce a more ecologically conservative attitude towards environmental/economic tradeoffs and greater concern for the social externalities of economic decisions than encouraged by pro-nuclear ideology. The material embodiment of these ideological and institutional predispositions has been a web of social networks that have served to channel information and organize political activity. Mazur notes:

"Several studies of recent social-protest movements indicate that recruitment often occurs along pre-existing social links, and that people frequently join in an organizational bloc rather than as isolated individuals. . . . The 30 leaders of the antinuclear movement whom I interviewed in 1973 showed this tendency . . . . [T]heir concerns about nuclear power developing largely in the context of local environmental groups which eventually affiliated with the anti-nuclear coalition. Half of these environmentalists explicitly reported that their concerns had been influenced by other anti-nuclear people with whom they had come into personal contact. A few non-environmentalists were introduced into antinuclear groups through friends. . . . Only a few respondents formed their anti-nuclear alignment completely independently of important social influences" (Mazur 1981, 58).

Commenting on the origins of pro-nuclear activism, he adds:

"Most activists on the establishment side of a controversy have become involved through the occupational activity of their workday jobs. . . . The establishment employee earns his livelihood from the support of the technology (directly or indirectly), his career may be tied to the viability of the technology . . . and his work day is spent among friends and associates who are like minded. The common pattern in this situation is to support the policy of one's organization" (44). Elsewhere Mazur adds: "Even an event as jarring to the rationale for nuclear power as the accident at Three Mile Island, produced little desertion of nuclear proponents to the opposition" (57).

Characterizing the social milieus that have defined the distribution of scientists in nuclear controversies, Mazur notes the cleavage between weapons scientists, such as Edward Teller, who have supported nuclear power, and a group of more leftist, biomedical scientists, such as George Wald, who have opposed nuclear power. Citing a number of statistical correlations, including a link between the degree of a scientist's support for the anti-ballistic missile system and support for nuclear power, he writes:

". . . the predictability of pro or anti-nuclear petition signing on the basis of one's scientific discipline, one's status in the hierarchy of science, and one's positions on prior issues which are ostensibly unrelated to the nuclear power controversy, is best explained as a consequence of the social networks which exist in the academic science community. The political judgments of scientists are shaped by their social milieus, just as are those of laymen . . ." (Mazur 1981, 81).

Participants in Disestablishment

The Professional Managerial Class (PMC)

By the PMC I refer loosely to independent professionals and salaried personnel who usually possess some form of specialized training. To some extent the term refers to the segment of the division of labor whose responsibility it is to coordinate abstractions or the work of others. In the context of

the nuclear industry, the term refers to nuclear scientists, engineers, administrators, economists, journalists, lawyers, etc.

The group possesses two powerful assets in political-economic contexts. Within the division of labor, its coordinating and conceptualizing function leaves its members with a fair degree of functional autonomy (that is,
the precise manner in which they carry our their assignments is to some
extent self-defined). The same workplace skills leave PMC members influential advocates in social movements. In effect, PMC members have the
ability to politicize an economic issue. They have the ability to transform a
closed planning context (such as that dominated by the nuclear industry and
highest levels of the AEC 1954–1970) into a more public forum.

As the technology of modern capitalism has become more sophisticated, the PMC has gained increased leverage over certain political-economic decisions. This is partially because it is responsible for conceptualizing the context within which technical (but potentially political) matters are
posed. It is also a product of the gradual expansion in the U.S. of the due
process and egalitarian aspects of political life into economic life. In particular, the democratization of access to information and increased opportunities
for direct citizen participation in regulatory proceedings in the 1960s and
1970s facilitated PMC led challenges to nuclear expansion. Much to the
nuclear industry's misfortune, its expansion coincided with the growth of the
PMC supported environmental and consumer movements, which along with
the anti-war movement comprise the roots of the anti-nuclear movement.

It is important to note that many PMC members actively promoted nuclear development, both in the context of their professional work and private
lives. The key point is not that the group as a whole took an anti-nuclear
position (though it was more critical of nuclear power than the AEC or
nuclear industry), but that a significant activist subset did. These PMC members were able to politicize nuclear policy making and thus dissolve the
closed confines of the OT planning context.

Environmentalist Roots of Nuclear Protest

PMC members played a central role in the growth of the environmental
movement,[7] which culminated legislatively in the passage of the National
Environmental Policy Act (NEPA) and symbolically in Earth Day in 1970.
The NEPA legislation,[8] a series of water pollution control acts, and the
social network and information channels established by an estimated 20,000
local environmental groups provided a fertile context for incubating anti-
nuclear pressures (Cook 1980, 11). Increased public interest in environmen-

tal issues in the late-sixties also spurred muckraking journalists' attention to nuclear hazards.

Although atomic energy was initially seen by many environmentalists as a benign alternative to fossil fuels, this view gradually changed. In 1965, for example, a Harris poll found that while most groups supported expanded nuclear power plant construction by a 2:1 margin, environmentalists opposed it by a 4:1 margin (Del Sesto 1979, 193). Public attention to nuclear issues was increased in the early and mid-sixties by conservationist concerns about nuclear plant sitings in scenic areas and fish kills around water intake structures for nuclear plant cooling.[9] As the environmentalists became more familiar with nuclear technology, their list of concerns widened. By the late 1960s they were spearheading objections to nuclear plants due to thermal pollution hazards (Mazur 1981, 114). Of the twenty-seven challenges to the ninety-eight construction permits for nuclear plants applied for from 1962 through 1971, more than half included waste heat complaints (Rolph 1979, 102, 105). Two-thirds of the leaders of the National Intervenors, a coalition of groups active in the emergency core cooling accident controversy in the early 1970s, were environmentalists (Mazur 1981, 58).

Most of these early protests involved legal interventions in the licensing process and reflected the strong PMC presence in the environmental movement of lawyers and academics. The direct access of academics to research resources and media attention facilitated intellectual challenge to the planning vision of corporate-military bureaucracies. The history of the anti-nuclear movement demonstrates how this potential can be actualized by a social movement which legitimates and motivates critical behavior.

While achieving some direct effects, recall the cooling tower agreements noted in chapter 4, the major impact of early environmentalist efforts was to politicize nuclear development and lay the groundwork for wider protests in the 1970s. Among the critical audiences whose nuclear skepticism appears to have been increased by the controversies were the decision makers of the *New York Times*, whose editorials took a noticeable turn against rapid nuclear development in May and August of 1968.[10]

Consumer and Public Interest Group Roots

The label "consumer movement" is probably less appropriate for the activism stirred by Ralph Nader in the 1960s and 1970s than the term "public interest group movement". Nader's organizations have frequently sought to open economic planning to direct citizen inputs. Beginning in late 1972, anti-nuclear organizing became one of Nader's chief foci. By the mid-seventies, a Nader-sponsored group, Critical Mass, was probably the largest national anti-nuclear group, with several hundred local affiliates and an estimated 200,000 supporters.[11] Similarly Nader-inspired campus based "public interest research groups" (PIRGs) provided key local research and large numbers of student activists to the anti-nuclear movement. Nader himself was able to attract significant media attention to nuclear hazards and alternative energy possibilities.

Nader's movement has traditionally relied heavily on PMC members' participation. Besides the key role played by campus members, the movement has had important contributions from lawyers. More traditional liberal advocacy groups, such as ADA and Common Cause, have also participated in anti-nuclear organizing efforts and appear to have strong roots in the PMC.

Nader's efforts to open the market and executive branch's planning process to public participation were aided in the late 1960s and 1970s by the political backlash against the closed planning context that had characterized the Vietnam War buildup. Among the key legislative measures aiding the anti-nuclear movement were the Freedom of Information Act, the Federal Advisory Commission Act of 1972, the Government in the Sunshine Act of 1976, and the afore mentioned environmental impact statement requirements of the NEPA legislation. In the judicial area, liberalized "standing" requirements facilitated public interest group court challenges to nuclear power. In the early 1970s, procedural changes by the AEC similarly appear to have increased the discovery powers available to intervenors during regulatory hearings (Ebbin and Kasper 1974, 160, 255). The 1978 Public Utilities Regulatory Policies Act facilitated public funding of intervenor activities. Similar open government reforms were introduced at the state level.

All of the above reforms tended to increase access to information and regulatory authority for those able to swim in legal and/or technical channels. In so doing, they significantly strengthened the potential clout of PMC activists and reduced the planning autonomy of corporate and federal bureaucracies.

Role of "the Left"

By the "left" I refer loosely to a general outlook and set of organizations sympathetic towards an anti-corporate, anti-big business ideology. In this definition I include both American populist and socialist perspectives. While the two viewpoints diverge sharply at times, they both oppose the concentration of economic and political power in large private bureaucracies. This antagonism and a common objection to the sacrifice of various public goods (like the environment and civil liberties), to the immediate demands of GNP maximization, provided the basis for a shared skepticism towards nuclear power.

One of the after-effects of the Vietnam War was an increased participation in "leftist" organizations and a greater cultural openness to leftist activity. This receptivity created the social context within which the expertise of the PMC group, the protests of environmentalists, and the activism of the anti-nuclear movement could come together. This is not to claim that the anti-nuclear movement was a socialist movement. It was not and is not. The left's explicit assertion of the possibility of an alternative planning context to that promoted by the momentum of corporate-military planning, however, encouraged new approaches to energy policy, such as that of the Ford Foundation's *A Time to Choose* (1974), Amory Lovins' *Soft Energy Paths* (1977), and the Harvard Business School's *Energy Futures* (1979). The impact of these works was similarly magnified by the social networks created by leftist organizing.

Although the most important "leftist" input to the anti-nuclear movement was the general replacement of the cold war ideology of the 1950s with the anti-war skepticism of the late 1960s towards military-industrial policy, there were a number of very direct links between the anti-nuclear and anti-war movements. The two leading anti-nuclear groups among the scientific community, the Union of Concerned Scientists (UCS) and Scientists Institute for Public Information (SIPI) both possessed leftist origins. The UCS grew out of the "March 4th Movement's" objection to the military use of technology in Southeast Asia.[12] SIPI was animated by the socialist perspective of its leader, Dr. Barry Commoner, who later ran for President on the socialist platform of the Citizens Party. Leftist ideology also infused the energy inquiries of groups like the Institute for Policy Studies, the Environmental Action Foundation, and Environmentalists for Full-Employment. Many, though not all, of the scientist-activists in these groups were led to transcend the boundaries of official discourse by their shared participation in a leftist-political culture.

The expansion of the anti-nuclear movement in the mid and late 1970s was facilitated by a rekindling of the leftist networks generated during the Vietnam War.[13] Footnote 14 illustrates the interactive linkages between the anti-nuclear power and anti-war movements and the overlaps across the anti-nuclear movement.[14]

Destabilizing Political-Economic Shocks

The success of the leftist-PMC challenge to the nuclear industry was facilitated by a combination of technical factors which destabilized the energy sector in the mid-1970s and prevented the nuclear industry from consolidating its OT advantages. Chief among these "technical shocks" were the 1970s inflation, the OPEC oil embargo, and subsequent oil price increases.

Utilities' Financing Problem

Prior to 1973 the utilities had little difficulty in financing new construction. They enjoyed both a relative independence from external financing[15] and low credit costs when they did borrow. They thus had no trouble financing the nuclear plants of the "great bandwagon" market 1966–1967. In the mid-seventies, however, inflationary pressures and the rising real cost of fossil fuels altered this situation dramatically. Inflation undermined the utilities' cash flow position in two ways. Regulatory lag retarded recovery of escalating operating costs and rate base regulations precluded rate increases to fund escalating construction costs before new plants came on line. The rising real cost of fossil fuels also hurt the utilities in two ways. The sensitivity of electricity demand to rising prices reduced utility revenue growth while an accompanying political backlash limited regulatory approval of utility rate increases. Quite unexpectedly, after decades of 7% annual demand increases, growth fell to 0% in 1974, 2% in 1975 (Gandara 1977, 31) and ~3% 1973–1977 (Cook 1980, 3).

When combined with escalating interest rates, which increased from an average of 4.9% on utility bonds in 1965 to 9.8% in 1975 (Gandara 1977, 29), the utilities' cramped cash flow resulted in a collapse of coverage ratios (the ratio of a utility's earnings before taxes to its interest payments on long term debt). The ratios fell from an average of 5.2 (1961–1966) to less than 3 in the mid-seventies (Ibid 30–31). Many utility debt agreements prohibited the issuance of new obligations if the ratio fell below 2 (Ibid 30; *Business Week* 8/19/72).

It was in this context that the utilities began postponing and canceling new construction in 1974 and 1975.[16] Although both fossil fuel and nuclear projects were curtailed, the emphasis was on nuclear cutbacks due to the plants' greater capital demands and longer construction periods. Amid a period of significant demand uncertainty, the latter was a serious liability as it reduced planning flexibility.[17]

Although the above account of the utilities' financing problems makes them appear quite severe, it would be incorrect to view them as the root cause of nuclear power's decline. Continued sympathetic regulatory treatment could have easily circumvented these obstacles through the granting of full CWIP charges (i.e., rate increases to cover construction work in progress costs), or the approval of any one of several credit channeling options proposed by nuclear advocates. Thus while financing constraints were one of the proximate causes of nuclear retrenchment, they are best viewed as partial reflections of nuclear power's changing political fortunes rather than simple macroeconomic phenomena.

Immediate Need for Oil Substitutes

One of the major impacts of the OPEC oil embargo was a national commitment to quickly reduce U.S. vulnerability to sudden oil cutoffs. Despite repeated portrayals of nuclear power as a key substitute for oil imports by the White House and nuclear industry, it was soon clear that atomic energy could not play this role due to the rising cost of nuclear plants, their long planning and construction lead time, and the inappropriateness of electrical energy for important oil markets. The vision of a gradual transition from an oil to a nuclear fueled economy was thus interrupted by the need to consider short term alternatives to dependence on oil imports. It was in this context that conservation and alternative energy technologies first received broad government and corporate attention, including the publication of Amory Lovins' famous "Road Not Taken" article in *Foreign Affairs*.

A superficial reading of the period would leave the impression that an external shock, (the oil embargo) and not an internal social movement was responsible for the decline of nuclear power. A dynamic view of economic constraints, however, suggests that regulatory means could have been found to reduce the cost and construction time of nuclear plants had the technology retained its OT status. Such was the promise, for example, of the Nixon administration's proposed Project Independence. The role of the anti-nuclear movement in denying such adjustments thus returns social phenomena to the forefront of the disestablishment process.

Nationalization and Nuclear Weapons Risks

By the mid-1970s, a number of special characteristics of nuclear power posed potential problems for its corporate and cold warrior backers. Chief among these was the risk of nationalization, which appeared one way to recapture public confidence in the nuclear industry's safeguards against reactor accidents and nuclear weapons proliferation.[18] Though a short term solution to the utilities' financing difficulties and a potential source of electricity for IOU retailing, nationalized nuclear power would have excluded private utilities from a major generating market and would be expected to dim their enthusiasm for the technology.

The evolution of military nuclear programs beyond the point at which further civilian reactor development could provide significant defense externalities, and the growing linkages between the anti-nuclear power and anti-nuclear weapons movements similarly dulled cold warrior support for the technology. India's testing of an atomic bomb built partially from materials diverted from their civilian power program raised new nuclear weapons proliferation concerns in 1974. In 1977 demonstrations fusing anti-nuclear power and anti-nuclear weapons sentiments were held in over 100 U.S. localities during the August anniversary of the bombing of Hiroshima (Gyorgy et al. 1979, 386). The Ford Foundation's *Issues and Choices* recommended against plutonium recycle and the Carter administration opposed the Clinch River Breeder project and fuel reprocessing in the late seventies.

Finally, the diversified nature of many key nuclear firms, and their ability to replace nuclear revenues with increased sales in competing energy markets (Institute for Energy Analysis 1979, 256), may have also muted opposition to disestablishment. While these firms had a strong interest in a successful nuclear industry, they were unwilling to bleed their companies indefinitely in defense of an ill nuclear industry.

The Anti-Nuclear Conjuncture: A Summary

Both the rise and fall of nuclear power as an Official Technology can be connected to the structural characteristics of modern American capitalism. The rise of nuclear power coincided with the interests of the dominant corporate and military bureaucracies in the energy area from 1950–1970 and the cold war outlook of the period. The decline expressed the logic of a different planning context, one strongly influenced by the left and segments of the PMC. Though it is usual for the market momentum of corporate planning to dominate the path of technical change, various characteristics of American capitalism allow conjunctures to occur within which PMC-leftist activism can politicize economic policy and reorient its direction. In the case of nuclear power, a combination of PMC-left activism and destabilizing external shocks disestablished an Official Technology.

The nature of "structural causality," i.e., the process by which the bias or logic of socially determined planning contexts affect economic decisions, is far subtler than commonly suggested by simple lobbying models of corporate power or studies of interest group electoral politics. In chapters 2–5 we looked at the diffuse manner by which corporate and military support for nuclear power improved its relative technical efficiency and market competitiveness. In the next section we examine how the social context created by the leftist-PMC alliance dissolved many of these advantages and created an alternative context for energy sector development.

The thrust of the analysis is that economic outcomes must be studied within a system of socially determined planning contexts in order to unravel the social basis for what in retrospect may appear the result of exogenously given technical coefficients. Sociology and political economy need complement engineering and the optimization theory of conventional neoclassical economics to understand the path of technical change. Future energy choices need similarly to be posed with attention to the dynamic implications of the consolidation of alternative planning contexts.

From Social to Technical Change

Opening a Closed Context

Although by 1967 the utilities had ordered forty-seven reactors and were expected to have nearly five hundred plants on-line by 1990, there had been minimal debate over nuclear expansion. The *New York Times'* annual summary indices for 1965–1967, for example, list only twenty-six articles including references to opposition to nuclear power.[19] There were scattered protests during the early OT years, but these actions lacked the critical mass necessary to assume significant social meaning. Curiously, the atomic testing debates (mid-1950s to 1963) did not spread to nuclear energy.[20] Thus while it is important to note the receptivity of post Hiroshima societies to anti-nuclear campaigns, the impact of this potential, like the impact of the utilities' financing problems in the late 1970s, was contingent upon the presence of an active social movement.

Although anti-nuclear intervenors managed to deter the construction of a few nuclear plants in the early 1960s, such as the Ravenswood, Bodega Bay, and Malibu plants, these events appeared site specific anomalies and did not alter investor expectations or energy sector planning. As is clear from table 6.1, which tallies the number of articles about nuclear power listed in the *New York Times'* annual summary index, and those containing references to opposition to nuclear power, nuclear energy did not become a significant public issue until about 1969.[21]

The impact of increasing nuclear protest was a gradual restructuring of

Table 6.1
Press Coverage of Nuclear Power

Year	Total Articles About Nuclear Power	Number Containing References to Anti-Nuclear Sentiment
1965	45	7
1966	82	7
1967	94	12
1968	69	16
1969	86	34
1970	148	65
1971	147	76
1972	161	77
1973	211	85
1974	208	112
1975	247	105
1976	378	210
1977	388	185
1978	232	141

Source: *New York Times* Annual Summary Index.

the nuclear planning context. Illustrative of the most important changes *directly* fostered by the environmental and anti-nuclear movements were:

- bureaucratic reorganizations within the AEC to increase the integrity and autonomy of safety R&D and nuclear hazard assessment (e.g., the establishment of a Division of Reactor Safety Research free from administrative control by the promotionally oriented Division of Reactor Development and Technology)

- abolition of the AEC in 1974 and divorce of its regulatory and promotional functions (currently split among the NRC and DOE).

- a modest shift of some executive branch authority over nuclear power from the AEC and its offspring (the NRC and DOE) to agencies and individuals with less of a history of collaboration with the nuclear industry (e.g., the transfer of some regulatory authority over radiation exposure standards to the EPA, very modest requirements to include participation by nuclear skeptics in government nuclear studies, and demands that nuclear projects file environmental impact statements).

- abolition of the JCAE and decentering of congressional oversight over nuclear power to at least two dozen separate subcommittees, some chaired by nuclear critics.

- weakening of the federal pre-emption doctrine, (which facilitated much greater regulation over nuclear power by states and localities critical of nuclear technology).

- increased access by the public to AEC documents and regulatory proceedings.

- legal requirements that utilities expand their planning process to include attention to conservation and other non-nuclear energy options (e.g., Integrated Resource Planning and Least Cost Planning-requirements).

Shifting Informational Environments

As membership in the NPC changed so did the data collected and methodologies used to conceptualize nuclear power issues. As strikingly demonstrated in tables 4.2 and 4.5 on nuclear power hazards and cost forecasting, and table 11.2 on energy demand forecasting, the reconfiguring of the NPC led to a paradigm shift in nuclear technology assessment.

Alongside restructuring the political, institutional, and scientific environments shaping public policy, the anti-nuclear movement was able to expand the focus of media attention from the official optimism of the AEC and nuclear industry. The line of causality runs from increased anti-nuclear organizing and information dissemination to increased media attention, rather than the reverse as is sometimes claimed.

The basis for the anti-nuclear movement's media success was the creation of an internal information network. The journals of national anti-nuclear organizations played an especially important role in downloading expertise to local anti-nuclear activists. Recipients of national newsletters, such as Friends of the Earth's *Not Man Apart*, Ralph Nader's *Critical Mass*, and the Environmental Action Foundation's *Power Line*, were often the reporters and editors of local anti-nuclear groups' newsletters and publications. These groups' meetings also served as instruments for self-education. Formal substantive presentations, literature reviews, book sales, etc. were regular events. It was also common for the organizations to possess a library and research files. Once having internalized various kinds of technical and historical information, the movement was very active in outreach and educational activities. Besides meeting with local political figures, regulatory bodies, religious leaders, and media representatives, anti-nuclear groups frequently staged public information events, such as teach-ins, debates, and symbolic protests. Letters to the editor appear to have been especially numerous. In all these educational activities, the movement was strongly aided by its PMC members.

Ultimately, the network created an alternative to the official lines of communication available to the AEC and nuclear industry through mechanisms like press conferences, government reports, utility advertising, and industry announcements. It thereby encouraged the evolution of an alternative planning context and attracted media attention. While it is true that the movement eventually managed to "create media events" (akin to AEC press conferences), it was able to mobilize such attention because of its social base. There was very little media muckraking of nuclear problems, for instance, during the 1965–1968 period.

From Increasing Nuclear Protest to Increasing Nuclear Costs to Collapsing Nuclear Orders

As discussed at the end of chapters 3–5, the anti-nuclear movement's political challenge to nuclear power significantly increased the cost of nuclear generated electricity. Protest-induced regulatory upgrades appear responsible for more than half of the $3 billion increase in plant construction costs for reactors coming on-line from 1984–1993 compared with those on-line by 1972.[22] Nuclear power's loss of OT status also meant: higher risk premiums in capital markets, reduced government subsidies, loss of numerous cost reductions dependent on sector size, and increased support for non-nuclear technologies.

The process by which the anti-nuclear movement increased nuclear costs is as diffuse as the manner by which OT status had reduced them. The impact is captured by a number of regression models and statistical studies of the determinants of nuclear plant capital costs. These models (Bupp et al. 1975; Mooz 1978, 1979, and Komanoff 1981) all contain proxy variables for the level of nuclear protest. The models' findings can be summed up by Bupp et al.'s conclusion:

> "Our interpretation of the relationship between nuclear reactor cost increases and licensing has highlighted the fact that the issue here is not merely technical or economical, but is inherently political: Present trends in nuclear reactor costs can be interpreted as the economic result of a fundamental debate on nuclear power within the U.S. community. Beyond its economic effects, the real issue of this debate is the social acceptability of nuclear power . . ." (Bupp et al. 1975, 25).[23]

By 1975 the closed planning context that had fostered nuclear expansion had dissolved in controversy. While the nuclear industry appeared poised to dominate U.S. energy development after the oil crisis in 1974, it was actually in crisis. From the mid-1970s forward there was a crescendo of nuclear protest, echoing in referendum, mass legal demonstrations, and large scale civil disobedience at nuclear facilities. The number of *New York Times* summary index references to opposition to nuclear power for the 1976–1978 period, was more than fifteen times the level of the 1966–1968 period.

It was amidst this history of protest that the Three Mile Island accident occurred on March 28, 1979. The event certainly exacerbated the nuclear industry's problems, but like other "technical shocks" its impact needs to be situated within a social context.[24]

Alternative Explanations for the Decline of Nuclear Power

The boom/bust pattern of nuclear development was the reflection of two different planning contexts. The expansion period, 1954–1974, reflected the priorities and planning imagination of key energy sector firms and cold warriors. The contraction period, 1974–present, involved increased influence from the left and segments of the professional-managerial class. The full theory of economic development underlying the thinking in this book runs from a structuralist analysis of the social origins of different planning contexts to an economic analysis of how these frameworks for thinking and acting influenced the competitiveness of different technologies. I have focused on the second task in this book. The challenge of tying the evolving characteristics of different planning contexts to a theory of the dynamics of American capitalism is beyond the scope of this project.

Two alternative explanations for the pattern of nuclear development to a planning context approach deserve attention. The first is an "external shocks" interpretation (noted briefly above) that ties nuclear decline to the impact of the 1970s inflation and OPEC oil embargo. This interpretation mistakes a facilitating condition for an underlying cause. While these shocks played a role in derailing nuclear power, the level of regulatory support necessary to transcend their obstacles was no greater than that which nuclear power had previously enjoyed. Thus the shocks are best viewed as a trigger rather than general cause for nuclear decline.

A second interpretation of nuclear history perceives escalating nuclear costs and renewed interest in non-nuclear energy options as "a-political," "rational," responses to new information about nuclear power and nuclear weapons, rather than as "politicized" products of an alternative ideological framework or new paradigm. This approach is consistent with conventional (neoclassical) economic theories of information which predict market adjustments when the costs of acquiring information become significantly less than the cost of potential or actual economic errors.

The choice between a "rationalist" and "paradigmatic" model of nuclear assessment (both with respect to early promotion and later rejection) is akin to many debates in social theory over whether societal outcomes need to be analyzed primarily in terms of the logic of social structures or in terms of individualistic behavior (with reference to "human nature", "rationality", and perhaps an ad hoc appeal to historically given institutional constraints). With respect to technological change, the question is whether there are multiple paths of potential technological evolution contingent upon the sponsoring characteristics of different planning contexts, or a single road which follows an objective logic akin to the unfolding of geometric theorems.

Most conventional neoclassical economists believe that long run energy sector developments are an expression of technical rationality. The market is perceived as a wonderful instrument that conforms economic outcomes to efficiency criteria, given existing scientific knowledge.[25] Corporate growth strategies and political "interventions" into market decision making are treated as second order effects, leaving the basic flow of market evolution determined by engineering and cost minimizing imperatives. There is also a tendency among neoclassical economists to portray political opinion in a methodologically individualistic light, such that it becomes a reflection of rationality or rational self-interest, defined with reference to an a-historical human nature.

Such views lead to a different explanation from the Planning Context - Official Technology framework for nuclear decline. The utilities' and public's turn away from nuclear power is treated as a rational response to new information about nuclear hazards, and/or the result of self-interested fears (Not In My Back Yard [NIMBY]), by a growing number of people living near nuclear facilities. In both cases the focus of explanation is on aggregated, individual behaviors rather than on how a social logic created a particular social context and ideological lens for individuals to use in processing information and organizing collective action.

Two major weaknesses of the rationalist interpretation of nuclear expansion and contraction are the approach's difficulty in explaining why debate persists about nuclear power and the theory's frequent jump from an allegedly "universalistic" and/or "rational" association of nuclear power with nuclear weapons, to the development of a powerful anti-nuclear movement. According to such logic one would have expected a potent anti-nuclear weapons movement long before 1982. From a planning context perspective, the "economic meaning" of nuclear imagery was and is mediated by social contexts. Just as popular opinion has accepted nuclear weapons facilities as "safe" and atomic bombs as "necessary," nuclear energy could have overcome its apocalyptic imagery. The evolution of private mushroom cloud anxieties into anti-nuclear power politics depended on the development of a social movement whose success was tied as much to social structural phenomena (such as the growth of the PMC in numbers and influence and the increased ideological resonance of the left in the late 1960s), as to the character of individual rationality or human nature.

The same kind of objection is raised from the PC-OT perspective to claims that scientific progress would have quickly led to more cautious nuclear regulation and nuclear decline. Chapters 4, 10 and 12 emphasize the paradigmatic nature of technology assessment and R&D decisions, and the potential for different "technological aesthetics" to generate different initial estimates of hazard burdens and assessments of the need for additional research. It is quite easy to imagine the postponement of hazard data collection, attention to alternative methodologies, and more stringent regulatory responses to hazard findings for 10–20 years. One need only look at the cigarette smoking controversy.

Implications for the Future

Like muscle memories of how to ride a bicycle or play a musical instrument, traces of the social network that disestablished nuclear power as an Official Technology lie dormant in the body politic. Groups like the Union of Concerned Scientists, Nuclear Information Resource Service, and the New England Coalition on Nuclear Pollution continue to circulate new technical findings critical of nuclear power to activists around the country. While mass protest against nuclear energy has declined significantly in the wake of the technology's collapse, the ability of nuclear critics to mobilize popular sentiment against renewed nuclear expansion persists. Any attempt to establish a second nuclear era will have to come to terms with this legacy.

Part II

The Future of Nuclear Power: Nuclear Sector Issues

Parts II and III of this book explore the future of nuclear power in America. Part II looks at the factors within the nuclear sector that will pace its development, such as expected nuclear power economics. Part III explores the issues external to the nuclear sector that will shape its future, such as the impact of greenhouse constraints on fossil fuel use.

Part II is divided into four chapters. Chapter 7 looks at the debate over future nuclear power costs for existing reactor designs, ones relying primarily on "engineered" rather than "passive" safety features. Chapters 8 and 9 analyze the public policy issues that will most influence nuclear development. Chapter 8 explores current nuclear R&D and subsidy issues while chapter 9 addresses regulatory debates. Chapter 10 explores the special economic and institutional issues raised by a potential shift to reactor technologies utilizing passive safety measures.

Chapter 7

Nuclear Power Cost Forecasts*

There continues to be a wide range of debate over future LWR generating costs, with optimists projecting costs of ~3.7–~4.6 c/kwh[1] for new nuclear plants and pessimists expecting costs of 8–12+ c/kwh.[2] I foresee future generating costs of 7.5–8.5 c/kwh, which would leave nuclear power more expensive than coal and natural gas fired electricity, many investments in energy efficiency, and a number of renewable energy technologies over the next ten to twenty years. While there are factors besides expected costs (such as fuel diversity and greenhouse concerns) that might promote nuclear investments, public skepticism about nuclear safety makes it unlikely that nuclear power can survive cost disadvantages.

The following discussion: (1) reviews the history of nuclear cost projections and the reasons for past forecasting errors; (2) outlines the qualitative issues underlying current debates between nuclear cost optimists and pessimists; (3) looks more quantitatively at a few specific cost forecasting controversies, and (4) summarizes the implications of nuclear cost forecasting experience for the future of nuclear power.

Historical Experience

As noted in chapter 4, the historical record of nuclear cost prediction by official government and industry participants in nuclear planning is dismal. The generating costs of the last forty-three plants completed are more than five times the constant dollar predictions of the 1960s. At least four different phenomena have contributed to cost underestimation:

—the promotion of misleadingly optimistic cost expectations by nuclear industry supporters in pursuit of corporate market share and industry expansion (what we have termed the economics of self-fulfilling prophecy)

---

*All cost figures are denominated in 1992$ (per the GDP deflator, *Economic Report of the President 1994*, 272) unless otherwise indicated.

—underestimation of the engineering problems posed by the novelty of nuclear technology and neglect of anomalous information and alternative perspectives (the problem of bounded rationality)

—the assumption of regulatory environments with less stringent safety requirements, greater tolerance of hazard uncertainties, and larger economic subsidies than recent environments (the OT assumption), and

—the assumption of excessively rapid nuclear expansion, resulting in overestimation of the industry's capture of scale economies, learning curve gains, and other sector wide efficiencies (the OT assumption).
Nuclear critics charge that many of these tendencies still bias nuclear industry cost predictions.

Methodological Debates in Nuclear Cost Forecasting

Five topics dominate current cost forecasting debates: the expected character of nuclear learning, the reproducibility of superior domestic and/or foreign nuclear performance across the industry, the likely economic impact of plant standardization, the degree of capture by the nuclear industry of system-wide efficiencies, and the payoffs to megawatt scaling.

Learning

The optimists foresee a relatively steep learning curve for new nuclear plants. They emphasize the youthfulness of nuclear technology and the continuing availability of classic cost cutting innovation paths.[3] They highlight the severe inefficiencies imposed on recently completed plants by the tightening of regulatory requirements in mid-construction and anticipate that new plants will meet existing requirements more efficiently than retrofitted ones. Because nuclear planning was originally oriented toward minimizing fuel costs, the optimists anticipate significant savings from reorienting planning to minimize capital and/or maintenance costs.[4] They also expect continued reactor operating experience to demonstrate the conservatism of existing safety systems and thereby permit some relaxation of regulatory requirements.[5] The optimists also assume there will be few unpleasant technical surprises.

The pessimists expect negative or very modest learning curves. They acknowledge the potential for novel solutions to many existing problems, but expect operating experience to continue to uncover new hazards with large financial repercussions. They also expect reactor aging to generate new sets of safety challenges.[6] Key to their thinking is a regulatory shift that occurred in the late-sixties and early-seventies. Until then, regulators assumed the existence of backstop safety technologies, such as inviolable reactor pressure vessels, unbreachable containment structures, and fail-safe emergency core cooling systems. Design base accidents were posited on single rather than multiple failure-initiated events. These assumptions minimized the need for individualized hardware responses to many imaginable accident paths. By the mid-seventies, however, the characteristics of larger reactors, the implications of plant operating experience, and shifting scientific and political judgments challenged these assumptions. Spending spiraled to contain newly perceived accident hazards, as regulators required back-up systems to back-up systems, and common-mode failure complications proliferated. Despite an impressive list of resolved safety issues, numerous unresolved and newly discovered safety issues remain (see ch. 9). The pessimists generalize the experience of escalating reactor construction requirements to the entire nuclear sector, including waste disposal and facility decommissioning. The pessimists also challenge the rapid growth rates assumed in optimistic learning curve projections. They argue that the current planning environment makes large numbers of new orders for nuclear plants unlikely, leaving nuclear costs in the relatively expensive portion of the learning curve.

Reproducibility

The optimists note the high variance among nuclear construction costs. For example, while ORNL's optimistic direct construction cost projections require a 45% decline from existing industry averages, the assumed costs are still *higher than the actual costs achieved by the four cheapest plants completed in 1984–1986* [ORNL 1987, 15, 31; DOE 1986, 109). The costs are also consistent with some estimates of French and Japanese construction costs.[7] Similar results obtain in the plant capacity and operation and maintenance areas.[8]

The key question is whether it is appropriate to project the better existing plants as future industry averages. ORNL analysts insist ". . . there is no fundamental reason why capacity factors of 70% or greater cannot be attained routinely by United States nuclear plants. Such capacity factors are currently attained by some United States nuclear plants and routinely in Europe" (ORNL 12/86, 6). Similar arguments are raised with respect to construction duration (p. 11) and capital costs (p. 22). Pessimists attribute industry variance to unique organizational capital or stochastic phenomena, minimizing the probability of industry-wide improvement.

Numerous explanations have been offered for variations in nuclear performance. Aware of the initial success of EDF in France, Ontario Hydro in Canada, and Duke Power in the U.S., early research explored the impact of size and prior nuclear experience on nuclear outcomes. Most studies found both variables had only modest explanatory power (Hansen et al. 1989, Thomas 1988). Subsequent discussion has emphasized managerial variables, appealing to differences in management quality, corporate culture, and the level of management involvement in day-to-day activities to explain relative performance.[9] Pessimists suggest that the chemistry of good management draws on corporate traditions and/or personality blends that are difficult to reproduce quickly (if at all).

It has been argued that during the early years of nuclear expansion, the utility industry was staffed by mediocre managerial and engineering talent (Kuhn 1966, 108). In the 1960s relative salaries and social prestige for utility executives were low. The regulated character of the industry may have discouraged talented entrants. The optimists argue that higher salaries and more institutional attention to managerial issues can produce high dividends. High payoffs are also expected from increased industry-wide research and cooperation.

Standardization

Standardization is still highlighted by the industry as the most important reason for expecting large future cost reductions. Savings are expected from the capture of scale economies in production and increased modularization in design. The latter should permit expanded factory rather than in-situ fabrication with accompanying cost reductions and increases in quality control and quality assurance.[10]

A 1986 study by the Atomic Industrial Forum (AIF) foresaw savings of 55% above "best experience" plants from standardization.[11] In contrast with actual costs of more than $3,750/KW for plants completed after 1982, and ORNL's estimate of ~$2100/KW (assuming regulatory stability, improved utility management, and economics akin to today's better existing plants), the AIF study projected costs of approximately $1350/KW for a standardized plant due on-line in 1992. Industry papers given at a 1990 MIT conference foresaw savings in the neighborhood of 30% (MIT 1990, p. 2–24). The AIF study also predicted lower O&M costs through savings from improved access to spare parts, reduced staff training costs, and greater industry-wide learning.

Cost pessimists note that standardization has been actively pursued by the reactor vendors since the mid-sixties and by regulatory authorities since 1972. These efforts have been sidetracked, however, by the fluidity of safety requirements, which the skeptics expect to continue due to the youthfulness of nuclear technology and the sensitivity of light water reactors to accident hazards.[12]

The skeptics also argue that the risk of unanticipated safety problems limits the degree of feasible standardization due to the fear that a single unexpected problem could disrupt national electricity supply (such concerns were briefly aired in France over problems with pressure vessel cracking and defective control rod pins).

The pessimists also note that the industry may be unable to approach standardization incrementally. The AIF study assumed a large number of simultaneous orders. Unless manufacturers and engineering/design firms were willing to speculatively offer standardized products in advance of the market (something they do not seem willing to do), it may be impossible to capture related scaling economies.[13]

Systemwide Efficiencies

The optimists also foresee cost reductions due to the industry's capture of systemwide efficiencies (that is, cost reductions accompanying technological maturity and industry expansion). Among the benefits projected are: scaling economies, multiple plant siting economies, better access to capital markets, spin-offs from complementary investments in interfacing technologies (such as robotics and long distance electricity transmission) and manpower economies.

Megawatt Scaling Effects

Nuclear optimists have traditionally projected plant scaling economies to contribute significantly to long-run cost reductions. Appeal to scaling cost reductions has been crucial to the feasibility claims of many new energy technologies (Phung 1987, 15). Most regression studies of actual nuclear capital cost behavior, however, have found only modest scaling savings for nuclear plants. The debate continues today. Scaling optimists foresee regulatory stability and construction learning permitting appropriation of the scaling economies forecast in engineering studies.[14] Scaling pessimists foresee diseconomies of scale. They emphasize the enduring management problems associated with massive, high-tech, on-site construction projects, and related capacity performance failures.

Key Current Cost Debates: Quantitative Dimensions

(This section focuses on the quantitative details of current nuclear cost forecasting debates. Readers more interested in the methodological issues underlying these debates than their empirical details may want to skip to the next section.)

Three topics dominate nuclear power economics: plant construction costs, capacity performance rates, and operation and maintenance costs. Disagreement about other topics, such as uranium prices or waste disposal costs, are unlikely to have major impacts on cost debates. Table 7.1 lists cost projections for evolutionary LWRs beginning construction 1/95, by nuclear optimists, pessimists, and myself. The text reviews the major cost forecasting controversies.

Plant Construction Costs

The debate over future nuclear plant construction costs has the largest implications for nuclear economics. Optimists foresee costs of ~$1590/KW to $1885/KW (U.S. CEA 6/92, 23), while pessimists project results closer to the $3,750+/KW cost of plants coming on-line after 1992.

Construction expenditures depend on direct construction [DC] (or "overnight" construction) costs and interest during construction [IDC] costs. The latter are quite sensitive to construction durations. Nuclear optimists foresee DC costs of $1230/KW–$1675/KW (U.S. CEA 6/92, 20–21), implying a dramatic 43%–59% decline from the $2819/KW cost of the forty nuclear plants coming on-line during 1981–1988 (National Research Council 1992, 31). The optimists project construction periods of five to six years, versus actual durations of ten to twelve years during 1980–1989 [Ibid., 33].

Many of the factors underlying disagreements over direct construction costs have been alluded to in the methodological discussion of the basis for nuclear cost optimism and pessimism. Especially important are assumptions about safety requirements. A characteristic issue, reflecting differing attitudes towards uncertainty, is contingency allowance. Optimists adopt rates of ~10%–15% while pessimists assume rates of 25% to more than 50%.

Table 7.1
Projected Nuclear Power Costs for New LWRs (1992$)*

Cost Category	Optimist Projection	My Projection	Pessimist Projection
Total Costs:	3.8–4.8 c/kwh	7.4–8.6+ c/kwh	~8–12+ c/kwh
Capital Costs	23.5–29.5 M/kwh	42–48+ M/kwh	43–85+ M/kwh
-Construction Costs	$1590–$1885/KW	~$2300–$2650+/KW	$2200–$4000+/KW
-Construction Duration	5–6 yrs.	8 yrs.	~10+ yrs.
-Capacity Rates:	75%–80%	65%	55%–60%
Non-Fuel Operation & Maintenance Costs	6.5–10 M/kwh	14–17+ M/kwh	15+ M/kwh
Capital Additions	.5 M/kwh	3–6 M/kwh	5+ M/kwh
Fuel Costs	6 M/kwh	7 M/kwh	7 M/kwh
Waste Disposal	1 M/kwh	3 M/kwh	3+ M/kwh
Decommissioning	.5–1 M/kwh	3.0 M/kwh	4 M/kwh
Miscellaneous**	0	2 M/kwh	2+ M/kwh

*References discussed in text. Calculations assume a real fixed charge rate of 10.3%
**Miscellaneous includes debit for higher risk premiums in capital markets, siting penalties, etc.

Until contradicted by empirical experience, it seems appropriate to add a significant margin to the optimists' cost expectations. Many of the optimists' assumptions, such as multiple orders and significant standardization economies, short construction periods, and no major new safety regulations, are open to serious question. I expect costs of $2300/KW–$2650+/KW or about 1.5 times the U.S. CEA's projections.

Post Operation Capital Additions

The U.S. CEA posits outlays of less than 1 M/kwh. Underlying this estimate is the assumption that *no retrofitting* will be required to meet changes in safety or environmental regulations once the plant is built (U.S. CEA 1991, 8; 1992, 8). The pessimists foresee continuing public pressure for higher safety standards and the need to address new safety problems uncovered in operation (see ch. 9).[15] The pessimists predict costs in the neighborhood of the 1986–1989 experience, ~6.5 M/kwh, noting this level is still less than the 9 M/kwh average rate experienced in the 1980s (Komanoff and Roelofs 1992, 20). I project costs of 3–6 M/kwh.

Capacity Performance

Industry and DOE forecasts project capacity rates of ~75%–80% (U.S. CEA 6/92, 13; National Research Council 1992, 134, 138). This represents a 25%–33% improvement over the industry's 59% average capacity rate 1968–1990 (Komanoff and Roelofs 1992, 18). Cost pessimists are skeptical of capacity projections higher than 65%.

The optimists argue that many of the reasons for past outages (such as material corrosion) have been eliminated through design changes (such as altered water chemistry, reduced steam generator vibration, and the use of lower carbon steel), increased maintenance efforts, better operator training, improved instrumentation and control systems, and longer fuel cycles.[16] The pessimists note that new problems continue to surface (see ch. 9) and highlight the potential for plant aging and tighter regulatory standards to retard capacity improvements (Komanoff, 4/90).[17] The shutdown of Yankee Rowe in 1992 due to uneasiness about reactor vessel embrittlement and the discovery of severe steam generator cracking in Maine Yankee in 1995 have reinforced these concerns.

While the industry's recent improvement in capacity rates has been impressive, I expect aging burdens and new difficulties, such as problems with cable fire retardants and BWR core water level measurement, to limit future capacity rates to ~65%.

Non-Fuel Operation and Maintenance Costs (O&M)

Cost optimists project O&M costs of about 6.5–10.5 M/kwh (1990$) (U.S. CEA 6/92, 43, 1991, p. 13).[18] These projections are significantly lower than the ~15 M/kwh level of recent years. A 1991 forecast by the U.S. Council for Energy Awareness sums up the rationale for O&M optimism, arguing,

> "New nuclear plants are designed for greater ease in operation and periodic maintenance. Increased use of automated monitoring and instrument control will reduce the operators' work and increase plant reliability. Fewer parts and simpler designs will require less replacement work, and larger work spaces will facilitate and expedite maintenance" (U.S. CEA 1991, 8).

Pessimists foresee O&M costs of 1.5c/kwh or higher.[19] Pessimists note that from 1970 to 1990 O&M costs escalated at a real rate of 10.9% (the rate was somewhat under 5% for 1985–1989) (Fertel 1992). They foresee similar pressures in the future, especially for: higher insurance premiums, higher utility payments for NRC services, aging related repairs,[20] and regulatory reactions to new information (e.g., responses to recent ICRP recommendations for tighter radiation protection standards and fluctuating levels of concern over pressure vessel embrittlement and plant security issues). Supporting the pessimists' outlook is the industry's recent inability to prevent escalating O&M expenditures from prematurely retiring some existing reactors. The pessimists also accuse industry forecasts of allocating certain nuclear-related O&M costs to overall utility overhead [Borson et al. 5/89].[21]

I find the pessimists' case relatively convincing and expect areas of O&M cost saving to be constrained by regulatory conservatism (as in the case of proposed staff reductions), offset by new O&M burdens (e.g., escalating low level waste disposal costs)[22] and undermined by lower capacity rates than assumed by industry optimists. A range of 14 M/kwh–17 + M/kwh seems a likely level for future O&M costs.

Fuel Costs

Fuel costs (excluding waste disposal) have been the one bright spot in nuclear cost forecasting and nuclear economics. The industry's impressive success serves as a model for optimists' projections in other nuclear markets. Current expenditures average about 6 M/kwh (DOE 0436(95), 47) and government and industry forecasts project this or a slightly lower rate through 2010. Pessimists tend to differ by only a few mills per kilowatt hour.[23]

Backend Costs: Decommissioning

Backend costs refer to nuclear plant decommissioning and high level waste disposal costs. Despite wide disagreement over expected backend costs, decommissioning is likely to have only a modest impact on nuclear economics. This is largely due to the effect of time discounting which deflates the present value of future expenditures. Escalating decommissioning costs are likely, however, to further erode industry cost forecasting credibility and to burden weak utilities who have set aide insufficient decommissioning funds.

In early 1993 NRC and industry decommissioning estimates ranged from about .5 to 1 M/kwh.[24] Pessimists foresee costs four to more than ten times higher.[25] As noted earlier, government and industry decommissioning costs have been embarrassingly overoptimistic and increased at a constant dollar annual rate of ~16% during 1976–1987 (Biewald and Bernow 1991, 235). This trend is likely to continue, as recent NRC and industry estimates tend to inappropriately assume few new regulatory requirements, few serious technical surprises (beyond those accommodated within 25% contingency margins), no labor or materials bottlenecks or problems with insufficient lead-time for specialized equipment, minimal difficulties meeting ALARA (As Low As Reasonably Achievable) radiation exposure requirements, and excessive MW scaling and standardization savings (DOE 0438(90), 27; Cantor 1991).

As a 1990 DOE report notes, the NRC and U.S. CEA cost estimates exclude the implications of potential federal or state regulatory requirements demanding return of the nuclear site to greenfield use (DOE 0438(90)). More importantly, the analyses tend to grossly underestimate low level waste disposal (LLWD) costs, which have escalated from ~$1/cubic feet (cf) for class A low level waste in 1975 to $41/cf in 1991, with expected future costs ranging from $30–$40/cf to $600–$700/cf (all $/cf costs in historical $) (Makhijani and Saleska 1992, 85).

The escalation in LLWD costs reillustrates the generic problems of public acceptance, risk averse safety regulation, and institutional uncertainty facing the nuclear industry. Continued LLWD cost increases are likely, for example, in response to the International Committee on Radiological Protection's recommendation that maximum annual occupational exposure limits be lowered from five rems/yr. to two rems/yr. (Makhijani and Saleska 1992, 114). Pressures for tighter regulation of waste transport and site management may also bring cost increases. The industry's loss of public trust has made it difficult to take advantage of the large economies of scale involved in LLWD technologies. Strong "Not In My Back Yard" opposition to nuclear waste sitings has lead to widespread refusals by states to accept out of state wastes. This has resulted in a proliferation of plans for regional or single state disposal sites instead of a few national disposal sites. Calculations at MIT, for example, estimate that storage costs would be three to four times higher for a Massachusetts only site (@40,000 cf) than for a joint Massachusetts, Connecticut, New York, and New Jersey site (@250,000–350,000 cf) (MIT 1993b).[26]

Given the failure of past decommissioning cost estimates and the methodological basis for excess optimism, I expect actual decommissioning costs to be at least two to three times higher than current industry projections.[27] While there might be avenues to lower costs (such as concentrating LLW at a few national waste sites),[28] these outcomes currently seem unlikely.

Backend Costs: High Level Waste Disposal (HLWD)

While a key focus of public attention due to hazard concerns, HLWD is not likely to have a major bearing on nuclear economics. Nuclear optimists, such as the U.S. CEA, project costs of 1 M/kwh for waste transportation and permanent disposal (U.S. CEA 6/92, 10). Although pessimists foresee costs several times higher, the difference seems unlikely to exceed 3–5 M/kwh.[29]

There are several reasons for expecting that current DOE and industry HLWD cost projections are too low. Industry assumptions about fuel performance (kwh/kg U) and nuclear sector size have tended to be overoptimistic, thereby inflating the kwh base over which to distribute waste repository costs. The price tags for siting and constructing a HLW facility have been consistently revised upwards. From 1989–1991, for example, the expected costs for military waste disposal more than doubled (Makhijani and Saleska 1992, 67). From 1983–1990 the DOE's projected costs for handling commercial HLW increased from $179,000/MTU to $325,000/MTU (Ibid., 66, 68), though curiously the DOE's charge for waste disposal services and industry cost projections remained fixed at 1 M/kwh. Simply adjusting the 1982 fee for inflation would produce costs of 1.4 M/kwh.

Many of the pressures behind cost escalation, such as higher site evaluation costs and increased bonus payments to host communities are unlikely to abate. Other cost categories, such as waste transport, may experience faster growth in the future (Resnikoff 1983). Former NRC Commissioner John Ahearne also warns that public distrust of nuclear power and declining research funds may discourage talented people from tackling waste disposal issues (MIT 1990, 7–9).

On the other hand, there appear to be practical limits to HLWD cost escalation. The amount of waste produced by a 1 GWe reactor, about 25–30 MT/yr., is relatively modest. While scientific uncertainties and local opposition to waste sitings may prevent the construction of a HLWD repository, it is difficult to imagine repository costs escalating indefinitely. It now seems likely that short term policy will be dominated by dry cask storage at reactor sites, with presumably modest cost impacts.

Indirect Costs

Nuclear critics tend to include more kinds of costs in their analysis of nuclear economics than nuclear advocates. The critics, for example, debit nuclear power for:

—reducing utility planning flexibility (due to nuclear plants' long construction periods and large MW size)

—increasing spinning reserve requirements (due to nuclear plants' large MW size and historically low capacity rates)[30]

—high siting costs, public relations burdens, and attendant demands on scarce management time (due to anti-nuclear sentiment among significant sections of the public)[31]

—higher electricity transmission costs due to remote siting

—high risk premiums and therefore higher financing costs (due to past prudency risks, accident risks, and general uncertainty levels).[32] These costs are the financial echoes of past nuclear failures, such as the $47 billion in sunk costs abandoned in canceled reactors (Komanoff and Roelofs 12/92, 15).

Nuclear advocates' economic analyses tend to ignore most of these cost categories. The U.S. CEA, for example, refuses to include a risk premium in its nuclear cost calculations, asserting

"no risk premium, in addition to the average cost of capital, is included in this study's base-case assumptions for the nuclear plants. It is believed that under a favorable regulatory environment, and given their high performance and operation standards, Advanced Light Water Rectors should not be treated differently than alternative large power plant projects" (U.S. CEA 6/92, 6).

Such assertions confuse wishful thinking with cost forecasting, as technical and financial uncertainties involve real economic costs and are genuine aspects of foreseeable nuclear investments.

Conclusions

(1) Future nuclear power costs for evolutionary LWRs will probably range between 7.5 and 8.5 c/kwh, with much higher costs more likely than much lower costs. Public concern about nuclear hazards and the emergence of new problems with increased operating experience will limit industry cost cutting success.

(2) Past experience recommends posing nuclear forecasting disagreement as a debate over expected cost trajectories, rather than a debate over static engineering cost estimates. Thus posed, the key issues become: the reproducibility of best plant performance, the expected behavior of scale and

systemwide economies, the expected magnitude of routine learning and novel innovations, and the impact of unexpected technical and regulatory problems. Posing the issues in this manner illuminates why it has been impossible to resolve the optimist/pessimist debate by recourse to the data. In effect, each paradigm has defended its projections by reference to the hypothetical future, rather than the empirical past.

(3) Attention to the dynamic aspect of cost forecasting heightens the relative attractiveness of reactor designs that rely on passive safety features and minimize population and occupational radiation exposure. Such designs would presumably be less sensitive to unexpected technical and regulatory surprises and more robust in the face of pessimistic cost assumptions. Chapter 10 explores the future of these designs in detail.

(4) The tendency for stylized realms of discourse to constrain forecasting analysis and for the dominant paradigm to resist empirical refutation suggests the usefulness of institutionalizing competing centers of cost prediction. Statistical techniques can perhaps be derived for estimating the degree of bibliographic insularity and self-referencing in forecasting discourse and the need for, and boundaries of, alternative forecasting paradigms.[33]

(5) The history of nuclear power cost forecasting challenges purely rationalist and technically deterministic conceptions of technological change. Nuclear power development suggests how social contexts can influence the direction of innovation by shaping cost forecasting expectations and thereby increasing the capture of scale and other path dependent advantages for different technologies.

Chapter 8

Public Policy and the Future of Nuclear Power: R&D and Subsidy Support

As demonstrated in chapters 3 and 5, favorable public policy has been crucial to past periods of nuclear expansion. This chapter analyzes the current status and likely future of government nuclear R&D and subsidy policies. Chapter 9 explores the regulatory issues that will most effect the technology's future. The chapters reillustrate the paradigmatic nature of nuclear controversies by tying current debates over energy policy to basic issues in technology assessment.

While trying to present both the pro and anti-nuclear positions, I am not neutral. I find the paradigm generating nuclear criticism more compelling than that generating nuclear advocacy. I think much can be gained, however, by dropping the "idiot theory" of nuclear debate and replacing it with paradigmatic explanations for disagreement.

Energy R&D Policy: Current and Past Nuclear Programs[1]

As noted in chapter 3, debates over energy R&D policy resemble paradigm debates in science over the fruitfulness of different research agendas. Final R&D outcomes reflect the "technological aesthetics" of decision makers, the political-economic ability of different industries to construct critical mass development paths (independent of technical arguments), and the character of existing engineering knowledge. Current conditions suggest that the nuclear industry will capture enough R&D to keep many existing facilities operating, but will be unable to mobilize the funds necessary to stimulate a second nuclear era.

163

Current Programs

Fission nuclear power remains both a needy and fertile technology with respect to R&D. On the needy-side, existing plants require about $100 million per year of NRC safety research to continue routine operation. The DOE is spending several times this amount on nuclear waste and decommissioning research for DOE reactors and overhead for the national labs.[2] These outlays are in addition to the several hundred million dollars spent annually for commercial nuclear waste disposal R&D that are funded from a 1 M/kwh surcharge on utility nuclear power generation. Other funds for nuclear power related research appear in the federal budget under categories like "Basic Energy Sciences", University and Science Education (e.g., university reactor fuel assistance) and Biological and Environmental Research (e.g., research on radiation hazards). Thus even if no R&D funds were approved for new reactor designs, nuclear power would continue to claim a major share of national energy R&D resources.

On the fecund-side, the youthfulness of nuclear power suggests the availability of many avenues to cost saving innovation. The Electric Power Research Institute, the reactor vendors, and the national labs, for example, have all offered long lists of R&D projects thought promising by nuclear industry planners.

Current nuclear power research has four tracks. The first track addresses existing LWR research needs (in areas such as plant lifetime extension, decommissioning, waste disposal, and hazard assessment) as well as DOE facility cleanup needs. The second track funds a potpourri of nuclear energy projects with differing degrees of relevance for the civilian power program. For example, the AVLIS uranium enrichment project ($100+ million/yr. in the early nineties; *Nuclear News* 3/91, 29) is primarily a civilian power project, while space reactor programs (~30+ million per year in the early-nineties [Ibid.]) appear to have limited civilian payoffs. The DOE also funds a large naval reactor development program (~$600 million/yr.; *Nuclear News* 3/91, 29), but its research affinities with the civilian power industry are uncertain.

The last two tracks of fission power R&D aim at developing "next generation" or "advanced reactor" technologies. Track three focuses on developing standardized reactor designs with precertified NRC license approval for large LWRs with active safety features and mid-sized LWRs with some passive safety features. Recent funding has been in the neighborhood of twenty to fifty million dollars per year.

Track four involves R&D for non-LWRs with passive safety features, principally the modular high temperature gas reactor (MHTGR) and liquid metal reactor (LMR). Spending in the early 1990s was in the neighborhood of $50–$100 million per year. Funding for the LMR was terminated in FY 1995 and funding for the MHTGR was ended in FY 1996. Both programs continued to have pockets of support in congress and may resurface in the future.

Shifting Priorities

As detailed in chapter 3, nuclear power has enjoyed the lion's share of federal energy R&D funding since World War II. From 1950–1990 it received nearly $50 billion in R&D assistance (1990 $) (see table 8.1). R&D funding has declined significantly, however, since the technology's loss of OT status. Earmarked DOE spending for civilian reactor development fell every year during the 1980s, from a high of 1.5 billion dollars in 1980 to .25 billion dollars in 1989 (see table 8.2). Spending has continued at modest levels in the 1990s (see table 8.3).

Because of nuclear technology's loss of OT status, the industry has been unable to win enough government R&D support to rapidly commercialize any of the targeted standardized designs. Instead of deferring to a "nuclear imperative," political leaders now defer to the "market." Federal policy has not generated analogs to the government financed Shippingport demonstration reactor, the AEC's Power Reactor Demonstration Program, or the early Clinch River Breeder Reactor program.[3]

Discouraged by nuclear power's loss of OT status, cheap fossil fuel prices, and uncertain competition from renewable energy technologies, the corporate sector has been unwilling to assume the risks tolerated by the

Table 8.1*
Federal Nuclear R&D Spending 1950–1990 (Billions of Dollars)

	mixed current $	*1990 $*
Conventional Fission	13.7	28.6
Breeder	4.3	9.6
Civilian Related Military	.8	3.5
General Programs	1.5	4.5
Waste (generic R&D, not covered by utilities' waste disposal fund)	1.0	1.5
Total	$21.2	47.7

*Tallies exclude fusion R&D of $9.4 billion and exclusively military R&D. Source: Komanoff and Roelofs 12/92, 53.

Table 8.2
DOE Expenditures: Civilian Reactor Development Program
Millions of 1989$

Year	80	81	82	83	84	85	86	87	88	89	90
Reactor Type											
Facilities	411	308	296	204	188	166	148	138	137	140	163
LWR	42	55	66	49	65	60	54	37	33	27	23
HTGR	65	55	46	44	36	37	34	22	24	20	22
LMR	592	512	512	466	366	137	110	60	59	54	35
Clinch River Breeder	276	257	241	280	101	20	0	0	0	0	0
Light Water Cooled Breeder	91	83	68	56	42	29	21	15	0	9	0
Totals	1477	1270	1229	1099	798	450	367	273	253	250	243

Source: U.S. General Accounting Office May 1990.

vendors in the turnkey plants or the utilities in de facto demonstration plant purchases in the 1960s. A 1992 study overseen by the National Academy of Sciences, for example, concluded:

"no first plant mid-sized LWR with passive safety features is likely to be certified and built without government incentives, in the form of shared funding or financial guarantees" (National Research Council 1992, 169).

A May 1990 GAO report on reactor development reported

"Utility officials said that they were not as familiar with MHTGRs and LMRs as they are with LWRs because they have no

Table 8.3
Recent Nuclear Power R&D Spending[1]

Fiscal Year Status:	1996 Clinton request	1995 Appropriation	1994 Net Appropriation	1993 Budget	1992 Enacted	1991
Total Civilian Reactor Development	50	91	106	209		
Total Nuclear Energy R&D		177*	236	342	332	304

1. Totals exclude indirect R&D assistance, such as that for improved laser enrichment technology or naval reactor development.
*Budget request, rather than actual appropriation.
Source: *Nuclear News*: 3/95, p. 15; 3/94, p. 25, 3/92, p. 28, 3/91, p. 29.

'hands on' experience with these reactors. . . . (thus) they would be hesitant to select these technologies unless they had first been demonstrated" (24).

The educational infrastructure supporting nuclear power research has also eroded. The number of nuclear engineering students at the masters and senior undergraduate level, for example, fell about 40% in 1978– 1988 (National Research Council 1992, 167). The number of universities with research reactors fell by two-thirds over the same period (Ibid. 167). Total enrollments in undergraduate nuclear engineering programs have continued to decline, falling ~30% in 1992–1995 (*Nuclear News* 9/95, 50; 9/96, 38). Some of the weakness in domestic enrollments in nuclear engineering is below the surface. In 1991, for example, 322 of the 699 students in doctoral programs were foreign students (*Nuclear News* 9/92, 53). There has also been a dramatic shift within some nuclear engineering departments away from fission power programs towards areas such as nuclear imaging.

Reflecting shrinking markets, the industry has seen a large number of mergers and joint ventures. The domestic light water reactor manufacturing industry has fallen from four to two firms, as Combustion Engineering was acquired by ABB, a large Swiss-Swedish electrical equipment and nuclear manufacturing firm, and Babcock and Wilcox was acquired by Framatome, a French nuclear firm. G. E. and Westinghouse have joint R&D projects with many Japanese firms. Similar mergers and international cooperation are occurring in other nation's nuclear programs (DOE (0438) 1990, 34–35). The global consortium financing of the International Thermonuclear Experimental (fusion) Reactor (ITER) may be a model for large fission power projects in the future.

Technological Aesthetics and R&D Competition

Nuclear power R&D advocates face severe challenges from proponents of increased funding for advanced fossil fuel, renewable energy, and energy conservation technologies. Chapters 10–12 look at the economic and technical *details* of some of the most promising nuclear and non-nuclear R&D options. The discussion below focuses on the *general* character of R&D competition, extending the paradigmatic metaphors developed in chapter 3 for analyzing the history of energy sector R&D policy to current R&D debates.

As noted in our discussion of nuclear cost forecasting, the questions asked during the early stages of technology assessment do not lend themselves to unique answers, falsifiable from existing empirical data. Judgments necessarily rely on historically conditioned intuitions, rules of thumb, or what I've termed technological aesthetics. R&D choices can thus reflect ideological habits of mind as well as more narrowly grounded scientific principles.

Much of the current technical debate over the promise of different energy sector options can be summed up in terms of different technological aesthetics about: (1) the merits of high versus low "power densities"; (2) the benefits of large versus small unit size; (3) the value of a technology's ability to supply virtually unlimited energy; and (4) the answers to questions like, "what is a simple technology?"; or "what is an acceptable level of uncertainty?"

Power Densities

Power densities refer to a technology's energy/space ratio. Nuclear technologies have high power densities while most renewable energy technologies (RETs) involve diffuse energy sources. Enthusiasts for high power densities prize their relatively modest land and material requirements, their need for few facility sites, and amenability to centralized management. They warn that technologies with low power densities, such as solar, wind, and biomass, will inevitably involve large materials needs and as a result potentially large environmental burdens (be it from PV materials like gallium arsenide, biomass inputs like pesticides and herbicides, or visual pollution from endless windmills). Illustratively, Terence Price, a former Secretary-General of the Uranium Institute, writes:

> "Although the total energy reaching the earth from the sun is enormous, . . . the amount falling on a given area is inconveniently low for large-scale applications . . . . [S]chemes for solar electricity generation require engineering on a scale which verges on the heroic" (Price 1990, 332).

> "The potential (wind) resource is large . . . but once again it is inconveniently 'dilute' . . . . [I]n contrast to the very compact and visually non-intrusive nature of nuclear power, a 1 GWe windmill farm would be huge, covering 10 square kilometres or more" (Price 1990, 334).

Former AEC Chairperson Dixy Lee Ray similarly argues:

"It is also possible to produce electricity by harnessing sunlight if—and here's the big 'if'—all you need is a few watts. . . . But to produce large amounts of electricity . . . solar generated electricity is not a practical alternative.

"Why not? Because, to begin with, sunlight is diffuse. . . . Two analogies help illustrate the point.

"First, suppose you wish to boil a pot of water and all you have is a bunch of matches. No matter how many matches are used, the water cannot be heated to boiling by holding them, one by one, under the pot. . . ."

"The other analogy is my all-time favorite, for it dramatically illustrates the importance of concentrated energy. It goes like this:

"In biology, there is a term, 'biomass,' which refers to the total amount of living material in any body or collection of living things. Thus, you can compare the biomass equivalents of different species; for example, there is the same biomass in the body of one elephant as there is in 100 million fleas. Now, if you need to pull a very heavy load, would you rather harness one elephant or 100 million fleas? Provided, of course, that someone builds flea harnesses at a price you can afford to pay, and provided, of course, that you can make all those fleas hop at the same time and in the same direction!

"And that explains the trouble with solar power. It is diffuse and like the fleas, it is difficult and expensive to organize and concentrate" (Ray 1990, 128–129).

Enthusiasts for diffuse energy sources prize their ease of siting (even if large numbers of sites are required) and their amenability to decentralized management. While acknowledging the technologies' relative land intensity, they find this disadvantage less significant when the technologies' reduced mining requirements are included in the calculations. They also find available land resources more than sufficient to the task of projected energy supply.

Proponents of diffuse sources judge the serious accident risks of concentrated energy sources, such as nuclear power or liquid natural gas technologies, far more troubling than the potential materials and land use requirements of diffuse technologies. They have much less faith than the defenders of high power densities in the ability of clever design, quality control, and human engineering to avoid serious accidents. Jan Beyea, staff physicist for the National Audubon Society, writes, for example:

". . . a major accident is sufficiently serious, and . . . the probability of occurrence sufficiently uncertain, that nuclear power cannot be perceived as a desirable technology from the perspective of safety" (Kaku and Trainer 1982, 107).

Unit Scaling

Many of the intuitions separating enthusiasts for large and small sized technologies parallel those involving power densities. Proponents of large scale technologies, such as 500–1100 megawatt (MW) nuclear and coal fired plants, prize: (1) the plants' expected engineering and construction economies of scale; (2) the need for fewer facility sites, and (3) the technology's amenability to centralized management. Nuclear physicist and nuclear power advocate Bernard Cohen argues:

"It would take 50,000 wind turbines of the type being used in California to replace the average electricity produced by a single nuclear or coal-burning plant, which is hardly an inviting prospect for an electrical utility. Management costs would be horrendous" (Cohen 1990, 263).

Alvin Weinberg, former director of Oak Ridge National Laboratory and "father" of the PWR, adds

"Why did most engineers gravitate toward supply enhancement rather than demand management? I can give at least two reasons. First, designing nuclear reactors seemed to be more glamorous than improving car efficiencies. Second, demand management usually requires millions of people to change their way of doing something. In some cases, such as lowering the thermostat, the change might affect life-style; in other cases, such as replacing an energy-inefficient refrigerator with a more efficient one, the change requires an additional outlay of money. In a broad sense, demand management, even when based on clever new technologies, is a social fix: many individual decisions are needed to achieve lower demand. By contrast, increasing supply was regarded, perhaps naively, as a purely technical fix: only a few people have to be convinced to build a nuclear reactor or a synfuel plant. The technical fix seemed to be simpler than the social fix" (Weinberg 1990, 27).

In contrast, enthusiasts for small unit systems (.3 MW–100 MW): (1) expect greater payoffs from the mass production economies and faster generational learning that are possible with small plants compared to the unit scaling economies anticipated with big plants; (2) emphasize the disadvantages imposed on large units by field rather than factory construction; and (3) prefer the decentralized management and greater planning flexibility offered by smaller units over the administrative simplicity of large units. Princeton Professor Robert Williams, writes:

> "The small unit size (50 to 300 kWe) and relative simplicity of wind and many other renewable energy technologies facilitates cost-cutting. Most renewable energy equipment can be constructed in factories. . . . The small scale of the equipment also makes the time required from design to operation short, so that needed improvements can be identified by field testing and quickly incorporated into modified designs. . . . In contrast, large conventional nuclear and fossil fuel energy facilities require extensive construction in the field where labor is costly and productivity gains difficult to achieve. The long construction periods of these large energy systems also make learning difficult" (Williams 10/93, 4).

Thomas Hughes has theorized that a centralizing tendency animated aspects of what he calls "modernist engineering". His work suggests that an emerging "post-modernist engineering" imagination may be more receptive to the messy complexity of a decentralized, multi-technology, multi-firm electricity sector.

Supply Abundance

Technologies can also be distinguished on the basis of their upper bound energy supply potential. Energy systems relying on breeder reactors, hot dry rock geothermal resources or fusion energy hold out the hope for virtually limitless energy. Other sources, such as wind and biomass, offer very large but bounded energy supply potentials. Some technological aesthetics, like those of former AEC Chair Dixy Lee Ray are fired by visions of infinite energy; other planning visions, like those of Amory Lovins, emphasize the economic payoffs to increased energy efficiency and give little *special* weight to energy supply. The former aesthetic preference will value nuclear technologies more highly than the latter.

Illustratively, Dixy Lee Ray argues:

> ". . . mankind's long path of progress out of savagery. . . . started with energy—the energy of fire.

". . . . the history of western civilization is to a considerable extent the history of learning about energy and its use.

". . . . Utilities could lead the way to the electric economy—just as they pioneered in introducing nuclear power . . . so now they must lead the way with advanced reactors. Reactors dedicated to: Charging batteries, Desalinating . . . Producing hydrogen fuel for the future of air travel. . . .

"We should dare to dream big. Perhaps we could learn from . . . Goethe's immortal Faust. . . . Faust's soul was saved, not because he reclaimed land, but because . . . power works. . . . In this sense and in the knowledge that we who believe in the technology and use of electrical energy are engaged in the struggle to improve the lot of every human being, we can still share Goethe's enthusiasm and get a taste of Faust's salvation" (Ray 1991, 1–7).

Alvin Weinberg adds,

"It is a Faustian bargain that we strike: In return for this inexhaustible energy source, which we must have if we are to maintain ourselves at anything like our present numbers and our present state of affluence, we must commit ourselves—essentially forever—to exercise the vigilance and discipline necessary to keep our nuclear fires well behaved. As a nuclear technologist who has devoted his career to this quest for an infinite energy source, I believe the bargain is a good one . . ." (Miller, 1980, 111).

In contrast, Lovins argues:

"People do not want electricity or oil, . . . but rather comfortable rooms, light, vehicular motion, food, tables, and other real things. . . . we are using premium fuels and electricity for many tasks for which their high energy quality is superfluous, wasteful and expensive. . . . Where we want only to create temperature differences of tens of degrees, we should meet the need with sources whose potential is tens or hundreds of degrees, not with a flame temperature of thousands or a nuclear temperature of millions—like cutting butter with a chainsaw" (Lovins 1976, 78–79).

The notion of technological aesthetics could also be used to analyze other aspects of energy technology assessment, such as judgments about the seriousness of intermittency limitations for wind and direct solar technologies or the seriousness of various energy related negative externalities, such as nuclear weapons proliferation hazards or greenhouse risks. We will return to issues of technological aesthetics in chapter 10's discussion of intra-nuclear industry R&D debates between advocates of different reactor designs.

R&D Recommendations and Likely R&D Outcomes[4]

When it was *assumed* that massive deployment of nuclear power was inevitable (the only question being when), it was relatively easy to justify nuclear R&D. With the absence of a nuclear imperative (i.e., the existence of energy alternatives), it is much more difficult. Whatever one's technological aesthetics, several characteristics of nuclear technology disadvantage it in competition for R&D dollars. Nuclear projects tend to require much more expensive prototype and demonstration plants than smaller scale technologies, often by an order of magnitude. Nuclear projects tend to have long gestation periods and sluggish learning curves due to the need for time-consuming safety precautions (e.g., any innovation with potential impacts on reactor safety may require years of safety tests, materials qualification in radioactive environments, and regulatory review before deployment). Nuclear research can also be hazardous.

Given these disadvantages and the poor economics of current nuclear power plants, only three kinds of nuclear R&D are likely to mobilize significant support: (1) R&D spending for the safe operation, decommissioning, and waste disposal associated with existing reactors; (2) "Cross-cutting" R&D that benefits both nuclear and non-nuclear energy technologies (such as R&D for high temperature materials, gas turbine technologies, or energy storage); and (3) research that supports nuclear power's potential role as a long run insurance policy with respect to greenhouse hazards and energy scarcity.

The first tack will be financed primarily by nuclear power consumers and will lead to plant shutdowns before large expenditures to improve existing plant performance. The second tack will be dominated by non-nuclear objectives. Only the third strategy holds out the hope for large new nuclear power programs directed by nuclear power enthusiasts. The "insurance" rationale for nuclear power R&D appears in two different forms: a *"preservationist"* tack, which aims to maintain existing expertise, and a *"revisionist"* tack, which aims to reconceive nuclear technologies.

The *preservationists* argue that the nuclear industry has accumulated hard won knowledge and practical experience. Some of this knowledge is incapable of transmission through the printed word as captured in scholarly papers, conference proceedings, text books, government regulations, industry materials specifications, etc. Some of the knowledge is "tacit knowledge", involving modes of problem solving, rules of thumb, intuitions about what not to do, as well as what to do, and memories of unrecorded deadends that elude the journals. This kind of knowledge is often transmitted by mentors and requires an ongoing R&D program to ensure its survival.

The problem with this reasoning is that an R&D program without a clear mission and frequent "reality checks" may flounder. Historical experience suggests that the absence of ongoing construction experience will discourage entry into the nuclear industry by the most talented young scientists and engineers. Those who do enter are in jeopardy of losing their bearings. The absence of feedback from actual reactors threatens to encourage the evolution of "fantasy" designs insulated from the reality check of operating experience and market criteria. The proliferation of fusion reactor designs that are cranked out by universities and national laboratories show how easy it is to fall into this trap and how dangerous the process is to the practitioners. The "preserved industry" may reduce to "true-believers", self-selected into an isolated fraternity. It thus may be impossible to nurture the benefits of our hands-on experience in the absence of a vigorous nuclear program.

In any case, it may well be that we do not want to preserve our current knowledge; it is not clear that current nuclear expertise will be relevant to nuclear projects thirty to fifty years from now. It is likely that materials breakthroughs, instrumentation advances, and other innovations from broader intellectual domains than nuclear engineering, such as mechanical engineering and computer science, will reshape nuclear technology. It is thus not clear what the payoffs will be to maintaining a sharply focused nuclear power engineering and scientist cohort. Nurturing existing nuclear expertise (e.g., in fuel cladding materials) may be akin to preserving hands-on experience with electric typewriters after the shift to personal computers.

The "value-added" of preservationist research is also reduced because some American nuclear R&D is already guaranteed for "technological maintenance" in areas such as decommissioning and waste disposal and because of the existence of foreign nuclear programs. The history of LWR development in Japan and France suggests that importing nuclear technology may be a viable route to nuclear expertise.

The preservationist case is also weakened by the need for any nuclear revival to break cleanly with the industry's history of insular discourse, excess technical optimism, and dominance by short-term commercial pressures. While some impressive advances have been made in the last fifteen years, institutional subcultures change slowly. In the absence of external corrections, it may be difficult to ensure that an intellectual version of

Gresham's Law does not preserve the least savory, rather than most useful, aspects of nuclear experience.

The *"revisionists"* argue that the insurance rationale for nuclear power and large increases in expected uranium resources, shifts the criteria for reactor selection from short term market competitiveness (favoring LWRs), to long-term viability (favoring passively safe reactors rather than breeder reactors). What is pre-eminent in backstop insurance is guaranteed availability. Thus revisionist R&D strategies focus on meeting public concerns about radiation hazards, reactor accident probabilities, nuclear weapons proliferations, and waste disposal. The revisionists promote: (1) R&D spending for passively safe reactor designs, such as the PIUS reactor and MHTGR; (2) Increased attention to weapons diversion issues in reactor design (minimizing the appeal of LMRs, especially designs involving reprocessing); (3) Increased scientific study of the mechanisms of radiation damage and large scale epidemiological studies to resolve statistical uncertainties in currently available data; and (4) Continued waste disposal R&D, without the pressures for immediate demonstration of long term disposal options.

While I find much of the revisionist program reasonable, the problem is that it can serve as a Trojan horse for supporters of traditional nuclear technologies and industry outlooks. Nuclear enthusiasts, for example, may use the rhetoric of passive safety to maintain an industry infrastructure intended to promote breeder and other non-passively safe reactor designs in the future.

Greenhouse Issues

Because the future of nuclear power is increasingly tied to arguments about greenhouse constraints on fossil fuel use, it is appropriate to explore briefly the implications of greenhouse concerns for nuclear R&D policies. (Chapter 13 looks at the general implications of greenhouse issues for nuclear power in more detail). The implications of greenhouse hazards for nuclear power depend on three factors: (1) scientific judgments about the physical impact of greenhouse gases on the environment; (2) the translation of physical outcomes into economic outcomes (i.e., damage assessment); and (3) the availability of non-nuclear greenhouse abatement options.

Uncertainty dominates all three areas and is likely to persist for at least a decade and probably much longer. Despite these uncertainties and sometimes because of them, certain conclusions can be drawn about the implications of greenhouse hazards for future nuclear power R&D:

(1) It will be difficult to mobilize public support for otherwise unpopular nuclear power research in the short run (0–10 years) on the basis of greenhouse hazards, due to persisting indeterminacies about the hazard.

(2) Options that are less expensive and less socially contentious than nuclear power are likely to remain available for at least ten to twenty years. Because the analyses that project high damages from global warming are driven by the same kinds of concerns (risk aversion, distrust of technological fixes, ecological conservatism, etc.) that motivate the anti-nuclear movement, it is unlikely that groups very concerned about greenhouse hazards will favor nuclear responses.

(3) The major value of nuclear power as a greenhouse option is long term. Given the wide array of potential backstop technologies alongside nuclear power (see chapter 12), this role does not justify large short-run R&D support.

Future R&D Prospects

Current DOE and private sector energy R&D strategies emphasize energy diversity. No single technology, such as nuclear power, synfuel or energy efficiency enjoys privileged status. For the near term, energy R&D competition is likely to be dominated by short term priorities and opportunities for marginal innovation. Nuclear power is likely to fare badly under these criteria. Gas turbine and clean coal technologies offer especially attractive fossil fuel research opportunities. Many renewable energy R&D options are much smaller in scale and require far less financial support per research project than nuclear power. RET technologies' modest size also fit more easily into corporate financial planning than large nuclear demonstration plants. Several longer term research options, such as hot dry rock or photovoltaic technologies, also challenge the assumption that only nuclear power can provide large amounts of future energy.

Robust nuclear renewal will require much larger federal R&D spending than current outlays and the assumption of more significant market risks by the private sector than current practice. Without a recapture of OT status for nuclear power, it seems unlikely that these R&D needs will be met.

**Nuclear Subsidies:
Economic Significance and Future Prospects**

Nuclear power remains a technology in need of government subsidy for economic viability. Besides demanding continued R&D expenditures, this dependency reflects: (1) the technology's need for high levels of infrastructural investments ahead of the market; (2) the burden of uncertain accident probabilities and decommissioning costs; (3) the sensitivity of nuclear economics to regulatory policy; and (4) the tough competition expected from coal, renewable energy, and natural gas technologies.

While public funding for nuclear power has fallen significantly since the OT years, continuing subsidies total about .75 c/kwh. Because many of the subsidies involve risk reduction rather than transfer payments, their monetary value is hard to quantify. The perceived cost of nuclear power is also artificially reduced by the underfunding of future decommissioning and waste disposal liabilities. Taken together, the subsidies and cost deferments total over 1 c/kwh.

The major subsidies and cost deferments are:

—Federal R&D spending:	~1 M/kwh
—Limited Liability Protection (Price Anderson Act):	5+ M/kwh
—Subsidized Enrichment Prices and Infrastructural guarantees:	~1–2 M/kwh
—Miscellaneous Regulatory and Support Services:	.2+ M/kwh
—Deferred Waste Disposal and Decommissioning Fees:	4 M/kwh
—Subsidized Credit:	no quantitative estimate
—Tax Subsidies:	no quantitative estimate

The following discussion analyzes the major active nuclear subsidies.

Risk Shifting

The public sector continues to support nuclear power with four kinds of risk sharing:

- acceptance of liability for catastrophic nuclear accidents (Price-Anderson Act)

- acceptance of financial responsibility for maintaining adequate nuclear power infrastructural facilities (e.g., adequate enrichment and waste disposal facilities)

- acceptance of liability for corporate defaults on decommissioning and waste disposal tasks

- acceptance of credit risks on many nuclear power loans (e.g., Export-Import Bank loans).

Price-Anderson Act

The Price-Anderson Act was renewed in 1988. The primary beneficiaries are the utilities and reactor vendors but all participants in the industry enjoy its protection. Under the act's fifteen-year extension, the utilities must purchase $160 million of liability insurance per reactor. If accident damages exceed this amount, each nuclear plant owner is additionally liable for a maximum of $63 million, capping the industry's collective liability at $8 billion. This represents a 275% real dollar increase over the 1957 liability limits.

The subsidy arises because many conceivable accidents could cause damages far in excess of $8 billion. Recent analysis indicates that the liability limits amount to an implicit subsidy of about .5 c/kwh.[5] Renewal of Price-Anderson past 2002 will face strong opposition, aided by Germany and Switzerland's adoption of unlimited liability in the 1980s (Price 1990, 249).

Uranium Enrichment Subsidies

Because the DOE is required by law to obtain full cost recovery for enrichment services, the General Accounting Office concluded in 1988 that it had undercharged its utility customers by $9.6 billion (Montange 1990, 5, 32–33). More recent estimates of the enrichment debt, including accrued interest, tally about $11 billion.[6] The latter figure ignores the exclusion from AEC and DOE enrichment charges of fees for decommissioning enrichment facilities and associated environmental clean-up activities. Cost estimates for these tasks range from a low of $4–$6 billion to well over $20 billion.[7] Utility liabilities would be about one-third the total clean-up bill.

Recent legislation appears to write off all but $3 billion of the enrichment debt and debits U.S. utilities $2.25 billion ($150 million per year for fifteen years) for enrichment decommissioning, implying a per kilowatt subsidy of about 1 M/kwh–2 M/kwh.[8]

A major reason for the high level of unrecovered enrichment costs is the DOE's write-offs of investments in surplus enrichment capacity. The DOE canceled the Portsmouth Gas Centrifuge Enrichment Project in 1986 after \$3.4 billion in outlays (Borson et al. 6/89, 10–11). It has also written off a billion-plus expansion of its gaseous diffusion plants and absorbed nearly \$2 billion in payments to the TVA for unused power (Ibid., iii, 5). The burden of these failed investments reflects the risk-shifting habits of the OT period. At the urging of the nuclear industry, the DOE replaced the utilities' risk of nuclear fuel shortages with the government's risk of excess enrichment capacity (Montange 1990, 5; Borson 6/89, 4).[9] Besides building ahead of the market, the DOE allowed the utilities to renegotiate their enrichment commitments after the cancellation of nuclear orders (Montange 1990, 4–10).

Similar infrastructural guarantees will be required to facilitate a second nuclear era. The current glut of global enrichment capacity and the recycling of enriched uranium from dismantled Soviet weaponry make new enrichment facilities unnecessary in the short run. Major nuclear renewal, however, will require either new government enrichment investments or public guarantees of private sector investment.

While the DOE has continued to support enrichment R&D, major spending for new government-owned enrichment facilities seem extremely unlikely. Industry efforts to secure government financing for a new enrichment plant using the experimental AVLIS process have been unsuccessful. Private sector enrichment initiatives will probably require profitability guarantees and regulatory environments that are no longer politically feasible.[10]

Other Infrastructural Subsidies

The nuclear industry continues to enjoy government bailout spending to clean up older nuclear facilities. By 1994 the federal government will have spent about one billion dollars cleaning up abandoned uranium mill tailings sites. State governments will have spent another \$100 million (Komanoff and Roelofs, 1992, 50). About one-half of these tailings appear to be associated with civilian nuclear power (Ibid., 52). Final clean-up costs could be significantly higher if the trend for tighter environmental safety standards continues. New Jersey, Pennsylvania, and the DOE have spent more than \$100 million to help clean up the Three Mile Island Accident (Komanoff and Roelofs 1992, 38).

Subsidized Loans and Loan Guarantees

As noted in chapter 3, nuclear power has traditionally enjoyed generous credit guarantees, especially from the Export-Import Bank. Public sector utilities, such as the TVA, have also been able to finance nuclear investments at reduced interest rates due to their access to tax-free financing. Current proposals for privatizing uranium enrichment similarly include multibillion dollar loan guarantees.

There has been, however, increasing congressional resistance to nuclear credit subsidies. Approval of the enrichment loan guarantee seems unlikely. Ex-Im Bank assistance will probably fare better, due to perceived export subsidies by foreign competitors. The Bank, for example, recently approved loan guarantees of $334 million for a Czech utility to finance Westinghouse's completion of a partially constructed Czech reactor (*Nucleonics Week* 3/17/94).

International Programs

In the last few years the industry has sought public funds for U.S. firms and national laboratories to aid former Soviet Union [FSU] states in their efforts to increase reactor safety and dispose of accumulated plutonium. In 1993, for example, the U.S. Agency for International Development earmarked $3 million for the NRC and $22 million for the DOE for reactor safety projects in FSU states (*Nucleonics Week* 1/28/93). In the fall of 1993 a consortium of firms proposed the DOE guarantee the financing of a multibillion project to build plutonium burning reactors in the U.S. and FSU (*Nucleonics Week* 9/16/93). Approval seems unlikely.

Waste Disposal and Decommissioning Cost Deferments

As explored in more detail in chapter 7, current utility payments for high level waste disposal (1 M/kwh) and set asides for plant decommissioning (less than 1 M/kwh) are unlikely to cover final clean-up costs. How large the gap will be is very uncertain. I've estimated a 4 M/kwh shortfall. If the nuclear utilities remain financially solvent, this shortfall will represent a transfer payment from future utility customers to current nuclear power consumers.

If some nuclear utilities go bankrupt, the U.S. treasury will likely pick up the waste disposal bill. Liabilities could reach several billion dollars.[11] The potential costs of bailing out utilities with insufficient funds for nuclear plant decommissioning are much higher. Most IOUs have not posted large decommissioning bonds or accumulated sinking funds able to finance large decommissioning cost overruns, though the latter are very likely. Even without cost escalation, many sinking funds will be insufficient to cover decommissioning costs due to the likely shutdown of dozens of nuclear plants (due to poor economic performance and safety failures) prior to the completion of their expected lifetimes. Partially due to uncovered decommissioning liabilities, a number of bond rating services anticipated declining utility credit ratings (and potential utility bankruptcies) (*Nucleonics Week* 11/4/93, 6). State and federal taxpayers are likely to pick up the check.

Tax Subsidies

The major tax subsidies enjoyed by nuclear power have historically involved the utilities' advantages in financing capital intensive projects. The most important tax aids have been the investor owned utilities' (IOUs) investment tax credit and accelerated depreciation options and the publicly owned utilities' use of tax exempt bond financing. The IOUs use of tax exempt pollution control bonds for nuclear projects and the uranium mining industry's depletion allowance have had minor impacts.

Since 1986, tax initiatives have generally worked against nuclear power, reducing the accelerated depreciation and Investment Tax Credits associated with new nuclear plant construction and offering tax breaks to renewable energy sources that do not extend to nuclear energy.[12]

Regulatory and other Support Services

The nuclear industry has traditionally paid only a small fraction of the AEC and NRC's costs of regulating nuclear power. Cumulative subsidies through 1990 (net user fees) total $7.5–9 billion (1990$) (Management Information Services 12/92, 13; Komanoff and Roelofs 1992, 32).[13] Congress began phasing out this assistance in the mid-eighties and terminated it in November 1990. Current regulatory costs are ~2/3 M/kwh. Should plans for new reactor designs increase the NRC's regulatory activities, these costs could rise to 1 M/kwh.

Nuclear power still enjoys some unreimbursed regulatory and support services from other government agencies. Heede (1991), for example, lists more than $100 million in support spending from non-DOE-NRC sources in his review of federal energy subsidies for 1984.[14]

Conclusion

The level of public subsidy of nuclear power remains a key part of nuclear economics. Important future battles are likely over: the direction of federal R&D spending, extension of the Price-Anderson Act, allocation of decommissioning liabilities for enrichment facilities, financing mechanisms to avoid public assumption of potential utility defaults on waste disposal and decommissioning liabilities, credit subsidies for domestic and foreign nuclear construction, and, perhaps, operating subsidies for nuclear plants as greenhouse abatement technologies.

While nuclear power continues to enjoy significant subsidies, the level of support has been falling and it seems unlikely that future policies will favor the nuclear option.

Chapter 9

Nuclear Regulatory Issues

The fate of nuclear power remains quite sensitive to regulatory decisions. This chapter discusses current policy debates with respect to low-level radiation hazards, reactor accident safeguards, and nuclear waste disposal. The chapter also explores the implications of recent regulatory changes in the utility industry that encourage increased competition in the electricity generating market. The discussion echoes themes developed in chapter 4's "sociology of knowledge"—analysis of the history of nuclear technology assessment. While recommending increased regulatory stringency, the analysis demonstrates why nuclear power enthusiasts favor stable or relaxed safety requirements without portraying nuclear supporters as apologists for corporate greed or professional self-interest. The chapter reemphasizes the impact of "technological aesthetics" on technology assessment.

Nuclear skeptics and nuclear enthusiasts bring different technological intuitions to nuclear hazard assessment. Nuclear critics tend to be: (1) risk averse in assessing nuclear hazard uncertainties and relatively sanguine about the hazard burden of small scale technologies, such as wind power; (2) worried about the impact of institutional biases on nuclear hazard data collection and assessment; (3) dismayed by a perceived tendency for nuclear hazards to have been underestimated in the past; and (4) bearers of technological intuitions that imply serious difficulties in containing nuclear hazard dangers (e.g., doubts about the ability of clever reactor design to contain the risks of human error in reactor operation).

Nuclear proponents tend to: (1) make optimistic assumptions in the face of nuclear hazard uncertainties and suspect equal or greater hazards from non-nuclear energy alternatives; (2) have great confidence in the objectivity and imaginative breadth of the institutional framework organizing nuclear hazard research; (3) find only modest or mixed trends over time for upward revision in the scientific community's assessment of nuclear hazards; and (4) have intuitions about technical matters that minimize nuclear hazard risks (e.g., faith in the ability of "human factors engineering" to eliminate the dangers of catastrophic human error in reactor operation).

The general public seems more sympathetic to the views of the safety

183

skeptics than safety optimists. Even if the technical case for increased regulatory vigilance were weak (which I don't think it is), political pressures for regulatory escalation would probably persist, due to the public's distrust of nuclear industry and nuclear regulatory officials. Continuing revelations of massive cover-ups and hazard mismanagement in the nuclear weapons complex and disclosure of radiation experiments on human subjects without informed consent have recently exacerbated the nuclear industry's long-standing credibility problem.[1] It is very unlikely that popular perceptions will be reversed soon. Nuclear proponents can thus expect more trouble than help from regulatory initiatives.

The Low-Level Radiation Hazard Debate

There continues to be vigorous debate about the seriousness of low-level radiation hazards. Among the factors perpetuating debate are: (1) data problems involving small sample sizes and long latency periods; (2) measurement problems involving uncertain radiation exposures and incomplete health follow-ups; and (3) confounding factors involving selection bias in sampling and the absence of information on non-radiation related phenomena that effect health levels among the sampled population.

The major focus of debate is currently on cancer hazards. Central tendency estimates differ by about 10x–20x. The major controversy involves the proper way to extrapolate from epidemiological conclusions about the hazards of high radiation doses to low radiation doses. Distinguished health physicist and nuclear power critic John Gofman projects 1 cancer (excluding leukemia) per ~400 rems of low-level radiation exposure (Gofman 1990, 25–12, 25–15). Noted health physicist and nuclear power advocate Bernard Cohen projects 1 cancer/~4,000+ rems (Cohen 1990, 58). Most "official" projections, such as those of the National Academy of Sciences BEIR V Committee (1990) or the United Nations Scientific Committee on the Effects of Atomic Radiation (UNSCEAR 1988) forecast 1 cancer (excluding leukemia) per ~2,000 rems–11,000 rems (Gofman 1990, 25–12). The most common range is ~2,000–4,500, with a recent U.S. Interagency Committee adopting a 2222 rem/cancer rate (*Nucleonics Week* 4/8/93, 2). The EPA and NRC assume about a 2,500 rem/cancer rate (*Science for Democratic Action*, spring 1995, 7–8).[2]

Nuclear optimists often argue that the cancer hazards for radiation exposures below .1 rem may be zero (threshold claim). They portray BEIR V

(1990) and other findings of ~2,500–4,500 rems/Cancer as upper bound estimates, rather than central tendencies. The range of debate between nuclear pessimists and optimists is therefore even larger than that suggested by the 400–4000+ rems per cancer disagreement between Gofman and Cohen.[3] In recent years nuclear proponents have also explored and publicized the possibility that low-level radiation may have beneficial health effects (hormesis).

Claims of serious low-level radiation hazards usually assert a "linear" or "supra-linear" relationship between low and high dose radiation effects.[4] Nuclear optimists reduce their high dose radiation hazard estimates by 2–10+ times for low dose exposures (Cohen 1990, 58; Gofman 1990, 25–12). There appear to be plausible theoretical arguments for both positions and data constraints make it extremely difficult to resolve the theoretical debate with empirical evidence.[5] While the Gofman/Cohen debate has only modest implications for assessing nuclear hazards during routine operation, it has major implications for assessing the hazards of serious nuclear accidents and may influence the stringency of waste disposal and decommissioning regulations.

Alongside debates over how to extrapolate from high-level to low-level radiation hazards, there are current controversies in radiation hazard assessment over:

(1) the implications of the Japanese bomb data for *high* level radiation exposure hazards[6]

(2) the impact of "healthy worker" effects on occupational hazard calculations[7]

(3) the impact of radiation on non-cancer related immune system disorders[8]

(4) the magnitude of radiation caused teratogenic effects (damage to the fetus) and mutagenic effects[9]

(5) the appropriate time horizon to measure radiation release impacts[10]

(6) the implications of the potential interactive effects of radiation exposure hazards with other hazards (such as the apparent multiplicative impact of radiation and smoking risks)

(7) the magnitude of internally absorbed rather than externally exposed radiation hazards.[11]

And in a slightly different vein

(8) the accuracy of existing radiation release monitoring around nuclear power plants.

While the evidence of the last five years is mixed, there have been numerous reports finding evidence of greater hazards than anticipated. Illustrative of such studies in the 1990s are:

(1) a 1990 report of the National Academy of Sciences' Committee on the Biological Effects of Ionizing Radiation (BEIR V, 1990), which increased the committee's past radiation-induced cancer hazard estimate by ~400% and also raised hazard estimates for mental retardation as a result of in utero radiation exposure (*New York Times* 12/20/89, Wolfson 1991, 72).

2) a 1990 review of the radiation hazard literature (Gofman 1990) which found low-level radiation hazards more than five times higher than BEIR V revisions.[12]

3) a 1990 study by Martin Gardiner which found elevated leukemia rates in the children of men exposed to radiation at a British nuclear fuel reprocessing plant.[13] (Interestingly, a similar finding, tying fathers' radiation exposure to children's incidence of neural tube defects, had been ignored due to a lack of parallel findings or known biological mechanisms for explaining the linkage (Sever 1991).

4) a 1991 study of occupational health at Oak Ridge National Laboratory that found the first evidence linking cancer rates at the lab to radiation exposure.[14]

5) a major 1992 British study of radiation hazards that adopted higher risk estimates than the International Commission on Radiological Protection and very large uncertainty bounds.[15]

6) a 1992 review of the DOE's radiation studies by Physicians for Social Responsibility (Geiger et al. 1992) that presented detailed critiques of the optimistic findings in many earlier DOE reports.

7) a 1992 study by Alice Stewart et al. that found higher radiation-induced cancer rates at the Hanford facilities than previously published DOE studies (*New York Times* 12/8/92).

8) a 1994 analysis of previously unreleased government data that found elevated cancer rates at the Fernald nuclear weapons facility (*New York Times* 4/13/94, A9).

On the other hand, the last five years have also seen the publication of numerous studies that are consistent with DOE and nuclear industry hazard estimates. Among these are:

1) a 1990 study funded by sources independent of the nuclear industry and DOE that found no excess cancers around TMI.[16]

2) a 1990 study by the National Cancer Institute that found no statistically significant increase in cancer rates around the nation's nuclear power plants.[17]

3) a 1991 study of naval shipyard workers servicing nuclear submarines that found no statistically significant evidence of elevated cancer rates.[18]

4) the appendix of a 1994 UN study that suggests a biological basis for positive benefits from exposure to low-level radiation and reinterpretation of data on Canadian women repeatedly fluoroscoped that found positive effects at low exposure levels (Pomeroy 1996, 2).

5) several new studies that found little linkage between indoor radon exposure and cancer rates (*New York Times* 9/6/94, B7; Cole 1993).

6) a 10/94 review of previously published epidemiological data on 96,000 nuclear industry workers (IARC 1994) that found it very unlikely that current BEIR V projections could seriously underestimate radiation hazards.

7) a 9/95 study of the low-level radiation hazard literature (Muckerheide 1995) that lent support to the threshold hypothesis and recommended increasing allowable exposure limits (26–34) and a March 1996 position statement by the Health Physics Society that included zero health risks in its plausible range for low level radiation hazards (*Nuclear News* 4/96, 18–19).

The import of these conflicting studies is that radiation hazard assessment is still surrounded by scientific uncertainties. When joined to a history of insular discourse, the literature invites continued tightening of occupational exposure and radiation release regulations. The International Commission on Radiological Protection (ICRP), for example, has recommended occupational exposure limits be lowered from 5 to 2 rems/yr. There is lively debate in the U.S. over this recommendation and the level of radiation exposures to the general public permissible at nuclear plant and nuclear waste site boundaries.

Regulatory Implications

It is unclear what the economic impact of tighter occupational exposure and radiation release standards will be. The industry has predicted different effects at different times. Some analysts foresee only minor consequences for power plant design and operation due to the tendency for existing operating procedures to be governed by ALARA (as low as reasonably achievable) principles rather than maximum release levels (*Nucleonics Week* 4/6/92). The industry is also hoping to reduce exposure levels through increased use of in-plant robotics.

Other analysts expect tighter radiation release standards to impose significant costs on older, more contaminated plants as they are forced to address aging problems. Pressures are also likely to continue for increased spending for radiation monitoring. Massachusetts, for example, is planning to funnel $322,000 from utility taxes to finance sensors around the Seabrook and Pilgrim nuclear plants (*Nuclear Monitor* 5/18/92, 5). Tighter radiation release regulations would also be likely to increase uranium mining and waste disposal costs.

Nuclear Power Plant Safety Debates

Judgments about the seriousness of the accident risks of nuclear plants depend on: (1) estimates of the probability of accidents involving partial or total core melting; (2) assessment of the ability of the plant's containment structure and radiation control mechanisms to trap fission products inside the plant after core damage; and (3) estimates of the ability of emergency preparedness to minimize population radiation exposure after a breach of containment. Disagreements on each of these topics can easily exceed an order of magnitude. Adding in debates over the risks of low level radiation exposure can generate assessments of nuclear plant accident hazards that differ by as much as 10,000 times.

Because judgments about reactor accident probabilities depend on a myriad of supporting judgments, deciphering the basis for difference can quickly exponentiate into a morass of overwhelming detail. The sheer magnitude of the data and expertise necessary to assess nuclear safety means that overall determinations require judgments on topics beyond the analyst's immediate expertise. Alongside judgments about piping corrosion, pump failures, and reactivity excursions, for example, nuclear safety engineers have to make safety assessments about potential saboteur activity, earthquake magnitudes, quality control breakdowns at large construction sites, and the degree of local emergency preparedness. While there is, of course, an expertise involved in meeting this challenge, it involves a generalist's skill in choosing amongst competing experts and basic intuitions or technological aesthetics about the behavior of complex systems. These kinds of determinations are not simple sums of available data; they are infused with subjective judgments, such as assessments of the dangers of human error or the risks of insular discourse. It is in these areas that safety optimists and pessimists most disagree, with optimists expressing a faith in technological fixes and pessimists a belief in Murphy's law (what can go wrong will go wrong) and O'Toole's corollary (Murphy was an optimist).

Because most public debate over nuclear safety has focused on the probability of core damage, we will illustrate the paradigmatic nature of safety assessment with respect to the meltdown controversy. Similar conclusions could be demonstrated with respect to the robustness of plant containment or the adequacy of emergency preparedness.

Core Damage Estimates

Current estimates of the likelihood of significant core damage vary by more than 300 times, from .01–3+ per 10,000 reactor years (RY).[19] Disagreements are even larger over the uncertainties accompanying these predictions. The debates continue because the nature of "defense in depth"-safety makes it impossible to unambiguously "prove" reactor safety (or nonsafety) through laboratory experiments, appeal to nuclear plant operating data, or theoretical argument.

Safety experiments are inconclusive because it is impossible to test reactor performance in all of the virtually infinite accident paths possible for a LWR. Analysis of plant operating experience is inconclusive because of the absence of enough accumulated reactor years to allow the data to discriminate between different accident probability estimates.[20] The changing character of nuclear power plants also leaves existing operating experience with ambiguous implications for future experience.

Paradigmatic Basis for Safety Debates

The indeterminacy of theoretical debates about reactor safety arises from disagreements about: (1) the treatment of uncertainty; (2) the dangers of insular discourse; (3) the ability of existing nuclear plant models to anticipate all significant accident paths; and (4) the adequacy of existing hazard assessment techniques to assess certain kinds of risks.

Safety skeptics argue that industry safety studies often transform "real" uncertainty into probability distributions with expected values, neglecting the difference between uncertainties where each single event is unpredictable but the pattern of outcomes is well understood and uncertainties where the underlying distribution of outcomes is unknown. The skeptics claim that nuclear hazards involve a larger percentage of "real" uncertainty than usually acknowledged. Attention to "real" uncertainty generally increases the public's safety concerns.

Safety skeptics fear the presence of bounded rationality and constrained realms of discourse in the nuclear industry's hazard studies. Supporting these concerns, the critics cite numerous cases of past excess safety optimism,[21] the tendency for safety problems to be discovered "ex-post" (in operation) rather than "ex-ante" in design review,[22] industry public relations efforts to manage or restrict hazard information,[23] and serious critiques of industry safety practices in official reviews.[24] Safety optimists respond by citing industry reforms (partially spurred by these official reviews), the large number of studies from diverse sources that find low accident probabilities, and a tendency for safety analysts to have a more favorable assessment of nuclear power the more technically focused their expertise.[25]

Nuclear critics link the latter correlation to the inbred character of traditional nuclear expertise and the sector's neglect of sociology of knowledge concerns.[26] The skeptics persuasively argue that there are too many technically expert critics of nuclear safety (though still a minority in the nuclear engineering profession) to explain hazard concerns as the product of uninformed naivete. The challenges to safety optimism are more Kuhnian (paradigmatic) than Luddite (irrational or anti-technological).

Reflecting on his professional experience as a geologist involved in siting controversies for nuclear power plants (most often on the pro-nuclear side), the concluding chapter of Richard Meehan's *The Atom and the Fault* offers an especially thoughtful discussion of the lack of necessary correspondence between technical expertise and sensitivity to the problem of bounded rationality. He writes,

". . . it is not obvious that the most creative scientists and technologists necessarily are experts on such important matters as the limits of scientific knowledge and inference . . . (148)." He adds, ". . . [A]re practicing scientists and engineers necessarily capable critics of their own or opposing witnesses' epistemology? More importantly do they have any more than a lay person's capacity to combine knowledge from several different disciplines to create sound composite knowledge? After all, few scientists have any formal training in the philosophy, history, or sociology of science or engineering, . . . (149)."

Meehan extends Edward Radford's observations from the radiation hazard debate to plant safety debates, quoting Radford's observation that

"(i)n any scientific controversy, when complex and poorly understood subjects are debated, subtle personal biases inevitably cloud the picture. These biases include personal leanings, often subconscious, derived from background, experiences, loyalties, and the like—subtle and involuntary factors to which every human being is subject. I do not refer to overt expressions of a position that will bring financial or professional gain to scientists; the issue is more subtle and by no means reprehensible" (Meehan 1984, 128).

It is these socio-institutional biases or habits of mind that most worry nuclear safety skeptics.

Unanticipated Accident Paths and Probabilistic Risk Assessment (PRA)

Many of the issues underlying theoretical debates over nuclear safety reemerge in debates over the applicability of probabilistic risk analysis to nuclear accident forecasting. Defenders of reactor safety generally rely heavily on probabilistic risk assessment [PRA] to organize their safety analysis and represent their conclusions. This technique uses fault trees and estimated occurrence rates for identified accident sequences to derive accident probabilities. Safety skeptics have criticized PRA projections for: (a) their inability to fully anticipate the gamut of potential accident paths, (especially those linked to human error, multiple equipment failures, and common mode failures); (b) insufficient attention to externally initiated events (such as earthquakes and saboteur activity); (c) the limited data available for projecting equipment failure rates (which often leads to the use of design assumptions that can underestimate failure rates); (d) the habit of assuming that plants are operating in compliance with NRC regulations, and (e) the neglect of some plant specific problems in order to inflate safety margins.[27]

Specific Nuclear Power Accident Hazards

Alongside general methodological critiques of industry hazard assessments, safety skeptics have raised serious concerns over numerous specific accident risks. The hazards fall into three categories: general hazards that can take many forms (such as plant aging hazards), more specialized concerns (such as O-Ring failures under accident conditions) and newly discovered hazards (such as inadequate BWR core water level measurement).

Among the most important general hazards are: equipment failures due to plant aging, sabotage/terrorism hazards, seismic hazards, operator error, quality control deficiencies, and maintenance related failures. The analysis below looks at the first three of these concerns, while note 28 briefly addresses the rest.[28]

Among the most serious aging related hazards are steam generator tube degradation, BWR pipe deterioration, pressure vessel embrittlement, emergency diesel generator failure, check valve failure, motor operated valve failure, electrical cable deterioration, and pump failures. Because there are many avenues to core damage and complex interactions among plant systems, redressing unanticipated aging effects can be tricky.

For example, oxygen levels in the circulating water of the Surry plant in Virginia were lowered in an effort to reduce steam generator tube aging and degradation (Riccio and Murphy 1988, 3). This reduction retarded the normal build-up of magnetite in the plant's main feedwater line. The absence of magnetite reduced the pipe's resistance to "erosion/corrosion" wear, and along with poor pipe configuration, led to its rupture in 1986. The pipe's failure released 30,000 gallons of superheated water and scalded eight workers, four of whom eventually died (Riccio and Murphy 1988, 3).

A similarly unexpected system interaction caused an accident at the San Onofre plant in California. Like many reactors, San Onofre 1 had been forced to operate at reduced power levels. At 85% power, the water flow through the main feedwater pipe was insufficient to prevent check valve fluttering. The latter appears to have caused the rapid aging and eventual failure of five check valves, leading to a severe water hammer accident in 1985 (Pollard 1992).

The lack of reliable detection techniques is an especially troubling aspect of some aging phenomena. Traditional methods for detecting pipe cracks (ultrasonic testing and pre-break leaking), for example, are unable to anticipate all significant pipe failures. Similar difficulties have frustrated efforts to test the ability of motor operated valves and electrical cables to perform under accident conditions.[29] Frequent testing of emergency power diesel generators is opposed by some utilities as it appears to decrease the machines' reliability (*Nucleonics Week* 11/26/92, 6–7).

Due largely to aging related degradation, Bob Pollard, senior nuclear safety engineer for the Union of Concerned Scientists, finds existing nuclear safety levels worse than in 1975 when he resigned from the NRC to protest lax safety regulations. He argues that the increasingly stringent competition offered by cheap natural gas and other nuclear power competitors has left the NRC loathe to impose new regulations on nuclear plants out of fear of being blamed for their shutdown and the industry's total collapse (Pollard 10/93).

Paul Blanch, formerly a senior nuclear engineering supervisor with the largest nuclear utility in New England, echoes similar concerns with respect to the non-enforcement of NRC regulations, inaction with respect to defective BWR core water measuring devices, and inaction with respect to the risks of feedback accidents between the reactor core and waste fuel pool (see below) (Blanch 10/93).

Despite an upgrading in NRC security requirements, skeptics continue to raise sabotage concerns. The International Task Force on Prevention of Nuclear Terrorism warned in 1986, for example, that terrorist threats to power plants were small but increasing. A 1990 paper co-authored by the president and Scientific Director of the Nuclear Control Institute in Washington D.C., urged the NRC to follow Europe and Japan's lead and protect plants from truck-bomb threats.[30]

Reactor vulnerability to earthquake damage is one of the largest risk drivers in PRAs. Safety skeptics emphasize current uncertainties with respect to seismic prediction and plant behavior under earthquake conditions. MHB analyst Jim Harding, for example, has noted that "earthquake-induced electric relay chatter and subsequent loss of electric power or signals" may be more of a risk than stress induced structural damage (Harding 1990, 97).

Among the more specialized hazards cited by safety skeptics are pressure vessel (PV) and reactor support structure embrittlement, PWR steam generator tube degradation, BWR pipe cracking, potential power oscillations at BWRs at low power and loss of emergency power. Note 31 briefly explores the nature of these problems.[31]

Perhaps even more disturbing than the persistence of unresolved safety issues is the continuing discovery of serious new safety problems. Among the major new hazards encountered (or significantly re-evaluated) in the 1990s were: deficient fire barriers, inadequate BWR core water level measurement, unexpected computer code interactions, possible problems with pressure vessels, feedback accidents involving interactions between core cooling accidents and overheating of the waste fuel pool, and core shroud cracking. Note 32 briefly explores the nature of these problems.[32]

While it is difficult to fully assess the safety significance of the hazards elaborated in note 32, their presence illustrates the impossibility of proving the safety of existing light water reactor's "defense-in-depth"-safety strategies. Also disturbing is the continued stonewalling, information management, and insensitivity to safety uncertainties by segments of the industry and NRC. Illustrative is:

- the aggressive dismissal of concern over measurement problems for BWR core water levels by the nuclear industry (based on what has turned out to be incorrect assumptions of minimal measurement error), the harassment of the utility engineer who initially raised BWR water level measurement concerns (which led to a proposed NRC fine of $100,000 [*New York Times* 6/1/93, *Nucleonics Week* 7/22/93]), and efforts by G. E. and BWR utilities to keep damaging test results proprietary information (*Nuclear Monitor* 6/7/93, 1; see also *Nucleonics Week* 1/28/93).

- the utilities and vendors' misleading assurances about the ease of license extension.

- recent revelations of ten years of inaction by the NRC with respect to deficient fire retarding materials at reactors.

- the NRC's decision to permit changes in standardized designs without serious public hearings (*Nuclear Monitor* 3/1/93).

- the NRC's permission to utilities to withhold formal responses to NRC safety notices in order to avoid releasing such information into the public domain.

- the NRC's apparent tolerance of incomplete safety reviews for plant specific PRAs (see note 27)

- continuing reports of harassment of whistleblowers, as illustrated by: a Department of Labor finding of retaliation against three workers raising safety concerns at the Millstone and Palo Verde nuclear plants,[33] a 1992 Department of Labor finding of management retaliation against an Oak Ridge worker for safety complaints,[34] a 1993 NRC Inspector General report finding that NRC policies provide insufficient protection for whistleblowers,[35] a December 1993 fine against the TVA for harassment and intimidation of an employee raising safety issues,[36] and a March 1996 expose in *Time Magazine* detailing pervasive intimidation of whistleblowers at Northeast Utilities' nuclear plants (*Time* 3/4/96, 47–54).

- ongoing revelations of enormous safety hazard oversights at the nation's nuclear weapons facilities.

Optimist Rebuttals

The vision driving LWR safety optimism is that of "asymptotic safety." The legacy of past malfunctions highlighted by safety skeptics is perceived by LWR defenders as an important part of the learning curve for LWR safety and a key reason for favoring evolutionary LWRs over more novel reactor designs. The safety optimists criticize the pessimists for overlooking or dismissing the safeguards in place to address identified hazards, including newly discovered ones. They note, for example:

- that new NRC regulations require the utilities to station human fire monitors every few yards in order to redress Thermo-Lag fire barrier deficiencies during high fire risk activities, like grinding, until new insulating material is installed.

- that BWR reactor operators have been warned of the potential for misleading water level indications under rapid depressurization conditions and instructed to attend to other available information about reactor conditions in making reactor control decisions.

- that existing computer control systems include independent codes to protect against unexpected system interactions.

- that even the engineers who identified the irradiated fuel pool accident path admit its probability of occurrence is very small.

LWR defenders also highlight the dramatic improvement in safety indicators that has occurred since the Three Mile Island accident. They note, for example, that:

- the average number of unplanned automatic scrams at reactors fell from 7.4 in 1980 to 1.6 in 1990 (National Research Council 1992, 52).

- that unplanned safety system actuations fell from 1.3 per plant in 1985 to .7/plant in 1990 (Ibid., 53).

- that collective radiation exposure per plant fell from 425–800 man rems/plant for PWRs and BWRs in 1985 to 294–436 man rems/unit in 1990 (Ibid., 55).

Proponents of evolutionary LWR reactors expect new plants to perform even better than existing retrofitted ones. The construction of pressure vessels without copper welds, for example, is expected to reduce failure risks dramatically. New emergency generators built by a French firm are expected to greatly increase back-up power reliability (*Nucleonics Week* 11/26/92). Active research in human engineering is expected to further reduce human error rates, and so on.

The safety optimists acknowledge that myriad minor malfunctions occur regularly at nuclear plants, but suggest that critics fail to appreciate the logic of defense in depth safety strategies in leaping from such malfunctions (enumerated for example in Licensee Event Reports) to serious accidents. They argue that existing PRAs incorporate these failures into their calculations and still demonstrate the miniscule probability of major accidents.

Industry backers also argue that while there are about 120 whistleblower complaints filed annually, this is a relatively small number in an industry with about 100,000 workers (*Nucleonics Week* 7/22/93).

Future Prospects

While I believe that the data strongly supports safety skepticism, it is unlikely that safety optimists will alter their hazard judgments. Recent support for this conclusion comes from an unlikely source—Bernard Verna, a nuclear industry safety expert who from 1975–1994 wrote 110 columns on operating experience at nuclear power plants for the American Nuclear Society's professional journal *Nuclear News*. In his last column, in September 1994, Verna concluded, "The industry continues to claim that tremendous progress in operations has been made. . . . I would have to disagree" (*Nuclear News* 9/94, 32). Citing an apparent tolerance of common mode failures, lengthy inaction with respect to fire hazards, and a persistent neglect of maintenance and repair issues, he finds the industry unable to focus on "the basics and the practicalities" of safety (Ibid. 33).

The public is likely to side with Verna. One of the lasting impacts of the anti-nuclear movement has been the creation of alternative sources of information to nuclear industry groups like the Edison Electric Institute or the U.S. Council for Energy Awareness. Safety skeptics have access to significant technical expertise (from organizations such as the Union of Concerned Scientists (UCS), MHB Associates, Tellus Inc., and the Rocky Mountain Institute) and are able to disseminate new safety concerns very quickly through advocacy journals like the *Nuclear Monitor* (published by the Nuclear Information Resource Service), and *Nucleus* (published by the Union of Concerned Scientists). Robert Pollard of UCS has been particularly effective in identifying accident hazards and translating technical information into a language accessible to educated lay persons. Mainstream media sources like the *New York Times* monitor skeptic groups, such as Ralph Nader's Critical Mass Energy Project, as well as official sources for nuclear safety information.

The optimists suffer from lost credibility (which short periods of accident-free operation will not reverse), associated fears of constrained realms of discourse, and a safety strategy that can not be fully demonstrated. The optimists also ask the tolerance of numerous uncertainties (about earthquake hazards, sabotage risks, human error, etc.), which many people find unsettling. If the public were convinced that there were no alternatives to nuclear energy, these misgivings might be overcome. In the present climate, however, they are likely to be insurmountable. The result will be continued social and political opposition to nuclear expansion and pressures for tighter safety regulation.[37]

Regulatory Format Debates

Alongside technical debate over the nature of accident hazards, there is controversy over the best way to organize nuclear regulation. Nuclear advocates favor changes that would: (1) replace existing adversarial NRC-industry relationships with more collegial relationships or self-regulation; (2) re-centralize nuclear regulatory authority in federal hands by limiting state and local nuclear oversight; (3) recentralize federal regulation in the NRC[38]; (4) reduce public participation in technical decision making; and (5) replace detailed prescriptive regulations with performance oriented requirements. Most of these changes seek to recreate the regulatory environment of the OT years.

Proponents of the above changes point to the activities of the Institute for Nuclear Power Operations (INPO) (such as INPO's plant inspection and evaluation programs and accreditation reviews of reactor operator training programs), as examples of successful industry self-regulation. They see the collaborative relationship between industry and government in France and Canada, and between the AEC and American firms during the OT period, as exemplary regulatory regimes. They assert that increased collegiality between regulators and industry will improve information flows about safety, while increased public participation in regulatory activities will discourage candid disclosures.[39] They link recent trends towards larger regulatory roles for state and local authorities to the triumph of parochial interests over the national interest (typified by the "Not In My Backyard" or NIMBY syndrome) and the elevation of short run over long run concerns.[40] Public participation in regulatory proceedings is treated as an invitation for obstructionism.

Proponents of performance oriented regulatory policies predict that a decline in detailed regulations will: (1) encourage safety innovation; (2) gear safety practices to local plant conditions rather than generic rules; and (3) increase industry attention to safety outcomes rather than regulatory conformity ("working to rules") (Weinberg et al. 1985, 70).[41]

Safety skeptics disagree with most of these regulatory recommendations. Critics of self-regulation argue that it is precisely the conflation of public and private interest and inattention to the dangers of insular discourse that produced past management and safety failures. Arguing that institutional cultures change slowly and pointing to past intervenor safety contributions,[42] the critics assert the need for external review to insure meaningful change.

Illustrative of safety skeptics' recommendations are calls for: (1) increased NRC on-site inspection of plant construction, operation, and radiation release; (2) the appointment of technical experts from the skeptical scientific community to key regulatory posts; (3) the establishment of an accident review board independent of the NRC to investigate serious reactor malfunctions; (4) increased public funding for intervenors; and (5) a wide array of measures designed to increase public access to nuclear hazard information.

Safety skeptics are also wary of delegating too much discretion to the utilities in meeting regulatory standards. The skeptics emphasize the need to gear regulatory regimes to the weakest utility, rather than mean or median firm, due to existing LWR designs' potential for catastrophic accidents.

The skeptics have also objected to the way in which the NRC uses cost-benefit analysis to decide the appropriateness of retrofit requirements. They challenge industry claims of excessive backfitting prior to the NRC's decision in 1983 to require cost-benefit justifications for retrofit requirements. The skeptics charge the commission with: (1) putting the burden of proof on retrofit advocates; (2) systematically underestimating the benefits and overestimating the costs of safety retrofits; and (3) using cost-benefit analysis to conceal the inevitable subjectivity of hazard assessment. The skeptics claim that the accident probabilities and accident damage assumptions the NRC employs in its cost-benefit analysis are so low that the maximum expenditure justifiable (one that would reduce "both the probability and the consequences of a meltdown to zero") is $19 million (Harding 1990, 102).[43]

Likely Regulatory Outcomes

Overall Regulatory Stringency

While some safety regulations will likely be relaxed in the future, such as the required number of security personnel at nuclear plants, other safety requirements will probably increase. Recent concerns over BWR power oscillations, for example, will require an extra day of downtime to repower the reactor. Steam generator tube repair will require extended downtimes and costly replacement. Pressure vessel embrittlement may require ameliorative measures and downtime for testing. Redressing Thermo-Lag deficiencies may cost billions of dollars. Net outcomes are unlikely to reduce generating costs.

Licensing Reform

Recent regulatory changes permit power plant site-banking, the licensing of standardized reactor designs, and 1-step, combined construction and operating licenses. Proponents claim these changes will significantly shorten construction and licensing time and reduce utility planning uncertainties. Critics charge that the changes will reduce public participation in licensing reviews, arbitrarily freeze reactor designs, and undermine plant safety levels.

A large number of uncertainties surround the implementation of the licensing changes, including: (1) how emergency planning issues, environmental impact reviews, and potential state intervention will effect long range site banking; (2) how well insulated precertified standardized designs will be from re-review; and (3) how contentious pre-operation hearings will be in ensuring that plants are built to specifications. Popular opposition to new nuclear plants has prevented the industry and NRC from enlisting a single volunteer utility to test the new siting procedures by "banking" a site for a hypothetical future nuclear power plant.

Licensing Extension

When NRC Chair Ivan Selin took office in 1991, he indicated that extending existing plant's operating licenses from forty to sixty years was his highest priority. The initial economics appeared very attractive, with industry projecting refurbishing costs in the neighborhood of 10% of the construction costs for new nuclear plants. Plant aging hazards however, have seriously undermined licensing renewal efforts. Rather than seeking license extension, up to twenty-five plants are currently facing premature retirement.[44]

In addition to aging problems, public doubts about reactor safety and the availability of cheap alternatives to nuclear power make it unlikely that licensing extension will be pursued very aggressively. Attempting extension on the scale initially proposed by the industry and DOE invited repetition of the poor economics and safety risks that accompanied the bandwagon market for nuclear plant construction in the 1960s and suggests that the nuclear industry has yet to fully appreciate the novelty of its technology.

Waste Disposal

In the eyes of many, failure to solve the nuclear waste disposal problem is the Achilles' heel of the nuclear industry. Current high-level nuclear waste policy is governed by the 1982 Nuclear Waste Policy Act, its 1987 amendments, and the 1992 energy bill. The policy's two major foci call for developing a long term geological repository at Yucca Mountain in Nevada and the construction of a monitored retrievable storage (MRS) facility.[45] In order to avoid delay on permanent disposal, the 1987 amendments conditioned MRS construction on the pace of progress on geological disposal.

Work at Yucca Mountain has progressed extremely slowly. The earliest projection for a functioning geological depository is 2010. Numerous polls indicate that waste mismanagement in the nuclear weapons complex, instances of incomplete information disclosure, previously unsuccessful siting initiatives, and the public's special dread of nuclear waste (Slovic 1990) have created enormous obstacles to new disposal sites.

Controversy also surrounds the regulation of low-level nuclear waste, where costs have increased by as much as one hundred times since 1970. Efforts by the NRC to designate a large percentage of materials from nuclear power plants as "Below Regulatory Concern," and therefore exempt from special disposal requirements, have been unsuccessful due to opposition by the anti-nuclear movement and numerous state governments. Current policy decentralizes low-level nuclear waste disposal, encouraging states to establish regional disposal sites. Because of technical problems and active local opposition to nearly every siting initiative, waste projects are stalled across the country.

As Slovic (1990) suggests, it is not clear how public confidence in the siting and oversight of nuclear waste can be restored. It does seem likely that the public will favor erring on the side of excessive caution as illustrated by recent developments with respect to rail transport of nuclear waste.[46] To the extent that nuclear renewal is contingent upon the successful demonstration of geological disposal, the current outlook for the industry is bleak. It seems likely, however, that the economic implications of gridlock on Yucca Mountain will be minimized by a shift towards a centralized, "interim" MRS or a shift towards "temporary" dry cask storage at power plant sites (a de facto decentralized MRS policy).

It seems unlikely that waste disposal costs will determine the competitiveness of nuclear power. While precedent suggests the DOE's cost projections are low, increasing them by 500% still leaves disposal costs at only 5 M/kwh.[47] Thus, while continued waste disposal uncertainty will increase popular opposition to nuclear power, it seems unlikely to single-handedly foreclose the nuclear option.

As in many other areas, popular images of nuclear power will indirectly condition the cost of waste disposal. There are large economies of scale in siting low-level waste facilities and modest scale economies with high-level waste disposal, though the technology is too young to forecast optimal site sizes. There are also sector-wide personnel economies that are currently working against the nuclear industry. As former NRC Commissioner Ahearne has observed,

> ". . . the weakness of nuclear power drives good people away from working on nuclear power issues. . . . In the absence of research moneys for professors or students interested in working in the field, talent is not going to be applied to any of the nuclear energy problems *including high level waste disposal*" (emphasis added) (MIT 1990 Conference Proceedings, pp. 7–9).

Paradigms and Nuclear Regulatory Debates

Many current regulatory debates reflect paradigmatic differences over how to assess nuclear safety. Both the optimist and pessimist perspectives are thus relatively immune to falsification by logical or empirical contradiction. I find the skeptics' perspective more convincing and would strongly recommend tightening safety regulations. It is important to acknowledge, however, that both safety optimism and pessimism are logically plausible.

There is a contrary tendency amongst the participants in nuclear debates to dismiss their opponents as either foolhardy or self-serving. Within the optimistic paradigm, safety skepticism tends to be understood as a product of ignorance, radiation phobia, irrational psychological linkages between nuclear power and nuclear weapons, and anti-corporate political agendas. This conception relieves many optimists of the need to take safety skepticism seriously. Within the skeptic community there is a tendency to dismiss industry safety claims as forms of corporate advertising. This relieves the skeptics of the need to investigate optimist claims of safety advances. There is a disturbing symmetry for both safety optimists and pessimists to define their critics by the more extreme expressions of the opposing paradigm. Thus the misleading public relations assurances of nuclear safety by the U.S. Council for Energy Awareness come to represent industry safety analysis for nuclear critics, while the more extreme claims of nuclear hazards by some anti-nuclear groups define safety skepticism for nuclear optimists.

I have tried to replace an "idiot" theory of nuclear safety debates with paradigmatic notions of debate. The substitution offers interesting conclusions. The paradigmatic approach, for example, implies that only passively safe reactor designs that permit more conclusive safety demonstrations offer any hope of allaying safety skeptics' concerns about reactor accident hazards. The paradigmatic approach also invites attention to the question of why different paradigms of technology assessment are popular at different times, a subject to which we will return in our concluding chapter.

Utility Regulation

The evolution of utility industry regulation and market structure will also influence the viability of nuclear power. Several measures have been suggested to decrease the financial risk of utility nuclear investments (most dramatically illustrated by the $35 billion cost of canceled nuclear power plants (Komanoff and Roelofs 12/92, 23) and more than $10 billion in prudency disallowals for nuclear construction in 1980–1988 (Anderson 1991, 24). Among the suggestions most popular with the nuclear industry are:

- restoration of the "regulatory bargain" (i.e., de facto guaranteed rates of return on new plant investment, per the expectations of the 1960s and early 1970s)

- and rolling prudency reviews (i.e., approval of construction costs as expended with only a modest lag)

These proposals are at odds, however, with strong trends in utility regulation towards more market oriented mechanisms. Besides signaling trouble for new nuclear plants, increased market competition threatens to retire many existing nuclear reactors whose operating costs (independent of sunk capital costs) exceed the price of replacement power. The Yankee Atomic, San Onofre 1, and Trojan nuclear plants have already been shut down for such reasons. Five studies released in January 1994 by nuclear industry sources found that only 25% of existing nuclear plants generated electricity more cheaply than available replacement power (*Nucleonics Week* 3/17/94, 1, 11–12). The studies concluded that many plants' survival depended on the terms of access to transmission grids given non-utility generators (Ibid.). The trigger for many shutdown decisions is likely to be the need to replace expensive steam generators on PWR plants more than halfway through their expected lifetime.

Even if the economics of future reactors were to improve dramatically, leaving the plants' total expected costs marginally competitive with available alternatives, the absence of risk shifting measures, such as guaranteed recovery of capital outlays, is likely to severely limit new utility nuclear investments. The most likely form of nuclear renewal would involve turnkey contracting (as in the early days of nuclear orders) or independent power producer [IPP] arrangements. Under the latter, independent corporations would own and operate nuclear power plants as wholesalers of electricity, paralleling the role played by cogenerators and small power producers within the PURPA (Public Utilities Regulatory Policy Act) framework. IPPs would make a profit if their generating costs were less than the price at which local utilities bought imported power.

While the concept of nuclear generating companies (NUGENCOs) is supported by the nuclear industry and DOE, many obstacles are likely to prevent IPP arrangements from spurring significant nuclear construction. The main problem is that without shifting the financial implications of nuclear uncertainties to ratepayers, as was expected during the OT period, the technology will bear a significant risk penalty in capital markets.

Under IPP arrangements, IPP debt holders are likely to require high rates of return, as the risk of construction cost overruns and poor plant performance are uncovered by other revenues. Furthermore, in order to avoid demand uncertainties, IPPs will probably require long term purchase agreements with the utilities prior to plant construction. Besides being reluctant to commit themselves to such advance purchases amidst electricity demand uncertainties, the utilities may be hesitant to rely on nuclear IPPs in their franchise planning due to past construction delays.[48] In the end, significant IPP initiatives will probably require high equity investments by the vendors and architect-engineer construction firms, shouldering risks analogous to the early turnkey plants.

Nuclear critics have raised other questions about the wisdom of using NUGENCOs to revive nuclear power. Public Citizen (a Nader group) notes that the limited corporate assets of NUGENCOs undermines the potential ability of the firms to meet their plant decommissioning, waste disposal, and accident liabilities under the Price Anderson Act. Bruce Biewald of the Energy System Research Group warns that the shift towards NUGENCOs would aggravate tensions between profitability (and even corporate viability) and plant safety (*Public Utilities Fortnightly* 6/7/90).

Several other regulatory changes have been proposed for the utility industry. Many ideas would conform utility rate structures to the logic of economic efficiency (these initiatives include replacing embedded-average cost pricing with marginal cost rates, expanded use of peak load pricing, decreased use of declining block rates, and expanded internalization of negative externalities). The National Association of Regulatory Utility Commissioners has endorsed Integrated Resource Planning which would increase attention to investments in energy efficiency as well as energy supply (National Research Council 1992, 26). The net effect of most of these changes would be a reduction in electricity demand and derived nuclear power demand.

A final industry shift that might significantly influence nuclear development is the potential for industry consolidation. Some analysts foresee an electric future dominated by a few very large utility companies. While the implications of this shift are unclear, nuclear power has traditionally done best in contexts managed by a few decision centers.

Conclusion

The direction of future regulatory policy is likely to increase the obstacles to nuclear renewal. Both tighter nuclear hazard regulation and more market oriented utility regulation will discourage private sector nuclear investments.

Chapter 10

Alternative Reactor Designs

In the aftermath of TMI a number of leading nuclear power advocates have urged shifting directions in reactor design.[1] They find nuclear renewal impossible for existing LWRs because of their inability to recapture public confidence in reactor safety. They fault LWR safety assurances for their inevitable reliance on subjective judgment by experts (as with Probabilistic Risk Assessment) at a time when nuclear industry credibility is low and expert opinion is not unanimous. They argue that only testable safety claims with results transparent to the public can reduce the political barriers to nuclear renewal and the economic costs of safety uncertainties. Among the latter are expensive redundancy requirements for safety systems, the threat of new retrofit orders (after the discovery of unanticipated accident paths), and slower industry innovation because of the arduousness of demonstrating safety to regulatory authorities. This chapter explores these claims, the nature of the new reactor designs they spurred, and the new technologies' likely market future.

Passive Safety Designs

There are basically two approaches to nuclear safety: either (1) tolerate the hypothetical possibility of major accidents, but include in the plant's design enough safeguards to make the probabilities of serious accidents approach zero; or (2) build reactors that are prohibited by design from having serious accidents (such as very small reactors with minimal amounts of nuclear fuel). LWRs follow the first approach, passively safe reactors follow the second.

To draw an analogy, imagine an electric stove with a tea kettle. In designs that follow the first approach, steam explosions are inhibited by a pressure gauge, an automatic feedback control on stove temperature, a kettle whistle and myriad other mechanisms that signal the user to remove the teapot from the stove and/or lower the burner's temperature. In designs that

205

follow the second approach, the maximum temperature the stove's electric coils can ever reach is insufficient to boil the water (though, presumably high enough to make the tea).

Following this second approach, the term "passive safety" refers to reactor designs that avoid serious accidents without relying on "actively" engineered safeguards. To accomplish this feat, the typical passively safe reactor has:

- a negative reactivity coefficient that precludes runaway chain reactions, that is, an inherent slowdown or shutdown of the core's nuclear reaction if anything momentarily accelerates it. This feature is also present in existing LWR designs, but was absent at Chernobyl.

- passive decay heat removal, that is, the dissipation of heat from the natural radioactive decay of the fuel rods (after a cessation of the core's chain reaction) through natural air circulation around the reactor or direct contact with the earth or a cooling pool.

- lower power densities than LWRs, that is, the ratio of reactor power to reactor vessel volume is lower than found in existing reactors. This reduction greatly facilitates the viability of passive measures for decay heat removal.

There are currently three major passively safe reactor designs under discussion: the Modular High Temperature Gas Reactor (MHTGR), the Process Inherent Ultimately Safe reactor (PIUS), and the Liquid Metal Reactor (LMR).[2] (The appendix to this chapter expands the brief description of each reactor given below.)

MHTGR: (~125–~150 MW modules) The Modular High Temperature Gas Reactor is a helium cooled, graphite moderated reactor. Its distinctive uranium oxycarbide fuel pellets are encapsulated in ceramic material designed to retain fission products at temperatures of more than 1600 degrees Centigrade (C). The reactor relies on its low power density (5%–10% of conventional PWRs) and several kinds of passive cooling mechanisms (chiefly air circulation and ground contact) to dissipate decay heat from the core before temperatures can approach 1600 degrees C.

PIUS: (~400–650 MW) The Process Inherent Ultimately Safe Reactor situates the core and its power generating steam cycle in a borated pool of water within a large prestressed concrete pressure vessel. Pressure differentials keep the borated water from poisoning the chain reaction during routine operation. Any disturbance of the reactor, however, ruptures this balance and floods the core with neutron absorbing water. This inflow chokes off the chain reaction and provides a week's reservoir for decay heat removal. Natural air cooling is also available.

LMR: (~150 MW modules) The Liquid Metal Reactor immerses the core in liquid sodium, which acts both as coolant and decay heat reservoir. This reactor is a variant of older breeder reactor designs and uses fuel with relatively high plutonium concentrations. It is capable of burning its own waste (as well as that of existing LWRs). Decay heat is passively removed from the sodium reservoir by natural airflow around the reactor vessel and ground contact.

Safety Issues

Because the rationale for passively safe reactors rests on their enhanced safety features, much of the debate over their future involves safety questions. The major issues raised by skeptics involve:

1) The Degree to Which Any Reactor Can Be Totally Protected Against Serious Accidents and Therefore Freed from Defense-In-Depth Safeguards

Critics from the anti-nuclear movement and proponents of other nuclear designs question the conceptual possibility of "inherent safety." A 1990 study of advanced reactor safety conducted for the Union of Concerned Scientists, for example, concluded, ". . . we do not believe that claims of 'inherent safety' are credible. . . . there is always something that could be done (or not done) to render the reactor dangerous" (MHB 7/90, 3–5). A 1992 National Academy of Sciences study of advanced reactor designs warned, ". . . dependence on passive safety features does not, of itself, ensure greater safety, especially given the potential effects of earthquakes, design errors, inspectability, manufacturing defects, and other subtle failure modes. Consequently, the Committee believes that a prudent design course retains the historical defense-in-depth approach" (National Research Council 1992, 136).

2) The Degree to Which Safety Can Be "Proved" and Reactors "Licensed-By-Test"

The issue here is whether it is possible to design a "worst-case" experiment for which safety success would demonstrate resistance to any conceivable accident hazard. Passive design advocate Lawrence Lidsky of MIT has suggested that an adequate test would involve the withdrawal of all control

rods, a simultaneous loss of reactor coolant, and transference of plant oversight to a "malicious operator" bent on frustrating the plant's safety systems.
Successful negotiation of Lidsky's criteria would probably satisfy many skeptics, though some critics have raised additional concerns over earthquake hazards for some designs and over the length of time and magnitude of resources assumed available to the malicious operator (especially with respect to fire hazards and strategies to overwhelm passive heat dissipation). Weaker tests, such as Lidsky's criteria minus the malicious operator, would probably be unconvincing to many nuclear critics.

3) The Degree to Which Diverging from Existing LWRs Invites Unknown Problems and an Imprudent Discarding of Invaluable Safety Information from Thousands of Reactor Years of Collective Operating Experience with LWRs

Proponents of existing LWR technology argue that it is prohibitively expensive to acquire as much safety insight about the new reactors as is currently available from operating experience with LWRs and from previous research by the vendors, NRC, ACRS, and the entire LWR complex (universities, architecture-engineering firms, materials manufacturers, etc.). They are deeply suspicious of nuclear power development strategies that attempt large innovations, preferring instead incremental change with ample time for feedback review.[3]

4) The Reasonable Level of Protection Required Against Externally Initiated Hazards Such as Earthquakes, Flooding, and Sabotage

Probabilistic Risk Assessments (PRAs) for LWR have found externally initiated events (along with small pipe breaks and loss of off-site power) to be the most important causes of core-melt (Harding 1990, 96–7). Similar concerns have been raised about some passive designs (e.g., fears of earthquake and saboteur hazards for the LMR and for any passive design involving an overhead, gravity fed water tank or pluggable air cooling ducts).

5) Issues of Operator Error and Quality Control for Plant Structures and Equipment

Uncertainties about quality control are especially salient for the MHTGR's fuel pellets, the PIUS's prestressed concrete reactor vessel, and the LMR's sodium carrying pipes. Should passive designs be deployed, it seems likely that the NRC will have a greater presence at manufacturing facilities than it does now.

6) Accident Hazards Specific to Each Design (See Chapter Appendix for Details)

7) Safety Hazards with Respect to Nuclear Waste Disposal, Accident Risks Along the Nuclear Fuel Cycle, and Nuclear Weapons Proliferation

While passive designs often involve the same kinds of hazards as LWRs in these areas, some designs have reduced or increased risks (see chapter appendix).

Economic Issues

In addition to these safety concerns, critics have raised economic considerations. While the preliminary nature of most passive designs ensures a large degree of uncertainty, proponents have offered fairly detailed cost projections. The 1992 National Academy of Sciences Advanced Reactors study reported vendor estimates of about 3–5 c/kwh (1989 $) for the MHTGR, PRISM, and PIUS reactors (National Research Council 1992, 134). Experience suggests that these estimates be treated as highly speculative until empirical cost experience is available. Even attending to relative rankings seems premature and an invitation for excess optimism.

The major debates about the economics of passively safe reactors involve:

1) The Magnitude of Unanticipated Technical Difficulties

Nuclear critics and proponents of traditional reactors expect the newer designs to encounter many serious unforeseen technical problems. They harken back to the classic distinction between "real and paper" reactors drawn by Admiral Rickover, the father of the nuclear navy, in the 1950s. "He noted that a paper reactor generally has the following characteristics:

It is simple.
It is small.

It is cheap.

It is lightweight.

It can be built very quickly.

Very little development is required: it will use off-the-shelf components.

It is in the study phase; it is not being built now.

By contrast, a real reactor has the following characteristics:

It is complicated.

It is large.

It is heavy.

It is being built now.

It is behind schedule.

It requires an immense amount of development on apparently trivial items.

It takes a long time to build because of its engineering development problems" (Rockwell 1992, 158–159).

Because history has borne out Rickover's prediction, "first of a kind"-engineering cost estimates that include contingency margins of less than 25% seem unrealistic.

2) The Degree to Which Demonstrations of Passive Safety Will Permit Relaxation of Existing Safety Requirements

This has especially important financial implications with respect to containment requirements, emergency planning requirements, emergency power requirements, various safety system redundancies, quality control and quality assurance requirements, and control room and operator quality requirements.

It seems likely that relaxation of major safety system requirements, such as containment, will require many years of safe operating experience with passive designs. First generation plants will thus be burdened with expenses for both passive and "defense-in-depth" safety systems.

3) The Magnitude of "Traditional" or "Static" Per MW Construction Cost Penalties for Smaller Plants

Popular debate ranges between scaling components of .85 and .4 for per MW construction costs, implying that a 125 MW plant would cost 40%–400% more to build per KW than a 1250 MW plant.[4] A priori engineering studies tend to assume larger scaling effects than empirically observed with nuclear construction. Enthusiasts of traditional LWRs tend to penalize passive safety designs heavily for their small size.

4) The Magnitude of "Dynamic" Cost Savings for Smaller Standardized Plants from Mass Production Economies and the Capture of Learning Curve Advantages

The economics of serial production asserts a counter to the a priori geometry favoring larger plants. Many observers (e.g., Phung 1984, 4; Stewart 1981, 191) suggest learning curves for nuclear plant construction of 15%–20% per each doubling of output.[5] This implies cost declines of about 50% from a tenfold increase in output (as might accompany a shift from 1250 MW plants to 125 MW plants). It may be inappropriate, however, to use a constant learning curve over a range of output as wide as a tenfold increase. The capture of volume economies could also be frustrated by lack of design stability, as happened with the LWR.

5) The Economic Credit Given Smaller Reactors for Their More Efficient Integration into Utility Grids

This advantage reflects several features of these reactors:

- their ability to match small increases in demand with small increments of supply without as many periods of excess capacity and as large a spinning reserve as large plants;

- their shorter construction periods, which increases planning flexibility and reduces necessary reserve margins;

- and their smaller debt burdens, which could increase utility coverage ratios and perhaps lower financing charges (see Clark and Fancher 1985, esp. 10–19).

Both Clark and Fancher (1985) and Coxe (1988) have attempted to quantify aspects of these benefits. Their results depend on assumptions about utility size and the degree of grid integration (more of each reduces the planning value of smaller plants), the stability of electricity demand behavior (more of which reduces the value of shorter construction times) and regulatory variables dealing with capital cost recovery. Clark and Fancher's results suggest a surprisingly large value for smallness, claiming, all other things being equal, a $750/KW premium for a 125 MW technology with a two-year construction period compared with a 1150 MW technology with a ten-year construction period (p. 9). Coxe's results suggest a more modest impact (~5%) (159, 166).

6) The Magnitude of Cost Savings from Faster Technical Innovation Due to Increased Regulatory Flexibility in the Absence of Catastrophic Accident Concerns

Among the strongest arguments for passive designs is their dynamic rather than static promise. Proponents of the MHTGR, for example, have highlighted the reactor's ability to take advantage of potential breakthroughs in new high temperature materials and gas turbine technology. Skeptics doubt, however, that regulators will permit quick integration of major innovations.

7) The Achievement of High Capacity Rates

Because most passive reactors have very high capital costs their relative economics is highly sensitive to capacity rates. Almost all of the vendors' cost estimates rely on availability rates that exceed 86%. Proponents often argue that quality control will be much better for passive designs due to their smaller size and amenability to shop floor rather than on-site fabrication. It is also claimed that the design's elimination of many defense-in-depth safety systems will increase capacity rates. These claims are likely to be greeted skeptically until demonstrated empirically.

8) The Economic Credit Given Passive Safety Designs for Potential Siting Advantages and Perhaps Superior Suitability for Deployment in Third World Markets

To the extent inherent safety can be demonstrated, it should ease domestic siting problems and reduce skilled labor constraints on exports.

Semi-Passive Reactors[6]

A third reactor type has recently emerged in between large evolutionary LWRs and passively safe reactors. The "semi-passive" reactor adds passive safety features to mid-sized (~600 MW) LWR designs. Its proponents claim it achieves most of the safety advantages of passively safe reactor concepts without as large a sacrifice of MW scaling economies. Supporters also emphasize that the design is less vulnerable to unpleasant technical surprises and regulatory conservatism because it builds on existing LWR technology.

The leading semi-passive designs are Westinghouse's Advanced Passive 600 reactor (AP 600) and G. E.'s Simplified Boiling Water Reactor (SBWR). Combustion Engineering (Safe Integral Reactor [SIR]) and a number of foreign suppliers are also developing similar designs (e.g., Hitachi and Toshiba).

Basic Design

Both Westinghouse and G. E.'s reactors are 600–640 MW. They rely on simplified designs and claim large reductions in material requirements from redesign efforts that meet newer safety regulations more efficiently than older retrofitted plants. They also incorporate significant learning from past LWR operation and the products of continuing LWR R&D.[7]

The reactors meld passive safety features with aspects of older defense-in-depth safety strategies. Their lower power densities than existing LWRs allows them to use semi-passive decay heat cooling systems. The AP 600, for example, utilizes a gravity fed core cooling system, a gravity fed containment vessel cooling system, and additional air cooling for the containment building. While these safety systems do not require any active pumping devices or external power sources once activated, they do rely on instrumentation to open air intake valves, reactor coolant system depressurization valves, and water feed valves in the event of a serious accident. The addition of passive safety features has allowed the designers to reduce some other safety outlays.

Safety Concerns

The reactor's semi-passive design has raised concerns about potential instrumentation failure, valve failure, and valve power source failure. There seems to be sufficient probability of potential problems with related equipment, such as check valves, to make it unlikely that the NRC will significantly reduce many defense-in-depth requirements.

The design's residual potential for serious accidents raises safety issues similar to those accompanying larger LWRs regarding externally initiated hazards such as earthquakes, floods, and sabotage, and internally initiated failures involving human error and fire. MHB Associates has also raised a number of special concerns specific to each design.[8]

As noted by the National Academy of Sciences in its 1992 study of advanced reactors, the preliminary nature of most semi-passive designs, the frequent lack of complete PRAs, and absence of operating experience makes comprehensive safety assessment impossible (National Research Council 1992, 136).

Economics

The vendors expect cost savings from design simplification, lower total safety expenditures (due to credit for passive safety features), continued feedback from LWR operating experience and R&D, and modularization to significantly reduce construction costs. Westinghouse is working with Avondale Industries to apply the modular techniques used in shipbuilding to reactor construction. James Cottrell, an Avondale vice president, estimates that most of the 30% cost reduction achieved by the AP 600 in comparison with traditional PWRs results from modularization (MIT 1990, p. 2–21).

The vendors project levelized generating costs, excluding waste disposal, of 3.9 c/kwh for the AP 600 and 3.5 c/kwh–4.1 c/kwh for the SBWR (1989$) (National Research Council 1992, 134). As the NAS report notes, these estimates are highly speculative (Ibid. 134). They seem troublingly similar to the promotionally oriented, misleadingly optimistic cost projections of the early days of the great bandwagon market. The calculations are based on assumptions at odds with historical performance, such as projected construction periods of 3 to 3.5 years (versus actual averages of ten to twelve years for the forty-seven plants completed in 1980–1989) (National Research Council 1992, 33) and availability rates of ~90% (MHB 7/90, 134) versus average capacity rates of 59.8% in 1968–1990.

As with passive designs, semi-passive capital costs will vary with the level of output and it seems unlikely that the vendors will enjoy a large volume of orders in the foreseeable future. Unfortunately, it is not clear from the vendors' presentations how dependent their cost projections are on high output levels.

Competing Nuclear Technologies: A Summary

Like the mid-fifties, when as many as one hundred different nuclear power technologies were conceivable, the current period is marked by an explosion of design creativity. At least seventy different passive reactor concepts, for example, have been proposed. Like broader debates about energy sector choices, current intra-nuclear power debates can be analogized to paradigm debates about the fertility of different research agendas. Unfortunately there is no simple algorithm for translating information about a youthful technology into assessments of its mature form. Judgments necessarily involve "technological aesthetics," as the questions addressed (for example, how valuable are the long run thermal efficiency advantages of MHTGR gas turbine technology compared with the greater operating experience of existing LWRs) do not lend themselves to immediately testable answers.

Supporters of large evolutionary LWR designs emphasize the technology's massive advantage in operating experience and cumulative research. Their technological aesthetic heavily favors incremental over discontinuous change in nuclear design. They accept the adequacy of existing reactor safety levels and safety assessment techniques (especially PRAs), and are confident that the geometry of reactor economics will ultimately demonstrate the optimality of large MW plants in a stable regulatory environment. They doubt that alternative designs can skip the learning by doing phase of reactor development and foresee disappointing technical surprises. They doubt that many nuclear critics' minds can be changed by the results of any conceivable reactor safety test.

Proponents of semi-passive reactors accept most of the above analysis, but see net benefits from adding some passive safety features to existing LWRs and cutting their size in half. The range of disagreement among LWR advocates is modest and not a paradigm difference.

Passive safety reactor proponents present a path challenge to LWRs. They see defense-in-depth safety strategies flawed at the level of design rather than detail, finding existing safety uncertainties intolerable from a hazard and/or public relations perspective. They anticipate long run diseconomies of scale with respect to MW size and perceive greater opportunities for innovation with passive than defense-in-depth safety strategies.

They find semi-passive reactors burdened with many of the same limitations as large LWRs and question the wisdom of attempting to balance safety and short run economic performance instead of maximizing safety and attempting to evolve economic competitiveness.

Paradigm debates also abound among passive safety reactor proponents.

Table 10.1 summarizes the key strengths and weaknesses of the three major passive reactor concepts detailed in the appendix to this chapter. Dozens of other passive safety reactor combinations of coolant, moderator, and fuel type have also been proposed, along with numerous new safety technologies for defense-in-depth LWR plants.

It is difficult to predict which designs will triumph within the U.S. nuclear power community. The preferred outcome depends upon what criteria are used to weigh the different attributes of the technologies. If the decision is based on risk averse R&D payoffs and short term economic prospects, for example, the likely winners are LWR designs. If the decision emphasizes the importance of guaranteeing long-term energy supplies, the probable winner is the LMR. If the decision prioritizes reactor safety, the probable winners are the MHTGR and PIUS, unless an incrementalist view of acceptable change is adopted, in which case the LWR is favored.

Which objectives dominate the decision process depends on the self-interest and technological aesthetics of the decision maker. The major actors with respect to reactor choice are the reactor vendors, utilities, and the federal government. The vendors have a strong interest in maintaining the value of their corporate capital (patents, production facilities, staff expertise, marketing networks, etc.) which is generally tied to particular reactor designs (e.g., Westinghouse: PWR; G. E.: BWR; General Atomics: HTGR), though the larger firms have also invested modestly in developing alternative designs (e.g., G. E.: LMR). This legacy imparts strong biases in favor of LWR designs.

Like the LWR vendors, the nuclear utilities have a corporate interest in preserving the market relevance of their management experience with the LWR. Skepticism towards new nuclear orders by Public Utility Commissioners and Wall Street, however, is likely to make it difficult to arrange financing for new LWR or passive safety nuclear plants. These problems are exacerbated in the short run by the presence of cheap natural gas.

The DOE also seems unlikely to undertake major new nuclear initiatives, constrained by the federal budget deficit and the massive cost of cleaning up nuclear weapons facilities. President Clinton has publicly linked wasteful government spending with nuclear power projects and targeted many nuclear programs for termination. Key Republican members of Congress have called for the abolition of the Department of Energy and would likely opppose large new nuclear development subsidies.

While passive reactor designs arouse less opposition among some nuclear power critics than traditional reactors, concerns remain about residual reactor safety hazards, waste disposal and other fuel cycle issues, and nuclear weapons proliferation problems. Equally pressing are fears that passive reactor projects could serve as Trojan horses for traditional nuclear designs

TABLE 10.1
Passive Safety Paradigm Debates

Pro-MHTGR	*Anti-MHTGR*
-Impressive safety characteristics including the possible survival of a Lidsky test -mass production and utility planning benefits due to small size -high energy conversion efficiencies due to gas coolant -potential for significant future technical change[1] -potential high temperature heat applications -potential for extending nuclear fuel base due to higher conversion efficiencies and shift to thorium cycles	-quality control uncertainties about fuel integrity -the loss of MW scaling economies in reactor vessel construction and instrumentation -relatively high construction costs due to helium's low density -Minimal experience with helium coolants and turbines,[2] and accompanying potential for unanticipated engineering problems -graphite combustibility

Pro-LMR	*Anti-LMR*
-nuclear fuel insurance value (due to potential use as a breeder reactor) -possible value as a nuclear waste burner -proponent's claims of passive and testable safety -mass production and utility planning benefits due to small size	-most of the standard objections to breeder technologies vis-à-vis reprocessing and Pu circulation -concern over technetium disposal problems -The increased uncertainties accompanying non-LWR design choices, past problems with LMR projects, R&D difficulties working with liquid sodium -the loss of MW scaling economies in reactor vessel construction and instrumentation -problems with sodium fires and reactivity surges from sodium boiling

Pro-PIUS	*Anti-PIUS*
-Impressive safety features, including potential survival of a Lidsky test -use of familiar materials -potential for deployment at high MW levels (600MW–1000MW)	-strong fears of very low capacity rates -the lack of any previous prototype plants and high first-of-a-kind demonstration plant costs -relatively high capital costs due to larger reactor vessel -non-US design -possible difficulties with underwater maintenance

Notes

1. Especially interesting is the MIT trajectory, which would initially replace General Atomics' steam turbine with a gas turbine, using a heat exchanger to link the helium coolant circulating through the reactor with a second helium loop running through the gas turbine. The design

by diverting funds from non-nuclear technologies and sustaining nuclear infrastructures for later redirection towards breeder reactor projects.

Given the above constraints, it seems doubtful that the U.S. nuclear industry will attempt major new investments. The AP 600 seems the most likely choice for a small number of new nuclear orders (should there be any) due to its popularity with some utilities and smaller investment risk than full-sized LWR reactors. One can imagine (under optimistic assumptions) one or two larger or more innovative projects as well, if they can spread investment risks across a consortium of firms (e.g., a vendor, architect-engineer, and group of utilities) and draw on EPRI and DOE subsidies.

Beyond these activities the U.S. nuclear industry will likely take a backseat to technical developments in foreign markets, where the lack of fossil fuels and absence of effective anti-nuclear sentiment make new investments more attractive. Tokyo Electric Power Company, for example, has had two ABWR plants under construction. South Korea has plans for as many as eighteen additional reactors by 2006 (*Nuclear News* 11/92, 41). Japanese (and perhaps Chinese) support for the MHTGR may revitalize that option.

Nuclear power exerts a pull on the imagination because of its enormous energy supply potential. This allure is dimmed by serious concerns about nuclear hazards and the technology's extremely high R&D costs. It is much easier to justify a $20 million expenditure for innovative wind power research than a multi-billion dollar demonstration-construction project for a new nuclear technology. In the absence of compelling short term reasons for large commercialization investments, long term oriented R&D on nuclear technologies that minimize hazard concerns seems the most productive development path.

Table 10.1 notes continued

would ultimately dispense with the heat exchanger, circulating the same helium through the reactor and turbine. The trajectory builds on recent advances in gas turbine technology (see chapter 12) and expected breakthroughs in high temperature materials.

There are of course "many a potential slip between the cup and lip." There are significant uncertainties, for example, about potential interaction problems between the nuclear and gas turbine systems inside the reactor vessel. Unexpected turbine maintenance problems would be complicated by the reactor vessel's radioactive environment.

2. First-of-a-kind construction of a helium turbine, for example, could prove fairly expensive, though it does not appear to involve any serious technological leaps.

Appendix: The Three Major Passive Reactor Designs

The Modular High Temperature Gas Reactor (MHTGR)

Several different kinds of MHTGRs have been proposed. The most common differences involve prismatic versus pebble cores and steam versus gas turbines. This discussion concentrates on the MIT design (MHTGR-GT) which is a pebble bed, gas turbine variant, as it seems the most promising.

If the reactor performs as designed, it could demonstrate its "inherent safety" features in a "Lidsky-test" (that is, it could endure a simultaneous loss of coolant, removal of control rods, and delivery into the hands of a malicious operator, without a significant release of radioactivity into the environment). A small German test reactor, the 15 MW AVR reactor, shut down safely after a loss of helium coolant in a 1988 experiment (*ORNL Review* 1988 #4), but no full Lidsky-test has ever been attempted with an MHTGR.

Design Issues

The distinctiveness of the MHTGR lies in:

(1) its helium coolant's:

- high temperature potential, which permits energy conversion efficiencies of 45%–50%, versus ~33% for LWRs,

- low corrosive characteristics, which is attractive for lowering O&M costs and raising capacity rates,

- chemical inertness, which reduces chemical routes to core explosions,

- lower cooling efficiency, which increases reactor volume and associated capital costs, and

- relative novelty, which threatens unexpected technical problems and licensing delays.

(2) its graphite moderator's

• large heat sink, which aids in passive cooling, and

• combustibility, which raises new safety hazards.

(3) its ceramic-coated fuel kernels

• (designed to retain fission products at temperatures of at least 1600 degrees C versus 1200 degrees for LWR zirconium cladding) which facilitates passive cooling and safety demonstration.

(4) its underground silo siting

• which aids passive heat removal.

(5) its small size (~150 MW vs. 600 MW for the smallest LWR and 400MW–600 MW for the PIUS)

• which permits passive cooling to prevent core temperatures from reaching 1600 degrees C and

• complicates economic assessment (due to the complex relationship between reactor size and generating costs)

Safety Issues

The main safety issues specific to the MHTGR design involve:

1) Residual uncertainties about the thermal integrity of the fuel kernels in accident contexts, especially with respect to quality control under mass production (National Research Council 1992, 149). While data from fuel performance at the Fort St. Vrain and the German AVR plants seem encouraging, the ACRS has indicated that higher levels of manufacturing quality will be necessary than have been achieved in the past.[1]

2) Fears of graphite water reactions leading to the production of combustible gases (CO and H).

3) Fears of graphite fires. Lidsky has suggested that the graphite be coated with fire retardant to eliminate this concern. Other less certain but cheaper measures, such as combustible gas relief valves, have also been proposed (MHB 7/90, 3–52).

4) Fears of reactivity surges (and perhaps chemical degradation of defective fuel kernels [MHB 7/90, 3–54]) due to water intrusion into the core.

As with most water-related hazards, this problem would be minimized by using a gas rather than steam turbine (as proposed in the MIT MHTGR design).

5) Fears of saboteur interference with passive heat removal and/or introduction of water into the core. It appears it would be extremely difficult to frustrate the reactor's passive capacities for decay heat removal. Malicious introduction of water into the core, or explosives into the cooling cavities (MHB 7/90, 3–52), however, seems a more realistic threat.

6) Seismic concerns. While earthquake concerns have been raised for some MHTGR designs due to potential core reconfiguration (*Nuclear News* 12/88, 26), there appear to be no potential disruptions of the core or reactor vessel that could increase reactivity or interfere with passive heat removal for the MIT design.

Overall, the MHTGR joins the PIUS reactor as the most promising designs with respect to reactor safety. The MHTGR's fuel pellets also offer extremely low worker radiation exposure. Despite all of the maintenance work required at the Fort St. Vrain plant, for example, its occupational exposure rates were about 2% of LWR rates (Lidsky 2–3/84, 53). The fuel coatings may also aid in waste disposal (National Research Council 1992, 143) though the graphite moderator appears to increase waste volume (MHB 7/90, 4–2).

Economic Issues

Economic projections by proponents of the MHTGR foresee generating costs of 4 to 5 c/kwh (Gas Cooled Associates 1993, Table 7-11; Lidsky and Yan 11/92). Skeptics assert costs could easily be more than 50% higher. The main debates involve:

1) The extent to which the design's passive safety features will permit relaxation of various defense-in-depth safety requirements. Prospects are brighter in the long than short run. It is unlikely that the ACRS or NRC will approve General Atomics' design which omits a containment structure (MHB 7/90 3–4, 3–23; *Nuclear News* 12/88, 26). Adding containment would probably increase plant costs by about ∼5% (MHB 7/90, 3–22). Higher expenditures for other defense-in-depth features than projected in General Atomics' proposals (such as increased quality assurance programs) are also likely for the first generation of MHTGR plants. Collectively, these additions could easily increase projected plant costs by 10%–20%.

2) The extent to which unexpected technical problems will increase construction costs. Current design studies employ traditional contingency

rates of 15%–20%. Given the novelty of the designs, skeptics might add at least an additional 10%.

3) The extent to which the MHTGR can achieve high capacity rates. Partly due to the MHTGR's small size and helium coolant, its per KW reactor construction costs are relatively high.[2] A drop in projected capacity rates from 90% (assumed by MIT) to 80% would increase generating costs by about 4 M/kwh or ∼10%. Lidsky has offered several plausible reasons for expecting the gas turbine variant of the MHTGR to achieve high capacity rates, including: the traditionally higher rates of gas rather than steam turbines, the reduced maintenance problems and thus lower forced outage rates expected from a helium as opposed to fossil fuel gas turbine, and the higher quality control expected from the MHTGR's replacement of on-site construction with factory production of many reactor components. Nevertheless, past nuclear performance, including experience with the HTGR, counsels skepticism until high capacity rates are demonstrated empirically.

4) The extent to which near-term MHTGRs can capture the learning and mass production economies made possible by the design's small modular characteristics. Given the obstacles facing nuclear plant orders in the foreseeable future, prospects for volume economies seem dim.[3]

5) The extent to which major technical innovations will reduce generating costs. As Lidsky has noted, the technology offers attractive innovation possibilities with respect to high temperature materials and gas turbine designs. Unfortunately, capture of this potential will take time.

6) The extent to which reactor accidents pose an investment, rather than safety risk (even if the design is able to reduce the probability of major fission releases to close to zero).

MHTGR: History and Future

Interest in HTGR technology dates back to the early days of nuclear power development, due to the potentially higher energy conversion efficiencies of gas over water coolants. The technology was at a severe disadvantage, however, due to its inability to merge development paths with the nuclear submarine. Its lower power densities also discouraged some early analysts due to expectations of high capital costs.

Two HTGR plants were constructed in the U.S., the 40 MW Peach Bottom plant (in operation from 1967–1974) and 330 MW Fort St. Vrain plant (∼1977–1989). The latter's 14% lifetime capacity rate discouraged further gas reactor investment. More recent experience with a 300 MW thorium HTGR project in Germany has also been disappointing. Although the primary difficulties in the latter two cases involved non-nuclear aspects of the plants (the helium circulator at Fort St. Vrain and cross duct piping in the German plant),[4] the failures reemphasized the likelihood of unanticipated problems within any nuclear development path and highlighted the need for very deep pockets in order to commercialize a nuclear technology.[5]

The strategic problem for the MHTGR is that its competitiveness requires long-term investment (in reactor safety and fuel quality control demonstrations, in R&D for high temperature gas turbine development, and in market building for the capture of volume and learning curve cost reductions), prior to any assurance that the investments will pay off. The history of nuclear power suggests that unanticipated technical problems and public opposition could easily undermine what might otherwise seem promising.

The most compelling argument for MHTGR investment is the technology's value as an insurance policy in the event of problems with other energy options. It is not clear, however, that successful corporate development of the technology would permit the innovating firm to enjoy large market advantages over later market entries, as evidenced by Westinghouse and G. E.'s failure to enjoy enduring advantages over later entries into the LWR market.

Thus it seems likely that corporate risk taking for MHTGR development will be modest and conditioned by matching or largely government subsidized research assistance. While the incentives for public spending for backstop technologies are greater than private incentives, the free-rider problem invites relying on foreign governments, with fewer long term energy options (such as Japan or Korea) to finance global energy supply insurance policies.

The immediate prospects for MHTGR development in the U.S. seem dim. A 1992 review of advanced reactor concepts by the National Academy of Sciences (NAS) recommended an end to the DOE's civilian funding for the MHTGR (National Research Council 1992, 192). The NAS study's major complaint appeared to be that the MHTGR offered no prima facie advantages over existing LWR technologies and therefore should be jettisoned in order to preserve scarce development funds for the next generation of LWRs and the breeder option. The study's mode of argument reillustrates the power of path dependency in technological decision making.

Congress terminated direct R&D funding for the technology in FY 1996. Plans to use the construction of a new tritium producing reactor as a demonstration vehicle for MHTGR development have been shelved due to a fall in demand for weapons material.[6] The technology also lacks a major corporate sponsor. Its main backer, the General Atomics Corporation, is no longer a subsidiary of Gulf and Shell Oil.

On the other hand, the MHTGR continues to have some reliable allies in Congress. The design also benefits from continuing research at M.I.T. and

ORNL and low level support by a consortium of nuclear industry firms. The MHTGR is also among the least objectionable nuclear options with respect to reactor safety in the eyes of the technically trained skeptic community. Perhaps most importantly, the Japanese are constructing a major MHTGR development complex and have included the technology in their most recent nuclear development program.

The bottom line appears to be that MHTGR technology will proceed slowly in the U.S. unless some dramatic agreement can be reached between the skeptic community and nuclear industry that prioritizes the MHTGR. Japanese initiatives and future LWR difficulties, however, could turn the global nuclear industry towards the technology. There also appear to be pockets of interest in other countries, such as Russia and China, and among major nuclear vendors, such as Siemens and ABB-CE.

The Liquid Metal Reactor

Safety and Economic Issues

The LMR is a passive variant of earlier breeder reactor designs and carries with it the strengths and weaknesses of that technology. Its leading variant is G. E.'s PRISM (Power Reactor Innovative Small Module) design. The reactor is designed to take advantage of the cooling properties of liquid sodium. The latter serves as a heat sink during accidents and dissipates fuel rod decay heat by passive means (thermal conduction, air currents, etc.) to the environment.

LMR promoters assert its value as a nuclear fuel insurance policy due to its potential use for fuel breeding. Critics dismiss this benefit with reference to current analyses of nuclear fuel supplies that see little economic rationale for fuel breeding for at least one hundred years. Critics indict the technology, however, for carrying the same severe nuclear proliferation and environmental risks as breeder cycles due to its use of fuel reprocessing and a plutonium fuel cycle (MHB 7/90, 2–7,2–50).

Promoters of the LMR praise the reactor for its ability to burn actinide wastes, which involve some of the most long-lived waste disposal problems. Critics warn that actinide burning produces technetium, another long-lived serious radioactive waste product (National Research Council 1992, 131).

The major safety concerns raised about the design involve:

• the potential for reactivity surges due to sodium boiling

- the routine hazards associated with liquid sodium due to its explosive potential in contact with water and air. Beside posing severe quality control and potential accident problems, this feature makes some R&D work more difficult. Sodium's opaqueness also "makes the assurance of satisfactory in-vessel inspections and operation more difficult" (National Research Council 1992, 150).

- the vulnerability of the reactor's passive air cooling to disabling acts of sabotage.

- the vulnerability of the reactor to earthquake and potential operator error.

General Electric has projected generating costs, excluding waste disposal, of 3.1–5.1 c/kwh (1989$) (National Research Council 1992, 134). The major economic uncertainties involve:

- the usual probability of unexpected technical problems when attempting to develop as novel a fuel cycle as that used in the PRISM design and to use as volatile a coolant as liquid sodium.

- the extent to which the NRC will permit relaxation of current defense-in-depth requirements in the light of asserted passive safety features. The NRC staff, for example, initially concluded that the design could not dispense with containment requirements (MHB 7/90, 0–5), though they were more sympathetic towards reduced offsite emergency planning requirements (MHB 7/90, 0–5–6). MHB associates have called for critical review of G. E.'s request for a reduced number of reactor operators and condensed quality assurance requirements.

- the uncertain costs of reprocessing

- the extent to which successful fuel cycle innovations can offset capital cost disadvantages (projected to be about 33% versus standard LWRs by the Electric Power Research Institute) (National Research Council 1992, 139).

LMR History and Future

Experience with LMRs has not been good. A LMR design was selected as the backup design for Rickover's submarine program and a G. E. prototype was constructed. The PWR's success and problems with the LMR's heat exchangers led to the latter's discontinuation (Creutz 6/70, 76). Two early U.S. reactors suffered partial meltdowns (EBR-I and FERMI I), and the Clinch River breeder was canceled after disastrous cost overruns. All three French LMRs have encountered serious technical problems involving sodium leaks or reactivity surges (National Research Council 1992, 126) and the head of France's regulatory commission has raised serious doubts about the future of the technology (*Nucleonics Week* 6/19/92, 1). Japan is sliding its breeder program towards the back burner, with fully commercial reactors not expected before 2030 at the earliest. A prototype plant (Monju) began low power tests in August 1995 and appears to have suffered a serious accident on December 8, 1995. Congress terminated funds for LMR development in FY 1995.

On the other hand, the LMR continues to enjoy support among the U.S. nuclear establishment's technical elite. Its supporters highlight 1986 tests of the EBR-II as demonstration of the design's ability to simultaneously withstand a control rod malfunction and the loss of some coolant capacities (National Research Council 1992, 125). It was the only non-LWR prioritized in the NAS's 1992 advanced reactor recommendations.

In the absence of major uranium fuel shortages and a consensus between the nuclear industry and its informed critics that the LMR is the preferred nuclear technology, it seems unlikely that any commercialization of LMR technology will occur in the foreseeable future. The barriers posed by the novelty of the design and extra risks accompanying reprocessing seem too daunting.

PIUS

A major problem in assessing the PIUS reactor is that no PIUS plants have ever been constructed. This generates even larger than average economic uncertainties. Like the MHTGR, however, the reactor appears safer than LWRs and LMRs and thus continues to attract policy attention

The design represents the Swedish nuclear industry's response to a Swedish referendum requiring the phase out of Sweden's current generation of nuclear plants by 2010. The major vendor for the PIUS is ASEA-Brown Boveri-Atom (ABB) (which now includes Combustion Engineering). The company has both the technical depth and financial resources to commercialize the technology. ASEA-Atom's 12 BWRs have had the highest availability average in the world. ABB projects overall generating costs of 4 c/kwh (1989$) for PIUS plants (National Research Council 1992, 134).

The most serious doubts about the concept involve its economic claims.

Because recent designs are in the 400 MW to 640 MW range, it will be expensive to resolve cost uncertainties with a demonstration project. The most serious economic concerns involve:

1) the reactor's ability to avoid frequent and unnecessary shutdowns and therefore low capacity rates,

2) the high cost of the pre-stressed concrete vessel

3) the degree to which the plant's passive safety features will permit regulatory relaxation of balance of plant safety requirements, such as containment vessel requirements.

Less serious questions have also been posed about potential maintenance problems caused by having to perform repair work in a submerged system, and the cost and performance characteristics of the submerged steam generator.

The main safety risk of the PIUS design is failure of the prestressed concrete vessel. Proponents find this risk negligible; skeptics worry about earthquakes, quality control, and terrorists.

At present the design seems on hold in the U.S. It is not receiving any major DOE funding and there appear to be no plans for a demonstration plant in the foreseeable future. A number of foreign nuclear programs appear to be discussing PIUS designs with ABB, including firms in Italy and China.

Notes

1. Demonstrating fuel quality is one of the major tasks for MHTGR licensing and development. The recent shutdown of several demonstration HTGRs (Fort St. Vrain, the AVR, and the German THTR) has deprived the technology of key fuel demonstration facilities.

2. The MIT design projects MHTGR capital costs of $2,000/KW (1990$) (Lidsky and Yan 11/4/92).

3. There is debate about the minimal level of output necessary to capture economies of scale. Projections based on shipyard experience imply that from (2–4) to 10 units per facility are necessary to capture 15% savings (MIT 1990, 2–24).

4. Along with difficulties with the piping connecting the reactor to the rest of the plant, the German HTGR suffered from problems caused by friction between the control rods and fuel balls.

5. See Stewart (1981, 184–189) for an interesting account of General Atomics's inability to transform its 8–10 orders for HTGRs in the early-seventies into a successful product line, despite outlays of upwards of a billion dollars.

6. Gas Cooled Reactor Associates has estimated that piggy backing MHTGR development on top of the construction of a new tritium production reactor could reduce development costs from $1 billion to $300–$600 million (National Research Council 1992, 197).

Part III

The Competitive Context

Several factors external to the nuclear sector will heavily influence the future of nuclear power by defining the context for nuclear choices. The three major factors are the level of future energy and electricity demand, the economics of alternative electricity generating options, and the character of public policy responses to potential greenhouse hazards. The next three chapters explore these topics.

Paralleling our discussion of nuclear technologies, chapters 11–13 will demonstrate that the strength of nuclear power's competition is very sensitive to path dependent phenomena, government policy, and judgments about future technological developments that are dependent on forecasters' technological aesthetics. Like earlier nuclear power controversies and paradigm debates in science over the fertility of different research agendas, disagreements about the viability of non-nuclear energy options involve untestable hypotheses about forward looking phenomena.

Forecasting versus Backcasting

Before turning to non-nuclear energy issues, it would be useful to emphasize the distinction between forecasting and backcasting. Forecasting is commonly equated with predicting. In the energy sector it frequently assumes a technologically deterministic tone. Energy supply and demand predictions are generated by optimizing models that translate assumed technical information about engineering relationships into forecasts about future market behavior. There is a tendency to abstract from socio-political contexts, usually by implicitly assuming the continuation of existing institutional arrangements, cultural habits, and public policies.

Backcasting identifies a possible outcome and the conditions under which it would occur. The approach often emphasizes the sensitivity of potential outcomes to societal decisions and implies the need for prediction to forecast both engineering potentials and socio-political developments. Backcasters are less interested in prediction, however, than persuasion, and portray energy sector outcomes as choices rather than exogenous probabilities. The reader is frequently urged to adopt measures that would actualize the potential outcome backcasted.

Inattention to the differences between forecasting and backcasting has frequently confused energy sector debates. Backcasts (analyses with highly stylized assumptions offered for purposes of illustration rather than prediction) have been mistaken for forecasts. "Predictions" have been adduced to assert policy imperatives that were avoidable if government programs other than those *assumed* in the prediction were implemented.

Among nuclear enthusiasts the mixing of forecasting and backcasting has often led to claims of a nuclear imperative. Nuclear advocates have tended to project high energy demand growth and minimal contributions from non-nuclear energy options, leaving no alternative to nuclear expansion. As with nuclear hazard assessment and cost forecasting, these projections reflected a particular planing vision and the constellation of institutions, self-interests, and ideological beliefs giving rise to that vision. The predictions were thus more reflections of the forecaster's "ideological present" than the energy sector's "necessary future". Stylized planning visions have similarly infused technical forecasts and energy sector modeling by nuclear critics.

The broadening of participation in energy planning in the last twenty years to include greater input from environmental and activist groups has thus altered "predictions" about the future as well as recommendations for public policy.

Chapter 11

Nuclear Competition: Demand Side

Recent Forecasting History

The demand for nuclear power derives from the broader demand for energy and electricity. The DOE's nuclear power forecasting model, WINES (World Integrated Nuclear Evaluation System), for example, assumes a fixed relationship among the three variables, such that any change in energy demand implies a specific change in nuclear power demand.[1] Nuclear enthusiasts generally expect higher energy demand growth than nuclear skeptics. This chapter explores the basis for differing energy demand expectations.

Since the early seventies, government and industry forecasts have tended to overestimate the level of future energy demand, resulting in large excess capacity in the electric utility industry from 1975–1990. Beginning with a Ford Foundation study (1974) and an essay by Amory Lovins (1976), an initially maverick and increasingly mainstream group of economists have asserted the cost effectiveness of energy efficiency investments. Their lower energy demand forecasts proved more accurate in the 1980s than conventional high energy growth scenarios. Many advocates of energy conservation believe that industry and to a lesser extent government sources continue to underestimate conservation potentials due to fixed habits of mind, relatively static information networks, and institutional inertia.

Under the WINES forecasting assumptions, recent debates over the level of future energy demand could alter the size of the nuclear sector by about a factor of two.[2] In 1994 the U.S. consumed 89 Quads of energy (DOE, *Annual Energy Outlook 1996*, Table A1). Projections for the year 2030 range from low estimates of 50–60 Quads to high estimates of 120–150+ Quads.[3] In 1994 the U.S. consumed ~3,000 TWH (terawatt hours, billion kwhs) of electricity. Conceivable levels of electricity consumption for 2030 range from ~2,500 TWH to more than 6,000 TWH.[4]

Because of anticipated improvements in plant capacity rates, the likelihood that non-utility generators (especially small independent power producers) will provide an increasing share of electricity output, and the possibility of increased electricity imports, utility capacity is not expected to grow as fast as electricity consumption. In fact, the DOE currently projects that utilities will order only 119–167 GW of new capacity 1994–2015 (AEO 1996, Table B9).

Even if one assumes an extremely high nuclear share for new orders (50%), the potential nuclear market is only ~3–~5 1000MW (1 GW) plants per year. This is far below the 31 GW rate of nuclear ordering 1970–1974 and implies that U.S. reactor vendors will need to supplement domestic orders with foreign sales to remain economically viable.

The task of energy demand forecasting is complicated by the need to anticipate social, economic, and technological behavior. The key technological projections involve the future cost of energy efficiency measures and the rate of technical change in energy conservation. The key sociological forecasts involve the direction of public policy, energy sector institutional design, and cultural change. The key economic predictions involve GDP growth rates, energy prices, and the future energy intensity of the economy's output mix.

The Energy Conservation Debate

The energy conservation debate reillustrates the impact of technological aesthetics and assumptions about future public policy on forecasting outcomes. Amory Lovins, the most well known advocate of increasing energy efficiency, argues that 75% of recent U.S. electricity production could be replaced at average costs of less than .6 c/kwh, and marginal costs of ~4 c/kwh (Lovins 7/90, 134, 136). These rates are well below current average production costs of ~7 c/kwh and my projected costs (7.5–8.5 c/kwh) for new nuclear power plants.[5] MIT economists Joskow and Marron find fewer opportunities for energy conservation and calculate that utility financed energy efficiency investments cost about 7.5 c/kwh, or three times Lovins' projections (Joskow and Marron 1992, 51,70).

Energy conservation skeptics generally use "top-down-econometric"-forecasting techniques, while Lovins and many energy efficiency enthusiasts use "bottom-up-technological costing"-models of energy efficiency potentials. Top-down econometric forecasts project future energy demand on the basis of past relationships between macroeconomic activity, energy prices, and energy demand. The models assume basic parameters (such as population growth and natural resource supply curves) and generate GDP predictions, energy demand levels, and so on, from a combination of historical behavior and optimizing assumptions.

Bottom-up forecasting models of energy demand use engineering cost projections for available (and in some case "anticipated") energy efficiency technologies to construct "conservation supply curves". The projections tend to assume fairly high levels of adoption for energy saving technologies (such as better insulation for homes and higher mpg cars) when they have lower life cycle costs than energy supply technologies.[6]

Top-down energy demand modelers criticize these bottom-up projections for allegedly ignoring the "hidden" costs involved with energy efficiency investments, in particular: the costs of acquiring information about energy efficiency, the utilities' costs for marketing and monitoring Demand Side Management programs, and the illiquidity costs of energy efficient investments due to their low resale value.[7] The top-down modelers also charge bottom-up forecasters with assuming overly optimistic costs and performance characteristics for some technologies (much like technological enthusiasts on the energy supply side),[8] ignoring the risk of technological obsolescence for expensive energy efficient equipment, using excessively low discount rates, ignoring subtle declines in consumer satisfaction associated with some energy efficiency substitutions (such as higher mpg autos, or shifting from incandescent to fluorescent lighting), and underestimating the durability of institutional obstacles (such as imperfect consumer access to capital) and consumer habits in estimating the market penetration of conservation technologies. Pessimists about conservation potentials suggest that these hidden obstacles explain why energy consumers have not adopted many conservation measures found to save money in engineering cost models.

Bottom-up forecasters reject most of these criticisms. They tie consumers' past neglect of energy savings to the logic of bounded rationality during times of cheap fossil fuels rather than the absence of opportunities for energy conservation. They argue that contextual changes, such as the OPEC price shocks and a cultural shift towards a conservationist ethic, leave past behavior a poor predictor of future behavior. They acknowledge that residual market imperfections, such as imperfect access to capital markets for homeowners, currently constrain energy efficiency investments, but expect these barriers to be reduced by institutional changes such as Demand Side Management (DSM) (which permits utilities to finance customer investments in energy efficiency measures at lower credit costs than available to private individuals).

While numerous bottom-up forecasters acknowledge that the transaction costs of energy conservation can be significant, they emphasize that many of these costs are sensitive to scaling economies. Energy efficiency information costs, for example, decline as technologies diffuse across the economy. Administrative costs for DSM programs fall as utilities capture scale economies and "learn" how to manage these programs with increased experience.[9] Illiquidity costs drop as speciality firms emerge that are able to certify residential energy efficiency levels for resale customers. Conservation enthusiasts also argue that the relative neglect of energy efficiency in the past augers well for R&D breakthroughs in the future.[10]

At least for the next few decades, an emerging consensus favors the energy efficiency perspective, implying that past industry and government conservation projections were too low. The consensus is greatest with respect to technological feasibility[11] and hardware engineering, and weakest with respect to institutional change and social engineering.

Policy Impact Debates

The level of U.S. energy consumption is surprisingly sensitive to public policy. Forecasters who assume aggressive government support for energy conservation project much lower levels of energy consumption than analysts assuming traditional government promotion of energy supply. Nuclear enthusiasts have generally assumed very limited government efforts to promote energy conservation.

The policy decisions that will most influence energy and electricity demand levels involve: tax and subsidy rates for energy supply and energy conservation technologies,[12] the treatment of energy sector negative externalities,[13] the level of energy efficiency requirements,[14] the shape of R&D policy,[15] the structure of electric utility regulation,[16] the character of government purchase decisions with respect to energy efficiency,[17] and the nature of infrastructural planning with respect to land use and transportation systems.[18]

It seems likely that public policies in the above areas will tilt energy consumption to the low side of conventional energy forecasts. Aggressive pursuit of the conservation options discussed above could reduce energy consumption by 30% from baseline levels. The persistence of low energy prices, however, could erode the current policy consensus in favor of energy conservation.

Cultural Directions

Future energy demand levels are sensitive to "cultural directions" because the latter influence political choices and people's tastes for energy efficient products. The marketability of activities and commodities such as recycling, "luxury cars" (or "gas guzzlers" depending upon cultural definition), and energy efficient buildings (with white roofs to reduce cooling needs, passive solar designs, and fluorescent lighting, for example) depends somewhat upon the degree of cultural support for energy conservation.

Cultural contexts will also influence the research interests of scientists and engineers, the education of architects and urban planners, the coverage by the media of energy efficiency opportunities, and long run decisions about land use and transportation systems. Commercial perception of cultural patterns will infuse market expectations and shape long run planning by industry.

The presence of path dependency in energy sector economics magnifies the impact of social factors on market outcomes. Scale economies seem especially important to the economics of energy efficiency with respect to information costs, management costs for DSM programs, the illiquidity costs of energy efficiency investments, and R&D. Normal scale and learning curve characteristics would also be assumed to accompany the production and evolution of most energy efficient products (such as automobiles or refrigerators).

The evolution of western societies since the 1960s suggests a broad shift in public opinion towards environmentalist and conservationist values. Whether this is due to the apparent income elasticity of these priorities or a discontinuous cultural change is uncertain, but the trend seems likely to continue.

Miscellaneous Economic Factors

The three major economic variables that will influence energy demand are GDP growth rates, fossil fuel prices, and the economy's energy/GDP ratio. The DOE's *Annual Energy Outlook 1995* foresaw annual real GDP growth averaging 1.5%–2.5% 1994–2015, with the reference case being 2.0% (Table 1). Assuming income elasticities of energy demand of ~.75, implies GDP fluctuations could add $+/- \sim.4\%$/yr. to energy and electricity demand.

Predicting energy prices is fraught with uncertainties. The DOE's projected energy prices to 2010, for example, have fallen by 29% for oil, 54% for natural gas, and 45% for coal over the last four years. The DOE currently expects moderate oil and natural gas price increases, falling coal prices, and stable electricity prices over the next two decades (table 11.1). The likely

Table 11.1
Energy Price Projections (1994$)

	actual 1994	reference case 2010		high ec. growth 2010	low ec growth 2010	high oil price 2010	low oil price 2010
		2010	2015				
Oil/bbl	15.52	23.70 *(33.40)	25.43	24.77 * (33.40)	22.60 *(33.40)	32.61 * (40.20)	16.02 *(22.60)
Domestic NG at Wellhead/tcf	1.88	2.15 *(4.65)	2.57	2.51 *(4.80)	1.82 *(4.62)	2.27 * (4.46)	2.01 *(4.00)
Coal/Mine short ton	19.41	17.43 *(31.63)	17.39	17.79 * (32.90)	16.96 *(29.98)	18.81 * (31.59)	16.59 *(31.40)
Electricity c/per kwh	7.1	7.0 *(6.99)	7.0	7.10 *(7.13)	6.7 *(6.96)	7.1 * (7.02)	6.8 *(6.74)

*To illustrate the volatility of energy price expectations, the DOE's 1992 forecast has been included in parentheses. The 1992 projections are priced in 1992$. All other entries are from the DOE's 1996 forecast.
Sources: DOE *Annual Energy Outlook 1996*, Appendix A, Tables A1, A8, B1, B8, C1, C8; *DOE Annual Energy Outlook 1992*, 3.

impact of fossil fuel price changes on nuclear power is ambiguous. While low fossil fuel prices help nuclear power by spurring energy demand, they hurt nuclear power by posing stiffer inter-fuel competition and dissolving the argument for a nuclear imperative. Conversely, while higher fossil-fuel prices improve nuclear power's relative competitive position, they contract energy demand. Given recent generating mixes, for example, a doubling of 1992 fossil fuel prices delivered to utilities would raise average electricity prices from ~7 c/kwh to ~8 c/kwh.[19] This price hike would be expected to reduce electricity demand by 10%–15%, and could wipe out enough new capacity needs to offset the benefits to nuclear power of higher fossil fuel prices.

Low energy demand forecasters expect continuing shifts in the economy from manufacturing to service employment (and within the manufacturing sector, from basic materials production to fabrication and assembly) to reduce the energy intensity of U.S. output.[20] Most high energy demand forecasters accept some of the structural decline argument with respect to overall energy demand (though they expect some offsetting trends, such as expanding air travel, to mute the decline) but balk at extending the slowdown to the demand for electricity. The DOE's WINES model for predicting nuclear power demand, for example, assumes electricity demand growth equal to GDP growth, explicitly rejecting analogies between falling energy/GDP ratios and electricity/GDP ratios (DOE (0438)(90), 10–11).[21]

Cross currents make it difficult to forecast the energy intensity of future

GDP. While the computer and electronic communications sector will certainly expand, their energy demands seem unlikely to offset the declining importance of and falling energy intensity in the manufacturing sector.[22] The widespread adoption of the electric car would be another matter,[23] but this seems unlikely in the foreseeable future. Overall, the energy intensity of GDP will likely continue to fall, while the ratio of electricity-use to GDP will remain constant or drop slightly. The uncertainties in this area are large.

Conclusions

Paradigmatic Nature of Demand Forecasting

The energy demand controversy reillustrates the paradigmatic nature of energy sector debates. Fundamental assumptions that are difficult to falsify empirically underlie many demand forecasting disagreements. Energy demand forecasts are especially sensitive to engineering intuitions because of the need for energy efficiency projections to aggregate applications across sites and activities that are too numerous, too specialized, and too rapidly changing to permit case by case review. Table 11.2 compares the technological aesthetics underlying the intuitions associated with high and low energy demand forecasts. The table also notes the different normative judgments that encourage analysts to prefer increasing energy supply or increasing energy efficiency in energy policy making.

As table 11.2 suggests, both energy efficiency enthusiasts and skeptics accuse each other of bounded rationalities and flawed forecasting methodologies. They have fundamentally different intuitions about the long run linkages between energy consumption and GDP growth. They also tend to assume different capacities for social and institutional change. The bottom line is that low energy demand forecasters assume a much more significant break with past energy consumption habits and relationships than high energy demand forecasters.

Probable Demand Levels

Future energy demand will probably be lower than anticipated by conventional forecasters. Assuming a continuing political tilt towards increased energy efficiency, a reasonable range for primary energy demand in 2030

Table 11.2
Energy Efficiency Enthusiasts and Energy Efficiency Skeptics

Enthusiasts   *Skeptics*

Technological Aesthetics

I) Role of Energy

Enthusiasts	Skeptics
Energy efficiency easily substitutable for energy supply	Energy relatively unique input, energy = power = affluence, energy efficiency desirable but mere footnote to energy policy

II) Sociology of Knowledge/Bounded Rationality Concerns

Historical inattention of skeptics to energy efficiency opportunities prevents existing technical assessments from capturing full potential of energy conservation; underestimation of impact of scaling and other path dependent cost reductions on energy conservation options	Tendency for energy efficiency advocates to assume excessively optimistic cost and performance characteristics, typical of most enthusiasts for new technologies; neglect of potential problem areas accompanying energy efficiency investments, such as transaction costs, unexpected environmental externalities & subtle product quality losses

III) Forecasting Methodologies

Heavy reliance on technology costing, engineering based models for assessing economic competitiveness and market penetration of energy efficient technologies; critical of econometric forecasting models for projecting past demand relationships into the future	Heavy reliance on econometric models for projecting energy demand; critical of technology costing models of energy efficiency potential for underestimating the cost of energy conservation.

IV) Social Dynamics

Anticipate social and institutional changes to facilitate adoption of cost effective energy efficiency opportunities	Expect social and institutional inertia to seriously interfere with deployment of new energy efficient technologies

---

Normative Judgments

I) Conservation

Concern about materials scarcity (especially potential fossil fuel scarcity), fear that market decisions deplete resources too quickly	Reject "Limits to Growth" fears, affirm faith in market rationing of scarce resources, greater fear of economic stagnation from regulatory burdens than fear of resource scarcity from excessive market depletion rates

II) Negative Externalities

Strong concern about enviornmental and national security externalities of energy consumption; presumption that energy conservation brings large environmental benefits	Fear energy externality regulation to be Pandora's box for politicizing energy pricing and dulling market efficiency; anticipate marginal costs exceed marginal benefits for many new environmental protection regs.; anticipate new environmental hazards from energy efficiency (such as indoor air pollution) to limit environmental payoffs to energy conservation.

Table 11.2 *continued*

Normative Judgments

III) Politics

Openness to social engineering to promote energy efficiency; preference for small, local economic units over large corporate entities	Skeptical about effectiveness of social engineering, respectful of productivity of large corporate entities, willing to accommodate corporate interests with public assistance

seems 80–125 Quads, with electricity demand varying between 3,000 TWH–5,400 TWH, (reflecting annual growth rates of -.0015% to + 1% for primary demand and 0–1.5% for electricity demand). Uncertainties about numerous factors (GDP growth rates, energy price levels, the behavior of technical change, the shape of public policy, the direction of popular tastes, etc.) leave the boundaries somewhat elastic, particularly on the upside. Lower than expected energy prices would especially encourage higher energy consumption, both through price effects and reduced political pressures for institutional changes encouraging energy efficiency.

A more certain conclusion is that energy and electricity demand are quite sensitive to public policy decisions and the capture of path dependent cost reductions for energy efficient technologies. Much of the energy efficiency vision seems achievable with sympathetic government action. Thus from a public policy point of view, backcasting claims seem more relevant than forecasting exercises.

In settling on energy demand forecasts that are lower than most DOE and industry projections, I have tended to accept bounded rationality criticisms of conventional forecasters, both with respect to the technical potential for increased energy conservation and the ability of public policy to capture this potential. The technical errors seem a legacy of past habits of mind, while the political errors reflect an underestimation of the clout of the energy efficiency movement at the national as well as the local level.

While national campaigns by groups like the Union of Concerned Scientists and Environmental Defense Fund are quite effective, the decentralized lobbying of state Public Utility Commissions, legislatures, local politicians, and local media by local energy efficiency groups is even more impressive. There currently exists a powerful flow of information and expertise between local and national environmental and energy efficiency activist groups. Journals such as *Nucleus* and *Amicus,* quickly introduce the newest findings of energy efficiency advocates into local utility and government planning debates. Representatives of The Natural Resources Defense Council (NRDC), for example, have worked closely with PG&E in California to reorient its generating mix towards demand side management. Environmentalists have similarly elected conservation oriented individuals to the board of directors of the Sacramento Municipal Utility District and they have made increasing consumer energy efficiency the utility's top priority (SMUD 1/94).

While lower than conventional forecasts, the 80–125 Quad and 3000–5400 TWH energy demand projections offered above are still higher than some conservation scenarios projected by energy efficiency enthusiasts. These lower energy forecasts seem to underestimate the intransigence of some institutional obstacles to energy efficiency in the absence of crisis environments. Some of the projections also seem prey to the same kind of excess technological optimism and neglect of implementation details (such as transaction costs) that plagued nuclear cost forecasts.

Implications for Nuclear Power

There are two major implications of the energy demand debate for nuclear power.

(1) The level of energy demand is likely to be somewhat lower than projected in industry forecasts with a corresponding reduction in the demand for nuclear output. While cheap fossil fuel prices could significantly increase energy demand, this would probably not aid nuclear power. Significant deployment of the electric car could help nuclear power.

(2) Energy efficiency investments are a threatening competitor for nuclear power, especially in an energy crisis environment. One of the largest uncertainties with respect to energy demand is the degree of public policy support for energy conservation. A surge of government aid large enough to win OT status for energy efficiency investments could dissolve many of the institutional barriers in the way of energy conservation. This support could arise in response to an OPEC price increase, pessimistic reassessments of world fossil fuel reserves, or severe greenhouse constraints. This scenario is important as it offers an alternative policy initiative to the renewed capture of OT status for nuclear power often adduced from such environments by nuclear power advocates.

Chapter 12

Nuclear Competition: Supply Side*

Overview

Nuclear power will face stiff competition over the next forty years from alternative energy technologies. This chapter begins with an overview of this challenge and then addresses each competing option in detail. Cheap fossil fuels are expected until at least 2015, with large reductions in renewable energy costs anticipated by 2030. As a result, expected nuclear costs will have to fall below 6 c/kwh in order to regain utility attention.

Fossil Fuel Competition 1995–2015–2030

In the absence of serious greenhouse constraints, nuclear power will probably face coal-fired generating costs of ~5.0–6.50 c/kwh and natural gas-fired generating costs of ~3.75 to 5.5 c/kwh during the 1995–2015 period. For at least the next dozen years (and perhaps as long as thirty to forty years) it appears gas will easily dominate nuclear power due to very low wellhead prices, new optimism about gas reserves, significant improvements in gas-generating technologies, and gas-fired plants' short construction periods. Without greenhouse penalties, coal generating costs could remain below 6.5 c/kwh over the next fifty years, due to coal's enormous resource base, flat long run supply curve, and anticipated technological improvements. Both the coal and natural gas industries have political allies and can expect some social support for the institutional infrastructure necessary to realize their technological potential.

*All costs denominated in 1992 $ unless otherwise specified.

241

Renewable Energy Competition

Technical innovations have also brought expected generating costs for renewable energy technologies (RETs) in 2010 down to the 4.5–6.5 c/kwh range for well-sited biomass, wind, hydroelectric, and geothermal projects. While various constraints appear to limit tapping these sources for more than 100 GW of new capacity (nuclear equivalent) over the next twenty years, with a modest increase in R&D, their thirty to forty year supply potential is as high as 300–500 GW/yr (nuclear equivalent) (SERI 1990, 40).

Because of the many different kinds of renewable energy technologies, it is difficult to generalize about RET economics. Nevertheless some summary judgments are possible:

- the youthfulness of most technologies suggests a large opportunity for cost declines and dangers of premature cost optimism due to neglect of institutional and other concealed obstacles.

- recent reductions in wind, biomass, and solar electric generating costs lend historical support for long run cost optimism.

- while there are large uncertainties accompanying each individual option, aggregate uncertainties are smaller. It is easier to predict that some RET technologies will generate electricity at less than 6 c/kwh in 2025, than which ones.

- future RET costs will be quite sensitive to government energy policy, especially with respect to R&D support, regulatory treatment, and risk-reducing assistance.

- future RET costs will also be sensitive to the technologies' scale of deployment, with potential cost declines accompanying mass production, learning curve cost reductions, and other path-dependent phenomena, such as breakthroughs in complementary technologies. Beyond a certain level of deployment, however, the intermittency of some renewable energy technologies, such as wind energy, may increase marginal costs due to the need for increased energy storage capacities.

As subsequent sections will detail,[1] the most promising RET generating options over the next twenty to forty years are:

—wind   4.00 c/kwh–5 c/kwh by 2010.
         15–35 GW new capacity (nuclear equivalent) by 2010.

Possible costs as low as ~3.5–5 c/kwh by 2030,
50–150+ new GW (nuclear equivalent) by 2030.

—biomass   4.5 c/kwh–7 c/kwh by 2010,
10–25 GW new capacity (nuclear equivalent) by 2010.
25–100 GW by 2030.

—hydro   ~6.5 c/kwh current costs.
0–8 GW new capacity by 2010.
0–45 new GW by 2030 depending on siting constraints.

—geothermal   ~5–7 c/kwh current costs (hydrothermal),
~6–10 c/kwh near term projected costs for hot dry
rock (HDR).
5–10 GW new capacity (all types) by 2010.
Potential costs for HDR as low as 3–6 c/kwh,
30GW-enormous supply by 2030 with successful
development of HDR technology.

Major contributions also appear possible from photovoltaics and solar thermal in twenty to forty years:

—photovoltaic   8.5–10.5 c/kwh by 2010.
0–2 GW new capacity by 2010.
Potential costs as low as 4.5–7.5 c/kwh by 2030,
40–100 new GW by 2030.

—solar thermal   5.5–~8 c/kwh, by 2010,
1–5 GW new capacity by 2010.
Potential costs as low as 5–6 c/kwh by 2030,
50–100+ new GW by 2030.

The economics of other energy options, such as tidal energy, wave energy, ocean-thermal energy, and fusion energy are more speculative at this point.

Supply Side Implications

In the absence of greenhouse constraints, utility planning would rely on natural gas in the short run and coal in the long run. The availability of cheap gas and coal-fired electricity would seriously limit investments in renewable energy and nuclear technologies until fossil fuel prices rose significantly or empirical evidence proved the competitiveness of non-fossil fuel options. Modest RET investments might continue at the most favorable sites since they would not expose investors to the massive risks of a new 1000

MW nuclear project. "Green"-oriented consumers might also choose to pay a premium for RET based kwhs if given the opportunity to choose their generating source under utility deregulation.

In an ungreenhouse-constrained world nuclear power would be a "shelved"-technology, awaiting demonstrable failures from other options before capturing renewed commercial (as opposed to research) investments.

Even in a greenhouse constrained world, nuclear power faces very stiff competition. Increased natural gas, coal, and RET generation would appear able to meet all electricity needs through 2010 without additional nuclear generating capacity if: (1) greenhouse ceilings permit increased coal and natural gas-fired electricity as long as total GHG emissions approximate 1990 levels (permitting fossil fuel fired kwhs to increase in tandem with higher energy conversion efficiencies and GHG offsets, such as tree planting); (2) annual electricity demand growth is ~1.5% or less (the high end of forecast demand in chapter 11); and (3) natural gas and renewable technologies expand at modest rates. Beyond 2010 the picture is brighter for renewables and more severe greenhouse constraints could be accommodated without pressures for increased use of nuclear power.

Technological Aesthetics

The following discussion explores the nature of alternative electricity-generating technologies in more detail, discussing each option's expected costs, resource base, potential environmental and other negative externalities, attendant public policy issues, and sensitivity to path dependent factors for economic viability. The implications of greenhouse constraints are analyzed in chapter 13.

The analysis highlights the impact on technology assessment of technological aesthetics and derived engineering intuitions about: (1) the long run fertility of different research agendas; (2) the payoffs to different kinds of energy system strategies, such as diffuse versus concentrated energy sources; and (3) the weights assigned to different energy sector externalities. Like nuclear power cost forecasts, fossil fuel and renewable energy cost predictions are dominated by assumptions about future cost trajectories, rather than calculations of current costs. Forecasters must predict:

- R&D payoffs (e.g., the return to genetic engineering research for biomass energy or deep drilling R&D for fossil fuel and geothermal energy)

- learning curve behavior (e.g., expected cost declines from routine learning from windmill siting experience or PV rooftop installation)

- the impact of standardization and mass production economies (e.g., the impact of scale economies on the cost of solar thermal or photovoltaic cells)

- the reproducibility of best current practices (e.g., the reproducibility of best windmill or low head hydro experience)

- the likelihood of investments in complementary R&D (e.g., investments in energy storage and transmission technologies for improved solar and wind economics)

- the evolution of congenial infrastructures for RET deployment (e.g., the reoptimizing utility generating mix strategies to include intermittents and the restructuring of utility regulation to accommodate dispersed producers).

While judgments about the above possibilities are not arbitrary, they permit disagreements based on broad intuitions about technological evolution that are not subject to simple empirical falsification or contradiction by engineering or economic theory.

Technological aesthetics also influence judgments about: (1) the significance of various indirect cost factors, such as planning flexibility; (2) the value placed on the size of a technology's resource base; and (3) the significance of different energy sector externalities.

(Readers uninterested in the details of non-nuclear energy development may wish to skip to section 10)

Natural Gas

Overview and Costs

Over the next ten to fifteen years natural gas seems the fuel of choice for firing new generating capacity. It is currently cheap, easily integrated into utility planning, and the most environmentally benign of the fossil fuels. The major uncertainties in the natural gas sector involve long run fuel costs and potential greenhouse constraints. Gas optimists foresee delivered gas costs to utilities remaining below $6.25 per million BTUs (/MMBTU) for many decades. This implies gas-fired generating costs of less than 6.0 c/kwh (see table 12.1) and would probably discourage utility investment in new nuclear plants. Pessimists expect fears of greenhouse constraints and steep natural gas price increases to limit the use of natural gas.

Resource Base

There have been major increases in natural gas reserve estimates over the last fifteen years. In 1995, for example, the U.S. Geological Survey nearly tripled its on-shore, conventional gas reverse estimates (DOE, *Annual Energy Outlook 1996* p. 9). These revisions reflect the youthfulness of research into the geology of natural gas in non-oil bearing strata, new search and forecasting techniques, innovations in unconventional gas recovery, and the erosion of downward forecasting biases after the lifting of price controls on natural gas. Recent projections of economically recoverable reserves *(using existing technology)* in the lower forty-eight states generally range from ~900–1200+ Quads, or about forty-five to sixty years supply at recent consumption rates (~20 Quads/yr). There appear to be promising R&D options that could trap massive new reserves from unconventional sources, such as Alaskan and offshore reservoirs, coal seams, tight sands and Devonian Shale, and more speculatively, gas from geopressured brines, ice bound methane, and perhaps "primordial" or inorganic sources.

World reserves appear to be at least 20 times the size of U.S. reserves and increased international trade is likely. The DOE foresees imports (mainly from Canada and Mexico) rising from ~1.5 Quads in 1990 to ~4.5 Quads in 2015 (DOE, *Annual Energy Outlook* 1996, Table A-1). While the relatively high costs of liquid natural gas (LNG) transport (~$2.50/mcf–~$3.50/mcf) will limit LNG imports in the short run, large growth is possible in the long run, should the U.S. and foreign exporters invest in expensive liquefaction, shipping, and regasification facilities.

Environmental and Other Externalities

Natural gas is the most benign fossil fuel from an environmental perspective.[2] The major environmental concerns about natural gas combustion arise from greenhouse gas emissions. While the best of the fossil fuels, an efficient gas-fired power plant still produces ~1/3 kg carbon dioxide (or ~.1 kg of carbon) per kilowatt hour of electricity. The greenhouse burden of gas-fired power plants is at least 25% higher, if the indirect greenhouse effects of gas production and use are included.[3] The most important non-environmen-

Table 12.1
Natural Gas-Fired Generating Costs Mid-1992 $

Technology	Capital $/KW	Cost M/kwh*	Conversion Efficiency	fuel costs (M/kwh) @ gas costs of 2.25, 3.50, 5.00 & 7.50/MMBTU	O&M M/kwh	Total Costs @ 2.25, 5.0 & 7.50/MMBTU
Current Gas Fired Steam Turbines[1]	$813	14.5	36%	21, 33, 47, 71	6.5	42, 68, 92
Gas Turbines[2]	$214–$321	4–6	30%	26, 40, 57, 85	6.0	37, 68, 96
Combined Cycle[3a]	$556	10	47%	16, 25, 36, 54	6.0	32, 52, 70
Steam Injected Gas Turbine[3b]	$439	8	40%	19, 30, 43, 64	6.5	34, 58, 79
Intercooled Steam Injected Gas Turbine[3c]	$428	8	46%	16, 25, 36, 54	6.5	31, 51, 69
Chemically Recuperated Gas Turbine[4]	$600	11	52.5%	15, 23, 33, 49	6.5	33, 51, 67

(*) Capital costs/kwh assume 65% capacity rates and .103 FCR unless otherwise specified. All dollars are 1992 $.

Notes

1. Fulkerson et al. 1990, 89 (original costs multiplied by 1.07 to transform presumably 1990 $ into 1992 $). The Congressional Research Service projected costs of 3.9 c/kwh (1985 $) in 1991 assuming natural gas prices of $2.25/mcf (CRS 6/91, 15) and 6.2 c/kwh for gas prices of $4.50/mcf. O&M costs from DOE *Annual Outlook for U.S. Electrical Power 1991*, 56.

2. Grubb et al. 1991, 96; O&M costs from DOE *Annual Outlook for U.S. Electrical Power 1991*, 56; both sources' cost estimates multiplied by 1.07 to transform presumably 1990 $ into 1992 $.

3a. Fulkerson et al. 1990, 89, "optimistic but achievable." The estimates of the National Research Council's Greenhouse Mitigation study are in a similar range: ~$500/KW and ~50+% conversion efficiency (National Research Council 1991, 6–6). Williams projects costs of $493/KW and a conversion efficiency of 42.5% (1987 $) (Williams 1990, 41). The Congressional Research Service projects costs of 3.3 c/kwh and 5 c/kwh (1985 $) assuming natural gas prices of $2.25/ mcf and $4.50/mcf (CRS 6/91, 15). The price drops to 3.1 c/kwh and 4.8 c/kwh for advanced CCs. O&M costs based on Williams 1990, 43.

3b. Fulkerson et al. 1990, 89, "optimistic but achievable." The Congressional Research Service projects capital costs of ~$600/KW and overall generating costs of 4.1 c/kwh and 6.2 c/kwh (1985 $), assuming natural gas prices of $2.25/mcf and $4.50/mcf (CRS 6/91, CRS-15). O&M costs assumed to be same as for ISTIG plants. Williams projects capital costs of $505/KW (1987 $) and a conversion efficiency of 47% (Williams 1990, 43). O&M costs based on Williams 1990, 43.

3c. Fulkerson et al. 1990, 89, "optimistic but achievable." Williams projects capital costs of $600/KW and overall generating costs of 3.7 c/kwh and 5.4 c/kwh (1985 $), assuming natural gas prices of $2.25/mcf and $4.50/mcf (CRS 6/91, CRS, 15). O&M costs based on Williams 1990, 43.

tal externality of natural gas use is the national security concern of potentially increased reliance upon imported energy sources.[4] LNG also raises
safety issues with respect to shipping and port facilities.

Opportunities for Technological Change

Recent breakthroughs with respect to combined cycle and steam injected gas turbine plants reillustrate the sensitivity of energy sector economics to R&D levels and commercial expectations. Combined cycle plants
burn natural gas in compressed air, relying on the mixture's expansion to
directly drive generating turbines. The turbine's hot outlet gases are then
used to boil water for traditional steam turbines. Overall energy conversion
efficiencies of 45%–60% are expected. Fears of natural gas scarcity appear
to have discouraged R&D and commercial development in this field until the
late-eighties.[5] Most forecasters now expect sharp increases in CC deployment in the near future.[6]

Steam Injected Gas Turbines [STIG] plants utilize recent breakthroughs
in aeroderivative gas turbine technology. Heavy DoD funding of jet engine
R&D (~$.5 billion/yr. during the last decade) has made possible steady
improvements in turbine blade materials and turbine cooling.[7] Several other
gas burning technologies have also experienced, and/or promise, rapid technical advance.[8]

Path Dependency, Public Policy, and Future Nuclear/Gas Competition

U.S. natural gas consumption will probably expand substantially for at
least twenty years, and perhaps much longer. Along with coal, gas will fuel
most new generating capacity through 2015, due to its low fuel and capital
costs, enhancement of utility planning flexibility, and relative environmental
benefits. Shifting an additional 2 quads of natural gas to electricity generation (a conceivable outcome) would permit the *growth* in natural gas-fired
electricity to entirely replace the nuclear sector's 1992 output.[9]

At average 1994 gas prices of ~$2.25/MMBTU delivered to utilities
and accompanying generating costs of ~3.25 c/kwh (historical $) (*MER*
5/95, 125) for combined cycle plants,[10] gas-fired electricity costs less than
one-half of my predicted costs for new nuclear powered electricity. Even at
twice the DOE's projected delivered price to the utilities of $2.95/MMBTU
in 2015 (DOE, *Annual Energy Outlook 1996* Table A-3), gas-fired plants

will probably produce cheaper electricity (5.5 c/kwh–6 c/kwh) than nuclear power.[11]

Utilities will also be drawn to new gas units because of their shorter and more predictable lead time (two to four years, versus six to ten years for nuclear plants), their availability in modest increments (100 MW for example, for a STIG unit versus ~1000 MW for conventional nuclear plants), and their modest capital costs. Gas generation is also likely to be a fuel of choice for non-utility cogenerators[12] and independent power producers, whose role in electricity supply is expected to grow rapidly in a deregulated electricity generating industry.[13]

The economics of natural gas-fired electricity is somewhat sensitive to the direction of public policy and degree of capture of path dependent economies we have associated with OT status. Because of the large economies of scale in the economics of pipeline transport (both in terms of pipe diameters and in-place utilization rates) and the high capital costs and long lead times involved with LNG gas transport, large investment commitments are required to capture the full promise of gas-fired technology. Clear demonstrations of government support for expanded natural gas use could facilitate capture of this potential. Perhaps most helpful would be minimum price guarantees for unconventional gas supplies as fear of competition from cheap coal and/or breakthroughs in renewable technologies seriously inhibits new initiatives in the gas industry (much as fear of cheap gas inhibits risk taking in other energy sectors).

Government leadership also seems important in the R&D area, where the inability to fully internalize the benefits of technical change can lead to underfunding by the private sector. Breakthroughs in aeroderivative gas turbines in the 1980s, for example, were the product of government military research.

While gas technologies would benefit significantly from OT status, they are also relatively well suited for marginal expansion. Congeniality with incremental, rather than system-wide deployment, gives gas technology a significant market advantage over options like nuclear power, which appear to require large deployment in order to approach competitive economics. Proponents of "soft energy paths" have highlighted this aspect of gas economics in urging that it be used as a "bridging fuel," in order to buy time for the successful development of renewable technologies. A similar argument could be made for expanding gas consumption as a bridge to a second nuclear era built around passively safe reactor designs.

Coal

Overview and Costs

Coal has been nuclear power's most direct competitor over the last twenty years and is likely to share this role with natural gas over the next twenty years. As a fuel, coal has three major advantages: (1) abundant supply (global reserves of about 1500 years at current consumption rates); (2) low current production costs (~$1.50/MMBTU) and a relatively flat long run supply schedule; and (3) domestic availability. Coal's major disadvantages involve environmental, health, and safety hazards.

Most forecasters expect new conventional coal power plant costs to range between 5 and 6.5 c/kwh, with more innovative technologies, such as fluidized bed combustion (FBC) and integrated coal gasification combined cycle (IGCC) plants, offering potentially lower costs (see table 12.2). As a rule, cost-saving technical innovations are expected to offset more stringent environmental standards. The relative maturity of many coal technologies and assurances of fuel supply make it unlikely that unexpected coal-fired generating cost increases could impart a large economic advantage to new nuclear plants. Coal thus seems to provide an insurance policy that minimizes the economic risks of a nuclear moratorium. The one wildcard qualifying this judgment (and it is a major qualifier) are greenhouse gas concerns. Limitations on CO_2 releases could sharply escalate coal generating costs and/or limit the quantity of coal burned.

Resource Base

Proven global coal reserves in 1990 were estimated at more than 21,000 Quads, representing more than 200 years use at current global consumption rates (World Resources Institute 1990, 144). Economically recoverable world reserves are projected in the neighborhood of 150,000 Quads (Fulkerson et al. 1990, 91). The U.S. has been nicknamed the Saudi Arabia of coal and has proven coal reserves 43% larger than the sum of the world's oil and natural gas reserves (World Resources Institute 1990, 144). This large and economically accessible resource base is expected to prevent significant coal price increases. In 1994 the delivered price of coal to utilities was $1.36/MMBTU (1994 $) (DOE, *Annual Energy Outlook 1996*, 78–79). The DOE's forecast price for 2015 is only $1.28/MMBTU (Ibid.).

Table 12.2
Coal-Fired Generating Cost Estimates mid-1992 Mills/kwh*

Summary Results

Advanced Pulverized Coal Plants	47–62
Fluidized Bed Combustors	51–69
Integrated Coal Gasification Combined Cycle Plants (IGCC)	45–~65
Coal Integrated Gasifier / Intercooled Steam Injected Gas Turbine (CIG/ISTIG)	~45–~48 +

Findings of Specific Studies

Source Date of study	New Steam Plants	AFBC or PFBC	OTHER
USCEA[1] 6/92	47–49		IGCC 49–51
DOE[2] 3/92		AFBC 51–61	IGCC 46–51
NRC[3] 6/91	~53		
Manne and[4] Richels 1990	59		Gasification Feasible at ~65
ORNL[5] June 1987	59		
CRS[6] 1991	60	AFBC PFBC 60 69	IGCC 65 Coal-gas fuel cell 62 M/kwh
Williams[7] 1990	62		CIG/ISTIG 45 M/kwh
Grubb[8] 1991			CIG/ISTIG ~48

Notes to Table 12.2

*Studies' forecasts converted to 3rd quarter 1992 $ using GDP deflator from table B-3, 1993 *Economic Report of the President*. No effort has been made to standardize other aspects of the studies' methodologies. Cost figures contained in the footnotes below have been left in the original dollars of the works cited.

1. U.S. CEA, 6/92 (1/92 $). Calculations assume 6.2% real interest rate, 10.6% fcr, nth of a kind plant, capital costs of $1302–$1394/KW (Pulverized Coal) and $1629–$1728/KW (IGCC), capacity rates of 80%, initial fuel costs of $1.46/MMBTU w/1.2% annual real escalation, ~35% energy conversion efficiency, $25–$29/KW fixed O&M costs, 4 M/kwh variable O&M (14, 20). Ranges reflect difference between 600 MW and 1200 MW plants.

2. DOE 3/92 (~1992 $). AFBC cost projection based on capital costs of $1200–$1400/KW and efficiencies of 35%–36% (p. 15). IGCC cost projection based on capital costs of $1100–$1400/KW and efficiency of 40%–42% (p. 25). (Numbers in table 12.2 assume 1/92 $).

3. National Research Council 1991, table I-2 (presumably 1991 $). NRC cost estimates based on: $1537/KW capital costs, 65% capacity rate, .106 FCR (implying capital costs of 28.6 M/kwh); Heat Rate of 9,080 BTU/kwh (37.6% eff), coal at $1.31/MMBTU (implying fuel costs

Environmental and Other Externalities

Coal energy's negative externalities are dominated by occupational and environmental hazards.[14] The main focus of regulatory policy has recently been on acid rain. While the 1990 Clean Air Act Amendments (CAA) significantly reduced allowable sulfur dioxide (SO_2) emissions, rapid technical change and institutional innovations, such as emission rights trading, are expected to moderate the Act's economic impact on coal-fired utilities. The DOE has predicted an average increase in coal-fired generating costs of only a few mills/kwh in response to the CAA amendments (DOE, *Annual Outlook for U.S. Electric Power 1991*, ch. 3).

There has been substantial achievement, but continued need for additional redress with respect to many other social costs of coal usage, such as mining hazards, the containment of land subsidence and acid runoffs from underground mining, land scarring, erosion and stream filling from strip mining, and non-SO_2 and NO_x air pollutants from coal combustion, such as particulate matter, hazardous trace elements, and VOCs (volatile organic compounds). The inconvenience and traffic hazards at rail crossings caused by coal transport can also be surprisingly large.

Notes to Table 12.2 continued

of 11.9 M/kwh), fixed O&M of $29/KW or 5.1 M/kwh and variable O&M of 5.7 M/kwh, for total costs of 51.3 M/kwh.

4. Manne and Richels 4/90, 60 (12/88 $). 20% Co_2 reduction feasible for coal gasification plants with less than 6 c/kwh generating costs and 93% Co_2 reduction feasible at ~7.5 c/kwh.

5. ORNL 6/87 (1986 $). Cost calculations for a 550 MW coal plant in vicinity of Chicago, on-line in 2000. Capital cost calculations assume $1310/KW construction costs, a capacity rate of 70%, and a real FCR .0961, for total capital costs of 20.6 M/kwh. O&M costs assume $24/KW fixed and 2.1 M/kwh variable (for plant w/FGD and 3.5% S) for total O&M costs of 5.9 m/kwh. Fuel costs assume delivered high sulfur coal at $1.60/MMBTU (1986) escalating at 1% per year, heat rate of 9,900 BTU/kwh for eastern coal, for fuel costs of 20.7 M/kwh. Decommissioning costs assumed to be .1 M/kwh (pp. 29–31, 36, 42, 46, 60).

6. Congressional Research Service 6/91, p. CRS-15.

7. Robert Williams 1990, 43, 45 (1987 $). Williams assumes a 500 MW pulverized coal plant w/FGD at $1410/KW, 75% capacity rates, and .103 FCR, for capital costs of 22.1 M/kwh; Heat Rate of 10,060 BTU/kwh (33.9% efficiency) and coal at $1.89/MMBTU, for fuel costs of 19.0 M/kwh, and O&M costs of 9.8 M/kwh, for total costs of ~51 M/kwh. The *Proposed* Coal-Integrated Gasifier/Intercooled Steam-Injected Gas Turbine (CIG-ISTIG) assumes a 109 MW plant, w/$1032/KW, 75% capacity rates, .103 FCR, for capital costs of 16.2 M/kwh; Heat Rate of 8,107 BTU/kwh and coal costs of $1.89/MMBTU, for fuel costs of 15.3 M/kwh and O&M costs of 5.5, for total costs of 37 M/kwh.

8. Grubb et al. 1991, 101, citing Larson (1989), assuming 100 MW plant and coal at $1.8/GJ (1987 $).

Table 12.3
Emissions Profile
New Coal Generating Technologies[1]

Technology	% So_2 Reduction	% NO_X Reduction	kG C per kwh*	Conversion Efficiency
Conventional Coal w/FGD	90	300**	.25	34%
AFBC[2]	90	70	.24	36%
PFBC	90	80	.19	42
IGCC	99	90+	.20	42
STIG	99	90+	.24	36
ISTIG	99	90+	.20	42

Notes

*kG Carbon as Co_2/kwh

**Conventional Coal w/FGD emits 300 mg No_x per million joules of electricity (.00108 kg No_x/kwh). Subsequent reductions treat this as a baseline figure.

1. Source unless otherwise specified: Fulkerson et al. 1990, 89.

2. DOE 3/92, 15. Carbon emissions unreported, assumed to be similar to STIG due to similar energy conversion efficiencies.

Greenhouse Issues

The major wildcard effecting the coal sector is the greenhouse effect. Serious efforts to curb CO_2 discharges will probably require reductions in coal-fired plant emissions, as they account for about one-third of U.S. CO_2 emissions. While uncertainties abound, it seems likely that:

- 20% to 25% reductions in coal plant CO_2/kwh emissions could be achieved relatively cheaply by shifting from conventional coal plants with energy conversion efficiencies of ~34% to newer designs with projected conversion efficiencies of ~42% (Fulkerson et al. 1990, 89; Williams 1990). Longer term goals of 50%+ energy conversion rates might double these gains.

- a substantial amount of coal-fired CO_2 could be offset by slowing deforestation and/or reforesting appropriate topography.

- a large amount of inexpensive greenhouse gas abatement could be achieved in non-coal related areas of the economy, but it is not clear that coal-fired plants will be able to buy offset credits from these abaters.

- mechanically capturing and storing CO_2 will probably be prohibitively expensive.

- more ambitious abatement initiatives, such as climatic engineering, are unlikely in the short and medium term.

Overall, it appears that inexpensive strategies are available to permit up to a 50% expansion of the coal sector without significant increases in CO_2 emissions. Significant reductions in U.S. carbon dioxide discharges, such as cutbacks of 20%, however, will require institutional innovations for trading CO_2 offsets, major abatement initiatives beyond current planning, or constraints on future coal use. These options are explored in more detail in chapter 13.

Opportunities for Technological Change

While coal suffered from a sense of technological satiation in the late-sixties, the DOE's large "Clean Coal" and "Combustion 2000" R&D programs have contributed to a renewed sense of technological optimism. Many new coal combustion technologies promise lower coal generating costs and higher environmental protection. The most important innovations involve fluidized bed combustion (FBC)[15] and integrated gasification combined cycle (IGCC) plants.[16] There are also numerous interesting R&D opportunities to address coal's environmental hazards, especially with respect to acid rain.[17]

Public Policy and Path Dependencies

Strong R&D support has recently been the most important government assistance to the coal sector. Since 1986 $2.75 billion in federal funds and somewhat more in required matching funds from private sources have been earmarked for clean coal research.[18] The pace of future coal sector technical change will be significantly influenced by the level of new R&D spending.

The key regulatory decisions shaping coal's future involve environmental policy, both with respect to the level of pollution reduction and the efficiency of abatement responses. Recent regulatory reforms that shift pollution abatement from mandatory equipment installation to a fee for pollution emissions rights allows for flexible abatement responses and may reduce the cost of any given level of pollution reduction significantly.

The full exploitation of coal power would require large infrastructural investments (for example, piping grids for combined heat and power cogeneration systems, new slurry pipelines, and railroad upgrades for coal transport). Fears of cheap natural gas, possible breakthroughs in renewable energy options, and environmental constraints on coal use will probably preclude private capital from taking advantage of some of these opportunities.

Nuclear vs. Coal: Conclusion

It is probably wise to expect coal generating costs in the high end of predicted ranges (5.0 c/kwh–6.50 c/kwh) due to the tendency for overoptimism on the part of a technology's sponsors. Even with this caveat, however, coal electricity could probably underprice nuclear power indefinitely if it were not for concerns about global warming.

As elaborated in chapter 13, the most likely range of government mandated greenhouse gas reductions over the next two decades is 0%–20%. Such reductions could be accommodated by the coal sector alongside a 10%–20% expansion in output without eroding coal's economic advantage over nuclear power.

While uncertainties about future coal regulation and the level of competition from natural gas and renewable energy sources are likely to discourage some coal investments, coal technology can probably evolve incrementally more easily than nuclear power. The compatibility of IGCC technology with existing gas-fired combined cycle plants offers a particularly attractive development path. It thus seems likely that coal power will continue to push nuclear technology to the edges of energy policy.

Petroleum

Nuclear power and oil compete directly in very few markets. Only 3% of U.S. electricity is currently oil fired and the DOE foresees no increase in this percentage over the next twenty years (DOE, *Annual Energy Outlook* 1996, 94–95). About two-thirds of oil consumption involves transportation demand. Nuclear-fired electricity can not compete with the internal combustion engine without significant constraints on auto emissions. If a portion of the light vehicle market is reserved for zero emission vehicles, nuclear power is likely to face stiff competition from non-nuclear produced hydrogen carriers and non-nuclear electrified vehicles (see Williams 1993). Nevertheless, OT status for the electric car could renew interest in nuclear technologies.

I have performed no independent analysis of the oil sector and rely on

DOE projections, which foresee oil prices rising from ~$15.52/bbl in 1994 to $25.43 in 2015, and oil consumption increasing from 35 Q in 1994 to ~42 Q in 2015 (DOE, *Annual Energy Outlook* 1996, Table A1).[19]

The tightness of the oil market affects nuclear power indirectly by altering the demand and price for oil substitutes, such as natural gas and biofuels. While cheap oil clearly weakens the demand for nuclear power, rapidly rising oil prices have ambiguous effects. To the extent price increases mobilize political efforts to develop alternative energy sources, such as unconventional gas and renewable energy sources, they hurt nuclear power; to the extent they lead to renewed interest in OT status for nuclear power, they benefit it.

Biomass Energy

Overview and Costs

Biomass energy technologies use terrestrial and aquatic plants as feedstocks for energy production. Biomass' potential contribution to energy supply is commonly underestimated. Possible applications include almost all markets served by fossil fuels, especially natural gas and liquid fuel markets. Existing biomass consumption (~3 Q) is dominated by wood burning stoves (~1 quad) and direct combustion in steam boilers for electricity and heat generation.[20] The U.S. currently has ~8 GW of biomass-fueled generating capacity (Williams 1994, 8).

The most serious short run competition between biomass and nuclear power is from emerging technologies that use biomass feedstocks for biogas production for use in electricity generation based on new natural gas generating technologies. Longer run competition might include the transportation sector where liquid biofuels or biomass-based hydrogen energy might compete with nuclear-based electric or hydrogen powered vehicles. Many studies project biomass electricity costs in the 4.5 c/kwh to 7 c/kwh range over the next forty years (see table 12.5). Recent innovations and opportunities for further technical change hold out hope for costs in the low end of this range.

Resource Base

The four major sources of biomass are waste vegetation, urban refuse, standing forests, and energy crops from dedicated energy plantations. While biomass resource assessment is still in its early stages, ten to twenty-five Quads is a reasonable order of magnitude for the resource base (see table 12.4). Policy analysts have frequently underestimated the potential size of a bioenergy sector due to neglect of the magnitude of excess cropland and a tendency to assume biomass production levels akin to average forest output (~4 dry tonnes per hectare per year) rather than production levels optimized to energy crops (15 dry tonnes/hectare/yr.) (Williams 1994, 10–11). The youthfulness of energy farming research suggests that R&D will expand the resource base.

Environmental and other Externalities

Biomass has attractive environmental features in combustion because of its very low sulfur content, manageable NO_x emissions (Williams and Larson 1993), and general absence of toxics. Potential problems with large particle-particulate matter and volatile organic compounds are also controllable

Table 12.4
Biomass Resource Base

Source, Year of Study	Quads	Type of Estimate
SERI, 1990[1]	55 Q	Year 2000, maximum theoretical potential using existing BM wastes excluding dedicated energy crops.
	15 Q	Currently recoverable energy from BM wastes
Brower 1992[2]	19–53 Q	Maximum production from energy crops
SERI 1990[3]	11 Q	Potential yield in 2030 from available crop land for energy farming, w/existing R&D levels
SERI 1990[3]	26 Q	Potential yield in 2030 from available crop land for energy farming, w/accelerated R&D
ORNL 1989[4]	28 Q	Potentially available at costs less than $4/MMBTU
Williams 1990[5]	10 Q	Immediately available from unused wood resources
UCS 1991[6]	20 Q	Available within reasonable environmental and economic constraints in 2030

Notes
1. SERI 1990, B-4
2. Brower 1992, 93, citing: Cook, James H., Jan Beyea, and Kathleen H. Keeler, 1991, "Potential Impacts of Biomass Production in the United States on Biological Diversity." *Annual Review of Energy and the Environment* 16: 401–431.
3. SERI 1990, B-18, B-29
4. Williams 1990, 46, citing: ORNL 5/89
5. Williams 1990, 44.
6. Union of Concerned Scientists 1992, E-3.

Table 12.5
Biomass Generating Costs*
3rd Qtr. 1992 $

Source/yr.	c/kwh and Nature of Prediction
Williams & Larson 1993[1]	5.0–5.4 c/kwh (BIG/ISTIG)
SERI[2] 1990	4.9 c/kwh–6.3 c/kwh, for new wood fired generation (by 2010)
National Research Council 1991[3]	5.6 c/kwh–7 c/kwh
OTA 1991[4]	~11.8 c/kwh for wood fired generation
Ostlie[5] 1988	~4 c/kwh, whole tree burner
UCS[6] 1991	5.0 c/kwh (5.9 c/kwh w/10.3% fcr rather than UCS assumed 5% fcr)

Biomass Feedstock Costs
3rd Qtr. 1992$

Williams[7a] 1989	Current delivered dry wood chips (~$5.4/MMBTU– ~$7.1/MMBTU. DOE target for 2000: $3.3–4.6/ MMBTU
Hall et al. 1993[7b]	~$3–~4.4/MMBTU production costs (current), ~$2– $3/MMBTU 2010
SERI[8] 1990	Currently: $3.50/MMBTU feedstock; w/existing technology, $2.70/MMBTU ($45/dry ton) possible, $2.14/ MMBTU expected 2010 (B-9)
Grubb[9] 1991	current costs ~$1.2/GJ–~$4.7/GJ , possibly falling to ~$2.30/GJ w/increased R&D

*Notes denominated in sources original dollars unless otherwise specified.
Notes
1. Williams and Larson 1993, 748, 744 (assuming original calculations of 4.14–4.89 c/kwh were in 1987$)
2. SERI 1990, B7, B9.
3. National Research Council 6/91, Table I.2.
4. OTA 7/91, 93.
5. Ostlie 1988.
6. Union of Concerned Scientists 1992, pp. E7–8, E-20.
7a. Williams 1989, 11, and Table 19.
7b. Hall et al. 1993, 626.
8. SERI 1990, B-27.
9. Grubb et al. 1991, 107.

with available technology.[21] The total greenhouse gas burden of biomass energy depends on the selection of farming techniques and the degree of replanting,[22] but could be minimal if renewables are used to power the agricultural sector (Brower 1992, 108).

Environmental concerns have also been raised about other potential side effects from biomass cultivation including erosion, water depletion, chemical pollution (from inputs like pesticides), and threats to biodiversity (due to potential transformations of forest ecosystems into monocultural energy plantations). While all of these problems appear avoidable (e.g., thoughtful biomass cultivation could actually reduce erosion risks), many analysts assert that existing market incentives will encourage harmful outcomes without government intervention. They call for the correction of existing market imperfections, such as improper water pricing and the failure to internalize the externalities of farm runoffs.

Other observers have raised concerns about the implications of potential competition between food and energy farmers. The fear is that affluent energy consumers will outbid less affluent food consumers for available land. Due to the presence of large excess capacity in the agricultural sector, however, the risks of scarcity-driven agricultural price increases seem small, at least for the foreseeable future.[23] Concerns have also been raised about the unknown side effects of introducing genetically engineered crops into the ecosystem and the persistently high rate of farm accidents.

Opportunities for Technical Change

Because of the newness of many biomass energy concepts and recent advances in bioengineering, coal gasification, and natural gas utilizing technologies, there is significant optimism about the potential for innovation in the biomass energy field. A 1990 SERI study, for example, estimated that biomass energy production could be increased from 6.3 to 9.6 Quads in 2010 and from 10.3 Quads to 19.1 Quads in 2030 through a very modest increase in federal R&D spending (SERI 1990, B19–21).

While there is much interest in biomass liquid fuel research (especially in technologies that would permit inexpensive fermentation of woody plants and herbaceous grasses), I shall concentrate on research related to electricity generation, as this is where current nuclear power-biomass competition is greatest. Potential innovations fall into two major areas: increases in agricultural and harvesting productivity,[24] and improvements in utilization technologies.[25] At least 33% reductions in biomass feedstock costs and 25% increases in energy conversion efficiencies are anticipated. There has been only modest government support for biomass R&D in the past. From 1974–1990, for example, biofuel research received $389 million in federal R&D funding compared with more than $14 billion for nuclear fission (Sisine 1991). Much of the basis for current optimism has come from spinoffs in related fields, such as natural gas and clean coal research. There is now a need to tailor these findings to biomass energy applications.[26]

Alongside innovative research, public financing for demonstration power plants could increase investor confidence in the technology and spur complementary investments necessary for sector development. The minimum two to eight year lead time for growing and harvesting short rotation energy trees, for example, will tend to discourage farm investments until the entire production process is well demonstrated and markets are relatively well assured (SERI 1990, B-27).

Public Policy Impacts

Alongside R&D spending, government tax, subsidy, and regulatory policies will have major impacts on biomass markets. The 1992 Energy Policy Act, for example, provided a ten-year federal subsidy of 1.5 c/kwh for biomass generating plants coming on-line during 1994–1999 (DOE *Annual Energy Outlook 1993*, 55). Broad based carbon taxes, which credited biomass energy sources for their displacement of carbon, could also have a large impact on biomass development.

Recent legislation increasing the access to utility grids of biomass electricity producers has also encouraged biomass cogeneration and independent power producers. Restructuring agricultural subsidies so they no longer discourage farmers from experimenting with new crops and reducing siting obstacles facing MSW, agricultural waste, and wood burning facilities might also expand biomass output.

One of the greatest barriers to biomass energy development is fear of potential competition from cheap natural gas, gasified coal, or unspecified new energy technologies. Government guaranteed minimum prices (for example, biomass electricity at 6 c/kwh, or biomass feedstock at $2.00/MMBTU) for specified quantities of biomass energy might be a cheap way of circumventing existing uncertainties.

Path Dependencies

Biomass technologies offer significant opportunities for the capture of economies of scale. Because of the small size of biomass generating facilities (20–100 MW), significant mass production economies and rapid generational learning are possible. Williams projects that the ~$2600 + /KW capital costs of a first-of-a-kind biomass-integrated gas turbine plant (BIG-GT) could be reduced to ~$1300/KW for the 10th unit through the capture of routine learning curve cost reductions (Williams 10/93, 7). Williams calculates that the capture of similar learning curve benefits for Westinghouse's AP 600 reactor would be twenty-four times as expensive, due to the nuclear plant's larger size and higher price tag.

Fully realizing biomass' economic potential would require the capture of system-wide efficiencies and necessitate infrastructural investments ahead of the market. A fully developed biomass sector, for example, might involve a network of rural biogas pipelines, new patterns of agricultural crops and crop rotations, and new harvesting and processing machinery. Like the minimum two to eight year lead time for growing and harvesting short crop rotation energy trees, these potential contributors to bioenergy efficiency illustrate the sensitivity of biomass economics to "preparation decisions" or path choices. A highly publicized government commitment to expand bioenergy might thus reduce bioenergy costs by spurring long term private investments in bioenergy infrastructures.

Bioenergy vs. Nuclear Energy

As with other energy options, technological aesthetics as well as technical information plays a key role in biomass energy assessment. Many nuclear power enthusiasts continue to dismiss biomass technologies as utopian daydreams. Their intuitions remain oriented towards more concentrated energy forms and are inherently skeptical of attempts to wring out of photosynthesis the energy necessary for industrial civilization.

Drawing comparisons more broadly, biomass energy enthusiasts tend to weigh heavily the technology's: (1) environmental promise; (2) renewability; (3) potential for large (though not abundant) supply; (4) decentralized and relatively small scale format; (5) domestic availability; (6) opportunities for technical change; and (7) potential benefits for farmers and rural economies. Biomass energy skeptics tend to highlight the technology's: (1) low sunlight conversion efficiencies and correspondingly large land (and potentially materials) input needs; (2) the associated possibility of significant environmental burdens from inputs like pesticides and herbicides; (3) lack of open-ended, long run growth potential (compared to fission or fusion power); (4) possible conflicts with global agricultural needs; and (5) presumed institutional messiness due to its decentralized format and lack of current integration with existing energy sector corporations.

Biomass Outlook

Should global warming concerns require large greenhouse gas reductions and supply scarcities limit natural gas expansion, biomass energy could become a major energy source. The resource base is large and convertible into many energy forms. The economics appear favorable enough to be made competitive by either significant carbon taxes or levels of R&D support equivalent to that enjoyed by nuclear power in the 1980s.

Anticipated biomass generating costs (4.5 c/kwh–7 c/kwh) compete favorably with my projection of costs of 7.5 c/kwh–8.5 c/kwh for new nuclear power plants. The major factors discouraging biomass expansion are very low natural gas prices, cheap coal, and general uncertainty within the energy sector. While the market security accompanying OT status for biomass would accelerate its development, biomass generating capacity is likely to grow even without OT status due to its ability to be added in small (20MW–50MW) increments.

The major uncertainties qualifying optimism about biomass generating costs involve questions about:

(1) biomass feedstock costs: especially with respect to future food acreage needs, and energy crop vulnerability to pests, pathogens, weather fluctuations, and soil erosion.

(2) generating plant capacity rates (with little supporting evidence presented for the assumption of 75%–84% performance rates).

(3) supply constraints due to competing demand for biomass stocks from liquid fuel needs.

Wind Energy

Overview and Costs

Wind electric energy is among the most promising renewable energy sources in the short and long runs. It is free of most environmental hazards and has a large renewable resource base. While wind turbines currently generate the equivalent output of only ~.5 GW of nuclear capacity, the technology appears on the verge of becoming a major option in the electricity sector. Costs for existing wind electric facilities averaged about 8 c/kwh in the early 1990s, falling to ~5 c/kwh at the best sites (OTA 7/91, 100). There has been a dramatic shift in judgments about wind energy potential since the pessimism of the 1970s. Reductions in wind generating costs have been spurred by standardization and mass production, learning curve based improvements in site selection and windmill maintenance, and technological innovations.[27] Wind economics is also buoyed by short lead times which enhances utility planning flexibility. New plants are expected to have generating costs of ~5.0–~5.5 c/kwh in the 1990s (see table 12.7). With vigorous R&D efforts, optimists foresee costs as low as 3.5–4.5 c/kwh by 2010 and ~3.0–~3.6 c/kwh by 2030.[28] The energy sector implications of

Table 12.6
Wind Energy Resource Base

Source/yr.	Magnitude of Wind Energy Supply
Abelson[1] 9/93	Long run: ~20% U.S. electricity needs.
DeMeo (EPRI) 1992[2]	Possibly 10% of U.S. electricity in ~2020.
Brower (UCS) 1992[3]	Long run potential to supply 20% or more of U.S. electricity.
SERI[4] 1990	1988: Actual consumption: .02 Quads (~.5 GW)
	2010: Business as Usual: 1.02 Quads (~17 GW)
	Accelerated R&D: 2.29 Quads (~39 GW)
	2030: Business as Usual: 3.3 Quads (~56 GW)
	Accelerated R&D: 10.65 Quads (~181 GW)
Williams[5a] 1990	Citing Thompson (1981), wind resources in US and Ca. with average wind density > than 400 watts/meter squared of turbine swept area = 16% land, potential output 7,900 TWh or 2.5 times 1988 generation.
Congressional Office of Technology Assessment 1991[6]	By 2000 market might be as high as 21 GW.
Alliance et al. 1992[5b]	~100 Quads available at sites w/wind speeds greater than 14.3 mph, under moderate siting constraints; potentially 28 GW on line by 2010, 160 GW by 2030.

Notes to Table 12.6
1. Abelson 1993, 1255.
2. *New York Times* 9/8/92, C-6. DeMeo is director of renewable energy research at the Electric Power Research Institute.
3. Brower 1992, 72. Brower is research director for the Union of Concerned Scientists.
4. SERI's Quad projections are in terms of primary energy. Assuming conversion efficiencies of ~33% and nuclear plant capacity rates of 65%, one additional Quad of primary wind energy equals the output of ~17 GW of nuclear power capacity.
5a. Williams 1990, 47.
5b. Alliance et al. 1992, pp. E-2, E-7, E-22.
6. OTA, 2/91, 90.

Table 12.7
Recent Wind Generating Cost Projections
(3rd qtr. 1992$)

Source/yr.	Current Costs	Future Costs
U.S. Windpower[1] 1992	~5 c/kwh	~4.3 c/kwh, expected costs for "soon to be commercial" model 33–300, sited in Altamont Pass
Cavallo et al. 1993[2]	~5.3 c/kwh	~3.8 c/kwh 2020–2030 (sites w/450 Watts per sq. meter wind power density)
Swezey and Wan[3] National Renewable Energy Laboratory 1996	5.3 c/kwh 1995	3.5 c/kwh by 2010
Brower/Union of Concerned Scientists[4] 1992	~5–8 c/kwh in Ca.	less than 5 c/kwh expected w/mass production of existing prototype w/16 mph wind; long run costs of ~3–5 c/kwh at sites w/15–19 mph wind
Williams[5a] 1990	less than 7 c/kwh	5.7 c/kwh by 1995–2000 4.6 c/kwh by 2010
Abelson[5b]	7–9 c/kwh	5 c/kwh soon, good prospects for 4 c/kwh by 2000
Congressional Office of Technology Assessment[6] 1991	Average Costs 1989 9.3 c/kwh; best sites: 5.8 c/kwh	4.1 c/kwh by 2010 for sites w/moderate wind resources (~14–16 mph)
Solar Energy Research Institute 1990	8.2–11.7 c/kwh 9.7 c/kwh at sites w/13 mph wind[7a]	6.2 c/kwh in 2000 at sites w/13 mph wind, 5.4 c/kwh w/accelerated R&D[7b] 4.4 c/kwh in 2010 w/accelerated R&D, 5.5 c/kwh w/o extra R&D[7b] 3.6 c/kwh in 2030 w/accelerated R&D[7b]
California Energy Commission 1990[8]	5.7–8.7 c/kwh, 1990 technology	
Edgar DeMeo EPRI[9a] 1992	~7–9 c/kwh	~5 c/kwh by ~1995 ~3–4 c/kwh by 2000 at windy sites
Dr. James Birk EPRI[9b] 1991		target ~5 c/kwh by 1994 ~3.5 c/kwh by 2005
DOE[10] 1991	9 c/kwh	less than ~4 c/kwh expected by 2030

Notes

1. *New York Times* 9/8/92, C-6; SERI 1990, F-10. U.S. Windpower is the largest U.S. wind turbine manufacturer. Their cost predictions need to be treated gingerly, as they may fuse optimistic hopes and marketing strategies with disinterested prediction.

this literature are difficult to interpret, however, because of a lack of reliable data on the quantity of wind electricity available at these prices. This ambiguity is probably due to the sensitivity of wind economics to site selection and a lack of detailed survey data about most locations.[29]

Because most U.S. wind resources are located in areas relatively far from load centers, such as the great plains, the economics of wind power is quite sensitive to assumptions made about long distance electricity transmission costs. Because wind is an intermittent source, its economic value also depends on how its variable supply is integrated into an energy system.

Despite the generally favorable outlook found in wind technology studies, there is a need for caution in assessing wind economics, as many of the detailed studies have been performed by wind enthusiasts. It is not clear that the excess optimism of many wind advocates in earlier periods is entirely gone.[30]

Resource Base

Meteorological data indicate that the physical resource base is huge.[31] In 1990 SERI projected that more than 150 GW of wind generating capacity could be competitive by 2030 with a modest increase in wind R&D spending.[32] Many analysts have suggested that wind could provide ~10%–20% of U.S. electricity needs.[33] Because of the youthfulness of wind resource assessment and the frequent sensitivity of site assessment to aesthetic judg-

---

Table 12.7 notes continued

2. Cavallo et al. 1993, 121, 152. The authors' 2.94 c/kwh–4.44 c/kwh range (per discount rates of 6% and 12%) has been condensed to 3.25 c/kwh using a single 10.3% FCR and adjusting the text's original dollars (assumed to be 1988$) to 3rd quarter 1992$.

3. Swezey and Wan 1996, 10.

4. Brower 1992, 78, 80.

5a. Williams 1990, 44–48 (assuming 10.07 FCR).

5b. Abelson 1993, 1255.

6. OTA 7/91, 100–102.

7a. SERI 1990, F-1, F-2.

7b. SERI 1990, F-5. All calculations assume 13 mph wind speeds, and a FCR of 10.07 percent.

8. Gipe 1991, 762.

9a. Edgar DeMeo, Director of Renewable Energy Research at the Electric Power Research Institute (EPRI), *Power Line* January-February 1992, 4–5. See also *EPRI Journal* 12/92.

9b. Dr. James R. Birk, Director, Storage and Renewables Department, Electric Power Research Institute. Testimony before Senate Committee on Energy and Natural Resources, hearings on "Renewable Hydrogen Energy Research and Development Act of 1991," 6/25/91, 47.

10. Department of Energy Secretary Watkins, written response to Senate inquiries; printed in hearings transcript on the "National Energy Security Act of 1991", before the Senate Committee on Energy and Natural Resources 2–3/91, p. 53.

ments of "acceptable appearance," large uncertainties accompany resource estimates. This is especially true with respect to potential energy contributions from offshore wind generating platforms. Table 12.6 lists some quantity estimates of wind resources.

Environmental and Other Externalities

Wind energy is among the cleanest energy sources, estimated to produce only a few percent of the environmental burden of coal-fired electricity (Ottinger 1990, 351, 398, 436). Negative externalities consist mainly of objections to windmill appearance, turbine noise, fears of interference with TV reception, and collision hazards for birds. Only visual concerns seem capable of posing serious barriers to windmill development.[34]

As with biomass and direct solar forms of energy, windmill technology involves relatively large land areas.[35] The impact of wind power's land requirements, however, is mitigated by the potential for joint use with ranching or farming.[36] The problem of visual clutter remains. There already have been a number of wind projects withdrawn due to local residents' aesthetic objections to wind farm sitings.[37] Recent survey research and wind farm design efforts are attempting to minimize the visual impact of windmill arrays.[38] The long run impact of aesthetic constraints on windmill deployment remains uncertain.

Opportunities for Technical Change

Among recent and continuing avenues for innovation in wind power are: advanced controls that orient blades for maximum wind capture, variable speed turbines that can operate in strong gusts of wind, improved materials (such as lightweight fiberglass turbine blades and more damage-resistant rotors), taller hubs, and larger unit size. Routine learning is also permitting better tailoring of turbine characteristics and array spacing to site characteristics and deriving better maintenance practices. Additional research on offshore generating platforms could perhaps expand the resource base.

Because of wind power's intermittency and geographic mismatch with electricity demand, delivered wind power costs are quite sensitive to energy storage and long distance transmission costs. Alfred Cavallo has emphasized the importance of advances in long distance, high voltage, direct current electricity transmission over the last decade (Cavallo 1993, 92). Relying on dc transmission lines and underground compressed air energy storage, he projects only a ~2 c/kwh transmission cost for bringing 3–4 c/kwh wind power from Kansas to California markets (Cavallo 1993, 94; Williams 10/93, 10).

Public Policy Impacts

Like almost all renewable energy technologies, wind systems have been given comparatively little federal R&D support. From 1974–1990 wind R&D totaled $460 million or about 3% of fission R&D spending over the same period (Sisine 1991). The Solar Energy Research Institute concluded in 1990 that modest increases in government R&D could reduce expected wind electric costs from 4.7 c/kwh to 3.8 c/kwh by 2010 (SERI 1990, F-5). One of the competitive advantages that wind systems have over nuclear technologies is their relatively low R&D and demonstration costs. An extremely important innovation, the development of variable speed wind turbines, for example, was commercialized for only $20 million (Williams 10/93, 5–6).[39] The absence of serious accident hazards also permits wind innovations to be deployed immediately, without the long period of testing and regulatory review common in the nuclear sector.

Government tax and subsidy policies have had large impacts on wind markets. Generous incentives in the 1980s were key to the growth of installed wind capacity from .3 GW in 1981 to 1.5 GW in 1988 (ORNL 1989, 81).[40] While some technologies were prematurely commercialized, leading to a period of equipment failures and battered industry reputations, the aid facilitated extensive hands-on experience with wind technology and laid the groundwork for learning curve cost reductions (*EPRI Journal* 12/92, 9). From 1987 to 1990, for example, capacity rates improved from 13% to 24% (Cavallo 1993, 83). The 1992 Energy Policy Act's 1.5 c/kwh subsidy for wind electric systems should facilitate further expansion.

The PURPA legislation's guarantee of access to utility transmission lines for independent power producers (IPPs) has been central to wind energy development. By 1989, 2,226 IPPs had qualified as wind electric generating sources (Sisine 1991, 7). The availability of long term contracts with attractive prices for at least ten years was a key spur to California's wind boom. As with many new technologies, risk minimization is central to market acceptance. Future wind success will be heavily influenced by the pricing schedules available to IPPs.

Regulatory treatment of environmental externalities will also play a key role in wind's future. As perhaps the most benign energy option (with 1 M/kwh in estimated environmental externalities compared to an estimated 20–30 M/kwh for nuclear and coal-fired electricity in a widely cited Pace

University study [Ottinger 1990, 31–36]), wind will benefit from increasing attention to externalities in Least Cost and Integrated Resource Planning reviews of utility generating options. Along similar lines, the Clean Air Act Amendments of 1990 gave utilities sulfur dioxide (SO_2) allowances for each ton of SO_2 abated through the use of qualified renewable energy sources, such as wind energy (Sisine 1991, 13).[41]

Because of the importance of mass production and standardization to wind economics, government purchase policy could help lower wind power costs. The Military Construction Appropriations Act of 1991, which includes plans for using DoD expenditures to promote renewable energy use, may help wind capture some scaling economies. Other bills have increased AID and Export-Import Bank support for renewable energy exports.

The recent shift of utility attention to wind energy options reillustrates the role of bounded rationalities in defining energy choices and the potential impact of social movements in broadening planning horizons. Until recently the utilities paid little attention to wind options. Growing political pressures, however, embodied in requirements such as "Integrated Resource Planning," have forced attention to wind systems. The most important developments have occurred in California, where the Public Utility Commission fined Pacific Gas and Electric $15 million and Southern California Edison $8 million for failing to give sufficient attention to alternative energy and demand management options (Gipe 1991, 757). Other state policies (such as the California Energy Commission's assessment of wind resources and the state's 25% tax credit) offered infant industry incentives for wind expansion. California now leads the nation in wind power generation.[42]

Technological Aesthetics

Assessments of the future potential of wind power inevitably draw upon technological aesthetics. Enthusiasts for wind energy emphasize the technology's: (1) environmental benefits; (2) domestic availability; (3) large (though not limitless) resource base; (4) decentralized small scale format; (5) opportunities for technological innovation; and (6) modular format (which permits increased factory rather than construction-site assembly, mass production economies, short project lead times, and rapid generational learning).

Wind skeptics highlight wind energy's: (1) intermittency; (2) bounded (albeit potentially large) resource base; (3) low energy intensity and accompanying large land demands; (4) visual obstructiveness; (5) potential management problems due to its decentralized format; (6) the likelihood of unexpected problems; and (7) the historical tendency for excessive optimism on the part of wind enthusiasts.

How you weigh and aggregate these attributes depends very much on one's technological aesthetics. Many judgments tend to cluster. Enthusiasts for concentrated energy technologies, such as nuclear power, also tend to highly value very large growth potentials and a technology's amenability to centralized management. They are especially troubled by wind's dispersed and intermittent supply (Price 1990, 344; Cohen 1990, 263).

Wind advocates tend to look favorably on dispersed energy systems, decentralized management structures, and energy strategies emphasizing energy efficiency (minimizing the allure of boundless energy supply technologies). While wind enthusiasts acknowledge intermittency as a problem, they suggest its economic costs can be reduced by increasing the number and type of intermittent producers,[43] expanding grid integration, and developing more sophisticated planning techniques for managing intermittent supply (such as interruptable service options and generating mix strategies that are optimized to include intermittency).[44]

Wind enthusiasts and skeptics often have different visual reactions to wind farms. Rather than perceiving windmills as eyesores, many wind advocates portray them as symbols of appropriate technology. Various studies of aesthetic responses to windmills indicate that along with classical notions of beauty, people's reactions are infused with social and political attitudes about energy policy (Gipe 1989, 15, 23).[45]

Wind vs. Nuclear Power: Likely Futures

The biggest obstacles to increased wind power are the current low costs of fossil fuels, uncertainties about future energy policy (e.g., greenhouse policy), and uncertainties about wind economics (such as wind system lifetimes and the magnitude of local wind resources). Besides offering stiff competition, cheap fossil fuels burden wind with higher risk premiums in capital markets (Sisine 1991, 4). As with many other alternative energy options, private sector risk aversion (which discourages risk taking R&D) conflicts with social risk aversion (which would proliferate energy options).

While wind power would benefit enormously from the capture of OT status by renewable energy development strategies (with payoffs ranging from R&D breakthroughs and altered utility planning contexts to more favorable aesthetic reactions), wind technology can also develop incrementally due to wind units' small size and modest R&D costs. First generation wind turbines can be limited to ideal sites and managed by the utilities most able to accommodate intermittent supply in their generating mix.

It seems likely that wind power capacity will increase by a minimum equivalent of 15–50 GWs of nuclear power generating capacity by 2015.

Wind's relatively low expected costs and large potential capacity leave it a major long run competitor for nuclear power, especially in an energy sector with serious greenhouse constraints.

Solar Energy

Overview and Costs

While many energy sources ultimately derive from the sun, the term "solar energy" usually refers to energy options involving relatively direct applications of current sunlight. There are three main kinds of solar energy systems: (1) building structures that capture solar radiation for heating and cooling; and (2) solar thermal (ST) and (3) photovoltaic (PV) systems that capture solar radiation for electricity generation.[46] Solar energy is popular with the public and has received the highest level of federal support among renewable energy options.[47]

Solar Building Technologies

Although among the least glamorous energy options, solar building technologies tap an important energy market, as at least 20% of U.S. energy consumption involves building related heating and cooling. Michael Brower of the Union of Concerned Scientists projects that 15%–25% of existing buildings' energy consumption could be economically replaced with low cost solar design features, such as orienting buildings to capture more of the winter sun, taking advantage of natural ventilation, and including "sensible landscaping" (Brower 1992, 45).[48] Because it is usually much more expensive to retrofit solar features to existing structures than to include them in new designs, the full potential for solar buildings will be approached slowly as old structures are retired.[49] As solar building technologies are basically energy conservation technologies, the debate over their economic potential is usually subsumed within energy demand forecasting debates.

Solar Electricity

There are two major strategies for producing electricity from solar energy, solar thermal systems that use sunlight as a heat source for eventual steam turbine generation of electricity, and photovoltaic systems that rely on the "photovoltaic effect" to transform sunlight directly into an electric current. For the next ten to fifteen years both solar thermal and PV technologies are likely to remain R&D rather than commercial options, except for speciality markets (such as consumer electronics products and remote site applications).[50] Current solar electricity costs generally exceed 10 c/kwh and PV costs will probably not fall much below 10 c/kwh for more than a decade. The short run outlook for solar thermal systems is slightly more promising (see table 12.8).

Resource Base

Interest in solar energy is due to the technology's longer run potentials. Over a twenty to thirty-five year horizon, ST and PV generating costs could fall as low as 4–7 c/kwh and play a major role in electricity generation. Solar thermal technologies appear the most promising option in the medium run, while photovoltaic systems dominate long run projections.[51] Optimists and pessimists foresee costs in the low and high ranges listed in table 12.8. The Solar Energy Research Institute (recently renamed the National Renewable Energy Laboratory) estimated that 15 quads of solar energy could be available by 2030 with an accelerated R&D program (SERI 1990, E-4, G-7). The most expansive visions foresee solar electricity as a key input for a hydrogen economy.

Environmental and Other Externalities

Both ST and PV technologies pose minimal environmental burdens from the standpoint of traditional fossil fuel pollutants (SO_2, greenhouse gases, etc.). Debates over potential novel externalities from ST and PV systems reflect the intuitions of different technological aesthetics. Skeptics about solar energy argue that the low energy density of ST and PV technologies implies that both systems will involve large material needs and huge tracts of land, resulting in potentially serious toxic material hazards and waste disposal problems. The pessimists note, for example, that some existing PV technologies involve toxic materials such as arsenic and cadmium. The optimists expect careful materials choice and recycling to minimize hazardous materials problems. Pace University's externality study projected solar environmental burdens of 0–4 M/kwh in comparison with nuclear hazards of more than 29 M/kwh (Ottinger et al. 1991, 34–36).

Table 12.8
Solar Electricity Costs

	Current Costs c/kwh	~2005–2010 c/kwh	~2030 c/kwh
Solar Thermal Costs (3rd qtr. 1992$)			
Parabolic Trough	14–20 ([1a] best sites, ~13 [2a]	9.3–12 [1b] Hybrid solar/gas 7.6–10.9	
Parabolic Dish	17.5–38.5 [1a]	6.4–12.4 [1c]	
Central Receiver	(1995) 9.3–18.7 [1d] ~9 c/kwh [2b]	5.4–7.6 [1b]	
Solar Thermal	less than 8[3a] trough technologies		~4.7 [3b]
Photovoltaic Costs			
Photovoltaics	~25–~50 [4]	~10.7–16.1 [5a] (before 2000) 8.2–10.5 [6a] less than 5.5 c/kwh (6c)	3.7–7.5 [5b] 4.7–5.8 [6b]

Notes

1a. Assuming typical southwest U.S. site, 7.8% fixed charge rate, 80 MWe "trough" plant, and a 3 MWe "dish" plant (De Laquil et al. 1993, 281).

1b. Per note 1a but 200 MWe plant.

1c. Per note 1a but 300 MWe plant.

1d. Per note 1a but 100 MWe plant.

2a. Brower 1992, 52, 68.

2b. Brower 1992, 56, assuming advanced equipment.

3a. *Renewable Energy Annual 1995*, U.S. Department of Energy, July 1995. Chapter 11, section F. URL: http://www.eia.doe.gov/cneaf/pubs_html/rea/chap11f.html

3b. SERI 1990, E-6.

4. Brower 1992, 64. SERI estimates late 1980s costs at 30 c/kwh (1988$) (SERI 1990, G-4). Johansson et al. 1993a, estimate early 1990s costs at 25–35 c/kwh (p. 21).

5a. Utility financed systems, moderate to good sunlight (Kelly 1993, 303). 5b) Mid to long term (Kelly 1993, 303).

6a. 8.2 c/kwh assumes "accelerated R&D"; 10.5 c/kwh assumes "business as usual" levels of R&D (SERI 1990, G-4).

6b. 4.7 c/kwh assumes "accelerated R&D", 5.8 c/kwh assumes "business as usual" levels of R&D (SERI 1990, G-4).

6c. Enron Corporation (*New York Times* 11/15/94).

Opportunities for Technological Change

Solar optimists note the impressive success of past R&D that reduced flat plate PV module costs by two-thirds in 1976–1990 and parabolic trough ST capital costs by over 50% during the 1980s.[52] Solar enthusiasts foresee continued technological change along traditional avenues for cost reductions, such as: (1) new materials design (e.g., replacing single cell crystal silicon with thin film polycrystalline PV cells); (2) equipment improvements (e.g., better stirling-cycle engines for coupling to solar thermal systems); and (3) manufacturing improvements (e.g., use of laser grooving for PV cells).[53] The Solar Energy Research Institute projected PV costs falling from an expected 9 c/kwh to 7 c/kwh in 2010 from an accelerated R&D program. By 2030 SERI projected an extra 190 GW of installed capacity in response to increased R&D spending (SERI 1990, G-4). Solar pessimists note the tendency for excess optimism on the part of a technology's practitioners and warn of the likelihood of unanticipated problems (such as higher than expected maintenance costs and shorter than anticipated lifetimes).[54]

Public Policy and Path Dependency

The expected cost and level of solar energy use in the future is highly sensitive to assumptions made about government policy and the technology's capture of path dependent cost reductions. The logic of many solar forecasts assumes that the positive externalities of solar energy (low expected environmental hazards, fossil fuel conservation, domestic availability, etc.) argue for actualizing backcasted possibilities. The goal of many projections, therefore, is to demonstrate the existence of routes to solar competitiveness rather than the probability of their adoption. Most of the avenues to competitiveness follow the classic modes of path dependency emphasized throughout this book. Among the key mechanisms are:

1) THE CAPTURE OF MASS PRODUCTION ECONOMIES

The DOE estimates that PV prices will fall 40% for every tenfold increase in factory production levels (Brower 1992, 64). Chamberlin of Sandia National Laboratories projects about a 50% cost reduction for annual output increases from 1 MW to 100 MW for a broad array of PV components (concentrator cells, cell assemblies, optics, housings, etc. [Boes and Luque 1993, 391]). De Laquil et al. (1993) foresee similar economies of scale with respect to collectors, receivers, and stirling engines for parabolic dish solar thermal systems (1993, 284). In November 1994 the Enron Corporation, the largest natural gas company in the U.S., predicted costs of 5.5 c/kwh for its newly announced *100 MW* photovoltaic plant in Nevada. The breakthrough was tied to the mass production of PV modules from an adjacent PV factory and new thin film designs (*New York Times* 11/15/94, C1).[55]

2) THE CAPTURE OF LEARNING CURVE ADVANTAGES

The DOE foresees 70% price declines for every tenfold increase in production experience (cumulative MWs produced over time) with photo-voltaics (Brower 1992, 64). Henry Kelly, senior associate at the Congressional Office of Technology Assessment, argues "Solutions to the practical and unglamorous problems that contribute substantially to system costs: site preparation, cable connections, site-specific design, etc. will only come about as the result of extensive field experience" (Kelly 1993, 328).

3) THE CAPTURE OF MW SCALING EFFECTS

Increases in megawatt size are deemed important for central receiver ST technology, probably the most promising solar thermal option (De Laquil et al. 1993, 282). MW economies have also been claimed for parabolic trough ST systems (Brower 1992, 56). The relatively high cost of building a 200 MW central receiver demonstration plant, however, nullifies some of the technology's attractiveness as an inexpensive R&D option.

4) THE CAPTURE OF R&D PAYOFFS

Capture of many of the technological opportunities noted above will likely require federal R&D support, as the current availability of cheap natural gas and the private sector's inability to capture many of the benefits of basic R&D discoveries will discourage corporate R&D efforts.

5) THE CAPTURE OF SYSTEM EFFICIENCIES

The competitiveness of solar energy is sensitive to developments in non-solar electric fields. As noted below, the burden of intermittency depends in part on the overall characteristics of utility grid systems. Increased grid integration and inexpensive back-up service, for example, would reduce intermittency penalties. Solar costs could be reduced by breakthroughs in complementary technologies, such as electricity storage systems and stirling engine design (for ST parabolic dish systems). Terrestrial solar technology has already benefited from solar space research. Integrating PV requirements into new building designs and glass manufacturing processes could also reduce solar electric costs.

6) INSTITUTIONAL FACILITATION

Among the institutional issues most important for solar energy development are access to low cost financing for dispersed unit installation (such as home mortgage or utility financing for rooftop PV installation) and regulatory guarantees of grid access for independent solar energy producers.

7) GOVERNMENT SUBSIDY, TAX, AND PROCUREMENT POLICIES

Policy initiatives in these areas could alter solar competitiveness by as much as 3 c/kwh. Among the major policies in place or under consideration are:
—The 1992 Energy Policy Act's permanent extension of a 10% tax credit for solar power (about a .5 c/kwh subsidy).
—Proposed externality credits for solar generated electricity in pubic utility commissions rate calculations. If regulators adopted the estimates of electricity externalities calculated in the Pace University study, for example, solar energy would enjoy a ~2.5 c/kwh boost in competition with nuclear power and the best coal-fired technologies, and a .5 c/kwh boost with respect to natural gas-fired plants (Ottinger et al. 1990, 31–36).
—Market spurring government purchases of PV and ST units for public buildings and low income housing units.

Technological Aesthetics

Among the most attractive aspects of solar energy are its: (1) non-depletability; (2) domestic availability; (3) environmental friendliness; (4) modest R&D costs (compared to larger scale options such as fission power, fusion power, and synthetic fuels); (5) short generational cycles (which facilitates learning); (6) opportunities for mass production; (7) short lead times between order and availability and (8) potential for reducing electricity transmission and distribution costs. Other benefits claimed by some analysts (depending on technological aesthetics) include its: (9) potential for small scale decentralized deployment; (10) more direct linkage between electricity use and externality burdens (due to local generation and consumption); (11) siting ease; and (12) fecundity for long term innovation.

Among the most unattractive aspects of solar energy are its: (1) intermittency (day/night, seasonal and weather related), (2) high current costs and uncertainty about future costs; and, depending on one's technological aesthetics, (3) low energy concentration (and potentially large accompanying materials and land needs), (4) small unit size (and potential loss of unit scaling economies); and (5) the need for a large number of generating sites.

Debates between advocates of nuclear and solar power hinge on the weightings given the above attributes. Nuclear enthusiasts tend to favor high density, centralized energy systems with limitless energy supply. Solar advocates prefer low density technologies with dispersed facilities and tend to place a higher value on minimizing negative externalities than on maximizing energy supply.

Debates over the cost burden of intermittency are especially interesting as they highlight the sensitivity of solar economics to "system-wide characteristics" and overall utility generating mix strategies. The burden of an energy option's intermittency depends on the character of the supply system receiving the electricity as well as the energy source's pattern of fluctuation. Among the system-wide factors that effect intermittency costs are: (1) the degree of grid integration (the greater the integration, the lower the burden of intermittency); (2) the variance amongst intermittent energy suppliers (the greater the diversity of supply, the smaller anticipated fluctuations in supply); (3) the costs of energy transmission and storage; (4) the presence of interruptable service options; (5) the character of backup power; and (6) the local correlation between energy supply and demand fluctuations. Problems are minimized, for example, where backup power is inexpensive and fluctuations in supply match well with fluctuations in demand, as with solar energy inputs to utility systems where peak demand is dominated by air conditioning loads.

Many recent technological developments have decreased the cost of intermittency, such as: (1) increases in grid integration; (2) advances with respect to long distance dc electricity transmission and compressed air energy storage; (3) the automation of electricity transmission and distribution; and (4) the availability of cheap natural gas turbines as a back-up technology. Solar advocates argue that older utility planning models give insufficient attention to these innovations and have not fully explored how to integrate intermittents into a generating mix. [56]

The intermittency debate reveals a tendency for path competition between intermittent energy sources, such as wind and solar power, and energy options with expensive capital outlays, such as nuclear and coal-fired plants. It is much more expensive to add intermittent energy supplies to a generating mix with a large percentage of its capacity committed to technologies with expensive fixed costs than one with large amounts of gas turbines and/ or pumped hydro. Managerial habits of mind nurtured by one path may also blind planners to opportunities available along another strategy.

Solar vs. Nuclear Power: Likely Futures

While the favorite of many "soft energy path" advocates and the symbol of renewable energy for much of the public, solar energy is unlikely to have as significant a market impact over the next fifteen to twenty years as wind, biomass, and hyroelectric forms of renewable energy. Neglect of many potential pitfalls (such as shorter than anticipated product lifetimes and higher than expected maintenance costs) and the assumption of unrealistically low discount rates in some solar cost calculations seem to tip many solar advocates' economic analyses towards excessive optimism.

Prospects are brighter, however, over the next twenty-five to thirty-five years. It seems quite possible that generating costs could be reduced to 6 c/kwh or less by 2020 with continued government R&D support and other kinds of assistance. The major current barrier to rapid solar development is the availability of cheap fossil fuels. Private sector interest in solar energy is likely to be muted in the absence of large natural gas price increases or greenhouse constraints.

Because of solar energy's positive externalities, public investment in the technology as one of a number of backstop energy options seems quite appropriate and reasonably likely. The emergence of 6 c/kwh solar electricity would further weaken notions of a nuclear imperative. One of the most haunting images for nuclear enthusiasts must be a recent picture of the shutdown Rancho Seco nuclear power plant, whose cooling towers now overlook a 2 MW array of photovoltaics (*Physics Today* 9/93, 23).

Geothermal Energy

Overview and Costs

Geothermal (GT) energy taps the earth's internal thermal energy for electricity production, district heating, and conceivably, industrial heat applications. Current GT energy projects are focused on hydrothermal systems, which tap relatively shallow hot water and steam reservoirs, and hot dry rock (HDR) systems that mine rocks for their heat by injecting and then recovering water from artificially created fractures in the rocks. Two other sources of GT energy, geopressured brines and magma, are also under study.[57]

Geothermal energy is of interest because of its enormous resource base, which potentially dwarfs the combined energy available from nuclear and fossil fuels (Tester et al. 1989, 6) and its minimal greenhouse gas emissions. Current systems rely on hydrothermal reservoirs and have only limited supply potential. The most promising long run option, HDR geothermal energy, must solve a number of technical problems before it can be commercialized.

Electricity from the Geysers' hydrothermal plants recently cost about 4.7–7 c/kwh (SERI 1990, C-1, 3rd qtr. 92$). Projected hot dry rock generating costs with existing technology range from 6.1 c/kwh at good sites, to 10 c/kwh at medium sites, to 31 c/kwh at poor sites (3rd qtr. 92$).[58] GT researchers are confident that R&D can reduce these costs and foresee long run costs of ~3–9 c/kwh depending on site characteristics (Brower 1992, 145).

Resource Base

The U.S. currently has about 2.5 GW capacity of hydrothermal GT energy, most tied to the Geysers in California. Estimates of recoverable hydrothermal resources tally ~380 Quads (at the surface) or enough to fuel 23 GW of generating capacity for thirty years (SERI 1990, C-2). Unidentified hydrothermal sources are thought to be about three to five times as large (Ibid.). The HDR resource base has been estimated at 650,000–2,000,000 Quads (SERI 1990, C-2, Brower 1992, 130). Resource base projections numbering in the hundreds of thousands of Quads have also been projected for magma and geopressured brines.

Environmental and Other Externalities

Geothermal energy involves relatively modest environmental burdens. Greenhouse gas emissions from open loop hydrothermal systems are about 5% of coal-fired plant emissions (SERI 1990, C-1). Closed loop HDR systems would be expected to have zero greenhouse gas emissions. Closed loop HDR systems that reinject circulating fluids are also expected to be free of air and solid waste disposal problems. Early concerns about land subsidence and human initiated earthquake hazards have also diminished.[59] Open loop systems have problems with hydrogen sulfide (H_2S) emissions and some heavy metal precipitates after steam condensation (Brower 1992, 150–153). Though the rotten egg odor of H_2S can be reduced by scrubbers, the residue creates some solid waste problems (Brower 1992, 151). The most promising disposal option for both scrubber wastes and precipitates seems to be reinjection into the geothermal well. The key task is to ensure that local aquifers are isolated from geothermal flows.

Aesthetic objections to locating geothermal facilities near wilderness areas and national parks will likely place some siting constraints on GT development, though the technology's land requirements are modest. Constraints on water availability for GT plant cooling may also limit plant siting (Brower 1992, 152).

Technological Agenda

Three main tasks dominate current GT research agendas: (1) the development of better drilling technologies to access HDR environments;[60] (2) the development of better fracturing technologies to create HDR reservoirs; and (3) the development of better analytical tools for characterizing the size and lifetimes of HDR reservoirs.[61] Other research projects involve multi-welled designs for HDR reservoirs (Tester and Herzog 1991, 58), and managing materials corrosion for hydrothermal GT systems.

Public Policy Impacts

The most important public policy influencing the rate of GT development will probably be federal R&D decisions. Exacerbating the normal disincentives for private R&D spending is the geothermal industry's current organization by small firms unable to fund significant research (SERI 1990, C-5) and the long time horizon likely before GT technologies have major payoffs. While GT energy has received significant federal R&D support relative to other non-nuclear, non-fossil fuel, technologies ($1.023 billion since 1974), funding during 1988–1992 averaged only $22 million/yr. (Brower 1992, 191). Many geothermal researchers feel that current spending levels are insufficient to master drilling and fracturing tasks (Tester, Brown, and Potter 7/89, 4). The 1992 Energy Policy Act aided geothermal energy by granting it a permanent 10% investment tax credit.

Technological Aesthetics

Enthusiasts about geothermal energy emphasize its enormous supply potential and low environmental burdens, including minimal greenhouse gas emissions. Of lesser significance is the technology's modular characteristics, permitting modest lead times of two to five years and incremental (100 MW) capacity additions (SERI 1990, C-1).

Skeptics about geothermal energy emphasize the technical obstacles in the way of commercialization. They are especially concerned about the obstacles posed by the high temperature, high pressure, and corrosive environments accompanying geothermal energy. They also anticipate unexpected problems due to the youthfulness of geothermal technology, especially if employment is attempted on a massive scale. The recent experience of unexpected drops in steam pressure (and thus plant capacity performance) at the Geyser hydrothermal facilities in California, for example, has increased investor concern about the uncertainties surrounding reservoir lifetimes (Brower 1992, 135). There are also fears of unexpected environmental problems.

Geothermal Futures

The near term future of geothermal energy options seems relatively modest. The DOE foresees little increase in hydrothermal generating capacity through 2015 (DOE, *Annual Energy Outlook 1996*, 114). The Solar Energy Research Institute projected GT energy contributions to remain under 1 Quad through 2010, even with accelerated R&D spending (SERI 1990, C-7). The long term prospects of the technology are much more open-ended due to potential R&D breakthroughs with respect to drilling technologies and the creation of HDR reservoirs. It is the technology's long run potential as an enormous source of energy and a greenhouse abatement option that is relevant for nuclear power assessment. These attributes contradict the notion of a long run nuclear imperative and undermine appeals for government support of nuclear power as a necessary insurance policy against energy scarcity or global warming.

Hydroelectric Energy

Overview and Costs

There are three major kinds of hydroelectricity: conventional hydroelectric, low head or small hydro (less than 30–80 MW), and pumped storage. Current capacity includes 78 GW of conventional hydro and 20 GW of pumped storage (DOE, *Annual Energy Outlook 1996*, 96, 114). While the latter consumes 1.25–1.4 kwh for every kilowatt hour returned, it smoothes out peak demands and is an attractive energy storage option for intermittent supply technologies (like wind and photovoltaic) and base load options like nuclear power. Total hydroelectric production in 1995 was 294 BKWh (DOE, *Annual Energy Outlook 1996*, 114), or roughly 1/2 nuclear power output. Opportunities for increased hydro generation seem modest, due to increasingly stringent environmental constraints.

Cost projections depend upon site conditions, but were predicted by the Solar Energy Research Institute to average about 6.5 c/kwh at new sites.[62] Further cost reductions are expected to accompany expanded R&D. Upgrading existing hydro facilities is the most economical hydro option, with projected costs of ~$100/KW and .8 c/kwh (SERI 1990, A-11).

Resource Base

Technical estimates of the size of potential U.S. hydropower resources are in the 500 GW range (SERI 1990, A-11). A 1988 study by the Federal Energy Regulatory Commission (FERC) found a practical resource base, given existing technology and siting constraints, of about 150 GW or roughly twice current capacity (Brower 1992, 113; SERI 1990, A-3). A 1989 study by Oak Ridge National Laboratory found 46 GW a more realistic upper bound limit for potential capacity growth (ORNL 1989, 29). While noting that increasingly stringent environmental restrictions aimed at protecting scenic river flows, fish resources, and dam integrity had further narrowed acceptable hydro sites, a 1990 SERI study estimated that 22 GW of untapped hydro generating capacity were still economical (A-3). By 1996 the DOE had cut this projection to less than 5 GW due to ever stronger regulatory protections of fishing stocks (DOE *Annual Energy Outlook 1996*, 31).

Environmental and Other Externalities

Hydroelectricity is extremely "clean" with respect to traditional fossil fuel pollutants (greenhouse gases, acid rain precursors, trace metals, etc.) and radiation hazards. It is, however, ecologically disruptive and the 1968 National Wild and Scenic Rivers Act precluded about 40% of untapped hydro sites from development (Brower 1992, 113). Under the 1986 Electric Consumer Protection Act, new hydro projects and license renewals must meet tighter ecological requirements. Brower indicates, for example, that hydro facilities along the Columbia River will likely suffer 1 GW declines due to increasing concern about their impact on salmon populations (Brower 1992, 116).

Dam failure is also a serious hydro risk and safety standards have been tightened in areas such as earthquake tolerance and spillway integrity (SERI 1990, A-2).

Perhaps the major indirect cost of many hydro projects is the loss of outdoor recreational opportunities such as white water rafting and salmon fishing. These costs may be offset, however, by the creation of new sporting opportunities such as boating and swimming. Calculating Hydro's overall recreational impact is quite site-specific and involves controversial estimating techniques.

Public Policies and Hydro Futures

The rate of hydroelectric expansion is fairly sensitive to public policy. The SERI study projects an increase of only 8 GW capacity during 1988–2030 in its "Business as Usual" (BAU) scenario. This addend jumps to 42 GW (excluding additional pumped storage) with a modest increase in R&D.[63] Among the most promising areas for research are refinement of free-flow turbines for in-river generation (+13 GW) and the development of technical fixes for environmental concerns (+11 GW) (SERI 1990, A-3–4).[64]

The SERI study projected an increase of 55 GW conventional hydro capacity by 2030 from a 2 c/kwh hydroelectric subsidy (or environmental credit, depending on the logic of justification) (p. A-5). Because of hydro's low capacity rates, this expansion would replace about 38 GW of nuclear power.

The pace of hydro expansion will also be influenced by the terms governing independent power producers access to utility grid lines and the public's general attitude towards "engineering nature". Low head hydro, for example, appears to have been suspended by licensing hurdles. Although the immediate outlook for hydropower is relatively static, with relicensing constraints likely to offset new growth, an additional ~50 GW of capacity remains accessible should greenhouse concerns or other energy crises emerge.

Conclusion

Stiff Competition

There is no nuclear imperative. Over the next twenty to forty years nuclear power is likely to face very strong competition from both fossil fuels and renewable energy technologies. The nuclear industry will have to resolve concerns about nuclear hazards and enjoy expected costs of 4.5–6.25 c/kwh to regain market attention.

One of the striking aspects of the aftermath of nuclear power's loss of OT status has been the positive reassessment of numerous other energy options. Among the noteworthy surprises are: (1) the large upward revision in natural gas reserves and emergence of new natural gas combustion technologies; (2) the end of technological pessimism in the coal sector and emergence of new combustion and pollution abatement technologies; (3) the elevation of biomass to a major energy option, aided by unexpected breakthroughs in biomass gasification technologies; (4) the emergence of wind power as a major energy source, aided by routinized learning and R&D advances, (5) the emergence of hot dry rock technology as a serious energy option; and (6) more sympathetic views of small scale and intermittent energy sources.

These new directions parallel previously discussed reassessments of future energy demand growth, nuclear hazards, and nuclear costs. The changes reillustrate the impact of shifting social contexts on technical realms of discourse. Once again, the point is not that engineers and scientists cook results to please corporate or political sponsors, but that planning contexts, constrained by phenomena like ideological and institutional habits of mind, politically determined R&D funding priorities, data limitations, and scarce opportunities for synergistic discovery, create bounded realms of discourse.

Current debates over the feasibility of non-nuclear futures reflect two different technological aesthetics, the pro-nuclear intuitions of the ~1950–~1970 period that tilted towards technologies with high power densities, large centralized plants, and boundless energy supply, and the anti-nuclear intuitions that followed, that tilted towards technologies with lower power densities, more decentralized inputs, and large but not necessarily limitless energy supply. The current abundance of cheap natural gas permits both perspectives to see the recent period as a bridge to their long run vision.

Path Dependencies

The economics of non-nuclear energy options reillustrates the large impact of path dependent phenomena (and by extension the impact of social contexts that influence path choices) on energy sector competition. In many cases, the capture of R&D payoffs (contingent upon government funding), learning curve and production economies (contingent upon sector size), and system-wide economies (contingent upon path choices), has been and remains critical to an energy option's competitiveness.

Nuclear power's loss of OT status opened the door to numerous new technological trajectories, such as the exfoliation of gas combustion technologies (spreading from breakthroughs in natural gas turbines to innovations in coal gasification and biogas technologies) to a proliferation of small scale, dispersed generating strategies (facilitated by IPP access to electricity grids, breakthroughs in solar and wind technologies, and a reorienting of utility planning to include intermittents). The possibility of future investments in alternative energy infrastructures (pipelines, electricity transmission and storage technologies, cogeneration facilities, etc.) illustrates how planning shifts can infuse material contexts to create new relative economic efficiencies. For energy sector planning, the suggestions of backcasting appear more relevant than the predictions of forecasting.

From a backcasting perspective, political support for renewable technologies seems capable of greatly expanding their potential contribution. From a forecasting perspective, nuclear power seems a suspended option. The nature of current energy sector competition suggests that technologies that can evolve incrementally (without capture of OT status) will dominate options like nuclear power that require aggressive government support and large investment commitments in order to achieve their economic potential. Assuming moderate energy demand growth, modest expansion of natural gas, coal, and well sited renewable technologies seems the most likely future of the energy sector. The major wild cards are possible greenhouse constraints, which are addressed in chapter 13.

Table 12.9
Nuclear Power's Competition*

	NATURAL GAS	COAL	BIOMASS	WIND	SOLAR ENERGY	GEOTHERMAL ENERGY	HYDROPOWER
Costs	~1995–2015, 3.75–5.5 c/kwh 2015–2030 probably less than 6.5 c/kwh	1995–2015 5–6.5 c/kwh 2015–2030 5.5–7.0	1990–2030: 4.5 c/kwh to 7 c/kwh	5.0–5.5 by 2000, 4.0–5.0 by 2010, w/vigorous R&D as low as 3.0–3.5 c/kwh at good sites by 2030	~2005–2010 ST: 5.5 c/kwh–8 c/kwh PV: ~10 c/kwh, 8 + c/kwh w/accelerated R&D, optimists as low as 5.5 c/kwh *Long run–* ~2030+ 4.5 c/kwh–7.5 c/kwh	Hydrothermal: near term ~5 c/kwh–7 c/kwh HDR: Uncertain, near term 6 c/kwh–10 c/kwh – 30+ c/kwh depending on site, longer term: ~3–9 c/kwh	near term new capacity ~6.5 c/kwh
Resource Base	~900–1200+ Quads, 45–60 years at existing use rates; Trend for upward revision in unconventional supplies Large potential reservoir in unconventional supplies	Enormous: U.S. alone more than 35,000 Quads	10–25 Quads, 25–100 GWe by 2030	Up to 150 GWe by 2030 10%–20% long run share of U.S. electricity	By 2030: up to 150 GWe, 15 Quads, significantly larger longer run possibilities	Hydrothermal: fairly modest (~20 GW for thirty years) HDR: Enormous, larger than fossil and nuclear fuels combined, uncertain access	~0–45 GWe new capacity
Externalities	Most benign fossil fuel Modest No_x problems Greenhouse im-	GHG problems; traditional air pollutants, including SO_2, NO_x, CO & VOCs; mining	Minimal air pollutants (low sulfur and toxics content, controllable particulates and	Minimal environmental externalities modest visual and noise pollution	Minimal traditional pollutants, potential hazardous materials problems	Relatively modest Possible earthquake concerns	Risk of dam failures Loss of some recreational resouces

Table 12.9 (*continued*)

	NATURAL GAS	COAL	BIOMASS	WIND	SOLAR ENERGY	GEOTHERMAL ENERGY	HYDROPOWER
	pact: .1kg C/Kwh Long run potential for import dependence and LNG hazards	hazards and land scarring	VOCs) Minimal GHG problems, Need for sustainable agricultural practices (potential problems w/herbicides, pesticides, monocropping, etc.) Unknown risks accompanying genetic engineering				
Recent and Future Opportunities for Technological Change	Recent breakthroughs in combined cycle plants and aeroderivative turbines. Significant potential for advances wrt unconventional gas recovery and transportation markets.	Numerous new combustion technologies, e.g., AFBC, PFBC and IGCC; pollution abatement technologies; mining technologies	Feedstock innovations (e.g., breeding and genetic engineering, use of micro algae and off-season crops) Utilization technologies (e.g., whole-tree burners, biogasgas turbine technologies, biomass-based fuel cells)	Development of: variable speed turbines, advanced electronic controls, improved blade materials and design, easier manufacturability, taller hubs, larger unit size, cheaper long distance transmission, potential development of offshore	Significant possibilities for materials, equipment and process improvements, especially re: PV cell materials and preparation	Attractive opportunities, especially w/respect to: drilling technologies, HDR fracturing, and reservoir characterization technologies	Refinement of free-flow turbines Technical responses to ecological concerns

		Joint product production processes		wind technology			
Major Public Policy Impacts	R&D funding, drilling access, NOₓ regulation, Greenhouse policies	R&D levels, environmental regulations, rail and slurry pipeline regs.	R&D policy, production subsidies, structure of agricultural subsidies, IPP rules for grid access, price guarantees, GHG credits	R&D funding, Grid access regulations (PURPA, etc.) Environmental credits and other subsidies and incentives	R&D levels, Subsidy rates, Procurement policies, Grid access terms	R&D levels, Subsidy rates, Terms of grid access	Licensing regulations, Externality credits, IPP grid access, R&D support
Path Dependencies	Scaling issues wrt pipelines, infrastructural lumpiness wrt LNG	Infrastructural lumpiness (CHP projects, pipeline and rail investments)	Opportunity for large learning curve-scale economies, presence of major system-wide economies	Importance of: R&D funding, Routine learning (windmill design, siting, size, materials, etc.) Production economies, Innovations in complementary technologies, System design to incorporate intermittents	Significant possibilities for mass production, learning curve and unit scaling economies. Importance of system-wide issues (especially re: intermittency)	—	Pumped hydro fits well w/intermittents
Head to Head w/Nuclear Power	*Plus Side* Cheaper next twenty years, Less uncertainty, Greater planning flexibility, Opportunities for	*Plus Side* Cheaper, less uncertainty, opportunities for incremental evolution, familiar technology.	*Plus Side* Probable economic edge, Large externality advantages, Regional/rural attractiveness	*Plus Side* Cheaper, Fewer negative externalities, More rapid learning *Minus Side* More limited	*Plus Side* More environmentally benign, Potential for more rapid learning *Minus Side* Intermittency	*Plus Side* Less serious negative externalities, Less expensive, R&D costs *Minus Side* Costs even more	Relatively modest competitor, due to modest potential for capacity growth. Most important in low electricity demand

Table 12.9 (continued)

	NATURAL GAS	COAL	BIOMASS	WIND	SOLAR ENERGY	GEOTHERMAL ENERGY	HYDROPOWER
	incremental evolution *Minus Side* Potential long run supply constraints Potential GHG problems	*Minus Side* Serious GHG burdens Serious non-GHG environmental costs	*Minus Side* Supply uncertainties Less data on actual costs	supply potential Intermittency Regional disparities	Large cost uncertainties Uncertain supply potential	uncertain than nuclear costs	scenarios.
Additional Features Sensitive to Technological Aesthetics	Small scale, familiar tech., requiring minimal institutional change, potential bridging fuel	Taps familiar institutions Centralized power source	Renewable energy source Low power densities Small unit size, decentralized format Outside existing energy sector institutional structure Domestic supply	Renewable Low power density Small unit size, decentralized format Domestic supply	Renewable energy source Low power density Small unit size and decentralized format Domestic supply	Enormous supply potential Domestic supply Technically challenging production environment	Ecologically intrusive to river systems

*All dollars 1992 dollars, references in text.

Chapter 13

Global Warming and Nuclear Power

The future of nuclear power is increasingly linked to arguments about greenhouse constraints on the use of fossil fuels. The greenhouse effect analogizes the behavior of certain atmospheric gasses to panes of glass in a greenhouse. These greenhouse gases (GHGs) permit sunlight to pass through them but trap part of the infrared radiation (heat) rebounding from the earth. Over half the greenhouse effect of human activities arises from the combustion of fossil fuels and their generation of carbon dioxide, nitrous oxide, fugitive methane, and tropospheric ozone.[1] Deforestation and select farming practices contribute another 20%–25% of current GHG burdens.

If present trends continue, popular forecasting models predict an increase in equilibrium global mean temperatures of 1.8–6.3 degrees Fahrenheit by 2100 (IPCC Working Group II: Summary, 2). The major adverse consequences anticipated from global warming are:

- sea level rise (with potential damage including: the flooding of low lying areas, erosion of beaches and coasts, destruction of wetlands, salt water intrusion into freshwater sources, and damaged fisheries).

- disrupted agricultural production (due to shifting temperature and precipitation patterns).

- increased weather extremes (stronger hurricanes, more frequent droughts, etc.)

- possible harm to global ecosystems and biodiversity.

- increased incidence of some infectious diseases, due to increased populations of carrier pests.

The challenge of climate stabilization is made more difficult by the trend towards increased greenhouse gas emissions and projected global population and GNP/capita growth rates of ~1.4% and 1.4–2.9% per year through 2025.[2] The need to continually expand energy services while reducing fossil fuel greenhouse gas emissions has led some analysts to claim an immediate nuclear imperative. For example, Alvin Weinberg, former head of Oak Ridge National Laboratory, asserts,

> "Carbon dioxide, I believe, has emerged and continues to emerge as perhaps the central environmental issue. It seems to me . . . [to be] the strongest incentive to get back on track with nuclear energy".[3]

This reaction parallels many research and government policy responses to the energy crises of the early 1970s. Nuclear power's lack of OT status in the 1980s and 1990s, however, has led to more careful consideration of these claims than in the OT period. To assess the merits of nuclear responses to global warming, it is necessary to compare the costs of substituting nuclear for fossil fuels with other abatement or adjustment options, including:

1) Economic and social adaptation to climate change (i.e., adjustment to temperature increases).

2) Climatic engineering (e.g., particulate injection into the atmosphere to increase reflectivity).

3) The capture and storage of greenhouse gases resulting from fossil fuel combustion.

4) Increased efficiency in energy use and fossil fuel combustion.

5) The substitution of non-nuclear renewable energy sources, such as solar and biomass, for fossil fuels.

6) The curtailment of non-fossil fuel contributions to climate change such as agricultural by-products.

The remainder of this chapter explores these comparisons.

Greenhouse Damage Estimates: The Cost of Non-Abatement

The dominant characteristic of damage estimates is the uncertainties surrounding them. The major scientific uncertainties involve the behavior of GHG reservoirs (or sinks), the likely feedback effects of increased heat trapping by greenhouse gases on the earth's climate system, and the impact of final temperature changes (initial effect plus feedback) on various natural systems (such as rainfall and ocean currents).

Uncertainties about greenhouse sinks make it difficult to predict the percentage of future GHG emissions that will remain in the atmosphere. No one is quite sure, for example, where at least 20% of existing carbon emissions go, which makes forecasting future atmospheric retention rates difficult.

Uncertainties about thermal feedback are even larger than those about greenhouse sinks. Feedback optimists foresee initial thermal shocks reversed or unmagnified, due to phenomena such as increased cloud formation and greater atmospheric reflection of sunlight. Feedback pessimists foresee positive feedback of 2–4+ times the initial thermal shock, due to phenomena such as increased snowmelt and reduced surface reflectivity.[4]

Uncertainties about the impact of temperature changes on the earth's natural systems, especially with respect to local weather, sea level rise, and ocean ecosystem behavior, make it difficult to estimate the social impact of a given level of temperature increase. Some climate models, for example, foresee changes in deep ocean currents and surface winds in response to global warming. These changes, independent of increases in global mean temperatures, could have major effects on local climate and agricultural conditions.

Unfortunately, many of the above uncertainties will likely persist for decades or far longer due to the complexity of the earth's climate system. Public policy and scientific recommendations will thus have to be made amidst imperfect information. The current consensus among climatologists and participants in recent global meetings on climate change appears to be that the dangers of global warming are high enough to merit serious policy attention.[5] Complementing the scientific uncertainties surrounding climate change are economic uncertainties about the social costs of any given temperature change, including:

- uncertainties about the economic consequences of alterations in the natural environment (such as the impact of higher temperatures on agricultural productivity)

- uncertainties about the value of phenomena affected by climate change that are not priced in markets (such as the value of lost biodiversity)

- uncertainties about the ability of future technical innovation to reduce or undo the impact of current GHG emissions

- uncertainties about the discount rate to use to translate the future damages caused by current activities into present value damages

- uncertainties about how to treat uncertainty (i.e., how to integrate risk averseness into damage estimates)

- uncertainties about whether to tally warming damages with respect to the U.S. or world economy.

Reflecting all of these social and scientific uncertainties, greenhouse damage estimates vary by as much as ten to twenty-five times, leaving greenhouse concerns either irrelevant or central to nuclear power's future.

One useful way to analyze the impact of greenhouse concerns on nuclear power's future is to translate greenhouse damages into a surcharge on fossil fuel use. This task requires monetizing the damages likely from global warming, linking these damages to increases in greenhouse gases, and debiting economic activities by the marginal cost of their greenhouse emissions. Because of the aforementioned uncertainties, there are few detailed dollar estimates of the economic damage of differing warming levels. Among the most thoughtful cost estimates are studies by William Nordhaus, an economist with the Cowles Foundation and Yale University, and research by William Cline, a senior economist with the Institute for International Economics. Nordhaus estimates that a doubling of CO_2 levels and accompanying increase in temperature of about 3 degrees C would cost the U.S. economy about .25% GNP per year (Nordhaus 1991a, 933). While acknowledging large uncertainties, he estimates that only 3% of U.S. GNP is very sensitive and 10% moderately sensitive to greenhouse dynamics. Eighty-seven percent of the economy is held relatively immune to warming damages (p. 930). He adds,

> "This figure (.25% GNP) is clearly incomplete, for it neglects a number of areas that are either inadequately studied or inherently unquantifiable. We might raise the number to around 1% . . . to allow for these unmeasured and unquantifiable factors, although such an adjustment is purely ad hoc. It is not possible to give precise error bounds around this figure, but my hunch is that the overall impact upon human activity is unlikely to be larger than 2% of total output. . . . These remarks lead to a surprising conclusion. Climate change is likely to produce a combination of gains and losses with no strong presumption of substantial net economic damages" (933).

While acknowledging that damage ratios might be slightly higher for the developing countries (due to larger agricultural sectors), and significantly higher for a few other countries, Nordhaus suggests that similar conclusions hold globally (935).[6]

Cline finds higher damages than Nordhaus, projecting costs of 1 + %– 4% GNP for a doubling of CO_2 levels (1992a, 6). Like Nordhaus, however, he uses a 1% GNP reference case for estimating the costs of CO_2 doubling. His major differences with Nordhaus (over forecasting periods of thirty-five years or less) involve moderately higher damage estimates for agricultural impacts, health effects, water resource effects, energy requirements, and species loss.

While most of the greenhouse literature discusses warming damages in terms of the economic costs of a doubling of CO_2 levels, it is possible to transform these numbers into estimates of the marginal cost (MC) of an additional ton of carbon emissions. The latter is often the relevant cost for policy decisions. The methodology for calculating the MC of GHG emissions is quite complicated.[7]

Using this methodology, Nordhaus transforms his greenhouse damage estimates of 1/4% GNP (low estimate), 1% GNP (medium), and 2% GNP (high) into costs per greenhouse gas emission. He standardizes all greenhouse gases by expressing their warming impact in terms of the amount of CO_2 needed to produce an equivalent thermal effect.

His low, medium, and high damage estimates for the costs of CO_2 doubling translate into marginal damage costs of $1.83/ton carbon emitted, $7.33/tC, and $66/tC (p. 934). Following conventional economic theory, he defines optimal GHG abatement as the level of GHG reduction at which the marginal benefits of reducing carbon emissions by another ton exactly equals the marginal costs of an extra ton of abatement. His medium damage case thus recommends carbon taxes of ~$7.33/tC. Those with cheaper abatement opportunities will reduce their carbon emissions. Those facing more costly abatement schedules will pay the tax and continue to emit GHGs.

At existing combustion and electrical conversion efficiencies, coal-fired electricity produces about .94 kilograms of CO_2 per kilowatt hour (.94 kg CO_2/kwh) or .25/kg carbon per kilowatt hour (.25 kg C/kwh).[8] Given Nordhaus' three damage estimates, this implies greenhouse damages from coal-fired electricity generation of .45 Mills per kilowatt hour (M/kwh), 1.8 M/kwh, and 16.5 M/kwh. Since the projected cost of new nuclear power ranges from 40M–100+ M/kwh, only the latter damage estimate has any significant effect on nuclear competitiveness. Because oil and natural gas are 20% and 40% less CO_2 intensive per BTU[9] than coal-fired electricity, the impact of greenhouse concerns on nuclear competitiveness with these fuels is correspondingly smaller. Another way of organizing this information is to note that at *current* energy conversion efficiencies, it takes a damage estimate of about $40/tC, $50/tC, and $70/tC to generate a 1 cent/kwh surcharge on coal, oil, and natural gas-fired electricity generation.[10]

Disregarding all other concerns than greenhouse damages and market prices,[11] my expected 1.0–3.5 cent/kwh nuclear/coal cost disadvantage implies a need for damage estimates in the range of \$50–\$175/tC to equalize the generating costs from *new* nuclear and coal-fired power plants.[12]

Should Nordhaus' damage estimates prove accurate, global warming will have a very modest impact on nuclear power. Many observers, however, attach higher costs to climate change. Nordhaus' critics can be divided into two groups: the "numerical critics" who accept Nordhaus' framework but offer higher quantitative estimates for the model's parameters, and the "methodological critics" who favor a different framework for assessing global climate risks.

The numerical critics, such as Cline, assume the high end of conventional climate models' temperature forecasts for a doubling of CO_2, the high end of conventional estimates of the economic cost of rising temperatures, and increasingly severe marginal costs for additional GHG emissions as temperatures rise. They either accept the higher damage forecasts or, because of risk averseness, favor adjusting "best guesses" towards pessimistic outcomes. They project damage estimates two to five times more severe than Nordhaus.[13]

In a variation on this theme, Cline argues that planning inertia requires attention to longer run outcomes than the benchmark of CO_2 doubling (~35 years). Extending his analysis to 2275 and worst case temperature changes of 18 degrees C and GNP losses of well over 50%, he calls for early active intervention.

The "methodological critics" argue that the complexity of global ecosystems elude scientific and economic modeling and urge avoidance of massive shocks to these systems. Their greenhouse policy recommendations tend towards climate stabilization with target levels set relatively independent of detailed estimates of economic costs and benefits. They are more concerned about potentially explosive thermal feedback effects or disruptions of complicated life support systems than they are about warming's impact on particular industries. Popular policy goals from this perspective include freezing global GHG emissions at 1990 levels, 20% cutbacks from 1990 levels, and 60%–70% cutbacks from 1990 levels. Only the last option would eliminate anthropogenic warming pressures according to most general climate models.

Proponents of ecological conservatism are often optimistic about "technology forcing." They suggest that posing environmental constraints will generate technological responses that reduce abatement costs. Rather than setting abatement levels where the current marginal cost of abatement equals the marginal damage of greenhouse gas emissions (as suggested by much of standard economic theory), the ecological conservatives urge abatement targets be set in order to maintain the stability of natural systems. The adjustment mechanism is technology rather than temperature.

A hybrid approach, combining preferences for quantitative limits on human disruption of natural systems with a sensitivity for abatement costs, posits the goal of limiting global warming to the maximum level experienced in the last 160,000 years (~2–3 degrees C), subject to some total expenditure constraint. A popular variant of this approach treats 2%–3% GNP as a maximally acceptable cost for GHG abatement and urges as much GHG reduction as possible within this constraint.

There is an irony for nuclear power in the current debate over greenhouse policy. The kinds of imaginations most worried about global warming tend to be similarly concerned about nuclear hazards. While this overlap theoretically could have muted some of nuclear power's ardent critics, it has tended instead to prevent greenhouse concerns from significantly increasing support for nuclear power. The major beneficiaries of global warming fears have therefore been renewable energy sources and energy efficiency options.

In the short run, 1996–2000, it seems likely that U.S. responses to global warming will be dominated by damage uncertainties. Among the most likely policy responses are inaction, increased funds for climate change and energy conservation research, and a token carbon tax (perhaps $5–$10/ton C). None of these measures would provide short run incentives for new nuclear orders. Greenhouse concerns might, however, increase support for nuclear R&D as a climate change insurance policy (though the problem here is the relative expensiveness of nuclear research in comparison with alternative energy options).

Over the longer run, the high range of greenhouse damage estimates are serious enough to sharply curtail coal use and erase natural gas's cost advantage over nuclear power. The low range of damage estimates would have little lasting impact on nuclear competitiveness. Whether the high damage estimates could reinvigorate the nuclear option depends upon the economics of alternative GHG abatement strategies, which are addressed in the next section. Whether the high or low damage estimates are correct will likely remain uncertain for decades or longer.

Alternative Abatement Strategies

The economic merits of nuclear power as a greenhouse abatement option depend upon nuclear costs, the level of greenhouse gas (GHG) emissions from nuclear power and its alternatives, and the economics of alternative abatement strategies, in particular on:

- the cost of energy efficiency investments (which reduce GHG emissions by reducing fossil fuel combustion)

- the cost of shifting from carbon rich fossil fuels, like coal, to less carbon rich fossil fuels, like natural gas

- the cost of non-nuclear energy alternatives to fossil fuels

- the cost of offsetting GHGs (through policies such as reforestation) and

- the cost of reducing non-fossil fuel generated GHGs (such as agriculturally released methane)

Nuclear Power's Greenhouse Gas (GHG) Emissions

Operating nuclear power plants release no carbon dioxide. Including the GHGs emitted during nuclear plant construction and nuclear fuel preparation, greenhouse gas burdens average only ~.002 kgC/kwh or less than 1% of those from coal-fired plants.[14]

GHG Abatement Schedules

In drawing cost comparisons, it's helpful to combine all non-nuclear abatement options into an aggregate abatement supply schedule. This permits easy estimate of the costs of reducing greenhouse gases, with or without nuclear generation, to any target level. There is wide debate over the shape of this schedule. Figures 13.1 and 13.2 represent estimated abatement cost curves by ICF Resources, a contractor for the EPA, and William Nordhaus.[15] The ICF study finds that GHG emission could be cut by more than 42% from "business as usual"-baseline projections for 2010, at zero marginal cost, without nuclear power (Lovins and Lovins 1991, 31). Amory Lovins argues that additional reductions could be purchased quite cheaply (Ibid. 31–35). Nordhaus is less optimistic. He foresees marginal costs of ~$90/tC, $120/tC, $172/tC, and $240/tC for GHG reductions of 40%, 50%, 60%, and 70% (Nordhaus 1991a 929; 1991b, 62–63).

Under Lovins' abatement supply schedule, greenhouse constraints add little incentive for nuclear expansion. Even if targeted GHG reductions were to reach 60%–70% (the level generally thought necessary to stabilize atmospheric GHG concentrations and a level far beyond what seems politically feasible), non-nuclear abatement options remain cheaper than nuclear based

Fig. 13.1

ICF/Lovins Marginal Cost for GHG Abatement

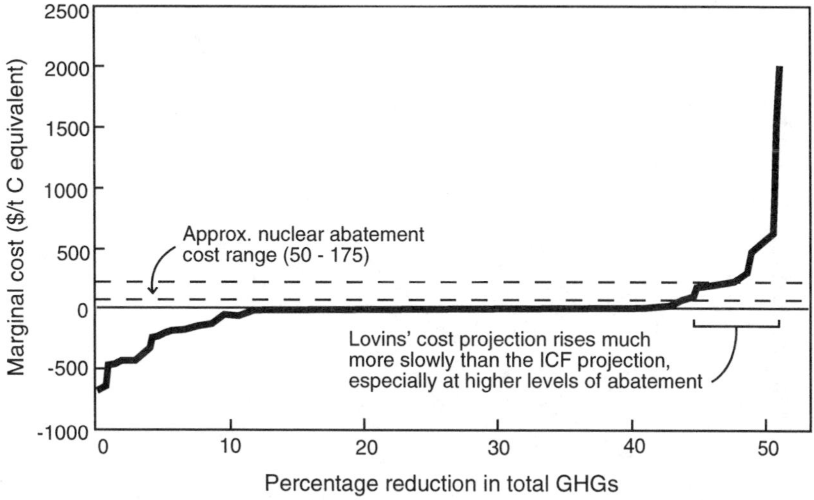

Source: Lovins and Lovins 1991, P. 31

abatement of $50–$175/tC.[16] Under Nordhaus' abatement schedule, nuclear power appears an appealing abatement option (even at a 3 c/kwh cost disadvantage with coal-fired electricity), once abatement targets pass 55% of current GHG emissions.

Underlying the Lovins-Nordhaus debate are differing estimates of the cost of substituting energy efficiency investments[17] and non-nuclear energy sources for fossil fuels and the cost of reducing GHG emissions in non-energy related fields. As chapters 11 and 12 and note 17 have addressed the first two topics in detail, this section focuses on the feasibility of three other non-nuclear abatement options: capturing and sequestering CO_2 (with trees or scrubbers), modifying non-energy sector activities (chiefly agricultural practices) to reduce GHG accumulation, and geoengineering to alter the earth's climate.

Biomass Capture and Storage of CO_2

Variants of this strategy include slowing deforestation, expanding or creating new forests (reforestation), the cultivation of special carbon capturing crops, altered agricultural practices, and the acceleration of ocean based photosynthesis and carbon retention. Slowing deforestation is an extremely

Fig. 13.2

Nordhaus Marginal Cost for GHG Abatement

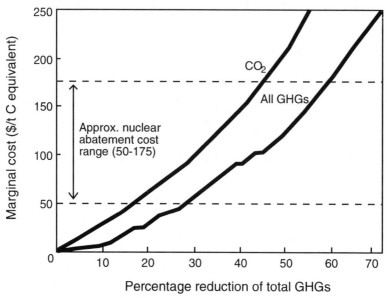

Percentage reduction of total GHGs

Source: Nordhaus 1991a, P. 929

promising GHG abatement option due to the meager economic benefits of many current forest destroying practices. Cline estimates that curbing de- forestation could reduce global GHG emissions by as much as 1 GtC/yr (~15% current global carbon emissions) for ~30 years at costs in the neigh- borhood of $10/tC (Cline 1992a 220–221).[18]

While more expensive than reducing deforestation, most analyses find reforestation relatively inexpensive at modest levels. Widely cited is the off- set experiment by Applied Energy Services, which intends to plant 194,000 acres of trees in Guatemala to offset the expected lifetime CO_2 emissions from an 80 MW fluidized bed coal-fired electricity generating plant in Con- necticut. The utility estimates it can recover its costs through a voluntary 5% surcharge on the plant's output (Lovins and Lovins 1991, 44).[19]

The key question with respect to reforestation is how fast the marginal costs of expanding aboreal carbon sinks turn upward. Nordhaus estimates that only ~.2 GtC/yr. could be sequestered in new tropical forests at a cost of ~45 tC/yr. (Nordhaus 1991a, 60). He foresees sharply rising expenditures if U.S. land is used, with marginal costs reaching ~115. tC/yr. for a se- questering of .28 GtC/yr. Cline and Lovins are more optimistic. Cline foresees costs of ~$18/tC for sequestering ~.4 Gt C/yr. in the U.S. and a global average cost of $11/tC for the capture of 1.6 GtC/yr. (Cline 1992b, 66–67, Lovins and Lovins 1991, 27).

Lovins also offers eye-opening suggestions for increasing the soil's carbon retention. One of Lovins' great gifts is an ability to expand realms of discourse by jumping from marginal changes within existing systems to new planning contexts. His analysis of the agricultural sector asserts the economic viability of much less energy and chemical intensive farming practices and the availability of a much wider range of GHG abatement options than usually imagined (Lovins and Lovins 1991, 22–28). He notes, for example, that the subsoil acts as an even larger carbon sink than terrestial forests and urges the adoption of revised farming techniques, such as low tillage and increased reliance on natural fertilizers, to increase the soil's carbon retention.[20]

CO_2 Capture and Storage Options: Engineered Systems

For existing plants, engineered capture and storage is prohibitively expensive. Researchers at M.I.T. have estimated that the cheapest existing systems would add ~6.5 c/kwh to ~11.5 c/kwh to coal generating costs (Drake 1993, table 5, 37). Long run prospects are more encouraging due to opportunities for innovations in CO_2 capture and disposal technologies and the ability to design and site new plants with an eye towards minimizing scrubbing penalties. The MIT team suggested that capture and disposal costs could conceivably fall to 2–4 c/kwh in ten to twenty years (Ibid.). While the systems proposed would still involve expensive abatement options (~$100–$200/tC) and residual carbon emissions of ~.05 kg/kwh (~15%–~20% current levels), they could serve as a backstop technology for greenhouse abatement in the electricity sector. Assuming long run coal generating costs of 5c/kwh without GHG abatement, implies backstop costs of 7c/kwh to 9c/kwh if optimistic CO_2 scrubbing forecasts prevail.[21] Because of uncertainties about CO_2 storage technologies, an interested skepticism seems appropriate.

Climatic Engineering

Numerous geoengineering technologies have been proposed for offsetting greenhouse gas accumulations; these include cloud seeding over the oceans, floating polystyrene atop the oceans, and sunlight screening (through the orbiting of 50,000 100-km squared space mirrors, the placing of aluminized hydrogen balloons in the stratosphere, the lowering of aircraft engine efficiency in order to generate a sooty exhaust, and the launching of tiny particulates into the stratosphere from 16" naval rifles (Grubb 1990, 12; NAS 1991, 5; Nordhaus 1991b, 61). Nordhaus cites preliminary cost estimates equivalent to $.1–$10/tC for some of these options (1991b, 61). While intrigued by their low cost, he notes that they carry unknown risks. The dangers would seem to raise the same kinds of concerns that greenhouse abatement is intended to avoid. Echoing this sentiment the 1991 National Academy of Sciences greenhouse policy study concluded, "Geoengineering options have the potential to affect greenhouse warming on a substantial scale. However, precisely because they might do so, and because the climate system and its chemistry are poorly understood, these options must be considered extremely carefully" (NAS 1991, 58–59). For the foreseeable future, geoengineering options are most likely to be pursued as insurance policies in the event a sudden and large abatement response is needed.

Ocean Carbon Storage

Nordhaus finds intriguing the idea of seeding the North Pacific and Antarctic Oceans with trace amounts of iron in order to accelerate photosynthesis there and increase accumulation of precipitated organic carbon on the ocean floor. He cites preliminary cost forecasts in the range of $.1 to $10/tC (1991b, 61). Like the geoengineering options discussed above for altering the earth's climate system, ocean seeding carries unknown risks and is likely to be viewed skeptically by many environmentalists.

Coalbed and Landfill Methane Capture

Lovins estimates that the fuel value of fugitive methane from landfills and coalbeds can nearly finance its capture, noting that 123 landfills already attempt methane recovery (Lovins and Lovins 1991, 29–30). Research by the Center for Clean Air Policy in Washington, D.C. finds coalbed methane capture self-financing at a price of $3/1000 cubic foot of natural gas, roughly equal to the DOE's projected delivered price of natural gas to utilities in 2015.[22] Other observers are more skeptical and anticipate unexpected technical problems to limit coalbed methane recovery.

CFC Reducing Strategies

Almost all greenhouse abatement analyses before late 1991 found CFC reductions to be among the cheapest GHG reducing strategies. Optimism about greenhouse abatement costs was aided by dramatic declines in the expected costs of phasing out CFCs.[23] Since late 1991, however, new research has suggested that CFCs' warming effects may be significantly offset by the gas' ozone destruction, due to the latter's role as a GHG. Pessimists about the costs of reducing greenhouse gases point to this reversal as the kind of negative surprises they anticipate.

Abatement Competition

Critics of nuclear power often note the inability of the technology to unilaterally solve the greenhouse problem and the availability of many low cost abatement options. These conditions are insufficient, however, to preclude greenhouse constraints from spurring nuclear expansion. On the cost side, what is important is not the existence of some cheaper abatement options, but the marginal cost of the last unit of abatement that new nuclear-fired electricity might replace. On the supply side, the issue is not whether nuclear power can unilaterally eliminate the greenhouse problem, but whether it can play a significant role.

The real difficulty for nuclear advocates is a Catch-22 dilemma. At low levels of GHG reductions there are cheaper abatement alternatives than nuclear power. At high levels of abatement, no plausible rate of nuclear expansion can significantly reduce GHG emissions without aggressive energy efficiency programs.[24] The latter, however, invites consolidation of OT status for energy efficiency and other institutional changes that devalue nuclear power's potential greenhouse abatement contribution.

Nuclear power's current status as a greenhouse abatement option seems best described as a "last resort" strategy. In the short run (five to ten years) there are much cheaper abatement options, led by energy efficiency, forestry initiatives, and the replacement of existing coal-fired electricity generation with advanced gas-fired plants. While there is some debate over the magnitude of these low cost abatement options, it appears very likely that they could reduce current U.S. GHG emissions by at least one-third at costs below $25/tC abated. This price tag is about one-seventh to one-half the projected cost of reducing GHG by replacing fossil fuel-fired plants with nuclear plants. GHG abatement optimists foresee continuing low costs for abatement levels of more than 50% or even 60% and it seems unlikely that unpopular options, like nuclear power, will be tried unless popular options like energy efficiency prove unable to achieve target GHG reductions.

In the longer run (thirty to fifty years), the nature of nuclear power's abatement competition is more uncertain and depends largely upon the rate of technical innovation with respect to energy conservation and renewable energy technologies, and the degree of public policy support for institutional changes to facilitate greenhouse abatement.

"Top down"-energy sector forecasting models[25] suggest there may be a large role for nuclear power if long run abatement targets attempt to freeze GHG emissions at levels 20% below 1990 emissions (which by 2050 implies a ~50% reduction from "business as usual" emission levels). Most of the models foresee costs in the neighborhood of $120–$250/tC by mid-century (Cline 1992a 150, 294). "Bottom up"-models of GHG reduction options[25] imply little role for nuclear power in greenhouse abatement, especially if greenhouse concerns spur increased support for energy efficiency initiatives and renewable energy technologies.

Conclusion: Will Global Warming Nourish Nuclear Power?

In the short- and mid-run, the impact of greenhouse concerns on nuclear power is likely to be minimal. Greenhouse hazards could resuscitate nuclear power in the long run, but only if high estimates of global warming damages are confirmed (or uncertainty continues, but public policy is governed by ecological conservatism) and alternative abatement strategies prove unsuccessful.

Over the next ten years greenhouse abatement responses are likely to be dominated by calls for further study, energy efficiency initiatives, the substitution of natural gas for coal in power plants, increased spending on R&D for renewable energy sources, and perhaps reduced deforestation and increased afforestation efforts.[26] Some minimal carbon taxes are possible ($5/tC–$20/tC), but it is unlikely that the taxes would approach the $100–$200/tC level necessary to alter nuclear power's large expected cost disadvantage with coal or natural gas-fired electricity generation.[27]

The impact on nuclear power of global warming concerns in ten to twenty-five years is a little more uncertain. It depends upon the desired level of GHG reductions and the mid-run effectiveness of alternative abatement strategies. There are several reasons to suspect serious limits to the public's willingness to pay for expensive GHG reductions: (1) the almost certain persistence of large scientific uncertainties about greenhouse dynamics;[28] (2) the lack of visible feedback from abatement actions; (3) the modest level of estimated economic damage from GHGs at current emission rates (~$5/ tC to $25/tC) and likelihood of damages only two to three times this level by the middle of the next century; (4) the more concentrated impact of abatement costs (fossil fuel industries) than abatement benefits (general public); and (5) the limited payoffs to unilateral U.S. action and difficulties inherent in obtaining global commitments to very high GHG constraints.

Weighed against these factors is the ethic of ecological conservatism and the symbolic potential of greenhouse politics. Should high GHG damages be confirmed or resistance to global warming become a litmus test for decent mindedness and global citizenship, stiff carbon taxes could be adopted. The imposition of a moderate carbon tax, perhaps as high as $50/tC by 2025, seems more likely. (Recall this would amount to a tax of about 1 c/kwh on high efficiency coal-fired electricity and .5 c/kwh on high efficiency gas-fired electricity.)

The mid-run attractiveness of nuclear power as an abatement option is modestly better than its short run prospects and especially sensitive to assumptions about the cost and availability of natural gas, the economics of energy efficiency, and the cost of non-carbon renewable energy sources. Most analyses predict that cheap energy conservation measures will be declining but still available. Other low cost abatement options, such as afforestation, will be nearing their quantity limits. The expected price of natural gas is controversial, but would probably still be low enough to leave gas-fired electricity cheaper than nuclear power.

It is really only in longer time frames that greenhouse concerns may spur nuclear expansion. It is in these years that damage uncertainties may be reduced and cheap abatement options (e.g., inexpensive conservation measures, expanded biomass carbon sinks, and low cost natural gas) may be exhausted by energy demand growth. The key question is whether R&D will generate attractive new energy efficiency and renewable energy options to compensate for constraints on fossil fuel use.

Projections over long time horizons are necessarily speculative and the distinction between forecasting and backcasting blurs (partially because predictions can change behavior and thus act like self-fulfilling prophecies.) Lovins' papers assert an existence proof of the possibility of non-nuclear greenhouse abatement, rather than a prediction of such abatement. In much the same way the nuclear industry's cost projections (based on "nth of a kind standardized nuclear plants, operated by experienced, high quality utility staffs and regulated by a friendly NRC) assert the possibility of cheap nuclear responses to greenhouse hazards. Lovins' vision assumes a societal commitment to institutional changes that would facilitate energy efficiency, renewable energy development, and decentralized greenhouse abatements. The nuclear vision assumes societal adjustments to facilitate nuclear expansion.

Skeptics about the potential magnitude of energy efficiency, such as Alvin Weinberg, argue that it is easier to develop new technologies than new patterns of institutional behavior. Lovins is more sanguine about societal change and wary of technical fixes that carry unknown side effects. As in the energy demand sphere, Lovins' greenhouse optimism rests on the claim of an evolving paradigm shift towards OT status for energy efficiency.

This argument is replayed in third world contexts when greenhouse issues shift from a domestic to global focus. The logic of industrialization and population distributions imply that the developing world will be the major emitters of GHGs. Because of more immediate concerns (which imply the use of high discount rates to depreciate long term hazards) and the reasonable claim that the developed world should bear the brunt of GHG reductions (because it is wealthier and largely responsible for the 25% increase in the atmosphere's stock of carbon from pre-industrial times), many developing countries will probably place a relatively low value on limiting their GHG emissions in order to reduce the risk of global warming. The case of China, with its enormous coal reserves, is especially important.

It is in this context that planners oriented towards technical fixes feel much more comfortable with the idea of finding a cheap energy alternative to coal, like nuclear power, than seeking to wring out of the Chinese economy all of the potential adjustments that could reduce energy demand and unnecessary GHG emissions. There are several problems, however, with attempting to construct large nuclear sectors in the third world. Among the most important difficulties are: capital constraints, foreign exchange constraints, skilled labor constraints, and small electricity grids. Because of these problems, small passively safe reactors (such as the MHTGR) would appear to have advantages over large evolutionary LWRs in developing economies. Even these reactors, however, would seem less appropriate than reliance on local resources, such as advanced biomass and wind technologies, unless nuclear power had a very large cost advantage.

Ultimately the debate over the long run implications of greenhouse constraints for nuclear power is similar to the general debate over the future of nuclear power. Once time horizons approach fifty to one hundred years, basic intuitions about technological trajectories, ecological risk taking, and societal dynamics govern forecasting outcomes. The underlying disagreements between those who perceive fission power as the logical next step for energy sector development (due to its large fuel supply and potential for continued technical change) and those who see it as a dead-end (due to its inherent hazards) is likely to continue.

At this level of abstraction, the impact of global warming hazards on the nuclear debate is ambiguous. Greenhouse concerns (and increased respect for ecological conservatism) raise the likelihood of both constraints on fossil use and increased support for energy efficiency and renewable energy technologies. Assuming that nuclear power remains an "option of last resort," greenhouse constraints will spur its expansion only if other strategies fail.

Part IV

Conclusion

It is time to summarize the implications of the history of nuclear power for the technology's future and for theories about the nature of economic activity and technical change in American capitalism. The first section of chapter 14 explores the implications of nuclear history for political-economic theory. The second and third sections predict the likely future of nuclear power in the U.S. and offer recommendations for public policy towards nuclear technology.

Chapter 14

Findings

Nuclear Power and Social Theory

The preceding chapters linked the implications of path dependency in economic competition to sociology of knowledge concerns about the nature of technology assessment. The analysis combined the concepts of path dependency, bounded rationality, and technological aesthetics to help explain the rise and fall of nuclear power development in the United States. The discussion below explores the implications of these three linked concepts for debates over what determines the direction of technical change and other issues in social theory.

The Debate Over Technical Determinism

One of the major debates in modern social theory is over whether the direction of market organized technical change is influenced by socio-political factors or simply reflects the logic of scientific discovery and market pressures for cost minimization. The distinction has important implications. The a-social perspective perceives the market as a medium for the assertion of technical rationality. The "social context"-approach perceives the market as a contested terrain whose outcomes may reflect socio-political phenomena *as well* as the imperatives of cost minimization. The former view implies an inevitability to the shape of technical change. The latter view allows technological evolution to be much more contingent and invites commercial interests as well as political and social movements to attempt to influence the direction of technological change.

The history of nuclear power in the U.S. generally supports the non-technically deterministic position. The intra-nuclear industry triumph of the light water reactor (LWR), for example, was more a product of the technology's appropriateness for naval use and its sponsors' promotional activities, than the inherent advantages of the LWR over alternative nuclear technologies, such as the gas-graphite reactor or passively safe reactor designs. The pattern of expansion and contraction of the U.S. nuclear sector has depended more on the shifting character of the nuclear planning context than the inevitable implications of a priori engineering efficiencies.

The logic of the Planning Context-Official-Technology (PC-OT) framework permits exploration of how social contexts can infuse market outcomes even as the latter conform to cost minimizing pressures. The framework demonstrates how least cost characteristics can be *created* as well as *discovered*. It suggests how technological outcomes that appear to have been dictated by the least cost characteristics of naturally given engineering imperatives can be the result, rather than the cause, of political-economic initiatives.

The PC-OT framework illuminates how social contexts can infuse technological outcomes by exploring: (1) the impact of path dependent cost reductions on the competitiveness of different technologies; (2) the tendency for bounded rationality to organize technology assessment; and (3) the impact of historically given technological aesthetics on judgments about the relative promise of different technologies. These phenomena permit sociopolitical variables, such as distributions of power and ideological belief, to shape technological outcomes by influencing the criteria for technology assessment and which technical options capture the cost reductions associated with increased sector size.

Path Dependency in Nuclear and Non-Nuclear Energy Economics

As noted in chapters 2 and 5, path dependent cost reductions have played a key role in nuclear planning and cost performance. Savings from phenomena such as mass production economies, learning curve cost reductions, and lower risk premiums in capital markets, for example, were more than an order of magnitude greater than the expected nuclear cost advantage over coal fired plants that justified many nuclear orders during the bandwagon market of the 1960s.

The tendency for technological momentum to channel energy sector R&D into extensions of existing commercial technologies, a practice that can be analogized to the logic of "normal science" within scientific paradigms, also aided nuclear power as the nuclear sector expanded. The market impact of technological momentum is reinforced by what economists call "first mover advantage". If a technology actualizes its R&D potential (through R&D spending) it gains a large advantage over hypothetical rivals. While the risks of failure remain constant for unfunded technologies, the payoffs to duplicate achievements are significantly reduced in the aftermath of a successful or even semi-successful R&D venture. Thus a pioneering technology can deny a promising alternative crucial R&D funding if it captures earlier research support. This appears to have been the case with the triumph of the LWR over the MHTGR within the nuclear sector and was nearly the case with respect to competition between nuclear and renewable energy technologies within the energy sector.

As demonstrated in chapters 11 and 12, path dependent factors are also critical to the competitiveness of non-nuclear energy technologies. Expected cost reductions of 10%–20% per doubling of cumulative output are common across a wide array of energy sector options. The cost of non-nuclear energy sources is also quite sensitive to infrastructural and institutional design decisions (such as the level of R&D support for energy storage technologies) and accomodation to the institutional needs of non-nuclear energy sources (such as access to electricity grids for independent power producers and access to credit at utility rates for energy efficiency investments by home owners).

Utility planners face similar "system" or "path choices" (rather than repeated marginal choices) in designing their generating mix strategies. An energy system relying heavily on large baseload nuclear and coal plants will find the costs of integrating intermittent energy sources into their generating mix much greater than a system with a high percentage of hydro, pumped storage, biomass, and gas turbine units. The implication of "cumulative causation" is that "history matters". Early decisions, made amidst large uncertainties can be self-fulfilling economic prophecies of the relative costs of different energy sector options. The PC-OT framework illuminates how socio-political factors can shape later economic calculations by influencing these early path choices.

Given the importance of path dependency and ambiguities of technical information, the PC-OT framework recommends economic theory adopt an "active" rather than "passive" theory of the firm with respect to technical change. Rather than treating the corporation as a "technology taker," inevitably following development paths determined in advance by technical imperatives, the PC-OT framework suggests that firms may attempt to shape technological change in the pursuit of special profits (economic rents) on their technologically specific assets. By extension the framework suggests that social movements can also influence the shape of technical change in pursuit of various socio-political objectives.

The Tendency for Bounded Rationality in Technology Assessment

One of the striking things about the history of technology assessment in the energy sector is the degree to which shifting planning contexts reoriented *technical thinking* about energy sector options. The reconfiguring of the nuclear planning context to include greater participation by environmentalists, public interest groups, and "the left", produced a shift in *technical thinking* akin to Kuhn's notion of a scientific revolution in fields as diverse as radiation hazard assessment, reactor accident probability forecasting, and nuclear cost forecasting.

Many earlier chapters used a common framework to illuminate the impact of social contexts on the type of information available about nuclear power. The discussion explored how socio-political phenomena effected the data available (or unavailable) for analysis, the conceptual frameworks used to analyze data, and responses to anomalous findings. The pattern of errant assumptions and mistaken forecasts governing early nuclear power planning and energy demand forecasting described in tables 4.2, 4.5 and 11.2 demonstrates the ability of bounded rationality to orient research findings by delimiting the questions asked and approaches taken to problem solving. It is simply too expensive "to doubt everything". Basic assumptions frequently go unchallenged and alternative ideas are left unexplored. The net result is that planning context biases can infuse technical discourse.

The history of bounded rationality in the nuclear sector highlights the role played by research groups like the Union of Concerned Scientists and Komanoff Energy Associates in disestablishing nuclear power as an Official Technology. The groups' ability to challenge the nuclear industry's monopoly of nuclear information production with less optimistic findings, reflected both the quality of the groups' research and the presence of social movements able to demand attention to the research. Similar, though sometimes less well developed, analyses were available earlier but were ignored.

The legacy of the nuclear industry's history of excess optimism is a widespread skepticism towards current nuclear industry predictions about new reactor designs. As Alvin Weinberg, father of the PWR, has conceded, a major increase in public confidence in nuclear industry claims will probably require their endorsement by some well known nuclear skeptics.

The Impact of Technological Aesthetics on Technology Assessment

Alongside bounded rationality, the history of nuclear power also highlights the importance of technological aesthetics in technology assessment. Debates about the promise of nuclear power have often turned on untestable intuitions about what characteristics of a youthful technology foreshadow future success. The technological aesthetics of participants in the NPC prior to nuclear power's loss of OT status tilted energy sector choices towards technologies with unlimited energy supply potential, high power densities, large unit size, and centralized administrative formats. The reorganization of the NPC to include greater participation by environmentalists, public interest groups, and "the left", brought with it a skepticism about large scale, centralized technologies with power densities threatening serious accident hazards. This skepticism devalued the appeal of nuclear options. The restructuring of the NPC also brought with it an uneasiness about the concentrations of political-economic power that nuclear technologies seemed to foreshadow, but this is a separate issue from revisions in engineering and economic judgment.

At the heart of many current nuclear debates are questions without objective answers, such as: (1) can "human factor engineering" eliminate serious error by reactor operators; (2) can "social engineering" alter energy consumption patterns and increase energy conservation; (3) will technologies offering economies of unit size be cheaper than smaller scale technologies offering mass production cost savings; (4) will centralized technologies be easier to manage than decentralized technologies; and (5) will generating mixes relying on large baseload technologies inevitably dominate generating mixes that include a high percentage of intermittent energy sources. How a planning context responds to these questions inevitably reflects the participants' technological aesthetics as well as concrete empirical data.

Holistic Alternatives to Technical Determinism

The PC-OT framework encourages a sociology of knowledge analysis of the character of nuclear power information. The approach suggests a "structuralist epistemology", wherein the character of technological knowledge is linked to both the "objective" character of the physical world and the structure of the social context producing the knowledge. The claim that social contexts infuse technical information raises the question of whether there is a logic or causal structure to the ensemble of social variables (e.g., distributions of power, patterns of technological aesthetics, character of institutional structures, forms of bounded rationality, etc.) that define planning contexts. I think there is a connectedness to the societal phenomena that influence technical change, but the task of demonstrating such linkages is beyond the scope of this book.

I anticipate that Althusser's concepts of "structural causality" and "overdetermination" will prove very useful to attempts to construct theories of technical change that tie planning context characteristics to the larger logic of a social structure. Structural causality implies that historically determined patterns of institutions and belief encourage some kinds of collective action more than others. The authoring institutions and beliefs are interconnected so that it is impossible to attribute causality to any one element of the social nexus. Overdetermination is a fancy way of claiming that social causality is holistic rather than additive. Thus there are many causes for the same event, or alternatively, only one cause that has many manifestations.

In this vein, I expect that the rise and fall of nuclear power can best be explained in terms of a shift in American capitalism after the mid-sixties that created a political-economic order more influenced by the world views of the PMC, "the left" (though only on issues that didn't fundamentally threaten underlying distributions of wealth) and environmentalism than during the OT period in which American economic planning was dominated by military and corporate imaginations.

While similar phenomena have been occurring in other advanced capitalist countries, each nation's particular history conditions how these tendencies are expressed. It appears that the impact of general tendencies (such as the increased political-economic influence of the PMC) on specific policies, (such as nuclear development), is highly contingent, depending on the exact combination of historical factors present. Thus modest historical difference, such as the greater centralization of science and politics in France than in the U.S., can lead to significant differences in nuclear trajectories. This contingency can be analogized to the ability of positive feedback in chaos theory to generate two very different outcomes from nearly identical initial positions. The net result is that predictions are difficult in social theory. Nevertheless, the following section will offer some guesses about nuclear power's future in the U.S.

The Future of Nuclear Power in the U.S.

The immediate prospects of nuclear energy in the U.S. are bleak, as symbolized by the TVA's cancellation of three of the last four nuclear plants still under construction in the U.S. in December 1994, despite previous expenditures of more than $6 billion on the plants (*New York Times* 12/15/94, DOE 0436(95), ix, 7). Increasingly strong competition from energy efficiency investments, cheap natural gas, innovative coal technologies, and renewable energy sources seems to preclude a large number of new nuclear plant orders for a minimum of ten to fifteen years. While idiosyncratic support for nuclear power may emerge among a few public utility commissions or independent power producers, it is highly unlikely that the nuclear sector will win enough orders to capture learning curve and other scaling economies for new reactor designs. Problems with plant aging are also likely to limit utility interest in plant lifetime extension and have raised the possibility of as many as twenty-five premature plant shutdowns.

Recent regulatory changes involving one-step licensing and site banking seem unlikely to unilaterally spur new nuclear orders. While opinion polls suggest that a majority of the public may be willing to tolerate new nuclear plants in the absence of alternatives, most people and political-economic decision makers believe there are alternatives to nuclear expansion. With choices, the public favors tapping non-nuclear over nuclear energy sources.[1] In addition, about 25% of the public appears adamantly opposed to new nuclear construction and it is not clear that their opposition could be overcome, even if the majority would tolerate nuclear expansion.[2]

The two major wild cards in nuclear power's future are the greenhouse effect and a possible large increase in the demand for electric cars. While the latter would help nuclear power, the technology would still face strong competition from innovative fossil fuel and renewable energy options. The real precondition for a nuclear renewal is the adoption of severe constraints on fossil fuel use in response to greenhouse concerns. This tack seems unlikely, however, due to uncertainties about greenhouse damages and the likelihood of cheaper greenhouse abatement options than expanding nuclear power.

For the time being the best hope for U.S. nuclear firms are export sales, especially to Asia. The South Korean nuclear program, for example, has been the most rapidly growing nuclear program in the world. Recent U.S. agreements with North Korea call for two new LWRs for that country. China has consistently flirted with the idea of a large nuclear program.

For the most part, however, nuclear power is also on the defensive overseas. As World Bank official Robert Saunders has indicated, "nuclear power appears to be uneconomic in most countries" (*Nucleonics Week* 10/7/93, 14). The capital intensity of nuclear energy is also ill matched for the labor rich and capital poor economies of the third world. Even in France which gets 80% of its electricity from nuclear power, there is increasing skepticism about the wisdom of additional nuclear investment and opposition to the country's expensive breeder reactor program.

Only under the most favorable assumptions, including: the absence of a serious nuclear accident anywhere around the world, a significant escalation in natural gas prices, large greenhouse constraints on coal use, the failure of most renewable energy technologies, an exhaustion of energy efficiency options, and resolution of concerns about nuclear waste disposal and nuclear weapons proliferation will nuclear power make a major comeback in the foreseeable future.

Recommendations for Public Policy

Long Versus Short Term Foci

The strongest rationale for government support of nuclear power involves treating the technology as an insurance policy that would minimize the economic costs of large unexpected fossil fuel price increases or severe greenhouse constrains on fossil fuel use in the presence of disappointing progress in the renewable energy field and rapid energy demand growth. While this rationale is not unreasonable, its implications for nuclear power funding are quite modest.

Treating nuclear energy as a backstop technology implies that nuclear funding should be geared towards long term development possibilities rather than the short term market issues that have dominated nuclear planning in the past. Among the projects that drift to the top of a long run nuclear development program would be: (1) assessment of nuclear radiation hazards, (2) design of passively safe reactor systems; (3) development of proliferation resistant reactor designs; (4) and resolution of nuclear waste disposal issues. The nuclear industry continues to pursue strategies largely at odds with these priorities, focusing on short term cost reducing measures (such as elimination of nuclear regulations deemed by the industry marginal to safety), the refinement of large light water reactors relying on active rather than passive safety systems; the immediate construction of a waste repository independent of thorough review of all outstanding waste disposal uncertainties, and minimal attention to proliferation issues. This focus reflects the needs of firms with sunk capital costs in current nuclear technologies and is inappropriate for public policy.

The Absence of a Nuclear Imperative

The loss of nuclear inevitability implies that nuclear power must compete with other potential backstop technologies for R&D funds and other forms of social support such as limited liability protection. Once the notion of a nuclear imperative is abandoned, several characteristics of nuclear power disadvantage it in competition for R&D dollars. For example, the large unit size of nuclear plants' (even small nuclear reactors) leave nuclear R&D projects among the most expensive R&D options. The prospects for success must be much higher to justify a billion dollar nuclear research project than a 20 million dollar wind power project. The technology's serious accident hazards also require thorough regulatory review before innovations can be adopted, which retards the pace of technical change and industry learning. In the face of such disadvantages nuclear research needs to shift from a construction to conceptual focus.

To many observers inevitable uncertainties about reactor safety, proliferation hazards, waste disposal, and uranium availability leave the technology a "last resort" option. This view recommends little government support for nuclear power until nearly all other options have been exhausted. I am sympathetic to this conclusion, but would de-emphasize the role of waste disposal and uranium scarcity concerns. While waste disposal is a serious problem, associated risks seem orders of magnitude lower than those posed by major reactor accidents. Global uranium resources also seem large enough to preclude serious pressures for breeder reactor designs for several decades and perhaps indefinitely.[3]

The Polarizing Implications of Path Dependency

The path dependent character of energy sector competition and the past behavior of the nuclear industry tend to polarize nuclear energy debates. Both supporters and opponents of nuclear power often perceive nuclear and renewable energy options as mutually exclusive development paths, due as much to the planning outlooks and socio-political dynamics they encourage as to the technical incompatibility of the energy forms.

Past deceptions and mistakes by the nuclear industry have led the public and anti-nuclear activists to distrust nuclear optimism. The disingenuous and misleading claims of groups like the Council for Energy Awareness (the nuclear industry's public relations arm in the early 1990s, whose name was chosen to give its pro-nuclear material a more objective appearance) have exacerbated rather than reduced the industry's public relations problems. Backlash against the CEA's promotional campaigns has overwhelmed thoughtful efforts by supporters of light water reactor technologies, such as Michael Golay of MIT (who has repeatedly tried to organize scholarly exchanges between nuclear and anti-nuclear experts), to find some common ground with nuclear skeptics for a continuing exploration of nuclear power options.

While I am generally supportive of scholarly conferences on nuclear power, the risk that conversation and explorations of more benign nuclear technologies, such as passive reactor designs, could serve as Trojan horses for the breeder reactor limits the potential for dialogue. Nothing better illustrates why nuclear skeptics are hesitant to participate in discussions of alternative reactor designs than the remarks of former DOE Assistant Secretary for Nuclear Energy A. David Rossin before the American Power Conference in 1987. As reported in *Power Engineering,*

> "Rossin said at the APC that the goal of DOE's nuclear program is to 'keep the infrastructure together so we can get from here to there.' His 'here' is the current state of the nuclear industry, which hasn't seen an order for a new plant in the U.S. for almost 10 years. 'There' is the breeder economy."
>
> ". . . Rossin does not believe in the concept of small, modular reactors. He said he still believes in the economies of scale: 'A good big reactor is better than a good small reactor.' He admitted, however, that work on small nuclear unit sizes is valuable if it helps keep the technology alive" (*Power Engineering* July 1987, 4).

Desert Sojourn

Like the Israelites' forty-year sojourn in the desert waiting for the old guard to pass away, it may be necessary to "dissolve" the nuclear industry in order to "save it." Many "true believers" in the industry seem little chastened by the pattern of safety lapses and cost overruns over the last twenty years. The reactor vendors and nuclear utilities, for example, continue to rush towards licensing extension with insufficient respect for the hazards of plant aging. Many leaders in the nuclear industry continue to oppose support for research on passively safe reactor designs due in part to fears of public relations problems for non-passively safe reactors. The DOE continues to limit full exploration of nuclear hazards (as illustrated by attempts in 1993 to limit access to a paper by Marvin Miller of MIT on the proliferation issues raised by some of the newer reactor designs). Many pro-nuclear cost forecasters and safety analysts continue to rely on the methodologies that produced the oversights of the 1970s and 1980s.

The sad conclusion from my perspective is that the nuclear dream has not worked out. The technology has failed and should be put aside until other energy options have been exhausted and the industrial subculture that nurtured the first nuclear era dismantled. I find this a sad conclusion because the nuclear dream was compelling, the imaginations behind it were talented, and the human energy and economic wealth mobilized to pursue it were enormous. It is crucial, however, that the energy sector take this opportunity to alter direction.

I would favor continuing some nuclear power research, but in contexts capable of a fresh start. I would give a large role to groups such as the Union of Concerned Scientists (who have worked tirelessly to improve the safety of existing reactors) and innovative reactor designers such as Larry Lidsky of MIT and Charles Forsberg of Oak Ridge National Laboratory. I would try to reform the subcultures of the National Laboratories by transferring many reactor designers to non-nuclear projects and hiring former skeptics from outside the nuclear industry.

An enormous amount of creativity and human resources have been tied up in the nuclear sector, and I expect that significant progress can made in the development of non-nuclear technologies if these resources are re-deployed for alternative energy development. Such initiatives have already borne fruit at MIT and Oak Ridge National Laboratory in response to funding shifts.

I would repeal the Price Anderson Act and use the threat of accident liability to discipline private sector nuclear activities. I would require the utilities and nuclear investors bear the full costs of any future nuclear power project and cost overrun risks.

Only time will tell whether new innovative nuclear reactor designs can compete with other energy technologies without burdening the energy sector with unacceptable proliferation and safety hazards. It is a question worth asking, but only as a modest part of a broader energy sector development strategy.

Notes

Chapter 1

1. Kuhn's key claims are contained in *The Structure of Scientific Revolutions* (2nd ed.) (Chicago: University of Chicago Press, 1970). Two other essays are especially helpful in clarifying his views: "Second Thoughts on Paradigms" in his *The Essential Tension: Selected Studies in Scientific Tradition and Change* (Chicago: The University of Chicago Press, 1977) and "Reflections on My Critics" in *Criticism and the Growth of Knowledge*, edited by Lakatos and Musgrave (New York: Cambridge University Press, 1970).

Chapter 2

1. Ideological belief refers to a general outlook whose retention is based on broad value judgments or sets of impressions that are not immediately sensitive to changes in empirical information. Such beliefs tend to limit or define realms of public discourse and impart an inertia to planning contexts.

2. In 1966, more than 55% of those surveyed expressed great confidence in the people running scientific institutions. By the early 1970s this tally had fallen below 30%. By the late 1970s it had rebounded to ~40% (Mazur 1981, 48).

3. The cited quote comes from a longer discussion in Spencer Weart's classic study of the cultural images spawned by nuclear energy (*Nuclear Fear*). Describing a particularly captivating image, that of a "nuplex" (a nuclear complex), consisting of ". . . a town centered on reactors," Weart writes,

> "Confident about safety, engineers figured the reactors ought to be right in the middle so that their output of heat could serve factories. . . . For some people this was not just a technical idea but a move toward social rebirth . . ."
> "Oak Ridge drew up detailed plans for a 'nuclear-powered agro-industrial complex'. . . . Supported by Senator Anderson and many others, the idea turned into serious plans. In 1965 President Johnson announced that if Israel and Egypt promised not to build nuclear weapons, the United States

321

would give them reactors to pour forth electricity and pure water, while the Palestinian refugees would be bought off with fertile new irrigated lands" (Weart 1988, 303).

4. Richard Hirsh writes,

"A nuclear system did not initially appear to require major new construction or operating skills, nor did its management. As noted by Philip Sporn in 1952, nuclear energy, 'will provide merely a new form of fuel, with the reactor taking the place of the boiler side of a thermal-electric generating station.' Likewise, at Commonwealth Edison, one of the earliest utilities to purchase nuclear plants, managers generally conceptualized fossil and nuclear technologies as identical . . ." (Hirsh 1989, 116).

5. In an excellent study of the technical evolution of nuclear reactor designs, Morone and Woodhouse write,

". . . once a particular reactor technology gained momentum, the monetary and organizational investment required to bring it to fruition led to a massive social and institutional complex . . ."

"Technical inertia gradually created intellectual inertia. The expanding organizational complex devoted to commercializing nuclear power brought with it trade associations, professional societies, and university departments. . . . The social and intellectual infrastructure associated with this organizational complex focused naturally on large light water reactors with engineered safety. Everyone who might have been a creative, countervailing force was essentially co-opted into the system, and large light water reactors built with engineered safety were the only game in town. University departments of nuclear engineering emphasized light water reactors to prepare their students for jobs in the nuclear industry. At the same time, members of the faculty consulted for the firms that were building and operating the current generation of technology. Any research contracts that university researchers won from government likewise focused on the dominant approach—or on alternatives like the liquid metal fast breeder that were expected to replace light water reactors in the long term" (Morone and Woodhouse, 1989, 126–128).

6. Mullenbach 1963, 110, 80–102, 185; Allen 1977, 32; DeLeon 1979, 53; Nelson and Eads 1971; Weinberg 1990, 22.

7. The study was also optimistic about nuclear power's economic potential, but as an avenue for achieving even lower energy costs, rather than as a response to fossil fuel scarcity. This optimism was the product of AEC and nuclear industry promotionalism, rather than empirical experience. It was a result, rather than a cause, of the nuclear planning context.

8. The Putnam report's case for nuclear investment rested on a risk averse strategy to protect energy consumers from the implications of enormous energy demand growth. The report sharply underestimated the ability of increased energy efficiency to provide similar insurance.

9. Nuclear power's role in energy planning was also limited by its electrical form, which made it difficult for the technology to compete in the oil fueled transportation sector. It also required that nuclear power compete directly with coal in the electricity sector where coal's abundant supply appeared to limit future cost escalation, as environmental concerns were relatively undeveloped (Perry 1977, 72).

10. In addition to uncertainties about nuclear plant costs, nuclear power economics was clouded by fears of uranium scarcities. Many believed that rapid development of speculative technologies, such as the breeder reactor, was necessary for a viable nuclear industry (AEC 1962, 22; Bupp and Derian 1981, 173; Ford 1982, 55).

11. Oak Ridge Lab Director Alvin Weinberg told the JCAE in 1954 that ". . . our potential in military nuclear explosives . . . would be greatly increased if we had a large-scale economic central nuclear power industry" (Hertsgaard 1983, 26). In 1955 the National Security Council argued, "If the United States fails to exploit its atomic potential, politically and psychologically, the USSR could gain an important advantage in what is becoming a critical sector of the cold war struggle" (Balogh 1991, 103). The Joint Committee relied on similar arguments in mobilizing congressional support for generous nuclear funding (Orlans 1967, 178). Support for the "peaceful atom" was also seen as a way of softening the militaristic image at home and abroad of the U.S. atomic energy program (Allen 1977, 32; Sommers 1978, 23–24; Ford 1982, 35; Mullenbach 1963, 264). Similar private sentiments mobilized support for civilian nuclear power among some nuclear scientists as a kind of "atonement" for creating the hazards of nuclear weapons. (See, for example, Lilienthal 1963, 108).

12. Appointed by the JCAE to study the peaceful uses of atomic energy, the McKinney Panel, for example, concluded in 1956 that "In the uncommitted areas of the world, American leadership in making atomic power available could be a strong influence in guiding these areas toward a course of freedom. . . . This consideration should strongly influence . . . the rate at which the development of atomic power suitable for such purposes is pursued" (Donnelly 1972, 32). For a general discussion of the impact of ideological rivalry on nuclear development, see also: Mullenbach 1963, 294–296, 19, 264; Allen 1967, 31–32, 76–77; Hogerton 1968, 23; Nau 1974, 71; Perry 1977; and DeLeon 1979.

Non-superpower nuclear efforts were also mobilized by symbolic nationalist dynamics. Like the Olympics or competition for Nobel Prizes in the humanities, nuclear proficiency became a symbol of national pride (DeLeon 1979, 55–61; Lonnroth and Walker 1983, 11; Nau 1974, 71). The JCAE, for example, reported that some developing nations sought Atoms for Peace reactors to demonstrate their coming of age, despite their lack of scientific personnel to manage the facilities (Donnelly 1972, 35). Henry Nau emphasizes the psychological dimension underlying the French and German nuclear efforts. Of the French program he writes, "Under the Fifth Republic technological progress became the expression of the country's independence in the widest sense . . ." (Nau 1974, 71). Describing the German reactor program, he quotes its director, "For us it is not a matter of military or political power. Nor is it a matter of prestige. But it is indeed a matter of asserting and securing the place of the German people among the industrial nations, a place which we have regained again with so much effort" (Nau 1974, 72).

13. DeLeon 1979, 268–271; Lindberg 1977, 330; Mullenbach 1963, 270; *Nucleonics* 3/55, 8.

14. See, for example, Bupp and Derian 1981, 15–42, 56–69; Lonnroth and Walker 1983, 25–29. The Euratom program was supported by both AEC and Export-Import Bank subsidies. The aid and persistently misleading AEC assurances about the economic promise of U.S. reactor technologies were instrumental in precipitating a key 1957 Euratom study ("A Target for Euratom"). The report urged European planners to defer to the greater resources that the AEC and American corporations could mobilize in the development process. As one of the three co-authors, Louis Armand, wrote, "One can see no country, even France, with its three reactors of the same type under construction . . . that could be capable alone of counterbalancing the U.S. which already has 30 different types of reactors manufactured" (Bupp and Derian 1981, 28).

Many years later similar arguments were offered by the director of the French national utility for rejecting renewed efforts to develop the French gas-graphite reactor. The official argued, "We have to acknowledge that a light water model is not more reliable than a gas-graphite model . . . But the world currently has around 80,000 MW under construction or on order from light water models, while there are 8,000 MW in service or on order from graphite-gas models. . . . For France, within our little borders, to continue pursuing a technology in which the world has no interest doesn't make sense today. The fact that the world market is now clearly oriented towards light water models means that our industrialists will only be able to enter the industrial world insofar as they have their own valid experience with the models that the world is interested in" (Gorz 1979, 12).

15. Krugman writes, ". . . in imperfectly competitive markets there is some monopoly rent for which firms are competing. Government action may enable domestic firms to seize a larger share of these rents than they would otherwise be able to get. Introducing technological competition into trade theory, then does seem to give some justification for the kinds of industrial policies which Japan is accused of following. Or at any rate, it offers support for the idea that protecting R&D intensive industries may really be a beggar-thy-neighbor policy, not simply a beggar-thyself policy" (*American Economic Review* 73, No. 2, 346).

16. The discussion in this section frequently draws on Morone and Woodhouse 1989 and Weinberg 1975.

17. As Morone and Woodhouse note, "There are no records of sustained deliberation over safety and acceptability in the available documents of the archives of the AEC; nor does the detailed account by the AEC's chief historian indicate any search in the 1950s for reactors that would be particularly safe or well suited to widespread use in society" (41). Instead, reactor R&D built on its own momentum.

18. The 1946 Atomic Energy Act, for example, required the AEC to pursue private sector solutions to nuclear development. The memoirs of AEC Chairman

Lewis Strauss demonstrate that it did (Strauss 1962, 319). When AEC policy deviated from this principle, the reaction from the private sector was swift and powerful. In 1961, for example, when the AEC proposed adding generating facilities to its Hanford weapons reactor complex, anti-federal power project sentiment defeated the proposal in Congress (Green and Rosenthal 1963, 263; Mullenbach 1963). In 1954 the Johnson amendment, and in 1956 the Gore-Holifield bill were both defeated when the technology's supporters tried to expedite its development through the construction of large federally owned demonstration projects. On the other hand, the Power Reactor Demonstration Program, which mainly subsidized investor owned utility projects, received $256 million (historical dollars) in the fifties and sixties (Dawson 1976, 101). While there were relatively minimal public controversies during the first fifteen years of nuclear development over nuclear health, safety, and environmental issues (Ford 1982, 41–44), there were very large congressional debates over patent issues and reactor and materials ownership rights (Mullenbach 1963, 159, 162, 324).

19. In most market studies, the reactor vendors are referred to as nuclear steam supply system (NSSS) suppliers. Though somewhat an elastic concept, the NSSS generally includes the reactor core, pressure vessel, associated heat transfer equipment (pipes, pumps, etc.) and control and safety systems. A major study of the nuclear industry by A. D. Little in 1968 estimated that the NSSS accounted for about 30% of plant construction costs (Little 1968, 17). Its share has fallen drastically since then. Many components of the NSSS are purchased rather than produced in-house by the NSSS suppliers.

20. In a study for the Brookings Institution, Harold Orlans writes,

> "At one time Westinghouse and at another time General Electric has appeared predominant in the private nuclear power industry . . . but at no time has a 'third echelon' company—Allis-Chalmers, Atomics International, Babcock and Wilcox, Combustion Engineering or General Atomics—superseded them . . . Speaking in 1965, at a time of apparent G. E. domination, an employee of one of the latter companies observed that the Commission was torn between its wish to promote these 'weaker sisters' and recognition that G. E. was best qualified to bring nuclear power to immediate commercial application. Repeatedly G. E. would proffer arrangements so attractive AEC staff called it the 'generous electric' company; but after contracting for them, they would bemoan the consequences for a competitive nuclear industry" (Orlans 1967, 47).

21. Admiral Rickover, for example, was instrumental in shaping the organizational structure of Westinghouse's nuclear division (Hewlett and Duncan 1974, 235–236). The latter frequently provided key personnel for the commission's staff. A recent chair of the NRC, for example, was a former Westinghouse engineer. A DOE chief of long term energy planning was a former Westinghouse market analyst (Hertsgaard 1983, 213). Richard Roberts sandwiched a period as the Energy Research and Development Administration's (ERDA) assistant administrator for nuclear energy amidst a G. E. career (Nader and Abbotts 1979, 277). Common Cause's study "Serving Two Masters" documents this tendency more generally, indicating that more than

half of ERDA's top 139 employees came from private enterprises involved with energy activities (Nader and Abbotts 1979, 277).

The commission frequently treated client staff as an extension of its own bureaucracy, often adhering to the principle of "self-regulation". The AEC relied heavily on industry studies for key safety information (*New York Times* 10/16/83; Rolph 1977, 40; Ford 1982, 52, 54, 180, 186). Borrowed or existing G. E. and Westinghouse personnel, for example, supplied key data and performed primary analyses for important AEC reactor safety studies. The vendors similarly provided the information for the AEC's widely cited and misleadingly optimistic cost estimates in the 1962 study *Civilian Nuclear Power: A Report to the President*.

The AEC reciprocally sought to protect the economic health of its contractors. In 1963, for example, a commissioner acknowledged, "We do feel some obligation to tide the industry over for a brief period of years by going forward with a reasonably aggressive development program" (*Nucleonics* 12/63 17).

22. Perry 1977, xii, 35, 94; Gandara 1977, 53; *Business Week* 12/25/78; Burness et al. 5/80, 188, 193, 200.

23. Stewart 1981, 186, 188; *Business Week* 12/25/78. Alongside its Fort St. Vrain turnkey contract (which included nuclear fuel cost guarantees and large penalties for failure to meet a seven year construction deadline), the company was forced to negotiate loss-leader contracts for later high temperature gas reactor sales (Stewart 1981, 186–188). The company currently lacks the deep pockets necessary for similar initiatives for its passive safety modular high temperature gas reactor.

24. In withdrawing from the NSSS market in 1966, for example, Allis-Chalmers cited its inability to absorb such development losses (Little 1968, 145). G. E. Vice President Wolfe argues similarly, ". . . it was the turnkey years that really did it [consolidated the industry]. A lot of companies . . . found out . . . that profits were way in the future. . . . You either had to be a big firm or one that was inherently tied to the utility industry . . ." (Hertsgaard 1983, 47).

25. For example, the commission relied heavily on industry analysis in designing reactor safety studies and tests of the emergency core cooling system (Ford 1982, 146, 163–164, 106–107). Subsequent review has challenged the companies' minimization of hazard uncertainties. The vendors also lobbied actively for more lenient safety regulations (Rolph 1977, 23). They urged approval of urban reactor sitings and reduced retrofit requirements (Rolph 1977, 23, 24, 34, 86; Okrent 1981, 146, 194, 310).

26. Describing Westinghouse's CAMPUS AMERICA program, for example, the president of Westinghouse's Power Systems Company wrote, ". . . young nuclear engineers journey on their own volition to campuses to discuss nuclear energy. They usually also appear on local television. . . . We have other programs to provide radio and television materials and guests anywhere in the country . . ." (Hilgartner et al. 1982, 81).

27. Ralph Sultan's two volume study, *Pricing in the Electrical Oligopoly*, is especially helpful in situating nuclear decisions within a history of rivalry dynamics

between General Electric and Westinghouse. Sultan analyzed the character of the turbine-generator (T-G) industry, which had traditionally accounted for approximately 10% of Westinghouse and General Electric's sales. He argued that the industry's large scale economies enabled G. E. to reproduce its early market dominance for over fifty years. If taken as a model for the expected behavior of the nuclear market, the history encouraged early nuclear investments.

Sultan suggested that relative costs in the T-G industry were a logarithmic function of the cumulative number of turbine-generator units produced (Sultan 1974, 176). He tied this relationship chiefly to the impact of learning curve efficiencies (Sultan 1975, 14), but noted that higher sales volume also reduced per unit R&D and marketing costs, and increased scheduling flexibility and specialization opportunities (1975, 15; 1974, 93). G. E.'s early market dominance in Sultan's view was self-perpetuating. In the absence of anti-trust concerns the industry would have become a monopoly.

The charm of Sultan's analysis was that it demonstrated how G. E.'s pricing, output, and R&D behavior enabled it to reproduce a dominant position without inviting anti-trust intervention. Sultan noted that although G. E.'s two rivals, Westinghouse and Allis-Chalmers, tended to match the company's high R&D to sales ratio, their smaller sales base prevented them from challenging G. E.'s technical leadership (1974, 226). When introducing new T-G innovations, G. E. simultaneously raised prices on older models. It also priced its new innovation high enough to permit a healthy market to continue to exist in the dying technology, wherein Westinghouse and Allis-Chalmers could enjoy company sustaining short term profits. As G. E. moved down the learning curve of the new technology, it gradually lowered its price. It was thus able to permanently undercut Westinghouse and Allis-Chalmers' market initiatives without eliminating its competitors (1974, 226–233).

28. Some observers have also speculated that Westinghouse perceived nuclear power development as a means for ending G. E.'s turbine-generator market domination and a more general strategy for resisting growing foreign competition in some linked markets (see, for example, Lonnroth and Walker 1983, 21–23).

29. See, for example, Hertsgaard 1983, Bodde 1975, Kuhn 1966, Sultan 1974, Bupp and Derian 1981, and Adato et al. 1987. In 1979, for example, the NRC's director of research asserted, ". . . much of the [backfitting] of regulatory requirements for the operating plants about which industry has complained has been a direct result of the fact that the unduly rapid push to larger sizes has resulted in what amounts to a generation of prototypes . . . this situation was almost inevitable given the substantial extrapolation from the early technology" (Adato et al. 1987, 39).

30. Hertsgaard writes, "Deddens of Babcock and Wilcox sees the AEC's move as a blessing. 'It stopped the horsepower race,' he says. 'We were extrapolating plants further and further out [in size] without the benefit of operating experience.' Deddens concedes that no vendor could have unilaterally taken such a decision, because 'the competition would not have allowed it.'" (Hertsgaard 1983, 64).

31. The fifteen utilities are: Commonwealth Edison, Consolidated Edison, Consumers Power, Detroit Edison, Duke Power, Duquesne Light, General Public Util-

ities, three New England utilities (Boston Edison, New England Electric, and Northeast Utilities), Northern States Power, Pacific Gas and Electric, Philadelphia Electric, Southern California Edison, and the Virginia Electric and Power Co.; selection based on level of overall nuclear participation 1950–1969, emphasizing early years. The list is not well defined at the margin. Among other utilities with significant nuclear projects, especially during the 1965–1969 period, are: the TVA, Florida Power and Light, Pennsylvania Power and Light, Public Service Electric and Gas, and Carolina Power and Light.

32. Sultan 1974, 24–25; Little 1968, 83.

33. See, for example, Gandara 1977, 19–20; Sultan 1974, 225, 1975, 199; Bupp and Derian 1981, 74–75; Hirsh 1989; and Sporn 1969, 75, 90–91, 101. While important to a few utilities, environmental concerns were relatively modest during nuclear power's early expansion (Perry 1977, 72).

34. Sultan and others employing a variant of the "managerial control" hypothesis have suggested that the strong presence of engineers in utility management also biased firms towards support for growth and technology promoting investments (Sultan 1974, 20; 1975, 199).

35. This bias, first formalized by H. Averich and L. Johnson (1962) is frequently referred to as the Averich-Johnson effect. Gandara (1977) finds evidence of such practice in the electric utility sector until the credit crunch of the mid-seventies (81). Scherer's work suggests a 25% excess capital investment (Brannon 1974, 112, 117). Other studies have found more ambiguous effects (Hirsh 1989, 81, 227). Nuclear plants have always been expected to be much more capital intensive than fossil fueled generating facilities.

36. Komanoff 1981, 200. The 5/2/66 issue of *Electrical World*, for example, projected declines from 10.7 M/kwh for a 50 MW plant to 5 M/kwh for a 500 MW plant to 4.2 M/kwh for a 1000 MW plant. The AEC (1968a) foresaw a further 20% decline between 1000 and 3000 MW. Wilbanks reports that the "FPC predicted that nuclear power plants would reach the size of 5,000 MWe by 1980 and 10,000 MWe by 1990" (Wilbanks 1984, 13). For evidence of earlier perceptions of scaling economies, see: JCAE 1955, 408; JCAE 1958, 347; Tybout 1957, 353; and AEC 1962. Besides having difficulty integrating large chunks of capacity into their grids, small utilities would also be expected to lack some of the specialized expertise available to large IOUs for managing nuclear power plants (Lester 1986a, 354).

37. See, for example, AIF, *Nuclear Industry* 9/65, 4.

38. Speaking before the Edison Electric Institute in 1958, the chairman of General Electric asked, "Will atomic energy provide a second chance for those who want to see investor owned electric utilities wither away, replaced by federal power plants?" (Mullenbach 1963, 104). The strongest supporters of an expanded government development program were powerful members of the JCAE. With their assistance, the Gore-Holifield bill calling for a $400 million federally owned reactor construction program passed the Senate in 1956, but died in the House.

39. The president of one early nuclear utility indicated "We acted because we needed to guarantee the position of private industry. The money spent was a gamble to preserve the private sector" (Kuhn 1966, 115). Notes from AEC Chair Lewis Strauss' files of 1957 echo similar observations (Balogh 1991, 110). Southern California Edison described its 1964 nuclear desalinization initiatives in a similar light (AIF, *Nuclear Industry* 12/64, 12–14). Memos from New England IOU planning meetings in 1965 indicate that a Maine nuclear plant was spurred by fear of the creation of a Maine Power Authority with nuclear construction assignments (Senate Judiciary Committee 6/70, 454–55). As late as 1970, the Atomic Industrial Forum reported that IOU support for Rockefeller's nuclear initiatives was spurred by the governor's promise to bar nuclear construction by the state's power authority (AIF, *Nuclear Industry* 4/70).

Rivalry dynamics also spurred some large scale public power nuclear initiatives, such as those of the New York State Power Authority in the early sixties (AIF, *Nuclear Industry* 3/61, 28). The TVA's 1966 Browns Ferry reactor, located at a site with expected fossil fuel cost of 2.83 M/kwh (1966$) and Nebraska's early nuclear projects, also seem, in part, technology accessing investments. Rockwell (1992) notes the TVA's very early fear that nuclear power would be monopolized in the private sector (159).

40. The project was conceived as an R&D exercise and eventually produced electricity at about 7–8 times the cost of a conventional plant in the same location. Duquesne agreed to purchase steam from the AEC reactor at prices 30%–40% higher than the expected cost of conventionally generated steam and to contribute $5,000,000 (1954$) to reactor construction (JCAE, 1963c, 225).

41. For a more detailed discussion of the history of utility nuclear investments, see Cohn 1986, 99–148.

42. The first four privately financed utility reactors were initiated by Consolidated Edison of NY, Commonwealth Edison of Chicago, Pacific Gas and Electric, and General Public Utilities. Consolidated Edison's president told the JCAE in 1955, "I am not particularly interested in just how economical the thing (the Indian Point nuclear plant) is within limits. I am interested in getting something done" (JCAE 1955, 403). Eight years later the chairman of the board told the JCAE, "So far as Consolidated Edison is concerned, as I think our investment activity to date clearly demonstrates, we look primarily to nuclear energy to meet the future thermal generating requirements in our territory, *and we are prepared to do all we can to contribute to its development*" [emphasis added] (JCAE, 1963a, 621). Incredible as it seems in retrospect, Consolidated Edison lobbied the AEC in the early 1960s to build a plant inside New York City! The company was simultaneously a foe of cogeneration (*Fortune* 12/31/78).

The leader in nuclear activism was Commonwealth Edison of Chicago, which pursued an aggressive growth strategy built around nuclear expansion. Following its 1955 Dresden plant, the company contracted for thirteen additional reactors in 1963–1972, accounting for 9% of the nation's nuclear orders (AEC 1974a). By the 1980s Commonwealth Edison appeared to enjoy significant learning curve cost advantages in managing nuclear construction (Bupp and Komanoff 1983). The company also pursued nuclear initiatives in the radioisotope, weapons material, fuel reprocessing, and nuclear manpower training markets. In 1974 Commonwealth Edison acquired the tenth ranked uranium milling company, the Cotter Corporation (Senate Committee on Energy and Natural Resources 1977, 327) and has been a leader in breeder reactor development, serving as the chief utility for the Clinch River project.

In the political sphere, the company has funded expensive pro-nuclear campaigns, contributing, for example, over $3 million to the Committee for Energy Awareness' pro-nuclear advertising efforts (*Power Line* 8–9/83). Commonwealth Edison executives have also testified frequently before congressional committees urging increased nuclear power support.

Complementing its nuclear supply side initiatives, the company fed its growth strategy with an aggressive advertising campaign on the demand side. *Fortune* (3/67) reported, "Much can be credited to Ward's [company chairman] marketing team, 'We tried to convince present and potential customers of new uses of electricity. We've been very successful . . .'" The *Fortune* article details the anxiety associated with the company's high risk expansion plans, quoting the firm's president, "'We have a construction program for the next five years of 1.7 billion dollars. Sometimes I wake up worrying if we will have enough demand for all the new capacity this program will provide.'" Later Commonwealth Edison executives have commented on the slowness of the company to adjust its demand forecasts downward in the light of changing empirical experience (Hirsh 1989, 129).

Pacific Gas and Electric's 1958 Humboldt Bay and 1962 Bodega Bay announced plants followed the company's junior partner role in Commonwealth Edison's 1955 Dresden project and a 1957 G. E. financed R&D reactor. In February 1963, PG&E released a seventeen year generating strategy calling for up to two-thirds of all new capacity to be nuclear (AIF, *Forum Memo* 3/63, 3–4). The firm was also an active nuclear lobbyist. It sponsored extensive pro-nuclear advertising (Berger 1977, 182) and sought to prevent the airing of an anti-nuclear documentary on California TV (Berger 1977, 179; Hertsgaard 1983, 200–201; *Power Line* 8–9/83). A company public relations officer, Hal Stroube, helped formulate the nuclear industry's early public relations strategies and campaigned against public release of updated AEC accident hazard studies (Hilgartner et al. 1982, 77–78, 119).

As late as 1978, PG&E had not initiated a single study comparing the economics of its nuclear expansion program with solar, wind, or conservation options (Stobaugh and Yergin 1979, 141, 302). Subsequent pressures from the environmental movement and California Public Utilities Commission have reoriented the company's generating mix strategy and made it a leader in energy conservation.

As early as 1953, GPU urged the rapid development of nuclear power, declaring, "We want atomic power if it is economical. We can absorb large quantities of it. The sooner we get it, the better we like it" (Hertsgaard 1983, 141). In 1956 the company asked for bids on a reactor for its Philippine subsidiary (JCAE 1957, 395–6). It followed its 1959 R&D reactor with the 1961 planning (*Electrical World* 7/20/64) and 1963 purchase of the first turnkey plant, Oyster Creek. In the ensuing months its spokesmen seemed to serve as G. E. sales representatives, making claims for the plant that exceeded the AEC's optimism and G. E.'s capital cost guarantees. During

1963 the president of its Pennsylvania Electric subsidiary served as head of the Atomic Industrial Forum. The company purchased additional reactors in 1966, 1967, and 1969, and indicated in the mid-seventies that its generating strategy called for an all-nuclear base load capacity (Gandara 1977, 64). The company has also been active in breeder reactor plutonium fuel cycle, nuclear desalinization, and enrichment policy research. GPU is the parent company that operates the Three Mile Island reactors.

43. In 1967 Niagara Mohawk projected 2300 MW of atomic capacity to complement its existing 2800 MW fossil fuel-hydro base (AIF, *Nuclear Industry* 3/67). Niagara Mohawk also became part owner of an in situ uranium recovery facility (Taylor and Yokell 1979, 14). Anderson (1981) indicates that the company's aggressive growth strategy left it in the forefront of groups opposing utility rate structure reforms aimed at replacing declining block rates with marginal cost pricing.

44. Niagara's "brand loyalty" caused it to purchase ten of its eleven turbine generators (1948–1962) from G. E. (compared with a national average of 58%) and to acknowledge that ". . . (the) principle goal of the 9 Mile Point project is to prove on our own system, that a nuclear power plant can be built and cost no more—at worst—than a coal fired plant. This has never been done yet" (*Nucleonics* 5/64).

45. Hertsgaard writes, "The Rockefellers got their start in nuclear in 1950, when they hired Lewis Strauss, recently resigned Atomic Energy Commission member, as their investment adviser. Strauss served them until 1953, when President Eisenhower called him back to chair the AEC. In 1954, Laurence and David Rockefeller founded the United Nuclear uranium company, and Chase Manhattan became the first bank to establish a nuclear power division. In 1955, Nelson Rockefeller, who was then serving in the White House as President Eisenhower's special assistant, persuaded Eisenhower to reinvigorate and expand the Atoms for Peace program to include more training for foreigners and increased funding for exporting U.S.-manufactured research reactors. As governor of New York between 1959 and 1973, Nelson worked hard and successfully to stimulate, through state subsidies, the private development of nuclear power in New York. And in 1975, as vice president, he pushed for creation of a federal Energy Independence Authority, a $100 billion program of government subsidies and loan guarantees intended to stimulate U.S. domestic energy production. Most of the money was targeted on such nuclear-related projects as breeder reactors, uranium enrichment, and fuel reprocessing" (Hertsgaard 1983, 133).

46. New York ranked seventh highest among all states in fossil fuel costs in 1952 (Mason 1957, 323). Downstate New York by itself ranked second highest in the early sixties among thirty-six fuel regions.

47. JCAE, 1961, 786. Illustrative of the intra-nuclear utility rivalries that helped spur nuclear development, Moses added, ". . . New York can beat other parts of the country to the punch, pioneer in bringing down power costs and regain a competitive advantage for its industry. . . . While we debate other areas of the country are growing faster not only in power production but in manufacturing. Southern and Western states actively seek to lure industry away. . . . In the long run the major advantage which other parts of the country can offer to industry is cheaper power. . . . [T]hose

who control fusion and fission will be the masters of population growth and location, industry, trade, commerce . . ." (JCAE 1961, 789–790).

Repeating these sentiments in a 1963 address to the Atomic Industrial Forum, Governor Rockefeller declared, "It is for these reasons, combined with our conviction that those who lead the scientific revolution are most likely to benefit from it, that we here in New York State . . . have been pursuing a vigorous program of atomic development" (Rockefeller 1963, 121).

48. For evidence of other state and local nuclear initiatives, see the monthly journal *Nuclear Industry*, subheading: "state and local governments." For accounts of nuclear strategizing in the South, see: Sugg 1957, 9–10 and Olson 1976, 202.

49. The companies were adamantly opposed to Robert Moses' efforts to build a nuclear plant through the state's power authority. From 1959–1963, ESADA sponsored about $25 million of nuclear research. Among the key projects funded were G. E.'s superheat R&D reactor, General Atomic's high temperature gas reactor, Atomics International's sodium graphite project, and G. E.'s breeder components project (JCAE 1963a, 784–5; AIF, *Nuclear Industry* 2/68, 53).

50. The state began searching for a reprocessing plant site in 1959, purchasing a 3300 acre plot in 1961. In its successful negotiations with Nuclear Fuel Services in 1963, it agreed to sweeten the site by funding the construction of an $8 million waste disposal facility. It also agreed to assume long term liability for the reprocessing plant's radioactive waste for a minimal fee (JCAE 1963b, 97; see also JCAE 1960a, 367). It now appears that this guarantee will cost state and federal taxpayers 1.5 billion dollars (*New York Times* 7/9/96, B15). To further sweeten the project, ESADA extended the $24 million plant a $2 million grant (JCAE 1963b, 108, 80). In 1968 the Atomic and Space Development Authority sought similar subsidies for the siting of a plutonium fuel reprocessing plant. Included were funds for the construction of a fast breeder prototype, "because, through it, there can be brought into being within the state . . . the plutonium fuel industry" (Oliver Townsend, chairman of the New York State Atomic and Space Development Authority; AIF *Nuclear Industry* 2/68, 53).

51. Under the PRDP, the AEC provided about 25% of the projects' costs. Because the commission's contributions were fixed in advance, the utilities (and vendors in the case of fixed price contracts) still bore the brunt of the plants' cost uncertainties.

52. New England has historically had the highest fossil fuel costs in the nation, enduring coal costs 43% higher than the national average in the late 1950s and early 1960s, and 66% higher in 1975 (AIF, 1964 Annual Conference Proceedings, Vol 2, 88; Gandara 1977, 25).

53. See, for example, Thomas 1988, 7; and Stobaugh and Yergin 1979, 195.

54. Stobaugh and Yergin 1979, 157–160; U.S. Congress, House Government Operations Committee 1977, 1161–1180; *Power Line* 10/81. When the city of Chicago indicated it might build a garbage burning cogeneration facility, Commonwealth Edison threatened to shift its headquarters and $140 million tax revenues out of the city (*Wall Street Journal* 10/23/85, 6). Robert Williams of Princeton University sug-

gests that such efforts successfully discouraged innovation in the cogeneration field. The declining block and all-electric discount aspect of utility rates also discouraged the expansion of passive solar and other alternative energy options.

55. The term "bandwagon market" was used by American Electric Power President Philip Sporn in a 12/68 letter to the AEC to characterize the dynamics behind the ~50 nuclear orders placed in 1966–1967 (JCAE 1968, 2–10). It is used here to refer to the 71 orders of the 1966–1969 period and the 144 orders of the 1970–1974 years. Bupp and Derian (1981) have given the metaphor wide circulation.

The cyclical-queuing character of utility capital equipment markets may have also encouraged a tendency for bandwagon dynamics (Sultan 1974). The utilities' felt need to "get in line" in order to avoid the danger of being caught in a supply bottleneck, for example, has traditionally fostered herd behavior in the turbine-generator market. Sporn notes that in the late-sixties the lead times for nuclear plant orders significantly exceeded expected construction durations (JCAE 1968, 16).

56. Bechtel has estimated the 1960 market value of partial insurance against these risks at about 50% plant costs. In a successful legal defense against liability for the poor economics of Portland General Electric's 1968 Trojan nuclear plant, the company noted that construction contracts typically imposed the risks of nuclear projects (which it characterized as ". . . extraordinarily variable, unpredictable, and uncontrollable") on the utilities (Hellman and Hellman 1983, 5).

57. Nuclear totals based on cumulative plant costs and projected figures as of 1969 for plants still under construction (AEC 1970b, 154–155). Due to overruns, actual investments exceeded projected levels.

58. Richard Hirsh, for example, writes, "'Where are the bright engineers?' asked a 1968 *Electrical World* editorial lamenting the fact that utility companies could not attract good engineering talent—talent that would find its way into management ranks. . . . (W)ith the onset of World War II . . . electrical engineering students gravitated to the more exciting electronics and aerospace industries. The move left the power industry with an image of being 'lethargic and plodding'. As a result, utilities lost their appeal as places to perform novel engineering work" (Hirsh 1989, 111–121).

In 1966 James Kuhn noted "(i)f salaries are taken as a rough indicator of ability, the average quality of engineers among utilities is noticeably lower than in industry in general. The median salary is 9% lower and in the upper decile about 20% lower" (Kuhn 1966, 108). Terence Price (1990) suggests that one reason for the better performance of nuclear plants in Sweden and Finland than in the United States might be the operating companies access to better engineering talent due to less competition from alternatives like NASA and Silicon Valley (158).

59. In 1955 the U.S. had 18,000 nuclear scientists and engineers; 1,400 were employed by the AEC and its prime contractors. The bulk of the remainder were former AEC employees (Kuhn 1966, 46, 133). For some time this pool served as the basis for industry manpower (Kuhn 1966, 133). Formerly high ranking AEC employees were especially attractive to utility managers, due to their ease of access to commission staff.

60. ORSORT = Oak Ridge School of Reactor Technology. NRTS = National Reactor Testing Station.

61. Philip Sporn, president of American Electric Power, was one of the few utility executives publicly skeptical of the vendors' nuclear cost projections. He urged the utilities to develop an independent capacity for assessing nuclear technology. In a 1967 letter to the AEC, he warned that "there is a clear indication that the utilities need very badly to cut the umbilical cord . . . that ties them to the manufacturers. . . . To paraphrase the late Mr. Charles Wilson, what is best for the electrical equipment manufacturers, or what they think is best, may not be best for the utilities" (JCAE 1968, 16–17).

62. See, for example, the Congressional Office of Technology Assessment 1984, 255; Hellman and Hellman 1983, 21–22 and Tomain 1987, 30–44; Rockwell 1992, 351–352.

63. A series of utility executive interviews conducted by Arturo Gandara of the Rand Corporation tend to confirm Hogerton's account. As one of Gandara's interviewees expressed it, "If the management of a utility company believes a particular type of generation is going to become a major factor in the long range generation picture, there is the desire to become a part of such technology" (Gandara 1977, 58–59). Sporn argues similarly (JCAE 1968, 7). Gandara also found that nuclear development was often perceived by ambitious utility presidents as the way to leave their stamp on company policy. It was the pioneer's path, with much the same social appeal as solar energy projects today (Gandara 1977, 68).

64. Sporn writes, ". . . 1966 witnessed an increase in coal prices that is being continued in 1967. While there is some economic basis for this development, the non-economic contributions were in all probability much more significant." He then cites as key, "(a) resignation to the inevitable," and notes the industry's resulting failure to take advantage of investment opportunities to further automate mining, reduce rail costs, innovate in slurry pipelines and increase fossil fuel utilization efficiencies (JCAE 1968, 5, 13–14).

65. Among the factors encouraging market concentration in the architect-engineering-construction industry are: (1) the scale, quality control requirements, and potential for learning curve cost reductions in plant construction; (2) the benefits of established client relations with the utilities and regulatory authorities; and (3) the cyclical character of utility purchasing behavior (which necessitates large market shares in order to avoid discontinuous work periods).

66. The company contributed $1 million (1958$) to a R&D fund for Commonwealth Edison's Dresden 1 plant in the mid-fifties and served as project A-E-C (JCAE 1956a, 239). It assumed multi-million dollar risks in 1958 when it contracted on a fixed-price basis to build the Humboldt Bay plant for PG&E. As the late fifties were marked by a struggle between the AEC and IOUs over who would bear the overrun risks associated with early nuclear development plants, Bechtel's sole exposure in the Humboldt Bay project is striking (Bowring 1980, 25; JCAE 1957, 246, 393; JCAE 1963c, 227–228). In the summer of 1958 the company made extensive

efforts to enlist utility support for high temperature gas reactor projects (JCAE 1960b, 70–71). Late in the year it negotiated a fixed price contract for the Peach Bottom HTGR plant. In 1959 former AEC Director of Reactor Development, W. Kenneth Davis, noted the apparently high risks involved with the contract (JCAE 1959, 186). The company also played a key role in building the N.S. Savannah, the nation's first nuclear merchant ship, in 1958 (McCartney 1988, 110).

By 1960 Bechtel had also assumed an A-E-C role for the Vallecitos, Consumers Public Power District, Big Rock, and San Onofre reactors. It was also prime contractor for the AEC's organic cooled reactor study and a nuclear power consultant for a number of clients (JCAE 1959, 176–177).

67. Bechtel took early action to win dominant market position in design services for fuel reprocessing. Besides serving as the A-E-C contractor for an early fuel reprocessing plant, it won the engineering-construction contract for Nuclear Fuel Services' West Valley plant by offering a turnkey contract for 90% of the facility and numerous engineering warranties. The company was also the driving force behind Uranium Enrichment Associates' 5 + billion dollar enrichment privatization proposal, which would have given it and its partners a monopoly over the nation's enrichment facilities.

68. Bechtel's major linkages to government nuclear policy makers began in 1958 when a former business partner of Steve Bechtel, John McCone, became AEC Chairman. About the same time the company hired W. Kenneth Davis, AEC Director of Reactor Development (1954–1958), to head its nuclear efforts. In the mid-seventies it hired Richard Hollingsworth, general manager of the AEC (1964–1974). Former Export-Import Bank Director John L. Moore became executive vice president of Bechtel Financing in 1984 (*Wall Street Journal* 10/16/84). His predecessor at the Bank, Henry Kearns, also found employment at Bechtel (McCartney 1988, 226). At a higher level of administration, former Secretary of State George Shultz served eight years as Bechtel president after terms as Secretary of the Treasury and Secretary of Labor. Former Secretary of Defense Casper Weinberger served as special counsel to the firm after his period as Secretary of HEW. Former CIA Director Richard Helms and former Secretary of the Treasury William Simon also became Bechtel consultants (McCartney 1988, 174).

Reflective of these linkages is the *Wall Street Journal's* report that Bechtel's privatization proposal for uranium enrichment received special attention due to its Bechtel authorship (*Wall Street Journal* 11/20/75). It was subsequently forwarded to Congress as a Ford Administration proposal. W. Kenneth Davis reputedly authored the Reagan administration's nuclear trade and proliferation policies (Hertsgaard 1983, 232–233). He is also said to have persuaded the Department of Energy to support a government insured program for Bechtel's takeover of the Barnwell reprocessing plant (Hertsgaard 1983, 241). Laton McCartney details how Steve Bechtel Sr. reputedly persuaded Export-Import Bank Director Henry Kearns to promote U.S. nuclear exports, especially those linked to Bechtel.

69. The biases affected the kinds of data collected, the abstractions used to organize the data, and the attention given to anomalous results. The conventions

adopted resulted in an underestimation of the engineering safeguards needed to contain the technology's hazards. Rand analyst Robert Perry has suggested that the narrow scope of the industry's safety research reflected the inherent limitations of a commercial perspective (Perry 1977, 60).

Some observers have suggested that the company was more than "inattentive" to anomalous information and safety warnings. Laton McCartney, for example, cites accusations of reprisals against safety-oriented whistleblowers within the company (201).

70. U.S., House, Government Operations Committee 1978, 44–45; Government Operations Committee 1977, 1803–4, 1574.

71. In 1984, it was estimated that Bechtel would have ranked around twenty-first on the 1984 Fortune 500 list had it been a publicly held corporation (*Wall Street Journal* 10/16/84).

72. See Cohn 1986, 165–166 for a detailed discussion of the oil companies' mid- and late-sixties nuclear fuel cycle initiatives.

73. Campbell asserts that "(i)n an effort to preserve future profit margins as best it could, the company [NSF] cut back on expensive safety features such as adequate ventilation systems and proper shielding around radioactive pipes, decisions that caused important political and economic problems later . . ." (Campbell 1988, 112). Although Campbell does not discuss the AEC's role in approving these safety decisions, tolerance of them would be consistent with the commission's tendency to adopt an infant industry attitude towards nuclear hazards (see chapter 4). Campbell also argues that the AEC's aggressive support for reprocessing was part of an overall strategy to lower reactor fuel costs by earning plutonium credits for LWR operators (Campbell 1988, 11).

74. The influential Arthur D. Little study of 1968 projected reprocessing plant capital costs to vary as the .35 power of plant size (Little 1968, 221). This projection was consistent with popular estimates that Allied's reprocessing plant would enjoy costs one-third as high as existing 1–2 ton/day plants (AIF, *Nuclear Industry* 3/68, 12).

75. In 1970, for example, the AEC decided to require solidification of reprocessing waste, disadvantaging would-be PUREX reprocessing facilities. Later in the 1970s, the Ford and Carter administrations imposed a moratorium and finally a de facto ban on fuel reprocessing (Campbell 1988, 114–119).

76. Based on a literature review and petroleum industry interviews, the Department of Interior concluded in 1956 that nuclear expansion would have little impact on oil industry markets over the next twenty years. The DOI's study noted, "If all incremental large power stations built after 1960 were to use atomic energy—an unlikely assumption—the estimated loss to the oil industry would amount by 1975 to . . . 1.3% of the anticipated domestic demand . . . trifling losses" (JCAE 1956b, 100). The study added that oil executives did not expect nuclear power to become competitive in transportation or heating markets, noting, "It appears more likely that some other source of energy might enter these fields before atomic energy does. Solar radiation,

for example, might very well compete with oil and gas in household heating ahead of atomic energy" (JCAE 1956b, 101).

The president of Standard Oil of New Jersey indicated in the same year that his company welcomed nuclear development as a way of accelerating third world economic growth and the derived demand for liquid fuels (AIF, *Forum Memo* 1/56, 35). The companies may have also thought of nuclear power as a post-petroleum medium for reproducing their dominance of the energy sector, as they possessed potential competitive advantages in many nuclear fuel markets.

77. The major fuel processing markets are enrichment, fuel fabrication, and reprocessing. Exxon and ARCO have been active in efforts to assume enrichment responsibilities. The $80 billion market thought available to U.S. firms during the 1970s through the year 2000 (AEC 1974c, 42) and its technically determined oligopoly character were especially alluring.

The dominant enrichment technique in the past has been gaseous diffusion. It is characterized by enormous economies of scale. A major AIF fuel study envisioned an industry initially composed of four plants. A 1968 GAO report foresaw a similar industrial structure and was critical of the oligopoly implications of private sector development. Subsequent technological developments suggest that smaller units may be feasible using laser or other techniques. High R&D costs and regulatory uncertainties may provide significant barriers to entry for this option as well.

Through 1976 Exxon had spent $20 million for centrifuge and $30 million for laser enrichment R&D. In 1975 the company began negotiations with ERDA for the construction of a privately designed and owned centrifuge plant. In contrast, the company had spent a total of only $9 million on all kinds of solar energy research through 1976 (Senate Judiciary Committee 1977, 170–171). ARCO was a partner with Electro-Nucleonics in a major enrichment R&D team in the mid-seventies.

The next step in the fuel processing cycle is fuel fabrication. By the early seventies it was expected to generate annual sales of $700 million (Dawson 1976, 144). By 1974 Exxon, with $1.4 billion in uranium and fuel assembly orders, had broken the vendors' collective monopoly on fabrication activities (Senate Energy and Natural Resources Committee 1977, 368).

Exxon has also aggressively entered the reprocessing market. Explaining the company's $25 million R&D outlays (1969–1977), Slick noted, "Reprocessing is both technologically and capital intensive. . . . [A] small change in regulatory requirements can carry large financial implications. . . . The demands of the fuel reprocessing sector combine many of Exxon's skills. . . . (The company) now has a license application pending . . . (for a facility large enough) to satisfy the fuel needs of 40 large nuclear plants" (Senate Judiciary Committee 1977, 169–170). Similarly motivated, Getty, ARCO and Gulf announced plans to enter the market in the late-sixties and early-seventies.

78. It is also likely that representatives of financial capital played an important role in nuclear planning.

79. Numerous observers have noted the closed character of the decision-making environment that oversaw nuclear development before 1970. Though many groups

testified at the JCAE's annual hearings on the "State of the Atomic Energy Industry," for example, only the voices of the NPC members identified above were heard. Their spokesmen repeated the cost optimism and nuclear world view created by the OT process. As Bupp and Derian write, "The voluminous record of the hearings is an impressive monument to the mutually reinforcing government-industry capacity for self-deception" (Bupp and Derian 1981, 227).

Through the early-seventies, participation in the AEC's licensing process was similarly circumscribed. As Ebbin and Kasper concluded in their widely cited National Science Foundation study, ". . . the only consensus among all the parties to the proceedings [Atomic Safety and Licensing Board hearings] appeared to be a general evaluation that the whole process as it now stands [circa 1972] is nothing more than a charade, the outcome of which is for all intents and purposes predetermined" (Ebbin and Kasper 1974, 246). Public involvement in the planning for a local reactor was precluded until the plant's formal hearing stage, which occurred years after coordinated efforts by the utility, vendor, architect-engineer, and AEC to design and promote the project. Subsequent to being granted intervenor status, non-industry groups were given only 30–60 days to review formerly inaccessible plant information in preparation for the hearings. The procedures were administered in an adversary context with the burden of proof on the intervenors to demonstrate why the plant should not be licensed (Ebbin and Kasper 1974, 244–253; Chubb 1983, 92–96).

Chapter 3

1. Perry 1973, 39–40; Holloman and Grenon 1975, 106, 108; DOE 2/81, 19; NSF 1969, 36.

2. The $23 billion figure includes expenditures for general nuclear energy programs and civilian related military R&D. It excludes funds earmarked for the fusion or the breeder reactor programs and military spending unrelated to the power reactor program. The total reaches $26 billion if research funds for the breeder reactor are included. Because there is no widely agreed upon set of categories for nuclear power or other energy systems' R&D expenditures, cumulative totals can differ markedly. Some tallies of LWR related R&D, for example, exclude fuel cycle R&D outlays and anything not explicitly earmarked for LWRs. The nuclear industry's current trade association, for example, disingenuously claims that R&D subsidies for existing nuclear plants total only $3.7 billion (NEI 8/17/96, 3).

3. For example, The *New York Times'* review of the Energy Research and Development Administration's 1976 "Inform" study found: ". . . corporations are waiting for the government to take the lead in deciding whether and how to pursue [alternative energy technologies] . . . the corporations involved were not prime movers in energy development. Most corporations were found reluctant to invest large sums in long range development . . . in five of the least advanced fields, solar power plants, wind generators, ocean thermal power plants, and the use of waste

heat—almost all corporate research is dependent on federal funds" (*New York Times* 7/4/76).

4. By 1961 the U.S. had sixty-four nuclear vessels in operation or various stages of design and construction (Mullenbach 1963, 132; Dawson 1976, 134). By 1972 one hundred eight nuclear powered ships were afloat (Dawson 1976, 134). Naval historians Hewlett and Duncan write, "Just as much of that technology (LWR) came directly from the naval propulsion project, so did the laying of a broad technical base in industry depend in large measure upon the techniques derived in building the nuclear fleet" (Hewlett and Duncan 1974, 382–384).

5. Many studies and observers have noted this impact. The Perry report, for example, concluded, "The Government's role in energy R&D at this time is crucial. The projects required are so large and expensive, and the risks so great, that Government will be the cornerstone of any program . . ." (Perry 1973, 23). See also: Commoner 1979, 39–40; Perry 1973, 17; *Business Week* 10/9/78; and *Congressional Quarterly* 1981, 71.

6. Under the PRDP the AEC provided lump sum R&D grants, supplemental R&D support, and free fuel usage for reactor projects. The last step in the light water reactor development program, the subsidized construction of commercial sized demonstration plants, began in 1962. In total, fifteen plants were built under various PRDP incentives (Dawson 1976, 94–95).

7. In 1980, for example, of the $69+ billion dollars allocated for R&D in the U.S., $33 billion was federally funded, $34 billion corporate funded, and only $2+ billion university/non-profit funded. Since many federal dollars support research in other sectors, performance statistics for 1981 look a bit different, with industry absorbing $49 billion and federal and non-profit projects $9 billion each (NSF 1981, 25).

8. Of the $8.7 billion in basic research performed in 1981, for example, $4.3 billion was campus based (NSF 1981, 22).

9. Nader and Abbots 1979, 277.

10. Holloman and Grenon 1975, 25. Galbraith asserts the principle more generally (Galbraith 1973, esp. 142–144). Hayes and Zarsky's 1984 study of Export-Import Bank policy reveals a similar dependence on corporate bureaucracies for planning data.

11. Among major energy studies finding a planning context bias against renewable energy options and energy conservation strategies were reports by: the Ford Foundation (1974); Lovins (1977, 1982); U.S. Council on Environmental Quality (1978); Stobaugh and Yergin (1979), and the U.S. Solar Energy Research Institute (1981).

12. As late as 1972, for example, after outlays of more than *$20 billion* for nuclear power R&D, the AEC's director of reactor development argued against spending $15 million for solar energy research, on the grounds that it was too speculative an investment! (JCAE 1972, 1087–1107, esp. 1107).

13. Edward Constant (1973) uses a somewhat similar framework to analyze the shift from piston-propeller driven planes to turbojets. The paradigm metaphor for technological trajectories is productively expanded by Dosi (1982) and Clark (1987).

14. Operating subsidies, like those associated with uranium fuel production, have been distributed over the lifetime of effected plants. Development subsides, such as R&D outlays, have been amortized over a thirty to seventy year span. For a detailed discussion of the methodology used to amortize development outlays and the sensitivity of subsidy estimates to different assumptions about amortization periods, interest rates, and risk premiums, see Cohn 1986, chapter 5, especially 264–272. Minor adjustments have been made to the tables in Cohn 1986.

15. Varying risk premiums and expected kilowatt hours within reasonable limits produces a wide range (1 M/kwh–60 M/kwh) of development subsidy estimates. See footnote 14 above. My base case calculation (3.33 M/kwh) distributes OT period development outlays over the lifetime kilowatt hour production of all reactors expected to be sold through 2004. For more detailed discussion of the methodology used to calculate the subsidy see Cohn 1986, chapter 5, Appendix A. Minor adjustments have been made to the tables in Cohn 1986.

16. See Cohn 1986, ch. 5, esp. 264–272.

17. Mullenbach 1963, 121, 154, 321.

18. A number of authors have emphasized the importance of the assumption of positive value for reactor Pu by-products in winning utility confidence in the competitiveness of nuclear power. Campbell (1988), for example, asserts, ". . . AEC officials felt that reprocessing offered benefits that would stimulate the sector's overall development because it created the chance to reduce fuel costs by recycling the recovered uranium and plutonium as fresh reactor fuel. . . . According to a spokesman for one reactor manufacturer, corporations and utilities believed that without the plutonium repurchasing program and the possibility of fuel recycling, the cost of fuel would have been high enough that nuclear power would not have been competitive with traditional fossil fuel plants. . . . Furthermore, from the utilities' point of view reprocessing essentially solved the waste management problem by providing someone else to take responsibility for the storage and ultimate disposal of spent fuel" (Campbell 1988, 111–112).

19. Under the "stretch-out" program and similar practices the AEC accumulated a 50,000 ton uranium surplus (enough to fuel all on-line reactors in 1983 for four years) (Bowring 1980, 47). The purchases cost more than $3 billion and were intended to provide a smooth mining transition from military to civilian markets (Bowring 1980, 49; Mullenbach 1963, 121–122). Programs like "stretch-out" lowered the level of uncertainty in the uranium industry and its required rate of return, thereby lowering long run nuclear fuel costs (Bowring 1980, 45–46).

20. See Cohn 1986, 245–247, 273 for detailed calculations of enrichment subsidy rates.

21. Komanoff and Roelofs 12/92, 47.

22. Through 1974 unreimbursed regulatory outlays totaled about $2 billion (Battelle Memorial Institute 1978, 145). Distributing this sum over cumulative kwh's through 1974 yields about a 5.5 M/kwh operating subsidy. Since some of these early expenditures, however, were geared towards resolving long term issues, only one-third have been treated as operating expenses, yielding an operating subsidy of ~2 M/kwh. The remaining sum has been added to the development subsidy totals in table 3.4. The same procedure was followed for 1974–1979.

23. *Nucleonics* 7/65 23; *Nuclear Industry* 11/67.

24. DOE 2/81, 25.

25. It is difficult to tally nuclear power's miscellaneous subsidies because of their diverse forms and numerous funding sources. I have assumed a ~2.75 billion total in table 3.4. As this sum is almost exhausted by the examples cited in the text, it probably underestimates the level of such assistance.

26. U.S. Senate Judiciary Committee 1970, 742–743.

27. The nuclear industry argues that only tax statutes that *single out* nuclear power should be considered nuclear subsidies (excluding, for example, all the tax breaks given the utilities for new generating plants). At another extreme, some analysts treat any divergence from regular tax liabilities as tax subsidies, including common practices, such as the deductability of business interest payments.

28. See Cohn 1986, 274–5 for calculation of the tax subsidy rate.

29. Komanoff and Roelofs 12/92, 52.

30. Green 1973, 483–4. The insurance sector, acting through various pools, was willing to write only $60 million (1957$) worth of coverage per plant, while AEC worst case scenarios projected accident liabilities in the $5–$7 billion (1957$) range. Though allegedly confident that serious accident probabilities were low, the leading nuclear firms threatened to withdraw from the industry if forced to assume multi-billion dollar risk exposures. The NRC found a similar situation in the early-1980s (NRC 1983). In 1987 A. David Rossin, DOE Assistant Secretary for Nuclear Energy, reiterated the impossibility of nuclear power without limited liability (*Power Engineering*, July 1987).

31. The Dubin-Rothwell subsidy rates are significantly higher than most previous government estimates, but consistent with the revealed preferences of private firms and popular expression of public concern (Dubin and Rothwell 1990, 78; DOE 11/92, 77–78).

32. Duffy and Adams 1978, 58.

33. Hayes and Zarsky 1984, 34.

34. Hayes and Zarsky 1984, 30–31.

35. Bello, Hayes, and Zarsky 1979, 9.

36. U.S. AEC 1973b, 15.

37. Nuclear power consumers also appear to have received implicit subsidies through public assumption of waste disposal costs for various abandoned nuclear sites, such as uranium mining sites (see, for example, Komanoff and Roelofs 1992, 49–50 and DOE 2/81).

38. U.S. House, Government Operations Committee 1977, 5.

39. DOE 5/80, 108–113.

40. Perry 1977, 37; Zimmerman 1982, 308.

41. Dawson 1976, 153.

42. This difficulty would be eased for a technology that could progress incrementally (i.e., one that could finance its R&D through a series of short term projects). Such a strategy works best for developed technologies capturing marginal improvements, it would have seemed difficult (and probably dangerous) to nurture a nuclear industry this way.

43. Duffy and Adams 1978, 60.

44. U.S. Senate, Committee on Banking, Housing and Urban Affairs 1976, 5–6.

45. Olson 1976, 202–204; *New York Times* 3/28/75, 44.

46. *New York Times* 11/3/74, 88.

47. *Power Line* 8/81.

48. Berger 1977, 335.

49. From 1945–1974, for example, there were only nine prudency cases in the United States challenging gas and electric utilities' recovery of investment outlays (Cantor, undated, 2).

50. The common choice of a "negative salvage" method for decommissioning accounting, for example, was due to its provision of a maximum cash flow for new construction (DOE 5/80, 174). Similar promotional concerns appear to have governed the accounting treatment given tax subsidies (Lanoue 1976, 22,24).

51. Until the mid to late sixties, declining block rates could be defended on the grounds of scale economies. By 1967, however, the industry faced a rising marginal cost curve (Anderson 1981, 70).

52. *Science* 4/19/74, 268

53. Rolph 1979, 77. See also Ford 1982, 65, 225; Komanoff 1981, 168; and DOE 5/80, 117.

54. Rolph 1979, 59,68,74,163; Komanoff 1981, 68; Perry 1977, 59; Wood 1983, 19–20, 66–67.

55. *New York Times* 10/16/83. See also: U.S. Congress, Office of Technology Assessment 1984, 144; Ford 1982, 52, 106; Rolph 1979, 158–9 and Gorinson 1979b, 3.

56. Taylor and Yokell 1979, 24.

57. In the early-sixties, for example, the AEC successfully pressured the Navy to allow Southern California Edison to utilize a portion of the Pendleton naval base for the San Onofre nuclear plant (Allen 1977, 72). The initiative was part of a larger plan favored by JCAE member Craig Hosmer to create national reservations for nuclear power plants (Balogh 1991, 193). In New York, Governor Rockefeller announced plans to locate nuclear facilities on state land in order to circumvent local siting opposition (*New York Times* 9/6/69, 23). In Rhode Island, an unused naval airstrip was improperly transferred to the New England Power Company for nuclear use (Gyorgy 1979, 392).

58. Through the early-seventies, the commission permitted utilities to contract for enrichment "requirements" without specifying specific commitment levels. This flexibility insulated the utilities from the risk of superfluous enrichment liabilities if plant construction was slower than anticipated (Ford Foundation 1977, 366). Even after requiring fixed commitments in the mid-seventies, the AEC allowed the utilities to renegotiate 135 contracts in August 1975 in response to reductions in fuel demand. The cancellations and postponements saved the utilities several hundred million dollars (Lanoue 1976, 20). The AEC similarly guaranteed a back-up supply of enriched uranium to utilities participating in private centrifuge enrichment projects as insurance against potential project failures and fuel shortfalls (AEC 1974c, 150).

59. Bowring 1980, 44.

60. JCAE: 1957, 106; 1963b, 238–9.

61. Although many states allowed a partial recovery of construction work in progress (CWIP) from ratepayers, the allowance was not high enough to fund the capacity expansion planned during the OT years (DOE 11/82, 41). Although the Federal Energy Regulatory Commission could authorize CWIP charges for utilities in financial distress, it did not use this authority to promote nuclear generation (Bowring 1980; DOE 5/80, 202). A number of "utility reform" bills were introduced in the mid-1970s with the aim of centralizing utility regulation at the national level in institutions friendly to utility financing needs. Virtually all the major proposals failed (Campbell 1988, 105).

62. In New Hampshire, for example, anti-nuclear movement efforts pressured the state legislature to repeal CWIP charges (Gyorgy 1979, 385). After New Hampshire Governor Thompson vetoed the repeal, CWIP became a central issue in the 1978 gubernatorial campaign and is widely considered a major reason for Thompson's defeat (*Wall Street Journal* 10/25/84). In Missouri, CWIP was banned by a statewide initiative referendum (Gyorgy 1979, 385).

63. Post TMI nuclear projects have suffered at least $9.8 billion in disallowed expenditures (Anderson 1991, 24). In Oregon, the utilities were precluded from recovering investments in abandoned plants by a statewide ballot initiative (Tomain 1987, 110).

64. Nader and Abbotts 1979, 353–366.

65. U.S. Congress, Office of Technology Assessment 1984, 216.

66. *New York Times* 9/1/80.

67. Nader and Abbotts 1979, 360–363.

68. The Environmental Defense Fund was especially important in gaining marginal cost pricing reforms (Anderson 1981, esp. 74, 88, 97, 110–113). See also *Science* 9/20/74, 1031.

Chapter 4

1. In 1957 the Academy recommended that a national registry be established to record individual radiation exposure and health histories. The suggestion was rejected at the time by the government as impractical (*New York Times* 7/5/79), and about thirteen years later as unnecessary (Lewis 1972, 94; Sternglass 1981, 100). The commission similarly opposed recommendations by the U.S. Public Health Service to install radiation monitoring equipment in uranium mines, due to fears that monitoring could alarm miners and halt production (*New York Times* 1/9/90, A-20). It was not until 1968 that the AEC established a registry to keep track of the health histories of plutonium workers (Nader and Abbotts 1979, 175), and not until the late-seventies that it was decided to keep a registry of the radiation exposure and medical experience of all uranium workers. Until the mid-eighties many companies' records did not include data on temporary hires ("jumpers") who have increasingly accounted for significant percentages of industry exposure levels, reaching 50% in the seventies (Gofman 1981, 586; Morgan 1978, 38; Gyorgy 1979, 92).

2. The first major epidemiological study of American nuclear industry workers was not undertaken until the mid-sixties. After its preliminary findings suggested higher than expected cancer rates, the study's oversight was transferred from a group of independent researchers at the University of Pittsburgh to the AEC's own laboratories (Geiger et al. 1992, 21). The Navy announced plans for epidemiological studies of the health histories of civilian workers at its nuclear shipyards only after a *Boston Globe* investigation reported elevated leukemia and cancer rates at the Portsmouth Naval Yard in 1978 (*Boston Globe* 2/18/79).

A major National Research Council review of DOE epidemiological studies in 1980 concluded ". . . that studies on human health effects of low doses of ionizing radiation are often not given high priority . . . Either the research has been inadequately planned and evaluated or the resources available in DOE to support it have been unsatisfactorily coordinated and directed" (Geiger et al. 1992, 82). The Council found it "noteworthy that the [DOE health research] staff does not exhibit strength in dosimetry, epidemiology and biostatistics . . ." (Geiger et al. 1992, 82).

Another major review of the low level radiation hazard literature in 1980 found that the occupational studies of radiation hazards at or around Oak Ridge ". . . are best noted for the insensitive methods employed. Large groups of unexposed persons, or recently hired persons were included with exposed persons when comparisons were made. In some, the healthy-worker effect was ignored. In all but the study by Patrick, there was no attempt to look at specific causes of death. In only one of them was consideration given to the latent period, i.e., the deaths for the years when no excess cancers from radiation could be expected were combined with the deaths for later years when some might be expected" (Archer 1980, 7).

3. During the atmospheric testing period, the commission funded only 30–50 technicians to monitor nationwide fallout levels (Metzger 1972, 103). Although a large number of soldiers were exposed to fallout hazards during U.S. bomb tests, minimal efforts were made to monitor their subsequent health histories (*New York Times* 12/25/77). It was not until 1978, in response to public pressures, that the Defense Department increased data collection efforts.

"Notes of AEC meetings in 1953, 1954, and 1955 show that the commissioners were concerned primarily about the public relations rather than health aspect of the fallout problem and the delay or increased cost it could have for the nuclear weapons development program" (*Washington Post* 4/19/79). A 1979 Senate Health Subcommittee hearing found a pattern of information suppression about fallout hazards by the AEC (ibid.). Documents declassified in the early 1990s indicate that the AEC knew that bomb tests in 1951 could contaminate residents near the sites, but resisted evacuating those at risk in order not to alarm the public (*New York Times* 3/15/95, A-22). The AEC's PR program sanctioned vacation viewing of bomb tests in order to buttress the image of the "friendly atom" (*Lies of Our Times* 4/94, 14).

The AEC did fund a series of epidemiological studies of populations downwind of the tests by the Utah Medical Center. Carole Gallagher, author of MIT Press's *American Ground Zero: The Secret Nuclear War* (1993), speculates that subtle methodological biases led these researchers to more optimistic conclusions than found in private studies (*Lies of Our Times* 4/94, 16).

4. Through the 1970s the NRC relied on the utilities to measure the level of radiation released by their nuclear plants (*Washington Post* 11/1/79). Similar policies were followed in uranium mines until 1979, after a federal study found mining companies under-reporting radiation levels by about 400% (*Denver Post* 9/2/79; see also Wasserman et al. 1982, 150–151). In 1980 the NRC began installing dosimeters around U.S. nuclear plants.

One of the difficulties in assessing the impact of the Three Mile Island accident is the paucity of information about the level of radiation released during the accident due to the inadequacy of plant monitoring equipment (*New York Times* 8/30/84 A-14; *Rocky Mountain News* 3/29/83).

5. A 1980 NRC sponsored study found that "'a significant percentage of the personnel dosimetry processors in the U.S. are not performing with an acceptable degree of consistency and accuracy'" (Caufield 1989, 221). An especially glaring weakness of existing radiation monitors is their inability to record the internally received radiation doses associated with clinging microscopic radioactive particles (called "radioactive fleas"). A 1992 review of the DOE's epidemiological studies by a Physicians for Social Responsibility task force detailed numerous technical flaws in

radiation measurement, cohort follow-up, and other areas (Geiger et al. 1992, esp. 35–40).

6. Especially important was the AEC's neglect of the hazards of Iodine 131 and Strontium 90 via milk contamination (Metzger 1972, 85–86, 103). Early studies also neglected uranium mining's radon decay avenue into the food chain (Ford Foundation 1977, 174).

Alongside errors of omission, the NRC now acknowledges that the AEC promoted misleading studies of fallout's food chain flow in order to minimize opposition to the atomic tests (*Washington Post* 11/11/79). According to the Post article, the AEC studies purposely selected soils that were the least absorbent of fallout materials. Experimenters subsequently heated the soil in order to destroy bacteria which otherwise aid in plant fallout absorption. Finally, radioactive particles were added to the test plant's environment right before harvest rather than during the vegetation's entire growing cycle.

7. Although many radiologists still assert that the linear hypothesis overestimates radiation health hazards at low dose levels, a modest number support an inverse non-linear hypothesis. Work by Drs. Stewart, Petkau, and Morgan suggest that because low level radiation is less likely to destroy cells, it has a higher probability of causing life-threatening alterations (Nader and Abbotts, 1979, 79; Pawlick 1980, 30; Morgan 1978; Kaku 1982, 66; Gofman 1990).

8. Because of the classified nature of the information related to the Hiroshima bomb blast, little or no independent analysis was undertaken of the methods used to determine the ratio of low/high level radiation caused by the explosion. It was not until 1977 that the credibility of the official figures was widely suspected. Current thinking assigns more of the bomb related cancers to low level radiation than initially acknowledged. The debate is especially significant because numerous radiation studies have relied on "constants" derived from the Hiroshima data in calculating hazard burdens.

Other methodological objections to Hiroshima-based hazard estimates have criticized: (1) the extrapolation of constant (or "absolute") increases in future cancer rates, rather than percentage (or "relative") increases (Gofman 1981, 315–323); (2) neglect of the uniqueness of the population (blast survivors) (Stewart 1990); and (3) inattention to the downward bias in cancer reporting amongst survivors, due to increased mortality from other radiation related immune deficiencies (Morgan 1978).

9. A 1974 EPA study found that previously ignored nuclear fuel cycle emissions of carbon 14 and tritium would produce sixty times the health effects of the acknowledged polluters in a hundred year period (Berger 1977, 76–78). Dr. Robert Pohl of Cornell University criticized the AEC-NRC for ignoring the thorium hazard in uranium tailings. Dr. Marvin Resnikoff criticized decommissioning research for ignoring the presence of radioactive nickel alloys in the reactor's steel infrastructure.

10. Cornell University's Dr. Robert Pohl criticized AEC-NRC hazard research for utilizing time periods of 1–30–100 years for calculating environmental burdens rather than the lifespan of the offending isotopes. The latter approach implies uranium tailings cancer burdens hundreds of times the NRC's projection of a fractional

death per nuclear plant. The escalation reflects the cumulative impact of thorium's 80,000 year half-life on morbidity rates (Berger 1977, 76–78; *Nucleonics Week* 5/25/78). In response to such criticism, the commission increased its open pit uranium mining hazard burden period from one to one thousand years (*Nucleonics Week* 5/25/78).

The debate raises important questions about the proper way to cost account future environmental burdens. If the impact of radiation hazards is expressed in terms of lives lost, there is a tendency to value a life in the future nearly as much as a life in the present. However, if a dollar value is placed on the lost life, and future fatalities discounted to their present value, the burden of long range radiation effects becomes trivial.

The logical justification for such discounting lies in the implicit assumption that medical-atomic science will deter deaths at a rate roughly equal to the discount rate; or that the resources freed in the present by reliance on nuclear power will deter such deaths at this rate. Since this is a probability statement, some weighted probability distribution should be used to reflect the accompanying uncertainties and social risk aversion. The more conservative the assumptions, the closer to Pohl's accounting one comes.

11. The "survivor bias" suggests that the Japanese bomb blast survivors may constitute an unrepresentative sample; e.g., the individuals who survived the bomb and other hazards of wartime Japan may have had stronger than average immune systems.

12. Like the "survivor bias", the "healthy worker effect" notes that working people are generally healthier than non-working people. How much one needs to adjust morbidity and mortality data for the "healthy worker effect" in nuclear power occupations is ambiguous.

13. Concerns have been raised, for example, about potential radiation damage to the immune system and increased vulnerability to a wide variety of illnesses.

14. Some of Sternglass' assertions, in particular, seem poorly conceived.

15. Ten years earlier the president of the National Academy of Sciences similarly stated, "It is essentially impossible to find more than a small handful of such experts who have not in relatively recent times, had significant support—either research grants or actual employment—from the U.S. Atomic Energy Commission" (Metzger 1972, 26).

16. Nobel Laureate Linus Pauling, for example, was called before the House unAmerican Activities Committee for circulating a petition calling for an end to atmospheric testing. A newspaper editor who ran editorials critical of the tests and their potential health hazards was visited repeatedly by AEC representatives who implied his opposition might suggest Communist sympathies (Hilgartner et al. 1982, 88). Labor Department efforts to raise uranium mining safety standards were criticized by the JCAE as potential threats to national defense (Metzger 1972, 132). The highlighting of optimistic voices as official radiation hazard spokesmen was part of the larger ideological context created by McCarthyism. Recall, for example, the replacement of

348 *Notes*

"dovish" scientists like Oppenheimer by cold war enthusiasts such as Teller as popular sources of information about the atom.

Dr. Herbert Abrams of the Harvard Medical School has generalized the AEC's lack of radiation research funding to include insufficient attention to radiation issues in doctor training (Wasserman et al. 1982, 128; see also Morgan 1978).

17. Documents obtained by the *Washington Post* under Freedom of Information review provide an insight into the process of selective attention. In 1965 a U.S. Public Health Service study linked elevated leukemia rates to bomb test fallout. The study was suppressed and follow up research blocked after AEC review suggested publication was not in the national interest (*Washington Post* 4/14/79; Wasserman et al. 1982, 65). Another twenty year study linking increased thyroid cancers to fallout levels was discontinued after federal officials reportedly "lost interest" in such work. Similarly downplayed was the observation of increased birth defects in fallout areas by local Utah physicians and claims of increased sheep deaths by local ranchers (*Boston Globe* 1/8/79). In 1980 a Utah judge reversed his own 1954 decision denying ranchers damage payments from the AEC. The judge attacked the commission for having "manipulated" and "intimidated" witnesses in perpetuating a "fraud on the court" (Wasserman and Solomon 1/83, 15).

The AEC's resistance to researching the health hazards posed by the use of uranium mill tailings-based building materials in Colorado illustrates the same selective attention to information. H. Peter Metzger writes, "After discovery of the indoor radon problem by the Colorado State Department of Public Health, the AEC, both on an unofficial level and on an official level, sought to impede investigations into the nature of the problem" (Metzger 1972, 176). The commission blocked Public Health Service funding for a study of home radon levels and denied AEC funds to the Colorado Medical Center for a study of chromosonal damage in tailings contaminated dwellings. After dismissing the recorded radon levels as insignificantly different from background radiation, the commission withheld contradictory results of a commission research project (Metzger 1972, 195–197).

When releasing studies in conflict with official optimism, the AEC also tended to append contradictory claims. This practice served to dull the public impact of anomalous findings.

18. Significant circumstantial evidence suggests that the commission sought on a number of occasions to terminate funding for projects and researchers at odds with its expansionist policies. Among the most famous cases are: the denial of access to hazard data about U.S. uranium miners to Wilhelm Hueper, a top scientist at the National Cancer Institute, after he publicly acknowledged the seriousness of uranium mining hazards (*New York Times* 1/9/90 A-1, 20), the recall of 92% of Dr. Arthur Tamplin's staff after his findings and public statements challenged the commission's radiation standards (Wasserman et al. 1982, 21); the recommendation that funding for Dr. John Gofman be terminated after he attacked exposure standards (Berger 1977, 72); the removal of Dr. Thomas Mancuso as director of the Hanford health study after he refused to release incomplete results that might facilitate AEC efforts to reduce public concern about radiation hazards, and continued exclusion of Mancuso from access to the Hanford data after his preliminary findings implied higher than

AEC expected cancer hazards (Morgan 1978; Gyorgy 1979, 92, Hilgartner 1982, 104–108).

The DOE appears to have continued aspects of the AEC's policy, Geiger et al. indicate:

> "In 1986, Dr. Gregg Wilkinson, an epidemiologist working for the DOE's Los Alamos National Laboratory, circulated the draft of a paper to be submitted to a respected peer-reviewed publication, the *American Journal of Epidemiology*, showing an excess of brain cancer among Rocky Flats workers and suggesting the possibility that radiation dose/cancer induction risks were greater than the DOE then maintained to be the case.
>
> "The DOE response was intense. . . . [O]ne supervisor at LANL told Dr. Wilkinson that his findings would 'shut down the nuclear industry.' Another told him he should do research 'to please the DOE, your sponsors, not satisfy peer reviewers.' He was pressured to withdraw the paper, a request that was canceled only when he threatened to resign. The DOE made no effort to publicize the findings—in marked contrast with a major public relations effort that had followed the earlier publication of a very preliminary Wilkinson paper on Rocky Flats that contained no positive findings.
>
> "Shortly after the paper appeared, the epidemiology group at LANL was downgraded, its functions fragmented and its budget reduced" (Geiger et al. 56).

A more important censoring device than direct reprisals was the nuclear establishment's ability to encourage self-censorship. AEC and nuclear industry favor meant publication credentials and job security. AEC veterans comprised the "old boy network" for job recommendations and the editorial boards of peer review journals. See, for example, Metzger 1972, 276 and Ebbin and Kasper 1974, 208.

Private industry similarly sought to discourage its critics. For example, mine owners in Wyoming sought to have the state's chief radiological officer fired after he revealed that a mine owner had falsified disclosure information (Metzger 1972, 127). A coalition of business groups forced the resignation of Jefferson County Health Department Director Carl Johnson in response to his aggressive monitoring and publicizing of radiation releases from the Rocky Flats nuclear facility (*Westword* 5–6/81; *Nuclear Monitor* 11(1), 9). Similar events occurred in Grand Junction Colorado (Metzger 1972, 183).

In assessing the impact of promotional objectives on scientific discourse, the key question is one of degree. Even during the height of the OT period, articles critical of AEC orthodoxy were published. The issue is whether or not ideological biases influenced the frequency of publication enough to discourage the growth of a critical mass of alternative scholarly work.

19. See note 5 in chapter 9.

20. It is common for statisticians to characterize an event as "statistically significant" if its possibility of random occurrence is less than ~5%. For example, imagine you were flipping a coin and thought you had learned how to make it come up heads. To prove your achievement you flipped the coin 100 times. Assume you came up

with 58 heads and 42 tails, could we conclude you had some facility at making the coin come up heads? The answer is complicated because even without learning a new skill there is a possibility of coming up with 58 heads out of 100 tries. Statistical theory predicts that such an outcome would occur slightly more than 5% of the time with random flips. Thus we would be forced to report that your performance had demonstrated no statistically significant ability to flip a head. We might also note, however, that it suggested you might have such a skill and the issue merited further research. The latter is the attitude of nuclear power critics towards radiation hazards.

Geiger et al. (1992) offer analysis of about a dozen studies where DOE-funded researchers dismissed potentially suspicious findings because of a lack of statistical significance (i.e., an inability to rule out chance fluctuations as the cause of elevated cancer rates [47–50]). They note:

> "The recent report of a large DOE-funded project on the health effects of low level radiation in shipyard workers is an example of how very suspicious findings can be presented in a way that emphasizes that they are not likely to be indicative of any health risk. The conclusion of the report states: 'the population does not show any risk which can clearly be associated with radiation exposure in the current analysis.' It then goes on to say that the follow-up is not long enough to evaluate risk adequately.
>
> "An outside reader might reformulate the findings to say that the current analysis demonstrates disquieting information on the relationship of work in nuclear shipyards and subsequent cancer risk, and that the short follow-up period precludes the possibility of statistically significant results" (Geiger et al. 1992, 48).

Some nuclear critics have also attacked the shipyard study for underestimating the "healthy worker effect." For similar arguments, see: Geiger et al.'s critique of Checkoway et al., Reyes et al., and Polednak et al. (Geiger et al. 1992, 76, 71, 73) and Bertell's critique of DOE's Hanford studies (Bertell 1985, 93–96).

21. When asked why the AEC did not penalize uranium mill operators for tailings contamination of local streams, a staff member of the commission testified at a Santa Fe hearing, "'. . . We will not [try] to put them out of business because that in turn would put us out of business'" (Cook 1984, 59). In 1959, at a time when the International Commission for Radiological Protection (ICRP) was tightening its regulations and U.S. fallout levels exceeded certain AEC-ICRP standards, U.S. regulations were relaxed (Rolph 1979, 108–9). In January 1990, the *New York Times* reported that recently released documents indicate the AEC opposed the installation of radiation monitors and better ventilation in uranium mines due to fears that the former might alarm miners and the latter add .005% to mining costs (*New York Times* 1/9/90).

22. Through the sixties nuclear power plants had been permitted to discharge up to 500 milirems (mr) at their boundary. 1977 EPA guidelines reduced this level to 5–25 mr under most circumstances (Nader and Abbotts 1979, 75–76). The permissible average population exposure rate from the entire nuclear fuel cycle was similarly

reduced from 170 to 25 mr. (Nader and Abbotts 1979, 75–76; Gofman 1981, 532–533) and subsequently raised to 100 mr. It should be noted that some of the impetus for tighter regulation came from technical innovations that made reduction less expensive. Actual release levels in the 1960s were also far lower than permissible release levels.

23. Illustrative of the AEC and its successor agencies' regulatory conservatism (given their technical assumptions) has been the use of a $1000/rem damage estimate for radiation hazards in cost/benefit studies of the merits of regulatory requirements. Given the AEC's radiation hazard assumptions in the 1970s, this decision rule implied a $5–$30 million value for an avoided cancer death, quite high by historical standards.

24. Foreshadowing later petition efforts by the Union of Concerned Scientists, Linus Pauling's mid-fifties petition for a test ban treaty collected over 2000 US scientist signatures (Wasserman et al. 1982, 98). The badly defeated Stevenson campaign raised the issue in 1956. About the same time, unsuccessful efforts were made to transfer the regulation of radiation standards from the AEC to the Public Health Service (Rolph 1979, 109). The greater strength of the environmental movement a decade later succeeded in shifting significant regulatory authority to the EPA.

In 1959 President Eisenhower established the Federal Radiation Council, and the AEC created the Office of Health and Safety to reassure the public that radiation issues received serious government attention. Both efforts were chiefly public relations gestures. The council was denied a research capability and the Health and Safety Office took minimal initiatives (Rolph 1979, 110, 45; Wasserman et al. 1982, 99).

In the early-sixties pressures for a test ban treaty escalated. Among the groups actively organizing public opinion were Women Strike for Peace, The Committee for Nuclear Information, and SANE. A treaty was initialed in 1962.

Despite fallout concerns the AEC retained dominance of radiation research and popular perceptions of the character of radiation hazards. The controversy appears to have been generally limited to the bomb test arena (Rolph 1979, 110). Pressures for regulation of uranium mining radon levels, for example, were successfully resisted. The threshold hypothesis was publicly retained by the AEC, JCAE, and nuclear industry well into the late-sixties (Rolph 1979, 110–11).

The scientific lineage of popular criticism of nuclear power radiation standards can be traced to studies by the National Academy of Sciences and a UN team that challenged the threshold hypothesis in the mid-fifties (Rolph 1979, 109). These studies were followed by papers by Alice Stewart in 1959 and Brian MacMahon in 1962 linking in-utero x-rays to elevated cancer rates (Gofman 1981, 745), a 1963 study by Ernest Sternglass linking fallout to increased childhood cancers, and a 1970 Sternglass paper linking infant mortality rates to nuclear plant radiation emissions (Sternglass 1981, 282; Lewis 1972, 61–63).

Popular political activity made it increasingly difficult for the AEC to ignore such findings. Sternglass' mid-sixties charges, for example, received significant media coverage in the context of the anti-ballistic missile debate, including a heavily promoted feature article in *Esquire*, an appearance on the Today show, and a lecture before a congressional seminar.

Increasing public concern forced the AEC to ask two of its radiation experts, Drs. Gofman and Tamplin, to review and rebut his work. Front page stories, congressional hearings, and escalating controversy accompanied their conclusion that Sternglass was partially right. Though significantly reducing his hazard claims, Gofman and Tamplin's findings indicated that the AEC's hazard calculations were more than twenty times too low (Gofman 1979, 7). The two recommended a tenfold reduction in permissible radiation levels.

In response, the secretary of HEW asked the National Academy of Sciences to review Gofman and Tamplin's findings. The academy's 1972 report and other research stimulated by Sternglass' claims, concluded that the dangers of low level radiation had been underestimated. The report termed existing AEC radiation exposure standards "unnecessarily high" (Nader and Abbotts 1979, 74). In 1978, Dr. Edward Radford, chair of the academy's radiation research committee, called for a tenfold decrease in permissible occupational exposure levels, stating, "'new evidence indicates that the risk of cancer is substantially greater' than thought just six years ago" (*Washington Post* 2/9/78). Calculations in the National Academy of Sciences 1990 update (BEIR V) raised hazard estimates again, coming near 50% of Gofman-Tamplin's figures (*New York Times* 12/20/89, 1).

25. The press' belated attention to the GIs' injuries was abetted by the organizing efforts of anti-testing advocates. Paul Jacobs, for example, did extensive investigatory reporting on individual exposure histories, which culminated in the movie *Paul Jacobs and the Nuclear Gang*. The film received an Emmy Award in 1979. The Atomic Industrial Forum engaged in an active nationwide campaign to limit its showings on television (Wasserman et al. 1983, 112). See also notes 2 and 3.

26. Alice Stewart's study of the Hanford Data was funded by a $1.4 million grant from the Three Mile Island Public Health Fund. The absence of alternative funding sources to AEC-DOE-nuclear industry pockets during the OT years significantly retarded independent epidemiological research.

27. In return for dropping a court challenge to the Palisades nuclear plant, for example, critics won utility agreement to an improved liquid rad-waste discharge system (Lewis 1972, 135–142; *Wall Street Journal* 3/17/71, 10). At Lagoona Beach, Michigan, Detroit Edison agreed to spend an additional $5 million to upgrade its liquid rad-waste disposal system and $10 million to reduce its radioactive gaseous releases to 1% of the AEC's permissible level (Lewis 1972, 143). Intervenors similarly managed to win upgrading concessions at the Point Beach reactors in Wisconsin (Lewis 1972, 266) and the Dresden II plant in Illinois (Keating 1975, 61).

One of the most famous cases involved the Minnesota EPA's attempt in 1969 to impose radiation standards 100 times stricter than the AEC's regulations on a local power plant. Although the Minnesota EPA lost its court battle with the utility over the state's right to impose stricter radiation standards than the AEC, it won the regulatory war. Under the threat of unfriendly state legislation in other areas, the utility agreed to "voluntarily" reduce its radioactive gaseous emissions by 80% (Lewis 1972, 133).

28. For a more detailed listing of specific upgrades with respect to: gaseous radwaste, liquid radwaste, occupational radiation exposure, solid wastes, uranium mining, and reprocessing, see Cohn 1986, 337–338 and Campbell 1988, 116, 124.

29. For an alternative interpretation of the same trend (the glass being half full rather than half empty), see Kocher 1991.

30. The commission's light water reactor safety budget during the bandwagon years of 1963–1968 was less than 5% annual AEC R&D outlays (Bowring 1980, 31; Rolph 1979, 93). From 1965–1968 8.5% of the budget went unspent, as safety research projects faced severe review (Rolph 1979, 93). From 1965 to 1974, AEC safety budgets averaged about 1.5% of commission expenditures (Campbell 1988, 56). Safety research also had low prestige in the technical community. Former AEC Commissioner Victor Gilinsky reports, "Hiring good staff was a problem initially because the safety job had low status. The work was considered necessary to meet public concerns, but basically dull and unproductive. Nuclear power's 'best and the brightest', in the U.S. at least, shunned the safety function. This was an additional factor contributing to timid and ineffective regulation" (Gilinsky 1992, 706).

31. Campbell (1988) notes that "(b)oth Oak Ridge and the Advisory Committee on Reactor Safeguards complained that this seriously compromised the AEC's ability to evaluate reactor safety" (59).

32. The NRC's Special Inquiry Group investigating the Three Mile Island accident, for example, concluded, "NRC and the industry have done almost nothing to evaluate systematically the operation of existing reactors, pinpoint potential safety problems, and eliminate them by requiring changes in design, operator procedures or control logic" (Komanoff 1981, 56; see also Gorinson 1979b, 3). Although the degree of this indictment is excessive, the direction of criticism is correct. The extreme language probably reflects the committee's irritation over the lack of NRC and industry attention to pre-TMI dress rehearsals. NRC official James Creswell, for example, tried unsuccessfully for five months prior to TMI to gain regulatory attention to problems similar to those that triggered the accident (Gorinson 1979b, 108–112). Babcock and Wilcox, the plant's vendor, had accumulated information on similar accident initiating experiences at like reactors, but neglected to forward the data to TMI's managers (Gorinson 1979c, 137). The utility had access to several sources of operating experience data but judged that it was not cost effective to review the material (Gorinson 1979b, 116).

It should be noted that prior to TMI, the commission maintained a system of bulletins and circulars on reactor operating experience. It also supported a nuclear safety information center and a bi-monthly safety journal that reported on reactor performance. Critics charge that these efforts were insufficient rather than non-existent (Pollard 1979, 1–2).

33. Few links were established between regulatory and safety personnel, as RDT Division Director Milton Shaw feared communication might alarm the regulatory staff. Gillette writes,

"Researchers at both Idaho and Oak Ridge National Laboratory say that as long ago as 1966, and as recently as 1971, they were expressly forbidden to speak with members of the regulatory staff about such controversial matters of reactor safety as fuel-failure and seismic research, except in meetings prearranged and closely supervised by RDT officials in Washington. During these formal meetings, researchers said, RDT officials allowed them to answer specific questions propounded by the regulatory staff, but discouraged them from volunteering their concerns about the safety of specific nuclear power plants. Under no circumstances were they allowed to discuss 'program planning' of future research with the regulatory staff or to collaborate with the regulatory staff to define technical uncertainties that might require new R&D."

"The regulatory staff, of course, could always read the monthly progress reports that researchers at Idaho turned out, but the same restrictions that applied to meetings also applied to the reports" (Gillette 9/22/72, 1081).

Shaw also prevented AEC safety researchers from meeting with foreign reactor experts on three occasions and attempted to block a symposium on reactor safety sponsored by the American Nuclear Society (ibid 9/22/72, 1080). Gillette concludes, "Several research administrators interviewed said they thought these barriers—combined with RDT's persistent reluctance or inability to carry out research the regulatory staff wanted—deprived the AEC of information urgently needed to judge the safety of plants coming up for licensing" (ibid., 1082). The policy result was a bias towards lenient hazard regulation.

34. Rolph 1977, 25, 34; Perry 1977, 59; Okrent 1981, 216,314; Wood 1983, 34.

35. As early as the 1950s, Westinghouse argued "industry has developed reactor systems and engineered safeguards that should permit the location of large nuclear stations in population centers" (Rolph 1979, 61). Throughout the 1960s the vendors and utilities unsuccessfully pressured the AEC and the Advisory Committee on Reactor Safeguards to approve urban sitings. Unsuccessful efforts were made, for example, to gain AEC OK for reactors in or very near New York City (Ravenswood), Boston (Edgar Station), Philadelphia-Trenton (Burlington), and the Los Angeles metropolitan area (Bolsa) (*Nucleonics* 5/63, 19–20; *Electrical World* 1/20/64; Okrent 1981, 58).

36. During the OT period, the commission and nuclear industry argued that meltdown scenarios were not credible events and therefore did not require analysis or containment responses. The vendors' vitriolic dismissal of ACRS recommendations for an expanded pressure vessel research program and rupture defense system typifies industry's position (Okrent 1981, 90). A similar lack of research interest undermined assessment of the emergency core cooling system (ECCS).

In the late-seventies major questions arose about the integrity of the containment structure. Debates surged about the adequacy of G. E.'s pressure suppression and Westinghouse's ice condenser containment systems, and containment building sump adequacy. TMI increased concern about hydrogen control during severe accident conditions. In 1987 new concerns arose about corrosion related problems with BWR containments.

As the memo below from Joseph Hendrie, former NRC chair (and at the time of the quote, Deputy Director for Technical Review of the AEC) suggests, doubts among the AEC's staff about the safety of small volume containments were overridden by deference to the momentum created by the industry's sunk costs in plants with these systems.

". . . Steve's idea to ban pressure suppression containment schemes is an attractive one in some ways. Dry containments have the notable advantage of brute simplicity in dealing with a primary blowdown, and are thereby free of the perils of bypass leakage.

"However, the acceptance of pressure suppression containment concepts by all elements of the nuclear field, including Regulatory and the ACRS [Advisory Committee on Reactor Safeguards], is firmly imbedded in the conventional wisdom. Reversal of this hallowed policy, particularly at this time, could well be the end of nuclear power. It would throw into question the operation of licensed plants, would make unlicensable the G. E. and Westinghouse ice condensor plants now in review, and would generally create more turmoil than I can stand" (Beyea and von Hippel 1982, 54).

The memo reached the public domain through a UCS Freedom of Information Suit.

Reflecting somewhat similar sentiments on why key safety issues were resolved in favor of immediate licensing, Okrent, (ACRS chair during the mid-sixties China Syndrome debates), writes, "Why was resolution accepted based on partial information . . . there was considerable pressure from the industry not to impose further delays (and) . . . the commission and the AEC regulatory staff were very sensitive to the question of delays arising from the regulatory process" (Okrent 1981, 114).

37. It was not until the early 1960s that the AEC seriously began to review seismic hazard issues (Okrent 1981, 215,279). Two small reactors built in the fifties (G. E.'s Vallecitos test facility and the Humboldt Bay plant) were subsequently retired due to their inability to meet upgraded seismic stress standards (Komanoff 1981, 52). Similar compliance difficulties regarding upgraded ECCS standards led to the early retirement of Indian Point I. After ten years of unheeded ACRS requests for increased earthquake hazard R&D, work completed at MIT and UCLA in 1977–78 suggested that seismic risks may be two or three orders of magnitude greater than previously estimated (Okrent 1981, 283,287–8). In 1979 an error was uncovered in the computer codes used for calculating seismic stress resiliency in components at five operating plants (DOE 5/80, 114; Okrent 1981, 288). Roger Mason, director of the NRC's Division of System Safety warned, "This could be serious because of the possibility that . . . hundreds of pipes vital to the reactor's safety system would break during an earthquake . . . The fact that the error was made and not caught by the system is the important thing" (*St. Louis Post Dispatch* 12/13/79; Okrent 1981, 288).

38. A Union of Concerned Scientists study of a serious fire at the Browns Ferry reactor in 1975 linked the accident to insufficient cable separation R&D and inade-

quate plant quality control and safety data collection. The study notes that in 1971 an industry spokesman blamed information gaps for the lack of cable separation design criteria (Ford 1976, 22). The guidelines eventually adopted were undermined by the AEC's failure to test their effectiveness experimentally. Poor utility data collection on safety and maintenance practices at Browns Ferry allowed the procedure of checking cable conduits for air leaks with a lit candle (and subsequent plugging of the leaks with inflammable polyurethane) to persist despite the previous occurrence of several small fires using the same procedure (Ford 1976, 16). (For a general discussion of quality control problems, see JCAE 1974, part 2, vol. 2, pp. 208–270.) Okrent argues somewhat similarly and reports that the ACRS unsuccessfully urged the AEC to review potential fire accident paths in 1971 (Okrent 1981, 204, 219–20,231). Review of both earthquake and fire hazards has tended to generate tighter regulatory standards (Komanoff 1981, 94–97,90–92; Okrent 1981, 262–264).

Major new fire hazard concerns surfaced in the 1990s when it was discovered that the primary fire barrier used in nuclear plants, Thermo-Lag, was defective. "Problems with the fire barrier material Thermo-Lag 330–1 went unnoticed for ten years because NRC staff relied upon utility assurances and did only paper audits of the commercial supplier for the material, according to a report of the NRC's Office of Inspector General" (*Nucleonics Week* 8/20/92). New concerns about roof cave-ins and other unanticipated fire related common mode failures were raised in an NRC circular to utilities 9/13/93 (NRC Information Notice 93–71) as a result of the commission's analysis of a 10/11/91 fire at Unit 2 at Chernobyl.

39. Consistent with its policy of "industry self-regulation", the AEC engaged in limited data collection concerning quality control and quality assurance. Commission officials reviewed company quality control records but did not dispatch on-site inspectors (Ford 1982, 150–153). Both the staff report of the Rogovin Commission and a 1978 GAO report were highly critical of the NRC for continuing this practice (Gorinson 1979b). Accumulating evidence of poor quality control has been a driving force for increased construction documentation and equipment upgrading (Komanoff 1981, 73–77).

40. Reviewing nuclear performance, a 1973 AEC task force concluded, "The large number of reactor incidents, coupled with the fact that many of them had real safety significance, were generic in nature, and were not identified during the normal design, fabrication, erection, and pre-operational testing phases, raises a serious question regarding the current review and inspection practices both on the part of the nuclear industry and the AEC . . ." (JCAE 1974, 483–486).

41. Problems with insuring back-up power persist to this day. See chapter 9.

42. Rolph 1979 134; DOE 11/82, 61; DOE 5/80, 85, 131.

43. For example, former NRC Commissioner Victor Gilinsky writes, "To make the new approach—relying on emergency cooling (rather than containment) as the last line of defence—logically consistent with the agency's design review process, and therefore defensible in the agency's public hearings, the AEC banned consideration of accidents in which emergency cooling failed to function. Such accidents were simply deemed 'incredible. . . . If you assume that emergency cooling failures are

'incredible,' then the reactor containment structure will only have to cope with (slightly radioactive) steam from a pipe break. This logic permits easing the rules on containment, and in fact it led to construction permits for about twenty plants with relatively weak containments. Then the 'incredible' happened during the Three Mile Island accident . . ." (Gilinsky 1992, 709).

44. This issue was formally addressed after TMI, when the NRC established a fifth safety unit called the Division of Human Factor Safety. The commission's attention was forced to the issue by heavy criticism from the Kemeny and Rogovin reports. Along a similar line, post-TMI safety analyses have found numerous weaknesses in the training of reactor operators (Weinberg et al. 1985, 131–135; Rockwell 1992, 351–352).

45. The AEC's limited safety research program and tolerance of numerous unresolved safety issues (USIs) reflected this perspective. Critics were dismissed as Luddites. As early as 1968 the Advisory Committee on Reactor Safeguards complained of the lack of research attention to USIs (Okrent 1981, 151). A 1970 AEC report listed 139 open safety questions, identifying 44 of them as "very urgent, key problem areas, the solution of which would clearly have great impact either directly or indirectly on a major critical aspect of reactor safety" (Bodde 1975, VI–16).

46. Earthquake hazard research in the late 1970s, for example, involved the vibration of target components along two axes rather than one as previously conceived (Komanoff 1981, 90–91). In addition a more realistic pattern of frequencies has been employed. Both adjustments have tended to increase hazard estimates. Reanalysis of the AEC's ECCS research in the early seventies identified three key oversights in the computer program's accident simulations. The codes failed to consider: the potential for steam binding (whereby the steam produced by a loss of coolant accident inhibits the flow of emergency cooling water), the full potential of fuel rod swelling (whereby rising accident temperatures or the effect of pellet shrinking and concentration during normal operation, inhibit cooling water flow) (Ford 1975, 98–103), or the dangers of fuel rod embrittlement (due to a high temperature zirconium-steam reaction) (Ford 1975, 97–99).

47. Similar methodological gaps or errors in other safety areas led to potential underestimations of a myriad of accident hazards. In the "fire-hazard" area, for example, it was arbitrarily assumed that cable combustion could only be self-initiated. Regulatory requirements were thus insufficient to contain the candle initiated fire at Browns Ferry (Ford 1976, 22). In the piping area the potential for flow induced vibration problems was underestimated. In the containment area the impact of asymmetric loading on reactor vessel supports was overlooked, such that the potential damage of pressure transients during loss of coolant accidents was underestimated (Komanoff 1981, 54). In the quality-assurance area aging effects were given inadequate attention.

48. Ford 1982, 77–79; Nader and Abbotts 1979, 114; Rolph 1979, 76. See Ford 1982 for a detailed use of Freedom of Information documents to demonstrate the commission's public relations oriented treatment of accident probabilities research.
Similar public relations concerns governed the legislative treatment of the 1954

and 1956 Atomic Energy and the Price Anderson Acts. Accident issues were not addressed in legislative debate in 1954 and only modestly discussed in 1956 (Ford 1982, 42–46). Former AEC attorney Harold Green notes, "'there is not a single reference in the legislative history'—the four thousand pages of reports, testimony and debates before Congress relating to the ('54) law—'as to what those health and safety considerations really were'" (Ford 1982, 41–2). Senator Anderson has acknowledged that the choice of a $560 million liability limit reflected a desire to provide the appearance of liability insurance without raising concern about the magnitude of risk (Ford 1982, 46).

49. Ford 1982, 150–153; Bupp and Derian 1981, 123; Nader and Abbotts 1979, 372–3.

50. In addition to the AEC's selection bias, the tendency for pro-nuclear attitudes among ACRS members reflected the social character of available contexts for acquiring reactor safety related experience, and the self-selection of researchers into a field dominated by the nuclear industry and weapons program.

51. For example, in the late 1960s, when the committee was questioning the AEC about pressure vessel integrity and potential China Syndrome problems, Craig Hosmer, for many years the ranking Republican on the JCAE, told a nuclear industry audience, "The Joint Committee might take a good hard look at the proposition of eliminating the Advisory Committee on Reactor Safeguards. . . . ACRS has no responsibility for the economics of the nuclear business and apparently could care less. . . . I cannot help but wonder if ACRS had outlived its usefulness . . ." Six months later Hosmer told a joint meeting of the AIF and American Nuclear Society, ". . . I called for burning the Advisory Committee on Reactor Safeguards at the stake. Since then it has moved slightly off cloud # 9 . . . So tonight I'm going to recommend that . . . instead of letting ACRS itself pick and choose what it wants to create fear and trepidation about, that in the future the commission designate to it the matters which AEC believes important enough for specific ACRS review. . . . it seems appropriate that the commission tell it what it wants to be advised about instead of ACRS telling AEC what advice it is going to get" (Okrent 1981, 184–5). Although such "reforms" were not adopted, the AEC did suggest such legislation, sending clear warning signals to the committee. The AEC's head of regulation Dr. Clifford Beck had likewise sought to constrain ACRS staff size and limit committee access to outside consultants in the mid-sixties (Ibid., 122). Similar battles had been fought in the fifties (Ibid.).

52. The licenses for Dresden 3 and Indian Point 2, for example, were approved on the condition that the committee could attach a list of safety issues needing attention between the construction permit and operating license stage to its public letter of approval. This concession was later exchanged for the AEC's agreement to establish the Ergen Committee's review of loss of coolant accidents. The latter group subsequently redefined its mission and neglected some of the ACRS' concerns.

The committee similarly refrained from publicly reporting its conclusion that urban reactors required stiffer safeguards than rural reactors, in order to avoid public relations problems for the commission in thinly populated areas (Okrent 1981, 191–198). It also desisted from sending a formal public note to the commission concerning quality assurance problems at reactor sites after the AEC indicated that an oral message would generate much less public "misunderstanding" (Okrent 1981, 231).

53. During most of the OT period, official optimism dominated public discussion of emergency cooling issues. Prior to 1966 no high pressure, high capacity, emergency cooling system existed. Attention to core cooling problems was forced in 1966 by the ACRS. The committee threatened to write a public letter to the commission spelling out its belief that the larger reactors of the sixties required increased "engineered safeguards" to complement the industry's previous reliance on containment integrity, siting distance, and passive cooling system responses to a loss of coolant accident. To avoid this embarrassment, the AEC agreed in 1966 to establish an independent task force to study the adequacy of existing accident safeguards (Rolph 1977, 39).

Because of this arrangement the public remained unaware of the serious concern a majority of the ACRS had concerning the possibility and implications of a core meltdown in the newly approved commercial sized reactors. Former ACRS Chair Okrent writes:

"The only thing on the public record which indicated that some new provision for full-scale core melt had been considered in any way was the amendment to the Preliminary Safety Analysis Report submitted for the Indian Point 2 reactor in late June [1966], in which Consolidated Edison proposed to put a core-retention structure under the reactor vessel. It is interesting to look at the Public Safety Evaluation published for Dresden Nuclear Power Station Unit 3 on August 31, 1966, by the regulatory staff. There is no hint anywhere in this report that the China Syndrome and the inability of the containment vessel to withstand core melt had been a major concern. . . . one might consider this a less than candid review . . ." (Okrent 1981, 125).

Although the task force's report was generally optimistic about the condition of reactor safety, it did express concern about the uncertainties associated with the reliability of the ECCS (Rolph 1979, 89). A second AEC study reached similar conclusions about the same time. The final committee report was a compromise between highly optimistic representatives of the nuclear industry and more skeptical committee members (Gillette 9/15/72, 972). The composition of the committee and definition of its agenda (both determined by the AEC), appears to have been tilted towards an industry perspective (Okrent 1981, 167; Ford 1982, 95).

Troubled by the muted doubts raised in the report, the AEC successfully sought to limit the study's visibility. Gillette notes that "The public version bore no date, price, or address of any place where it might be obtained, nor did it bear the identification numbers customarily assigned to such reports" (Gillette 9/15/72, 972). The AEC with industry's support also rebuffed new ACRS efforts to resolve the technical uncertainties identified by the task force (Rolph 1979, 89; Gillette 9/15/72, 972).

It should be noted that the AEC did adopt what it believed were conservative ECCS guidelines in response to perceived uncertainties. What Ford and other critics charge is that it underestimated the implication of the uncertainties and disingenuously refused to research them.

In July 1971, the first mass media treatment of cooling system problems occurred (five years after the ACRS privately raised concern over related core-melt problems). Two networks aired a Union of Concerned Scientists' press conference analyzing the implications of a 1970 ECCS test failure (Primack and von Hippel 1974, 214). In an attempt to allay public concern and formally exclude ECCS issues from discussion in local licensing hearings, the AEC agreed to hold public rule-making hearings on ECCS standards. The proceedings revealed the depth of concern that the commission had suppressed amongst its technical staff. Dr. Morris Rosen indicated that system standards were inadequate and inconsistent with the opinion of the "majority of the knowledgeable people available to the regulatory staff . . ." (Primack and Von Hippel 1974, 219).

Testimony also revealed that findings at Oak Ridge contradicted the commission's assumption that accident-related fuel rod behavior could not interfere with coolant flow (Primack and von Hippel 1974, 216). These findings were not pursued. Indeed, the manager of the ECCS test facility, Curtis Haire, indicated that research announcements were regularly censored by the AEC "to avoid the problems or burden, if you will, of having to spend a lot of time answering public inquiries . . . (on) general questions of nuclear safety" (*New York Times* 11/10/74). Reminiscent of the AEC's behavior during the radiation controversy, Rosen, Haire, and Rittenhouse were subsequently transferred from their positions (Ford 1982, 128).

Gillette argues that the AEC's policy of intimidation minimized public dissent. Representing the American Academy for the Advancement of Science, he was forced to rendezvous with lab personnel in back streets for secret interviews. He writes, "That men nationally recognized in their profession should feel impelled to such maneuvers suggests how far relations between the commission and the Idaho installation have deteriorated" (Gillette 9/1/72, 773). Congressional testimony, the Presidential Commission's review of the Three Mile Island accident, and numerous AEC-NRC-nuclear industry staff interviews indicate that the closed environment at the Idaho Falls lab was reproduced in varying degrees at other public and private nuclear enterprises.

Four years after the ECCS hearings, for example, the following exchange took place during a congressional hearing called to investigate the charges of three senior G. E. engineers who resigned in protest over company and industry safety practices:
Representative Hinshaw: ". . . are you expressing the view that . . . General Electric's policy would be that you [as an employee] would have to be an advocate [of nuclear power] to the exclusion of expressing concerns about safety?"
Mr. Bridenbaugh: "I think that is an unwritten kind of policy that perhaps is self-imposed by many of us in the industry. That certainly is the attitude; yes."
Rep. Hinshaw: "Is that a common attitude with your associates at General Electric?
Mr. Bridenbaugh: "Yes, it is."
Rep. Hinshaw: Do you think it is a common attitude among people in similar positions in other companies?"
Mr. Bridenbaugh: "I am sure it is" (JCAE 1976, 35–36).

The Presidential Commission's review of the Three Mile Island accident found significant support for this viewpoint. NRC Commissioner Gilinsky testified,

> "(o)ne of the problems we have is that industry has taken the view that
> they will do just what the NRC requires and not more . . ." NRC Chair

Henrdrie indicated "vendors are reluctant to propose a modification to a plant for fear that the NRC will mandate that it be supplied to all other like plants." ACRS member Ebersole added, "A finding made by an individual deep in an organization which implies heavy costs which is not a regulatory requirement is not likely to be encouraged by what I call the shell of middle management" (Gorinson 1979b, 100–102).

Robert Pollard, a former NRC official in charge of safety review for the Indian Point III reactor and six other plants, has described a parallel atmosphere inside the commission:

> " '. . . many of the dedicated government employees in the NRC are deeply troubled about the pervasive attitude in the NRC that our most important job is to get the licenses out as quickly as possible and to keep the plants running. . . . Until you have been part of the agency at a level where the technical work is performed, it is difficult to appreciate the kind of pressure that inhibits your staff from doing its job. . . . [B]y the use of highly effective pressures, middle management totally suppresses most of the dissent within the NRC. In addition to outright threats of adverse consequences for one's job, pressures are applied by the device of requiring numerous rewritings of proposed position papers which conflict with rapid licensing and continued operation of reactors—even though there are no identified technical errors in the papers' " (Nader and Abbotts 1979, 113).

Numerous NRC reports and interviews confirm Pollard's charges. The NRC's inspector general, Thomas McTiernan, recorded similar comments in his 1976 study of the safety review process (Ford 1982, 181, 198, 214). A November 1978 study by Opinion Research of NRC inspection and enforcement officials found "six in ten employees believe that many managers practice a 'don't-rock-the-boat' philosophy" (Gorinson 1979b, 112; see also *New York Times* 6/4/79).

An interview between TMI inquiry Chairman John Kemeny and James Creswell (the NRC staffer who had tried unsuccessfully to obtain NRC attention to the kinds of problems that triggered TMI) reported similar sentiments:

Kemeny: Is the kind of experience you had in trying to follow up the two Davis-Besse incidents unique in your opinion or is it fairly typical?

Creswell: There has been a certain history of individuals that have worked for NRC that have had problems with dealing with safety issues. That is well documented, Mr. Pollard, Mr. Conrad and others, some to the extent that they have left the commission.

Kemeny: Are you suggesting there that individuals who raise fairly consistently serious safety issues may, in the long run, find that they cannot work for NRC?

Creswell: That they cannot work for NRC or that they would be placed in other organizations (Gorinson 1979b, 112).

As in the radiation hazard field, the AEC and nuclear industry constituted the basic funding source for hazard research. Internal criticism or testimony on behalf of anti-nuclear intervenors was often perceived as harmful to one's long run career (Ebbin and Kasper 1974, 207–211). Ebbin and Kasper concluded in 1974, "The AEC's role as the major funding source for research in the nuclear sciences over the last twenty-five years has created a situation in which almost every nuclear scientist and engineer of worth is under grant or contract to AEC, or in the employ of the AEC, the nuclear industry, or a national laboratory" (211). Earlier they note, "Such experts, out of concern (real or imagined) for their positions and reputations, find it difficult to support or testify on behalf of opponents of nuclear power plants" (207).

Some staff members at Oak Ridge National Laboratory believe that Alvin Weinberg lost his job as lab director for encouraging ORNL technical experts to engage in frank discussion in public hearings on the ECCS.

Organizational loyalty and administrator control of the coordinating function within research bureaucracies also tended to militate against individual challenges to organizational positions. Safety judgments often required the integration of technical results from a number of projects. Though the acquisition of the appropriate knowledge for this coordination would not appear to be beyond the ability of practitioners in any one field (as the administrators are often less technically trained than their staffs), there seem to be psychological and sociological barriers to individual initiatives in this area.

Ebbin and Kasper stress the strong inclination among professional scientists and engineers against becoming involved in controversies outside their relatively narrow realm of expertise (16, 17, 205–223). Fear of embarrassment and notoriety reinforce the credibility of what might be called "organizational expertise" and the power of administrators to pursue institutional objectives in conflict with technical findings. Administrative leverage was heightened in many areas of nuclear safety by the lack of fully specified theoretical models. As in the radiation hazard area, resulting ambiguities permitted promotional interpretation.

54. Dawson 1976, 262, 250; Rolph 1979, 130–134. See also: Okrent 1981, 313–14; Ford Foundation 1977, 234. Pressures for increased administrative freedom for safety researchers had been growing for some time. In 1969 the ACRS urged greater cooperation between the regulatory and research staffs, implicitly attacking the limitations on safety discussion imposed by Shaw (Okrent 1981, 311). In 1971 the ACRS suggested that the regulatory staff be given its own budget for safety research and in 1972 it orally advised the AEC to establish a separate safety research division (Okrent 1981, 312). It was not until the storm created by the ECCS controversy, however, that these suggestions were adopted.

55. Earlier political pressures had forced the JCAE to direct the AEC to include participation by environmentalists in its safety study of 1971. Though input from anti-nuclear groups was not included in the original draft, UCS and SIPI representatives were asked to comment on a preliminary version of the report. While most of the groups' recommendations were ignored, their criticisms did spur an extra chapter on previously neglected hazard problems such as operator error, poor quality control, sabotage, and breeder reactor meltdown. The level of public concern generated by the UCS and SIPI interventions also helped ferment the JCAE's 1973–1974 reactor safety hearings, which further escalated safety debate (Del Sesto 1979, 173–4).

56. In Virginia, for example, local intervenors discovered the existence of a fault near the nearly completed North Anna plant. A subsequent Justice Department investigation indicated that the utility and NRC had collaborated to suppress knowledge about the fault during the licensing process (*New York Times* 10/2/77–22). Intervenor activity similarly expanded seismic hazard inquiries in the Malibu, Bodega Bay, Diablo Canyon, and Seabrook licensing process.

Adato et al., citing "Reactor Safety Improvements Resulting from the Hearing Process", a list submitted by the Atomic Safety and Licensing Board Panel to the Advisory Committee on Reactor Safeguards, notes intervenor safety contributions with respect to:

- offsite power grid instabilities (St. Lucie plant)

- steam generator problems (Prairie Island)

- turbine related issues (North Anna)

- emergency planning (San Onofre)

- effluent treatment systems (Dresden and Palisades)

- control room improvements (Kewaunee)

- quality assurance breakdowns (Zimmer, Midland & South Texas)

- steam generator tube leaking (Beaver Valley)

Adato also lists several generic safety contributions arising from intervenor efforts (Adato et al., 1987, 59–60).

57. The AEC and nuclear industry's concern over such intervenor-ACRS linkages is illustrated by the repeated requests of both parties that the ACRS communicate its safety concerns orally rather than through formal public letters. Bridenbaugh reports a similar preoccupation prevailed during the investigation of containment integrity problems by G. E. and the utilities in the mid-seventies (JCAE 1976).

58. Like the WASH-740-update, this study highlighted the uncertainties surrounding nuclear hazards and the troubling implications of previous operating experience.

59. The file lists the most serious nuclear accidents from the mid-sixties to the mid-seventies. It was compiled by an NRC safety expert. The UCS became aware of the file's existence through references in other FOI documents (Pollard 1979, 1–3).

60. A set of internal memorandum and letters, the documents undermined the perceived objectivity and thus credibility of the report's principal designers. For example, the papers revealed the authors' decision not to address quality control issues for fear of undermining public confidence in the AEC (Ford 1982, 141, 150–153).

61. Adato et al. (1987) indicate that a 1982 NRC staff report on equipment qualification (i.e., demonstration of the ability of safety related equipment to operate in accident conditions) found that, "44.6% of the electrical equipment in operating

plants had to be replaced, physically modified, relocated, shielded, or further tested and that 31.1% lacked documentation to determine whether it was environmentally qualified . . ." (p. 27).

62. The information released undermined the reliability of the commission's use of ultrasonic tests to insure pipe integrity and revealed an alarmingly high level of attempted sabotage at nuclear power plants (*New York Times* 3/30/76).

63. As indicated in note 53, important information about ECCS problems surfaced in this manner. Additional open government requirements, such as the Federal Advisory Committee Act of 1972 and the Sunshine Act of 1976, increased the access of perceptive nuclear critics to internal disagreements within the AEC. Other information became public due to political pressures on Congress to investigate nuclear safety. At the initiative of Congressman Hughes, for example, the GAO investigated the NRC's safety-environmental evaluation of Westinghouse's proposed floating nuclear power plants. The study found that the commission's optimistic review omitted contradictory findings from some major environmental impact laboratories (*New York Times* 10/31/77, 65). Other congressional initiatives required the NRC to publish a list of abnormal occurrences, unresolved safety issues, and current plans to rectify outstanding safety problems.

64. One of the earliest whistle-blowing incidents by scientists and engineers was an anonymous letter to the ACRS that revealed serious design deficiencies at the Prairie Island reactor and precipitated regulatory upgrades costing as much as $20,000,000 for some plants in the early seventies (Ford 1975, 111–112; Okrent 1981, 235). The UCS case against the AEC's ECCS criteria was buttressed by a flow of leaked documents during the rule making hearings. This material appears to have been especially effective in shaking the confidence of the *New York Times* in the reliability of the cooling system. The intervenors in the Shoreham plant hearings were similarly endowed with a bundle of engineering documents that raised serious questions about plant safety (*Seven Days* 10/26/79).

In the mid-seventies the industry suffered a series of highly publicized protest resignations, including that of AEC safety expert Carl Hocevar, Indian Point safety manager Robert Pollard, the three G. E. engineers noted earlier, and NRC engineer Ronald Fluegge. At least seventeen separate *New York Times* articles covered their safety charges.

The same pattern of escalating whistle-blowing occurred on site, initiated by construction workers. Komanoff identifies the reporting of numerous deficient welds at the Surry nuclear plant in 1971, as the first of these incidents (Komanoff 1981, 61). By the late-seventies local anti-nuclear groups were strong enough to insure the disclosures received serious public attention. Intervenors in the Shoreham plant licensing hearings, for example, publicized worker charges of damaged pipes, deficient welds, and quality assurance violations (*Seven Days* 10/26/79). Clamshell Alliance opponents of the Seabrook plant interviewed site construction workers who raised similar safety questions. Opponents of the Marble Hill plant transformed the allegations of a concrete finisher's helper into a broad NRC investigation and confirmation of widespread quality control deficiencies. Similar events took place at the Callaway and

Zimmer plants. The Institute of Policy Studies' Government Accountability Project was especially helpful in supporting whistle-blowing (Tomain 1987, 32).

In 1979 security personnel at the Indian Point Plants attacked the facility's lax security procedures, citing poor personnel training, the falsification of personnel qualification records, and the cushion of advance warning before NRC inspector visits (*New York Times* 10/17/79). Other whistle-blowing incidents occurred at the Wolff Creek and South Texas plants.

65. An AIF study on the impact of NRC regulatory policy noted in 1978: " '(I)t is insufficient to identify the cost of material and labor as, for example, an added pipe, or pump or valve . . . (S)ignificant ripples caused by such changes affected not just the changed system but also, for example, supporting structures, normal or emergency power supplies, ventilation systems, rad-waste, etc.' " (Komanoff 1981, 68). See also DOE 5/80 and OTA 1984.

66. See, for example, Nelkin (1971, 92–116).

67. Along with reduction in radiation emissions, the 1966 Palisades agreement between Consumers Power Company and local intervenors called for the construction of a $15,000,000 cooling tower (Olson 1976, 77; Walker 1989, 987). Detroit Edison agreed to construct two cooling towers and a cooling pond for Fermi II (Lewis 1972, 143). Commonwealth Edison agreed to build a $30,000,000 thermal pollution reduction system (Lewis 1972, 296). In April 1969 New York State Electric and Gas withdrew its plans to construct a plant on Cayuga Lake due to protests over thermal pollution.

68. A 1975 review of industry behavior by Barber Associates for ERDA concluded, "We noted a distinct tendency in the nuclear energy industry to underestimate nuclear power costs by simply omitting some costs, or neglecting the potential effects on costs of practical or operational experience such as significantly lower capacity factors than theoretical projections would suggest" (*New York Times* 11/16/75, 1).

69. See for example, Bupp and Derian 1981, 227, 81.

70. Mullenbach 1963, 54–55, Kuhn 1966.

71. Lilienthal 1963, 98–99; Dawson 1976, 40; Ford 1982, 33–35. See also Mullenbach 1963, 55.

72. By assuming a 90% capacity rate for the Bodega Bay plant (~50% higher than the industry's subsequent performance), the firms projected a 1% nuclear cost advantage over oil fired generation (Mullenbach 1963, 69). Commenting on the specious precision suggested by such comparisons, Harold Orlans reported in a Brookings Institution study, "Some of the assumption upon which these calculations are based are so gross, the decimal places are a 'joke in the fraternity,' one reader observes" (Orlans 1967, 47).

73. AEC 1974b 29; Montgomery and Quirk 1978, 15; Perry 1977, 37.

74. AEC 1968a, 1–27, 1–29, 2–4.

75. AEC 1968a, 3–1 to 3–3. One of the most optimistic learning forecasts was offered in August 1968 by James Lane. At an AEC co-sponsored symposium, the Oak Ridge scientist foresaw scale and learning curve efficiencies reducing nuclear capital costs to $170/KW by 2010 (Lane 1968).

76. AEC 1969, 130.

77. Bupp and Derian 1981, 82; Gandara 1977, 62; see also Cohn 1986, 367, 399.

78. A familiar pattern of official neglect, OT optimism, anti-nuclear movement criticism, and rising cost estimates characterizes waste disposal projections. Despite the fact that the AEC gave waste disposal issues minimal attention before the mid-seventies, cost optimism prevailed. "An illusion of certainty was created . . . technological optimism embedded itself in the attitudes and thoughts of important agency policy makers. It became, in a sense, an official doctrine at AEC" (OTA 1985, 202).

Industry and commission representatives repeatedly minimized the uncertainties surrounding waste disposal. Their optimism helped induce New York State to agree to assume perpetual care liability for W. R. Grace's West Valley reprocessing project, in the event the company withdrew from the industry. As a safeguard Grace was required to post a $7 million (1992$) bond for funding decontamination expenses. Recent clean-up cost estimates have ranged as high as $2.4 to $3.4 billion (Makhijani and Saleska 1992, 120). Testifying in 1977, Peter Skinner of the NY State Attorney General's Office said, "New York State originally welcomed the so-called back-end of the nuclear fuel cycle . . . It has taken fourteen years for us to realize this early optimism, urged upon us by industry and the Federal Government . . . had no basis" (House, Government Operations Committee 1977, 757).

In 1971 the AEC predicted waste disposal costs of .09M to .19 M/kwh (Dawson 1976, 145; AEC WASH 1971b, 92). Significant efforts were made to manage the information environment about nuclear waste in order to avoid raising public concern (Berger 1977, 100). The anti-nuclear movement began to attend to nuclear waste issues in the early-seventies, beginning with protests against a poorly conceived proposal for a nuclear waste depository in Lyons, Kansas. By the end of the seventies, cost estimates more than fifteen times the AEC's 1971 projections were offered by a group of former nuclear industry-government engineers (DOE 2/81, 54). In 1976, the EPA's top radiation official acknowledged that serious attention to disposal questions had just begun. He tied the new interest to public pressure (*Wall Street Journal* 7/26/76).

A similar information vacuum surrounded nuclear facilities' decommissioning costs until the mid-seventies. Government spokesmen, for example, were forced to rely on figures supplied by the nuclear industry's trade association (the Atomic Industrial Forum [AIF]) in 1977 congressional hearings due to the absence of independent government cost studies. Practical experience was virtually non-existent.

Despite a paucity of information it was assumed that inexpensive decommissioning techniques would be found and that public funds would "bail-out" facilities' owners should decommissioning expenses be significantly greater than expected. A June 1977 General Accounting Office study reported.

"The Commission has done relatively little to plan for and to provide guid-
ance for decommissioning of commercial nuclear facilities. Studies sponsored by the Commission on acceptable alternative methods to decommis-
sion are several years from completion. It does not require owners of
nuclear facilities—except uranium mills—to develop plans or make financial provisions to cover the cost for future decommissioning. Consequently,
the true cost of nuclear power is not being reflected in the cost to the
consumer of nuclear power. Without this financial provision, the Federal or
State Governments can be asked to pay for problems that rightfully should
be paid by private industry" (House, Government Operations Committee
1977, 1529).

The AIF's widely cited 1976 study undergridded popular optimism, projecting
costs of $12.0 million for mothballing, $21.3–$27.8 million for entombment and
$84.2–$97.1 million for dismantling an 1150 MW reactor (Ibid., 427). The recommended procedure, a hybrid entombment-dismantling, was predicted to cost $43.5
million–$50 million. Based on these figures the NRC projected a .09M/kwh decom-
missioning cost (Ibid., 391).

Displaying an air of relaxed confidence, NRC spokesman Clifford Smith assured
the House Government Operations Committee in 1977, "The decommissioning of
nuclear reactors has been relatively well developed and is routinely considered in the
licensing process" (Ibid., 329). Characteristic of an OT frame of mind, he added, "It
should be mentioned that advances in technology might improve the economics of
decommissioning" (Ibid., 335).

The official optimism of the AEC-NRC and nuclear industry strongly influenced
"independent" cost analyses. The Ford Foundation's influential 1977 report, *Nuclear
Power: Issues and Choices*, for example, gave virtually no attention to decommissioning costs. The Massachusetts Energy Policy Office and Arthur D. Little nuclear
cost studies of the mid- to late-1970s merely adopted the AIF's figures, as did many
utilities.

Once again, however, increased research and anti-nuclear movement criticism
began to push estimates upwards. As early as August 1975, Friends of the Earth
analyst Jim Harding projected a $148/KW decommissioning cost. In December of
1977 Peter Skinner, of the New York State Attorney General's Office, foresaw costs
7–34 times ERDA's estimates, based on the state's traumatic experience with the
West Valley clean-up (House, Government Operations Committee 1977, 808). In
1980 a DOE study found $231/KW to be "representative of the most current disman-
tling assessments" (DOE 5/80, 172). In 1992 the nuclear industry's Council for Energy Awareness projected costs of $275/KW for 600 MW plants and $221/KW for
1200 MW plants (U.S. CEA, 6/92, 11).

Dr. Marvin Resnikoff's work demonstrates anew how the insularity and promotional purpose of early AEC-NRC-industry decommissioning analyses encouraged a
selective misperception of uncertainty. Resnikoff questioned, for example, the legit-
imacy of past studies' linear extrapolations from test reactors to commercial sized
plants, citing a case where the scaling exercise altered the nature of the dismantling

problem. His research also found that a previously neglected radioactive nickel product in reactor infrastructures would require much more complex handling than officially assumed. Resnikoff comments, ". . . there is a need for an independent evaluation of the nuclear industry. Because of the 'old boy' network that exists, decisions—very costly decisions—are being made based on incomplete information. When four undergraduate engineering students and myself can find what tens of thousands of technicians in industry and the federal agencies have missed concerning decommissioning, something is not right" (House, Government Operations Committee 1977, 261).

Other work by Pohl and Stephens, concerning trace elements, revealed greater uncertainties about the likely radioactive conditions in a thirty-year-old commercial reactor than previously projected from decommissioning experience with a six-year-old test reactor (House, Government Operations Committee 1977, 231). Their findings suggested that more expensive burial procedures than the surface techniques recommended by the AIF study will be necessary (Ibid., 247).

79. Stewart 1981, 192. Learning curve effects are commonly expressed in terms of percentage cost experienced per doubling of output. A 90% learning curve implies a cost function with the following form:

$$Yn = Y1 \times (n)^{-.152}$$

where Yn equals the cost of the nth plant and Y1 equals the cost of the first plant. An 80% learning curve implies a learning curve exponent of $-.322$.

80. Tybout 1957; AEC 1968a, 1–33, 3–2; Little 1968; Bupp 1975. For example, the reactor vendors assumed learning cost reductions of 20%–50% over the 1963–1966 period in their turnkey cost calculations (Perry 1977, 33). The AEC reported in 1968, "Experience gained in the various activities of the nuclear industry . . . has already led to cost reductions. . . . The effects of this trend to standardization, taken in conjunction with design repetition, experience gained in manufacturing, and the improved techniques of mass production will probably lead to cost reductions which have in the past in similar industries generally followed a 90 per-cent learning curve relationship. A major reactor manufacturer uses the learning curve technique to analyze and forecast progress in cost reductions in the manufacture of nuclear components" (AEC 1968a, 3–2).

Treating the first sixteen commercial plants as de facto R&D projects, about six sector doublings were required to reach the AEC forecast of 1000 nuclear plants online by the year 2000. Assuming a 90% learning curve implies expected cost reductions of 47%.

81. The technological inertia imposed by nuclear power's unprecedented accident hazards continues to retard technical change in the nuclear sector. Recent planning discussions for the MHTGR, for example, shied away from using new materials out of concern for the long testing period necessary to demonstrate the material's ability to endure radioactive environments without significant performance declines (private discussions with MHTGR planners). The fragmentation of the U.S. nuclear industry, especially in the utility sector, has also been adduced by some observers to explain the industry's modest learning curves (see, for example, Thomas 1988, 242–246).

82. Campbell 1988, 31–49.

83. Okrent's account of the licensing debates for Dresden 2 & 3 and Indian Pt. 2 indicates that many ACRS members felt that larger plants necessarily required a higher level of containment integrity, and accident response systems (Okrent 1981, 87–88, 101, 137). These sentiments were reinforced by the results of the Brookhaven safety study, which noted the increased potential damage from larger reactors. The AEC regulatory staff indicated in 1967, "'The increase in this potential hazard (from larger reactors) must be matched by corresponding improvements in the safety precautions and requirements if the safety status is to keep pace with advancing technology. The protective systems must have shorter response times, larger capacities and grater reliability to cope with the more rigorous demands presented by the large reactors'" (Komanoff 1981, 49).

84. Data from Cantor-Hewlett (1988) provide the most comprehensive account of these relationships. The authors found a savings of about 65% in per KW direct construction costs from a megawatt doubling [p. 331], but they also found a 60% lengthening in construction duration and an associated 78% increase in overall construction costs [p. 331]. The cost increase was tied to: (1) managerial diseconomies of scale in coordinating large construction projects with high quality control standards; (2) the greater regulatory scrutiny invited by larger MW plants; and (3) the tendency to stretchout the construction period of larger plants due to excess capacity concerns. The net effect of these phenomena was decreased labor productivity and increased safety expenditures. The addition of interest during construction costs (purposefully ignored in Cantor-Hewlett) would have increased the cost disadvantage of larger plants.

85. Testimony drawn from court report for: The Application of Arkansas Power & Light Company for Approval of Changes in Rates Applicable to Residential, General Service, Industrial and Other Retail Electric Service, July 30, 1985, A/M Reporters, Inc., Little Rock, Arkansas.

86. Among the key "movement" groups generating alternative economic information were: Komanoff Energy Associates (see *Power Plant Cost Escalation*); Business and Professional People for the Public Interest (see David Comey's "Will Idle Capacity Kill Nuclear Power?"); the Environmental Action Foundation (see Richard Morgan's *Nuclear Power: The Bargain We Can't Afford* and the group's periodical *Power Line*); the Environmental Defense Fund (see W. R. Z. Wiley's "Alternative Energy Systems for Pacific Gas and Electric Company—An Economic Analysis"); Friends of the Earth (see Jim Harding's "The Deflation of Rancho Seco 2", John Berger's Nuclear Power the Unviable Option, Amory Lovins' *Soft Energy Paths*, and the group's journal *Not Man Apart*); various Ralph Nader affiliated projects such as Critical Mass & The Center for the Study of Responsive Law (see Nader and Abbotts' *The Menace of Atomic Energy*, Ron Lanoue's *Nuclear Plants: The More They Build: The More You Pay*, and the journal *Critical Mass*); various Barry Commoner affiliated projects, such as the Scientists Institute for Public Information and the Center for the Biology of Natural Systems (see Richard Scott's "Projections for the Cost of Generating Electricity in Nuclear and Coal Fired Plants", and various issues of

Environment); the Nuclear Information Resource Service (see *Groundswell* and *The Nuclear Monitor*); the Investor's Responsibility Research Center (see "The Nuclear Alternative"); Environmentalists for Full-Employment (see Grossman and Daneker's "Jobs and Energy"); and the Union of Concerned Scientists (see Daniel Ford's "Nuclear Power Some Basic Economic Issues").

More traditional social action groups like the American Friends Service Committee and the Council on Economic Priorities also made important contributions.

The anti-nuclear movement's local organizations also produced some excellent economic analyses. The Clamshell Alliance put together *NO Nukes*. The New York Public Interest Research Group released an important study of nuclear plant decommissioning costs. Lengthy critiques of the economic assumptions underlying numerous specific plants were compiled by local activists. (See, for example, Dr. Harold Cassidy's analysis of the economics of the Marble Hill Plant prepared for the Save the Valley organization; Russel Love's analysis of the economics of the Palo Verde plant, prepared for Arizonians for Safe Energy, and Miles Males & Marvin Cooke's analysis of the economics of the Black Fox Plant, distributed by the Environmental Action Foundation.

87. Important contributions were made by university professors such as Irvin Bupp of Harvard (see "The Economics of Nuclear Power"), and Duane Chapman of Cornell (see "Decommissioning, Taxation, and Nuclear Power Cost"). State agencies frequently provided independent review of utility generating choices and funding for anti-nuclear research. New Jersey's Department of Public Advocate funded a Komanoff study of comparative nuclear and coal generating costs. California's Energy Resources Conservation and Development Commission funded Jim Harding's critical review of the economics of the Sun Desert nuclear plant. The California Energy Commission funded a Chapman decommissioning cost study. New York State's Attorney General's Office, Bureau of Environmental Protection, challenged the optimistic waste disposal and decommissioning cost estimates of the AEC.

88. Komanoff began his research as an analyst for the New York City Environmental Protection Administration. Subsequently he directed the energy projects of the Council on Economic Priorities. In the late-seventies he established his own energy consulting firm, preparing analyses for anti-nuclear groups (such as the Environmental Action Foundation), state bodies (such as the Wisconsin and Kentucky Attorney General offices), and sympathetic journals (such as the *Bulletin of the Atomic Scientists*). His expertise and increased media interest in non-AEC-nuclear industry perspectives enabled him to tarnish formerly unchallenged industry claims. Two examples follow.

In the mid-seventies, New York City's Consolidated Edison Company argued that operation of its Indian Point nuclear station had saved its New York customers $95,000,000 in 1974. Komanoff's reanalysis demonstrated that the utility's carefully worded claim compared the cost of owning the plant and operating it, with owning the plant and not operating it. Had Con Ed built and operated a coal plant at the same site, Komanoff's figures demonstrated that it could have saved 25% of its Indian Point costs.

An almost identical ploy on the part of Commonwealth Edison, the nation's most nuclear oriented utility, was successfully challenged by anti-nuclear critic David Comey in the February 1975 issue of the *Bulletin of the Atomic Scientists*. In this case the utility had claimed a $100 million rate payer savings by citing the relative fuel costs of nuclear and coal fired plants. Comey forced the company to acknowledge that including relative capital costs in the calculations eliminated nuclear's alleged savings [Nader and Abbotts 1979, 216].

In 1979 Komanoff discredited the AIF's widely circulated and definitively quoted 1978 study of relative nuclear and coal generating costs. By detailing the non-randomness of the study's sample, he demonstrated how the Forum had transformed a nuclear cost disadvantage into a 33% cost edge.

89. Jim Harding of Friends of the Earth, for example, was very influential in shifting the Sacramento Municipal Utility District [SMUD] (a publicly owned utility) away from new nuclear commitments (Olson 1976, 205). The election of nuclear critic Ed Smeloff to the board of directors of SMUD eventually forced a review of the economics of the utility's operating nuclear plant, Rancho Seco. The study found it was cheaper to shut down the unit than continue its operation. The plant was closed by public referendum in 1989. In 1976, an anti-nuclear law suit led to the revocation of the Midland nuclear plant's construction permit on the grounds that inadequate attention had been given to the relative economics of conservation. In 1978 an Environmental Defense Fund intervention before the California Public Utilities Commission spurred PG&E to investigate and subsequently promote conservation programs (Stobaugh and Yergin 1979, 141, 302). In 1984 the Congressional Office of Technology Assessment gave greater credibility to Komanoff's nuclear cost projections than to the continuing optimism of the Department of Energy (OTA 1984, 65).

Chapter 5

1. The meaning of learning curve cost reduction is ambiguous in the nuclear literature. The term sometimes refers to the cost savings embodied in improved production techniques at existing output levels. On other occasions the savings involve the benefits of standardization and the capture of production economies at higher output levels. For purposes of maintaining a conservative estimating bias and avoiding possible double counting, we shall collapse the two effects in our calculations. These gains are independent of and additional to, however, any improvements resulting from increased R&D expenditures.

2. See, for example: Tybout 1957; AEC 1968a, 1–33, 3–2; Little 1968; Bupp et al. 1974. In 1962 the AEC observed: "Efficiency of operation and low cost construction are to a considerable extent brought about through construction and operating experience. After more than half a century of experience, fossil fueled steam electric plants are still achieving very worthwhile increases in efficiency and reductions in real dollar construction costs. It seems almost certain that part of the improvement in

nuclear electric plants will come in the same manner. Consequently, nuclear generation in the year 2000 will be more efficient and lower cost if a number of large nuclear plants are built during the next ten to fifteen years, than if the acquisition of this experience is delayed" (AEC 1962, reprinted in: JCAE 1968, 220).

3. Mooz found a 10% decline in construction costs for each doubling of architect-engineer construction experience (Mooz 1979, v). Joskow and Rozanski found learning improvements in plant capacity rates through the mid-seventies, projecting ~5% increases in plant performance per year (Joskow and Rozanski 1979, 167). After reporting 1981 results similar to Mooz, Komanoff's 1984 analysis vested learning in the sponsoring utility. Plant costs were found to decline by 7% per new nuclear site (Komanoff 1984a, 11).

Lester cited findings from a 1984 EPRI study indicating shorter construction periods for more experienced A-E-C-firms for older but not younger plants, and a 1985 study linking construction cost reductions to utility construction experience (Lester 1986, 371). He also cites an NRC study emphasizing the positive impact of utility nuclear plant construction experience on plant outcomes (Ibid. 372). Cantor and Hewlett found no evidence of lower construction costs for utilities employing more experienced A-E-Cs, though increased utility experience may have had positive effects (Cantor Hewlett 1988, 330–332).

Komanoff (1991) reported that plant capacity rates were 5% higher for plants receiving construction permits after the 1971–1972 Calvert Cliffs licensing delay. Each doubling of the cumulative number of reactor years managed by a utility raised capacity rates by 2%. Multiple unit sites enjoyed a 1.68% capacity rate increase for the second and third units.

Learning gains may have been larger in the nuclear fuel industry, though regulatory conservatism may have also inhibited evolutionary change.

See also Cowan September 1990 for an interesting discussion of learning curve studies.

4. A major Arthur D. Little study in 1968 estimated that an increase in vendor output from three to six nuclear steam supply systems per year would reduce overhead and R&D costs by about 15% and direct production costs by about 3%–5% (Little 1968, 156–158). Bodde (1976) found that the nuclear steam supply vendors were able to deflect design changes to other parts of the plant and achieved significant standardization.

Since the mid-fifties scaling theory has also been applied to nuclear fuel cost projections. Tybout (1957) and Little (1968), for example, emphasized the cost reductions expected from scale economies in fuel fabrication and reprocessing.

The AEC's 1968 nuclear cost study assumed a 90% learning curve for the first two doublings of fuel fabrication output, followed by a 95% rate for the next four doublings. The result was a projected 33% cost reduction from 1970–2000 (AEC 1968a, ch. 5, 83). Larger scale and learning curve cost declines were assumed for fuel reprocessing costs (AEC 1968a, chapter 5, 101–105).

Little (1968) assumed a reprocessing scaling coefficient of .35 (p. 221), projecting a two-thirds decline in costs for 6 ton versus 1 ton/day reprocessing plants (245). A 6–7 ton/day size was estimated to be optimal (245). As the latter plant would meet the reprocessing needs of 60 1000 MW reactors a year, it presumes a large nuclear sector. The failure of the reprocessing industry erased these potential savings. Scaling economies will probably arise in waste disposal.

Standardization became an official regulatory goal in 1972 when the AEC announced licensing preference for standardized designs. Westinghouse's offshore power system project was the major standardization initiative (OTA 1981, 36). Severe public opposition to many of the coastal plants, utility financing difficulties, and TMI ultimately forced abandonment of the project (Price 1982, 46–49; Olson 1976, 200–205).

A consortium of utilities organized the Standardized Nuclear Unit Power Plant System (SNUPPS) and contracted for six units at four sites. Although two units were subsequently canceled, the utilities claimed that standardized procedures brought 10% cost savings to the remaining plants (OTA 1981, 46–48). Commonwealth Edison's four Bryon-Braidwood plants also appear to have benefited significantly from standardization (Komanoff and Bupp 1983, 11). Campbell indicates that Duke Power claimed cost savings from scale economies associated with its multiple Oconee plants (1988, 35).

The reactor vendors may have been on the edge of capturing larger production economies in the mid-seventies, just as the industry collapsed. Babcock and Wilcox, for example, had won orders for nine identical plants; over 50% of the construction permits issued in 1974 and 1975 contained some standardized sections (Campbell 1988, 35, 41). Most of these plants were subsequently canceled.

5. Oak Ridge National Laboratory, for example, has done significant research on robotics for general and nuclear applications.

6. Billion dollar efforts were made to link reactor expertise to air and merchant marine transport. Although these and other nuclear projects, such as the "Plowshare" and "Gasbuggy" programs designed to use nuclear explosives for excavation and fossil fuel recovery, proved unsuccessful, they tended to stimulate private nuclear investment by portraying atomic experience as a valuable by-product of nuclear initiatives.

7. Lane's conclusion illustrates the planning vision associated with nuclear power's OT status. He writes:

> "It appears that I have painted a very optimistic picture of the future outlook for low-cost nuclear power; however, in all probability it may be too conservative. First of all, the projected per capita use of electricity in the year 2000 represents merely a saturation of current applications, such as home heating, air conditioning, and color television, and makes no allowance for the introduction of new applications. If, for example, because of shortages of petroleum the U.S. transportation industry converts to electricity-powered vehicles, this would increase the per capita consumption of electricity by 10,000 kw-hr/yr with resulting decreases in costs.
> ". . . The overall result may lead to fulfillment of the age-old dream of electricity too cheap to meter" (Lane 1968, 25).

8. The relevance of institutional accommodation to nuclear needs can be illustrated by the adjustments required for viable nuclear parks. The latter would likely necessitate the creation of mega-utilities and modification of anti-trust policy. Also needed would be aggressive exercise of eminent domain in order to create extensive transmission corridors. The lack of similar land-use initiatives may have helped stall the growth of slurry pipelines.

9. The technology's support from diversified corporations like General Electric and Westinghouse also endowed it with a source of internally generated funds. Its utility sponsorship gave it easy access to bank and insurance company credit. Real dollar IOU credit costs in 1955–1977 averaged only 2.8%.

10. Several studies have sought to determine whether nuclear utility financial instruments bore higher credit costs than coal utility offerings after the late-seventies. Through the early-eighties the results were inconclusive (DOE 11/82, 114; OTA 1984, 70). The failure to find significant difference was partially due to the methodology used. Adequate distinctions were not always made between nuclear utilities with plants completed during the OT years and those with nuclear plants still under construction after disestablishment.

Nevertheless, the New York State Public Service Commission found a .25% risk premium attached to nuclear utility offerings in 1979, a month before TMI. This margin increased to .65% immediately after the accident. An even larger differential was suggested by J. Hugh Devlin, managing director of Morgan Stanley, in his 1979 testimony before the House Interior Committee. *Devlin blamed regulatory escalation before and after TMI, rather than the accident itself, for higher credit costs.* He warned,

> ". . . the confidence of investors is extremely fragile . . . If they see actions which they regard as unduly burdensome—an extended moratorium on the licensing of nuclear plants, for example—their confidence will vanish abruptly . . . and make it difficult if not impossible for these companies to raise additional capital at reasonable costs . . . We therefore urge you to move cautiously and to carefully consider the capital-raising implications of any legislative actions you may take" (House Committee on Interior and Insular Affairs 1979, 115).

More in line with Devlin's assessment of the importance of nuclear power's de facto "insured" status than the one-half percent increase in financing costs observed in the aftermath of TMI, was the extraordinary drop in Combustion Engineering's stock in May 1974. On May 7th the *Wall Street Journal* reported that the company had entered into reactor contracts "allowing power utilities considerable freedom to back out of deals they had made with Combustion, and extending broad warranties that even cover equipment changes that may be required by future revisions in Atomic Energy Commission rules." The article noted, "Normally contracts provide that any AEC-caused cost overruns are to be divided, usually with the utility paying at least two-thirds . . ." Combustion's stock, which stood at 75 and 1/8 on May 6th plummeted to 46 1/2 on May 8th. The bulk of the near 40% decline reflected investor concern over company liability for nuclear uncertainties.

Similar investor caution greeted private sector efforts to fund enrichment ventures without government guarantees (*Barrons* 7/7/75).

Six months after the Three Mile Island accident, Equitable Life Insurance Vice President Carleton Burtt told the House Interior and Insular Affairs Committee, "We at the Equitable are proceeding cautiously at this moment regarding further commitments in nuclear power. We cannot commit further without a clearly defined policy framework and adequate regulatory protection" (House Committee on Interior and Insular Affairs 1979, 111).

In August of 1981 *Barrons* noted there had been extensive nuclear-related declines in utility bond ratings (*Barrons* 8/24/81). In December 1981 Merrill Lynch found that only 26% of the utilities with nuclear construction projects had "A" or "Aa" ratings. This compared with more than 50% for utilities without nuclear construction (Hyman and Kelley 12/3/81, 23, 24). Hewlett estimated that nuclear utility financing bore a 1%–2% risk premium in 1979–1982 (DOE 5/84, VIII). Komanoff estimated that in May 1984 nuclear risk premiums on common stock exceeded several percentage points (Komanoff 1984b, 72).

11. The potential interactive effect between social accommodation to nuclear power's institutional needs and lower credit costs in capital markets can be seen with respect to the politics of rate base determination in the utility sector. After nuclear power's loss of OT status, the utility industry attempted to circumvent local public utility commissions' refusal to include construction work in progress funds in utility rate bases, by promoting legislation that would shift control over rate base decisions to more sympathetic federal authorities. These efforts failed. See Campbell 1988, ch. 6 for an excellent discussion of the interaction between politics, utility rate base regulations, and nuclear power's treatment in capital markets.

12. See chapter 3, especially tables 3.4 and 3.5, for derivation of the 2.0–2.5 c/kwh subsidy range.

13. The 3 c/kwh construction cost differential assumes regulatory insulation of $1525–$1775/KW per discussion in chapter 4.

14. The 1 + c/kwh differential assumes:

1) roughly half the difference between current actual O&M costs (~20 M/kwh) and expected costs (~2.5 M/kwh) was due to earlier regulatory protection.

2) roughly half the difference between my projected waste disposal and decommissioning costs (~6 M/kwh) and expected backend costs (~.2 M/kwh) during the OT period was due to early regulatory protection.

3) a 5% capacity rate improvement due to regulatory protection during the OT period

15. Cost underestimation assumes:

1) roughly half the difference between current actual O&M costs (~20 M/kwh) and expected costs (~2.5 M/kwh) was due to excess optimism about O&M requirements (independent of escalating safety standards)

2) roughly half the difference between my projected waste disposal and decommissioning costs (~6 M/kwh) and expected backend costs (~.2 M/kwh) during the OT period was due to excess optimism about backend costs (independent of escalating regulatory standards)

3) neglect of a nuclear risk premium of about .5% in fixed charge rates

4) excess capacity forecasts of 15%

5) construction cost forecasting errors of $650/KW or ~ 1 c/kwh independent of escalating standards. The $650/KW figure derived as follows:
a) aggregate construction cost forecasting error: $3100/KW ($3750 + [cost of reactors on line after 1982] minus $650/KW [expected costs])
b) minus errors due to escalating safety standards (1525/KW) = 1575/KW
c) minus errors due to macroeconomic related increases in interest rates ($600/KW) = $975/KW
d) minus cost increases due to voluntary stretchouts of nuclear power construction due to demand slowdowns, and other peculiarities accompanying recently commissioned plants (adjustment assumed to be one-third of residual cost overrun)

Chapter 6

1. DOE 0438[91], 106–110.

2. DOE 0438[91], 107–110.

3. The concept of ideology used here does not involve the notion of illusion. It refers to a particular world view or conceptual framework for organizing political-economic analysis. From this perspective there are no neutral or non-ideological, "objective" starting points.

4. Drawing on interviews with nuclear critics, Mazur writes:

"(Anti-nuclear activists) express their opposition to the technology in the context of larger ideological concerns . . . (they) are concerned about the degradation of the environment and corporate control of society" (46). "The left orientation of the opponents of nuclear power plants could be observed as early as 1956. . . . Once these initial lines were drawn, liberals were more likely than conservatives to find the anti-nuclear issue appealing, and they were more likely to be recruited by the early liberal activists . . ." (Mazur 1981, 47).

After a careful analysis of anti-nuclear testimony during congressional hearings, Del Sesto (1979) writes:

". . . much of the debate over nuclear energy can be traced to important ideological considerations. . . . opposition to nuclear energy seemed to be an arm of the environmental movement (192–3). . . . The second ideological position . . . we call the 'anti-centralization and political accountability plank.' . . . The primary focus of these concerns was an outspoken opposition to political and administrative centralization of any kind, which, at the same time, displayed a clear preference for such ideas as the value of participatory politics, emphasis upon due process and political accountability" (198).

5. The "social limits to growth" refers to a skepticism about the market's ability to maximize the quality of life for most participants by simply following individual utility maximizing decisions. Hirsch (1976) argues that as average income grows, the collective consumption of material goods (such as the environment) and collective experience of social life (such as the shared satisfaction of a sense of community) play an increasing part in individual happiness. Hirsch also claims that there is a growing perception of the aggregate futility of competition for positional goods (such as a *better than average* college credential).

Ebbin and Kasper (1974) include among the major reasons for anti-nuclear activism, "anger with the trade-off of diminishing natural resources for economic growth. . . . The physical ecology is a major issue; but the human ecology, the intangibles of quality of life, the realization that having more may mean enjoying less, . . . also contribute to their concern" (32). See also Cook (1980, 10) and the general tone of the two leading anti-nuclear texts of the period, *The Menace of Atomic Energy* by Ralph Nader and John Abbotts and *No Nukes* by Clamshell Alliance activist Anna Gyorgy & Friends.

6. While some anti-nuclear activists have held neo-Luddite views on technology, most have not. Many opponents of nuclear power, such as Amory Lovins, have been active promoters of technological change in non-nuclear energy fields.

7. See for example: Cook 1980, 12; Mazur 1981, 46; and Berger 1976, 327.

8. The NEPA legislation's Environmental Impact Statement (EIS) Requirements were especially important to a suit against the breeder reactor program by the Scientists Institute for Public Information. The legal challenge significantly expanded public controversy about plutonium fuel cycles (Del Sesto 1979, 165–168). EIS requirements also increased licensing hurdles for nuclear power plants. Other sections of NEPA created the EPA and the Council on Environmental Quality, thereby providing an alternative planning environment within the executive branch of government to the AEC and DoD for analyzing energy issues.

9. Of the forty-five articles about nuclear power in the 1965 *New York Times* annual summary index, seven contained reference to opposition to the technology; of these, three involved concern over fish-kills, and two, objections to power plant sitings in scenic areas. Of the eighty-two articles about nuclear power in 1966, another seven contained oppositional references, with three of these involving fish-kills. Of the one hundred and sixty-three nuclear power related stories in 1967 and 1968, twenty-eight included oppositional references with more than one-third involving environmentalist activities.

10. While backing Governor Nelson Rockefeller's pro-nuclear development policy, a 5/7/68 *Times* editorial supported a SIPI recommendation for hearings on nuclear hazards. The call for hearings was repeated on 5/10/68. In August (8/15, 8/21) and October (10/12) the *Times* called for a nuclear moratorium pending hazard study. David Burnham, a *New York Times* reporter who covered the UCS spurred controversy on the emergency core cooling system, writes:

> "Henry Kendall and Dan Ford came up with a brilliant way of using the media in their nuclear safety work. They knew that a reporter—not being a physicist or an engineer—could not directly challenge the assertions of organized physicists and engineers that the nation's nuclear power program was a dream come true. But a reporter could write about the administrative problems of the nuclear program, providing there was documentary evidence. So Dan and Henry filed Freedom of Information Act requests that eventually forced the Atomic Energy Commission to disclose documents showing that the government had repeatedly tried to suppress news about the technical failings of nuclear power.
>
> "These documents gave me—as a reporter for the *New York Times* the hook that was required to persuade the editors that there might be a problem with nuclear energy. Since the *Times* has always been a true-blue believer in science, technology, and progress, Henry and Dan's achievement—finding the evidence that persuaded the paper to print stories questioning nuclear power—was a prodigious feat—. . ." *Nucleus* Spring 1994, 2).

11. Olson 1976, 233; Cook 1980, 11.

12. Primack and von Hippel 1974, 210; *Nucleus* Spring 1994, 1.

13. Gyorgy et al. 1979, 388; Cook 1980, 14; Mazur 1981. Groups, such as "Another Mother for Peace" (which actively opposed the Diablo Canyon reactor) and individuals such as Fred Branfman (former director of Solar-Cal) and Michael Mariotte (current director of the Nuclear Information Resource Service) for example, were very active in opposing the Vietnam War. The "participatory democracy" and "direct action" spirit of the Clamshell Alliance in New England and its dozens of sister alliances across the country and the campus based activism of groups, such as the Student Coalition Against Nukes Nationwide (SCANN), was similarly animated by the legacy of Vietnam protest.

14. In the late 1960s Cornell University appears to have had an especially active anti-war movement. Cornell faculty members, for example, established the nationally recognized Indochina Resource Center in Washington, which served as an anti-war think tank. About the same time a number of university members became involved in the successful drive to block the location of a nuclear plant on Cayuga Lake.

It was in this context that David Comey, then head of the Research Institute on Soviet Science in Ithaca, became director of the Citizens Committee to Save Cayuga Lake. He subsequently moved to Chicago where he became the director of environmental research for Business and Professional People for the Public Interest (BPI). While at BPI he helped lead the local intervention against the Palisades nuclear plant which resulted in the first negotiated agreement concerning radiation releases and thermal pollution between a utility and an anti-nuclear group (Nader and Abbotts 1979, 215; Comey 2/75b, 14).

Comey was also successful in generating significant media attention for his economic and technical criticisms of nuclear power. In this area he was aided by the environmental movement's success in passing the National Environmental Policy Act of 1969 which created the EPA. In 1972, the Joint Committee on Atomic Energy had sought to dismiss Comey's criticism, with perhaps its most powerful member, Chet Holifield, declaring, "As far as I am concerned, and in the view of most of the members (of the committee), he was completely discredited as being an expert in the field" (Rolph 1979, 101). In contrast, in 1974, the EPA selected Comey for its first Environmental Quality Award, "for services that have immeasurably improved the design and safety review of nuclear reactors" (Nader and Abbotts 1979, 215).

The Union of Concerned Scientists' intervention in the ECCS controversy was sparked by notification from BPI that the Idaho tests of the ECCS had failed. (Recall that the UCS had grown out of the March 4th movement at MIT which had objected to the use of military technologies in Southeast Asia.) The long public airing of the ECCS controversy helped legitimize the private doubts of many technocrats within the AEC and nuclear industry and helped induce a flow of leaked documents and protest resignations.

Comey's inquiries into nuclear plant capacity performance also sparked very important work in the economics of nuclear power by Charles Komanoff, himself an opponent of the war in Vietnam and veteran of the environmental movement.

A similar history could be constructed for the social roots of the anti-nuclear movement in New England and other areas of the country. The history illustrates the importance of creating an alternative realm of discourse and context for synergism for a social movement's success. The "left's" presence in the 1960s helped create this context for nuclear criticism.

15. In the mid-sixties utility capital expenditures were nearly matched by retained earnings (Gandara 1977, 28).

16. In total, 130GW of planned nuclear capacity and 60GW of fossil fuel fired capacity were canceled or delayed in 1974 and 1975 (Gandara 1977, 33–34).

17. Only a two year construction time was required for installing a gas turbine system in the mid-seventies compared to an average of five years for coal-fired plants and six and a half for nuclear plants (Komanoff 1981, 229). The differentials would be considerably greater if licensing time were included.

18. Nationalization was prominently raised, for example, in a government sponsored study of nuclear power (Allison et al. 1981) co-authored by the Dean of the J. F. Kennedy School of Government at Harvard University, and discussed in congressional testimony in 1979 by the Chairman of Consolidated Edison of New York.

19. Listings cited under the heading "Atomic Energy-U.S.-Electric Light and Power."

20. Mazur (1981) similarly notes the contingent aspect of the impact of nuclear accidents on the level of public opposition to nuclear power, citing the minimal effect

at the time of the Chalk River (1952), Windscale (1957), Idaho Falls (1961), and Fermi (1966) accidents (110).

21. Mazur (1981), using an index based on nuclear power citations in the Readers Guide also dates the rise in protest from the late 1960s. His index shows a slight decline in media attention in the early 1970s before a renewed interest in nuclear power in 1973. He suggests that a similar slow down occurred in protest activities, though he does not support this claim with any evidence (106–110).

This picture differs somewhat from the picture that emerges from the *New York Times* data, which implies a continuous growth in anti-nuclear protest from 1965–1973, though the rate of growth does diminish during the 1971–1973 period.

22. See chapters 4 and 5 for derivation of the $1.5+ billion estimate of hazard containment cost increases.

23. David Montgomery and James Quirk of the California Institute of Technology reach similar conclusions through a descriptive rather than statistical analysis, writing, "The conclusions of the study are that . . . (p)rior to 1970, (nuclear) cost increases are related to bottleneck problems in the nuclear construction and supplying industries and the regulatory process; intervenors play only a minor role in cost escalation. After 1970, generic changes introduced into the licensing process by intervenors (including environmental impact reviews, anti-trust reviews, more stringent safety standards) dominate the cost escalation picture . . ." (Montgomery and Quirk 1978, ii).

24. Relatedly, Merril Lynch Vice President Leonard Hyman wrote in 1981, "Did TMI kill nuclear power? I doubt that TMI did much beyond what was happening anyway. . . . In my opinion, for the utility industry and for the investor, TMI was not a catastrophe that broke a chain of development such as the unknown catastrophe that led to the extinction of the dinosaurs and the rise of the mammals. It was simply one more link in the chain of development. We would have ended up the same place, just later" (Hyman 1981, 7).

25. Applying the logic of conventional economic theory the Ford Foundation's influential study, *Nuclear Power: Issues and Choices* (1977), for example, asserted, "For the purpose of estimating how resources should be allocated and how the economic and political processes of society will allocate them in the long run, the competitive market model is of great value—even in the face of market defects. . . . in summary markets work well enough to allow us to predict trends on the basis of real costs and scarcities, and then to use long run cost minimizing models to predict responses to these prices" (46–47).

Chapter 7

1. U.S. CEA 6/92, 6; National Research Council 1992, 134, 139.

2. See, for example, Kriesberg 11/87, E-10, and D-30 and Kriesberg 3/87, 3.

3. Included among expected cost cutting innovation paths are:

- the mechanization of manual operations, especially in hazardous (radioactive) environments (e.g., robotic weld repair)

- equipment innovation (e.g., guided wave bore probes for steam generator tube inspection)

- design improvements from operating experience (e.g., containment modifications to facilitate maintenance)

- training improvements (e.g., upgraded simulators)

- materials improvements (e.g., weldless ring forgings).

4. Design changes that would increase containment space and reduce cobalt use, for example, are expected to substitute minor increases in construction costs for larger decreases in O&M outlays and improved capacity performance. Westinghouse foresees large reductions in fuel loading downtime in response to modest increases in regular O&M expenses.

5. Illustrative of these hopes was the NRC's 1992 decision to allow FERMI-2 to operate at 4.2% higher power. G. E. is attempting to win generic upgrades for many of its reactors (*Nucleonics Week* 10/15/92, 4–5).

6. See, for example, Riccio and Murphy 1988, and Kriesberg 10/87.

7. French costs: Thomas 1988, 232–234; Japanese costs: Navarro 1988, 4–5.

8. Within the U.S., the standard deviation of capacity performance for PWRs was a startling 22% in 1980–1984. While U.S. PWRs availability averaged only 60.2% in 1975–1984, the best six U.S. PWRs (with over ten years operating experience) had rates of over 75% (Hansen et al. 1989).

9. See, for example, *Electrical World* 202(7), 15–16, Weinberg et al. 1985, 387, Hansen et al. 1989, 40.

10. See, for example, MIT 1990, Cottrell and Keene papers.

11. Because the AIF study is expressed in nominal dollars, some of the claimed cost savings are exaggerated, especially those associated with shortened construction. To avoid confusion, the AIF's results have been re-expressed in real dollars.

12. The most recent manifestation of the technology's immaturity have been recommendations for design changes in the light of decommissioning experience. Analysts skeptical of the massive economic savings claimed from standardization also warn: (1) that standardization might raise safety problems if administrative centralization interferes with quick responses to local plant safety issues by plant personnel (as suggested by three audits of the French standardization program by the International Atomic Energy Agency [*Nucleonics Week* 9/19/92, 11–12]); and (2) that modularization might increase maintenance costs if modular designs substitute unit replacement for minor equipment repair.

13. Analysts at a 1990 MIT conference on the future of nuclear power estimated

that it would take from six to ten modular units a year to achieve significant economies (MIT 1990, 3–17). It was felt unlikely that new orders would approach this level (Ibid., 3–17, see also 2–24). In April of 1993 Framatome Chairman Jean-Claude Leny indicated it would take at least eight to ten simultaneous orders of the same reactor to achieve competitive power (*Nucleonics Week* 4/29/93, 1, 6). He also stressed the need for a "commitment by safety authorities that they won't ask for changes" after designs are approved (Ibid.).

14. The engineering designs underlying the ORNL studies, for example, project a 30% saving for each MW doubling (though the ORNL studies warn against mechanically applying the projected scaling coefficients to megawattage significantly different from the reference case). The U.S. Council for Energy Awareness cost projections foresee about a 15% savings from a doubling in plant size from 600 MW to 1200 MW (U.S. CEA 6/92, 20–21).

15. Virtually every few months new problems surface at operating reactors. Among those identified in the early 1990s were: new fire hazards from defective insulation, insufficient emergency cooling for spent fuel pools, inadequate water level monitoring in BWR cores, unexpected computer code interactions, BWR core shroud cracking, reactor vessel head penetration cracking, and new problems with old trouble spots, such as motor operated valves, pressure vessel embrittlement, and steam generator tube cracking.

16. The optimists highlight recent improvements in performance, citing the industry's average capacity rate of 72.2% for 1992–1994 and record high of 78.8% for 1995 (NEI 8/96, 3). They note that the median downtime for refueling has fallen from eighty-three days in 1989 to fifty-two days in 1995 (NEI, 8.96, 3).

17. Komanoff (1991) found capacity rates to fall after the ninth year of service. A May 1991 *Nuclear News* article reported a leveling off of capacity improvements in older plants. The DOE found large plants twelve years or older had 24% lower capacity rates than younger plants (DOE 0436(95), 47). Whether this reflects improved design in the newer plants or aging effects in the older plants is unclear.

18. It is difficult to take the low end of optimistic O&M cost forecasts seriously. Despite continuing O&M escalation in 1990, the U.S. CEA's 1992 cost forecast lowered projected fixed O&M costs from $67/KW in its 1991 forecast to $42/KW and lowered variable O&M costs from 1.2 M/kwh to .5 M/kwh. Skeptics note the convenience of these dramatic declines at a time when many operating nuclear plants are facing shutdown pressures due to high O&M costs.

New problems needing O&M attention to continue to surface at on-line plants. A February 1993 incident in which a former mental patient crashed a station wagon through a security gate at Three Mile Island, for example, prompted the NRC to increase plant security requirements (*Nucleonics Week* 7/15/93). Continuing problems with motor operated valves caused the NRC to increase valve testing requirements in July 1993 (*Nucleonics Week* 7/8/93). A 1993 study of O&M costs since 1990 found staffing expenses continuing to escalate (though at a slower pace) (*Nucleonics Week* 7/8/93, 11).

19. Biewald and Marion 1989, 6; Kriesberg 11/87, D-10.

20. Data limitations make it difficult to project the future impact of aging on O&M outlays. A 1989 study by Critical Mass found significant increases in repairs as plants aged (Borson et al. 5/89, 4). When controlling for the impact of increasing NRC regulations, however, Hewlett found an inverse relationship (presumably because of utility learning) between age and O&M outlays (DOE 1991 [0547], 9). He warns, however, that aging effects may assert themselves later in the lifecycle of nuclear plants than discernible in his sample, which had an average age of only thirteen (p. 23). Hewlett (1992) repeats this warning, with the additional caveat that the results of a multimillion dollar NRC study of plant aging are likely to introduce new regulatory requirements (p. 613).

21. Hewlett (1992) indicates that O&M reporting errors for overhead costs appear to have understated O&M costs by about 30% (p. 608). He finds median 1989 O&M costs of about $112/KW (3rd qtr. 1992$) or nearly 2 c/kwh at 65% capacity rates (608).

22. In response to skyrocketing low level waste disposal costs ($270/cf as of 1/93 at Barnwell (*Nucleonics Week* 12/10/92), the utilities have dramatically reduced their LLW volume. BWR LLW output, for example, fell from 1,113 cubic meters (cm) in 1980 per plant to 219 (cm) in 1992 (National Research Council 1992, 54, *Nucleonics Week* 4/15/93). It is not clear, however, that all of the remedial actions taken (including materials reuse and perhaps increased on-site washing and additional drainage disposal of minute amounts of radioactivity) will be able to escape regulatory or public relations backlashes.

23. Nuclear fuel costs can be disaggregated into three categories: uranium costs, uranium enrichment costs, and miscellaneous fuel fabrication costs. Several factors are expected to discourage price increases in all three areas. The maturity of the fuel fabrication industries is expected to generate relatively stable prices. The current slowdown in nuclear plant construction and recent uranium discoveries (such as the large Canadian find in Saskatchewan) are expected to discourage short run uranium price increases. Upward revisions in uranium resource assessments since the late-seventies have also relaxed longer run price pressures. Mid-eighties projections find global uranium resources sufficient to fuel existing world nuclear capacity ($\sim$325 GWe) for 100–500 years at less than $60/lb (1986$). Increasing foreign competition, the U.S.-Russian agreement to recycle enriched uranium from old Soviet bombs in American reactors, and falling DOE enrichment costs imply stable or modestly falling uranium enrichment prices. More dramatic cost reductions, such as a 1988 ORNL forecast of declines of $\sim$60%–75% (ORNL 9/88, 39) rely on optimistic assumptions about the development of Atomic Vapor Laser Isotope Separation (AVLIS) and seem vulnerable to the industry's habit of excess optimism about technological change.

There are some pressures for enrichment price increases. Current and projected DOE enrichment prices have been found by the General Accounting Office to violate the DOE's statutory requirement to recover the government's capital investment in enrichment facilities. Uncertainties over the total cost and distributional burden of decommissioning U.S. enrichment facilities (frequently estimated to be ~$4–$6 billion and as high as $20+ billion) also cloud enrichment costs.

The most pervasive pressure for fuel price increases involves the potential for tighter safety and security regulation of fuel sector activities, such as nuclear mining and fuel transportation, due to increased concern about nuclear weapons proliferation, occupational radiation exposure, and uranium tailings disposal. There do not appear to be detailed estimates of the potential impact of these concerns. The literature's silence seems to imply the improbability of major escalation, though it might also reflect bounded discourse as has been the case with many cost projections.

24. As of early 1993, the NRC's generic decommissioning cost estimates were $119/KW for PWRs and $154/KW for BWRs (*Nucleonics Week* 2/4/93, 7), or about .4 M/kwh–.7 M/kwh (assuming a thirty-year sinking fund, 3% real interest rate and 65% capacity rate). The U.S. CEA forecast decommissioning costs of $220–$275/ KW for new nuclear plants (U.S. CEA 6/92) or costs of about .7–.8 M/kwh (given its optimistic 80% capacity rate projections).

25. Joseph Kriesberg of the Critical Mass Energy Project foresaw costs as high as $1000/KW–$3000/KW (1986$) in 1987 (Kriesberg, 11/87, D-24). The Critical Mass Energy Bulletin predicted cost overruns two to four times industry expectations in its spring 1991 issue (p. 7).

26. Low level waste disposal cost estimates vary from costs of ~$30–$40/cf (Makhijani and Saleska 1992, 85) to $100/cf (MIT 1993b) for large sites with inputs of ~230,000/year–350,000 cf/year; to $150/cf–$200/cf for sites with 100,000– 150,000 cf/yr. (MIT 1993b), to $330/cf–$400/cf for sites with inputs of ~40,000cf/ yr. (MIT 1993b) to $600/cf–$700/cf for small sites with inputs of ~10,000 cf/yr. (all $/cf costs in historical $) (Makhijani and Saleska 1992, 85). Total U.S. LLW volume in 1992 equaled 1.6 million cubic feet.

DOE decommissioning studies project about 18,000 cubic meters (486,000 cf) of LLWD for immediate decommissioning activities (Makhijani and Saleska 1992, 112). This suggests that LLWD costs by themselves could easily range from about $20 million (@ $40/cf) to nearly $200 million (@ 400/cf), exceeding the NRC's current estimate of total decommissioning costs!

27. The tendency for actual costs to more than double predicted rates in nuclear cost forecasting was reillustrated in early 1992 when decommissioning cost projections for the shutdown 167 MW Yankee Rowe plant leaped to $247 million, twice earlier predictions and four times the operating utility's collected decommissioning funds (*Nuclear Monitor* 6/15/92, 1). Later in 1992 decommissioning costs were tripled for the Fort Calhoun plant, whose management indicated that the Yankee revision had caused them to recalculate their expected costs (*Nucleonics Week* 11/5/92, 1–2). In 1994, utility cost projections for decommissioning Yankee Rowe increased to $370 million (*New York Times* 11/4/94).

28. Other factors that might lower costs include: delaying decommissioning by fifty or more years from plant closing, staggering decommissioning to permit industry

learning, and restoring public confidence in nuclear hazard regulation to the point where symbolic regulations (such as zero emissions are unnecessary).

29. Kriesberg offers one of the highest projections 4.8–12 M/kwh (1987$) (Kriesberg 11/87 D-21). Komanoff and Roelofs (1992), and Makhijani and Saleska (1992) imply lower waste disposal costs.

30. Kriesberg 11/87.

31. Illustrative of nuclear power's demands on scarce management time was the relief expressed by the chair of Portland General Electric after the utility retired its only nuclear plant fifteen years early. Chairman Ken Harrison indicated that although the nuclear plant "represented only 25% of the company's resources, 'it took 80% of my time'" (*Power Engineering* 4/93, 13).

32. Stephen Farber (1991) found a .8% increase in equity cost attached to a utility's first adoption of a nuclear plant (p. 81). In mid-1993, Moody's Investor Service found that "'the potential for future risk volatility and rating downgrades' is greater for those utilities that have 'significant' nuclear investments . . .'" due to uncertainties about aging problems at older reactors, regulatory requirements, and other phenomena (*Nucleonics Week* 5/20/93, 8).

Many of the special risks accompanying nuclear investments involve complications attendant with radioactive environments. For example, *Nucleonics Week* reported on March 4, 1993, "The U.S. nuclear industry and its insurers are anticipating a flood of tort claims from older workers . . . While direct employers are shielded from employee lawsuits by participation in the workers compensation program, employees may sue third parties, so contractor workers, for instance, could sue utilities whose plants they worked in. The current $400 million pool for such third party claims, which is shared by 115 U.S. utilities and nuclear-related businesses like fuel fabricators, may not stretch to cover all tort claims . . ."

33. The call for competing centers of forecasting, parallels more general arguments in favor of "adversary science" in the area of technology assessment. Surveying the history of nuclear power related radiation research John Gofman asserts, "A technology under current circumstances is practically guaranteed to find itself burdened with a group of 'think alikes' throughout its technical staff, for the simple reason that those who speak out are shortly weeded out. . . . The early establishment of reprisal-free, fully funded centers for adversary criticism of technology can correct this serious situation" (Gofman and Tamplin 1979, 255–256).

Hugh Folk, a past director of a University of Illinois program on the social implications of science and technology, has argued the case more generally, asserting ". . . experienced experts will usually be drawn from the interests involved in a problem . . . Institutional and professional biases are at least as potent as financial conflicts of interest in distorting one's conception of the problem. . . . people used to thinking about a certain area will tend to see it in the context of a large set of implicit technological, social and political assumptions" (*Technology Review* 3–4/73).

Chapter 8

1. Calculating civilian nuclear power R&D support is tricky due to the diverse budget categories under which civilian nuclear power assistance can occur. Because different analysts include different categories in their totals, the text's R&D tables are not fully comparable and differ at times in their annual R&D entries.

2. FY 1994 Budget of the United States Government, Appendix, p. 573; DOE 11/92, 46.

3. For example, proposals attempting to piggy back civilian demonstration plants on top of the DoD's requests for new tritium producing reactors have failed.

4. Much of the discussion below is quoted directly and/or paraphrased from Cohn & Lidsky 1993. For ease of exposition, I have not included specific citations.

5. Analysis by Dubin and Rothwell (1990), endorsed in a November 1992 DOE study, calculated an implicit subsidy of about $22 million per utility per reactor year or about 4 M/kwh (Dubin and Rothwell 1990, 73). Dubin and Rothwell's calculations appear biased downwards as they include only property damage and exclude health effects. The subsidy calculations also refer only to the benefits accruing to the utilities, though the legislation protects all firms in the nuclear industry in all accidents. The calculations also rely on official NRC accident probabilities and damage estimates rather than higher estimates by some private analysts. I have added 1 M/kwh to Dubin and Rothwell's 4 M/kwh subsidy estimate to reduce its downward bias.

Ken Bossong (7/87) cites a number of other subsidy estimates congenial with Dubin and Rothwell's projection (pp. 7–10). Koplow (1993) calculates a $2.75 billion/year Price-Anderson subsidy for ~4.4 M/kwh subsidy rate. See also *Nucleonics Week* 12/17/92, 9.

6. Phone conversation with representatives of the National Taxpayer's Union 9/17/92.

7. Montange 1990, p. i, 1 and phone conversation with National Taxpayers Union 9/17/92.

8. The legislation does leave open the possibility of further charges if the cost of decommissioning enrichment facilities exceeds DOE expectations (*Nucleonics Week* 9/30/93, 9). Subsidy calculations assume: (1) accumulated enrichment liabilities of $8 billion and $.5 billion–$4.5 billion in underpayment for decommissioning costs, for a total subsidy of $8.5–$12.5 billion; (2) a recovery period of fifteen years and a real interest rate of 5.5%, for a capital recovery factor of ~10% and annual charges of $850 million to $1.35 billion; (3) annual nuclear output of ~625 Bkwh.

9. In 1974, for example, the utilities' major trade association, the Edison Electric Institute, testified before Congress that "the economic penalties that would be imposed by a shortfall of enrichment capability far exceed the costs that would be associated with temporary oversupply" (Montange 1990, 5). Montange adds, "When

GAO [the General Accounting Office] warned against incurring the high costs and risks of building new enrichment plants in the face of uncertain demand, it was harshly criticized by spokesmen for the nuclear utility industry for raising these doubts. In their testimony supporting the $10 billion federal centrifuge program in 1978 against GAO objections, the nuclear utilities testified that 'the need to proceed rapidly with the planned . . . plant is urgent and cannot be overemphasized'" (Montange 1990, 5–6).

10. Efforts to build a private enrichment plant using centrifuge technology in Louisiana, for example, have encountered:

(1) active local opposition and careful monitoring by national anti-nuclear groups. Especially important is the ability of consumer groups to challenge efforts by the utility consortium proposing the enrichment plant to include their enrichment investments in the companies' rate base. The latter strategy would have offered investors another avenue for public assumption of investment risk.

(2) public pressure to ensure that company stockholders assume liability for plant decommissioning and environmental clean-up costs.

(3) public concern about proliferation hazards.

(4) Watchdog efforts by the National Taxpayers Union to minimize hidden public subsidies (such as the transfer of DOE uranium stockpiles to new enrichment entities at below market prices).

(5) general skepticism about optimistic enrichment cost claims.

(6) political opposition to attempts to license the facility without public hearings and an Environmental Impact Statement (E.I.S.). In December 1996 an NRC licensing board upheld environmentalist challenges to the project's E.I.S. and financing arrangements, making it unlikely that the enrichment facility will be built (nirsnet@igc. apc.org 12/5/96).

11. A 1990 report by the DOE's Inspector General found that the DOE had permitted seventeen utilities to defer several billion dollars of waste disposal payments. The report identified eleven utilities, with liabilities of $2.1 billion, whose debts might never be paid due to the companies' poor financial condition (*Nucleonics Week* 4/12/90, 8).

12. For example, the 1992 Energy Policy Act gave a 1.5 c/kwh production credit to wind and closed-loop biomass energy systems and permanently extended Investment Tax Credits for solar and geothermal energy systems (Koplow 1993, 31).

13. Komanoff and Roelofs' subsidy totals are about 15% higher than estimates by Management Information Services.

14. The major areas of expenditure involved: international atomic energy activities ~$25 million, uranium mining support services ~$25 million, nuclear energy-related health issues ~$30 million, and the Federal Emergency Management Agency ~$10 million.

Chapter 9

1. The *Columbia Journalism Review* (March–April 1994) contains a fascinating account ("The Radiation Story No One Would Touch" by Geoffrey Sea) of the 23-year history of efforts to investigate and publicize suspicions and findings about radiation experiments on human beings. The history redemonstrates how social contexts influence the use made of technical information.

2. Gofman and other nuclear power critics have strongly criticized the "official committees" for their insularity, historic linkages to the nuclear establishment, and past tendency to underestimate radiation hazards. Caufield, for example, indicates that since World War II less than fifty scientists, all of them men, have served on the International Commission on Radiological Protection (ICRP), a body whose recommendations have been extremely influential in determining U.S. and other nations' radiation exposure standards. The commission is self-perpetuating. It appoints its own members, much like a college board of trustees (Caufield 1989, 167–176).

3. In the aftermath of the Chernobyl accident, for example, the president of the American Nuclear Society, Bertram Wolfe (a high ranking executive in General Electric's nuclear power division), reasserted the threshold hypothesis, claiming that "no clear effects on health have been found (for low-level radiation) despite more than forty years of trying to find them . . ." (Gofman 1990, 34–8, citing *Denver Post* 9/27/86, p. 4-b).

4. See, for example, Gofman 1990, ch. 14.

5. The Hanford data set, for example, is one of the largest data sets on radiation hazards. It covers about 35,000 workers, exposed to ~78,000 rems. Expected lifetime excess cancers range from ~20 (per Cohen's assumption of 4000 rems/cancer) to ~195 (per Gofman's assumption of 400 rems/cancer). Given the normal variance of cancer in the population, one would expect to observe about 7000 $+/-$ 135 cancers. As the difference in prediction between Gofman and Cohen is only 175 cancers, measurement error and other "noise" (such as debates over how to correct for the "healthy worker" effect) could easily leave observed results consistent with either hypothesis.

   Because most of the impact of radiation on cancer rates is expected to occur in older age groups, there were very small differences in expected cancer death rates through 1986 (the latest data available in 1992) between radiation hazard optimists such as Dr. Edith Gilbert, and hazard pessimists, such as Dr. Alice Stewart (10–15 excess cancers expected versus fifty excess cancers) (*New York Times* 12/8/92). It is nearly impossible for epidemiological studies to resolve hazard debates within such narrow boundaries.

6. Stewart (9/90), for example, has raised questions about survivor bias and Gofman (1990) has questioned the cohort design in bomb assessment calculations. The debates over high level radiation hazards appear relatively modest, however.

7. Stewart (1990) has raised healthy worker issues with respect to DOE interpretations of the Hanford data. Irwin Bross (1991) has raised similar soncerns with respect to DOE studies of cancer rates among nuclear shipyard workers. Geiger et al. (1992, pp. 45–47, 71, 86–87) have raised the same issue with respect to several DOE hazard studies. Muckerheide (1995) has challenged these interpretations from a pronuclear perspective.

8. See, for example, Stewart 9/90.

9. See, for example, Fairlie 1991 and Stewart 9/90. There also seems to be increasing attention to the role of in-utero radiation exposure in causing childhood cancers. See, for example, Knox, Stewart, Gilman, and Kneale 1988.

10. Anti-nuclear analysts have criticized the government and industry's tendency to ignore the long term accumulation of radioactive materials by arbitrarily limiting hazard horizons to short time periods. See, for example, Gofman 1990, ch. 24.

11. In 1994 a former NRC nuclear plant inspector sued several nuclear industry firms for exposing her to "radioactive fleas" (microscopic particles) that are not detected by existing dosimeters (*Nuclear Monitor* 1/17/94). Several distinguished radiation scholars supported her claim that existing radiation monitors are unable to account for internally absorbed doses.

12. A 1994 paper by Gofman raises potential links between high current breast cancer rates and radiation exposure (*Nuclear Monitor* 3/28/94).

13. McCally 1990, 14; Fairlie 1990, 3–5; *Nucleonics Week* 2/4/93, 2/27/92. A 1994 paper by Sir Richard Doll in the British journal *Nature* has challenged the Gardiner hypothesis, lending support to an alternative explanation of the cancer clusters near British fuel reprocessing facilities that involves viral causes (*New York Times* 3/8/94). The Nuclear Energy Institute, the latest name for the nuclear industry's trade association, cites several other follow up studies that it asserts also challenge the Gardiner hypothesis (NEI 6/96). See also *Nuclear News*: 12/94, 37, 9/94, 113–114.

14. *New York Times* 3/20/91; *Technology Review* 2–3/93, *Journal of the American Medical Association* 3/20/91. The authors of the study noted that their hazard estimates were an order of magnitude higher than those based on the Hiroshima data and add, "Because the observed effects have clearly emerged from the most recent period of follow-up (at Oak Ridge National Lab, ed.) and because of long delays of the apparent radiation effects, it is essential that mortality follow-up continue in this population and in other populations with protracted exposures to chronic low doses of external penetrating ionizing radiation . . ." (Wing et al. 1991, 1402).

15. *Scientists for Democratic Action*, spring 1992; *Nuclear News* 3/92.

16. Radiation hazard pessimists have noted that the data only included cancers diagnosed within six years of the accident (*Nuclear News* 10/90, 28). Other official studies have been criticized for ignoring suspicious cancer clusters and poor statistical methodologies (Doroshow 1994, 6).

17. The study's methodology has been heavily criticized by anti-nuclear groups for comparing counties with nuclear power plants to counties without nuclear power plants, rather than comparing populations downwind from a nuclear plant with populations free of plant emissions. Nuclear skeptics have also emphasized the relative youthfulness of the plants in the sample (average operating life equaled nine years) compared with the long latency for cancer hazards.

Similar debates surround the adequacy of epidemiological studies of the health impact of the Three Mile Island accident. See, for example, Doroshow (1994, 6).

18. *Nuclear Energy* 30(6) Dec. 1991, 328. The study has been criticized by anti-nuclear skeptics for underestimating the "healthy worker" effect.

19. It is somewhat difficult to find comprehensive and comparable core melt probability projections. Many calculations ignore external events (such as earthquakes and sabotage), include only "design based"-accidents (a limited definition of accident paths), refer to new plants rather than existing plants, or assume plants are built to design specifications and operated in accordance with all NRC regulations, biasing accident probabilities downwards. Other studies fail to include safety improvements from plant retrofits and learning from the studies themselves, biasing probabilities upwards.

There has been some tendency for expected accident frequencies to increase over time. During the 1960s the expected probability of serious core damage was in the neighborhood of 1 per million reactor years (RY). The 1975 Reactor Safety Study (RSS) (WASH 1400 or the Rasmussen study) projected core damage risks of about .5/10,000 RY. While path breaking as well as helpful for prioritizing safety upgrades, the study's aggregate safety assessment was heavily criticized, especially for underestimating the uncertainties accompanying its projections. The NRC ultimately disavowed the study's conclusions in 1979. A 1982 study of actual reactor performance from 1969–1979 projected core damage probabilities of 17–45/10,000 RY (Weinberg et al. 1985, 113). Through the late-1980s, about two dozen plant specific Probabilistic Risk Assessments (PRAs) had been performed with average core melt probabilities estimated at ~3/10,000 RY (Harding 1990, 99). The NRC's follow-up to the RSS, NUREG 1150, released in draft form in 1987, found core melt probabilities of .082/10,000 RY to 1.5/10,000 RY (excluding externally initiated events) (Harding 1990, 97). Subsequent attempts by the NRC to include hazards like earthquakes increased expected core melt frequencies to slightly more than 1/10,000 RY (National Research Council 1992, 65). While these rates are generally higher than those contained in the RSS, the expectation of fewer containment failures after a meltdown than forecast in the RSS (due to increased confidence in containment integrity and chemical suppression of radioactive emissions), has left most recent NRC and industry forecasts of the probability of serious radioactive releases from nuclear accidents less than predicted in the RSS.

Safety skeptics offer many reasons for suspecting that these projections underestimate true accident probabilities and even more likely underestimate accident uncertainties. Especially important is the need to focus on the poorest performing plant, rather than the average plant. If ninety-nine plants have an expected accident rate of one in a million years and four plants have rates of 1/100 years, the average accident rate will be about 1/2,500 years and the sector rate will be about one accident per twenty-five years.

This points to one of the causes of the nuclear industry's economic problems; namely, the related tendency of the NRC to design regulations with the weakest utility in mind.

20. Using the Binomial or the Poisson distributions, it can be shown that it would take more than one hundred years of accident-free operation for existing U.S. reactors before one could reject the pessimistic assumption of accident probabilities of one per three thousand reactor years at a 2.5% significance level.

21. See chapter 4 for a more detailed discussion of previous hazard assessment problems. Among the areas having serious oversights in the past are: assessment of utility management capabilities, BWR pipe cracking, construction site quality control problems, control room layout, cooling water chemistry, emergency core cooling, fire hazards, loss of off-site power, small pipe break accidents, pressure vessel embrittlement, reactor operator training, sabotage risks, seismic hazards, steam generator tube degradation, and water hammer problems.

22. Illustrative of the industry's tendency for ex post rather than ex ante safety review was: the AEC's modest safety R&D budget and the limited attention that was given to potential hazards such as seismic stress, pressure vessel embrittlement, core melt damage control, or containment integrity until actual accidents or social protest demanded attention.

23. Among the more well known controversies about "managed information" are debates over: the design and use of the Reactor Safety Study (WASH 1400), the withholding of the results of an earlier safety study (WASH 740 update), the suppression of AEC staff doubts about the emergency core cooling system, the avoidance of criticism of pressure suppression containment techniques, the discouragement of linkages between AEC safety researchers and AEC staff regulators, the semantic rather than substantive resolution of many unresolved safety issues, Westinghouse's insufficient candor about potential steam generator tube problems, G. E.'s reticence about potential difficulties with BWR containment integrity, numerous utilities' lack of candor about seismic hazards, quality control problems, and likely cost overruns, the NRC and utilities use of private rather than public channels to discuss safety issues, and the NRC's habit of allowing nuclear plants to violate licensing conditions deemed unnecessary by the NRC without holding public hearings on the de facto licensing amendments (*Nuclear Monitor* 5/9/94, 3).

24. For examples of such official criticism, see: the *Report of the President's Commission on the Accident at Three Mile Island*, the report of the Nuclear Regulatory Commission's Special Inquiry Group: *Three Mile Island, A Report to the Commissioners and to the Public*, a key NRC safety official's list of major nuclear accidents (the *Nugget File*), the National Research Council's review of safety practices in the nuclear weapons sector, and various NRC reviews of particular hazards, such as the Office of Inspector General's report on Thermo-Lag (August 1992).

25. As argued in Cohen (1990) ". . . these Rothman-Lichter surveys show that scientists have been much more supportive of nuclear power than the public or the TV reporters, producers, and journalists who "educate" them. Among scientists, the closer their specialty to nuclear science, the more supportive they are. . . . The pattern is very clear—the more one knows about nuclear power, the more supportive one becomes" (43–44).

26. Safety skeptics suggest a similar blindness by highly specialized scientists and engineers to quality control problems in the construction and utility industry. While Oak Ridge National Laboratory might be able to permanently operate research reactors without serious accidents, maintaining such high standards across a large commercial nuclear industry is judged a different matter. Even at ORNL, post-Chernobyl reviews of Lab practices led to a shutdown of five reactors due to newly perceived safety complacencies (*ORNL Review* 22:4, pp. 14–23).

Echoing similar concerns about insular discourse, the AEC's first director, David Lilienthal, argued against the AEC and industry's plans for siting a nuclear plant inside New York City in the mid-sixties. He commented, "No, I don't have detailed knowledge. I think one of the best ways to get confused is to get detailed knowledge . . ." (*Nucleonics* 5/63, 21).

27. In March of 1995, for example, a nuclear safety engineer employed by the NRC to review utility data for plant specific PRAs indicated that he had been "told by NRC staffers not to 'look so hard and don't ask so much' " in assessing utility claims (*Nuclear Monitor* 5/1/95, 1–2). The engineer highlighted the NRC's unwillingness to let him visit the plants under review in order to investigate actual plant conditions. He also criticized the commission's tolerance of the use of generic failure rates for emergency power diesel generators at a reactor that had a history of poor performance from one of its diesel generators.

28. Safety skeptics' concern about potential human error, maintenance failures, and quality control deficiencies illustrates the pessimists' general distrust of existing LWRs' reliance on complex engineered safeguards. The critics note that despite advances in "human engineering," human error remains responsible for about half of all "Licensee Event Reports." Actions by "disgruntled" employees also continue to threaten plant operation. In August of 1996, for example, three safety switches were found glued shut at the St. Lucie nuclear plant (PORTZLINES88@delphi.com, 8/17/96). Especially disconcerting to safety skeptics is the potential for operators to override automatic accident safeguards as occurred at TMI and Chernobyl. Other cases of operator overrides have been reported at the Peach Bottom plant in 1986 (with respect to control rod withdrawal) and the Oyster Creek plant in 1987 (with respect to vacuum breakers) (Boley et al. 3/89, 19, 21). The Peach Bottom plant operators were also found to have been regularly sleeping on the job (Ibid., 19).

Skeptics continue to raise concern about industry problems with quality control hazards such as poor welds, construction site carelessness, and deficient operator training. The Union of Concerned Scientists has drawn special attention to "equipment qualification" problems, finding insufficient guarantees of safety equipment's ability to perform in accident conditions. In 1989, Critical Mass, a Nader group, highlighted the use of substandard parts and the discovery of fraudulent supply contracts in the utility industry (Boley et al. 3/89, 23).

Because some nuclear plants are being retired early and others are far enough along in their useful life to limit the amortizing period for expensive repairs, some utilities are reluctant to fund major maintenance activities. Skeptics fear this could compromise nuclear safety. This issue is especially acute for PWRs with serious steam generator tube problems. As financial pressures have increasingly squeezed nuclear economics, incentives have also grown for performing maintenance simultaneously on systems intended to offer independent backup capabilities. This practice undermines the rationale of defense in-depth safety strategies. In April 1990, for example, the NRC cited three incidents during which unwise concurrent maintenance took place (*Nuclear News* 3/92, 44–45). Emergency power seems especially compromised by economizing maintenance policies. In December 1994 the NRC voiced similar concerns over the utilities increasing tendency to perform preventive maintenance on safety systems while plants are in operation rather than during scheduled outages in order to increase plant capacity rates. In a letter to utility executives, the NRC complained of "a lack of understanding concerning the relative importance of safety systems or combinations of equipment that would have risk significance if taken out of service" (*Nuclear News* 12/94, 24).

Safety skeptics have also raised concern over the potential for declining quality in utility and vendor staffs due to the perception of nuclear power as a dying technology by talented engineers in graduate study. There has been significant declines, for example, in the number of university research reactors and enrollment in nuclear engineering masters programs.

29. Pollard 10/93; *Nucleonics Week* 10/15/92, 6; Pollard, 1992.

30. Leventhal and Hoenig 1990. New security concerns were raised in the aftermath of the World Trade Center bombing and a former mental patient's intrusion at TMI in February 1993. New NRC regulations requiring increased physical barriers to vehicle penetration are expected to cost $500,000 to $1,000,000 per nuclear plant (*Nuclear News*: 4/95, 36, 4/93; *Nucleonics Week* 2/11/93, 16, 7/15/93).

31. *Pressure Vessel (PV) and Reactor Support Structure Embrittlement* (exacerbated by thermal shock during emergency cooling): Until the mid-sixties PV failure was not considered a credible fear (Okrent 1981, 85). While most current analyses confirm the robustness of PV safety in youthful reactors, uncertainties are much larger for aging reactors. This was dramatically illustrated by the 1992 decision to permanently shutdown the Yankee Rowe reactor after its selection as the lead plant for NRC license extension, due in part to pressure vessel concerns (*Nucleonics Week* 2/27/92, 1). There is especially sharp debate over the ability of existing detection techniques to assess PV cracks. In April 1993 the NRC staff raised special embrittlement concern about fifteen reactors (*New York Times* 4/2/93).

PWR Steam Generator Tube Degradation: Despite more than twenty-five years of concentrated attention, steam generator tube degradation continues to plague Westinghouse reactors. The high costs of replacement (~$100–$200 million) and the relatively advanced age of some reactors (which makes renovation uneconomical), has

generated pressure for regulatory approval of reactor operation with marginally defective tubes. U.S. guidelines currently permit reactor operation with more defective
tubes than tolerated in many European nations (*Nuclear Monitor* 2/13/95, 1).

BWR Pipe Cracking (especially due to inter-granular stress corrosion cracking):
Of special concern here is the growing rejection of the adequacy of ultrasonic testing
and leak before break assumptions.

Potential Power Oscillations at BWRs at Low Power Levels: In August of 1992
the Washington Public Power Supply Unit 2 plant experienced oscillations in reactor
power from 23% to 47% every two seconds. This was the sixth incident of oscillation
at BWRs since 1988. NRC investigators worried about insufficient reactor control
and potential damage to reactor fuel and fuel rod cladding. Proposed remedies include new instrumentation and more gradual repowering from shutdowns (*Nucleonics
Week* 8/20/92, 9/3/92). Safety skeptics have found it disturbing that reactor behavior
as irregular as this should continue as late into LWR development as 1992. The
accident also raised concern about operator training, as though low power oscillation
risks were addressed in operator training, none of the operators remembered the material (*Nucleonics Week* 9/3/92).

Loss of Emergency and Potential On-Site Power: There have been several thousand incidents of at least partial failure of emergency power systems in the last
twenty years. In August 1991 an especially severe accident left the 9 Mile Point 2
plant with a common mode loss of instrument power. Operators lost feedwater system controls and monitoring capability in numerous areas, including control rod position, fire alarm indications, and most computerized monitoring functions (*Nuclear
Safety* 33 (1) January/March 1992, 103–107). Post-accident analysis found design
deficiencies, gaps in operator understanding of how to respond to the accident, and
maintenance errors (Ibid.). Plant aging is expected to exacerbate emergency power
concerns. A 1990 NRC report warned against a utility practice of reducing back-up
power redundancies by simultaneous maintenance activities (*Nuclear News* 3/92, 44–
45). The potential for unanticipated accident risks during non-standard reactor states,
such as refueling, low power, and selective maintenance is a general area of safety
concern.

A number of other hazards, such as "Anticipated Transients Without Scram"
(i.e., problems with reactor shutdown) and the loss of feedwater at Babcock and
Wilcox plants, are also cited by safety skeptics.

32. • *Fire Hazards*: The discovery of serious deficiencies in the fire barrier
material used to protect against cable tray fires (as occurred at Browns Ferry) raised
major fire hazard concerns. Echoing safety skeptic charges, a 1992 report by the
NRC's Inspector General sharply criticized the commission for failing to detect
Thermo-Lag problems earlier, noting the oversight exposed many plants to potential
common mode failures (*Nucleonics Week* 8/20/92, 9/3/92; *The Nuclear Monitor*
7/27/92, 8/28/92, 3/15/93; *Nuclear News* 3/93, 4/93). It is estimated that redressing
the hazard could cost several billion dollars.

• *The Inadequacy of Existing Monitors for Measuring BWR Core Water Levels*:
The risk here is that under certain accident conditions, reactor operators can be led to

believe that the core is covered with cooling water when it is not. A similar kind of error led reactor operators to turn off the emergency core cooling system at Three Mile Island, thereby seriously exacerbating that accident (*Nuclear Monitor* 6/7/93, *New York Times*, 6/1/93, 7/30/92, *Nucleonics Week* 1/28/93, 11/5/92 *Nuclear News* 9/92, 33).

• *The Presence of Unexpected Computer Code Interactions*: Problems at Canadian and French reactors appear to have raised new concerns about unexpected computer code interactions that can disable some computer controlled functions.

• *Rising Concern about Pressure Vessel Integrity*: New concerns surfaced as a result of serious French problems with reactor vessel head cracking at the point of control rod penetration.

• *Feedback Accidents*: This problem involves a loss of coolant accident accompanied by a loss of off-site power to the plant. The latter raises the risk of a loss of coolant to the irradiated fuel pool outside the protective enclosure of the containment building. Besides risking direct release of radioactive materials to the environment from the waste fuel pool, a fuel pool accident could interfere with the emergency cooling of the reactor core.

• *Core Shroud Cracking*: New concerns over core shroud cracking in BWRs forced the NRC in 1994 to require that all BWRs be checked for cracking (Riccio and Grynberg 1995, 16–19). Problems have been found in at least eleven plants. While the shrouds themselves have little direct safety significance, their cracking and shifting could interfere with control rod functioning and cause a meltdown (Ibid.). The shrouds deterioration has also raised new concerns about the integrity of other BWR components.

33. *Nucleonics Week* 2/27/92, *Nuclear News* 12/92, *Nucleonics Week* 8/26/93.

34. *New York Times* 2/5/92.

35. *Nucleonics Week* 7/22/93.

36. *Nucleonics Week* 12/9/93, 6.

37. The high cost of reviewing LWR safety, even for sympathetic audiences, such as the NRC, is also likely to force some operating plants into early retirement or a retreat from license extension (e.g., Monticello and Yankee Atomic). A recent probabilistic risk assessment for a PWR reactor in Germany, for example, cost more than $50 million (*Nucleonics Week* 11/12/92).

38. Especially helpful from the pro-nuclear perspective would be limitations on the EPA's influence on radiation exposure regulations, since the EPA has tended to propose stricter regulations than the NRC (see, for example, NRC 11/6/96).

39. Industry sources, for example, argue that releasing INPO's site visit and evaluative reports for specific nuclear power plants would discourage utilities from sharing current safety problems with INPO evaluators and safety experts.

40. One of the classic NIMBY examples is the problem of siting low and high level radioactive waste dumps. While the logic of eminent domain and the principles

of federalism can justify some federal pre-emption of local authority, the use of these powers to shift real economic costs (such as the perceived disamenities of radwaste disposal) to drafted shoulders is a form of nuclear subsidy. Generators of nuclear waste should offer fees large enough to induce voluntary acceptance of the waste.

41. Allison et al. (1981) provide the classic view of this debate. While lauding the theoretical payoffs to performance style regulations, they emphasize the barriers to successful implementation, noting: the difficulty of measuring performance or safety outcomes, the need for explicit safety rules in order to reassure a skeptical public of the integrity of the regulatory process, and most importantly, the problems posed by the wide variance in safety performance and management quality across the utility industry. The latter encourages regulatory designs geared towards minimizing the errors of the weakest utilities rather than towards maximizing the performance of the average utility.

Echoing Allison's skepticism, David Ward, chairman of the Advisory Committee on Reactor Safeguards has noted, "Everybody talks about performance base regulation including the (NRC) commissioners. But it's one of those things that when you say it fast sounds good, but when you get down to figuring out exactly what it is, it is proven to be very difficult . . ." (*Critical Mass* 5/93).

Recognizing the "weak-link in the chain" problem, proponents of performance regulations frequently recommend mechanisms for upgrading utility management. Most popular from the industry's point of view are self-regulation proposals. Less popular are disciplinary suggestions like those of former NRC Commissioner John Ahearne, who recommends that the NRC be permitted to divest poorly managed utilities of their nuclear plants.

Those interested in the advantages and disadvantages of performance based regulation may want to participate in an NRC internet discussion group on the application of performance based principles to fire regulation. The NRC's home page can be accessed on the internet at http://www.nrc.gov.

42. While industry generally portrays public participation, especially intervenor participation in licensing, as uninformed and obstructionist, there is much evidence to the contrary. The NRC's Special Inquiry Group report on TMI, for example, found "Intervenors have made an important impact on safety in some instances—sometimes as a catalyst in the prehearing stage of proceedings, sometimes by forcing more thorough review of an issue or improved review procedures on a reluctant agency" (Adato et al. 1987, 59). The Union of Concerned Scientists offers numerous examples of intervenor safety contributions at specific plants, for example:

- upgrades in the steam generator system at Prairie Island,

- additional requirements for turbine blade inspections at North Anna,

- improvements in the NRC's site-review process at Pilgrim 2,

- discovery of quality assurance collapses at the Zimmer, Midland, and South Texas plants,

and intervenor contributions to generic safety regulation, e.g.,

- increased attention to earthquake hazards,

- improved fire protection standards,

- improved plant security and quality control regulations (Adato 1987, 59–61).

In June of 1992 NRC Chair Ivan Selin credited nuclear watchdog groups for pushing the commission to take needed safety action at the Yankee Rowe power plant and Sequoyah nuclear fuels facility (*New York Times* 6/23/92).

43. Jim Harding, a senior technical staffer with MHB associates offers an impressive list of methodological criticisms of NRC cost benefit analyses of safety proposals, including:

- neglect of avoided site damage benefits (of potentially more than $1 billion) in calculating safety benefits,

- neglect of potential avoided accident costs beyond a fifty-mile radius in calculating safety benefits,

- underestimation of accident costs due to excessive optimism about prompt and effective accident clean-up,

- underestimation of possible spillover costs due to potential regulatory shutdowns of similar reactors (including others at the effected site),

- the assumption of containment integrity in an excessively high percentage of meltdown accidents.

Illustrating the unreasonableness of the NRC's cost/benefit accounting, Harding asserts that the commission's decision rules would make it impossible to add a containment structure to existing plants if they lacked one (assuming plants exactly like current plants except for the absence of a containment structure) (p. 104).

44. The difficulties facing licensing extension are typified by the permanent shutdown of Yankee Rowe due to concerns about pressure vessel embrittlement, after its selection as lead reactor for PWR license renewal. Efforts to demonstrate the ability of existing electrical cables to perform adequately in accident environments forty to sixty years after installation have similarly precipitated new problems for existing plants, due to the discovery of the cables' tendency to degrade after twenty or fewer years of service (Pollard 10/93). An especially contentious regulatory issue for licensing extension in the future is the degree to which newer and stricter safety regulations will be applied to older plants as a condition for license renewal.

45. A third initiative, near Carlsbad, New Mexico, pertains chiefly to defense wastes.

46. Although opposed by the nuclear industry, there has been increasing pressure from the railroads for the transport of radwaste in dedicated trains (Glickman and Golding 1991). The latter entails safeguards such as: the use of buffer cars, speed limits of 35 m.p.h., constraints on adjacent track travel, attempts to minimize train

time in switching yards, and easier route monitoring. The costs appear about 25% to 50% higher than standard service (Ibid., 12). Dedicated train requirements were imposed on TMI waste transport despite DOE opposition.

47. In 1984 the DOE projected high level waste system costs of $24 billion (1988$). By 1990 government projections had increased to $34 billion (1988$). Makhijani and Saleska argue that if declines in project scope are included, cost increases approach 100%, as projected fuel disposal costs rose from $179,000/mt to $325,000/mt (Makhijani and Saleska 1992, 65–68). While cost projections are likely to continue to rise, the per kwh impact of escalation is still likely to be modest. A 1000 MW nuclear plant generates about 25–30 mt of high level waste per year, implying a price tag of about 1.5 M/kwh (assuming 65% capacity rates). Thus even a 100% increase in costs would only add 1.5 M/kwh to total generating costs.

Not everyone agrees with this conclusion. Former NRC Commissioner John Ahearne, for example, has suggested that waste disposal planning be shifted from its current deep burial/geological strategy to surface storage with expensive compensation to the localities willing to accept the waste. He notes this may be a costly option (though how costly is not addressed) (MIT 1990, p. 7–10).

48. The EUA Power Corporation's inability to secure long term contracts for its Seabrook capacity illustrates the reluctance of customers to engage in long terms sales agreements with nuclear facilities until construction and licensing uncertainties are eliminated. This problem helped precipitate EUA Power's bankruptcy in early 1991 (DOE/EIA 0438(91), 25–26).

Chapter 10

1. Most nuclear industry supporters of passively safe reactor designs emphasize the public's unwillingness to accept LWR safety claims, rather than objective concerns about LWR safety, in arguing for design changes. Some, such as MIT Professor Lawrence Lidsky, appear to share the public's misgivings about existing reactor designs. He writes, ". . . we can draw our own lessons [from Chernobyl]. The first is that large nuclear accidents are not tolerable. . . . The second is that systems that depend on human beings consistently behaving rationally and intelligently will ultimately suffer an 'impossible' accident. . . . beyond a certain level of redundancy, defense-in-depth is worse than useless. Nuclear plants have come up against the limit. . . . Nuclear reactors require such a high level of safety that defense-in-depth becomes untenable" (Lidsky 4/91, 74).

2. Passive versions of many other reactor concepts, such as heavy water and molten salt reactors, have also been proposed, but most are in such a preliminary stage of discussion that they are unlikely to influence current debate.

3. The importance of feedback from reactor operating experience to reactor design has interesting implications. It suggests that nuclear plants should be thought of as producing a joint product, electricity and information (nuclear learning). Optimizing reactor choice thus involves the familiar goal of minimizing nuclear power costs and the additional goal of maximizing the value of new information. This shifts design attention towards evolutionary logics.

4. Assuming a .85 scaling coefficient implies that the marginal cost of unit 10x is:

[$10^{.85}$] divided by 10 as expensive as the xth unit or ~71%. While engineering studies suggest greater savings, Phung's (1984, 1987) reviews of empirical experience are consistent with a .85 MW scaling component. He is careful to note, however, that historical experience is confounded by temporal trends which may conceal larger scale economies (1984, 3). These relationships can also be very technology specific so it is somewhat risky to generalize across technologies. A gas turbine variant of the MHTGR, for example, would probably exhibit much smaller construction economies than steam cycle plants [Coxe 1988, 84).

5. In exploring the implications of learning curves for the MHTGR, Coxe (1988, 81) cites learning curve cost projections for various industry processes. Treating Cn as the cost of the nth unit produced and C1 as the cost of the first, he represents learning with the exponent $-L$, such that:

$$Cn = C1 \times N^{-L}$$

He finds typical learning exponents of:

.4 for design and management,   (25% cost reduction per and licensing and supervision doubling of output)

.15 for manufactured equipment   (10% reduction per doubling)

.07 for construction craft labor   (5% reduction per doubling)

6. Over time the terms "passive safety" and "passively safe reactor" have become increasingly imprecise. Some analysts argue that the term should only apply to reactors with natural cooling systems that require no engineered activation. Others extend the term to safety systems that need instrumentation to begin operation (such as opening valves) but no additional engineering devices (such as pumps) to continue operation. The reactors discussed in this section are of this hybrid type. I have chosen to call them semi-passive reactors.

7. Among the improvements claimed for the reactors are reduced steam generator (SG) tube corrosion due to improved tube material, easier SG maintenance due to greater access space (PWRs), the use of improved pump seals and improved control room instrumentation for the AP 600, and the removal external recirculation piping for the SBWR (*Nuclear News* 9/92, 70).

8. MHB Associates has raised technical questions about the AP-600's depressurization system, seismic sloshing of the containment spray pool, and the integrity of the spent fuel pool cooling system (3–51). The SBWR, like its big brother, the ABWR, has potential problems with core water level measurement (*New York Times* 7/29/92) and possible reactivity surges at low power levels.

Notes

Chapter 11

1. The demand for nuclear power is probably more sensitive to changes in energy and electricity demand than implied by the DOE's forecasting model. Very high energy consumption invites path choices in the direction of limitless energy sources like nuclear power. Low energy scenarios invite greater attention to renewables.

2. In the economics literature debates over energy demand projections tend to focus on three statistics: (1) the price elasticity of energy demand (the percentage change in energy demand for a percentage change in energy price); (2) the income elasticity of energy demand (the percentage change in energy demand for a percentage change in GDP) and (3) the autonomous (that is non-price related) rate of decline in the economy's BTU/GDP ratio.

Many energy demand price elasticity estimates appear to range from ~ −.4 (e.g., Manne and Richels 4/90, 58) to ~ −.9 (e.g. Williams 1990, 38). Income elasticities often range from ~.6 (e.g., Williams 1990, 38) to .9 (DOE 1990, 0438(90), p. 10). Projected rates of annual decline for the BTU/GDP ratio range from ~ −.85% (DOE 1993, 0383(93) p. 13) to −2.9% (climate stabilization case) (Alliance et al. 1991, 5). Hyman (1992) estimates the price elasticity of electricity demand at ~ −1 and the income elasticity of electricity demand at ~.8 (p. 54).

Price and income elasticity conclusions for energy and electricity demand seem very tentative in the literature. This is due to the difficulty involved with isolating the impact of these effects on past behavior. The need to distinguish between long and short run elasticities for commodities like energy that are used in conjunction with long lived capital assets seriously complicates the estimating task. Structural shifts in the way energy is used in the economy (especially in the aftermath of the OPEC price shocks and environmental movement) have weakened the inferences that can be drawn from past behavioral data. The long time horizons involved with many energy demand forecasts also undermines the ability to base predictions on past relationships.

3. Alliance et al. 1991, 44; Goldemberg et al. 1988, 166–179; ORNL 1989, 37.

4. Low estimate (2,453 TWH) from Alliance et al. 1991, 91–94, "aggressive climate stabilization case"; high estimate (6,200 TWH) from the Bush administration's National Energy Strategy, "frozen policies case." Debates over projected changes in annual electricity use range from declines of .5%/yr to increases of 2.5%/yr.

5. While often not as optimistic as Lovins, many other engineering studies also find large conservation potentials. The Electric Power Research Institute, for example, found that energy efficiency investments could replace 25% of current kwhs at costs less than 4 c/kwh (Fickett et al. 1990, 15). Similar assessments of conservation potentials are found in recent studies by the EPA, Congressional Office of Technology Assessment, National Academy of Sciences, and numerous environmental groups.

6. Using the bottom-up approach Lovins and/or EPRI analysts Fickett and Gellings estimate that: (1) 20% of recent U.S. electricity-use could be saved at costs of less than 1 cent/kwh by replacing 80%–90% of lighting electricity with energy efficiency measures (Fickett et al. 1990, 15); (2) another 15%–20% of current use could be saved at costs less than 4 c/kwh through energy efficiency investments to reduce heating and cooling needs (Lovins and Lovins 1991, 5); and an additional 12% of current use could be saved at costs of less than 1 c/kwh, by using more efficient electric motors (Ibid, 6–9).

7. For good examples of top-down criticisms of bottom-up approaches, see Joskow and Marron 1992, Sutherland 1991, and Katzman 10/89.

8. Joskow and Marron (1992), for example, argue that utility estimates of the costs of existing DSM projects probably understate program costs by a factor of at least two (p. 70). They note also that analyses of residential weatherization programs in the Pacific Northwest showed energy savings of only 50%–80% of estimations from engineering models (p. 63).

9. For example, Amory and Hunter Lovins report that Southern California Edison's energy conservation program had administrative costs (.5 M/kwh) that were one to two orders of magnitude less than smaller and/or poorly managed efficiency programs (Lovins and Lovins 1991, 3).

10. A 1989 Oak Ridge National Laboratory study, for example, concluded:

"The technical potential for economical improvements in the efficiency of energy use is large, and an expanded R&D effort can increase the potential significantly" (ORNL 1989, xxi).

Fickett et al. found in 1991 that:

"in the past five years the potential to save electricity has about doubled, whereas the average cost of saving a kilowatt-hour has fallen by about two-thirds. . . . [M]ost of the best efficient technologies are less than a year old" (p. 13).

11. See for example, ORNL 1989; Katzman 1989, 11, and Cherfas 1991, 155.

12. Led by declines in the utilities' investment tax credit and accelerated depreciation allowances, energy supply subsidies have fallen modestly from their $30–$50 billion/year level in the mid-eighties. The most important energy tax outcome in the last several years has been the defeat of the Clinton administration's proposed BTU tax, which would have reduced energy consumption by several percent. Major new initiatives in energy tax and subsidy policy seem unlikely in the foreseeable future.

13. The environmentalist pressures that culminated in the 1990 Clean Air Act Amendments (which highlighted energy sector pollution) are likely to continue. Both Pace University's study, *Environmental Costs of Electricity*, and later reports by the Union of Concerned Scientists and a number of environmental groups (Alliance et al. 1991, 1992), for example, recently found large negative externalities persisting in the energy sector. There is a growing backlash, however, that finds negative cost/benefit

ratios for many environmental protection measures. (See for example the environmental series in the *New York Times* 3/21–3/26/93.) The most likely policy outcome is stricter environmental standards in the energy sector, but a moderation in externality driven energy cost increases due to efforts to meet environmental objectives more efficiently. The DOE's Office of Energy Research has estimated that new externality adjustments could add "5% or more" to electricity costs. The National Coal Council has projected potential cost increases of 10%–24% (*Nucleonics Week* 3/25/93, 9, 13).

The forecasting implications for electricity generation would seem to tilt demand predictions modestly (perhaps −5%) towards lower consumption levels than DOE/industry projections. The major wild card in the externality area is global warming. The uncertainties it introduces into energy forecasting are discussed in chapter 13.

14. Government regulations currently require minimum levels of energy efficiency for a number of products. There is vigorous debate over the merits and effectiveness of such regulations, especially "technology-forcing-regulations" that set future requirements beyond existing capabilities. Corporate Average Fuel Efficiency (CAFE) standards have probably spurred the most controversy. Supporters of CAFE, like the Union of Concerned Scientists foresee the possibility of increasing new car fuel efficiency from the current average of 28 mpg to 46 mpg over the next ten years at a cost of ~50 cents per gallon of gas saved (i.e. a net financial gain to the motorist) (Alliance et al. 1991, 20). Skeptics call for MPG outcomes to be left to the market. Efforts by environmentalists to increase mpg requirements in the 1992 energy bill were blocked by the auto industry.

In 1987 the National Appliance Energy Conservation Act (NAECA) set minimum energy efficiency standards for thirteen appliances. The requirements were expected to reduce energy demand by 2.8 Quads per annum by 2015 (OTA 1991, 56). The American Council for an Energy Efficient Economy estimated that the Act would reduce U.S. residential electricity demand by 21 GW or .9 Quads by the year 2000 (Ibid.). The 1992 Energy Policy Act upgraded energy efficiency requirements for incandescent and fluorescent lamps, utility transformers, heating and cooling equipment for commercial buildings, and electric motors (*Power Line* 11–12/92, 9). The legislation also contained new energy efficiency requirements for federal and state building codes. Future initiatives might further reduce energy demand.

15. From 1974 to 1990 energy supply R&D received fifteen times the funding support of energy conservation R&D (Congressional Research Services Issue Brief 87140, R&D outlays table). Narum (1992) indicates that the Reagan administration also replaced staff members at DOE who wished to intervene in energy markets to promote increased energy efficiency with analysts touting a more free market and/or energy supply side focus.

Partially due to past neglect, energy efficiency enthusiasts foresee large payoffs to increased R&D for energy conservation. The Union of Concerned Scientists, for example, calls for two-thirds of all energy R&D to be allocated to energy efficiency research by the year 2000 (Alliance et al. 1991, 113). Conservation enthusiasts also hope that changes in federal policy will alert the private sector to the potential benefits of energy efficiency research (much like the impact of federal endorsement of nuclear power on private research agendas). One manifestation of this possibility is the "golden carrot" program. The latter involves the EPA and about two dozen utilities that have banded together to fund a $30 million bounty program for the development of a refrigerator that could reduce electricity consumption by half (*Amicus* Spring 1993, 49; *Technology Review* 2–3/93, 13). The payoffs to the utilities involve potential Demand Side Management credits as noted below.

16. The demand for electricity and new generating capacity is especially sensitive to the structure of utility rate regulations. Within the traditional "regulated monopoly"—framework of electricity generation, the most important issues involved: (1) the incentives or disincentives for new energy supply investments (through inducements such as guaranteed Construction Work In Progress funding, or disincentives such as aggressive prudency review); (2) the incentives for energy efficiency investments created by Demand Side Management programs and "Least Cost" and/or "Integrated Resource Planning" requirements; and (3) rate reforms that would have shifted electricity pricing from average to marginal cost pricing (and taken advantage of peak load pricing to reduce generating capacity needs).

Due to recent regulatory changes which allow electric utilities to earn profits on expenditures that increase the energy efficiency of customers' electricity use, Demand Side Management (DSM) has become a major factor in reducing the level of future electricity demand. In 1992, the DOE projected annual utility DSM expenditures of $3 billion by the year 2000, with 6% projected reductions in the utilities' required generating capacity (*DOE, Annual Energy Outlook 1992*, 40). By 1993 the DOE had increased its estimate of expected DSM savings to 10% capacity reductions (*DOE, Annual Energy Outlook 1993*, p. x). Eric Hirst, a researcher at Oak Ridge National Laboratory, has suggested that aggressive DSM programs could leave electricity consumption in 2010 19% below earlier DOE projections (*Public Utilities Fortnightly* 7/1/91, 32). Impacts are likely to be greatest on peak load demands.

There remain, however, some unanswered questions about the economics of energy efficiency investments (see for example, Joskow and Marron 1992, McCaughey and Meyers 1993). It is similarly unclear if aggressive DSM programs such as that of PG&E of California should be treated as state-of-the-art programs, to be adopted within a decade by the rest of the industry, or idiosyncratic outliers. Within the emerging "market oriented"-structure of electricity generation, the regulation of negative externalities and the terms of grid access for cogenerators are among the major factors likely to influence energy demand levels.

17. As the nation's largest energy consumer, the federal government can effect national energy demand by its own energy efficiency practices. Through the early 1990s, most government agencies had not pursued energy efficiency opportunities very aggressively (OTA 5/91, 3). There appears to have been little participation in utility DSM programs and minimal direct investment in energy efficient options (Nader et al. 11/8/91, 3–4). While a 4/91 executive order called for a 20% reduction in energy use in federal buildings by the year 2000, no funds were provided to finance initial adjustments (Alliance et al. 1991, 111). Many observers anticipate large long-run payoffs to modest short run outlays. Many energy efficiency enthusiasts have also urged that government procurement policies be used to stimulate the market

for state-of-the-art energy efficient products (Alliance et al. 1991, 111). Dr. Arthur Rosenfield of Lawrence Berkeley Laboratory, for example, has emphasized the importance of government purchases of energy efficient equipment for capturing critical mass economies (*Power Line* 5–6/92). Representatives of the Energy Efficiency Clearinghouse have pointed to the key role of early government purchases in spurring markets for air bags, less noise polluting equipment, and generic drugs, in urging similar pump priming for energy efficient products (Nader, Lewis, and Weltman, 11/8/91).

18. The most important infrastructural planning decisions involve policies towards mass transit and the automobile. A coalition of environmentalist groups have forecast that greater government support for mass transit, incentives for ride sharing and bicycling, disincentives for auto travel (such as higher parking fees and mileage-based insurance rates) and "Mixed-Use Infill"-land development strategies could cut vehicle miles traveled by nearly 20% by 2030 (Alliance et al. 1992, C7–C14). High speed intercity trains are also cited as potential conservation options. Major initiatives in this area seem unlikely.

19. The increase in electricity costs from 7 c/kwh to 8 c/kwh from a doubling of fossil fuel prices assumes: utility delivered coal costs of ~$1.42/MMBTU, natural gas costs of ~$2.10/MMBTU, coal and natural gas generating efficiencies of 38%, a 54% coal share of electricity output, 10% natural gas share, and 5% oil share (w/oil assumed to mirror natural gas in price and generating efficiency). All of the above numbers reflect averages for the first six months of 1992 (DOE, *Monthly Energy Review* 10/92).

20. Robert Williams, for example, estimates that nearly half of the 3.5% per year decline in industrial energy/GDP (1973–1985) was due to structural shifts within the industrial sector towards less energy intensive activities and expects such declines to continue (Williams 1990, 36–39). A Union of Concerned Scientists' energy study reaches similar conclusions (Alliance et al. 1991, 60).

21. Among the evidence cited for maintaining the GDP/Electricity link are: (1) the historical record from 1973–1991 during which time GDP grew 48%, total energy consumption 10%, non-electric energy consumption −6% and electricity consumption 61% (Fertel, 3/16/93 M.I.T. seminar); (2) the continued electrification of industry; (3) the development and wide diffusion of new electronics products based on computer technology, high speed electronic information networks, and robotics; and (4) the growth of interest in the electric car.

22. A high end estimate by the Electric Power Research Institute, for example, of the electricity needs of information technologies by 2010, would add less than 1 GW/year to required generating capacity (*EPRI Journal* 4–5/92, 15).

23. Electrification of light vehicle transportation would open a large new market for the electricity sector. Williams calculates that 270 GW of nuclear capacity would be necessary by 2010 to meet the derived demand for light vehicle power if all of those miles (~2.67 trillion per DOE projections) were driven in nuclear-generated electric powered cars and light trucks (Williams, 10/93 draft, 16).

California's environmental statutes requiring that 10% of all cars sold by a manufacturer in California be zero emission vehicles by 2003 is currently the major force propelling the electric vehicle market. If we assume a 5% national share of light vehicle miles for electric cars in 2010, this translates into a potential nuclear market of 13–14 GW. As Williams (10/93) makes clear, there are good reasons for suspecting that nuclear power will have very strong competition in a gasoline constrained transportation sector from wind, photovoltaic, natural gas, and biomass powered vehicles (see chapter 12). Nevertheless, the growth of electric cars could provide a major impetus for reexamining nuclear power.

Chapter 12

1. See subsequent sections of this chapter for the calculations and references supporting the overview's cost and capacity estimates.

2. Natural gas combustion produces minimal sulfur dioxide and particulate emissions. Although uncontrolled NO_x discharges can be relatively high, they can be reduced by 85%–90% (to about 15% of a contemporary coal-fired plant), with available technology. While gas combustion generates a few other pollutants, the hazards accompanying projected emission levels appear modest. Concerns have also been raised about pipeline and drilling disruption of wilderness areas and the general impact of hazardous drilling fluids.

3. Grubb et al. 1991, Appendix 1.

4. Fears of dependence on suppliers such as Algeria generated regulatory opposition to expanded LNG imports in the 1970s (Stobaugh and Yergin 1979, 70; Pirog and Stamos 1987, 128).

5. Grubb et al. 1991, 93; National Research Council 1991, 6–16. The National Research Council's 1991 Greenhouse Mitigation report noted that "Combined cycle systems have not been considered a serious option in the planning of future power generation until very recently, largely because of the uncertainty in the availability of natural gas and the poor reliability of GTCC systems in the past. The latter was not due to inherent technical barriers but to a lack of attention from the industry" (6–6).

6. The DOE, for example, projects utility CC capacity to increase from ~6 GW in 1990 to ~55 GW 2015. Further CC growth may be part of the projected increase in non-utility natural gas capacity from 19 GW to 75 GW over same period (DOE, *Annual Energy Outlook 1993*, 87; *Annual Energy Outlook 1996*, Table A9).

7. Williams 1989, 5, 1990, 41; ORNL 1989, 73; *EPRI Journal* 4–5/88, 8.

8. Among the most promising technological options are Intercooled Steam Injected Gas Turbine [ISTIG] plants, chemically recuperated gas turbines, and the development of the Kalina cycle. In the spring of 1993 the DOE announced a new four-

year program to "leapfrog the 1990s class of gas turbines" and achieve 60% or higher energy conversion efficiencies.

9. Assuming 45%–50% conversion efficiencies for new natural gas plants, implies 23–25 GW of replaced nuclear power capacity per quad of natural gas consumed in the electricity sector. Assuming gas consumption levels of 27 Quads in 2010, would allow recent revisions in projected natural gas consumption to replace the entire electrical output of the nuclear sector (assuming nuclear capacity rates of 65%). In practice, of course, all of the gas would not be used for electricity markets.

10. Cost calculations based on assumptions detailed in table 12.1.

11. 2015 gas price forecast from DOE *Annual Energy Outlook 1996*, Table A3. The per kwh calculations assume a Combined Cycle plant in 2015 and/or a Chemically Recuperated Gas Turbine plant, per table 12.1.

12. Chris Flavin of Worldwatch suggests that widespread shifts to gas-fired micro-cogeneration may significantly reduce the economy's reliance on central power stations in the future (private communication 11/96).

13. Competition from gas-fired IPPs is also expected to become more intense after many of these smaller companies have paid off relatively high priced mortgages on newly constructed plants (private conversation with IPP producer).

14. Analyses of inter-fuel competition often stress the occupational health and accident burdens of coal-fired power generation. While conventional neoclassical economic theory maintains that these occupational "costs" of mining are internalized in the cost of coal (as they implicitly enter into labor market outcomes), various market imperfections, such as, imperfect information and institutional barriers to labor mobility, and unequal inheritances across families leave such assumptions questionable guides for policy. Thus it is proper to add additional charges to coal use to reflect uncompensated accident and health burdens.

15. FBC technologies suspend crushed coal with limestone atop jets of air and can remove more than 90% SO_2 and ~80% NO_x, with potentially lower generating costs than conventional coal power plants. While atmospheric FBC technology is the most well developed FBC option, pressurized FBC plants hold out the most promise. Because of the opportunity for combined cycle applications, PFBC plants can achieve higher energy conversion efficiencies (up to 45%) than AFBC plants. PFBC boilers can also be factory manufactured and shipped by barge due to their smaller size (*Chemical and Engineering News* 6/17/91; ORNL 1989, 76–7). Among current R&D challenges is to insure that the hot gas from the combustor is clean enough to avoid corroding turbine blades.

16. IGCC plants are projected to operate at 42% energy conversion efficiencies, remove 99% SO_2, produce one-sixth the NO_x emissions of a conventional coal plant with scrubbers, and produce electricity at costs as low as 4.5–5.5 c/kwh (see tables 12.2 and 12.3). As noted earlier, some utilities are reserving space in new natural gas plants for coal gasifiers as insurance against unexpected natural gas price increases. There are several potential variations for burning gasified coal including Steam In-

jected Gas Turbines (STIG), and Intercooled Steam Injected Gas Turbines (see tables 12.2 and 12.3) that mimic their natural gas cousins.

Other coal R&D options include research on: magnetohydrodynamic generation, the Kalina cycle, carboniferous fuel cells, a coal-fired combined cycle plant relying on hot air as the turbine inlet gas, mining innovations and land restoration technologies.

17. See, for example: DOE 3/92; Fulkerson et al. 1990, and Torrens 7/8/90.

18. Some states have also funded coal R&D. Montana, for example, has appropriated $50 million for the development of a magnetohydrodynamic coal generating plant (*Chemical and Engineering News* 6/17/91).

19. The widespread expectation of rising oil prices has been strongly criticized by Michael Lynch of MIT's Center for International Studies ("The Fog of Commerce: The Failure of Long-Term Oil Market Forecasting," Sept. 1992). Lynch argues that current modeling and forecasting exercises *assume* rather than deduce rising prices and are largely driven by Malthusian hypotheses rather than by empirical evidence. He argues that herd behavior in oil price forecasting imparts the illusion of scientific consensus to interdependent rather than independent studies. (See *New York Times* 9/26/95, B-5, B-38 for recent evidence consistent with Lynch's optimism about oil reserves.) Despite Lynch's warning, risk aversion counsels assuming oil scarcity.

20. Biomass sources are also employed in "waste to energy" projects, such as landfill-generated biogas projects and over 125 municipal waste burning projects. Biomass serves as the feedstock for gasahol.

21. The constant high temperature of gas turbine combustion minimizes the release of incompletely burned organic pollutants. Existing wood stoves can raise problems with respect to particulate emissions, though design measures appear able to minimize most hazards.

22. The National Research Council's greenhouse mitigation study (1991) for example, found that existing ethanol production produces about 80% of gasoline's CO_2 emissions due to the use of CO_2–producing inputs in its production (especially diesel fuel for planting and harvesting, natural gas for nitrogen fertilizer preparation, and coal power for grinding and processing) (p. 6–8).

23. Hall et al. (1993) note that more than 20% of U.S. farmland (33 million hectares) is currently idled to reduce erosion and/or maintain agricultural prices. This total is projected to increase to 52 million hectares by 2030 due to increasing agricultural productivity, despite a doubling in export of corn, wheat, and soybeans (638). Excess capacity is also projected for European markets. The Solar Energy Research Institute noted that "The New Farm and Forest Products Task Force report to the Secretary of Agriculture indicates that new crops will be needed for 150 million acres of existing cropland that will be surplus as the result of improving productivity of current crops and slowing demand during the next twenty-five years. Based on the 1982 National Resources Inventory, an additional 150 million acres of land are now in pasture, range, and forest that are capable of supporting crop production." (SERI 1990 B-5).

24. Among promising avenues for biomass feedstock research are: (1) characterization, breeding, and genetic engineering projects on short-rotation trees and fast growing grasses; (2) exploration of micro algae resources; (3) inquiries into the availability of off-season energy crops (Brower 1992, 94); and (4) the development of harvesting equipment for energy crops.

25. Among the most promising areas for research in biomass utilization are: (1) whole tree burners; (2) turbine blade cooling and hot gas clean-up for biomass gasification generating systems; (3) fluidized bed gasifiers; and (4) biomass-based fuel cells, which are projected by some observers to approach 55% energy conversion efficiencies by 2020 (Williams and Larson 1993, 760). Another promising research agenda involves joint product optimization, that is the design of production processes to use the waste vegetation attendant with the production of products like alcohol and sugar for energy production.

26. There are some aspects of biomass systems that are different from their fossil fuel cousins and so require more specialized attention. Hot gas clean-up problems, for example, are dominated by alkalis rather than sulfur contamination (Williams and Larson 1993, 744–749).

27. OTA 7/91, 101; Williams 1990, *EPRI Journal* 12/92.

28. Swezey and Wan 1996, 10; SERI 1990, F-5, F-3; Williams 10/93, 6; Cavallo 1993, 65.

29. Wind power varies as a cube of wind velocity. The latter is quite sensitive to small differences in site characteristics. This leaves the economics of wind energy very site specific.

30. The current variance in wind system performance makes assessment of empirical data difficult. It is extremely tempting for wind optimists to treat successful wind farms as statements of future industry averages. Paul Gipe writes, for example, ". . . the industry produced a capacity factor of 16% during 1987. At least one-fourth of the industry delivers capacity factors of about 20%. And one wind plant has consistently achieved a capacity factor of 30% indicating what is reasonably attainable from turbines already in place at good sites during coming years with normal winds and no unexpected downtime" (Gipe 1989, 11). As in the nuclear industry, only time will tell whether such reproducibility is possible.

31. A 1990 SERI study finds that accessible resources are capable of providing more than ten times current electricity output (F-1). Also see: Williams 1990, 47 and Cavallo 1993, 74.

32. SERI 1990, F-9; assuming 33% energy conversion efficiency and 5.694 Bkwh/yr. per nuclear plant (i.e., 65% capacity rates).

33. See, for example: Abelson 1993, 1255; *New York Times* 9/8/92, C-6; and Cavallo 1993, 98.

34. Noise pollution has fallen significantly since the mid-seventies, with new designs offering only slightly louder sounds than background wind sounds (Grubb

and Meyer 1993, 173; Weinberg and Williams 1990, 109). Technical fixes such as cable television connections or local amplification can protect television reception. While some concern has been raised in Altamont pass over bird kills, the problem seems modest (e.g., one golden eagle and one other bird of prey killed per month), in comparison with the 1 to 1.25 million birds killed annually from collisions with radio and television towers (Gipe 1989, 18). U.S. Windpower, the leading U.S. windmill manufacturer, has been experimenting with painting turbine blades with stripes to reduce bird collisions (*New York Times* 9/8/92, C-6).

The Pace University study of the environmental hazards of electricity generation equates the non-radiological hazards of nuclear plant construction with those of windmill construction (442), which seems to involve conventional materials without special hazards.

35. Estimates of wind power's land needs vary widely. A mid-seventies study implying ~135 acres/MW seems to have been widely cited (Brower 1992, 84). Other studies imply significantly lower ratios, for example: Ottinger 1990: 15–45 acres/MW (p. 437) and Paul Gipe: 15–80 acres/MW, with most projects occupying less than 15 acres/MW (California data) (Gipe 1989, 15, 1991, p. 763).

36. Gipe (1991) finds that dual use wind systems typically absorb less that 5%– 15% of the land defined by wind arrays (p. 764). Grubb and Meyer (1993) note that in Europe, as little as 1% of the land involved in wind farming is actually occupied by wind generating equipment (p. 173). See also Abelson 1993, 1255 and Williams 10/93, 10.

37. Jim Manwell, a leading windmill technologist, indicates that siting problems have been very serious in New England (private communication, 1993). Recent protests against siting a wind farm on a barren ridge in Washington State echo these problems. Many participants in the latter protests were partisans of nuclear power (Asmus 1994, 30–31).

38. Survey results suggest that wind farms with homogeneous kinds of windmills arrayed in geometric patterns are more popular with the public than heterogeneous machines scattered about the landscape. The sight of stagnant blades in varied positions seems especially objectionable to many viewers (Gipe 1989, 1991, 7). Danish and Dutch experience suggests large numbers of windmills can be assimilated into the countryside without aesthetic insult (Grubb 1990, 171), though even in the Netherlands there have recently been bitter controversies over windmill sitings (*World Watch* 3–4/93, 35).

39. The adaptation of variable speed drive technology to wind applications was facilitated by the small scale of wind technologies (their optimal unit size appears .2–.5 MW (Cavallo 1993, 81) and recent breakthroughs in similar technologies in other fields (Williams 10/93, 5). A key step in the development process was a $20 million joint venture involving two private utilities (PG&E and Niagara Mohawk), EPRI, and U.S. Windpower. Before anti-nuclear shifts in political and regulatory climates, both utilities had been aggressive backers of nuclear power.

40. For a short time in the 1980s, the wind industry enjoyed 15% National Energy Act tax credits, 10% Investment Tax credits, and 25% California state tax credits (Gipe 1989, 3–4).

41. A 1995 ruling by the Federal Energy Regulatory Commission (FERC) nullifying California's plan to include environmental burdens in avoided cost calculations for different energy options may weaken the market payoffs to wind power's environmental friendliness. The DOE, for example, reduced its 1996 wind capacity forecast by 927 MW due to the FERC ruling (Zucchet 1996, 3; DOE, *Annual Energy Outlook 1996*, 36).

42. An interesting aside, several years after a ballot referendum shut down the Sacramento Municipal Utility District's Rancho Seco nuclear plant, which had been generating electricity at ~8 c/kwh in the mid-eighties (excluding amortization of sunk capital costs!), the utility was offered a guaranteed 4.2 c/kwh power contract by an independent wind power producer (Ed Smeloff, 3/26–27/94 conference remarks).

43. Nix (1996) suggests that improvements in wind forecasting "can potentially result in a situation in which the output of one wind plant can increase when the output of another decreases because of wind fluctuations" (p. 6). He cites recent research that found a payoff as high as one to two cents/kwh from smoothing out wind power fluctuations through better siting choices (p. 6).

44. The economics of intermittency is still in an early stage of analysis. The issue is complicated by many factors, including a need to examine the match between supply and demand variability and the character of complementary supply options. Kelly and Weinberg (1993) argue that intermittents can supply up to one-third of a utility's electricity with minimal intermittency penalties (1011). A 1991 study coauthored by the Union of Concerned Scientists projected a 1.5 c/kwh cost penalty for very high reliance on intermittents due to increased energy storage costs (Alliance et al. 1991b, p. E-11). Intermittency issues are addressed in more detail in section 7's discussion of solar energy.

45. Paul Gipe writes, ". . . viewers see wind plants through more than their aesthetic eye. They incorporate a set of values which they use to judge the view. Several researchers have noted that social values play a role . . . 'windfarms can be seen as symbolic of "higher" concepts, such as "stewardship," "renewable energy," . . . or "ugly technology"'" (Gipe 1989, 23; citing Thayer 1988).

46. There are a few other kinds of solar energy systems, such as solar ponds and satellite solar, but these are not expected to have significant short or long run impacts.

47. From 1974 to 1990 PV systems received $990 million, ST systems $842 million, and solar building systems $651 million in R&D support (mixed current dollars, Sisine 1991). Nuclear fission received ~$14 billion over the same period (Ibid.).

48. Solar hot water heating is another popular option, but generally involves much higher costs than the structural changes cited above.

49. The major factors determining the level of deployment of solar building technologies are likely to be government policy and energy price expectations. Public policy is likely to influence adoption rates through building codes, cultural movements that influence architectural training and imaginations, public information programs, the tax treatment of solar additions, and DSM treatment of residential solar investments.

50. PV applications for remote sites may be a larger market than anticipated. In March 1991, for example, the Electric Power Research Institute's journal (*EPRI Journal*) estimated that the utilities could cost effectively install 40,000 PV units for a combined capacity of 11.5 GW on their systems (p. 35).

51. The greater long run popularity of PV technologies seems partially a reflection of a technological aesthetic that finds the elegance of direct solar conversion to electricity more promising than thermal-steam systems. PV technologies, for example, hold the hope of incorporating solar collectors into regular roofing materials. Some interesting commercial projects are already under way with solar roofing tiles (Private communication with Chris Flavin 11/96).

52. Flat-plate PV module costs fell from from $20/peak watt in 1976 to $6.20 peak watt in 1990 (Kelly 1993, 300). Capital costs for solar thermal's parabolic trough technology fell from ~6,000/KW to ~3,000/KW, with 20% gains in expected efficiencies in the 1980s (Brower 1992, 51–52).

53. See Johansson et al. 1993b for excellent discussions of various research options. The December 1992 *EPRI Journal* and Flavin and Lenssen (1994), chapter 8, also offer optimistic analyses of R&D avenues to competitive PV power.

54. Among recent unexpected problems has been the degradation of high concentration PVs after initial illumination. Though most of the problem has been overcome, current solutions still involve some reductions in PV efficiency. (*EPRI Journal* 12/92, 19). There may also have been more persistent maintenance problems with rooftop moisture than expected.

55. The Enron plant will be more than twelve times the size of the largest existing PV plant. Its low costs are tied to: (1) economies of scale in PV production from a linked PV factory; (2) new thin film PV cell technology; and (3) government incentives (including access to government land, current RET tax breaks, and a guaranteed market (i.e., long term contracts) for the plant's output (*New York Times* 11/15/94, C1). "Size is key, says Sigurd Wagner, a professor of electrical engineering at Princeton University. 'If a good group of people puts a plant of that scale in, it will have a real consequence on costs . . . It's not going to go down by just a little bit, but by a factor of two'" (Ibid., C2).

56. Challenging traditional rules of thumb that limited the efficient use of intermittents to 10% electricity generation, Kelly and Weinberg argue that intermittents can supply up to 33% of a utility's electricity without significant intermittency penalties (Kelly and Weinberg 1993, 1011). They offer a detailed analysis of PG&E's supply options to back up their claims. Michael Grubb maintains that large integrated power systems could rely on intermittents for over half of their energy without suffer-

ing large cost burdens (Grubb 1990, 170). Grubb finds that more pessimistic assessments reflect a priori intuitions rather than concrete analysis (Grubb 9/91).

57. Both geopressured brines and magma (partially or fully molten rock) offer enormous long run energy supplies. The conventional energy portion of geopressured brines (dissolved natural gas) was alluded to in the discussion of natural gas. The GT part consists of the brine's high temperatures (130–260 degrees C) and hydraulic pressure (2,500–3,500 pounds per square inch) (Brower 1992, 138). If 5% of the geopressured brines found in sandstone could be recovered, the resource base would be as large as the U.S.'s proven oil and natural gas reserves (Brower 1992, 139). Shale laden brines are thought to hold ten times the energy of sandstone reservoirs but would be harder to mine.

58. Good sites defined as sites with thermal gradients of 80 degrees C/km); medium sites- 50 degrees C/km, and poor sites- 30 degrees C/km (Brower 1992, 145).

59. Tester and Herzog 1991, 37; Brower 1992, 139; *Power Line* 9–10/92, 8.

60. The use of thermal spallation (gas jets to penetrate rocks) rather than conventional bit drilling is one of the most promising avenues of drilling research.

61. Brower 1992, 146–7; Tester and Herzog 1991, 57–58.

62. SERI 1990, A-11, based on capital costs of ~$2335, capacity rates of 45%, and O&M costs of 6 M/kwh.

63. Funding for low head hydro R&D averaged only $300,000/yr. over the 1987–1991 period (Sisine 1991, 6). The 1990 SERI study foresees a potential increase of 5 GW/yr. from low head hydro with small increases in R&D (A-5). The EPA suggests a potential resource of about 10 GW (EPA 1989, vii–156). Brower notes that despite these claims, recent experience with low head hydro has been disappointing (Brower 1992, 116).

64. Oak Ridge Lab, for example, saw attractive payoffs to research on stream flow and dam bypass technologies that would maintain fish populations in rivers with hydro facilities (ORNL 1989, 81).

Chapter 13

1. Statistics on fossil fuel contributions to global warming are sensitive to the time frame considered. The longer the period, the more important are fossil fuels, due to the long atmospheric lifespan of CO_2.

2. *ORNL Review* 22(4) 1989, 128.

3. Keepin and Kats 1988a, 31. See also Grubb 1990, 67. Greenhouse concerns were similarly one of the reasons cited by the Trilateral Commission in September 1996 for urging expanded use of nuclear power (*Nucleonics Week* 9/12/96).

4. The issue of thermal feedback is probably the central issue in climate change debates. As greenhouse optimist Richard Lindzen of MIT notes, there is a popular consensus that a doubling of CO_2 would cause temperature increases of .5–1.2 degrees C without feedback effects (Lindzen 3/92, 4). While non-trivial, these increases are significantly smaller than the 1.5–4.5 degree C range commonly cited by the same authors after feedback effects. Among the major uncertainties in feedback debates are:

A) Uncertainties about the dynamics of atmospheric feedback, especially whether the increased cloud formation expected to accompany global warming will dampen or exacerbate warming.

B) Uncertainties about ice cap behavior; for example, will ice cap size decrease due to melting (and offer positive feedback by reducing surface reflectivity) or will ice cap size increase due to accelerated evaporation, higher air moisture, and increased snowcover?

C) Uncertainties over the likelihood of warming induced methane releases from permafrost and submerged oceanic clathrates.

D) Uncertainties about the behavior of carbon sinks, (for example, uncertainties about the impact of increased CO_2 on forest growth or the impact of global warming on nitrogen levels in the ocean and phytoplankton growth).

5. Close study of major scientific analyses of greenhouse hazards, such as the Intergovernmental Panel on Climate Change's report in 1990 or the U.S. National Academy of Sciences' study of the "Policy Implications of Greenhouse Warming" in 1991, reveals greater technical uncertainty about the impact of GHG emissions than the studies' language of consensus might suggest. The same curious divergence seems to accompany public and private discussions of climate change. The reconciling feature may be the risk aversion of climatologists which leads to presentations that highlight the potential dangers lurking in the uncertainties. Observers like Richard Lindzen of MIT have attacked the language of climatology reports as alarmist for this style of presentation. The charge resurfaced with a vengeance in mid-1996 after the second IPCC report on global warming was released (see, for example, *New York Times* 7/6/96). The majority of researchers strongly reject Lindzen's dismissal of warming dangers, but seem to acknowledge that uncertainties are larger than frequently emphasized.

The policy recommendations of the major global conferences on climate change have called for serious cutbacks in GHG emissions. The 1988 Toronto conference on global warming, for example, called for 20% reductions in CO_2 by 2005, and 50% reductions in the long run. The 1992 Rio Environmental Treaty called for capping industrial nations' GHG emissions at 1990 levels by the year 2000. The Berlin accords of early 1995 set a two-year deadline for setting stricter global emission standards.

6. Nordhaus concludes that damages from sea level rise dominate the cost calculations. Because some regions are expected to benefit from higher temperatures, shifting rainfall patterns, and increased ambient CO_2 levels, and because technical fixes are assumed for many weather-related problems in negatively affected regions, greenhouse impacts on agriculture are found to be minimal (Nordhaus 1991a, 932).

Risks such as ecosystem disruption and reduced biodiversity are not addressed. Also excluded is the impact of climate change on the pleasantness of everyday life. Nordhaus suggests, however, that warming may bring "major amenity benefits" (932).

7. The calculation requires estimates of: the retention rate of GHG emissions in the atmosphere, the equilibrium temperature change caused by a change in GHG concentrations, the adjustment path from an initial state to a new equilibrium temperature (i.e., the lag structure), a decay function for the atmospheric lifetime of GHGs, a damage function linking temperature changes to economic costs, and a discount rate that translates future damages into current dollars. Combining these estimates, it is possible to differentiate a damage function for changes in GHG concentrations. (See Nordhaus 1991a and Cline 1992a.)

8. The claim of .256 kgC/kwh coal-fired generation assumes: (a) one metric ton of coal [mt] = ~27.8 million BTU; (b) .694 mt carbon/mt coal; (c) coal electric energy conversion efficiency equals 33.3% (implying 10, 239 BTU/kwh). See chapter 12 for a discussion of projected technological innovations that would reduce Carbon emissions to .2 kg C/kwh.

9. ORNL 5/89, Appendix C, p. C-6. Looking at the 40% CO_2 savings accompanying shifts from coal to natural gas, one need note that a 3% to 4% leakage during methane transport and use would nullify the greenhouse advantage of natural gas, as the latter is twenty times as potent a GHG as coal over a one-hundred-year time horizon.

10. For purposes of comparison, a \$40/tC tax implies about a 11.5 cents per gallon gasoline tax.

11. The analysis also ignores greenhouse gas emissions from other aspects of coal and nuclear-fired electricity production than power plant fuel use (such as energy inputs to uranium and coal mining and uranium fuel enrichment). It would be necessary to employ an input-output matrix to derive a complete kgC/kwh ratio.

12. This assumes an increase in coal conversion efficiencies for new plants from 33% to 42%, per discussion in chapter 12.

13. For example, assuming a 3.5 degree Centigrade temperature increase from CO_2 doubling (the high end of the IPCC's 1995 projections), and Cline's "high" rather than "baseline" estimate for the economic consequences of temperature increases, implies warming damages about four times Nordhaus' estimate.

14. Ottinger 1990, 25–26; *Critical Mass Energy Bulletin, 3/90*, 5. While some nuclear critics warn that GHG burdens could increase dramatically if nuclear sector expansion required the mining of high cost uranium reserves, current uranium supply projections make this unlikely.

15. Lovins and Lovins 1991, 31; Nordhaus 1991a 929; 1991b, 62, 41. The ICF GHG projections are for the U.S. in the year 2010. The study foresees total "business as usual"-greenhouse gas emissions of 3.3 GtC (billion metric tons). Nordhaus' analysis is based on U.S. data for 1989, but generalized for the global economy.

16. The methodology for calculating nuclear power's GHG abatement costs is as follows:

A) 1 kwh of coal-fired electricity currently generates ~.256 kgC (see note 8 above). New high efficiency coal units are expected to generate ~.2 kgC/ kwh.

B) Nuclear Cost Disadvantage = 1 c/kwh–3.5 c/kwh (given expected nuclear power costs 7.5 c/kwh to 8.5 c/kwh, and expected coal-fired electricity costs 5.0 c/kwh to 6.5 c/kwh).

C) Nuclear GHG Abatement Costs = (NP costs/kwh) - (Coal Power Costs/ kwh) divided by kg/C saved per kwh

    = (1–3.5 c/kwh)/.2 kG C; or $50–$175/mt

17. The energy efficiency debate with respect to global warming recalls the contrast between "bottom-up" and "top-down" economic modeling discussed in chapter 11. The bottom-up researchers take a "technology costing" approach to GHG abatement options. Their analyses produce an impressive list of technologies that could in principle replace current practices at minimal cost and generate large GHG savings. Top-down abatement cost models use econometric techniques to estimate the sensitivity of the demand for carbon-rich fuels to the price of those fuels, based on past behavior. The studies find much more reluctance to abandon carbon-rich fuels than suggested by the technology costing approach.

The top-down modelers criticize the bottom-up forecasters for ignoring hidden costs (such as information costs, illiquidity costs, and subjective costs) in forecasting future levels of energy efficiency investments. The top-downers argue that econometric projections based on past behavior (perhaps adjusted for a few structural changes in the economy) are more reliable predictors of future energy demand and energy efficiency investment than engineering analyses based on technological opportunity. The bottom-up modelers attack the econometricians for projecting past behavior into the future despite large shifts in social contexts. They argue that the transaction and psychic costs overlooked in their analyses are small and more importantly subject to economies of scale, such that societal commitments to greenhouse abatement or energy efficiency significantly reduce their impact. The energy conservation debate also hinges on the assumptions made about the rate of energy efficiency innovation and the level of public policy support for energy conservation.

Figure 13.3, drawn from a National Academy of Sciences study, illustrates the tendency for more expensive abatement cost projections in top-down than bottom-up forecasting models.

18. Despite a general skepticism about cheap abatement opportunities, Nordhaus reports that deforesting may be contributing .5 to 3 billion tons of CO_2/yr. (~7% to ~40% of non-forest related GHG emissions) with little economic payoff (Nordhaus 1991b, 54–55).

19. Pacific Power and Light has projected costs of $375/KW to $750/KW (or about .65 c/kwh to 1.3 c/kwh) for a similar program (Cogan 1990, 86). Dudek and LeBlanc project costs of ~$37/tC or ~1 C/kwh (1985$) (Dudek and LeBlanc 1990, 36). Lovins cites reports by the U.S. Forest Service and National Academy of Sci-

Fig. 13.3

NAS GHG Mitigation Cost Comparison

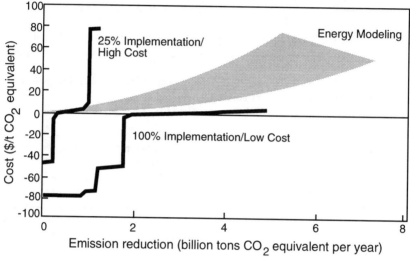

Source: National Academy of Sciences 1991, P. 62

ences that project costs of $10/tC for forest carbon sinks (Lovins and Lovins 1991, 28).

20. Lovins also calls for altered forest management practices, innovative forms of urban forestry (that besides sequestering CO_2 in new biomass, offset greenhouse emissions by reducing urban cooling needs through increased shading), and other measures that would reduce N_2O and CH_4 emissions (Lovins and Lovins 1991, 22–28).

21. Lovins and Lovins (1991, 2); Fulkerson et al. 1990, 93; and OTA 7/91, 95, also cite relatively optimistic scrubbing projections, but note that these claims have yet to be demonstrated in practice. The most attractive options for CO_2 storage are CO_2 injection into abandoned oil and gas wells and piped transport to deep ocean waters. Less promising are injections into mined caverns (salt and rock) and deep aquifers.

At existing natural gas and oil production rates, about 1/2 of the current level of CO_2 emissions from U.S. power plants (~1.7 Gt CO_2) could be accommodated in recently depleted reservoirs. For larger quantities and power plants distant from abandoned wells, ocean disposal is the key to economics of CO_2 scrubbing. The challenge is to sequester the CO_2 deep enough in the ocean that it does not resurface. Current thinking calls for deep water injection, shallower injection amidst downswelling currents, or chemical transformations that would cause the CO_2 to sink.

Research interest in engineered storage seems to be expanding. The DOE increased funding for the Office of Coal Technology's CO_2 capture and storage R&D budget from $100,000 in 1993 to about $1 million for 1994. The Japanese have an especially ambitious program, with government funding of ~$22 million and additional monies supplied by the utilities and industry. Norway and the Netherlands also have significant research programs.

22. Greenberger 8/91, 27; DOE, *Annual Energy Outlook 1996*, 109.

23. In 1987, for example, EPA analyses projected a $1.8 billion cost for U.S. compliance with the CFC reductions mandated by the Montreal Protocol. Recent technological change, however, has reduced projected costs to $500 million (Grubb 1990, 260–261), or less than $3.00/tC abated (Lovins and Lovins 1991, 29). Lovins and others have pointed to this decline as illustrative of the potential payoffs to greenhouse abatement R&D. Expected sulfur dioxide abatement costs have also declined dramatically.

24. Keepin and Kats (1988a) and Komanoff (1988a, 1988b, 1989) demonstrate that nuclear expansion cannot curb GHG emissions without a slowdown in energy demand growth. Keepin and Kats, for example, show that under Nordhaus and Yohe's 1986 high energy growth case (36 TW world energy demand in 2025), global GHG emissions would grow from 5.2tC/year in the late 1980s to 8.29 GtC/year in 2025 even if nuclear energy replaced all coal-fired electricity plants and one-half of all non-fossil fuel energy sources (Keepin and Kats 1988b, 10). This substitution would require the construction of *8000* new 1000 MW nuclear power plants by 2025 and is extremely implausible.

Under Edmonds and Reilly's 1983 medium energy demand growth case (21 TW world demand in 2025), 5200 new nuclear plants would be necessary worldwide to replace all coal-fired electricity (Keepin and Kats 1988b, 11–12). This expansion would require the construction of one nuclear plant every 4.5 days in the developed countries and one plant every 5.7 days in the third world and would only stabilize CO_2 emissions. Like the 8000 plant case, this growth rate is unlikely. Barriers include financing constraints on the program's enormous capital costs, the lack of appropriate infrastructures in the third world, and concern about the nuclear proliferation risks accompanying such a large nuclear sector.

It is only under Goldemberg's high energy efficiency scenario, where energy demand has been scaled back to 11.2 TW in 2020 that a plausible nuclear expansion path (600% increase in 1988–2025 for 1596 GW in 2025) could make a significant contribution to GHG reductions (38% cutbacks in emissions) (Keepin and Kats 1988b, 21, 28, 37).

25. For review of the distinction between "top-down" and "bottom-up" forecasting models, see note 17 above.

26. Many of these policies, such as increased spending for energy efficiency R&D, are often termed "no regrets" policies. They are felt desirable independently of global warming hazards. Nuclear power expansion is generally not viewed in such a favorable way.

27. Clinton's failed BTU tax, for example, amounted to ~$10/tC carbon tax. It seems unlikely that existing political climates would tolerate taxes ten to twenty times larger.

28. Illustrative of the impact of such uncertainties, in 1995 the Intergovernmental Panel on Climate Change, perhaps the most influential source of information on climate change, lowered its projected increase in global mean temperatures for the year 2100 by one-third from its 1990 estimate. The change reflected greater attention to the cooling effects of aerosols, improvements in modeling the carbon cycle, and lower emission forecasts for some greenhouse gases.

Chapter 14

1. For optimistic interpretations of the public's potential tolerance of new nuclear plants, see Nealey 1990, 3, 58; Wolfe 1990, 3–7, 3–8, 3–14; *Nuclear News* 10/90, 111–112; Cohen 1990, 40, 41, 45; and Ahearne 1993, 31.

On the pessimistic side, *Critical Mass* reported in May 1993 that 87% of those surveyed felt the U.S. should triple its use of renewables by 2010, while only 11% felt nuclear power should be the top priority of government funded R&D (p. 2). In February of 1994, *Critical Mass* reported that only 10% of the utility executives polled indicated they thought their company would ever consider ordering a new nuclear plant (p. 8). Popular images of nuclear energy remain unfavorable and generally deteriorated during the 1980s. Psychometric studies suggest that nuclear power is tarred with the ashes of Hiroshima and Nagasaki and the public's special dread of certain kinds of radioactive hazards (Slovic 1990). The technology is also burdened by the novelty and uncertainty of its risks and their imposition by social rather than individual decisions.

2. See, for example, Nealey 1990, 63 and *Time Magazine* 4/29/91, 55, and Beyea 1990, 3–13.

3. While power plant fuel consumption depends on several reactor design parameters, 150 metric tons (mt) uranium per GWe year (or ~4,500 mt U/1000 MW plant lifetime) is a popular ballpark estimate of fuel consumption (Weinberg 1986, 695). In the mid-eighties, reasonably assured global uranium resources available at prices less than $130/kg (~$59/lb.) were estimated to be ~6 million mt, jumping to $24 million mt's if speculative resources were included (Weinberg 1986, 695). Counting speculative resources, uranium supplies are thus large enough to support ~1,300–5,000 plant lifetimes. Given that global nuclear capacity is current ~325 GWe there are no immediate scarcity constraints on nuclear expansion.

The picture is even brighter if lower quality uranium deposits are mined. Weinberg et al. (1985) project a 65% increase in available U.S. uranium resources if the ceiling price is raised from $59/lb. to ~$118/lb (411). Weinberg et al. also foresee the availability of 10–20 million mt of uranium at less than $200/lb from shales and phosphates and virtually unlimited uranium from the oceans at perhaps $227–$554/lb. (415).

As nuclear generating costs increase by only ~1 M/kwh for every $10–$15/lb. increase in uranium prices, it would take an increase of $100–$150/lb. to raise nuclear power costs by 1 c/kwh.

Bibliography

Abelson, Philip H. 1993. "Power From Wind Turbines." *Science* 9/3/93, 1255.

Adato, Michele, James MacKenzie, Robert Pollard, and Ellyn Weiss. 1987. *Safety Second: The NRC and America's Nuclear Power Plants*. Bloomington, Indiana: Indiana University Press.

AEC. See U.S., Atomic Energy Commission.

Ahearne, John. 1993. "The Future of Nuclear Power." *American Scientist*, vol. 81 (1–2/93).

Allen, Bruce, and Arie Melnik. 1970. "Economics of the Power Reactor Industry." *Quarterly Review of Economics and Business* 10, no. 3.

Allen, Wendy. 1977. *Nuclear Reactors For Generating Electricity: U.S. Development From 1946 to 1963*. Rand, R-2116-NSF. Santa Monica, CA: Rand Corporation.

Alliance to Save Energy, American Council for an Energy Efficient Economy, Natural Resources Defense Council and the Union of Concerned Scientists. 1991. *America's Energy Choices: Investing in a Strong Economy and a Clean Environment*. Cambridge, MA: Union of Concerned Scientists.

———. 1992. *America's Energy Choices: Investing in a Strong Economy and a Clean Environment*. Technical Appendixes. Cambridge, MA: Union of Concerned Scientists.

Allison, Graham, Albert Carnesale, Paul Zigman, and Francis DeRosa. 1981. "Governance Of Nuclear Power." Study submitted to The President's Nuclear Safety Oversight Committee.

Anderson, Douglas. 1981. *Regulatory Politics and Electric Utilities: A Case Study in Political Economy*. Boston: Auborn House Publishing Co.

Anderson, John. 1991. "Are Prudency Reviews Necessary?" *Public Utility Fortnightly* (2/1/91).

Archer, Victor. 1980. "Effects of Low Level Radiation: A Critical Review." *Nuclear Safety* 21, no. 1.

Asmus, Peter. 1994. "Hot Air, Hot Tempers, and Cold Cash: Clashes of Ethics and

Clashes of Interests in the Controversy over Wind Power." *The Amicus Journal* (fall 1994).

Atomic Industrial Forum, Study Group on the Practical Application of Standardized Nuclear Power Plants in the United States. 1986. "Standardization of Nuclear Power Plants in the U.S." Bethesda, MD: Atomic Industrial Forum.

Atomic Industrial Forum, Inc. *The Forum Memo to Members.* Monthly 1954–1964. Retitled *Nuclear Industry* 1964–present. New York: Atomic Industrial Forum.

―――. 1965. *1964 Annual Conference Proceedings.* Vol. 2. New York: Atomic Industrial Forum.

Averch, H., and L. Johnson. 1962. "Behavior of the Firm Under Regulatory Constraint." *American Economic Review* 52, no. 5.

Balogh, Brian. 1991. *Chain Reaction: Expert Debate and Public Participation in American Commercial Nuclear Power, 1945–1975.* New York: Cambridge University Press.

Battelle Memorial Institute. 1978. "An Analysis of Federal Incentives Used to Stimulate Energy Production." PNL-2410 Rev. Richland, Washington: Pacific Northwest Laboratory.

Bello, Walden, Peter Hayes, and Lyuba Zarsky. 1979. *500-Mile Island: The Philippine Nuclear Reactor Deal.* Mountain View, CA: Pacific Research.

Berger, John. 1976, 1977. *Nuclear Power: The Unviable Option.* Rev. ed. 1977. New York: Dell.

Bertell, Rosalie. 1985. *No Immediate Danger: Prognosis for a Radioactive Earth.* Summertown, TN: The Book Publishing Company.

Beyea, Jan. 1990. "United States Panel Presentations," contained in MIT 1993.

Beyea, Jan, and Frank von Hippel. 1982. "Containment of a Reactor Meltdown." *The Bulletin of the Atomic Scientists* (8–9/82).

Biewald, Bruce, and Stephen Bernow. 1991. "Confronting Uncertainty: Contingency Planning for Decommissioning." *The Energy Journal*, vol. 12 (1991) (Special Decommissioning Issue).

Biewald, Bruce, and Donald Marion. 3/89. "Nuclear Power Economics: Construction, Operation, and Disposal." Boston: Energy Systems Research Group.

Blanch, Paul M. 1993. Open letter to Senator John Kerry. Distributed at the "New England Safe Energy Conference: Energizing the Grassroots Grid." 10/24/93. Bedford, New Hampshire.

Bodde, David. 1975. "Regulation and Technical Evolution: A Study of the Nuclear Steam Supply System and Commercial Jet Engine." Ph.D. diss., Graduate School of Business Administration, Harvard University.

Boes, Eldon C., and Antonio Luque. 1993. "Photovoltaic Concentrator Technology," contained in Johansson et al. 1993a.

Boley, Kenneth, with Daniel Borson, Ken Bossong, Joshua Gordon, Nancy Rader, and Scott Saleska. 1989. "Nuclear Power Safety: 1970–1989: An Assessment of Nuclear Reactor Safety Since Three Mile Island." Washington, D.C.: Public Citizen.

Borson, Daniel, with Kenneth Boley, Ken Bossong, Nancy Rader, and Scott Saleska. 6/89. "Forever In Its Debt?: The $9 Billion Debacle of the U.S. Uranium Enrichment Program." Washington, D.C.: Critical Mass.

———. 5/89. "Runaway Costs: Rising Operating and Maintenance Expenses at U.S. Nuclear Power Plants." Washington, D.C.: Critical Mass.

Bossong, Ken. 7/87. "The Price-Anderson Act: A Multi-Billion Dollar Annual Windfall For The Nuclear Industry." Washington, D.C.: Critical Mass.

Bowring, Joseph. 1980. "Federal Subsidies to Nuclear Power: Reactor Design and the Fuel Cycle." Pre-publication draft. Revised and subsequently published as: "Federal Support for Nuclear Power: Reactor Design and Fuel Cycle" by U.S. Department of Energy. Washington, D.C.: Government Printing Office. 2/81.

Brannon, Gerard M. 1974. *Energy Taxes and Subsidies*. Cambridge, MA: Ballinger.

Bross, Irwin. 1991. Talk presented at the "No More Chernobyls Conference." 4/27/91, Washington, D.C.

Brower, Michael. 1992. *Cool Energy: Renewable Solutions to Environmental Problems*. Cambridge: MIT Press.

Bupp, Irvin, and Charles Komanoff. 1983. "Prometheus Bound: Nuclear Power at the Turning Point." Cambridge, MA: Cambridge Energy Research Associates.

Bupp, Irvin, and Jean-Claude Derian. 1981. *The Failed Promise of Nuclear Power*. New York: Basic Books. Originally published as *Light Water: How the Nuclear Dream Dissolved*. New York: Basic Books, 1978.

Bupp, Irvin, Jean-Claude Derian, Marie-Paule Donsimoni, and Robert Treitel. 1975. "The Economics of Nuclear Power." *Technology Review* 77, no. 4.

———. 1974. "Trends in Light Water Reactor Capital Costs in the United States: Causes and Consequences." Cambridge, MA: Center for Policy Alternatives, Massachusetts Institute of Technology. Sections reprinted in: U.S. Congress. House Committee on Government Operations. 1977: 1730–1751.

Bupp, Irvin. 1972. *Priorities in Nuclear Technology: Program Prosperity and Decay in the United States Atomic Energy Commission 1956–1971*. Ph.D. Dissertation.

Burn, Duncan. 1967. *The Political Economy of Nuclear Energy: An Economic Study of Contrasting Organizations in the UK and USA, with Evaluation of their Effectiveness*. London: The Institute of Economic Affairs.

Burness, H. Stuart, W. David Montgomery and James P. Quirk. May 1980. "The Turnkey Era in Nuclear Power." *Land Economics* 56, no. 2.

———. June 1980. "Capital Contracting and the Regulated Firm." *American Economic Review* 70, no. 3.

CRS. See U.S., Congressional Research Service.

Cambel, Ali. 1964. *Energy R&D and National Progress*. Washington, D.C.: Government Printing Office.

Campbell, John L. 1988. *Collapse of an Industry: Nuclear Power and the Contradictions of U.S. Policy*. Ithaca, NY: Cornell University Press.

Cantor, Robin. 1991. "Applying Construction Lessons to Decommissioning Estimates." *The Energy Journal*, vol. 12 (Special Decommissioning Issue).

———. (undated) "Prudency Hearings and Management Audits: Instruments to Investigate the Management Process of Public Utilities." Mimeo. Oak Ridge, TN: Oak Ridge National Laboratory.

Cantor, Robin, and James Hewlett. 1988. "The Economics of Nuclear Power: Further Evidence on Learning, Economies of Scale, and Regulatory Effects." *Resources and Energy* 10: 315–335.

Caufield, Catherine. 1989. *Multiple Exposures: Chronicles of the Radiation Age*. New York: Harper & Row.

Cavallo, Alfred, Susan M. Hock, and Don R. Smith. 1993. "Wind Energy: Technology and Economics," in Johannson et al. 1993a.

Cavallo, Alfred. 1993. "Wind Energy: Current Status and Future Prospects," contained in *Science & Global Security* 1993, volume 4.

Chapman, Duane. 1983. *Energy Resources and Energy Corporations*. Ithaca, NY: Cornell University Press.

Cherfas, Jeremy. 1991. "Skeptics and Visionaries Examine Energy Savings." *Science*, vol. 251 (1/11/91).

Chubb, John. 1983. *Interest Groups and the Bureaucracy*. Stanford, CA: Stanford University Press.

Clark Jr., Charles, and Richard Fancher. 1985. "The Economics of Generating Unit Size and Lead Time." A paper presented at a Conference on Nuclear Power Plant Innovation. MIT, January 1985.

Clark, Norman. 2/87. "Similarities and Differences Between Scientific and Technological Paradigms." *Futures* (2/87).

Cline, William. 1992a. *The Economics of Global Warming*. Washington, D.C.: Institute for International Economics.

———. 1992b. *Global Warming: The Economic Stakes*. Washington, D.C.: Institute for International Economics.

Cogan, Douglas, (ed.). 1990. *The Greenhouse Effect: Investment Implications and Opportunities*. Washington, D.C.: Investor Responsibility Research Center.

Cohen, Bernard L. 1990. *The Nuclear Energy Option: An Alternative for the 90s.* New York: Plenum Press.

Cohn, Steven, and Lawrence Lidsky. 1993. "What Now? An Examination of the Issues Raised in 'The Outlook for Renewable Energy' by Robert Williams on the Nuclear Power Research and Development Agenda." Paper delivered at the Second MIT International Conference on the Next Generation of Nuclear Power Technology, 10/93.

Cohn, Steven. 1991. "Paradigm Debates in Nuclear Cost Forecasting." *Technological Forecasting and Social Change*, 40: 103–130 (1991).

———. 1990. "The Political Economy of Nuclear Power (1945–1990): The Rise and Fall of an Official Technology." *Journal of Economic Issues* XXIV (3).

———. 1986. The Political-Economy of Nuclear Power, 1946–1982. Doctoral Dissertation, University Microfilms, 1986.

———. 1980. "The Political-Economy of Nuclear Power, 1950–1978: The Rise & Fall of an Official Technology." Paper delivered at Allied Social Science Meetings, September 1980, Denver, CO.

Cole, Leonard A. 1993. *Elements of Risk: The Politics of Radon.* Washington, D.C.: AAAS Press.

Comey, David. 1978. "Fundamental Conflict between Nuclear Power and Civil Liberties." *In These Times* (10/25–31/70): 17.

———. 10/75. "On Cooking Curves." *The Bulletin of the Atomic Scientists* (10/75).

———. 2/75b. "A Critic Looks at Industry Credibility." Talk delivered at the conference "Nuclear Power and the Public" February 1975, recirculated by the Safe Energy Communication Council.

———. 2/75. "Chasing Down the Facts." *The Bulletin of the Atomic Scientists* (2/75).

———. 1974. "Will Idle Capacity Kill Nuclear Power?." *The Bulletin of the Atomic Scientists* (11/74).

Commoner, Barry. 1979. *The Politics of Energy.* New York: Alfred Knopf.

Congressional Quarterly. 1981. *Energy Policy.* Washington, D.C.: Congressional Quarterly, Inc.

Constant, Edward. 1973. "A Model for Technological Change Applied to the Turbojet Revolution." *Technology and Culture* 14(4) (October 1973).

Cook, Constance. 1980. *Nuclear Power and Legal Advocacy.* Lexington, MA: Lexington Books.

Cook, Earl. 1984. "The Role of History in the Acceptance of Nuclear Power in the U.S. and Canada," contained in Pasqualetti and Pijawka.

Cowan, Robin. 1990. "Nuclear Power Reactors: A Study in Technological Lock-in." *The Journal of Economic History*, vol. L, no. 3.

Coxe, Raymond Jr. 1988. *Electric Utility Capacity Planning with Modular Generating Technologies*. Ph. D. Dissertation, Dept. of Nuclear Engineering, Massachusetts Institute of Technology.

Creutz, E. 1970. "Nuclear Power: Rise of an Industry." *Bulletin of the Atomic Scientists* (6/70).

DOE. See U.S., Department of Energy.

Dawson, Frank. 1976. *Nuclear Power: Development and Management of a Technology*. Seattle: University of Washington Press.

De Laquil, Pascal, David Kearney, Machael Geyer, and Richard Diver. 1993. "Solar-Thermal Electric Technology," contained in Johansson et al. 1993a.

DeLeon, Peter. 1979. *Development and Diffusion of the Nuclear Power Reactor: A Comparative Analysis*. Cambridge, MA: Ballinger.

Del Sesto, Steven. 1979. *Science, Politics and Controversy: Civilian Nuclear Power in the United States, 1946–1974*. Boulder, Colorado: Westview Press.

Donnelly, Warren. 1972. *Commercial Nuclear Power in Europe: The Interaction of American Diplomacy with a New Technology*. Report prepared for the Subcommittee on National Security Policy and Scientific Developments of the House Committee on Foreign Affairs. Washington, D.C.: Government Printing Office.

Doroshow, Joanne. 1994. "A Decade of Delay, Deceit, and Danger: Three Mile Island 1979–1989, A Retrospective, Plus 15th Year Supplement." Harrisburg, PA: Three Mile Island Alert.

Dosi, Giovanni. 1982. "Technological Paradigms and Technological Trajectories." *Research Policy* 11: 147–162.

Drake, Elizabeth. 1993. "Sequestering Power Plant Carbon Dioxide." MIT seminar presentation, 3/29/93.

Dubin, Jeffrey A., and Geoffrey S. Rothwell. 1990. "Subsidy to Nuclear Power Through Price-Anderson Liability Limit." *Contemporary Policy Issues* 8(3).

Duchesneau, Thomas. 1975. *Competition in the U.S. Energy Industry: A Report to the Energy Policy Project of the Ford Foundation*. Cambridge, MA: Ballinger.

Dudek, Daniel, and Alice LeBlanc. 7/90. Offsetting New CO_2 Emissions: A Rational First Greenhouse Policy Step." *Contemporary Policy Issues*, vol. VIII (July 1990).

Duffy, Gloria, and Gordon Adams. 1978. *Power Politics: The Nuclear Industry and Nuclear Exports*. New York: The Council on Economic Priorities.

Ebbin, Steve, and Raphael Kasper. 1974. *Citizen Groups and the Nuclear Power Controversy: Uses of Scientific and Technological Information*. Cambridge, MA: MIT Press.

Fairlie, Ian. 1990. "Canada's Radiation Scandal." Toronto: Greenpeace.

———. 1991. "New Estimates of the Genetic Risks of Radiation." Unpublished mimeo.

Farber, Stephen. 1991. "Nuclear Power, Systematic Risk, and the Cost of Capital." *Contemporary Policy Issues* (January 1991).

Fertel, Marvin. 1993. "Current Issues and Future Opportunities for Commercial Nuclear Power Development in the USA." Presentation to the Department of Nuclear Engineering of the Massachusetts Institute of Technology, 3/16/93.

———. 1992. "Issues Surrounding the Management of O&M Costs." Paper presented at the American Nuclear Society's "Executive Conference on Controlling Nuclear Plant Operation and Maintenance Costs: A Matter of Survival." May 4, 1992.

Fickett, Arnold P., Clark W. Gellings, and Amory Lovins. 1990. "Efficient Use of Electricity" in *Energy for Planet Earth*, a collection of readings from *Scientific American* 9/90.

Flavin, Christopher, and Nicholas Lenssen. 1994. *Power Surge: Guide to the Coming Energy Revolution*. New York: W.W. Norton & Company.

Ford, Daniel, and Henry Kendall. 1975. "Catastrophic Nuclear Reactor Accidents." In *The Nuclear Fuel Cycle: A Survey of the Public Health, Environmental, and National Security Effects of Nuclear Power*. Prepared by the Union of Concerned Scientists. Cambridge, MA: MIT Press.

Ford, Daniel. 1982. *The Cult of the Atom*. New York: Simon and Schuster.

Ford, Daniel, Henry Kendall, and Lawrence Tye. 1976. *Browns Ferry: A Regulatory Failure*. Cambridge: MA: Union of Concerned Scientists.

Ford Foundation. Energy Policy Project. 1974. *A Time to Choose: America's Energy Future*. Cambridge, MA: Ballinger.

Ford Foundation. Nuclear Energy Policy Study Group. 1977. *Nuclear Power Issues and Choices*. Cambridge, MA: Ballinger.

Ford Foundation. Energy Study Group. 1979. *Energy—The Next Twenty Years*. Cambridge, MA: Ballinger.

Freeman, S. David. 1974. *Energy—the New Era*. New York: Vintage.

Fulkerson, William, Roddie R. Judkins and Manoj K. Sanghvi. 1990. "Energy from Fossil Fuels," in *Readings from Scientific American: Energy for Planet Earth*. New York: W. H. Freeman and Company. 1991. (Reprint of 1990 article, cited as Fulkerson et al. 1990).

Fulkerson, William, et al. 5/89. *Energy Technology R&D: What Could Make A Difference"* ORNL-6541/v1 (5/89). Oak Ridge, TN: Oak Ridge National Laboratory.

Fuller, John. 1975. *We Almost Lost Detroit*. New York: Reader's Digest Press.

Galbraith, John. 1973. *Economics and the Public Purpose*. Boston: Houghton Mifflin Company.

Gandara, Arturo. 1977. *Electric Utility Decisionmaking and the Nuclear Option.* Rand, R-2148-NSF. Santa Monica, CA: Rand Corporation.

Garvey, Gerald. 1977. *Nuclear Power and Social Planning.* Lexington, MA: D.C. Heath and Company.

Gas-Cooled Reactor Associates. 1993. "Modular High Temperature Gas-Cooled Reactor Commercialization and Generation Cost Estimates (DOE-HTGR-90365 Final Draft), September 1993.

Geiger, H. Jack, David Rush, and David Michaels (eds.). 1992. *Dead Reckoning: A Critical Review of the Department of Energy's Epidemiological Research.* Washington, D.C.: Physicians for Social Responsibility.

Gilinsky, Victor. 1992 "Nuclear Safety Regulation: Lessons from U.S. Experience." *Energy Policy* 20(8) (August 1992).

Gillette, Robert. 1972. "Nuclear Safety (IV): Barriers to Communication." *Science* 9/22/72.

———. "Nuclear Safety (III): Critics Charge Conflicts of Interest." *Science* 9/15/72.

———. "Nuclear Safety (I): The Roots of Dissent." *Science* 9/1/72.

———. "Nuclear Reactor Safety: At the AEC the Way of the Dissenter Is Hard." *Science* 5/5/72.

Gipe, Paul. October 1991. "Wind Energy Comes of Age: California and Denmark." *Energy Policy* (October 1991).

———. July 1989. "Wind Energy Comes of Age in California." Tehachapi, CA: Paul Gipe & Assoc.

Glickman, Theodore S., and Dominic Golding. 1991. "New Perspectives on Transporting Nuclear Wastes in Dedicated Trains." *Resources*, no. 104 (summer 1991).

Gofman, John W. 1990. *Radiation Induced Cancer From Low-Dose Exposure: An Independent Analysis.* San Francisco: Committee for Nuclear Responsibility.

———. 1981. *Radiation and Human Health.* San Francisco: Sierra Club Books.

Gofman, John, and Arthur Tamplin. 1971, 1979. *Poisoned Power.* Rev. ed. 1979. Emmaus, PA: Rodale Press.

Goldemberg, Jose, Thomas B. Johansson, Amulya K.N. Reddy, and Robert H. Williams. 1988. *Energy for a Sustainable World.* New Delhi, Wiley Eastern Limited.

Gorinson, Stanley. 1979a. *Staff Report to the President's Commission on the Accident at Three Mile Island. Reports of the Technical Assessment Task Force, vol. 1.* Washington, D.C.: Government Printing Office.

———. 1979b. *Staff Report to the President's Commission on the Accident at Three Mile Island. The Nuclear Regulatory Commission, Report of the Office of Chief Counsel.* Washington, D.C.: Government Printing Office.

———. 1979c. *Staff Report to the President's Commission on the Accident at Three Mile Island. The Role of the Managing Utility and Its Suppliers.* Washington, D.C.: Government Printing Office.

Gorz, Andre. 1979. "Nuclear Energy and the Logic of Tools." *Radical America* (May–June 1979).

Green, Harold. "Nuclear Power—Risk, Liability and Indemnity." 1973. *Michigan Law Review* 71(3).

Green, Harold, and Alan Rosenthal. 1963. *Government of the Atom.* New York: Atherton Press.

Green, Harold. 1957. "The Strange Case of Nuclear Power." *Federal Bar Journal* 17 (April–June).

Greenberger, Leonard. 1991. "Trading Coalbed Methane for Carbon Dioxide." *Public Utilities Fortnightly* (8/15/91).

Grubb, Michael J., and Niels I. Meyer. 1993. "Wind Energy: Resources, Systems and Regional Strategies," in Johannson et al. 1993a.

Grubb, Michael. 9/91. "The Integration of Renewable Electricity Sources." *Energy Policy* 19(7).

Grubb, Michael, with Peter Brackley, Michele Ledic, Ajau Mathur, Steve Rayner, Jeremy Russel, and Akira Tanabe. 1991. *Energy Policies and the Greenhouse Effect, volume Two: Country Case Studies and Technical Options.* Brookfield, Vermont: Dartmouth Publishing Company.

Grubb, Michael. 1990. *Energy Policies and the Greenhouse Effect, volume One: Policy Appraisal.* Brookfield, Vermont: Dartmouth Publishing Company.

Gyorgy, Anna & Friends. 1979. *No Nukes: Everyone's Guide to Nuclear Power.* Boston: Southend Press.

Hall, David O., Frank Rosillo-Calle, Robert Williams, and Jeremy Woods. 1993. "Biomass for Energy: Supply Prospects," contained in Johansson et al. 1993a.

Hansen, K., D. Winje, E. Beckjord, E.P. Gyftopoulos, M. Golay, and R. Lester. 1989. "Making Nuclear Power Work: Lessons from Around the World." *Technology Review* (2–3/89): 31–40.

Harding, Jim. 1990. "Reactor Safety and Risk Issues." *Contemporary Policy Issues* 8(3) (July 1990).

Hayes, Peter, and Lyuba Zarsky. 1984. "Nuclear Electric Futures in Developing Countries of Asia-Pacific." Photocopy.

Hays, Samuel P. 1987. *Beauty, Health, and Permanence: Environmental Politics in the United States, 1955–1985.* New York: Cambridge University Press.

Heede, Richard. 1991. Personal communication 12/3/91.

Hellman, Richard, and Caroline Hellman. 1983. *The Competitive Economics of Nuclear and Coal Power.* Lexington, MA: Lexington Books.

Herman, Stewart W. 1977. *Energy Futures.* New York: Inform Inc.

Hertsgaard, Mark. 1983. *Nuclear Inc.* New York: Pantheon.

Hewlett, James. 1992. "The Operating Costs and Longevity of Nuclear Power Plants: Evidence from the USA." *Energy Policy* (July 1992).

Hewlett, Richard, and Francis Duncan. 1974. *Nuclear Navy, 1946–1962.* Chicago: University of Chicago Press.

Hilgartner, Stephen, Richard C. Bell, and Rory O'Connor. 1982. *Nukespeak: Nuclear Language, Visions, and Mindset.* San Francisco: Sierra Club Books.

Hirsch, Fred. 1976. *Social Limits to Growth.* Cambridge: Harvard University Press.

Hirsh, Richard F. 1989. *Technology and Transformation in the American Electric Utility Industry.* New York: Cambridge University Press.

Hogendorn, Jan, and Wilson Brown. 1979. *The New International Economics.* Reading, MA: Addison-Wesley.

Hogerton, John. 1968. "The Arrival of Nuclear Power." *Scientific American* 218, no. 2.

Holden, Constance. "Low-Level Radiation: A High-Level Concern." *Science* vol. 204, April 13, 1979.

Holloman, J. Herbert, and Michael Grenon. 1975. *Energy Research and Development.* Cambridge, MA: Ballinger.

Hyman, Leonard S. 1992. *America's Electric Utilities: Past, Present, and Future* (4th ed.). Public Utilities Reports, Inc.

———. May 1981. "Three Mile Island Two Years Later: The Consequences of TMI for the Utility Industry." New York: Merrill Lynch.

Hyman, Leonard, and Doris Kelley. 1981. "The Financial Aspects of Nuclear Power: Capital Credit, Demand and Risk. New York: Merrill Lynch, Pierce, Fenner and Smith Inc.

IARC. See International Agency for Research on Cancer, Study Group on Cancer Risk among Nuclear Industry Workers.

IPCC. See Intergovernmental Panel on Climate Change.

Institute for Energy Analysis. Oak Ridge Associated Universities. 1979. *Economic and Environmental Impacts of a U.S. Nuclear Moratorium, 1985–2010.* Cambridge, MA: MIT Press.

Intergovernmental Panel on Climate Change, Working Group II. 1995. "Summary for Policymakers: Scientific-Technical Analysis of Impacts, Adaptations, and Mitigation of Climate Change, IPCC Working Group II 1995." URL: http://www.unep.ch/ipcc/sumwg2.html.

Intergovernmental Panel on Climate Change (IPCC). 1990. *Climate Change: The*

IPCC Scientific Assessment. Edited by J.T. Houghton, G.J. Jenkins, and J. J. Ephraums. New York: Cambridge University Press.

International Agency for Research on Cancer, Study Group on Cancer Risk among Nuclear Industry Workers (IARC). 1994. "Direct Estimates of Cancer Mortality Due to Low Doses of Ionising Radiation: An International Study." *Lancet,* vol. 344, 10/15/94.

Johansson, Thomas B., Henry Kelly, Amulya K.N. Reddy, and Robert Williams. 1993a. *Renewable Energy: Sources for Fuels and Electricity.* Washington, D.C.: Island Press.

————. 1993b. "Renewable Fuels and Electricity for a Growing World Economy: Defining and Achieving the Potential," contained in Johansson et al. 1993a.

JCAE. See U.S., Congress, Joint Committee on Atomic Energy.

Joskow, Paul L., and Donald B. Marron. 1992. "What Does a Negawatt Really Cost? Evidence from Utility Conservation Programs." *Energy Journal* 13, 4.

Joskow, Paul, and George Rozanski. 5/79. The Effects of Learning by Doing on Nuclear Plant Operating Experience." *The Review of Economics and Statistics,* vol. 161, no. 2.

Kaku, Michio, and Jennifer Trainer. 1982. *Nuclear Power: Both Sides.* New York: W.W. Norton and Company.

Katzman, Martin T. 1989. "How Far Can The World Get on Energy Efficiency Alone"? Paper presented to the International Association of Energy Economists, Los Angeles, October 1989.

Keating, William. 1975. "Politics, Energy and the Environment: The Role of Technology Assessment." *American Behavioral Scientist* 19, no. 1.

Keepin, Bill, and Gregory Kats. 1988a. "Greenhouse Warming: Comparative Analysis of Two Abatement Strategies." *Energy Policy* 16(6), 538–561 (12/88).

————. 1988b. Manuscript copy of 1988a.

Kelly, Henry. 1993. "Introduction to Photovoltaic Technology," contained in Johansson et al. 1993a.

Kelly, Henry, and Carl Weinberg. 1993. "Utility Strategies for Using Renewables," contained in Johansson et al. 1993a.

Knox, E.G., and A.M. Stewart, E.A. Gilman, and G.W. Kneale. 1988. "Effects of Background Radiation," contained in *Health Effects of Low Dose Ionising Radiation—Recent Advances and their Implications.* London: Thomas Telford Ltd.

Kocher, D.C. 1991. "Perspective on the Historical Development of Radiation Standards." *Health Physics* 61(4) (October 1991).

Komanoff, Charles, and Cora Roelofs. 12/92. "Fiscal Fission: The Economic Failure of Nuclear Power." Washington, D.C.: Greenpeace.

Komanoff, Charles. 1991. "U.S. Nuclear Plant Capacity Factor Data Base." New York: Komanoff Energy Associates.

———. April 1990. Personal communication.

———. 1989. "Energy Use Efficiency and Nuclear Generation as Competing Supply Sources." *Public Utilities Fortnightly* (2/2/89).

———. 1988a, b. "Greenhouse Effect Amelioration—Efficiency vs. Nuclear," memos 8/24/88, 12/19/88.

———. 1984b. "Testimony before the Washington Utilities and Transportation Commission." Photocopy. New York: Komanoff Energy Associates.

———. 1984a. "Assessing the High Costs of New U.S. Nuclear Power Plants." Paper presented at the 7th Annual National Conference of Regulatory Attorneys, 6/84. New York: Komanoff Energy Associates.

———. 1981. *Power Plant Cost Escalation: Nuclear and Coal Capital Costs, Regulation and Economics.* New York: Komanoff Energy Associates.

———. 1980. "Power Propoganda: A Critique of the Atomic Industrial Forum's Nuclear and Coal Power Cost Data for 1978." New York: Environmental Action Foundation.

Koplow, Douglas. 1993. *Federal Energy Subsidies: Energy, Environmental, and Fiscal Impacts.* Washington, D.C.: Alliance to Save Energy.

Kriesberg, Joseph. 11/87. "Too Costly to Continue: The Economic Feasibility of a Nuclear Phase-Out." Washington, D.C.: Critical Mass Energy Project.

———. 10/87. "Fading Fast: The Rising Costs, Declining Performance and Increasing Problems at Older Nuclear Reactors." Washington, D.C.: Critical Mass Energy Project.

———. "Shifting to Shutdown." 1987. Washington, D.C.: Critical Mass Energy Project.

Krugman, Paul. 1983. "New Theories of Trade Among Industrial Countries." *American Economic Review* 73, no. 2.

Kuhn, James. 1966. *Scientific and Managerial Manpower in Nuclear Industry.* New York: Columbia University Press.

Kuhn, Thomas. 1970. *The Structure of Scientific Revolutions* [1962] 2nd ed. Chicago: University of Chicago Press.

Lane, James A. 1968. "Rationale for Low-Cost Nuclear Heat and Electricity." Contained in *Abundant Nuclear Energy*, proceedings of a symposium held at Gatlinburg, TN, August 26–29, 1968. Sponsored by U.S. AEC and Oak Ridge Associated Universities.

Lanoue, Ron. 1976. *Nuclear Plants: The More They Build, The More You Pay.* Washington, D.C.: Center for the Study of Responsive Law.

Lester, Richard. 3/86. "Rethinking Nuclear Power." *Scientific American*, vol. 254, no. 3.

———. 1986. "Organization, Structure and Performance in the U.S. Nuclear Industry." *Energy Systems and Policy*, vol. 9, no. 4.

Leventhal, Paul, and Milton M. Hoenig. 1990. "Nuclear Terrorism: Reactor Sabotage and Weapons Proliferation Risks." *Contemporary Policy Issues*, vol. VIII (July 1990).

Lewis, Richard. 1972. *The Nuclear Power Rebellion: Citizens vs. the Atomic Establishment*. New York: Viking Press.

Lidsky, Lawrence, and X.L. Yan. 1992. "Design Options of MGR Gas Turbine Power Plants." (Photocopy). November 4, 1992.

Lidsky, Lawrence. 1991. "Rotten at the Core." *Technology Review* (4/91).

———. 1988. "Nuclear Power: Levels of Safety." *Radiation Research* 113: 217–226.

———. 2–3/84. "The Reactor of the the Future?." *Technology Review* (2–3/84).

Lilienthal, David. 1963. *Change, Hope, and the Bomb*. Princeton, NJ: Princeton University Press.

Lindberg, Leon. 1977. *The Energy Syndrome*. Lexington, MA: Lexington Books.

Lindzen, Richard. 3/92. "Global Warming: The Origin and Nature of Alleged Scientific Consensus" (unpublished manuscript) (3/11/92).

Little, Arthur D. 1968. "Competition in the Nuclear Power Supply Industry." Report to the U.S. Atomic Energy Commission and U.S. Department of Justice. Washington, D.C.: Government Printing Office.

Lonnroth, Mans, and William Walker. 1982. "The Viability of the Civilian Nuclear Industry," contained in Smart.

———. 1983. *Nuclear Power Struggles: Industrial Competition and Proliferation Control*. Boston: George Allen and Unwin.

Lovins, Amory, and L. Hunter Lovins. July 1991. "Least-Cost Climatic Stabilization." Old Snowmass, CO: Rocky Mountain Institute.

Lovins, Amory. 1990. "Four Revolutions in Electric Efficiency." *Contemporary Policy Issues*, vol. VIII (July 1990).

Lovins, Amory, and Hunter Lovins. 1982. *Brittle Power: Energy Strategy for National Security*. Andover, MA: Brick House Publishing Co.

Lovins, Amory. 1977. *Soft Energy Paths: Toward a Durable Peace*. Cambridge, MA: Ballinger.

———. 1976. "Energy Strategy: The Road Not Taken?." *Foreign Affairs* (October 1976).

MER. See U.S., DOE, *Monthly Energy Review*.

MHB Technical Associates. 1990. *Advanced Reactor Study*. Cambridge, MA: Union of Concerned Scientists.

MIT. 1990. *Proceedings of the First MIT International Conference on the Next Generation of Nuclear Power Technology*, October 4–5, 1990, MIT-ANP-CP-001.

MIT. 1993. *Proceedings of the Second MIT International Conference on the Next Generation of Nuclear Power Technology*, October 25–26, 1993, MIT-ANP-CP-002.

MIT. 1993b. Class notes from "Nuclear Energy Economics and Policy Analysis," spring 1993, Massachusetts Institute of Technology.

Makhijani, Arjun, and Scott Saleska. 1992. *High-Level Dollars Low-Level Sense: A Critique of Present Policy for the Management of Long-Lived Radioactive Waste and Discussion of an Alternative Approach*. New York: Apex Press.

Management Information Services, Inc. 12/92. "Federal Commercialization of Nuclear Energy: A Success Story." Washington, D.C.: U.S. Council for Energy Awareness.

Manne, Alan, and Richard Richels. 1991. "Global CO_2 Emission Reductions—The Impacts of Rising Energy Costs." *Energy Journal* 12 (1).

———. 4/90. "CO_2 Emission Limits: An Economic Cost Analysis for the USA." *Energy Journal* 11(2).

Mansfield, Edwin. 1968. *Industrial Research and Technological Innovation—An Econometric Analysis*. New York: W.W. Norton.

———. 1975. "Firm Size and Technological Change in the Petroleum and Bituminous Coal Industries, contained in Duchesneau.

Mason, Edward. 1957. *Economic Concentration and the Monopoly Problem*. Cambridge, MA: Harvard University Press.

Mazur, Alan. 1981. *The Dynamics of Technical Controversy*. Washington, D.C.: Communications Press.

McCally, Michael. 1990. "What The Fight Is All About." *Bulletin of the Atomic Scientists* (September 1990).

McCartney, Laton. 1988. *Friends in High Places: The Bechtel Story. The Most Secret Corporation and How It Engineered the World*. New York: Simon and Schuster.

McCaughey, John, and Richard Meyers. 1993. "Demand: Finding the Right Balance." *Nuclear Energy* (1993 First Quarter).

Meehan, Richard. 1984. *The Atom and the Fault*. Cambridge: MIT Press.

Metzger, H. Peter. 1972. *The Atomic Establishment*. New York: Simon and Schuster.

Miller, G. Tyler. 1980. *Energy and Environment: The Four Energy Crises* (second ed.). Belmont, CA: Wadsworth.

Miller, James. 1987. *Democracy in the Streets*. New York: Simon and Schuster.

Miller, Saunders, and Craig Severance. 1976. *The Economics of Nuclear and Coal Power*. New York: Praeger Publishers.

Montange, Charles. 9/90. "Stopping a Budget Meltdown: Reorganizing the Federal Uranium Enrichment Program." Washington, D.C.: National Taxpayers Union Foundation.

Montgomery, W. David, and James Quirk. 1978. "Cost Escalation in Nuclear Power." EQL Memo. No. 21. Pasadena, CA: Environmental Quality Laboratory.

Mooz, William. 1978. *Cost Analysis of Light Water Reactor Power Plants*. Rand R-2304-DOE. Santa Monica, CA: Rand Corporation.

———. 1979. *A Second Cost Analysis of Light Water Reactor Power Plants*. Rand R-2504-RC. Santa Monica, CA: Rand Corporation.

Morgan, Karl. 1978. "Cancer and Low Level Ionizing Radiation." *Bulletin of Atomic Scientists* 34, no. 7.

Morone, Joseph G., and Edward Woodhouse. 1989. *The Demise of Nuclear Energy? Lessons for Democratic Control of Technology*. New Haven: Yale University Press.

Muckerheide, Jim. 1995. "The Health Effects of Low-Level Radiation: Science, Data, and Corrective Action." *Nuclear News* (9/95): 26–34.

Mullenbach, Philip. 1963. *Civilian Nuclear Power: Economic Issues and Policy Formation*. Philadelphia: Twentieth Century Fund.

NAS. See U.S. National Academy of Sciences.

NEI. See Nuclear Energy Institute.

NSF. See U.S., National Science Foundation.

NRC. See U.S. Nuclear Regulatory Commission.

Nader, Ralph, Eleanor J. Lewis, and Eric Weltman. 11/8/91. Testimony on The Effect of Government Procurement on the Environment, before the Senate Governmental Affairs Committee, Subcommittee on Oversight of Government Management. (Reproduced by Government Purchasing Project, P.O. Box 19367, Washington, D.C. 20036.)

Nader, Ralph, and John Abbotts. 1979. *The Menace of Atomic Energy*. New York: W. W. Norton.

Narum, David. 1992. "A Troublesome Legacy: The Reagan Administration's Conservation and Renewable Energy Policy." *Energy Policy* (January 1992).

Nash, Hugh, ed. 1979. *The Energy Controversy: Soft Path Questions and Answers*. San Francisco: Friends of the Earth.

National Research Council. See U.S. National Research Council.

Nau, Henry. 1974. *National Politics and International Technology*. Baltimore: Johns Hopkins University Press.

Navarro, Peter. 1988. "Comparative Energy Policy: The Economics of Nuclear Power in Japan and the United States." *Energy Journal* 9(4): 1–15.

Nawab, Syed. 1980. "Nuclear Export Financing: The Role of the Export-Import Bank of the United States." Unpublished paper.

Nealey, Stanley M. 1990. *Nuclear Power Development: Prospects in the 1990s*. Columbus, Ohio: Batelle Press.

Nehrt, Lee. 1966. *International Marketing of Nuclear Power Plants*. Bloomington: Indiana University Press.

Nelkin, Dorothy. 1971. *Nuclear Power and Its Critics: The Cayuga Lake Controversy*. Ithaca: Cornell University Press.

Nelson, Richard, and George Eads. 1971. "Government Support of Advanced Civilian Technology: Power Reactors and the Supersonic Transport." *Public Policy* 19, no. 3.

Nix, R. Gerald. 1996. "Wind Energy as a Significant Source of Electricity." National Wind Technology Center. URL: http://nwtc.nrel.gov/publish_papers/at1pap2. html.

Nordhaus, William. 1991a. "To Slow Or Not To Slow: The Economics of the Greenhouse Effect." *The Economic Journal* 101(6) (1991): 920–937.

———. 1991b. "The Cost of Slowing Climate Change: A Survey." *The Energy Journal* 12(1): 37–65.

Nuclear Energy Institute. 8/96. "Economic Issues and Nuclear Energy: How Nuclear Energy Fits in a Competitive Market." URL: http://www.nei.org/main/ pressrm/facts/economic.htm.

———. 8/17/96. "Myths & Facts About Research on Advanced Nuclear Power Plants." URL: htpp://www.nei.org/main/cip/invest/myths.htm.

———. 6/96. "Radiation and Health." URL: http://www.nei.org/main/pressrm/facts/ radiatn/htm.

ORNL. See U.S. Oak Ridge National Laboratory.

OTA. See U.S., Congress, Office of Technology Assessment.

Okrent, David. 1981. *Nuclear Reactor Safety: On the History of the Regulatory Process*. Madison: University of Wisconsin Press.

Olson, McKinley. 1976. *Unacceptable Risk: The Nuclear Power Controversy*. New York: Bantam Books.

Orlans, Harold. 1967. *Contracting for Atoms*. Washington, D.C.: The Brookings Institution.

Ostlie, L. David. 1988. "The Whole Tree Burner: A New Technology in Power Generation." Minneapolis: Energy Performance Systems, Inc. (Xerox).

Ottinger, Richard, David Wooley, Nicholas A. Robinson, David R. Hodas, and Susan E. Babb. 1990. *Environmental Costs of Electricity*. New York: Oceana Publications. Also cited as Pace University, 1990.

Pace University Center for Environmental Legal Studies. 1990. *Environmental Costs of Electricity*. New York: Oceana Publications. Also cited under Ottinger 1990.

Paley Commission. 1952. "Resources for Freedom." See President's Materials Policy Commission. Washington, D.C.: Government Printing Office.

Pasqualetti, Martin J., and K. David Pijawka (eds.). 1984. *Nuclear Power: Assessing and Managing Hazardous Technology*. Boulder, CO: Westview Press.

Pawlick, Thomas. 1980. "The Silent Toll." *Harrowsmith* 4, no. 28.

Perry, Harold. 1973. *Energy Research and Development—Problems and Prospects*. See U.S. Congress. Senate. Committee on Interior and Insular Affairs 1973.

Perry, Robert. 1977. *Development and Commercialization of the Light Water Reactor, 1946–1976*. Rand, R-2180-NSF. Santa Monica, CA: Rand Corporation.

Phung, Doan L. 5/87. "Theory and Evidence for Using the Economy-of-Scale Law in Power Plant Economics." ORNL/TM-10195. Oak Ridge, TN: Oak Ridge National Laboratory.

———. 1984. "Are Very Small Reactors Really Cheap? An Investigation of Bradshaw's Arguments," Draft 1. Oak Ridge, TN: PAI Associates.

Pirog, Robert L. and Stephen C. Stamos (eds.). 1987. *Energy Economics: Theory and Practice*. Englewood Cliffs, New Jersey: Prentice Hall.

Pollard, Robert. October 1993. Remarks at New England Safe Energy Conference: Energizing the Grassroots Grid, 10/24/93, Bedford, New Hampshire.

———. 1992. "Accident Risks in Aging Nuclear Power Plants." *Nucleus* 14(2) (summer 1992).

Pollard, Robert, ed. 1979. *The Nugget File*. Cambridge, MA: Union of Concerned Scientists.

Pomeroy, Paul W. 1996. Letter to the Nuclear Regulatory Commission on "Health Effects of Low Levels of Ionizing Radiation," July 10, 1996. URL: http://www.nirs.org/radiation/acnw7106.txt

Price, Jerome. 1982. *The Antinuclear Movement*. Boston: Twayne Publishers.

Price, Terence. 1990. *Political Electricity: What Future for Nuclear Energy*. New York: Oxford University Press.

Primack, Joel, and Frank von Hippel. 1974. *Advice and Dissent: Scientists in the Political Arena*. New York: Basic Books.

Pringle, Peter, and James Spigelman. 1981. *The Nuclear Barons*. New York: Holt, Rinehart and Winston.

Ray, Dixy Lee. 1991. "Electricity." A talk delivered at the 1990 CIGRE Opening Session, Paris France. Reprinted in *IEEE Power Engineering Review* (March 1991).

Ray, Dixy Lee (with Lou Guzzo). 1990. *Trashing the Planet: How Science Can Help Us Deal With Acid Rain, Depletion of the Ozone, and Nuclear Waste (Among Other Things)*. New York: Harper Perennial (1992 ed.).

Resnikoff, Marvin. 1983. *The Next Nuclear Gamble: Transportation and Storage of Nuclear Waste*. New York: Council on Economic Priorities.

Riccio, James, and Michael Grynberg. 1995. "A Roll of the Dice: NRC's Efforts to Renew Nuclear Reactor Licenses." Washington, D.C.: Public Citizen.

Riccio, James, and Stephanie Murphy. 1988. "The Aging of Nuclear Plants: A Citizen's Guide to Causes and Effects." Washington, D.C.: Nuclear Information Resource Service.

Rockefeller, Nelson. 1963. Address to Atomic Industrial Forum—American Nuclear Society Banquet. Contained in: *Proceedings of the 1963 Annual Conference of the Atomic Industrial Forum*.

Rockwell, Theodore. 1992. *The Rickover Effect: How One Man Made a Difference*. Annapolis: Naval Institute Press.

Rolph, Elizabeth. 1977. *Regulation of Nuclear Power: The Case of the Light Water Reactor*. Rand, R-2104. Santa Monica, CA: Rand Corporation.

———. 1979. *Nuclear Power and the Public Safety*. Lexington, MA: Lexington Books.

Rosenberg, Nathan. 1972. *Technology and American Economic Growth*. White Plains, NY: M.E. Sharpe.

SERI. See U.S., Solar Energy Research Institute.

SMUD. See Sacramento Municipal Utility District.

Sacramento Municipal Utility District. 1993. *1993 Demand-Side Management Resource Plan*. 10/11/93 (draft). Sacramento: SMUD.

———. 1/94. *Demand-Side Management Resource Plan: Cornerstone for Sacramento's Energy Future 1994–2013*. Sacramento: SMUD.

Scientific American (eds.). 1991. *Energy for Planet Earth*. New York: W.H. Freeman and Company.

Sever, Lowell E. 1991. "Low-Level Ionizing Radiation: Paternal Exposure & Children's Health. *Health and Environment Digest* 5(1) (February 1991).

Sisine, Fred J. 1/22/91. "Renewable Energy: A New National Commitment?" CRS Issue Brief 87140. Washington, D.C.: Congressional Research Service. Also cited under Congressional Research Service.

Slovic, Paul. 1990. "Perception of Risk and the Future of Nuclear Power," contained in MIT 1990.

Smart, Ian (ed). 1982. *World Nuclear Energy: Toward a Bargain of Confidence.* Baltimore: Johns Hopkins Press.

Smeloff, Ed. 1994. Remarks at Three Mile Island 15th Anniversary Conference, March 26–27, 1994.

Sneddon, James. 1974. "Nuclear Webb Series." *Beaver County Times* (12/23–31/1974).

Sommers, Paul. 1978. "The Diffusion of Nuclear Power Generation in the United States." Ph.D. diss., Yale University.

———. 1980. "The Adoption of Nuclear Power Generation." *Bell Journal of Economcs* 11, no. 1.

Sporn, Philip. 1969. *Technology, Engineering, and Economics.* Cambridge: MIT Press.

Sternglass, Ernest. 1981. *Secret Fallout.* New York: McGraw Hill.

Stewart, Alice. 1990. "Low-Level Radiation: The Cancer Controversy." *The Bulletin of the Atomic Scientists* (September 1990).

Stewart, Hugh. 1981. *Transitional Energy Policy.* New York: Pergamon.

Stobaugh, Robert, and Daniel Yergin, eds. 1979. *Energy Future: Report of the Energy Project at the Harvard Business School.* New York: Random House.

Strauss, Lewis. 1962. *Men and Decisions.* Garden City, NY: Doubleday.

Sugg, Redding, ed. 1957. *Nuclear Power in the South.* Baton Rouge: Louisiana State University Press.

Sultan, Ralph. 1974. *Pricing in the Electrical Oligopoly, vol. I: Competition or Collusion.* Cambridge, MA: Harvard University Press.

———. 1975. *Pricing in the Electrical Oligopoly, vol. II: Business Strategy.* Cambridge, MA: Harvard University Press.

Sutherland, Ronald J. 1991. "Market Barriers to Energy-Efficiency Investments." *Energy Journal* 12(3).

Swezey, Blair G., and Yih-huei Wan. "The True Cost of Renewables: An Analytic Response to the Coal Industry's Attack on Renewable Energy." URL: htpp://syssrv9.nrel.gov/research/analytic_studies/projects/ceed/ceed.html (accessed 8/29/96).

Taylor, June, and Michael Yokell. 1979. *Yellowcake: The International Uranium Cartel.* New York: Pergamon Press.

Teitelbaum, Perry. 1958. *Productive Uses of Nuclear Energy: Report on Nuclear Energy and the U.S. Fuel Economy, 1955–1980.* Washington, D.C.: National Planning Association.

Tester, J.W., and Howard Herzog. 1991. "The Economics of Heat Mining: An Analysis of Design Options and Performance Requirements of Hot Dry Rock (HDR) Geothermal Power Systems." *Energy Systems and Policy*, vol. 15: 33–63.

Tester, J.W., D.W. Brown, and R.M. Potter. July 1989. "Hot Dry Rock Geothermal Energy: A New Energy Agenda for the 21st Century." Los Alamos, New Mexico: Los Alamos National Laboratory.

Thomas, S.D. 1988. *The Realities of Nuclear Power: International Economic and Regulatory Experience*. New York: Cambridge University Press.

Tomain, Joseph P. 1987. *Nuclear Power Transformation*. Bloomington: Indiana University Press.

Torrens, Ian M. 7–8/90. "Developing Clean Coal Technologies." *Environment* (July/August 1990).

Tybout, Richard. 1957. "The Economics of Nuclear Power." *American Economic Review* 47, no. 2.

UCS. See Union of Concerned Scientists.

U.S. CEA. See U.S. Council for Energy Awareness (USCEA).

Union of Concerned Scientists (UCS). (See Allliance to Save Energy et al.).

U.S. Council for Energy Awareness (USCEA). January 1991. "Advanced Design Nuclear Energy Plants: Competitive, Economical Electricity." Washington, D.C.: U.S. Council for Energy Awareness.

———. 6/92. "Advanced Design Nuclear Energy Plants: Competitive, Economical Electricity." Washington, D.C.: U.S. Council for Energy Awareness.

U.S., Atomic Energy Commission (AEC). 1974c. *The Nuclear Industry 1974*. WASH–1174–74. Washington, D.C.: Government Printing Office.

———. 1974b. *Power Plant Capital Costs Current Trends and Sensitivity to Economic Parameters*. WASH–1345. Washington, D.C.: Government Printing Office.

———. 1974a. *Nuclear Power Growth, 1974–2000*. WASH–1139 (74). Washington, D.C.: Government Printing Office.

———. 1973. *The Nuclear Industry 1973*. WASH 1174–73. Washington, D.C.: Government Printing Office.

———. 1972. *Pressurized Water Reactor Plant: 1000–MWe Central Station Power Plants Investment Study*. WASH–1230, vol. 1. Washington, D.C.: Government Printing Office.

———. 1971b. *The Nuclear Industry 1971*. WASH–1174–71. Washington, D.C.: Government Printing Office.

———. 1971a. *Reactor Fuel Cycle Costs for Nuclear Power Evaluation*. WASH–1099. Washington, D.C.: Government Printing Office.

———. 1970b. *The Nuclear Industry 1970.* WASH–1174–70. Washington, D.C.: Government Printing Office.

———. 1970a. *Trends in the Cost of Light Water Reactor Power Plants for Utilities.* WASH–1150. Washington, D.C.: Government Printing Office.

———. 1969. *The Nuclear Industry 1969.* WASH–1174–69. Washington, D.C.: Government Printing Office.

———. 1968b. *The Nuclear Industry 1968.* WASH–1174–68. Washington, D.C.: Government Printing Office.

———. 1968a. *Current Status and Future Technical and Economic Potential of Light Water Reactors.* WASH–1082. Washington, D.C.: Government Printing Office.

———. 1967b. *The Nuclear Industry 1967.* WASH–1174–67. Washington, D.C.: Government Printing Office.

———. 1967a. *Civilian Nuclear Power: The 1967 Supplement to the 1962 Report to the President.* In *Nuclear Power Economics 1962 through 1967.* See U.S. Congress. JCAE 1968.

———. 1966. *The Nuclear Industry 1966.* WASH–1174–66. Washington, D.C.: Government Printing Office.

———. 1962. *Civilian Nuclear Power: A Report to the President—1962.* Washington, D.C.: Government Printing Office.

———. 1960. *Civilian Power Reactor Program.* Washington, D.C.: Government Printing Office.

U.S. Congress. Joint Committee on Atomic Energy (JCAE). 1976. *Investigation of Charges Relating to Nuclear Reactor Safety, Hearings.* Vols. 1&2. 94th Cong., 2nd session. Washington, D.C.: Government Printing Office.

———. 1974. *Nuclear Reactor Safety, Hearings.* Part 2 vols. 1&2. 93rd Cong., 2nd. session. Washington, D.C.: Government Printing Office.

———. 1973. *Nuclear Reactor Safety, Hearings.* Part 1. 93rd Cong., 1st session. Washington, D.C.: Government Printing Office.

———. 1972. Energy, Hearings on "Civilian Nuclear Power Program" 2/22–23/72. Washington, D.C.: Government Printing Office.

———. 1968. *Nuclear Power Economics—1962 through 1967.* Report. 90th Cong., 2nd session. Washington, D.C.: Government Printing Office.

———. 1963c. *Cooperative Power Reactor Demonstration Program 1963, Hearings.* 88th Cong., 1st sesson. Washington, D.C.: Government Printing Office.

———. 1963b. *Chemical Reprocessing Plant, Hearings.* 88th Cong., 1st session. Washington, D.C.: Government Printing Office.

———. 1963a. *Hearings on the Development, Growth and State of the Atomic En-*

ergy Industry. 88th Cong., 1st session. Washington, D.C.: Government Printing Office.

———. 1961. *Hearings on the Development, Growth and State of the Atomic Energy Industry.* 87th Cong., 1st session. Washington, D.C.: Government Printing Office.

———. 1960b. *Hearings on Authorizing Appropriations for the Atomic Energy Commission.* 86th Cong., 2nd session. Washington, D.C.: Government Printing Office.

———. 1960a. *Hearings on the Development, Growth and State of the Atomic Energy Industry.* 86th Cong., 2nd session. Washington, D.C.: Government Printing Office.

———. 1959. *Hearings on the Development, Growth and State of the Atomic Energy Industry.* 86th Cong., 1st session. Washington, D.C.: Government Printing Office.

———. 1958b. *Comments of Reactor Designers and Industrial Representatives on the Proposed Expanded Civilian Nuclear Power Program.* Committee Print. 85th Cong., 2nd session. Washington, D.C.: Government Printing Office.

———. 1958a. *Hearings on the Devlopment, Growth and State of the Atomic Energy Industry.* 85th Cong., 2nd session. Washington, D.C.: Government Printing Office.

———. 1957. *Hearings on the Development, Growth and State of the Atomic Energy Industry.* 85th Cong., 1st session. Washington, D.C.: Government Printing Office.

———. 1956c. *Hearings on Accelerating the Civilian Reactor Program.* 84th Cong., 2nd session. Washington, D.C.: Government Printing Office.

———. 1956b. *Peaceful Uses of Atomic Energy: Background Material for the Report of the Panel on the Impact of the Peaceful Uses of Atomic Energy.* Volume 2. 84th Cong., 2nd session. Washington, D.C.: Government Printing Office.

———. 1956a. *Hearings on the Development, Growth and State of the Atomic Energy Industry.* 84th Cong., 2nd session. Washington, D.C.: Government Printing Office.

———. 1955. *Hearings on the Development, Growth and State of the Atomic Energy Industry.* 84th Cong., 1st session. Washington, D.C.: Government Printing Office.

U.S. Congress, House Committee on Banking, Housing and Urban Affairs. 1976. Hearings on the "Energy Independence Authority Act of 1975," April 12–14 and May 10, 1976. Washington, D.C.: Government Printing Office.

U.S. Congress. House. Committee on Government Operations. 1977. *Nuclear Power*

Costs, Hearings. Parts 1 and 2. 95th Cong., 1st session. Washington, D.C.: Government Printing Office.

U.S. Congress. House. Committee on Interior and Insular Affairs. 1979. *Oversight Hearings on Nuclear Economics.* 96th Cong., 1st session. Washington, D.C.: Government Printing Office.

U.S. Congress. Congressional Office of Technology Assessment. 7/91. *Energy Technology Choices Shaping Our Future.* Washington, D.C.: Government Printing Office.

———. 5/91. *Energy Efficiency in the Federal Government: Government by Good Example.* Washington, D.C.: Government Printing Office.

———. 2/91. *Changing by Degrees: Steps to Reduce Greenhouse Gases, Summary.* Washington, D.C.: Government Printing Office.

———. 1985. *Managing the Nation's Commercial High-Level Radioactive Waste.* Washington, D.C.: Government Printing Office.

———. 1984. *Nuclear Power in an Age of Uncertainty.* Washington, D.C.: Government Printing Office.

———. 1981. *Nuclear Plant Standardization: Light Water Reactors.* Washington, D.C.: Government Printing Office.

U.S., Congress, Congressional Research Service. 6/91. *Electricity: A New Regulatory Order?.* Prepared for House Committee on Energy and Commerce. Washington, D.C.: Government Printing Office.

———. 1/22/91. "Renewable Energy: A New National Commitment? CRS Issue Brief 87140. Washington, D.C.: Government Printing Office. Also cited under Sisine.

U.S. Congress. Senate. Committee on Energy and Natural Resources. 1977. *Petroleum Industry Involvement in Alternative Sources of Energy,* Committee Print. 95th Cong., 1st session. Washington, D.C.: Government Printing Office.

U.S. Congress. Senate. Committee on Interior and Insular Affairs. 1973. *Energy Research and Development—Problems and Prospects.* Committee Print. 93rd Cong., 1st session. Washington, D.C.: Government Printing Office.

U.S. Congress. Senate. Committee on the Judiciary. 1977. *Energy Industry Competition and Development Act of 1977, Hearings.* 95th Cong., 1st session. Washington, D.C.: Government Printing Office.

———. 1970. *Competitive Aspects of the Energy Industry, Hearings.* Parts 1 & 2. 91st Cong., 2nd session. Washington, D.C.: Government Printing Office.

U.S. Council on Environmental Quality. 1978. *Solar Energy Progress and Promise.* Washington, D.C.: Government Printing Office.

U.S., Department of Energy. AEO. See *Annual Energy Outlook.*

———. *Annual Energy Outlook (annual) DOE/EIA-0383(yr.)* Washington, D.C.: Government Printing Office.

————. *Annual Outlook for U.S. Electric Power (annual)* Washington, D.C.: Government Printing Office.

————. *Commercial Nuclear Power.* (1990, 1991) DOE/EIA–0438(yr.). Washington, D.C.: Government Printing Office.

————. *Monthly Energy Review* (monthly). Washington, D.C.: Government Printing Office.

————. *World Nuclear Capacity and Fuel Cycle Requirements.* (annual) DOE/EIA–0436(yr.). Washington, D.C.: Government Printing Office.

————. *Federal Energy Subsidies: Direct and Indirect* 11/92 *Interventions in Energy Markets* SR/EMEU/92–02. Washington, D.C.: Government Printing Office.

————. 3/92. *Clean Coal Technology: The New Coal Era* Washington, D.C.: Government Printing Office.

————. 1991. *An Analysis of Nuclear Plant Operating Costs: A 1991 Update* DOE/EIA–0547.

————. 3/88. *An Analysis of Nuclear Power Plant Operating Costs* DOE/EIA–0511. Washington, D.C.: Government Printing Office.

————. 1986. *An Analysis of Nuclear Power Plant Construction Costs*, DOE/EIA–0485. Washington, D.C.: Government Printing Office.

————. 5/84. *Investor Perceptions of Nuclear Power.* DOE/EIA–0446. Washington, D.C.: Government Printing Office.

————. 11/82. *Projected Costs of Electricity from Nuclear and Coal-Fired Power Plants.* Vol. 2. DOE/EIA–0356/2. Washington, D.C.: Government Printing Office.

————. 2/81. *Federal Support for Nuclear Power: Reactor Design and the Fuel Cycle.* DOE/EIA–0201/13. Washington, D.C.: Government Printing Office.

————. 5/80. *Nuclear Power Regulation.* DOE/EIA–0201/10. Washington, D.C.: Government Printing Office.

U.S., Environmental Protection Agency (EPA). 1989. *Policy Options for Stabilizing Global Climate*, Draft Report to Congress (1989). Washington, D.C.: Government Printing Office.

U.S., General Accounting Office. 5/90. *Nuclear Science, U.S. Electricity Needs and DOE's Civilian Reactor Development Program* GAO/RCED-90-151. Washington, D.C.: Government Printing Office.

————. 1979. *Nuclear Power Costs and Subsidies.* Washington, D.C.: Government Printing Office.

U.S., National Academy of Sciences (NAS). 1991. *Policy Implications of Greenhouse Warming: Report of the Mitigation Panel.* Washington, D.C.: National Academy Press. Also cited as National Research Council.

U.S., National Research Council. 1992. *Nuclear Power: Technical and Institutional Options for the Future.* Washington, D.C.: National Academy Press.

———. 1991. *Policy Implications of Greenhouse Warming: Report of the Mitigation Panel.* Washington, D.C.: National Academy Press.

U. S., National Science Foundation (NSF). 1981, 1982. *National Patterns of Science and Technology Resources* (1981,1982). Washington, D.C.: Government Printing Office.

———. 1958,1963,1967,1969. *Research and Development in Industry.* (1958,1963, 1967,1969).

U.S., Nuclear Regulatory Commission. 1995. "Briefing on Risk Harmonization Recommendations" 11/6/95. URL: HTTP://WWW.NIRS.ORG/RADIATION/NRCEPARD.TXT (accessed 8/13/96).

———. 1983. *The Price Anderson Act—The Third Decade.* NUREG 0957. Washington, D.C.: Government Printing Office.

U.S., Oak Ridge National Laboratory. 5/89. *Energy Technology R&D: What Could Make a Difference* ORNL-6541/V1. Oak Ridge, TN: Oak Ridge National Laboratory. Also cited under Fulkerson et al.

———. 9/80. "Nuclear Energy Cost Data Base: A Reference Data Base for Nuclear and Coal-Fired Powerplant Power Generation Cost Analysis" DOE/NE-0095. Oak Ridge, TN: Oak Ridge National Laboratory.

———. 6/87. "Nuclear Economics 2000: Deterministic and Probabilistic Projections of Nuclear and Coal Electric Power Generation Costs for the Year 2000" ORNL-6368. Oak Ridge, TN: Oak Ridge National Laboratory.

———. 12/86. "Nuclear Energy Cost Data Base: A Reference Data Base for Nuclear and Coal-Fired Powerplant Power Generation" DOE/NE 0078. Oak Ridge, TN: Oak Ridge National Laboratory.

———. 9/83. "Trends in Nuclear Power Plant Capital Investment Cost Estimates— 1976 to 1982" NUREG/CR-3500 ORNL/TM 8898. Oak Ridge, TN: Oak Ridge National Laboratory.

U.S., Solar Energy Research Institute (SERI). 1990. *The Potential of Renewable Energy. Interlaboratory White Paper* SERI/TP-260-3674, March 1990. Golden, CO: SERI.

———. 6/81. *New and Renewable Energy in the United States of America.* Washington, D.C.: Government Printing Office.

———. 1981. *A New Prosperity: Building a Sustainable Future.* Andover, MA: Brick House Publishing.

Walker, J. Samuel. 1989. "Nuclear Power and the Environment: The Atomic Energy Commission and Thermal Pollution, 1965–1971." *Technology and Culture* 30(4) (Oct. 1989).

Wasserman, Harvey, and Norman Solomon. 1983. "New Light on the Dangers of Radiation." *The Nation* (1/1–8/83).

Wasserman, Harvey and Norman Solomon, Robert Alvarez, and Eleanor Walters. 1982. *Killing Our Own.* New York: Delacorte Press.

Weart, Spencer. 1988. *Nuclear Fear: A History of Images.* Cambridge: Harvard University Press.

Weinberg, Alvin. 1990. "Energy in Retrospect: Is the Past Prologue?." Contained in *Energy: Production, Consumption, and Consequences*, edited by John Helm. Washington, D.C.: National Academy Press, 1990.

————. 1986. "Are Breeder Reactors Still Necessary?." *Science* (5/9/86).

Weinberg, Alvin M., Irving Spiewak, Jack N. Barkenbus, Robert S. Livingston, and Doan L. Phung (Russ Manning Editor). 1985. *The Second Nuclear Era: A New Start for Nuclear Power.* New York: Praeger.

Weinberg, Alvin. 1975. "The Maturity of Nuclear Energy." Paper presented at the International Symposium on Nuclear Power Technology and Economics, Taipei, January 13, 1975.

Weinberg, Carl J., and Robert Williams. 1990. "Energy from the Sun," contained in *Energy for Planet Earth.* New York: W.H. Freeman. 1991.

Wilbanks, Thomas. 1984. "Scale and the Acceptability of Nuclear Energy," contained in Pasqualetti and Pijawka.

Williams, Robert. 1994. "Roles for Biomass Energy in Sustainable Development." Scheduled for publication in *Industrial Ecology and Global Change.* R.H. Socolow et al. (eds.). Cambridge: Cambridge University Press.

————. 10/93. "The Outlook for Renewable Energy" (Draft). Final version contained in MIT 1993.

Williams, Robert, and Eric D. Larson. 1993. "Advanced Gasification-Based Biomass Power Generation," contained in Johansson et al. 1993a.

Williams, Robert. 1990. "Low Cost Strategies for Coping with CO_2 Emission Limits. (A Critique of 'CO_2 Emission Limits: An Economic Cost Analysis for the USA' by Alan Manne and Richard Richels)." *Energy Journal* 11(3).

————. 1989. "Biomass Gasifier/Gas Turbine Power and Greenhouse Warming." Paper presented at IEA/OECD Expert Seminar on Energy Technologies for Reducing Emissions of Greenhouse Gases (4/89). Paris.

Wing, Steve and Carl Shy, Joy Wood, Susan Wolf, Donna Cragle, and E.L. Frome. 1991. "Mortality Among Workers at Oak Ridge National Laboratory" *JAMA* 265(11) (March 20, 1991).

Wolfson, Richard. 1991. *Nuclear Choices: A Citizens Guide to Nuclear Technology.* Cambridge: MIT Press.

Wood, William. 1983. *Nuclear Safety Risks and Regulation.* Washington: American Enterprise Institute.

World Resources Institute (in collaboration with The United Nations Environment Programme and the United Nations Development Programme). 1990. *World Resources 1990–91: A Guide to the Global Environment.* New York: Oxford Univerity Press.

Zimmerman, Martin B. 1987. "The Evolution of Civilian Nuclear Power." Contained in *Energy Markets and Regulation,* edited by Richard Gordon, Henry Jacoby, and Martin Zimmerman. Cambridge: MIT Press.

————. 1982. "Learning Effects and the Commercialization of New Energy Technologies: The Case of Nuclear Power." *Bell Journal* (13)2.

Zucchet, Michael J. "Renewable Resource Electricity in the Changing Regulatory Environment." Contained in *Renewable Energy Annual 1995* (DOE July 1995). URL: http://www.eia.doe.gov/cneaf/pubs_html/rea/feature2.html (accessed 8/30/96).

Index